THE HISTORY OF
THE BRITISH COAL INDUSTRY

VOLUME I

BEFORE 1700: TOWARDS THE AGE OF COAL

THE HISTORY OF
THE BRITISH COAL
INDUSTRY

VOLUME I

Before 1700: Towards the Age of Coal

BY

JOHN HATCHER

CLARENDON PRESS · OXFORD
1993

Oxford University Press, Walton Street, Oxford OX2 6DP

Oxford New York Toronto
Delhi Bombay Calcutta Madras Karachi
Kuala Lumpur Singapore Hong Kong Tokyo
Nairobi Dar es Salaam Cape Town
Melbourne Auckland Madrid
and associated companies in
Berlin Ibadan

Oxford is a trade mark of Oxford University Press

Published in the United States
by Oxford University Press Inc., New York

British Library Cataloguing in Publication Data
Data available

Library of Congress Cataloging in Publication Data
Data available
ISBN 0-19-828282-6

1 3 5 7 9 10 8 6 4 2

Typeset by Joshua Associates Ltd., Oxford
Printed in Great Britain
on acid-free paper by
Biddles Ltd., Guildford and King's Lynn

Acknowledgement

The research for this book was undertaken with the assistance of Stephen Roberts, John Swain, and Mark Nicholls.

Preface

In 1975 the National Coal Board, under the chairmanship of Lord Ezra, initiated a project to sponsor the writing of a comprehensive *History of the British Coal Industry*. This volume belatedly brings that ambitious undertaking to a conclusion. It has the dubious distinction of being the last volume to be published in a five-volume series of which it is volume 1. While part of the explanation for this tardiness lies in the fact that I was the last author to be commissioned, and was not in post until 1980, this is by no means the whole story. The writing of a comprehensive history of the British coal industry from earliest times to the eighteenth century has proved to be a daunting task for a medievalist, and one which, despite the length of time that has elapsed, has not been fully performed. A further major obstacle to speedy progress was the fact that in these early centuries there was no British coal industry; rather there was a large number of regional industries, each one firmly rooted in its locality. The Bibliography of Manuscript Sources reveals that the records of coalmining and the coal trade within this period are both voluminous and widely scattered, as befits an industry which flourished in fifteen coalfields located in more than a score of counties. The diversity of experience, as well as the eventual scale of the production and trade of coal, posed many problems of exposition and eventually necessitated a good measure of selective treatment.

I should like first to acknowledge the special role of British Coal in supporting this volume. Generous financial provision funded research assistance for a period of almost three man-years and innumerable trips to archives around the country. But more than this, the central secretariat of the corporation, led first by David Brandrick and subsequently by Martin Shelton, offered unflagging encouragement and tolerance through the long years of gestation. Peter Mathias, the adviser to British Coal and editor of the series, provided an abundance of astute guidance and practical help, and he also read a complete draft of the text and made many helpful suggestions. I obtained much useful advice from the authors and researchers of other volumes in this series, most notably Roy Church, Barry Supple, John Kanefsky, and the late Michael Flinn. Additional financial support was provided by the Economic and Social Research Council, which funded a research assistant for seven months. In 1986–7 I was granted a fellowship at the Huntington Library, California, and was privileged to be able to begin the writing of this book in the ideal environment of an excellent research library, stimulating colleagues, and superlative gardens.

The research for this volume commenced early in 1980, and the arrival of Stephen Roberts later that year ensured a most productive start. From the outset it had been my intention to base the study firmly upon the records produced in the coalfields by coal-owners and colliery managers, and Stephen's talents were focused primarily upon the location and evaluation of sources scattered in a score or more archives stretching from Bristol to Edinburgh. This he did with such skill that, during a period of less than two years, when my own participation was necessarily limited by other commitments, famine was transformed into feast. The knowledge of the seventeenth century which Stephen Roberts possesses, and his enthusiasm for the coal industry, did much to inform me and to ensure that subsequent research was based upon secure foundations. John Swain, who worked with me for a year, as well as continuing with the collection of local mining records began the extraction of data from colliery accounts, the processing of customs accounts, and the creation of an index of British collieries. These were time-consuming and painstaking tasks, requiring attention to detail as well as knowledge of the priorities of economic history; he performed them with exemplary expertise and dedication, and played a substantial role in the building of the quantitative backbone of this book. A grant from the Economic and Social Research Council enabled Mark Nicholls to be employed for a period of seven months in 1984 on the seemingly interminable business of producing accurate and meaningful statistics from colliery accounts, and in addition his outstanding palaeographical skills were put to good use in reviewing records from the fifteenth to the eighteenth century. I count myself fortunate in having had the support of three such able scholars in the formative stages of the project, and I benefited immeasurably from their knowledge of sixteenth- and seventeenth-century Britain as well as from their views on the position of the coal industry within it. I also cherish fond memories of joint excursions to many archives where, added to the excitement of discovering important records, were the experiences of hiring wellington boots in Newcastle, being mistaken for policemen at a local government officers' party in Durham, and digging our car out of a snowdrift at Marley Hill colliery.

In the course of researching and writing this book I accumulated many further debts, and it is a pleasure to be able to record them formally. I am grateful to all the archivists and librarians who gave liberally of their time and knowledge, and without whose co-operation the gathering of many of the records upon which this book is based would not have been possible. Richard S. Smith generously loaned me a copy of his manuscript 'Mining around Nottingham, 1500–1600', which proved of immense value to my work on the East Midlands, and John Langton made available for my use some of his notes on the south-west Lancashire coalfield. Thanks are also due to Malcolm Wanklyn and Peter Wakelin who supplied me with data from the Wolverhampton Polytechnic Gloucester Port Book project; to David Farmer who supplied me with information on coal purchases recorded in manorial accounts; and to Marianne Kowaleski who supplied me with information on the shipment of coal in south-west England in the Middle Ages. I owe a special debt to Oliver Rackham who on many occasions shared with me his unrivalled knowledge of English woodlands, to David Hartland who taught me much about accounting methods and business management, and to Donald Woodward, who in addition to reading and commenting upon draft chapters, supplied the long-run price series from Hull contained in Appendix B. Among those colleagues who kindly read draft sections and offered valuable advice were John Harris, W. J. W. Bourne, and Brian Outhwaite.

Finally, I am deeply grateful for the kindness shown to me by my long-suffering family. It was a great comfort to me that Melissa and Zara, who have never known a life without the history of the coal industry and whose eyes grew ever wider as first the notes and then the typescript expanded beyond all believable bounds, none the less managed to retain a touching faith that some day their father would be capable of finishing it. To Janice, who has supported me in so many ways, I dedicate this book.

J.H.

June 1992

Contents

List of Plates

(Between pages 302 and 303)

List of Figures

List of Maps

List of Tables

Abbreviations in Notes and Bibliography

AA	*Archaeologia Aeliana*
AgHR	Agricultural History Review
AHEW	*Agrarian History of England and Wales*
APC	*Acts of the Privy Council*
APS	*Acts of Parliament of Scotland*
BL	British Library
BoL	Bodleian Library
BoRL	Bolton Reference Library
BrRL	Bristol Reference Library
CCR	*Calendar of Close Rolls*
CChR	*Calendar of Charter Rolls*
CIPM	*Calendar of Inquisitions Post Mortem*
ClRO	Clwyd Record Office
CoRO	City of Coventry Record Office
CPR	*Calendar of Patent Rolls*
CSPD	*Calendar of State Papers Domestic*
CSPV	*Calendar of State Papers Venetian*
CuRO	Cumbria Record Office
DeRO	Derbyshire County Record Office
DN	Duke of Northumberland's Archives, Alnwick
DuCL	Durham Cathedral Library
DUDP	Durham University, Department of Palaeography
DUPK	Durham University, Prior's Kitchen
DuRO	Durham County Record Office
EcHR	*Economic History Review*
EHR	*English Historical Review*
EJ	*Economic Journal*
GHL	Corporation of London Records Office, Guildhall
GPL	Gateshead Public Library
GRO	Gloucestershire County Record Office
HCA	Hull City Archives
HCJ	*House of Commons Journals*
HH	Hatfield House
HL	Huntington Library, California
HLJ	*House of Lords Journals*
HMC	Historical Manuscripts Commission

HRCM	*Historical Review of Coal Mining* (Mining Association of Great Britain)
HRO	Hertfordshire County Record Office
HTH	Hull Trinity House Archives
HUA	Hull University Archives
JEBH	*Journal of Economic and Business History*
KAO	Kent Archives Office, Maidstone
KC	King's College, Cambridge
LaRO	Lancashire County Record Office
LCA	Leeds City Archives
LPL	Lambeth Palace Library
LSE	British Library of Political and Economic Science
NCH	*Northumberland County History*
NEI	North of England Institute of Mining and Mechanical Engineers
NeUL	Newcastle University Library
NLS	National Library of Scotland
NLW	National Library of Wales
NoRO	Nottinghamshire County Record Office
NorRO	Norfolk County Record Office
NoUL	Nottingham University Library
NuRO	Northumberland County Record Office
P. & P.	*Past & Present*
PCR	*Privy Council Registers*
PRO	Public Record Office
PTRS	*Philosophical Transactions of the Royal Society*
RPCS	*Registers of the Privy Council of Scotland*
SCL	Sheffield City Library
ScRO	Scottish Record Office
ShRO	Shropshire County Record Office
SoRO	Somerset County Record Office
StRO	Staffordshire County Record Office
TNS	*Transactions of the Newcomen Society*
TWRO	Tyne and Wear County Record Office
UCNW	University College of North Wales
VCH	*Victoria History of the Counties of England*
WaRO	Warwickshire County Record Office
WiRO	Wigan Record Office
WSL	William Salt Library

Conventions Adopted in References to Sources

Manuscript sources. A list of the collections used and the locations of the record offices in which they are housed are given in the appropriate section of the Bibliography. Abbreviations of names of record offices are given in Abbreviations in Notes and Bibliography. In the notes the abbreviation of the name of a record office is followed normally by the name of the collection, and the reference number of the collection (where one has been allocated). Thus, the Hesketh of Rufford collection in the Lancashire Record Office at Preston is referred to as LaRO Hesketh of Rufford DDHe. The letters and/or numbers which follow are those allocated by the record office to the document which is being cited; these are followed, if appropriate, by folio or membrane numbers. Thus, DDHe 40/69 is the reference for an agreement concerning the getting of coals in Shevington, 1666. Of course, precise methods of identification vary from office to office.

Printed books and articles. Secondary works listed in the Bibliography are cited in notes by author's name and date of publication only, followed by page numbers where relevant. Contemporary printed material listed in the Bibliography has been referred to in the notes by the author's or editor's name and a short title, followed by page numbers where relevant. Works listed in the Bibliography are generally those to which a number of references have been made in the notes. For other works a full reference is given in the notes. London is the place of publication unless otherwise indicated. For abbreviations of journal titles see Abbreviations in Notes and Bibliography.

Unpublished theses. The full references for all theses used are set out in the theses section of the Bibliography. Theses have been cited in the notes by the author's name followed by the word thesis, the date of submission, and the page number where relevant.

Quotations. The spelling in quotations from contemporary sources has been modernized in order to render the sense more accessible to the reader. Modernized spelling also helps to provide a measure of consistency between those quotations which have been drawn from manuscripts and contemporary printed sources and those drawn from modern editions whose editors have adopted a variety of conventions. Punctuation has also been modernized, and abbreviations have been expanded where there is no doubt of their meaning.

PART I

TOWARDS THE AGE OF COAL

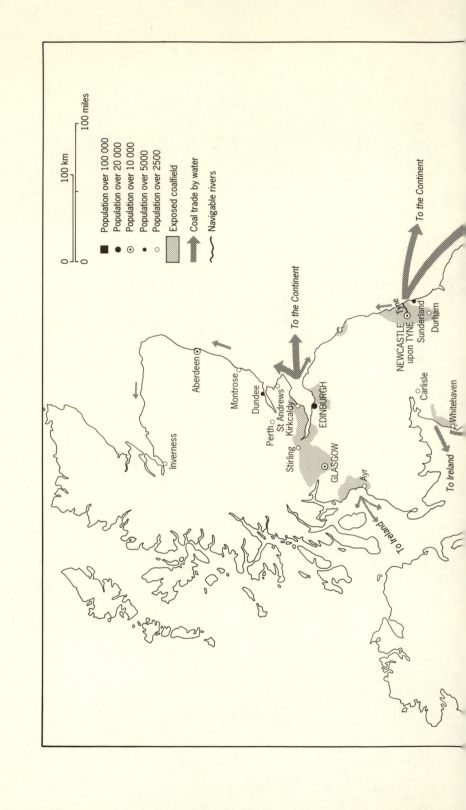

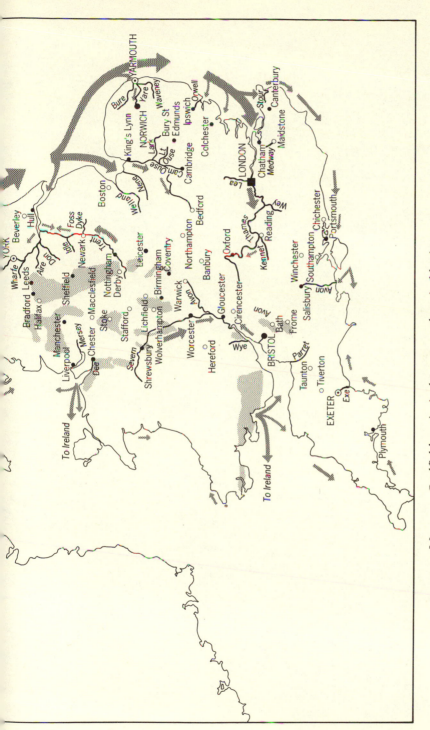

Map. 1.1. Coalfields, principal towns, and navigable rivers, c.1700

CHAPTER I

Towards the Age of Coal

Sea coal and pit coal is become the general fuel of this Britain island

John Stow, *Annales*, 1612

Between the mid-sixteenth century and the later seventeenth century coal was transformed from an occasional or specialized source of heat, endowed with consequence in a scattering of localities and industries, into the habitual fuel of much of the nation. In the context of these pre-industrialized centuries the expansion of coal consumption was truly spectacular, and its rate of growth far outstripped that of the general run of major commodities. British coalmining, with its output soaring well in excess of tenfold in the century and a half after 1550, and perhaps attaining around three million tons a year by the 1700s, rose from virtual insignificance to become one of a select group of staple industries. By the dawn of the eighteenth century coal output in Britain was many times greater than that in the whole of the rest of the world, and the firm foundations which were to underpin the fuelling of the industrial revolution had been laid.

The reasons for this early advance are in essence simple rather than complex. The demand for fuel of all types increased sharply as a consequence of rising population, with the numbers of people in Britain more than doubling between the early sixteenth century and the mid-seventeenth. Moreover, the strains this growth in numbers imposed on traditional fuel supplies were heightened by the increasing proportion which lived in towns, and by the disproportionate expansion of fuel-consuming industries.[1] In a society which depended directly upon the products of the land for its food, clothing, and warmth, and for the leather and wood which furnished its basic raw materials, such population growth inevitably intensified competition for the land and its

---

[1] It is thought that the proportion of the population of England which lived in towns of any substance approximately doubled from 10 to 12 per cent to just under a quarter between 1500 and 1700 (Clay 1984, i. 165). This would have constituted a quadrupling of the numbers of urban dwellers from, say, a quarter of a million to more than one million.

produce. Without colonization and advances in agricultural productivity on a scale sufficient to increase supply in line with rising numbers, inflation was inevitable in Tudor and Stuart England. But coal, unlike wood, did not compete for space with grain and animals, and it was not a scarce resource. Although coal reserves are now known to be finite, albeit vast, in Tudor and Stuart England they often gave the appearance of being an infinite resource, as ever greater quantities were able to be raised to the surface.

Fuel is a necessity in any society, but it is often available in a variety of forms. The allocation of the total demand for energy between the various alternative fuels is largely, though not exclusively, determined by relative prices. In the Middle Ages, away from the immediate vicinity of collieries, coal was normally prohibitively expensive relative to wood, turves, or other locally obtainable combustible materials, and was thus used only in a narrow range of processes for which its qualities were ideally suited. However, from the middle of the sixteenth century traditional fuels became progressively more scarce and thus more costly in many parts of Britain. Such scarcity was most acute in centres of population, and coal very soon became the most economical fuel in those towns of eastern England which enjoyed good water communications with Tyneside. As time passed, and as the demand for fuel rose ever higher, the price advantage enjoyed by coal became ever more pronounced, and the quantities burnt ever more substantial. In London and Cambridge, for example, the average price of coal delivered to the consumer rose scarcely at all between the 1580s and the 1610s, yet over the same period in Westminster the abbey college had to pay in excess of 80 per cent more for each bundle of firewood that it burnt, and in Cambridge already by the 1580s wood had ceased to be cheap enough for general consumption in the colleges and during the next two decades the price of turves doubled and even the cost of humble sedge rose by 40 per cent.[2]

The notion that there was a 'timber famine' in Tudor and Stuart England has a long pedigree, but recent generations of historians have cautioned against placing much reliance on the lamentations of contemporaries about the dearth of trees and wood, and many have urged the rejection of the notion of the existence of any but localized shortages.[3] They have warned that hard cases make bad generalizations, and in this connection we must not forget that John Stow's continuator, whose

[2] For these and other price data see below, Figs. 3.1, 3.2, and App. B.
[3] For further discussion and references see below, Ch. 3.

assertion that coal by the early seventeenth century had become the general fuel of Britain has been placed at the head of this chapter, was a citizen of London where reliance upon coal came exceptionally early and was soon dominant. Much of the scepticism concerning the existence of a widespread scarcity of wood has been generated by studies of the fuel supplies of the charcoal–iron industry, but when the matter is viewed from the perspective of the energy needs of the whole economy there are clear indications that this scepticism has proceeded too far. Despite the frequency and strength of protestations to the contrary, there is strong evidence that an accelerating shortfall in the supply of wood was under way in many of the towns of eastern England early in Elizabeth's reign, and that by the opening decades of the seventeenth century broad swathes of the country were facing a lack of affordable local firing.

The only national wood price index to have been attempted, that constructed by Dr Bowden, exhibits a rise of almost 400 per cent between the 1540s and the 1620s, while over the same period the general cost of living rose by less than 300 per cent. The massive simultaneous increase in the supply of fuel, which occurred through the growth of coalmining, makes the scale of the inflation in wood prices all the more dramatic.[4] Dr Bowden's 'national' price index is in fact heavily reliant upon southern sources but, as will be revealed later, the scarcity of tradi-tional fuels and the advance of coal were by no means restricted to the south and east of England and the immediate vicinity of coalfields. Expressions of acute anxiety about the diminishing availability of fire-wood and timber, as woodland suffered the twin depredations of consumers and cultivators, were to be heard from the far west and the far north as well as well as from the heartlands of England and the tradi-tionally thinly wooded and thickly peopled southern and eastern regions. Coal offered timely compensation for the insufficiency of conventional fuels and, in some instances, salvation from a prolonged energy crisis.

As the map at the beginning of this volume illustrates, the widespread distribution of coalfields and the relatively cheap transport offered by the sea and the extensive network of navigable waterways in early modern Britain, meant that coal was accessible to most of the leading towns of Britain and many of the more populous parts of the realm. As the rudimentary principles of human geography teach, settlement tends to flourish where communications are good. Accordingly, by the opening decades of the seventeenth century substantial parts of Britain

[4] *AHEW* iv. 846–50; Phelps Brown and Hopkins 1981, 28–31.

were far advanced along the road to dependency upon coal, and by the opening of the eighteenth century the country was on the way to becoming a coal-based economy. Calculations of the output of coal and of the extent and productivity of woodland suggest that by the close of our period fossil fuel had eclipsed plant fuels as the leading provider of the nation's heat.

The reputation for massive expansion during the later sixteenth and seventeenth centuries with which J. U. Nef endowed the British coal industry is thus lent ample support by this study. Where we can measure the growth rates achieved in coalmining, or speculate with some confidence on their dimensions, they are formidable indeed for a pre-industrial economy. In an almost ideal environment serving fast-growing dependent markets, the coasting trade of the north-east grew at an average annual compounded rate of 2.3 per cent between 1564 and 1685, and the amount of coal shipped from Northumberland and Durham was around fourteen times greater at the close of the seventeenth century than it had been at the start of the boom 140 years before. These are rates of growth which bear comparison with those achieved by the British coal industry during the industrial revolution.

Possibly of even more significance, and certainly of greater novelty, is that this sustained and spectacular growth in output was accomplished with relative ease. The early modern coal industry was blessed with a huge and seemingly constantly rising appetite for its product, yet supply seems only rarely to have lagged behind demand. Impressive as the achievements of the coal industry were in continuously raising output during most of the later sixteenth and seventeenth centuries, there can be no doubt whatsoever that far more coal could have been produced had there been a market for it.

All students of the pre-modern coal industry owe an immense debt to *The Rise of the British Coal Industry* which has, according to persuasion, for decades stood bestride the subject like a colossus or throttled it with 'massy coils'. The sheer breadth of Nef's two-volumed history, and the essays on the progress of technology and the growth of large-scale industry which complemented it, commands admiration.[5] Equally impressive is the depth of learning which Nef brought to bear upon his

---

[5] See in particular, J. U. Nef, 'The Dominance of the Trader in the English Coal Industry', *JEBH* 1 (1929); id., 'The Progress of Technology and the Growth of Large-Scale Industry in Great Britain, 1540–1640', *EcHR* 5 (1934); id., 'Prices and Industrial Capitalism in France and England, 1540–1640', *EcHR* 7 (1937); id., *Industry and Government in France and England, 1540–1640* (Philadelphia, 1940).

chosen themes; each one embellished by a veritable torrent of citations and footnotes which reveal the scale of his researches in the inner reaches of central government and legal archives, and in the records and literature of political economy, science, technology, commerce, and finance. *The Rise of the British Coal Industry* deserves to rank high as a contribution to the history of Britain's economic development. Yet it has proved to be a work as controversial as it is monumental, and its reputation has suffered grievously at the hands of successive generations of historians. It is hoped that the present work will assist in the formulation of a more equitable judgement of J. U. Nef's contribution to this field.

The story of coal usage rising strongly against the background of a mounting scarcity of wood will have a familiar ring to readers acquainted with the theses of J. U. Nef, and, notwithstanding that this present volume is based upon a wider range of sources, suggests new dimensions for weights and measures, and adopts different methods of analysis, the estimates it produces of the scale and chronology of the development of the coal industry and trade are broadly comparable to those of its predecessor. Yet it also contains many alternative explanations and differences of interpretation, some of a fundamental character. In the force of their arguments *The Rise of the British Coal Industry* and associated publications provide a powerful exposition of the credo that the coal industry lay at the centre of a revolution in industry and related sectors of later Tudor and early Stuart England. Nef believed not only in a revolution in the production, trade, and consumption of coal, affecting all stages from technology, through labour and capital, to transport, but that the ramifications of these advances extended far and wide beyond the boundaries of the coal industry itself. It is in the consideration of these themes that the present work deviates most starkly from its notable predecessor.

Many of the differences of emphasis and interpretation stem from the sources which have been studied. Nef relied for his knowledge of the operation of the coal industry, the scale of its units of production, the profits it generated, and the capital it consumed, almost exclusively upon records housed in London which emanated from the centre of government and the law rather than those compiled by the men in the coalfields who owned and ran collieries and dealt in coal. Many of the major collections of local colliery accounts were not easily accessible in the 1920s, and Nef scarcely consulted them. Dominant among his favoured sources were the records of litigation in central courts, especially Star Chamber Proceedings, Exchequer Depositions, Proceedings of the Court of Augmentations, and Duchy of Lancaster Pleadings and Depositions. Although Nef attempted to supplement legal proceedings with surveys of collieries commissioned by central government, including Duchy of Lancaster Special Commissions and Parliamentary Surveys made during the Interregnum, the documents he relied upon had an ineluctable bias towards the exceptional. Prodigious ventures, extraordinary losses and profits, mighty outputs and inputs, all abound in those law suits which were worthy of the attention, and costs, of a London action. Even if all the testimony given in such actions was truthful, which it was not, it would still be liable to mislead since it is derived overwhelmingly from exceptional circumstances and the operations of the very largest collieries. Moreover, it needs no stressing that the claims made by litigating partners and contending business associates are frequently extravagant and often designed to oppress the opposing party.

By contrast, this present study relies heavily upon the profusion of records emanating from the coalfields, and in particular upon those generated by the owners and operators of collieries, including deeds, correspondence, estate records, and, above all, colliery accounts. While undoubtedly providing more trustworthy evidence, this approach also has its pitfalls. To choose it is to desert the security of a manageable body of central records in favour of an almost overwhelming torrent of local experience. It is no simple task to unravel the typical from the untypical and construct a balanced and coherent narrative from the diversity of experience thrown up by the pits and collieries of fifteen well-scattered coalfields across a span of 500 years.

On a priori grounds alone it is tempting to believe that such a massive expansion of coal production could have been achieved only through equally massive changes in the structure of the industry and the scale of its collieries, and that such rapid progress must have depended upon huge doses of capital investment raised in novel ways from hosts of new investors, and have necessitated comparable revolutions in management and labour practices and in the technology of mining. Perusal of the luxuriant sources left by the industry and its trade, however, soon show that reality was often far less sensational. In the ensuing pages it will be proposed that, whereas the achievements of the industry were truly spectacular, the processes whereby they were accomplished frequently verged on the prosaic, and that the rise of the British coal industry depended as much if not more upon established practice, improved by *ad hoc* pragmatic embellishments, as it did upon thoroughgoing innovation.

Indeed, there was little necessity for revolutions in the production of coal since there were normally few formidable barriers to the achievement of progressive increases in output. Britain before 1700 possessed vast accessible reserves, and it is a central tenet of this book that there were few enduring physical restraints upon the ability of proprietors to extract this coal. Although due weight in any history of coalmining must be given to advances in the methods used to discover workable deposits, to improvements in the technology employed to exploit them, and to the provision of the capital and labour required to establish and operate collieries, the major constraints on the industry in this period were not on the production side. Collieries might be abandoned because the flow of water overwhelmed the engines and soughs employed to drain them, or because shallow and cheaply exploited deposits had been exhausted, but alternative mining sites often existed in the vicinity. While production in any individual colliery might be a discontinuous and unpredictable process, the industry overall displayed a commendable ability to mine ever greater quantities of coal and deposit them for sale at the pithead or on the river bank at prices which often fell in real terms.

Early modern coalmining has often been characterized as a highly capitalized industry. But to describe it thus is to create a misleading impression of its appetite for investment funds, and not only because such a view fails to give true weight to the hundreds of coal-mines and collieries which were no more demanding of capital than artisans' workshops. Even the great collieries, which undoubtedly dwarfed all but a few contemporary industrial structures and rivalled in scale many of those of later centuries, were financed mainly from within the industry itself and through the retention of profits. Moreover, far from placing extraordinary demands upon contemporary credit markets, most of Britain's collieries were adequately financed by the profits of farming and landholding. The principal coalmining entrepreneurs were the gentry, who acted in a traditional rather than a novel fashion by developing the resources of their estates, and raising any capital which they needed by pledging that most secure and time-honoured of assets, their lands. Even on Tyneside, which was in many ways a special case, there was much in the environment within which the paramount branch of the coal industry flourished that was more redolent of medieval than of modern times.[6]

[6] The sources and scale of mining capital are considered in Chs. 7 and 10 below.

In an article written in the early stages of a distinguished career, Hugh Trevor-Roper sketched a case for seeing the creation of the Grand Lease and the transfer of the greatest collieries of Tyneside, and indeed of Europe, from the bishop of Durham to the merchants of Newcastle, as a 'remarkably pure' example of the 'capitalist reformation'. Examining the episode, he wrote, was like 'studying a laboratory experiment or the resolution of a mathematical formula', in which 'The forces and structure of medievalism were thus united in the person of the bishop, the new forces of capitalism in northern England were also concentrated ... in coal'.[7] But the case will not stand. For the 'forces of capitalism' had at their heart a monopoly which was essentially medieval, being founded upon the sort of grants which were commonly given to medieval guilds and boroughs. Far from being stimulated by untrammelled competition, with free entry into mining and free trade in coal, the Tyneside industry strengthened and expanded at a pace virtually unknown outside of the eighteenth and nineteenth centuries, under a monopoly of the trade in coal and an informal but virtual monopoly of its production exercised by the Hostmen of Newcastle.[8]

Study of the technology of mining and the management of mines also reveals a fruitful marriage of conservation and innovation, in which formidable advances were accomplished without the wholesale supplanting of traditional frameworks. In the development of the technologies for mining coal, for managing collieries, and for transporting and selling the product, we discover adaptation and amendment in greater measure than sheer novelty. The methods by which collieries were laid out and maintained, and by which coal was cut from the seam and raised to the surface, benefited from continuous improvement, but the advances were normally the result of multitudes of small steps taken with the aid of the pragmatic ingenuity of generations of working miners rather than giant leaps facilitated by scientific breakthroughs. None the less, the cumulative accretions of successive betterments, minor or even trivial though they might appear in isolation, can cumulate over decades and centuries to constitute substantial progress. In the coal industry of the sixteenth and seventeenth centuries we have an exemplar of the potency of evolutionary progress achieved largely without discontinuities. When on occasion the industry faced major impediments to its prosperity, such as the high cost and difficulty of transporting large quantities of coal in carts over short distances from pits to rivers, or the ineffectiveness of prospecting, then innovation was

[7] Trevor Roper 1945–6.   [8] See Chs. 5 and 15 below.

often forthcoming, in these instances through the invention of railed waggonways and boring rods.

At the same time, spectacular as it was, the rise of coal was far from being entirely unimpeded. In particular, the lack of supply-side restraints did not extend to transport. With the apposite exception of firewood and turves, coal was worth far less by bulk and weight than virtually any other commodity which was regularly traded, and there were strict limits to the distances over which it could be economically transported. More than this, because coal consists of lumps of differing sizes and irregular shapes, it is particularly awkward and time consuming to handle. Measuring it and transferring it from boat to ship, ship to boat, boat to cart, and cart to cellar added mightily to its ultimate price. Before the coming of the railways, water was the only means by which coal could reach a distant market in quantity. In the late seventeenth century the sea voyage from Newcastle to London, a distance of around 300 miles, commonly resulted in less than a quadrupling of the Tyneside price, even though coal was subjected to heavy duties by the Crown and the City of London. Sir Robert Southwell, speculating on the impossibility of conducting such a vital trade overland, reported to the Royal Society in 1675 that 'the carriage of coals from Newcastle [to London] by wheels would be intrinsically sixty times dearer than the present sea-carriage'.[9]

In 1667, when the Dutch were ravaging North Sea shipping, the feasibility of providing alternative supply routes for London's fuel came under urgent consideration, and the costs of making the journey inland from King's Lynn were investigated. It was found that each chaldron of coal, which was expected to cost 30s. in Lynn, could be carried by river to Cambridge, a distance of some forty-four miles, for a mere 4s. But thereafter costs would escalate. A further 20–25s. was thought to be required for the thirty miles or so land carriage from Cambridge to Ware, and a further 6–7s. for the final twenty-five miles or so water carriage from Ware to London.[10] Taking each chaldron to be just under 1.5 tons, the costs of transport by river, land, and river would have averaged 0.7d., 5–6.7d., and 2–2.25d. per ton mile respectively. At a time when coal was sold for no more than 3s. 6d. a ton on the staithes at Newcastle, carriage from King's Lynn to London by these means would have multiplied the cost up to tenfold, while the overland journey from Cambridge to Ware added as much as the original Newcastle price every six to eight miles.

[9] Birch 1756–7, iii. 207–8.   [10] CSPD 1667, 268.

Overland transport costs of this order help to explain why, even as late as the mid-eighteenth century, as the Swedish botanist Peter Kahn found, coal gave way to wood for common usage no more than fourteen miles from London.[11] Spatial factors thus lie at the very heart of this volume. On the other hand, regions which could not enjoy the benefits of cheap coal happily often had less need of it. For the very inaccesibility of most of the parts of the country which were remote from coal meant that their woodlands were often left relatively unplundered by the demands of industry and of outsiders. The same inadequacies of transport which made coal expensive to carry into such parts made local wood even more expensive to carry out. The consequences of high and variable distribution costs, when combined with the location of coalfields, trees, and population, effectively segmented Britain into a series of heterogeneous markets. Thus, throughout the period covered in this volume there were regions of cheap fuel and regions of expensive fuel; regions where coal reigned supreme and regions where scarcely any coal was burnt.

Returning to the coalfields, at the other end of the chain of supply, it can be seen that it was very frequently the ease of communications with markets and the size of those markets, rather than the costs of raising the coal, which were pre-eminent in determining the scale of exploitation of reserves and the fortunes of individual collieries. Coal was not mined in significant quantities simply because it was there, or even because it was cheap to do so. The size attained by individual collieries, and the output of whole coalfields, was determined by the markets which they were capable of serving, and this in turn was primarily a function of location.

Such constraints, as well as the abundance of potential mining sites, help to explain why, away from the major arteries of water-borne trade, the vast bulk of collieries were modest in size. Relatively few regularly produced more than 5,000 tons a year and, outside of Tyneside and Wearside, only a handful ever produced more than 20,000 tons.[12] Small units were comparatively easy to finance and to manage, and it was their numbers which were precocious rather than their structures. Under exceptionally favourable conditions collieries could expand to capacities of 50,000 to 100,000 tons, but within our period those that did remained prodigies. The trade in coal, though massive in aggregate, was likewise broken down into multitudes of small manageable parcels. At the close of the seventeenth century around 700,000 tons of coal costing £125,000

[11] Eveleigh 1983, 3.   [12] See Ch. 4 below.

to £130,000 were shipped from the north-east annually. But this tonnage was carried in some 5,000 separate cargoes, of which even the largest was likely to be have cost the shippers less than £100 to purchase.[13] Conducted in such a fashion the production and trade of coal did not place unbearable strains upon the resources and enterprise of the age.

Describing and attempting to explain the development of the British coal industry and trade across fifteen scattered coalfields and more than 500 years of history is not a project which lends itself to efficient and economic exposition, and sadly the ensuing pages are both voluminous and, in part, repetitive. In mitigation it might be pointed out that historians of coal are not noted for their brevity. J. U. Nef took two volumes and almost 1,000 pages to complete his task, and Aster Moller's neglected D.Phil. thesis on an identical subject, coincidentally written at the same time as Nef's study, contains over 800 pages. Yet, as this introduction has stressed, the reader of the present work cannot even be promised much prospect of an encounter with the thrills of revolutionary change or iconoclastic hypotheses. It is therefore to be presumed that few will embark upon reading this present volume from cover to cover, and fewer still having begun such a daunting venture can be relied upon to persevere to the end. Accordingly, an attempt has been made to break the bulk of the text into a series of semi-discrete sections, which hopefully may still prove intelligible if read in isolation. By these means it is hoped the convenience of access may outweigh the inconvenience of repetition.

[13] See Ch. 13 below.

CHAPTER 2

The Era of Cheap Fuel
From Early Times to the Mid-Sixteenth Century

Coales in former times was onely used by smiths, and for burning
of lime

William Gray, *Chorographia* (1649)

Adequate supplies of fuel were cheaply, even freely, available throughout much of the early Middle Ages. Firewood could be gathered almost
everywhere from trees and hedgerows, and in addition turves, sedge,
thack, furze, heath, coal, and other local specialities might also provide
useful supplements. There were few people and many acres and, with a
population of perhaps two million in later eleventh-century England,
there was as yet little pressure on natural resources. In these spacious
times when extensive tracts of the country were thinly settled and
under-utilized, and most villages had expanses of commons, waste, or
woodland within their boundaries or on their borders, sufficient
supplies of fuel for domestic fires could usually be gathered locally. The
rights of villagers to take wood for building, fencing, and fuel from
common woodlands often became enshrined in the customs of 'house-
bote, haibote and firebote'. Tenants might also be permitted to use the
trees which grew on the holdings which they occupied and sometimes,
in return for a small rent or the performance of services, lords might
grant rights to collect dead wood from seigneurial woodlands and
forests.[1] When the commerce in domestic fuel was clearly so limited,
coal was never a consideration for the vast majority of people.

Nevertheless, coal had long since been burnt in small quantities by
those living close to outcrops, and the special qualities of mineral fuel
created a limited but widespread demand from artisans engaged in
specialist processes for which coal was the most suitable fuel. What is
perhaps the earliest indisputable example of the use of coal was indeed
esoteric, namely as the source of heat for a Bronze Age cremation in

[1] For the economic and social history of woodland see in particular Birrell 1987 and Rackham
1980.

South Wales. Similarly, in the second or third century AD, Solinus marvelled at the perpetual fire at the temple of Minerva in Bath which 'never whitens into ash but as the flame fades turns into rocky lumps'. Yet archaeological evidence from Roman Britain suggests that coal was no mere novelty, and that it was systematically dug and carted.[2] It was apparently used to provide heat for garrisons serving in a number of northern forts, on the Antonine Wall, Hadrian's Wall, and elsewhere, most of which were close to outcrops. On some of these sites, including Risingham and Housesteads, the quantities of coal found are such as to suggest regular usage. Elsewhere, grouped in three distinct clusters, excavations have revealed coal-burning on civil as well as military sites, urban as well as rural, and domestic as well as industrial. One cluster of coal-burning sites occurs in the north-west around Flint and Chester, and a larger cluster is located in the south-west, around the Bristol Channel and extending south-eastwards as far as Silbury Hill. Much of the coal was doubtless used for domestic heating, but there are also a large number of instances where it was used by smiths to work iron. Not all of the identifications are equally convincing, none the less it is evident that most of these sites could have been relatively easily supplied from nearby outcrops.

The use of cheap locally obtained coal is readily understandable, and it is clear that Romano-British smiths fully appreciated the superiority of mineral coal over charcoal for working iron, yet the final cluster of coal-burning sites is not at all easy to explain. For it is centred in East Anglia, with sites mostly located between Cambridge and the Wash, over 200 miles by sea or forty to seventy-five miles by land from the nearest coal. However, water communications with many of the sites were good, if the Car Dyke was as efficient as archaeologists believe it to have been, and it has been suggested that coal was brought to the Fens by barges from coalmining regions seeking grain and pottery. This may well have been the case, but the further suggestion that coal was commonly used in East Anglia for the drying of unripe grain is unconvincing; it is far more likely that coal made its long journey to be used on the forge.

Compared with these Roman enigmas, and with the spectacular developments of the later sixteenth and seventeenth centuries, the history of the medieval coal industry is largely prosaic. With the final departure of the Romans early in the fourth century evidence of most forms of economic and social activity ceases, and coalmining is no

[2] Webster 1955; J. Liversedge, *Britain in the Roman Empire* (1968), 200–1.

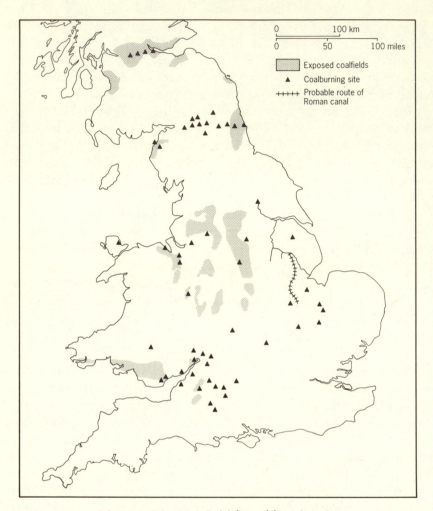

Map 2.1. Romano–British coal-burning sites

exception. It is more than likely that all commercial production or long-distance trade in coal ceased, and that it did not revive for centuries. There is no mention of coal in Domesday Book and no reason to believe that its consumption was other than negligible before the thirteenth century. Yet the long era from the eighth or ninth centuries to the opening of the fourteenth was one of massive expansion, and in its latter stages it brought increasing pressure on resources. Population between the Norman Conquest and 1300 rose steeply, perhaps threefold, thereby stimulating the colonization and settlement of vast tracts of hitherto uncultivated land. As settlement advanced so hundreds of thousands of acres of forest, woodland, moorland, heath, and marshland were converted into arable and pasture, and as a consequence supplies of fuel eventually contracted.[3]

England, by later Saxon times, was by no means a well-wooded country, and even if the 15 per cent of the country recorded as woodland in Domesday Book is an underestimate, succeeding centuries witnessed a dramatic contraction to around 10 per cent by the Black Death of 1348–9.[4] Almost everywhere the frontiers of agriculture advanced in the quest for subsistence to feed the mounting population. Woodland was the most important source of new farmland, and in many parts of the country it was destroyed on a prodigious scale, largely by the piecemeal nibbling of tens of thousands of land-hungry peasants. In the short term the destruction of woodland could actually increase the supplies of fuel and timber, as trees were felled for clearance, but in the longer term the base of supply was inexorably narrowed. Trees cut down for firewood regrow, but trees grubbed up to make way for grain and livestock permanently diminished the availability of fuel. Under the advance of colonization and the quest for food to nourish the rising population, the days of abundant fuel inexorably drew to a close. By the mid-thirteenth century clear signs were beginning to emerge of a growing awareness of the need to conserve woodlands, and some parts of the country began to experience wood and timber shortages. Nor were such signs confined to the hinterlands of thriving towns or to regions of dense settlement. For example, in 1250 the monks of Kelso were permitted to take timber for building repairs from the woods of Richard of Lincoln only on condition that they subsequently allowed those woods twenty to thirty years to recover, and when the abbey wanted to cut wood to make shelters for their sheep, Richard insisted that they did so only under view of his servants who would ensure that no unnecessary waste would be caused.[5]

Even in Staffordshire, which was far more heavily wooded than most regions, concern over the management and conservation of woodland manifested itself. Ancient customary rights to take wood became the object of strict definition, covering the amounts of wood by size, type, and quantity that were reasonable for the tenants of each size of landholding to take. As rights to take wood were curtailed, so prosecutions

[3] Miller and Hatcher 1978, 27–49.
[4] Rackham 1980, 111–21.
[5] J. M. Gilbert, *Hunting and Hunting Reserves in Medieval Scotland* (Edinburgh, 1979), 236.

for the 'theft' of wood multiplied, and as the assarting of woodland proceeded apace so disputes over woodland proliferated, between communities as well as between lords and tenants. Inevitably, in less well-endowed counties, pressure upon essential fuel resources was even greater. At Hecham (Suffolk) tenants were allowed only three small bundles of firewood at Christmas, and at Gransden (Cambs.) those holding a virgate of land were permitted two bundles for fencing, but smallholders and cottagers only one.[6]

Inevitably, the greatest impact on woodland resources occurred in areas with good water communications, or close to centres of population. The influence of the rising demand for wood, especially for fuel, on the forests of Kent has recently been traced in detail.[7] In the later eleventh century most Kentish woodlands had exiguous value, and were sized in Domesday Book according to the numbers of pigs they could support with their pannage. Two centuries later the values of woodland in the north of the county, accessible to London, and in the south of the county, accessible to the sea, had been transformed. Such was the voracious appetite for kindling in London, that the rental of well-managed coppiced woodlands in Eltham and Bexley rivalled that of decent arable land, while the demands of consumers in southern England and across the Channel, produced annual returns on coppice at Rainden near Folkestone as high as $9\frac{1}{2}d.$ an acre. In the southern Weald, especially where the Rother provided cheap access to the sea, coppicing triumphed over cattle pasture. However, further inland at Wye the abundant woodland continued to be used for rough pasture, with difficult transport ensuring that the ready supply of fuel provided merely a local benefit. But not all inland woodlands stagnated; at Chartham, close to Canterbury, entry fines for woodland were already as high as those for arable land by the early thirteenth century, and eventually matched those paid for meadow. Here, the point had been reached where the rising demand for fuel, even in an age of acute food scarcity, was sufficient to ensure the preservation of well-located woodland. By contrast in the central Wealden fastness, isolated from consumers, the greatest destruction of woodlands occurred.

It is important not to underestimate the contribution which peat turves made to meeting fuel needs in many parts of Britain in the Middle Ages, as well as through the early modern centuries. Huge quantities were dug, for example, from the great turbaries of Lancashire, York-

---

[6] Birrell 1987, nn. 30–1.

[7] K. P. Whitney, 'The Woodland Economy of Kent, 1066–1348', *AgHR* 38, (1990).

shire, Cumberland, Devon, and Cornwall, and the marshlands and fenlands of East Anglia. Inclesmoor, in the West Riding, lay conveniently close to navigable rivers and was a major source of fuel for its region, just as the Norfolk Broads were for theirs. But turves have an extremely low calorific value in relation to their weight, and were exceptionally expensive to transport overland. Once again location was all.[8]

Although the reserves of conventional fuel were contracting almost everywhere, and demand was rising almost universally, it would be wrong to see a national crisis occurring in the early fourteenth century. Yet there were regions which were beginning to experience severe difficulties in satisfying their mounting needs for both food and fuel from their hinterlands. The severity of local shortages, especially in London and other large towns, was recognized and exports of firewood were prohibited.[9] A sustained rise in the prices of arable and pasture and of agricultural products had been underway since the late twelfth century, and inevitably there came a time when the prices of wood and woodland were forced up. A multitude of references to growing scarcity and rising fuel prices exists, but reliable price series are hard to construct. However, Oliver Rackham's index of the price of standing underwood in eastern England, which manages to overcome many of the problems, indicates that a rise from 3d. to 6d. per acre for each year of growth occurred between 1250 and 1270, while frequent observations of purchases in Surrey suggest an increase in price there for cut firewood of more than 50 per cent between the 1280s and the 1330s.[10]

Such circumstances were propitious for an advance in the use of coal. For seven centuries after the departure of the Romans there is scarcely a mention of coal, yet by the opening decades of the fourteenth century mining was taking place on every British coalfield excepting perhaps Cumberland, and by the close of the Middle Ages pits abounded on all coalfields.[11] Mentions of mines in surviving documents are inevitably a poor guide to the scale and chronology of activity, for they depend upon chance survival. But first mentions do enable us to be confident about

---

[8] M. W. Beresford, 'Inclesmoor, West Riding of Yorkshire', in R. A. Shelton and P. D. A. Harvey (eds.), *Local Maps and Plans from Medieval England* (Oxford, 1986); J. Hatcher, *Rural Economy and Society in the Duchy of Cornwall, 1300-1500* (Cambridge, 1970), 186–8; C. Gill (ed.), *Dartmoor: A New Study* (Newton Abbot, 1970), 129–31; M. Bailey, *A Marginal Economy? East Breckland in the Later Middle Ages* (Cambridge, 1989), 163–4.

[9] Brimblecombe 1987, 17.

[10] Rackham 1980, 133–6, 167. Surrey firewood prices calculated from data in Rogers 1866–1902, ii. 393–7. [11] See Maps 5.1–5.10, Ch. 5.

the latest date that coalmining began and the absolute minimum number of mines that were opened up. A significant growth of production after the mid-thirteenth century is indisputable, albeit taking place from an extremely low base. At the same time it is evident that the vast majority of medieval mines ranged only from the intermittent scratchings of peasant farmers a few feet underground for a couple of hundredweight of coal for their cottage fires, to modest partnerships or undertakings employing at most a handful of labourers. We can also be certain that the bulk of their output was destined for consumption in the immediate vicinity.

Commercial mining and a trade in coal did exist, however, and from at least as early as the first half of the thirteenth century many of the uses to which coal was to be put in later centuries were already in evidence. In the reign of Elizabeth when coal was becoming the accustomed fuel of much of the realm, it was often remarked upon that in former times it had only been used by smiths and for the burning of lime. There is much truth in this belief, for it had long been appreciated that coal was the best fuel for working iron and burning lime, and this led to its widespread dissemination to consumers remote from collieries. Of the two specialist uses, lime-burning almost certainly consumed the largest amounts of coal, while the smaller quantities used in high-value smithing may well have led to a wider dissemination. Large-scale building works, where lime was used primarily for mortar and for plaster, provide us with many of the most spectacular examples of medieval coal consumption. Where building was not on a grand scale lime might be purchased from local burners, who might use wood to fire their kilns, but in great building projects both the desire for quality and the appetite for fuel often necessitated the transportation of coal to the site. The prodigious quantities of coal burnt during the building of Beaumaris, Conway, and Caernavon castles in the 1290s, for example, sent the output of a number of Flintshire collieries soaring to levels which may not have been surpassed until the later sixteenth century. In the spring and summer of 1295 Beaumaris castle alone consumed around 2,500 tons.[12] In these instances coal was close at hand, being ferried along with building stone from Bagilt and Whelston, but distance and cost rarely proved insurmountable obstacles for royal building sites, where in the course of the thirteenth century coal ousted oak brushwood as the fuel for on-site kilns.[13]

[12] H. M. Colvin (ed.), *The History of the King's Works, i. The Middle Ages* (1963), 349, 399.
[13] L. F. Salzman, *Building in England down to 1540* (Oxford, 1952), 149–50.

Although it resulted in a better end product, coal was far from essential for the production of lime, and for those of lesser means cheap local wood of necessity continued to be favoured over expensive coal. It was likewise with the working of iron. Coal burnt slowly and at relatively low temperatures, and the varieties which caked were ideal for the forge, where it was subjected to constant watering and blowing. Coal was therefore the favourite fuel for smiths wherever supplies were not excessively expensive or difficult to obtain, or whenever quality prevailed over cost. A surviving account book reveals that the forge serving the farm and community at Beaulieu Abbey burnt more coal than charcoal in 1269–70, although it cost 8*d.* per quarter compared to 3*d.* per quarter for charcoal. The Crown could also afford to be relatively unconcerned with expense, and coal was very frequently used in royal iron-founding, as at Dundee in the making of siege engines and at the Tower in the manufacture of guns. Coal was also purchased for use in the forges making and repairing ironware for use in the royal silver mines at Bere Ferris in distant Devon in 1480. It was also often one of the fuels used in casting bronze and bells.[14] The overwhelming majority of smiths, however, worked on a small scale, making and repairing everyday ironware for local customers who possessed limited purchasing power, and very few were able to use coal regularly, and most used it not at all. Archaeological excavations of medieval sites have found coal in association with ironworking close to the sea in Sussex, as well as at Coulsdon (Surrey), where it was used in addition to charcoal, but to judge from the rarity with which coal features in documentary records of purchases for manorial smithies, it is safe to conclude that even landlords normally found it too expensive. At Weston (Herts.), where small quantities of coal were regularly purchased in the 1290s for the repair of seigneurial ploughs, it cost 1*s.* 4*d.* a quarter, while charcoal made from wood collected from the lord's woodlands was a mere 1½*d.* a quarter.[15]

While lime-burning sometimes resulted in the shipment of sizeable quantities of coal direct to building sites, it was the modest needs of smiths which largely accounted for the distribution of tiny parcels of coal around the coasts of Britain and, more surprisingly still, into some inland locations. In addition to an export trade from many coastal

[14] S. F. Hockey (ed.) *The Account-Book of Beaulieu Abbey*, Camden Society, 4th Ser. 16 (1975), 265; Blake 1967, 4–5; Lewis 1965 edn., 196.

[15] *Medieval Archaeology*, 6–7 (1962–3), 339; 11 (1968), 218; 17 (1973), 187. I am extremely grateful to David Farmer for information on the frequency of coal purchases in manorial accounts.

coalfields, it is possible to trace a tiny re-export trade from ports remote from the source of coal. Thus, when the survival of records permits, we find the odd few tons of coal appearing with frequency in the major southern sea ports from the first years of the fourteenth century. Coal is among the commodities featuring in Southampton's customs records when they begin in the 1300s, and it was despatched thence in small consignments overseas, coastwise and inland. In the Southampton Brokage Books, which survive from the fifteenth century, we can trace consignments of a hundredweight or two being carted inland to nearby towns, such as Romsey, Twyford, Hursley, Nursling, Stoneham, Michelmersh, and Winton, sometimes in conjunction with iron.[16] While Southampton's coal came from Northumberland, Bristol's probably came from South Wales. The first certain mention of coal in this west country port dates from 1347, and later in the century it was sent overseas to Harfleur and La Rochelle. Yet these trades were notable for their existence rather than their scale; the quantities involved were almost invariably minuscule. Southampton's inland trade in the mid-fifteenth century, for example, usually totalled less than 10 tons, and coastal shipments might struggle to exceed 100 tons. Exports were little if any more substantial; some 60–70 tons were exported from Southampton in 1308–9, just £2 worth from Winchelsea in 1323–4, and 37 weys, worth £7. 8s., from Bristol in 1479–80. In the far west a thorough investigation of the customs records of Exeter has revealed a regular but tiny trade in the later fourteenth century.[17]

Consumption was of course far more substantial in the vicinity of coalfields, especially in the north-east, but London was also precocious in its use of coal. If recent estimates which place its population in the early fourteenth century as high as 75,000 to 100,000 are correct, it is easy to appreciate why.[18] Among the very earliest of mentions of coal in the capital are the duty of one farthing which was payable on every two quarters of coal unloaded at Billingsgate in Henry III's reign (1216–72),

---

[16] C. Platt, *Medieval Southampton: The Port and Trading Community, A. D. 1000-1600* (1973), 83, 159–60; P. Studer (ed.), *The Port Books of Southampton, 1427-30*, Southampton Record Society (1913); B. D. M. Bunyard (ed.), *The Brokage Book of Southampton, 1439-40*, Southampton Record Society (1941); H. S. Cobb (ed.), *The Local Port Book of Southampton, 1439-40*; Southampton Record Series (1961); B. Foster (ed.), *The Local Port Book of Southampton, 1435-6*, Southampton Record Series (1963); O. Coleman (ed.), *The Brokage Book of Southampton, 1443-4*, Southampton Record Series 2 vol., (1960–1).

[17] N. D. Harding (ed.), *Bristol Charters 1153-1373*, Bristol Record Society (1930), 103 (p. 113); E. M. Carus-Wilson, *The Overseas Trade of Bristol in the Later Middle Ages* (1967 edn.), 222, 237, 247, 286. Information on Exeter kindly supplied by Professor Maryanne Kowaleski.

[18] D. J. Keene, *Cheapside before the Great Fire* (1985), 19–20.

the name 'Sacoles Lane' given to a street near Ludgate Circus sometime before 1228, and the death of Robert le Portour, who was drowned in 1236 while unloading coal from a vessel in the Thames.[19] By the late thirteenth century the quantity of coal arriving in the city warranted the appointment of an official measurer, called a coal meter, and by 1330 London coal meters were numerous and significant enough to have formed themselves into a fraternity.[20] But perhaps of even more note was the concern displayed in the city over pollution caused by coal smoke, particularly from the kilns of lime-burners. In 1283 the first of a long series of complaints was made against coal on environmental grounds. In 1288 a commission was instituted to investigate the protests made by the citizens of Southwark against lime-burners whom, they alleged, had formerly burnt their lime by logs but now use sea coal 'so the air is infected and corrupted'. Ten years later men were refusing to work at night because of the pollution caused by coal fires, and in 1307 the 'prelates and magnates of the realm' joined with the Commons to complain that kilns in Southwark, Wapping, and East Smithfield, which had previously used brushwood and charcoal, now used coal with the result that 'an intolerable smell diffuses itself throughout the neighbouring places and the air is greatly infected to the annoyance of the magnates, citizens and others there dwelling and to the injury of their bodily health'. Though lime-buring was the major source of pollution, other complaints drew attention to the harmful activities of smiths, and to brewers and dyers who were also progressively turning from wood to coal for heating their vats.[21]

Despite being over 300 miles from the collieries of north-east England, London was favoured with direct water communications, and in the course of the thirteenth and fourteenth centuries references proliferate to merchants and shipowners making plans and securing licences for the shipment of coal to the capital and other east coast ports, and to the successful accomplishment of voyages. The trade became sufficiently large to attract the avaricious attention of the Crown, and duties were imposed upon coal shipments and complementary legislation was passed to monitor weights and measures and minimize evasion.[22] Middlesbrough, Scarborough, Hull, Grimsby, Yarmouth, King's Lynn, and many other smaller ports received supplies of coal for

[19] Galloway 1898, i. 29–30; Brimblecombe 1987, 7.
[20] Dale n.d., 1; Dale 1912, 11.
[21] *CPR 1281–92*, 29, 296; *CCR 1302–7*, 537, 549; Galloway 1898, i. 30; Brimblecombe 1987, 9–12.
[22] For surveys of the later medieval east coast coal trade see Blake 1967 and Fraser 1962.

their inhabitants and for re-export and, as we have seen, the channels of supply did not stop at London but continued round to the south coast.[23] Nevertheless, in spite of these signs of activity, we would be unwise to antedate the beginning of a routinely organized large-scale coal trade from the north-east. Certainly coal was despatched from the Tyne with frequency, but before the sixteenth century the organization of the trade was immature and its pattern somewhat haphazard, and the quantities which trickled around the coast were normally very small.

In sum, coal could normally be bought in many parts of the country remote from coalfields, but only in tiny parcels and at high prices. Large-scale consumers, even those close to London, were often obliged to make their own arrangements for purchase and delivery, as in 1298 when the bishop of London sent a ship to Northumberland to obtain coal for his building works at Gravesend, and in 1364 when the sheriff of Northumberland was ordered by the king to buy coal for the reconstruction of Windsor Castle and arrange its shipment from Winlaton.[24]

There was a significant export trade in the later Middle Ages from Newcastle to the ports of Flanders, Holland, Zeeland, France, and the Baltic, where coal served to dry madder and smoke and dry fish, as well as to burn lime and work iron. The fortunate survival of a series of customs accounts reveals annual exports averaging around 7,000 tons between 1377 and 1393. Though these exports were tiny in comparison with exports of wool, cloth, and metals, it is worth noting that they constituted a far more substantial part of the total coal trade of the time than exports were ever to constitute thereafter. It is also worthy of note that there was a significant trade with Scotland. The needs of the Scots also drove them to seek a ransom of 1,000 chaldrons of coal for Peter Bard, who had been captured while on royal service.[25]

Paradoxically, because coal was subjected to duties when it was transported by sea, evidence of coal consumption in the vicinity of coalfields is often harder to obtain than evidence of consumption farther afield. At Nottingham, which was well placed for coal with productive mines close to the city at Wollaton Park and at Cossall, the first mention arises from the discomfort of Queen Eleanor, who in 1257 found the coal smoke at the castle so offensive that she cut short her stay, left the king, and adjourned to Tutbury.[26] It is possible that lime-burners supplying

---

[23] Blake 1967, 9–11; D. M. Owen (ed.), *The Making of King's Lynn* (1984), 15, 127, 342–9, 365, 441, 454–5; E. Gillett, *A History of Grimsby* (Oxford, 1970), 37.

[24] *CPR 1292–1301*, 337; Taylor 1858, 208–9.   [25] Blake 1967, 12–21.

[26] H. R. Luard (ed.), *Annales Monastici*, Rolls Series (5 vols., 1864–9), iii. 203.

builders on the site were to blame, but coal was certainly widely used in the city by the later fourteenth century, for in 1395 no less than nineteen persons were presented before the borough court as 'common fore-stallers and gatherers of coal'.[27] Nottingham was also well served with wood from Sherwood Forest, and it was in the north-east of England, where an abundance of coal was combined with a scarcity of trees, that conditions most favoured high levels of consumption. From the earliest records, dating from the thirteenth century, widespread evidence is encountered of the use of coal in Northumberland and Durham for heating and cooking, as well as for lime-burning and smithing, and with the contraction of the forests and woods of Alnwick, Heworth, Bywell, Chopwell, and elsewhere adjacent coal-pits were inevitably utilized. Away from the coalfields it was exceedingly rare for coal to be used for domestic heating, but the monks of Durham priory, who owned collieries almost on their doorstep, burnt 162 chaldrons (c.200 tons) of coal in 1306-7 in addition to 420 cart-loads of kindling, 55,000 logs, and 613 cart-loads of peat. Before mid-century, Durham priory's coal consumption had risen to around 300 tons annually. The monks at the monastery of Jarrow installed two iron grates or chimneys in their hall to enable them to burn coal more efficiently, and some 50 tons of coal a year sufficed for the needs of their modest household.[28]

It was of course the cheapness of coal which lay behind its popularity in the north-east. At Durham the bursar usually paid less than 1s. 3d. for each chaldron, weighing in excess of a ton, delivered to the priory; while Jarrow priory paid less than 1s. a chaldron in the 1340s.[29] At these prices coal could be put to a wide range of uses. It was burnt in the brewhouse, bakehouse, and lime-kilns of Lindisfarne priory, as well as in the prior's chamber, the hall, the kitchen, and the infirmary.[30] At Berwick castle in the winter of 1302-3 coal fires were kept burning to keep the wine in the cellars from freezing, and at Newcastle in 1327-8 they were used to protect victuals stored for a forthcoming campaign in Scotland.[31] As in Roman times, it is the compactness of coal which gave it an advantage over wood in storage, which may explain its presence in many castles and garrisons remote from collieries.

[27] Stevenson and Baker (eds.), Records of the Borough of Nottingham, i. 273.
[28] Frazer 1962, 211; Raine (ed.), Jarrow and Monk-Wearmouth, 8, 28, 29.
[29] There are problems concerned with inconsistent recording of carriage costs and misuse of the long hundred in the price series constructed in the LSE Beveridge Collection (boxes C1, C5, C8) and the original manuscripts in the Prior's Kitchen, Durham, have been consulted instead.
[30] Simpson 1909-10, 580.
[31] Ibid. 582; Blake 1967, 8.

In the course of the thirteenth and early fourteenth centuries, there-fore, coal had emerged from obscurity, and in favoured parts of the the north-east it was close to becoming an habitual fuel. But progress there-after was no longer favoured by an expanding demand for fuel. For the long era of rising population was first halted and then decisively reversed in the course of the fourteenth and fifteenth centuries. The numbers of people in Britain probably fell by at least a half between the pre-Black Death peak and the late fifteenth- or early sixteenth-century trough, amounting in all to a contraction of perhaps in excess of three million persons.[32] Fewer people meant a lower consumption of fuel and also increased supply. Though agricultural retrenchment did not set in immediately after the arrival of plague in 1348, shrinking population eventually created an age of relative land abundance, in which settlement contracted, much arable was turned over to pasture, and much pasture retreated into rough grazing or waste. In such condi-tions there was a recovery in the extent of natural woodland, and in the numbers of non-woodland trees. The exportation of firewood was once again permitted, and much circumstantial evidence points to the easing of access for villagers to cheap or free local supplies of fuel.[33] A general sufficiency of fuel is also strongly indicated by price evidence. The best available charcoal index, from Oxford, shows the price falling gently from 10–11d. a quarter at the close of the fourteenth century to 8–9d. over most of the period from the 1400s to the 1540s, while the price of a year's growth of underwood in west Cambridgeshire fell persistently from well over 1s. per acre before 1380 to less than 6d. after 1450.[34] Such individual price movements accord well with both the index of timber prices compiled by Bowden and the general fuel price index compiled by Phelps Brown and Hopkins.[35]

The sources are simply too poor to support a detailed or confident survey of the fortunes of the coal industry in the later Middle Ages. Random notices of mining activity abound, but rarely are there any data capable of underpinning estimates of trend or scale. What evidence we have is best considered in a local context, and this has been attempted in Chapter 5. Prevailing conditions of general economic contraction and fuel sufficiency were undoubtedly unfavourable for the rapid progress of coal, and, if coal output followed the patterns of the rest of the

---

[32] J. Hatcher, *Plague, Population and the English Economy, 1348-1530* (1977).
[33] Brimblecombe 1987, 17.
[34] Rogers 1866–1902, ii. 397; iii. 255–72; Rackham 1980, 167.
[35] *AHEW* iv, 846–50; Phelps Brown and Hopkins 1981, 45–9.

economy, after enjoying a resurgence in the later fourteenth century it would have declined through much of the fifteenth. In the north-east there is certainly evidence of vitality in the second half of the fourteenth century. By an extraordinary lease granted by the bishop of Durham in 1356, just seven years after the Black Death, the collieries of Whickham and Gateshead commanded a rent of £333. 6s. 8d. a year. The terms of the lease permitted an output of 30,000 to 35,000 tons, which was almost certainly wildly optimistic, but the rent alone was equivalent to almost 10,000 tons of coal at prevailing pithead prices.[36] Although output even at this latter level from individual collieries was almost certainly unsustainable, as the sharply reduced rents subsequently fetched by Whickham and Gateshead confirm, fortuitous notices of deals made by Newcastle and London merchants comprising thousands of tons are suggestive of the persistence of a significant trade, as are the exports already noted.[37] Substantially all of the coal traded around the coasts of Britain and exported in the later Middle Ages came from Tyneside. In the later fourteenth century such shipments probably exceeded 20,000 tons annually. When account is taken of coal burnt locally, it is possible to envisage a total output of more than 50,000 tons in the north-east each year. In terms of the value of many other branches of trade at the time, and by the standards of the coal trade of later Tudor and Stuart times, this is a tiny amount indeed, but in comparison with the outputs of other medieval British coalfields it was very large.

Even in an era of general economic contraction some favourably sited and easily worked collieries could thrive. Although in the north-east there are some signs in the fifteenth century of recession, of falling rents, and abandoned mines, and from time to time of entrepreneurs displaying a reluctance to venture into coalmining which drove both the bishopric and the priory of Durham into direct management, some collieries continued to flourish.[38] In the mid-fifteenth century Whickham, on the Tyne, was producing over 2,000 tons, as was Railey, a land-locked colliery in south Durham. In the 1500s Railey's output rose to over 100,000 corves, perhaps 8,000 tons.[39] Though collieries of this scale were more numerous in the north-east a few significant collieries arose elsewhere. At the close of the fourteenth century in Glamorgan a colliery at Kilvey was yielding possibly 5–6,000 tons. Of more lasting

[36] *DUDP* Church Commission box 203, 244071.
[37] *DUDP* Church Commission, Receiver General's Accounts 189810, 190184; Blake 1967, 12.
[38] Lomas thesis 1973, 134–7.
[39] *DUDP* Church Commission box 79.

significance was the development of deep mining around Nottingham; by the close of the fifteenth century Wollaton colliery was producing around 5,000 tons annually. Very recent archaeological investigations have suggested that a colliery of equivalent size may have existed at Coleorton (Leics.).[40] Although such collieries were wholly exceptional, indeed they were large even by the standards of later centuries, their very existence does point to the security of the role enjoyed by coal in some parts of the country in an age of retrenchment, and of the existence of secure foundations for further expansion when conditions improved.

[40] Reported in the *Daily Telegraph* (21 Feb. 1991).

CHAPTER 3

From Abundance to Scarcity
Fuel Shortage and the Rise of Coal, 1550–1700

wood being grown to dearth and the severity of it felt more every day, causes many of the said coals to be used for fuel in London and in other places in this realm by those who in time past used nothing but wood for fuel

'A discourse touching the stapling of Newcastle coals' (1575)

The relative abundance of fuel which most parts of Britain enjoyed in the later fourteenth and fifteenth centuries was due to the collapse of demand, not to any permanent improvement in supply. In earlier times, when numbers had pressed upon the ceiling of resources, sufficiency had been threatened by scarcity, and history was to repeat itself, with redoubled impact, during the next long demographic upswing which began in the early sixteenth century. The latest and most scientific estimate points to a virtual doubling of English population between the 1530s and the 1650s, from around 2.75 million to approximately 5.25 million, and we may be justified in assuming comparable rates of increase in the substantially smaller populations of Scotland and Wales.[1] Britain once again experienced a massive expansion of the area under crops and animals, and with it the destruction of hundreds of thousands of acres of woodland. As before there was a build-up of pressure upon resources, and this was greatest upon the products of the land: food-stuffs above all, but also a wide range of raw materials such as wool, flax, hemp, dyestuffs, and leather, and of course wood and other surface fuels. As a result the prices of these commodities soared. The demand for wood was, of course, not restricted to those who burnt it. Wood was perhaps the most widely used raw material in the pre-industrial world, and a late seventeenth-century estimate would see less than half by value of all the wood that was cut going into fires, with the greater part going into the building of houses and ships, and the making of furniture, carts, mills and machines, tools, tableware, and other household items.[2] The

---

[1] Wrigley and Schofield 1981.
[2] King, *Natural and Political Observations* (1804 edn.), 53.

inevitable consequence of a strong rise in the demand for wood in excess of any increase in production, was scarcity and inflation. The great inflation in food prices is a commonplace of early modern history, but the scarcity of wood and the inflation of its price is both less well documented and less well understood.

It used to be believed that Britain experienced a wood and timber famine in these centuries.[3] But much scorn has been heaped upon such a notion by a succession of historians, and we are now invited instead to see 'the much vaunted fuel shortage as a strictly local and limited phenomenon' and the 'timber famine and the high prices [as] largely an illusion'.[4] It is perhaps time to engage in a reassessment, but this does not mean that a case should be made for a simultaneous nation-wide famine. Whereas a national market in grain has a long pedigree, because of its high value relative to bulk and the virtual universality of production, market conditions for wood and timber, particularly when they were not served by water transport, varied widely over short distances. As a consequence the relationship between the extent of woodland resources on the one hand and the demands placed upon them on the other, was often an intensely local one. Both woodland and population were unevenly distributed throughout the country with, for obvious reasons, high densities of population tending to coincide with low densities of woodland. The notion of a universal wood and timber famine thus does not fit well with such circumstances. But this is far from denying that large areas of the country and large sectors of its population came to suffer from an acute scarcity of wood. The presence of expanses of unexploited and under-exploited woodland in remote regions, of which there were many in Tudor and Stuart England, is not in conflict with the existence of real scarcity elsewhere. A fuel crisis can be said to occur when demand in a particular location greatly exceeds supply, and it is none the less a crisis because there is ample wood growing in some other inaccessible locations. When the numbers of markets suffering from a shortage of firewood multiply, that crisis can be said to be extensive. That was the situation from the later sixteenth century onwards.

For a balanced contemporary judgement written in the 1570s, we

---

[3] Nef made much of a national wood crisis, and a scarcity of fuel was also made a major factor in the declining fortunes of the charcoal iron industry (Nef 1932, i. 156–64; T. S. Ashton, *Iron and Steel in the Industrial Revolution* (Manchester, 1924)).

[4] Hammersley 1957, 158; Rackham 1980, 153. See also Hammersley 1973; O. Rackham, *Trees and Woodland in the British Landscape* (1976), 92; Flinn 1958, 149–53; M. W. Flinn, 'Timber and the Advance of Technology: A Reconsideration', *Annals of Science*, 20 (1959); D. C. Coleman, *The Economy of England, 1450–1750* (Oxford 1977), 85–6.

have the views of William Harrison of Radwinter in Essex, who is well respected as an astute observer of his times. In his reflective description of the state of England he took occasion to comment at length on 'the great sales yearly made of wood, whereby an infinite quantity hath been destroyed within these few years'. He went on:

thus much I dare affirm, that if woods go so fast to decay in the next hundred years of grace, as they have done and are like to do in this . . . it is to be feared that the fennie bote, broom, turf, gale, heath, firze, brakes, whins, ling, dies, hassocks, flags, straw, sedge, reed, rush and also sea coal will be good merchandise even in the city of London, whereunto some of them even now have gotten ready passage, and taken up their inns in the greatest merchants' parlours.

Yet Harrison was careful not to overstate his fears, or to turn the threat of dearth into a universal problem, for he noted that 'there is a good store of great wood or timber here and there, even now in some places of England'.[5] On the other hand, it is pertinent that he was writing when the process of deforestation had most of its course still to run.

The motives of those who grubbed up woodland in an age of rising population and impending food scarcity are not hard to comprehend. Woodland, as a general rule, was generally incapable of competing successfully with arable or even pasture farming for the use of the land in early modern times. Whatever the longer term returns from well-managed woodland might have been, when a thriving and profitable market existed for foodstuffs, as it did through most of the sixteenth and seventeenth centuries, the temptation to take a windfall gain by felling all the trees, selling the resultant timber and firewood, and then converting the land to crops or animals, was often too great for many land-owners to resist. In this way much of the woodland was destroyed in the vicinity of towns, in just those locations where there was the heaviest demand for fuel. A substantial part of the woodland of early modern Britain owed its survival either to lax estate management or to its remoteness from the market. What is more, even when owners nurtured their woodland, price trends often made the growing of timber more profitable than firewood.[6]

It has become almost conventional to dismiss the fears of hosts of contemporaries who observed, from the peripheries of the country as

[5] Harrison, *Description of England*, 276, 280–1.
[6] Hammersley 1973, 608–9; Rackham 1980, 169–70.

well as from the centre, from Scotland and Wales, Cornwall and Staffordshire, from the forests of Trawden, Rossendale, and Pendle and the peaks of Derbyshire, as well as from the pavements of the major towns, the relentless contraction of woodland and the increasing scarcity and cost of wood.[7] Admittedly many of these commentators, after the fashion of the age, mixed hyperbole with objective comment, but the sheer volume, uniformity, and persistence of their fears command attention. However overwhelming this contemporary testimony is, it must of course be scrutinized for bias or simple lack of judgement, but it should not be rejected from a distance of more than 300 years without powerful cause. Nor was the fear of timber starvation restricted to pamphleteers and lobbyists. From early in the sixteenth century it found concrete expression in a stream of national and local legislation designed to improve the supply of fuel and preserve woodlands.[8]

As Harrison intimated, there was a multitude of distinct market areas for fuel. The largest potential market of all for coal was the towns and cities within reach of the east coast of England. In the early sixteenth century the east coast and its hinterland contained over half of the wealthiest and most populous towns in the realm and, of course, London itself. The eastern coastal regions seem never to have been generously wooded, and there can be little doubt of the growing insufficiency of wood supplies to these towns and cities from woodlands within easy reach. London was exceptionally well placed to be supplied by water, using barges on the Thames as well as coastal shipping, and in this way it gained relatively cheap access to distant extensive woodlands in the Thames valley and the Sussex and Kent Wealds, as well as to the trees of coastal Essex, east Kent, and Suffolk.[9] In addition firewood was carted overland from the woodlands of the suburbs and Home Counties. Yet London, whose population may have approached 100,000 by 1550, had a voracious appetite for fuel. Moreover, the woodlands which furnished the capital with firewood had also to supply her with timber. At Mettingham in north-east Suffolk it was claimed in 1562 that the woods 'are sold at high prices because the same may be conveyed to London by water'. Although close to the River Waveney, Mettingham is almost 120 miles from London.[10] Closer to London there are many signs

---

[7] Swain 1986, 162; *VCH Derbyshire*, ii. 353; see also below, pp. 50, 98.

[8] e.g. *Statutes of the Realm*, 35 Henry VIII, c. 17; 7 Edward VI, c. 7; 1 and 2 Philip and Mary, c. 5.

[9] Willan 1976, 19, 27, 33–7.

[10] Rackham 1980, 144.

of farmers and landowners responding to the inflation of food prices by switching from the production of wood to agriculture.[11]

The fuelling of a major city, like its victualling, was a matter of prime concern to inhabitants and city authorities alike. Fuel, like food, was a basic necessity and, in pursuit of the goal of abundant supplies at reasonable prices, the trade was subjected to considerable interference and regulation. The first mention of a company with rights to organize the trade, the mystery of Woodmongers, occurs in 1375, though it was undoubtedly founded long before this.[12] In 1379 the City acted to eliminate forestalling and unfair profiteering by prohibiting the purchase and storage of wood by wholesalers, and ordering instead that wood brought into London by water should not be bought for resale but sold direct to the public from the vessels. Attempts were also made to fix prices and to regulate the measures used for the sale of wood and charcoal. In 1445, for example, it was decreed that faggots should be sold at 4s. the hundred, or two for a penny, and charcoal for 10d. a quarter.[13] While such orders alone do not prove that there were difficulties in securing adequate supplies, that proof was increasingly forthcoming as the sixteenth century progressed. In 1542–3, when the *Grey Friar's Chronicle* noted 'a great dearth for wood and coals', the Lord Mayor visited the wood wharves daily and distributed such fuel as he was able to find to the poor at reasonable prices, although 'it caused the wood merchants loss'. It is perhaps not a coincidence that the will of Sir John Allen, a wealthy Londoner who died the next year, contained provision for 500 marks to establish a stock of sea coal for the poor. This London fuel crisis was swiftly followed by an Act for the Preservation of Woods, in which 'The King our Sovereign Lord perceiving and rightwell knowing the great decay of timber and wood universally within this his realm of England to be such, that unless speedy remedy in that behalf be provided there is great and manifest likelihood of scarcity and lack as well of timber for building making, repairing and maintaining houses and ships, as also for fuel and firewood'.[14] Henry VIII and Parliament were no doubt greatly influenced by the heightened problems of the capital, but the legislation was a long and careful measure which

[11] e.g. M. K. McIntosh, *Autonomy and Community: The Royal Manor of Havering, 1200–1500* (1986), 227, 230; P. D. Glennie, 'A Commercializing Agrarian Region: Late Medieval and Early Modern Hertfordshire' (Cambridge University Ph.D. thesis, 1983), 134.

[12] Dale n.d., 3.

[13] Riley 1868, 487, 560.

[14] Brimblecombe 1987, 26; John Stow, *A Survey of London*, ed. C. L. Kingsford (2 vols., Oxford, 1971), i. 112; *Statutes of the Realm*, 35 Henry VIII, c. 17, 18.

emphasized a general alarm with the increasing cost and declining availability of firewood and charcoal elsewhere in the kingdom.

Ten years later, in 1554, the Common Council of the City followed the precedent set by the Fishmongers' Company in 1446, by levying a tax on all citizens 'towards provision of sea coals from time to time to be provided and brought to this city to be kept in a stock for ever as well for the succour of the poor when need shall require as for all other inhabitants', and Parliament passed another act, which as well as attempting to eradicate practices whereby 'fuel coals [charcoal] and wood runneth many times through four or five several hands or more before it cometh to the hands of them that for their necessity do burn or retail the same', laid down in detail not only the requisite dimensions of sacks of charcoal, but the length and girth of every type of firewood. And in the following year Parliament passed an act to restrain the carrying of corn victual and wood over the sea, 'by reason whereof the said corn victual and wood are grown into a wonderful dearth and extreme prices'.[15]

Price indices for wood and charcoal provide a stark context for this anxiety with fuel, echoes of which abound in many of the cities and towns of the realm. Composite indices constructed from discontinuous observations in a variety of different locations and at different links in the chain of supply from the tree to the hearth, are of limited value for a commodity like firewood, although the most recent attempt at a national index does show fierce inflation from the 1550s.[16] Local indices based upon a single link in the chain, by contrast, have far greater validity but narrower application. Such an index, derived from sales of standing underwood in Norfolk, Suffolk, Essex, Cambridgeshire, Huntingdonshire, and east Hertfordshire, which has a direct bearing on London's fuel supplies, displays an almost vertical ascent from c.1540, during which time it soared far above the general rate of inflation, taking the average price of a year's growth per acre from around 8d. to around 4s. by the opening decades of the seventeenth century. When this index is broken into its constituent parts, we find that a year's growth of underwood in west Cambridgeshire, which cost between 3½d. and 4½d. per acre in the last quarter of the fifteenth century, leapt from 8d. to 2s. 6d. during the 1540s and fetched 5s. and even 10s. an acre by 1625. Meanwhile in west Suffolk the price of an acre rose progressively from 8d. c.1540, to 16d. c.1550, to 2s. 4d. c.1560, to 7–10s. c.1620. In these

---

[15] Nef 1932, i. 196–7; *Statutes of the Realm*, 7 Edward VI, c. 7; 1 and 2 Philip and Mary, c. 5.
[16] *AHEW* iv. 846–50.

lightly wooded regions in an inflationary era the price of standing wood thus rose at a truly phenomenal rate, many times faster than that of prices in general, or of any other major commodity.[17]

For the retail price of wood in London before the last quarter of the sixteenth century we have only occasional references, but thereafter the purchases made at Westminster comprise a virtually continuous series up to the Civil War. The inflation of the retail price of firewood was, of course, less rampant than that of standing wood, for only a small part of the retail price of firewood in most centres of consumption was accounted for by the cost of the wood on the trees. The bulk was made up of the cost of the labour of cutting and carting it, and of the margins charged by those who handled it on its journey between landowner and consumer. Labour costs in the sixteenth and early seventeenth century rose at substantially less than the general rate of inflation, but even so the Westminster series demonstrates the severity of the increases in the price of firewood in London, compared with commodity prices in general and with coal prices in particular. As the price competitiveness of coal progressively improved, so levels of consumption rose. When the Westminster College accounts begin in 1574 no coal whatsoever was being purchased, the fuel needs of the institution and its brewery were served by tallwood (long logs), bavins (brushwood/faggots), and charcoal. The brewery burnt tallwood only until 1585, when it was completely and permanently superseded by coal. The college itself began to consume coal irregularly the following year, and from 1604 scarcely a year passed without substantial purchases. Between the later 1580s and the late 1630s the consumption of coal by college and brewery rose to more than 50 chaldrons (c.75 tons) a year, while that of bavins plummeted from around 100 loads to 10–20 loads, and that of charcoal from 40 loads to 8 loads or less. This pattern of fuel purchases at Westminster is readily explained by price movements, for over the same half-century the price of a chaldron of coal delivered to Westminster rose from an average of 16.87s. per chaldron to 20.77s., an increase of less than a quarter, whereas the price of a load of bavins more than doubled and the price of a load of charcoal, by far the most expensive of all fuels, rose by almost 30 per cent.[18]

Relative price movements, however suggestive, do not provide conclusive proof that coal came to enjoy a substantial price advantage over wood and charcoal. For this we need to know the cost of each unit

[17] Based on data in Rackham 1980, 167.
[18] Based on data given in Beveridge 1939, 153–202.

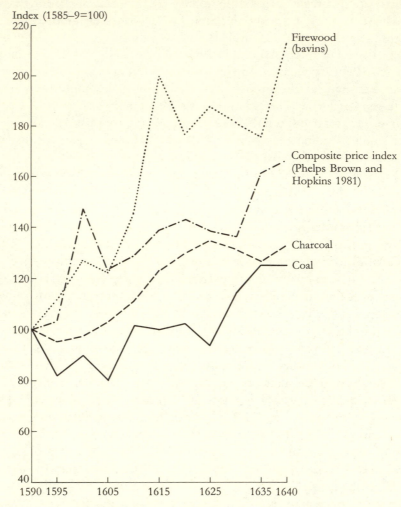

Fig. 3.1. The prices of fuels purchased by Westminster College, 1585–1640
Sources: Beveridge 1939, 193–4; Phelps Brown and Hopkins 1981, 28–30.

of heat which the respective fuels generated. Tim Nourse, who was an outspoken critic of the deleterious effects of coal-burning on London's environment, accepted in his essay upon fuelling the capital, published in 1700, that 'one chaldron of coal would yield more heat than three or four loads of wood'.[19] It is most unlikely that Nourse exaggerated the

[19] Nourse, *Campania Foelix*, 357–8, 360.

energy generated by coal, for he was attempting to demonstrate that it was both possible and preferable for London to meet its fuel needs with wood. Moreover, his ratio is broadly in line with modern scientific calculations which accord to coal at least twice the calorific value of dry wood, as well as with the likelihood that a load of wood weighed no more than a ton. Even if we take the lowest estimate of one chaldron of coal being equivalent to three loads of wood, then already by the beginning of coal purchases by Westminster College in 1585, the heat generated from burning bavins was more expensive than that from coal, and by the eve of the Civil War it was half as expensive again as coal. The heat generated by charcoal cost still more. A load of charcoal could not have weighed more than a ton, yet it was costing more than 21s. at Westminster at the close of the 1580s. The calorific value of coal and charcoal are very similar, yet a ton of coal in the late 1580s cost less than 13s. By the close of the 1630s charcoal was virtually twice as expensive as coal.

Coal had been used in London by industries for centuries, but increased consumption is indicated by the resurgence of concern over industrial air pollution in Elizabethan and Jacobean times, with brewers located in central London and Westminster taking over from lime-burners as the prime offenders.[20] Traditional coal-burning industries grew rapidly in this era and, as the relative price of wood rose inexorably, more and more industries turned over to coal whenever technology permitted. Without doubt, however, the most important transition of all was the progressive adoption of coal for domestic heating. Adam Smith remarked that 'coals are a less agreeable fuel than wood; they are said to be less wholesome. The expense of coals therefore, at the place where they are consumed, must generally be somewhat less than that of wood.'[21] Yet a simple price advantage, however great, was often not sufficient by itself to convert a consumer to the new fuel, since coal was ill-suited to traditional hearths and fireplaces designed for wood. Efficient coal-burning required the adaptation of hearths and flues, and the provision of functional chimneys. In their absence coal could certainly give off the 'horrible thick' smoke and 'virulent or arsenical vapours' that contemporaries so often complained of. Well might the President of the Council of the Marches of Wales plead with Queen Elizabeth to be allowed to cut wood in the royal Forest of Deerfold, since the supply of firewood was so diminished that they were

[20] Brimblecombe 1987, 40–2; *CSPD 1547–80*, 612.
[21] Adam Smith, *An Inquiry into the Nature and Causes of the Wealth of Nations* (2 vols., 1776), i, ch. 11.

'compelled to burn that noxious mineral pit-coal'.[22] The poor, however, could not afford to pander to such sensibilities, and had to put up with coughing and smarting to avoid freezing. Their ample ranks provided the first domestic consumers to become dependent on coal.

If a man were wealthy enough, even in London, he might long postpone the burning of coal in his own apartments. At first the London household of Lionel Cranfield, one of the capital's richest merchants, burnt only wood and charcoal, with just a little of the best Scotch 'pit-coal' purchased from time to time. But even here by 1621, small amounts of Newcastle sea coal began to creep into the kitchen. In 1637 the steward of the earl of Rutland laid in his master's London mansion the 'usual provision' of 30 tons of sea coal, 6 tons of Scotch coal, 26 loads of Kentish faggots, and 12,000 billets.[23] While the rich might deign to use only charcoal or wood in their own rooms, it was a needless extravagance not to use coal for cooking, or for heating the servants' quarters. Coal was also made more acceptable by changes in domestic architecture, by improvements in the fireplace and hearth, and by the provision and design of flues and chimneys, as well as by greater controls over the quality of coal. Well before the close of the sixteenth century William Harrison could write of 'the multitude of chimneys late erected' and of the trade in coals from the north which 'beginneth now to grow from the forge into the kitchen and hall, as may appear already in most cities and towns that lie about the coast, where they have but little other fuel'. In London, always setting the fashion, there were at least 200 chimney-sweeps in 1618.[24]

By the opening decades of the seventeenth century, therefore, coal had become the staple fuel of the capital, and even those who could afford not to burn it depended upon a plentiful flow to keep wood prices from escalating still higher. In the Civil War, when the Scots blockaded Newcastle and Sunderland and starved London of coal, a mischievous scribe mocked how, in happier times:

some fine nosed City dames used to tell their husbands: 'O Husband! We shall never be well, we nor our children, whilst we live in the smell of this city's sea-coal smoke; Pray a country house for our health, that we may get out of this stinking seacoal smell' [yet] how many of these fine nosed dames now cry, 'Would God we had Seacoal, O the want of fire undoes us! O the sweet Seacoal fire we used to have, how we want them now, no fire to your Seacoal!'.[25]

---

[22] Rees 1968, i. 67.   [23] Nef 1932, i. 198.

[24] Harrison, *Description of England*, 363–4; Nef 1932, i. 199.

[25] *Artificiall Fire, or Coale for Riche and Poore* (1624), quoted in Nef 1932, i. 198.

It is possible to put broad dimensions to the growing dependence of the capital on the coal of Tyneside and Wearside by using records of shipments to London, and these are presented in full below in Chapter 14(iii). Statistics of the early modern coal trade have been a source of contention for over fifty years, and any new protagonist must proceed with extreme caution. If the rate of increase is not to be understated there is great merit in seeking to establish a statistical baseline as early as possible in the sixteenth century in order to include the time when London's fuel-supply problems first became acute and the unremitting, irreversible shift from wood to coal began. But this is not an easy task. The earliest indications, and they are little more than that, must be derived from a few scattered and defective Newcastle port books. In one major respect these port books are unusually informative since they give the destinations of vessels as well as the cargoes which they carried, but sadly they do not cover full years. If full twelve-month periods are created by combining accounts, or by estimating the shortfall caused by the gaps they contain using the seasonal patterns contained in full accounts, it may be suggested that London received around 14,000 to 16,000 tons a year from the north-east in mid-century. The shipping data available subsequently are thankfully far more secure and point to imports of around 50,000 tons in the later 1580s, around 150,000 tons in the opening years of the seventeenth century, and as high as 300,000 tons on the eve of the Civil War. By the close of the century London was burning an average of 400,000 to 450,000 tons of north-eastern coal each year.

Although knowledge of the dimensions of London's surging population is far from precise, it is possible to probe more deeply into the scale and timing of the rise in per capita coal consumption in the capital by placing best estimates against the pattern of coal imports. London is thought to have had a population of 80,000 to 100,000 in the mid-sixteenth century, when coal imports probably averaged less than 20,000 tons. The result was a mere 0.2–0.25 tons per head. By the 1610s, when London's population is thought to have risen to more than 200,000, the per capita consumption would have been in the region of 0.75 tons per annum. The indications are that thereafter it increased more slowly, although total consumption continued to rise strongly as the population of the metropolis passed beyond 500,000 in the third quarter of the century, and 600,000 in the fourth quarter. Although consumption may have reached around one ton per head per annum in the best years of the final quarter, it intermittently stalled or fell in the war-blighted years at the close of the century under the combined impact of high prices and fitful supply.[26]

The failure of per capita consumption to rise higher than one ton should not be taken to indicate that at this level the fuel needs of Londoners were being fully met. Despite high wage rates in London a large proportion of the inhabitants had low disposable incomes, and coal was a relatively expensive commodity. There is reason to believe that only a minority could afford to keep themselves comfortably warmed, especially with the onset of the so-called 'little Ice Age' from the mid-sixteenth century. The succeeding 150 years experienced the coldest regime at any time since the last major Ice Age had ended 10,000 years before, and the incidence of extremely cold winters was abnormally high in the seventeenth century, especially in the latter half when the Thames froze over at least eleven times.[27] For the poor, coal had to compete for priority with food and clothing, and in those years when war or other interruptions cut the lines of supply with Tyneside and Wearside, effective demand was severely curtailed by spiralling prices. Overall, between the 1590s and 1700, a building craftsman in London had to work for at least seven to eight days to buy a ton of coal, and a labourer for ten to twelve days.[28] Although London building workers earned in excess of 50 per cent more than their fellows in, say, Newcastle or Derby, they had to pay four or five times as much for their coal.

Customs records further highlight the massive impact which London had on the north-eastern coal trade, and the increasing mutual dependency of the capital and the coalfield. In the mid-sixteenth century not much more than a fifth of all coal shipped from the north-east was destined for London; in the first half of the seventeenth century London's share reached 60 per cent, and by the close of the century it hovered between 70 and 80 per cent. The main reason for London's gargantuan share was that its population quadrupled between 1550 and 1700 while that of the country at large doubled. None the less, while exports were unimportant and showed little inclination to rise, sharply increasing quantities of Northumberland and Durham coal were also welcomed in a host of east coast and south coast ports. Well in excess of 200,000 tons a year by 1650 were being shipped to provincial ports, where it was burnt by

[26] Estimates of London's population are critically reviewed in V. Harding, 'The Population of London, 1550–1700: A Review of the Evidence', *London Journal*, 15 (1990). The figures quoted here relate to the total urbanized area, including suburbs.

[27] H. H. Lamb, *Climate, History and the Modern World* (1982), 201–2, 222–3.

[28] London wages from Beier and Finlay (eds.), *Making of the Metropolis*, 171.

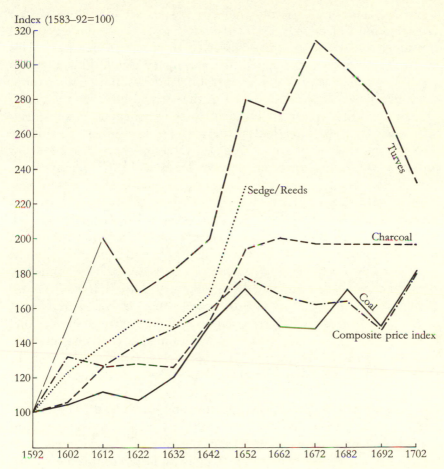

Fig. 3.2. Prices of fuels purchased by King's College and other colleges in
Cambridge, 1583–1702

Sources: Rogers 1866–1902, v. 404; KC Mundum Books; Phelps Brown and Hopkins 1981, 28–30.

the inhabitants and fed thence, via an efficient burgeoning network of
waterways, into the hearths of thousands of inland consumers.[29]

'Pitcoals commonly called seacoals, which grow near the sea or
navigable rivers, are the chiefest fuels for common fire to serve your
Highness' City of London, and all other cities and towns situate near the
sea in all parts of your realm', wrote an anonymous petitioner in the
later sixteenth century. He continued, 'all the country villages round

[29] See Ch. 13 below.

about the land within twenty miles of the sea are for the most part driven to burn of these coals for that the most part of the woods are consumed and those grounds converted to corn and pasture'.[30] This writer may well have overstated his case, for he was seeking a ban on exports, but the rise of coal in eastern England was indisputable, early, and cumulative. The need for coal in the virtually treeless regions of eastern England was scarcely less acute than in the capital itself.

William Harrison remarked in the 1580s, of Cambridge, that 'Only wood is the chief want to such as study there, whereof this kind of provision is brought them either from Essex and other places thereabouts, as is also their coal [charcoal] . . . and seacoal, whereof they have great plenty, led thither by the Grant [Granta or Cam]'.[31] Harrison's veracity is confirmed by the Mundum Books of King's College, which contain a virtually continuous record of that institution's fuel purchases. It was in 1580 that coal first became a significant and regular purchase at King's, and by this time wood had virtually ceased to be bought, the fuel needs of the college being largely met by sedge, *thacke* [reeds], turves, and charcoal. At first 25–30 chaldrons (c.40 tons) of coal were bought each year, at a cost which represented around a quarter of the total college fuel bill. Thereafter, as at Westminster, coal consumption increased rapidly at the expense of other fuels, until from the 1620s to the outbreak of the Civil War around 200 tons were burnt each year, accounting for approximately three-quarters of King's fuel bill. Once again the pattern of purchases is explained by price trends. The average cost of turves between 1583–92 and 1643–52 increased by 180 per cent, that of reeds or sedge by 130 per cent, but that of coal by 71 per cent, which was slightly below the rate of increase in prices in general. The inflation in charcoal prices was less than that of other non-fossil fuels, but it was already by far the most expensive, and the quantities purchased fell rapidly away. The pattern of fuel purchases at nearby Trinity College, though less fully documented, was very similar.[32]

Shipments from Northumberland and Durham have the potential to reveal the scale of consumption of coal in eastern England. It is to be regretted that attempts to measure them have aroused so much hostility and induced so much scepticism, for this branch of economic activity was not only of profound importance to the nation, it is one of the best documented. Much of the contention has centred on Nef's

---

[30] PRO SP 15/41/85.
[31] Harrison, *Description of England*, 67.
[32] KC Mundum Books; LSE Beveridge G2.

determination to take the mid-sixteenth century as the base for his calculation of rates of growth, despite the patent inadequacy of the data from this period that he could gather. As has already been mentioned in regard to London's imports, in order to reflect the true scale of increase, it is, of course, essential to gain a foothold at an early stage; yet Nef was able to muster only five isolated accounts prior to 1591–2 which recorded either total shipments from Newcastle, both overseas and coastal, or coastal shipments alone. In fact, his base was even less substantial than appeared at first sight, since three of the five accounts he used are seriously incomplete. Fortunately, it has proved possible to compile a new series of shipments based upon more than twice as many accounts as Nef was able to gather, and in particular we now have eleven complete years of total shipments prior to 1591–2. The recent discovery of a previously unknown clutch of Newcastle Borough Chamberlains' accounts provides total shipments for the years between 1508 and 1511, thereby extending knowledge back a full half-century. Moreover, we now have no less than eight complete years of total Newcastle shipments between 1564 and 1575, which constitute an excellent foundation upon which to build a quantitative assessment of the progress of the coal trade over the ensuing century and a half. Full statistical data, and details of the methodology applied to them are contained in Chapter 14 below.

It is hoped that the statistics of the Northumberland and Durham coastal and overseas coal trade which are now able to be presented will command greater respect than has been accorded to previous figures. From a base of around 45,000 tons annually between 1508 and 1511, shipments grew but slowly over the next half-century, and between 1564 and 1570 an annual average of a little over 60,000 tons was sent coastwise and overseas. But thereafter the rate of growth accelerated ferociously. By 1595–1600 over 220,000 tons were being shipped each year, and by 1655–60 over 500,000 tons. In peak years in the early 1680s the north-east may have shipped almost 800,000 tons. Thereafter, however, trade remained sluggish, and in the 1690s customs accounts record annual shipments of 600,000 to 650,000 tons. The rate of increase between the later 1560s and the 1690s was therefore in excess of tenfold, with a possible peak of thirteenfold in the early 1680s. Taking 1509–11 as the base produces rates of increase of over fifteenfold and nineteenfold respectively.

By any yardstick these are exceptional rates of growth for a major sector of a pre-industrial economy. Moreover, they are especially

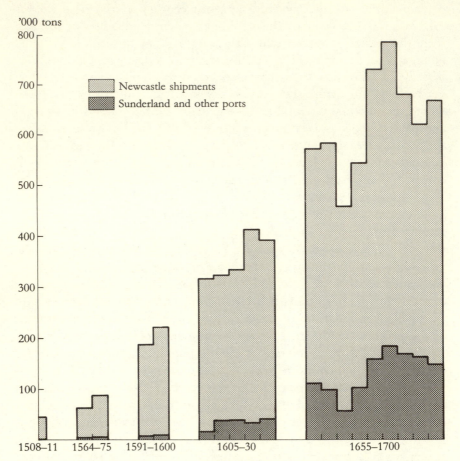

Fig. 3.3. Coal shipments from north-east England, 1508–1700 (in quinquennial averages)

significant because by the sixteenth century the north-eastern coal industry was already substantial, and the baselines therefore have meaning. When the achievement is viewed from the perspective of tons of output it is no less impressive. Taking the sea coal trade alone, and making no allowance for the undoubted growth of consumption within the north-east, the increase in shipments between the mid-sixteenth and the late seventeenth centuries translates into average annual increments of 5,000 to 6,000 tons. This was equivalent to the opening up of a good-sized colliery every single year.

When in 1612 the continuator of John Stow's *Annales* wrote that 'Sea coal and pit coal is become the general fuel of this Britain Island, used in the houses of the nobility, clergy and gentry, in London and in all other cities and shires of this kingdom, as well for dressing of meat, washing, brewing, dyeing, as otherwise', his perspective was undoubtedly coloured by the experience of his native city.[33] Although it is not impossible to find places where coal made as much impact as it did in the coastal towns and cities of eastern England, nowhere was there a market in any way comparable in size. Likewise the scale of the Tyneside industry was wholly exceptional, and it may have accounted for almost half of national output at the turn of the sixteenth and seventeenth centuries.

Yet as the regional surveys of Chapter 5 reveal, the rate of growth of output in Northumberland and Durham, though exceptional, was not unparalleled. Coastal and export trades from other coalfields also grew rapidly. Starting from a few thousand tons in the late sixteenth or early seventeenth centuries, shipments from the seasale coalfields of Wales, Scotland, and Cumberland matched the rate of increase of north-eastern shipments. The forces which stimulated the coal industry of the northeast were felt to some degree and at some time in all other British coalfields. None could hope to match the scale of its gains, but many achieved rates of expansion which were exceptional for any major industry or trade in the era. Indeed, a growth in national output of more than tenfold between 1550 and 1700 is a strong possibility.

Though variable in scale and pace the advance of coal-burning over these centuries was virtually nation-wide, long delayed in some places but precocious in others. As always progress depended primarily upon the relative scarcity and expense of alternative fuels, and pressure was most often felt first and most acutely in towns. While the demands of iron-smelting had a limited impact on the supplies of firewood for domestic hearths because it was primarily located in remote heavily forested areas, the demands of industries located close to towns or within their walls were of more significance for the advance of coal. Among such industries was glass-making, whose product was fragile and difficult to transport far overland, and whose furnaces used wood of a type suitable for domestic hearths.[34] Glasshouses were of necessity frequently located close to centres of population, or water transport. It was asserted by Leland that the Droitwich salt-boilers consumed 6,000 loads of wood each year, and were forced to repair far afield for their

---

[33] *Annales*, 210.   [34] See below Ch. 12(ii).

supplies,[35] and it is possible, since much of Worcester's firewood was shipped down the Severn from the Wyre forest, that these salters seriously exacerbated the fuel problems of that city. As early as 1496 complaints had been made of the 'greatly enlarged' price of wood and timber in Worcester, and thereafter we can discern very many indications of concern. City authorities passed a long series of laws which attempted to alleviate fuel shortages by forcing barge-owners coming down the Severn to unload their wood in Worcester rather than sailing on down to Gloucester and Tewkesbury, by restricting the activities of wholesalers and profiteers, by freezing prices in times of acute scarcity, by limiting the consumption of wood by bakers, brewers, and tile-makers, and by preventing a rising tide of thefts of wood not only from hedgerows and trees, but from 'bridges, stiles, gates'. On a more positive note, the city authorities purchased wood for distribution to the poor in the great scarcities of 1565 and 1574, and set about providing a supply of coal from the city's own mines.[36]

In many respects Worcester provides an exemplar of the experiences of the generality of British towns and cities as wood and other traditional forms of fuel became ever more expensive and difficult to obtain. Towns almost everywhere struggled against the odds to keep fuel supplies plentiful and prices low. Where some chance of success existed, and in some instances even where it did not, towns searched for coal, and when it was found they mined it. Among those towns which searched were Newcastle, Edinburgh, Nottingham, Shrewsbury, Liverpool, and Coventry.[37] Although these towns were all conveniently sited on or near coalfields, such was the cost of transport that a pit a mile or more nearer to the walls was likely to prove of great benefit. Deprivation during wartime even drove Londoners to prospect for coal in Windsor forest. When Richard Gardner, a Shrewsbury dyer, found a great store of coals hard by his town he was deemed by the grateful citizens to be 'not only worthy of commendation and maintenance, but also to be had in remembrance for ever'.[38] Similar motives led town after town to establish subsidized fuel stocks for their needy inhabitants.[39] In London the size of the stock provided by the Corporation had increased

---

[35] Leland, *Itinerary*, ii. 94.

[36] Dyer 1973, 53–6.

[37] Nef 1932, i. 19, 326 n.; ii. 73; Stevenson and Baker (eds.), *Records of Borough of Nottingham*, iv. 239–40; v. 144, 264–5, 272; J. A. Picton (ed.), *Selections from the Municipal Archives and Records from the Thirteenth to the Seventeenth Century Inclusive* (Liverpool, 1883), 289; below, Ch. 5.

[38] *VCH Shropshire*, i. 450.

[39] e.g. King's Lynn, Bath, Bristol, Hull, Lincoln.

to 4,000 chaldrons (c.6,000 tons) by 1603, while in Dorchester the stewards of the municipal fuel house purchased £50 to £60 worth of turf and furze.[40] The earl of Huntingdon in 1572 undertook to give £6 annually for seven years, together with free carriage by his tenants, to provide coal for the poor of Leicester, and continued thereafter, in collaboration with the city authorities, to be concerned with the provision of their fuel.[41] Even Exeter followed suit, despite being far from coalfields. In December 1609, 'whereas the price of wood doth increase to the great burden of the poor', an order was made for 10 tons of coal to be purchased for distribution as alms.[42] Funds for the distribution of fuel to the poor also became an increasingly frequent bequest in private wills.

Fuel was an essential commodity, and its increasing scarcity hit the urban poor very hard, especially during an era of sharply falling real wages. In more spacious times wood could often be had for the taking, but in the sixteenth century the taking of wood came to be punished severely. In Coventry in 1529 it warranted the stocks for the first offence, and expulsion from the city for the second, while at Leicester even the first offence was punishable by expulsion. As time passed such petty thefts came to be treated seriously even in well-wooded regions. The earliest indication of concern in Ludlow dates from 1591, but by 1602 a regular watch was being kept to apprehend those who attempted to return to the town with wood pilfered from the surrounding countryside.[43] A parallel policy was to punish those who did not lay in sufficient stocks of fuel for the forthcoming winter, presumably because they were more likely to be tempted into stealing combustible material.[44] At the same time, while the insufficiency of traditional sources of fuel showed itself most frequently in towns, the problem was by no means confined to them, even in the sixteenth century. The burning of straw and cow dung on domestic fires was widespread enough for fears to be raised in the Commons that the practice was depriving cattle of their fodder and the soil of its manure.[45] 'Hedge-stealing' became a crime common throughout the land. Offenders in rural Essex, at Ingatestone, were to 'be whipped till they bleed well'.[46]

[40] Nef 1932, ii. 261; Dyer 1976, 600.
[41] Stocks (ed.), Records of the Borough of Leicester, iii. 149–50, 178, 278, 414, 441, 448.
[42] Hoskins 1935, 101.
[43] Dyer 1976, 599–600.
[44] E. Gillett, A History of Grimsby (Oxford, 1970), 112.
[45] A. Standish, The Commons' Complaint (1611), 2, 7.
[46] Rackham 1980, 168.

If we are to place any credence upon the testimony of eyewitnesses the localities affected by shortage were very numerous and widespread by the close of the sixteenth century. John Leland, while on his travels in the later 1530s and early 1540s, observed that almost all of Pembroke-shire was 'somewhat barren of wood', and that in Staffordshire wood was scarce and expensive. In both instances he also remarked on the extensive use made of coal.[47] Pembrokeshire around 1600, according to George Owen, 'groaneth with the general complaint of other countries of the decreasing of wood'. The fuels burned by the inhabitants included 'wood, seacoal, turf, furze both french and tame, broom, fern and heath', and although Owen found that most of the gentlemen of the shire were well served with wood for their fuel from their own wood-lands 'those that dwell near the coal or that have it carried by water with ease, use most coal fires in their kitchens and some in their halls'. Richard Carew, a contemporary of Owen, tells us that furze and broom were also burned in Cornwall, and that 'timber hath in Cornwall, as in other places taken an universalle downfall'. Although he noted that there were woodlands in the east of the county, in the west 'either nature hath denied that commodity, or want of good husbandry lost it', and the inhabitants instead used dried turves or 'stone coal fetched out of Wales'.[48] The Scots parliament as early as 1503–4 proclaimed that the wood of their country was 'utterly destroyed', and visitors to the land frequently remarked on its treeless vistas. Accordingly a series of statutes was passed with the aim of preventing the destruction of wood-land, the excessive felling of trees, and the export of coal.[49] Of course, the fears were exaggerated, but a serious problem was emerging in the Lowlands where population and industrial activity were densest. Fortunately, this region also possessed rich coal reserves and water transport along the Firth of Forth.

A substantial early advance in the consumption of coal was not, however, a universal experience. Where there were ample local supplies of wood or other combustibles the adoption of coal was inevitably delayed, even when it lay close at hand, as in south Lancashire and north Cheshire. In both Kendal and Carlisle turf remained a popular domestic and industrial fuel into the eighteenth century, despite the soaring productivity of the Whitehaven collieries.[50] In the south of England the

---

[47] Leland, *Itinerary in Wales*, 115; id., *Itinerary*, ii. 102–3.

[48] Owen, *Pembrokeshire*, 86–7; R. Carew, *The Survey of Cornwall* (1769 edn.), 21.

[49] J. M. Gilbert, *Hunting and Hunting Reserves in Medieval Scotland* (Edinburgh, 1979), 238–9; Guy thesis 1982, 143; *RPCS* i. 340; Lythe 1973, 66, 69.   [50] Hughes 1965, ii. 133–4.

contrast between the fuels consumed by Oxford and Cambridge colleges was dramatic. Those in Cambridge became heavily dependent on coal before the close of the sixteenth century, but Oxford colleges, in a well-wooded region and a difficult and costly journey by land and water from London or overland from inland collieries in Warwickshire and Staffordshire, relied solely upon wood and charcoal for their firing right through to the 1650s, and in some cases far later still. Some Oxford colleges possessed their own proximate woodlands, but others were deterred by the excessive price of coal, which was at least double that ruling in Cambridge.[51] Oxford felt the lack of affordable coal, and in the preamble to a bill presented to the Lords in 1624 the main reasons given for extending the navigability of the Thames to Oxford were the conveyance of Heddington stone down river and 'the conveyance of coals and other necessaries thereto'.[52] Coal took even longer to penetrate to the hearths of Eton College. The college was for a long time adequately supplied with fuel from its own woodlands, and coal was purchased for the brewery for the first time in 1652, for the Audit Room in 1693, for the kitchen in 1714, and for the Long Chamber in 1774. The Registrar managed to avoid coal fires until 1797.[53] Nor is it surprising that the Toke family, with their seat and estates close to the Weald of Kent, managed to survive quite comfortably throughout the seventeenth century without purchasing a single ton of coal.[54] Perhaps more striking is the rarity of domestic coal-burning in central rural Essex where inventories of household possessions reveal few grates suitable for this fuel, though it is in accordance with the observation made by Peter Kahn in 1747.[55]

The axiom that spatial factors loom especially large in the history of the coal trade can bear repetition, and to provide us with a cross-section of the markets for coal in Britain at the close of the seventeenth century we have the price data collected by John Houghton, a London apothecary, from a host of correspondents.[56] These give us the ruling prices of a chaldron of coal in fifty-five locations, from 1692 when Houghton began his weekly journal until 1703 when he abandoned it. Moreover, for many of the locations Houghton was provided with regular and frequent observations spanning a number of years. The

[51] Rogers 1866–1902, v. 387–8; vi. 360–84.
[52] Brimblecombe 1987, 29.
[53] Beveridge 1939, 116–27, 143–8.
[54] E. C. Lodge (ed.), *The Account Book of a Kentish Estate 1616–1704* (1927).
[55] Steer (ed.), *Farm and Cottage Inventories*; Eveleigh 1983, 3.
[56] John Houghton, weekly newsheets. See also App. B below.

extremes of the price spectrum revealed in his collections span a factor
of almost ten, from the 5.83s. which would buy a chaldron of coal in
Derby in 1691–2 to the 54s. which it cost in Hitchin (Herts.), some forty
miles overland north of London and twenty-seven miles overland
south-west of Cambridge, in 1695–7. The inhabitants of Hitchin had
little alternative but to rely upon wood but, symbiotically, Hitchin's
landlocked remoteness meant that it was comparably difficult to
transport wood out of the locality.

Map 3.1 includes only those places for which five years of data are
available. The stark contrast between prices ruling close to the coalfields
or with good water access to them and those prevailing in inland
locations remote from mines, like Oxford, Dunstable, and
Berkhamsted, or far distant coastal locations like Chichester and
Shoreham is clearly revealed. Interestingly, we can observe that coal in
Northampton was somewhat cheaper than it was in Dunstable or
Hitchin, despite being appreciably farther from London. The answer
lay, of course, in the fact that Northampton did not draw its supplies via
London. Coal could be delivered to Northampton more cheaply from
the mines around Coventry and Nuneaton than the coal from Tyneside
or Wearside could be delivered via London or King's Lynn. Coal sent
inland from London had also to bear in 1695–6, and from 1698 onwards,

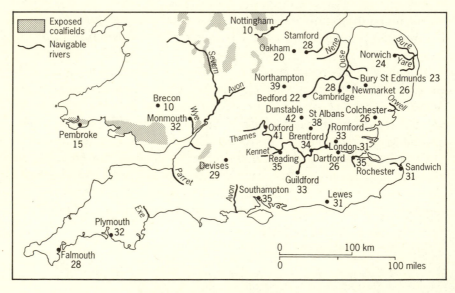

Map 3.1. Retail coal prices south of the Trent, 1691–1702

a duty of 5s. per chaldron imposed on coastal shipments. We can also observe the outer limits of the penetration of north-eastern coal along the south coast of England. By the time that Northumberland and Durham coal reached Sussex its price had risen steeply; at Chichester a chaldron averaged almost 50s. from 1692–7. But farther west in Falmouth and Plymouth coal was often cheaper, for these ports were served from South Wales.

Informative as Houghton's data are for historians, they could prove even more useful to contemporaries. William Gilpin, the principal steward of Sir John Lowther, the great Cumberland coal-owner, when considering how to dispose of the excess capacity of the productive collieries around Whitehaven in 1698, surmised whether coal might be sold elsewhere than in Dublin. He went on 'Some of Haughton's weekly papers have of late given us such an account of the prices of coals at Falmouth and other places in that channel that (if they be to be depended on) seem to give good encouragement to us to send coals thither'. Though Gilpin was well informed enough about the coal trade to hesitate and add, 'though it is not to be conceived they can be ill-supplied considering how near they are to Wales'.[57]

When late Elizabethan and early Jacobean men took stock of the changes which had taken place in the provision of fuel within their lifetimes, they marvelled at the progress of coal 'from the forge into the kitchen and hall', and from an esoteric combustible into 'a commodity so common and useful that people cannot live without the same'.[58] They gloried in its ascent from being a despised substance fit only for the hearths of the destitute into a commodious mineral utilized by 'Noblemen, knights, country and common people' alike. Whereas once coal had been of little moment it was now proclaimed as 'one of the most important commodities of the realm' and Newcastle was fêted as the new Peru, its prosperity founded upon black gold.[59] By 1600 the Hostmen felt confident enough to utter the proud boast that coal had already become a commodity 'of like condition with food and victuals'.[60]

For William Gray and William Harrison it was the progress of coal

[57] Hainsworth (ed.), *Sir Christopher Lowther*, 471.

[58] Harrison, *Description of England*, 363; Moller thesis 1933, 30 (quoting State Papers Domestic, James I, clxii. 20).

[59] Moller thesis 1933, 7 (quoting Star Chamber Proc., James I, 56/10); 'News from Newcastle', a poem 'Upon the Coale-Pits about Newcastle upon Tine' (1651).

[60] Dendy (ed.), *Hostmen*, 8.

from industrial to domestic use which was most worthy of note, but they did not mean to suggest that coal had lost its significance for industry. On the contrary, cost-conscious manufacturers and processors were driven by the same motives as private households to seek the cheapest practicable fuel, and consequently coal consumption soared. The sixteenth and seventeenth centuries were an era of industrial expansion and, as may be seen in Chapter 12, the greatest increase in demand in this sector came from the growth of consumption by industries which had been capable of utilizing coal in the Middle Ages, most notably salt-boiling, lime-burning, ironworking, brewing, and dyeing. Over a wide range of fuel-intensive processes, few significant technical barriers to coal had existed since early times. Accordingly, the improving price competitiveness of coal led not only to increasing usage in traditional coal-burning industries, but to its successful adoption in a long succession of industries in preference to wood. Boilings did not normally require particular species of fuel, and soap and sugar manufacture, as well as the production of alum, copperas, saltpetre, and paper were reliant primarily upon coal. Where technical problems erected a hurdle to the use of mineral fuel, the scale of the savings that could be made by overcoming them frequently inspired invention and improvement and, in the making of glass, bricks, tiles, and pottery, coal soon came to supplant wood and charcoal. By the close of the seventeenth century, lead, tin, and copper were being successfully smelted with coal, and only the smelting of iron, the greatest prize of all, resisted its advance.[61]

The cumulative impact of all these developments in domestic and industrial consumption called forth an increase in the total production of coal from all British coalfields of perhaps in excess of 2.5 million tons between the mid-sixteenth century and the close of the seventeenth. Inevitably, any estimate of national production must of necessity rest largely upon supposition rather than hard evidence, but the sheer scale of rising output cannot be disputed. Undoubtedly, many contemporary observers were prone to exaggeration, either because they dwelt in those parts of the country where coal's ascendancy was triumphant, or simply because they delighted in the reporting of novelty. Yet, as some simple but effective arithmetic will demonstrate, the transformation to which they bore witness was substantial rather than fanciful.

The relative importance of coal in meeting the fuel requirements of the nation may be indicated in the broadest of terms by a calculation of

[61] See Ch. 12(ii) below.

the potential yields of other types of fuel, of which the most notable was wood. The best estimate of a leading expert on the history of English woodland is that in 1700 rather less than 10 per cent of the country was covered by trees and hedgerows, which occupied in total less than three million acres.[62] Since it is most unlikely that in the seventeenth century the annual yield of an acre of well-managed coppice devoted to fire-wood could have consistently much exceeded one ton of dry wood, and since dry wood by weight produces no more than half the heat of coal, it follows that the absolute maximum energy that could have been gathered annually from all the trees and hedgerows in England could not have matched that produced by two million tons of coal. The best estimate of English coal output in 1700 is somewhat in excess of 2.25 million tons, of which all but a small fraction was burnt within the country. In assessing the relative contribution of coal due account must be taken, of course, of many additional non-mineral sources of heat, of which turf was by far the most important. On the other hand, whereas all the coal which was dug was consumed, only a fraction of the annual growth of wood was cut, and of that which was cut only a fraction was burnt. Much woodland was not managed efficiently, much of the annual growth lay untouched in regions remote from markets, and a very substantial proportion of the wood which was harvested was used as raw material in shipbuilding, construction, and manufacturing. On these assumptions, therefore, it would seem safe to conclude that by 1700 coal was supplying over half of the nation's fuel needs, and that coal may have become the leading source of supply well before 1650.

---

[62] I am indebted to Dr Oliver Rackham for giving me his estimates of the extent of woodland, hedgerows, and non-woodland trees in England and Wales before the 18th cent.

PART II

REGIONAL DEVELOPMENTS AND NATIONAL TRENDS

CHAPTER 4

Regional Developments and National Trends

Local causes are very frequently no more than local effects of general factors

M. M. Postan (1975)

i. The general and the particular

The title of this book is misleading. There was no British coal industry before 1700. Nothing which remotely resembled a national industry ever existed within our period. At best there was a series of regional industries, at worst a torrent of local, even individual, mining operations. Depending upon how the boundaries are drawn, there were at least fifteen coalfields stretching from Scotland to Somerset, and many had distinctive subregions within them. As the immense power of the forces of localism are increasingly recognized by the political and social historians of the Tudor and Stuart ages, how much more powerful were they destined to be in determining the patterns and processes of development of an extractive industry whose product had far less value by bulk and weight than almost any other traded commodity? Yet localism and particularism can be pushed too far. Not only is it the function of the historian to sift the singular in search of the general, even the local sources themselves quickly reveal how false it is to see only contrasts and diversity in the production of coal.

Following the methodology of spatial analysis and location theory, it would be possible to construct elaborate theoretical models in an attempt to aid an understanding of the history of British coalfields and the individual collieries within them. The major components of these models would include communications: proximity to the sea or navigable rivers, quality of roads and tracks; coal resources: the distribution of seams, their accessibility and thickness, the quality of the coal; markets: the density and distribution of population, the location and size of towns and industrial consumers, export markets; capital: the availability of investment and amounts required; labour: the supply and cost of labour, its training and skills; entrepreneurial behaviour: the supply and efficiency of mining adventurers, the levels of business and management skills. We could go on considerably lengthening this list, but it would still be a gross oversimplification of reality. For the model to be sufficiently robust and to possess adequate explanatory power, we would need to know not just the forms of transport available to producers, but their relative costs; not just the location, depth, and richness of coal-seams, but the extent of the awareness which contemporaries had of them, the state of technology, and the costs of mining; not just the size and location of markets, but intimate details of consumer behaviour in each of them, the availability and the price of alternative fuels, the elasticity of demand for coal. Once more we could proceed with a counsel of perfection, but it is manifest that the evidence which can be mustered from medieval and early modern documents falls far short of the minimum requirements of elementary location theory.

Instead we must approach the same goals via the unprepossessing route of empirical evidence. Studying the surviving documentation of each of the fifteen coalfields of Britain, and the throng of subregions within them, over the half-millennium from the thirteenth century to the eighteenth is a laborious and at times tedious undertaking. But it has resulted in the accumulation of a mass of material, including information on the experience of almost 1,000 collieries. Each item in the cornucopia of data that can be harvested from colliery account books, estate surveys, law suits, title deeds, correspondence, topographical writings, customs accounts, and so on might by itself possess a pronounced local, even antiquarian, resonance; yet when garnered together, winnowed, and graded, some patterns and tendencies of a general nature emerge. The sorting of data into categories of greater and lesser significance helps to differentiate the typical from the untypical and, among the luxuriant profusion of diversity, it is possible to discern that mining operations frequently possessed some common characteristics and were frequently subjected to some common influences. There were important general tendencies at work in medieval and early modern coalmining, and they are best identified and validated via the study of local and regional experience. The next chapter provides a survey of that experience; here we offer some broad conclusions derived from it.

Inevitably, as has already been stressed, one such general tendency bestowed a critical role upon location. Variations in costs of production frequently paled into insignificance against the expense of overland haulage. Time and again the evolution of whole coalfields, as well as the individual collieries within them, depended fundamentally upon access to markets: the proximity of the sea, of navigable rivers, of large towns. However cheap it might be to dig coal, and however good that coal might be, the quantity that could be sold imposed an iron constraint upon the numbers of pits that were sunk and the amounts of coal that were raised from them. While the richness of the coal deposits on the Tyne and the Wear was an important element in the precocious development of the Northumberland and Durham coalfield, it was the ready access to hundreds of thousands of fuel-starved consumers in London and other east coast towns which enticed production to soar to over one million tons by 1700. But not all collieries on this coalfield were equally well placed to share in this boom. Not only did the quality of coal and the cost of working it vary, distance from the Tyne was often even more crucial. Thus the colliers of Chopwell (Durham) testified in 1611 that although the seam they mined was good fire coal, a yard thick and a mere seven fathoms deep, only one pit was currently being wrought, and that at no great profit, 'by reason the carriage is far from the water'. They also offered the prescient speculation that there was enough coal for the colliery to continue for a hundred years. At the close of the century Chopwell, with its waggonway to the Tyne, was one of the larger collieries of the region, producing almost 40,000 tons each year. For inland collieries like Chopwell, located some miles from the Tyne, the cost of leading coal to the water could substantially exceed all the costs of working it. But at the close of the seventeenth century, for Chopwell as well as for collieries like Gibside and Hedley Fell, the combination of low production costs and waggonways rendered their coal competitive on the Tyne. At the same time high-cost collieries virtually at the water's edge, like Benwell and Newburn, were able to remain in production despite the necessity to sink deep shafts and drain copious flows of water, because they enjoyed the benefits of negligible transport costs.

So, too, the nearness of navigable rivers could provide inland collieries with cheap access to distant markets which, when combined with strong local demand, allowed them to grow far beyond the common dimensions. The output first of Wollaton and then of Strelley was stimulated by the proximity of the city of Nottingham and a whole string of communities rendered accessible by the Trent, while, in the Severn Gorge, Madeley, Broseley, and Benthall throve upon a combination of buoyant local demand and the existence of cheap water transport to consumers throughout the Severn valley. For truly landlocked collieries, market size was even more tightly constrained by transport costs. Output was restricted to supplying those consumers who could be reached by packhorses or carts before rising costs choked off demand. Yet on occasion the numbers of accessible consumers could be large. It may be seen from Map 4.1 that the proximity of large towns frequently stimulated collieries to grow beyond the average. Bedworth in Warwickshire and Coleorton in Leicestershire owed much to the proximity of Coventry and Leicester, as well as to broad hinterlands which lacked alternative sources of fuel supply. Conversely, of course, in the absence of such stimuli, development could be stunted, as it was in the Denbighshire, Lancashire, north Derbyshire, and Somerset coalfields. While even in landlocked areas which did experience a substantial rise in output, such as much of Yorkshire and parts of Staffordshire, the absence of large towns dictated that growth took place through the proliferation of smaller collieries, each supplying a restricted though often bustling hinterland, rather than through the emergence of giants.

The proposition that coal will tend to be mined in quantities that can be profitably disposed of borders on the banal, yet the experience of British coalfields and collieries before 1700 demonstrates that the relationship between markets, transport, and output was frequently far from straightforward. Being sited by the sea did not of itself guarantee limitless opportunities for growth, even for collieries where coal could be worked cheaply. Those of the Firth of Forth were simply too far from London and the east of England to compete effectively with the collieries of Tyneside and Wearside, despite the fine quality of much Forthside coal. Likewise collieries on the western seaboard did not enjoy such great advantages as those on the eastern, for settlement there was far lighter with far fewer coastal towns of any size, and Dublin was the sole major overseas market. For most of the seventeenth century Ireland was served primarily by South Wales and Flintshire collieries, and the coalfields of Ayrshire and Cumberland were painfully slow to develop. When, thanks largely to the entrepreneurial skills of Sir John Lowther, Cumberland coal reserves were finally exploited on a large-scale, the output of the most favoured colliery, Howgill, quickly soared to 20,000 tons or more. But the market had not grown commensurately, and as Howgill came to dominate the Irish coal trade so shipments from the collieries of South Wales and Flintshire contracted. Cumberland's growth in the closing decades of the seventeenth century harmed the Welsh coalfields. But even Howgill was capable of far greater outputs than Sir John Lowther could sell, as he frequently lamented. The very cheapness of water transport brought seasale collieries in far-flung coal-fields into competition with each other.

For landlocked collieries, even the presence of a large market in the immediate vicinity offered no guarantee that high production levels could be maintained. Lucrative markets attracted energetic competition, and competition between adjacent landlocked collieries seeking to supply the same markets was often very fierce. Bedworth colliery, close to Coventry, had captured the bulk of a market capable of consuming some 20,000 to 30,000 tons a year at the opening of the seventeenth century, but when nearby Griff or Hawkesbury was also in production this market grew scarcely at all, and severe difficulties for all the operators ensued. Entry into the industry was, as we shall see, relatively easy, and mineable outcrops were abundant on many coalfields. Even when formidable technical obstacles loomed to threaten profitability, the lure of a large market could seduce speculators into battling against the odds, even unto bankruptcy. In this way the supply of coal could be pushed above its rational level, to the detriment of soundly based collieries. The various ill-fated attempts to mine at Hawkesbury, close to the walls of Coventry, severely harmed the fortunes of the two more securely founded collieries of Bedworth and Griff. Faced with potentially ruinous competition, entrepreneurs might seek to ameliorate their trading environment by buying up rival pits or bribing their proprietors to close them down. Huntingdon Beaumont's ultimately disastrous attempts at rigging the market in the East Midlands are notorious, but in many respects his strategy was simply a particularly ambitious and reckless instance of the commonplace. Policies instinctively interpreted as hostile to consumers were, of necessity, frequently conducted covertly, and as such must often have left few traces. Yet there are no shortage of references to the deliberate closing of productive collieries. It was a policy followed, for example, in Leicestershire by Thomas Beaumont and, allegedly, by John Wilkins, in Cumberland by Sir John Lowther, in Warwickshire allegedly by John Bugges and Anthony Robinson, and in Kingswood Chase by Arthur Player. Nor was it rare for commercial rivalry to degenerate into industrial sabotage and violence. Instances and allegations abound of the deliberate destruction of collieries by the causing of floods and roof-falls, of the cutting of ropes and the damaging of headgear, of the poisoning of horses and the tearing up of waggon-ways, and of the intimidation and wounding of colliers.

Such behaviour was a consequence of the recurrent propensity, in most of the coalfields over most of the period, for supply not only to

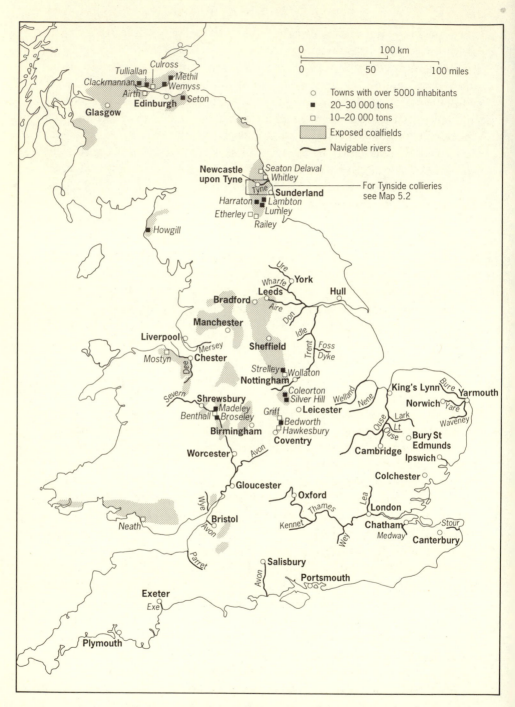

Map 4.1. Principal British collieries before 1700

match demand but outrun it. Given the soaring appetite for coal this was at first sight an extraordinary achievement. It resulted in a general tendency for pithead prices not only to rise less than the prices of competitive fuels, but actually in many places to fall in real terms. The occasions when a shortfall in production occurred were relatively few and short lived, while those when the market was overhung by a glut, or the threat of one, were far more numerous. As the regional histories in Chapter 5 demonstrate, the threat of a glut of coal was as real in the seasale coalfields of the north-east and the north-west as it was in the landlocked coalfields of the Midlands. The description of and the reasons for the vigorous performance of coalmining are major themes of this book, and the implications which they have for our general understanding of the potential for growth in pre-industrial economies are touched upon in the concluding chapter. Here we will concentrate upon the impact which this latent capacity, and the efficiency of transport and distribution, had upon the size and location of collieries.

ii. The size of collieries

As the regional surveys of British coalfields, supported by index cards of almost 1,000 collieries, clearly demonstrate, there were very few genuinely large units of production before the eighteenth century, and the great majority of those that did exist were to be found concentrated in the north-east, predominantly on the banks of the Tyne. The estimation of colliery size is, of course, not an easy undertaking. For most mining ventures we have only the indirect indications of scale provided by rents, profits, or valuations rather than statements of output, and then only on an intermittent rather than a continuous basis. Occasional observations are apt to be misleading, since few collieries enjoyed anything like continuous production over the long term, and levels of output were apt to fluctuate markedly, even over the short term. Yet greater confidence may be placed in the completeness and quality of the information which has survived on the larger collieries, not least because they were the objects of much contemporary comment.

If we follow Nef and take 25,000 tons capacity as signifying a large colliery, then it cannot be stated with absolute confidence that there was a single operation outside of Northumberland and Durham which produced this quantity of coal at any time before 1700. It is probable, however, that at their peak Clackmannan and Seton on the Forth, Strelley and Bedworth in the Midlands, Howgill in Cumberland, and

Madeley and Broseley on the Severn may just have qualified to join more than a score from the north-east in this élite. Placing the definition of a large colliery as high as 25,000 tons thus excludes the vast majority of the leading collieries of seventeenth-century Britain. Nor are numbers of qualifying collieries significantly affected by reducing the output limit to 20,000 tons. Clackmannan, Seton, Strelley, Bedworth, Howgill, Madeley, and Broseley would be firmly rather than tentatively in the top category. There is a possibility that both Coleorton and Silver Hill in Leicestershire may just have reached 20,000 tons in short bursts, though not contemporaneously, and we have also to allow for the possibility of adding the Forthside collieries of Tulliallan, Methill, and Wemyss. All in all, therefore, barely a dozen collieries outside the north-east produced more than 20,000 tons a year at any time before 1700, and not one produced substantially more.

Even when we scale down to 10,000 tons relatively few collieries qualify. It would seem possible to identify no more than ten in England and Wales with outputs of between 10,000 and 20,000 tons, and perhaps a further three or four at most from Scotland. Even collieries which at some time operated at between 5,000 and 10,000 tons capacity were a great rarity in most parts, and perhaps little more than a further dozen were scattered throughout English and Welsh coalfields. In the whole of the great Yorkshire coalfield there was perhaps Kippax alone which, for a time, produced more than 5,000 tons in a year, while in Lancashire even the famous Haigh colliery appears not to have yielded more than 4,000 tons in its most productive years. This is why contemporaries found collieries which produced more than 5,000 tons, and in some regions even less, worthy of special notice.

Since we have been dealing with collieries which at some time or another during the later sixteenth and seventeenth centuries produced the tonnages we have ascribed to them, our figures cannot be taken to indicate the numbers of collieries of that size which were actually in operation at any one time. Indeed in any given year, even towards the close of our period, only a fraction of these collieries would be producing the maximum tonnages ascribed to them. Very many would be producing far less, while others might not be in production at all. For example, it appears that Bedworth could only have exceeded 20,000 tons in the 1620s and 1690s; Howgill from the 1680s, Strelley on occasions in the 1610s and 1620s, and so on.

Although precision is elusive, and there were many notable exceptions, there does seem to have been a significant tendency towards increasing scale over time, and once again the north-east was in the vanguard. But throughout most British coalfields the great surge in output was primarily effected through the proliferation of collieries which in historical perspective must be viewed as small. The bulk of British coal output over the greater part of her coalfields continued to be produced by small-scale operations which had far more in common with the typical artisan workshops to be found in their thousands throughout the cities and towns of seventeenth-century Europe than with capitalist enterprises emblematic of an industrial revolution. Capital requirements of one or two hundred pounds at most, a full-time work-force of less than a score, and an annual turnover of a few hundred pounds, these were the numerically dominant units of production of the early modern British coal industry.

iii. Regional and national trends in output

Historians occasionally find themselves compelled to face the prospect of carrying out unpleasant tasks, even ones which are likely to prove damaging to their reputations. Attempting to put dimensions to the vast increase in British coal output between the later sixteenth century and the opening of the eighteenth, on a regional as well as a national basis, is just such a task. The reception accorded to the only previous full-scale attempt to accomplish this, by J. U. Nef in 1932, has been stridently ambivalent. On the one hand, his estimates have been almost universally disparaged, while, on the other, they have been voraciously consumed by generations of historians seeking to implant a quantitative backbone into their studies of early modern England. It has been repeatedly and forcefully contended that not only were Nef's statistical methods seriously defective, the mission he set himself was impossible to accomplish satisfactorily and should therefore never have been embarked upon. The total absence of any statistics whatsoever for some places and some times, it has been maintained, necessitated an excess of pure guesswork. Consequently, it might well seem more prudent not to embark upon a vainglorious attempt to conjure numbers and thereby impart spurious precision to what in most cases must be little more than informed guesswork. Instead this survey of the coalfields of Britain could be left resonant with the deceptively secure vagueness of such expressions as 'less than', 'faster than', 'relatively modest', 'exceptionally rapid', and growth and decline could be qualified by a wide range of dimensional adjectives, such as 'soaring' and 'plunging', 'substantial' and 'marginal', 'phenomenal' and 'prosaic', 'significant' and 'negligible', 'rapid' and 'slow', 'precipitous' and 'vertiginous'. Indeed such words recur in the pages which follow, and inevitably the reader is apt to be left wondering by how much, if anything, a 'soaring output' exceeded one which expanded 'extremely rapidly'. Adjectives cannot satisfactorily take the place of numbers and percentages, any more than precise numbers and percentages can be conjured from the records of the majority of British coalfields before 1700. The dilemma is that quantification is demanded but can never be supplied with confidence.

One purpose of the detailed historical surveys of each of the British coalfields in Chapter 5 is to enable the reader to assess the quality of the evidence which supports the quantities and growth rates hazarded in Table 4.1. It will be seen that most are at best based upon informed guesswork. Moreover, whereas the estimates of production at the close of the seventeenth century are in general founded upon a fair quantity of direct information, those for the mid-sixteenth century have had to be

Table 4.1 *The estimated output of British coalfields from 1560s to 1690s*

Area	1560s (tons)	c.1700 (tons)	Growth rate (fold)
North-east	90,000	1,250,000	14
Scotland	30,000	300,000	10
Cumberland	2,000	40,000	20
Lancashire	7,000	80,000	11
Staffordshire	15,000	150,000	10
Shropshire	12,000	230,000	19
Warwickshire	3,000	45,000	15
Forest of Dean	5,000	50,000	10
Bristol	5,000	60,000	12
Somerset	3,000	30,000	10
Leicestershire	5,000	40,000	8
Nottinghamshire/Derbyshire	15,000	75,000	5
Yorkshire	15,000	150,000	10
South Wales	15,000	100,000	7
North Wales	5,000	40,000	8
TOTAL	227,000	2,640,000	12

Note: Output figures are of necessity estimates of coal produced for sale, and do not include small-coal waste, colliers' allowances, coal burnt at the colliery, etc.

fabricated from a ragbag of indications of varying degrees of indirectness and inadequacy. In the round, and even in the context of the total production of coal in Britain, it would seem to matter little whether two, four, or even six thousand tons of coal were produced on a particular coalfield in the mid-sixteenth century. Yet growth rates are critically dependent upon the chosen baselines and, in the case of those in Table 4.1, upon the date which is chosen and the amount of development which had taken place prior to it. Thus, somewhat paradoxically, the small Cumberland and Warwickshire coalfields probably achieved among the fastest rates of growth of all, quite simply because production was so exiguous before the mid-sixteenth century. Yet we can have little confidence in such rates for, not only are the sources scanty, the approximate level of production itself is difficult to estimate with any confidence simply because it was so tiny. Where production was a few thousand tons the opening or closing of a single colliery could make a material impact. Perhaps the aggregation of regional estimates into national estimates lessens rather than multiplies the deficiencies of the data. Certainly these estimates should be used only as the broadest of indications of dimensions, and of the differing pace of development and relative standing of British coalfields.

The absence of precise quantification does not, however, obscure a broad symmetry in the patterns of change and development which are discernible across the sweep of British coalfields. From the widespread stirrings of mining in the thirteenth century to the surge of interest and investment experienced from the later sixteenth or early seventeenth centuries, there is a strong measure of conformity. The timing and pace of the advance varied, of course, not only between but within coalfields, for Britain in the early modern era consisted of a series of interdependent regional and local economies, rather than a national economy. Yet the broad trends of demographic and industrial development had ramifications in all parts of the country, not least upon the demand for coal and those who sought to meet it.

CHAPTER 5

The Coalfields of Britain

i. The north-east

Throughout the medieval and early modern eras the Northumberland and Durham coalfield was paramount among the coalfields of Britain, accounting at the end of the seventeenth century for around a half of Britain's output. In earlier times the share it contributed to national output was quite possibly higher still, and it was to remain the most productive coalfield up to the eve of the First World War, when it was eventually matched by South Wales.[1] The north-eastern coalfield was blessed with a multitude of assets, not least the vastness of its reserves and the ease with which they could be reached. The boundary of the exposed coalfield extends from the River Coquet in the north almost as far as the River Tees in the south, a distance of approximately fifty miles. From east to west above the Tyne the exposed portion stretches from the shores of the North Sea as far as twenty miles inland, and in Durham it begins a few miles from the sea and extends inland also for some twenty miles. In addition there is a small detached segment just to the south of Berwick. Not only did much of the coal lie close to the surface in seams of pleasing thickness, many of the relatively shallow deposits lay conveniently close to the Tyne and the Wear, along which coal could be ferried to sea-going vessels.[2] These vessels in turn carried the vast bulk of this coal cheaply to the fuel-hungry markets of eastern England. What is more, most north-eastern coal was good house coal, well suited to the consumers whom it served, while much 'small' and low-grade output found a ready use in local salt-pans.

The boundaries of the intensively exploited sector of the coalfield shifted over time, but were typically determined by a combination of geological and transport considerations. A series of major faults running mainly east-north-east to west-south-west, including notably the Ninety Fathom Dyke, effectively set the northern limits to large-scale mining in Northumberland before the nineteenth century. In Durham

[1] Church 1986, 3.   [2] See Map 5.1.

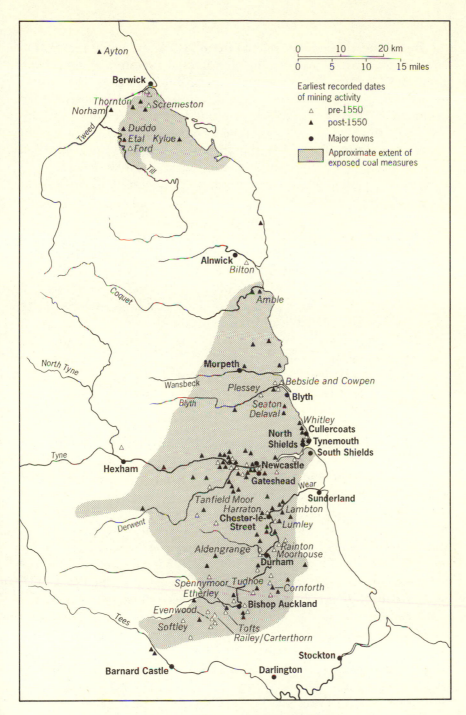

Map 5.1. The north-east coalfield

the Butterknowle fault set the southern boundary, while the eastern
limits were set by a thick covering of magnesian limestone running from
South Shields towards the southern limits of the coalfield. The clustering of collieries in the river valleys close to navigable water amply
demonstrates the primacy of water transport in colliery development.
The lie of the land as well as simple distance from water was also of
prime importance. Even after the advent of waggonways a downhill
route from colliery to staithe was essential, because horses were
incapable of hauling full wains or waggons up steep or long inclines.

The middle ages

That the north-east coalfield was as exceptional in the Middle Ages as it
was at the close of the seventeenth century is readily apparent from Map
5.1, with its profusion of medieval mining sites. The comprehensiveness
of the coverage charted there depends upon the fortuitous survival of
manuscripts, and the large numbers of early coal-mines which can be
found in Northumberland and Durham are all the more significant
because the region is in general poorly documented. Moreover, there are
clear indications of medieval mining operations which were extraordinary by the standards of the times. Rents and profits on this coalfield were frequently reckoned in pounds rather than the shillings and
pence typical elsewhere, and the outputs of a number of northern
collieries comprised thousands rather than hundreds of tons.

Despite the proven existence of a significant trade in Tyneside coal
from the early thirteenth century, disappointingly few traces of mining
are preserved in surviving records, and we must rely heavily upon the
archives of the bishopric of Durham. Although it is unlikely that coal
did not make some contribution to revenues totalling more than £500
received by the bishop of Durham from 'issues of mines' over a four-
year period in King John's reign, lead-mines were undoubtedly of far
more value. In fact, it is not until the 1270s that the coal-mines of the
bishopric of Durham are specifically mentioned in the Pipe Rolls. Even
by this date they cannot have been very substantial, for in 1274 the
combined lease of all the coal-mines, kilns, and fisheries of the bishop
was worth less than £30 a year.[3] Gradually, during the fourteenth
century, we are permitted to view more of the mining which was
undoubtedly taking place. Indeed, in 1356 a lease granted by the bishop
of Durham reveals that there was a colliery of truly extraordinary
dimensions on the Tyne. Sir Thomas Gray and John Pulhore, rector of

[3] DUDP Church Commission box 204, 244159–72.

Whickham, agreed to pay 500 marks a year for a twelve-year lease of Whickham. In return the bishop covenanted that he would win no new mine on the Tyne, or elsewhere in those parts, excepting those currently in operation at Gateshead, which would be offered to Pulhore and Gray when the present tenants' lease expired. There were five pits working at Whickham, and under the lease the bishop limited the output of each pit to one keel of coal per day, approximately 20 to 25 tons, 'according to use and wont in times past'. The lease therefore resulted in a rent of £333. 6s. 8d., and a maximum annual output of some 30,000 to 35,000 tons, both extraordinary amounts, especially so soon after the Black Death.[4] It would be most unwise to take the maximum permitted output as attainable, but the rent alone at prevailing pithead prices translates into almost 10,000 tons. It seems likely therefore that Gray and Pulhore were hoping to achieve an output of at least 20,000 tons. Sadly, it is not possible to follow the history of this lease, but the suspicion must be that the lessees were far too optimistic. None the less, it is interesting to note that the richness of the reserves of Whickham, and the ease with which they could be extracted and transported, were recognized by visionary if impractical men more than 200 years before the Grand Lease.

Subsequently, the bishop took Whickham and Gateshead into his own hands. In 1372 he appointed Nicholas Coke of Newcastle as 'keeper and vendor of our coals', and a couple of years later, to combat the labour problems occasioned by population decline, Bishop Hatfield secured royal approval to appoint commissioners to seize colliers and coal-bearers to work in these collieries, with the power to imprison or otherwise punish those who might resist impressment. The bishop consequently became a major supplier of coal, and in 1393, for example, the citizens of Newcastle purchased from him thirteen score keels (c.6,000 tons) for £312, no doubt intending to resell most.[5]

The Tyne valley around Newcastle seems to have always been the focus of mining activity. It is known that Winlaton, Heworth, Ferger-house, Wardley, and Gateshead were in production on the south bank, and on the Newcastle side we can identify Wylam, Elswick, and various pits in the vicinity of the city walls, including Castle Field, Forth, and Fenham.[6] Of course, production was rarely continuous, and the fortunes of individual collieries waxed and waned, but some were of

[4] Ibid., box 203, 244071. See also discussions in *VCH Durham*, ii. 322; Galloway 1898, i. 44–6.
[5] DUDP Church Commission box 204, 244134, 244173, 244182.
[6] Informative maps are contained in Simpson 1909–10, opp. 598, and Wilcock 1979, 7, 15.

significant proportions. Winlaton colliery supplied 1,000 tons for building work at Windsor Castle in 1362, while Elswick was leased for £4 in 1330, and the manor of Fergerhouse, including a coal-mine, commanded a rent of £24. 13s. 4d. in mid-century.[7]

There was also intense mining activity in south Durham around Bishop Auckland where the bishop had a number of productive mines. The most notable colliery in this region was Railey, which lay to the south-west of the town, and other sizeable operations also existed close by at Evenwood, Grewburn, Tofts, and Caldhurst, and to the north at Hargill, Lindsay, Tow Law, and Woodifield. Few details of these collieries can be found before the early fifteenth century, but thereafter mentions are frequent and their importance is fully attested. In 1416 the bishop leased all his south Durham mines to William de Eure, a prominent member of the gentry, for £112. 13s. 4d. It was the beginning of an association that was to endure for centuries. In 1424 on the death of William the lease passed to his son Ralph, and in 1443 on Ralph's death the lease passed at the same rent to his son, William.[8] By this collective lease, the Eures gained control over much of the buoyant coal trade of the region. The rent which they paid indicates very high levels of output for the times, and this is confirmed by production figures given in accounts surviving for periods when the collieries reverted to the bishopric. Railey, for example, produced around 4,000 tons between April and Christmas Day 1460, 8,000 to 9,000 tons in 1502–3 and again in 1503–4, and some 5,000 tons from January 1509 to January 1510. From the same set of accounts we learn that in the early sixteenth century Grewburn produced around 3,000 tons annually, and Hargill and Woodifield around 1,000 tons each.[9]

Such outputs could only have been supported by extensive markets which had to be reached by overland transport. Fortunately independent confirmation of the existence of such distant markets can be found. In 1463–4, the sheriff of Durham was directed by the bishop to arrest and detain certain men of the county of York, as well as of the county of Durham and the wapantake of Sedberge, who had been employing carts and horses to take coal from a pit worked by Sir William de Eure at 'Les Toftes' and had caused damage to the bishop's

[7] Simpson 1909–10, 578; Galloway 1898, i. 50; *VCH Durham*, ii. 322.

[8] DUDP Church Commission, Receiver-Generals' Accounts 189809–12, 189782, 190184. It is interesting to note that the Eures were leasing Railey, then known as Carterthorne, in 1635 from the bishopric (Nef 1932, i. 154).

[9] DUDP Church Commission, 189700, 190023, 190024, 190026, 190028.

land.[10] The trade into Yorkshire was still thriving in the 1530s, and when John Leland visited Richmond he observed that although some coal was being mined 'in the upper part of the west mountains of Richmondshire ... they be not used for the incommodity of the carriage to the lower part [instead] most of the coal that be occupied about the quarters of Richmond town be fetched from the Railey pits towards the quarters of Durham'.[11]

There was also considerable activity around the city of Durham, part of which is revealed in the records of Finchale and Durham priories. Finchale priory mined coal throughout the fifteenth century at Moorhouse, a few miles to the north-east of the city, both for its own fuel needs and for profit. Although pits at Moorhousefield were rarely worth more than a few pounds a year, those at Moorhouseclose prospered in the 1460s, producing annual receipts in excess of £20, and sometimes as high as £40. The importance of mining to Finchale is evidenced by the considerable investments which it made. In 1427–8, for example, £60 was invested in the construction of a drainage adit at Coxhoe, to the east of Durham. This venture was not a resounding success, however, for although £15, £54, and £24 were received in the ensuing three years, thereafter receipts plummeted and the mine was soon abandoned. It is of interest to note that for a time in the 1360s and 1370s pits flourished on the priory's manor of Lumley, later to be the site of one of the great Wearside collieries, but prosperity at this time was short lived.[12] Despite the evident interest which they displayed in mining, and the large quantities of coal which they consumed in their priory and its ancillary buildings, the monks of Durham were not endowed with rich collieries. The priory's mines were located at Rainton, Ferryhill, Heworth, Spennymoor, Aldengrange, and Broom, but of these only Rainton operated on a large scale, and then but intermittently. In the later fourteenth century the monks generally leased their mines out for others to work, but falling rents in the early fifteenth century drove them into direct management. The forced move proved moderately successful, however, and between 1410 and 1440 Rainton rarely produced profits of less than £20 a year, while Ferryhill's averaged £10. Mining was also resumed in the 1440s, after a lengthy break, at Aldengrange and Broom.[13]

[10] Galloway 1898, i. 73.   [11] Leland, *Itinerary*, v. 140.

[12] Raine (ed.), *Finchale* pp. lxxxv, cxcvii–ccx.

[13] Fowler (ed.) *Account Rolls of the Abbey of Durham*, 708–13; Morimoto 1970, 55–84; Lomas thesis 1973, 134–7; R. B. Dobson, *Durham Priory, 1400-1450* (Cambridge, 1973), 278–9. It seems

There was a substantial demand for coal in later medieval Durham, but even so abundant supply often threatened to outrun it. Severe competition for markets, for example, took place among the profusion of landlocked pits around Bishop Auckland. Softley was for a time the prime colliery of Finchale Priory, but it lay too close to the collieries of the bishops for its long-term prosperity to be assured. Between the 1360s and 1420 Softley returned regular profits of £6–7 annually, but, coincident with the entry of the Eures into coalmining, production flagged and then ceased. When Softley subsequently reopened, its profitability was both lower and less certain than it had been formerly.[14] The threat of overproduction and ruinous price competition also restriced output at landlocked pits owned elsewhere by Finchale and by Durham Cathedral Priory, its main rival. So plentiful were potential mining sites around the city of Durham that, before prospective tenants would agree to take a mine, lessors often had to pledge not to grant leases to other mines in the vicinity or to work them themselves. Thus, when in 1399 John Fossour and Richard Cowhird leased Broom colliery, they extracted a promise from the prior of Durham that he would not permit coal to be won or sold 'within the boundaries of Aldin Grange and Baxterwood', and in 1418–19 we learn that the prior of Finchale was paid by his counterpart at Durham to cease working pits at Baxterwood. Eventually, Durham Priory was driven to purchase four acres of coal-bearing land in Baxterwood from Finchale, although the latter in turn insisted on a covenant that any coal raised there should be solely for domestic consumption in the monastery at Durham and not for sale.[15]

During the later Middle Ages, in an era characterized by economic retrenchment, the coal industry of Northumberland and Durham consolidated and advanced modestly. Newcastle local customs accounts reveal an average annual seasale of between 40,000 to 45,000 tons from 1508–11 and, although shipments from elsewhere in the north-east were negligible, internal consumption and landsale were precociously high. By the later fifteenth century there was a profusion of collieries some of which were substantial. As we have noted, Railey was capable of producing more than 10,000 tons in its best years, and even though the full

likely that receipts given in the *Rotuli de Mineris Carbonum* are net of expenses in some years but not in others.

[14] Raine (ed.), *Finchale, passim*.

[15] Walton (ed.), *Greenwell Deeds*, xiv. 269, 278; Raine (ed.), *Finchale*, pp. clxxvi, clxxix, cxcvi; Galloway 1898, i. 70.

promise of Whickham, that had flickered dazzlingly but briefly in the mid-fourteenth century, was not realized during the remainder of the Middle Ages, it produced some 2,500 tons between February and August 1458 and 6,000 to 7,000 tons during twelve months of 1461–2.[16] All in all the total output of the whole coalfield before the close of the Middle Ages may well have exceeded 60,000 to 70,000 tons a year.

The 'take-off' of the north-east

There are scant signs of rapid growth in the north-east coalfield before 1570. A comparison of the shipments of 1508–11 with the next available data from the later 1560s, reveals that total coastwise and overseas shipments would seem to have risen by just 15,000 tons.[17] Although some new collieries were founded between 1500 and 1575 many established collieries for which we have records stagnated or even declined. This was the case with Gateshead which, after a fitful performance in the later fifteenth century, was periodically shutdown in the early sixteenth before being finally abandoned in 1546. Gateshead remained 'in decay and unoccupied' right up to the making of the Grand Lease thirty years later. Nor did Whickham prosper; before 1550 its rent invariably lagged behind the later fifteenth-century peak of £66. 13s. 4d., and did not rise consistently higher until the 1560s.[18] Elsewhere on the Tyne, however, there is some evidence of growth. It is in the 1520s and 1530s that we first hear of mining at Benwell, Ravensworth, Stella, and Chopwell. In 1530 a single pit at Elswick was realizing a rent of £20, and eight years later there were three pits working, for which a combined rent of £50 was paid. Close by, Denton colliery was commanding a rent of £20. To the east of Gateshead, at Heworth, leases made in 1546 and 1550 imposed an upper limit of around 10,000 tons in a year, though actual production was likely to have been lower.[19]

On the Tyne away from Newcastle and on the North Sea coast such mining as there was produced little coal. Bebside and Cowpen, for example, warranted a rent of only 22s. 8d. when leased in 1530, and revenues derived from pits at Tynemouth were insignificant. Likewise, on the Blyth and the Tweed rents were reckoned in shillings rather than

[16] TWRO 543/212; DUDP Church Commission, 190022, 190318.

[17] See Ch. 14 below.

[18] Rent receipts are recorded in the accounts of the Receiver-General of the bishopric of Durham in the Dept. of Palaeography, University of Durham.

[19] Simpson 1909–10, map opp. 598; NCH xiii. 33; Galloway 1898, i. 86–8, 90–1; Taylor 1858, 167; Brand 1789, ii. 265; Green 1866, 184; DUPK Dean and Chapter, Reg. 1A, fos. 61–61v, 158v–159.

pounds.[20] Faced with increasing competition from mines now owned by the dean and chapter of Durham at Rainton, Moorsley, Pittingdean, and Moorehouse, and from mines in north Yorkshire, even the south Durham collieries of the bishop struggled to maintain previous levels of output and, after a peak of £188. 10s. 0d. between 1514 and 1524, rents inched remorselessly downwards for the rest of the century. Moreover the mines that the bishop leased from the earl of Westmorland at 'Cockfield, Mawefeldes, Wodyfeldes and Fulcye' appear to have performed even worse. In 1569 the bishop refused to accept any liability for arrears of rent since 'the pits and mines are wrought out and no coals there to be gotten nor any pits in work within the places at this present'.[21]

The shattering of the slumber of the northern coalfield can be pinpointed precisely in time. From all perspectives we are driven unerringly to the 1570s and 1580s as the turning-point. Between the later 1560s and the later 1590s shipments of coal rose almost fourfold. Such a rate of growth necessitated the creation of an additional 160,000 tons capacity over a thirty-year period, and this was for the seasale trade alone. In the ensuing twenty-five years shipments virtually doubled again to reach an average of over 400,000 tons a year in the early 1620s. It is also possible to pinpoint where the growth in capacity took place. Shipping records tell us that over 97 per cent of coal sent overseas or coastwise was despatched through Newcastle, and coalmining records reveal that the vast bulk was produced by a battery of great collieries on the banks of the Tyne, clustering almost cheek by jowl within a few miles of the cities of Newcastle and Gateshead. Among the greatest were Whickham, Winlaton, Blaydon, Stella and Ryton, all on the south bank to the west of Gateshead, while further south on the Team lay Ravensworth, and in and around Gateshead itself lay a further cluster of productive collieries. There were fewer great collieries on the north bank of the Tyne, but Benwell is worthy of special note.

Whickham in the later sixteenth and early seventeenth centuries was, as it had been for a brief time in the mid-fourteenth century, a colossus. It dwarfed even the other giant collieries of the region. Although no colliery accounts survive for Whickham, we are fortunate in having many other indications of its size and value. Its rental began to rise strongly in the 1560s, leaping from £50 in 1558 to almost £200 by 1570. Under the Grand Lease granted to Thomas Sutton and subsequently to the Hostmen of Newcastle, mining within Whickham's borders soared

[20] Green 1866, 183; Galloway 1898, i. 73–4.
[21] DUDP Church Commission, Receiver-General's Accounts; VCH Durham, ii. 325–6.

ever higher. When the Hostmen in 1596–7 denied the charges levied by the Mayor and Aldermen of London, that the Grand Lease was responsible for the shortage and high price of coal in the capital, they attempted to belittle its contribution by asserting that the mines it included 'amount not in quantity to the 5th part of the coalery wrought about Newcastle'. Twenty per cent of the output of the Tyne valley in the mid-1590s probably exceeded 50,000 tons. Ralph Gardiner claimed after the Civil War that the Grand Lessees at the end of the sixteenth century reaped annual profits of at least £50,000, but we should treat this prodigious sum with considerable scepticism for he was both an enemy of the Hostmen's monopoly and writing from a distance of time.[22] A further valuation is obtainable from the Ship Money assessment of 1636, in which Whickham colliery was deemed to be worth £4,500 annually, which was nearly 30 per cent of the combined value placed upon an admittedly incomplete list of Durham collieries. Yet even this exalted valuation took no account of numerous pits located on freeholds within the parish of Whickham, or adjacent to it, which were to all intents and purposes part of the same colliery district but not part of the Grand Lease. Whickham was not a colliery, but a collection of collieries within legal rather than industrial boundaries. Some like Farnacres and Fugerfield were sizeable operations, valued in 1636 at £800 and £300 respectively. Fawdonfield, otherwise known as Greenlaw, was valued at just £200 in 1636, but it was said to have produced more than 6,000 tons annually from 1619–22. This is not all, there were important Crown freeholds within Whickham which were not listed in the Ship Money assessment, including Brinkbourne, which was estimated to be worth £400 a year to its proprietor in 1611.[23] Mining followed the seams rather than manorial or parish boundaries, and in regions like Tyneside where there were tracts of virtually continuous mining activity, the boundaries of collieries from our perspective are often indeterminate. At its peak before the Civil War more than 100,000 tons of coal were probably produced each year within the boundaries of Whickham parish.

Just across the Derwent, a mile or so from Whickham, lay Winlaton colliery. A rare glimpse of its capacity is granted by a legal dispute between its partners, which reveals that 23,602 fothers of coal, at 120 to the hundred, were raised between Martinmas 1581 and Martinmas 1582, and that they were all led to Blaydon and Derwent staithes between 25 May and 11 November 1582. Assuming a fother to be equal

[22] BL Harleian 6850(39); Gardiner, *England's Grievance*, 14.
[23] Nef 1932, i. 146–8; ii. 413–16; PRO E. 178/5037, m. 4d; Galloway 1898, i. 132.

to a wain-load of 17.5 cwt, Winlaton produced around 25,000 tons during this year.[24] Less than a mile to the north lay Blaydon colliery, which may have been of modest size at the turn of the sixteenth and seventeenth centuries but in 1636 was valued at £2,200 per annum, which placed it equal to Stella and second only to Whickham. Stella itself was scarcely less complex than Whickham in its tenurial structure, and in 1636 Stella 'Grand Lease' colliery was valued at £1,700 yearly, and Stella glebe land at £300. It is likely that Stella too grew fastest in the second, third, and fourth decades of the seventeenth century rather than earlier. The most westerly of the great collieries which lined the south bank of the Tyne at this time was Ryton, which lay about seven miles from the walls of Gateshead. It had grown rapidly under the ownership of Sir Thomas Tempest, although to judge from the Ship Money assessments it was only a quarter the size of Stella or Blaydon.[25]

Finally, there was Gateshead colliery, or rather the pot-pourri of collieries which clustered around the city, and which were variously and confusingly named in the course of time. Within Gateshead itself were the pits included in the Grand Lease, valued at £300 a year in 1636, and there was also a Crown freehold at Gateshead valued at £133. 7s. 4d. in 1611. To the west, close to the borders of Whickham lay Saltwellside and Wilson's Field collieries, said to be worth £200 annually.[26]

Collieries were both fewer and smaller on the north bank of the Tyne in the first half of the seventeenth century. Elswick, the closest large colliery to Newcastle, was leased by the Crown for just £21 a year in 1611, although it was thought to be worth £120 a year in profits for its lessees; and the same figure was put upon the profitability of Benwell. Neither colliery would seem to have produced more than 10,000 tons a year at this time, although we know that Benwell grew rapidly thereafter for it was reported in 1636 that as many as forty pits had been worked in an area of some twenty acres. Production at Benwell in 1636 was variously estimated to have amounted to between 100,000 and 300,000 tons over the previous decade.[27] The scale of mining within the city of Newcastle can only be guessed, but output is unlikely to have exceeded 10,000 tons in a year. Some five miles westwards, however, lay the earl of Northumberland's colliery of Newburn, which briefly in the

---

[24] PRO E. 134, 29 Elizabeth, Easter 4.

[25] Nef prints the Ship Money assessments for Darnton and Chester wards in Durham (1932, ii, app. I, 413–16).

[26] Ibid., i. 146–7; ii. 413–16.

[27] Moller thesis 1933, 71; Nef 1932, i. 362 n.

second decade of the century eclipsed all other Northumberland collieries. The lessee, James Cole of Newcastle, paid royalties on a production of 28,000 tons and 23,000 tons in 1612 and 1613 respectively. The earl's advisers, however, accused Cole of fraud, and one maintained that Cole had raised at least 1,000 tens (35,000 tons) from the colliery in 1616. Output slumped, however, when the earl evicted Cole and attempted to run the colliery using his steward, Captain Whitehead.[28]

Most of these Tyneside collieries were ideally located for seasale, and the great bulk of their output went into the ships which plied the Tyne. Winlaton coal was still competitive with leading costs of 5 d. per fother to Derwent Staith in 1582 and 4 d. per fother to Blaydon. Ravensworth, acquired by Thomas Liddell in 1607, was further still from the water, and, in addition to overland transport costs, payments had to be made to the copyholders of Whickham for leave to drive wains through their lands. Crawcrook, situated inland from Ryton, over seven miles from Gateshead, was valued at £500 a year in 1636, which suggests an output perhaps as high as 10,000 tons in good years. In times of booming demand and high prices for coal, even less favourably sited collieries could flourish, if their production costs were low enough. There were limits, however, and, although Chopwell possessed a seam of good fire coal a yard thick at only seven fathoms, it was judged in 1611 that 'there can be no great profit gotten by reason the carriage is far from the water'.[29]

The boom produced exceptional profits for many operators, profits which in a number of cases were further boosted by a liability to pay rents which had been rendered derisory by soaring outputs. The Crown, never to be ranked among efficient landlords, suffered greatly from the consequences of having granted long leases at fixed rents, which it compounded by lack of diligence thereafter. An attempt was made in 1610–11 to staunch the losses, and a series of inquisitions were undertaken of royal coal-mines in order to assess their true worth. In many cases rents were found to be tiny in relation to profits, and, while some discrepancies owed much to recent rapid expansion and the successful efforts of enterprising proprietors, others were held to be the result of dishonesty. John Lyons, a Yarmouth merchant, found himself charged with defrauding the king by securing a lease on Greenlaw freehold in Whickham for a rent of £5, when in fact it was worth £400 annually in profit to him. Lyons and his partners managed to escape prosecution by

[28] DN Syon CX 2(c); QVI 66, 109. See also below ch. 15 (i).
[29] PRO E. 134, 29 Elizabeth, Easter 4; Lewis 1970, 88; PRO E 178/5037, m. 4d.

speedily agreeing to pay a rent of £40, and a fine of 1,000 marks (£666. 23s. 4d.) 'to avoid law'. The Hostmen gained enormously from the Grand Lease as well as from leasing Crown mines, and although it would be foolish to take at face value the charges made in 1621 by Robert Brandling, a mortal enemy of the Hostmen, that Newcastle burgesses were renting the king's mines at a thirtieth of their true worth, they might well have contained more than a grain of truth.[30]

It was from such collieries, and from the efforts of such entrepreneurs, that the massive surge in output sprang. Expansion was heavily concentrated on the most favourably located portions of the exposed coalfield along the Tyne, and such was the productivity of this stretch of water that the Newcastle market could become glutted even when demand was soaring. What is more, even an era of massive growth could be punctuated by periods of stagnation or recession. Shipments from Newcastle marked time for at least a decade from c.1607–8 to 1617–18, and there was a major setback in the mid-1620s.[31] The richness of the Tyne valley coal reserves set limits on mining activity elsewhere, and even the waterside collieries of the Wear were slow to develop. Harraton, it was claimed, had shipped only 6,000 to 10,000 tons per annum between 1629 and 1638, even though 'the coals may be even from the pit almost put into the keels for a very small matter of leading'. Total shipments from the Wear before 1625 fell short of 40,000 tons annually, and it is certain that Lambton and Lumley collieries, though well established, were as yet modest in size.[32]

The Crown surveys of 1610–11 pinpoint decline and failure as well as vitality and success. Many of the mines that were surveyed were deemed to be unworked and without value, while others were in difficulty or without prospects. Away from the Tyne rich coal veins remained untapped for want of a market. At Amble, on the Northumberland coast at the mouth of the Coquet about seven or eight miles from Alnwick, only one pit was being wrought despite the great quantity of 'caking coal fit for fire or salt pans' to be won there. At Preston, a couple of miles to the north of North Shields, working had been abandoned because the water could not be drawn 'without any competent charge'; in recent times one pit had been worked full-time, and on occasion

---

[30] Nef 1932, i. 147–8. Lyons was also a partner in running Denton colliery (PRO E. 178/5037, m. 1d).

[31] See Ch. 14.

[32] Nef 1932, i. 30; Welford (ed.), *Records of Committees for Compounding*, 262; Beastall 1975, 13–15.

another had been set on work, but not fully. At Hartley, to the south of Seaton Sluice, a mile or so from the coast, mining had ceased in 1603 or 1604. Even when worked the coal there was said to be of poor quality, 'neither was there vent or utterance for any quantity'. In south Durham, the inquisitions went on, at Softley 'no work has been set on these last 20 years'; at Raby 'the mine is wrought out in ancient times'; at Thornley there was coal to be won cheaply but 'the vend is not great and uncertain'; at Brandon, two miles south-west of Durham, the profit was only five marks yearly 'by reason the vent or sale of coal is but little and the coal is a pan coal'; and at Cocken, although the coal was good and the seam five-quarters or rather more in thickness, the work was given over 'by reason there was no utterance whereby profit might be made'.[33] Elsewhere in south Durham few signs of growth were revealed by the Ship Money assessments of 1636, though Carterthorn (Railey) remained a substantial colliery, and Tudhoe, Bitchborne, and Spennymoor kept up a modest output.

Here was no Klondike. Success was not guaranteed, and the prospect of corpulent profits sometimes seduced adventurers into foolhardy speculations in ill-located mines, with catastrophic consequences. We are not forced to rely upon the infamously optimistic Huntingdon Beaumont for examples of the ever-present possibility of large-scale losses in an era of general advancement, but his project for breaking the monopoly of the Tyne valley collieries and their Hostmen proprietors by supplying the London market from mines on the Northumberland coast is most instructive of the power of prevailing market constraints. The chosen site for Beaumont and his partners was Cowpen colliery, on the coast between Bedlington and Blyth, about ten miles north of Newcastle, for the development of which they raised £6,000 to 7,000 by their own testimony. But in spite of Beaumont being 'a gentleman of great ingenuity and rare parts, and his many rare engines, not known then in these parts; as the art to bore with iron rods to try the deepness and thickness of the coal; rare engines to draw water out of the pits; waggons with one horse to carry down coals from the pits to the staiths, to the river etc.', the venture was an utter failure and one which buried the fortunes of Beaumont and those who had invested in him. It was not until the eighteenth century that Cowpen prospered. Beaumont was nothing if not adventurous, and in 1606, contemporaneously with his project at Cowpen and Bebside, he organized a group of investors to take over the remainder of a lease on nearby Bedlington colliery. There

[33] PRO E. 178/5037.

are few details of how this scheme fared, but we may presume that it too failed, for Beaumont defaulted on his obligations and suffered the indignity of being kidnapped by irate creditors in 1612.[34] There are few men in any age with either the vision, energy, or breathtaking reckless- ness of a Huntington Beaumont, and by no means all ultimately unsuccessful ventures were so evidently risky from the start. Robert Bowes, John Smith of King's Lynn, and the earl of Huntingdon, who attempted to establish a major colliery and saltworks at Offerton, close to the Wear on the outskirts of Sunderland, blamed their lack of success on a collapse underground which blocked the main drainage channel, but it was more probably due to a lack of demand for their coal and salt.[35] There was more to making a profit than digging coal out of the ground at a reasonable cost.

The Civil War and after

The Civil War was just one of a series of major catastrophes which struck Newcastle and its region in the middle decades of the seven- teenth century.[36] The first catastrophe was an exceptionally severe epidemic of plague in 1635–6. North Shields was devastated before Christmas 1635, and by October 1636 as many as 5,000 persons may have died in Newcastle. John Fenwick lamented of his city, with melancholy exaggeration, 'almost desolate, thy streets grown green with grass, thy treasury wasted, thy trading departed'. Hard upon the heels of bubonic plague came the pestilence visited by a bankrupt monarch. In 1637–8 Charles I embarked upon an attempt to monopolize the coal trade, but succeeded only in producing confusion and collapse in short order. The trade was boycotted by shippers who feared the loss of their livelihood, with the result that coal-owners could not dispose of their output. An already weakened coal trade faced ruin. In December 1638 the Privy Council wrote to the Lord Mayor of London warning him that many Hostmen had been forced 'for want of sale . . . to give over their works and discharge their workmen', and John Marley, Hostman and mayor of Newcastle, excused his inability to discharge debts incurred by him in the abortive contract with Charles I by pointing out that his staithes were so full that 'they are like to fire'.[37]

[34] Moller thesis 1933, 180–4; Smith 1957; Nef 1932, i. 32–3; ii. 16; Gray, *Chorographia*, 24–5.

[35] *CSPD, Addenda 1580-1625*, 327; Galloway 1898, i. 103–4.

[36] In compiling this section on the Civil War much use has been made of Howell 1967 and Terry, 1899 146–258.

[37] Nef 1932, ii. 282–3.

Newcastle's initiation into the traumas of war and hostile occupation came a matter of months afterwards. The victory of the Scottish army at the battle of Newburn had effectively given them control of Northumberland, and the remaining English forces evacuated Newcastle and retreated south on 29 August. Although the Scottish commanders did not set out to hinder the coal trade, 'since the free traffic of coal is so necessary to the city of London and other places of England', much harm was inevitably done. Gaining a balanced view of the impact of these momentous occurrences on the economic life of the region is no easy matter. Gloom inevitably pervaded the sentiments of those closest to the events. John Rushworth wrote of the complete collapse of the economic life of the city and its environs: 'Newcastle and the coalmines that had wont to employ ten thousand people all year long about their coalery, some working underground, some above, others upon the water in keels and lighters, now not a man to be seen, not a coal wrought.' Sir Benjamin Rudyard prognosticated that the north would not regain 'its former state these twenty years' and that 'the coalmines of Newcastle will not be set right again for one hundred thousand pounds'. There was some deliberate destruction of property, and Sir Thomas Riddell claimed that his coals were spoiled, his mining machinery broken, and the best part of his pits destroyed. But Riddell may well have been victimized because of his outspoken anti-Scottish sentiments. Clearly, Rudyard's and Rushworth's judgements were overly pessimistic, but it is important to stress that the trade was already weakening before the first Scottish occupation occurred.

If the coal industry had been harmed by the events of the 1630s, it was to suffer further severe injury during the Civil War. The coal trade was a prime target of the combatants, and both sides were well aware of the nourishing revenues which could be milked by those who controlled it, and of the 'great and pressing necessities of coals; which will so pinch the poor, that the consequences thereof will be full of horror and danger'.[38] The economy of the city of Newcastle and its region had nothing to gain from the war, and although its sympathies lay with the king it was in practice a hostage to the wills of both sides, and those wills were driven hard by necessity. Charles sought to use his control of Newcastle and the coal trade to raise revenues, and immediately reimposed all those duties of which he had recently been deprived by Parliament. In addition he levied a further huge charge of £30–50 on

[38] Alderman Adams of London to the House of Commons in July 1643 (quoted Howell 1967, 154).

every laden collier leaving the Tyne, which amounted to about 20s. on every chaldron. By these impositions the king threatened to raise in excess of £150,000. The response of Parliament was as inevitable as it was destructive, for unable to contemplate such sums flowing into royal coffers, and buoyed by assurances from Scottish allies that the collieries on the Firth of Forth could compensate for those on the Tyne, the Commons forbade trade with Newcastle, Sunderland, and Blyth on 9 January 1643.[39]

Within days the dependence of London on north-eastern coal forced prices there to intolerable levels in anticipation of scarcity. There was, of course, scant possibility in the short term of supplies from Scotland and Wales making up much of the shortfall, and ordinances seeking to restrain the price of coal were soon in force, but to little avail. So successful was the blockade, and so doleful its impact, that by the following May Parliament was already examining ways of lifting it; proposals were even made to equip an army using forced loans from shippers and consumers to take Newcastle. By the early months of 1644 the coal trade, and indeed the whole trade of the north-east, had virtually ceased to exist. In January 1644 only nineteen ships left Newcastle, in February just nine, in March three, April five, and between May and November 1644 just one ship set sail. In 1641 3,043 ships had cleared the port; in the twelve months after Michaelmas 1643 there were just 188 sailings. Sadly, there are few details of the collapse of mining, but it could not have been far short of total.[40]

London and Parliament looked towards the Wear for their salvation, and in March 1644 the Scots obliged by taking Sunderland. Colliers hastened northwards and in April some 120 were reported waiting in Sunderland harbour laden with coals. The output of Wearside collieries had undoubtedly grown rapidly prior to the outbreak of war, and Lumley, Harraton, and Lambton had developed into great collieries, the latter yielding £800 a year in rent. Records from the Wear show almost 64,000 tons being sent southwards in 1633–4, and some contemporary estimates put Sunderland's coal trade on the eve of the war as high as 100,000 tons, so the prospect of significantly improved supplies to London and other east coast ports was real enough. But a complete solution was not at hand, and on 10 June 1644 a royalist garrison carried out a destructive raid on Wearside mines, with the intention of inflicting

[39] See also the discussion in Nef 1932, ii. 284–300, in which it is claimed that the new taxes could have accounted for almost 20s. on each Newcastle chaldron.
[40] CSPV 1642-3, 229, 235; Terry 1899, 242.

long-term damage on the Tyne's main rivals as well as hindering the relief of the fuel crisis.[41]

For the severity of that crisis, and of the importance of coal to the life of the south-east, one need look no further than the proceedings of the Commons during the summer of 1644, in which the coal trade, the Wear collieries, and the prospective capture of Newcastle loomed exceedingly large. When, after a lengthy siege, the Scots entered Newcastle on 19 October 1644, they found extreme distress: 'the rich town, in which ten [sic] of the Aldermen are Knights, and as malignant as honourable, [is] to be an object of pity, if malignants are to be pitied, there being in view nothing but many hundreds of almost naked people, wanting all things but misery'. The capture of Newcastle was to mark a turning-point in the fortunes of the coal trade and the industry which supported it. Having gained control from the royalists the very indispensability of coal made the restoration of trade the overriding priority. Work on clearing the Tyne of sunken vessels was started and the coal ships began sailing again. No less than 145 colliers set sail from Newcastle in December, almost all destined for London and other stricken east coast ports. Between December and the following Michaelmas over 330,000 tons of coal left the Tyne, and the House of Lords was told in May that 'there is plenty of Newcastle coal' and that emergency ordinances encouraging the production of wood could be revoked.[42] By December 1645 emphasis had switched from satisfaction with the supply of coal to satisfaction with the amounts of money that taxes upon its shipment had yielded. So quickly did trade recover that a considerable proportion of early shipments must have come from stockpiles rather than new production, and we know that Sir Nicholas Cole was thought to have profited greatly by buying up and storing during the war 'a great stock upon his staithe, which he got cheap when others had no means to do the like', and which he was able to dispose of at 10s. a chaldron when trade restarted.[43]

Although all parties—Parliament, the Scots, colliery owners and their work-forces, shipmasters, and the long-suffering consumers—wished to get production and trade back to normal as soon as possible, there were many obstacles to be overcome. Some colliers had been deliberately sunk to block the Tyne, while others had been sequestered by the Scots.

---

[41] Newcastle coal-traders resented the absence of duty on coastal shipments of coal from Sunderland.

[42] *HLJ* vii. 388; viii. 34.

[43] Terry 1899, 253–4.

Collieries had deteriorated while they had lain unworked, or only intermittently worked, for many months. Much fighting had taken place on
the Northumberland and Durham coalfield, and some pits had been
damaged. The earl of Northumberland claimed that Tynemouth colliery
had been wasted by the fighting in 1643 and 1644. Harraton colliery lay
damaged and lost from 1642 to 1647, and it was asserted that £2,000 had
to be spent to put it to rights. Yet, despite the many threats that had
been uttered, few mines had actually been fired, since they were far too
valuable to both sides for that act to have been widely perpetrated.[44]

When the treatment of the delinquent colliery owners came to be
decided, expediency once again triumphed over principle. Whereas, on
the one hand, many coal-owners had been so 'malignant' that they
deserved to be punished severely, and the sequestration of their estates
was the obvious means of doing so, on the other they possessed indispensable expertise in the management of collieries and the prosecution
of the coal trade. If the question had ever been seriously in doubt, the
balance was decisively tipped by the fact that a flourishing coal trade
was likely to prove the best source of the money which had to be paid to
the Scots in recompense for their military exertions. Thus, royalists
were allowed to remain in control of their coal-mines and of the coal
trade. A further dilemma was posed, albeit of a more familiar character,
by the conflicting aims of shipping the maximum amount of coal at
reasonable prices in order to alleviate the sufferings of the poor in the
south-east, and extracting the maximum amount of taxation from the
coal trade in order to pay off the Scots and finance the war. In the event,
parliamentary commissioners settled on a huge tax of 10s. per chaldron,
with the owners' selling price fixed at 10s. per chaldron and the shipmasters' buying price at 20s. There can be no doubt the poor were
oppressed and recovery hampered by this burden, and it was soon
lightened.[45]

The north-east coalfield in the later seventeenth century

In spite of being gravely impaired during the hostilities, the north-east
coalfield made a speedy and complete recovery from the Civil War. But
the days of seemingly effortless acceleration of output that had characterized the pre-war era did not return. Records of shipments from
north-eastern ports reveal that there was no sustained growth between

[44] Howell 1967, 281–2; Welford (ed.), *Records of Committees for Compounding*, 392–3.

[45] Terry 1899, 253–8; Nef 1932, ii. 293–4. The 4s. duty was briefly reimposed under the threat of
a further Scottish invasion of the north of England in 1648.

the later 1650s and the early 1670s and that, after a surge to new peaks in the ensuing decade, the industry experienced many setbacks during the war-torn years at the close of the century. Fortunately, the documentation of mining as well as of shipments is excellent in this period, and much can be learned about the leading collieries in the coalfield, as well as about many of those in the second rank. For the turn of the century it is also possible to ascribe outputs to most leading Tyneside collieries by using an extensive range of complementary sources, including a series of vend or output limitation agreements between major producers, two contemporary listings of Tyneside collieries with their supposed outputs, and a large range of complementary colliery accounts.[46]

It would be tedious to recount the histories of all those collieries for which information is available, but a survey of some of the more important can illuminate the forces of continuity and of change which lay behind the overall development of the coalfield. It is appropriate to begin with the Grand Lease collieries, and more especially with Whickham, which in the 1630s had dwarfed every other colliery in Britain. A detailed survey was made of Whickham in 1652, and it revealed the extensive mining that had taken place within the manor. The surveyors reported that coal had been worked in no fewer than twenty-one distinct locations, with evidence of multiple sinkings in most places. In Eastfield, for example, fourteen pits had been sunk in the top coal, around nine pits in the five-quarter coal, and twenty-five in the main coal. Yet the surveyors forecast that 'three new pits may be sunk and wrought in the main coal. And that the five and twenty pits may and will yet cast in the several seams very considerable quantities of good and merchantable coal'. Likewise in thirteen of the remaining twenty mining sites on the manor the surveyors were credibly informed by 'skillful and knowing workmen' and by 'men judicious in collieries' that there remained rich reserves which would last for many years. The survey conducted of the lesser colliery, Gateshead, was much less thorough, but the surveyors felt able to report with confidence that 'there would be collieries left for many ages'.[47]

Coalmining at Whickham and Gateshead was indeed to continue on a large scale well into the eighteenth century, yet they were well past their peak. For all their optimism the surveyors of 1652 valued the Grand Lease at only £2,500 above the negligible rent which the bishop of

[46] NuRO Cookson ZCO/iv/47/; HRO Cowper D/EPT 4858; Hughes 1952, 167, 168; Cromar thesis 1977, 168; NEI Buddle 14/212; GPL Cotesworth CK/3/135.

[47] Kirby (ed.), *Parliamentary Surveys*, 132–41.

Durham received for it. Exactly ten years later Bishop Cosin's investigation of the economic state and prospect of the bishopric put the value to the lessees at £2,000 a year, although it was acknowledged with a mixture of nostalgia and expectation as 'having been worth heretofore and so may hereafter, £5,000 and sometimes £8,000 per annum'.[48] Even these latter figures were a far cry from the 'at least £50,000' yearly which the Grand Lease was held to be worth soon after its enactment.[49] For decades reality and mythology had fruitfully intermingled, but by the time that the bishops could look forward to regaining possession the productivity of the prize collieries was in steep decline.[50] At the turn of the seventeenth and eighteenth centuries around 35,000 tons a year were being produced within Whickham 'Grand Lease' and 15,000 tons within Gateshead.[51] Yet there were other potential compensations within the bishop's extensive and rich coal-bearing estates. Most notably Ryton colliery, which, with the neighbouring properties of Tallow and Kyo, was said to be worth over £2,400 a year in 1662, although Bishop Cosin received only £20. 13s. 4d. for it in rent.[52]

One of the most significant developments in the later seventeenth century was the spectacular growth in the output of collieries located some distance from the south bank of the Tyne, which was made possible by the provision of wooden waggonways along which coal could be cheaply transported. Foremost among these was Gibside, whose output rose meteorically under the enterprising management of Sir Charles Montagu; by the close of the century it was producing well over 60,000 tons annually.[53] Gibside was situated some four miles from the Tyne; even further away was Chopwell with an output of over 40,000 tons. The rich reserves at Chopwell had been noted in 1611, but judged to be virtually worthless 'by reason the carriage is far from the water'. In 1641 Chopwell had been purchased by the Vane family for a mere £404. 18s. 2d., but by the close of the century it had been transformed by a waggonway into one of the most productive collieries of the region.[54] To the west of Chopwell, located on a spur of the waggonway, lay Hedley Fell colliery, with a capacity of over 15,000 tons.[55] Just

---

[48] DuCL Sharp 167, 170 (Bishop Cosin's 'State of the Bishoprick', 1662).

[49] Gardiner, *England's Grievance*, 14.

[50] See e.g. the dispute about the valuations of Whickham and Gateshead collieries in 1647–8, when the corporations of London and Newcastle squabbled over the reversions of the manors (Howell 1967, 297–8; Dodds (ed.), *Newcastle-upon-Tyne Council Minute Books*, 84).

[51] Hughes 1952, 150.   [52] DuCL Sharp 167, 172.

[53] DuRO Strathmore D/St vol. 36.   [54] PRO E. 178/5037, m. 4d; PRO E. 121/2/4.

[55] HRO Cowper D/EPT 4877–8.

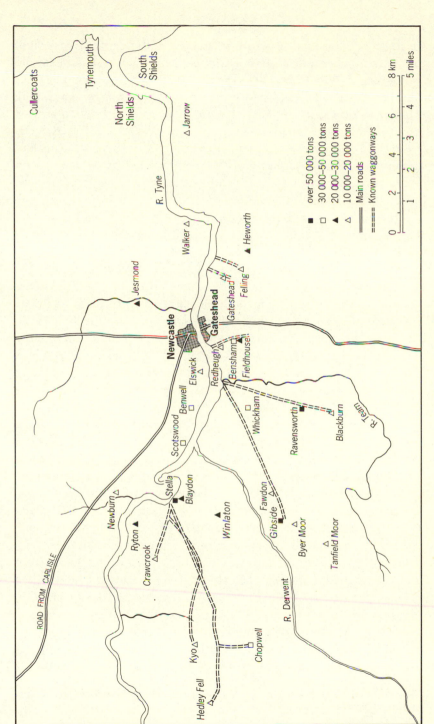

Map 5.2. Principal Tyneside collieries, c.1700

Legend:
- ■ over 50 000 tons
- □ 30 000–50 000 tons
- ▲ 20 000–30 000 tons
- △ 10 000–20 000 tons
- —— Main roads
- ==== Known waggonways

Scale: 0 1 2 3 4 5 miles / 0 2 4 6 8 km

Place names: Cullercoats, Tynemouth, North Shields, South Shields, Jarrow, R. Tyne, Walker, Heworth, Jesmond, Newcastle, Gateshead, Gateshead, Felling, Redheugh, Bensham, Fieldhouse, Elswick, Benwell, Scotswood, Whickham, Ravensworth, Blackburn, R. Team, Stella, Blaydon, Newburn, Ryton, Crawcrook, Winlaton, Fawdon, Gibside, Byer Moor, Tanfield Moor, R. Derwent, Hedley Fell, Kyo, Chopwell, ROAD FROM CARLISLE to the south of Gibside lay Byermoor colliery, with a capacity of around 5,000 tons. A further mile away lay Tanfield Moor, which had been sold for just £109. 2s. 8d. in 1648;[56] by 1700 it was producing around 15,000 tons a year. These collieries had been liberated by waggonways, and, together with others in similarly distant locations, they added at least 150,000 tons to the annual capacity of Tyneside. Moreover, Ravensworth in the Team valley went from strength to strength on the back of a waggonway first installed in 1669. By 1700 it was one of the very largest collieries in Britain, with an output of 65,000 tons. Close by, but even further from the Tyne, some 5,000 to 10,000 tons a year were raised from Blackburn colliery, while another colliery of similar dimensions was located at High Park, some three and a half miles inland from Gateshead.

Scarcely less significant was the expansion of mining on the Northumberland side of the Tyne. We have noted how in the earlier part of the seventeenth century collieries on the north bank had been both fewer and smaller than those on the Durham side, but by the last quarter there were a number of extremely productive areas, on or close to the river. In the hands of Charles Montagu, Benwell colliery, which had lain unworked stricken by a furious underground fire for much of the century, throve to outputs of at least 35,000 tons, while just to the west at Scotswood, where mining was relatively new but exceptionally vigorous, output matched that of its older neighbour. Although outputs at Elswick and Walker were relatively modest, Jesmond to the north of Newcastle was booming with a capacity of 25,000 to 30,000 tons. Most remarkable of all, perhaps, was the rise and decline of mining on Whorlton Moor, which lay about a mile and a half from the Tyne in Newburn parish, five miles to the west of Newcastle. In 1676–7, the first full year's account that we have, no less than 67,078 wain-loads (fothers) were led from the pits, all except 2,000 of which went to Lemington and Denton staithes, amounting in total probably to just under 60,000 tons. A peak was reached in 1684–5 when almost 100,000 tons of coal were led from Whorlton to the Tyne. Between 1676–7 and 1691–2 production averaged 60,000 tons annually, before tailing off and finally ceasing in 1698–9.[57] It is therefore not to be wondered at that Charles Montagu, when seeking reassurance for his 'ridiculous' (the word is his) computations of what Gibside might be capable of producing and selling after the

---

[56] Kirby (ed.), *Parliamentary Surveys*, 175–6; G. Allan, *Collectanea ad statum civilem et ecclesiasticum comitatus Dunelmensis spectantia* (Darlington, 1774), 201.

[57] DN Syon, CX 2a(1).

construction of a waggonway, drew comfort from the thought that 'Mr Rogers did actually work at Whorlton Moor 3,000 tens a year . . . and all the coals were sold at the highest price upon the river'.[58]

The output of collieries on the Northumberland coast also assumed greater moment in the closing decades of the seventeenth century. There was a cluster of ventures between Blyth and Tynemouth. The prospects of Whitley colliery, with its adjacent salt-pans, were so enticing that its owner, Lady Elizabeth Percy, was inspired to share with the lessee, John Rogers, the costs of dredging Cullercoats harbour and building a pier. Her money was well spent, for annual output frequently exceeded 20,000 tons in the remaining years of the century. Rogers also mined nearby at Monkseaton.[59] So buoyant was the output of Plessey that it justified the construction of a waggonway in 1689. If we may judge from the claim by Sir Ralph Delaval that he stood to lose £7,000 when Seaton Delaval flooded in 1676, this was also a colliery of great moment. In the event he was overly pessimistic, for it had been flooded by freshwater not the sea, and it was restored to production at a fraction of the cost.[60]

Significant as these new developments were, however, we must be careful neither to overstate nor antedate the migration of mining away from the banks of the Tyne. While in theory there was an ineluctable Ricardian tendency for the most accessible seams to be both worked and exhausted first, and for new mines to be both deeper and less favourably sited than the old, in practice the time-scale of the process could be very long indeed. In traditional mining areas many rich seams were very durable, and new sites were constantly being opened up which were both cheap to mine and conveniently located. Moreover, the lives of ancient collieries were extended, and their profitability improved, by advances in the technology of mining. We have noted the slow decline of Whickham, but output at Stella, where mining can first be noted in 1566, continued to soar, averaging an unsurpassed 80,000 tons in the 1680s and 1690s.[61] Winlaton colliery, which dated from at least as early as the mid-fourteenth century, was still producing over 20,000 tons at the close of the seventeenth; and Ryton, which dated from the early fifteenth century, yielded a similar quantity. Mines close to Derwent staithes at the estuary of the River Derwent, were producing

[58] NeUL Montagu, Montagu to Baker 10/7/97.
[59] *NCH* viii. 20; DN Syon, CX 4*b*(2).
[60] Lewis 1970, 112; North, *Life of Francis North*, 138.
[61] NoRO Cookson ZCO IV/47/1–33.

well over 40,000 tons a year, and the productivity of neighbouring Blaydon, though lower than earlier in the century still approached 20,000 tons a year. Moreover, while the Gateshead area witnessed the decline of some older collieries it also had many enduring successes. Most notable among the latter were Bensham, Fieldhouse, and Heworth, whose combined outputs must have exceeded 80,000 tons.

When developments in the north-eastern coalfield in the later seventeenth century are assessed in the round, it becomes evident that capacity soared above output. The sea coal trade stagnated after the Restoration, and although shipments rose strongly between 1675 and 1685, they suffered many setbacks in the remaining years of the century. Total shipments in the later 1650s had averaged 570,000 tons annually; in the last forty years of the seventeenth century they were to average 630,000 tons, despite reaching almost 800,000 tons on occasion in the 1680s. Many factors combined to trouble the shipment of coal, including a succession of wars with the Dutch, the reversal of England's long era of rising population, a slowing of London's growth, and, in the closing years of the century, the imposition of heavy duties by London and the Crown on the coastal trade.

Shipments of coal, of course, take no account of trends in local consumption, and both domestic and industrial coal consumption had for centuries been high within the vicinity of the coalfield. Moreover, the persistent dislocations which marred the east coast trade and the oppressive new duties which had been placed upon it, gave further encouragement for coal-intensive industries to locate themselves close to the mines. According to the author of a pamphlet entitled *The Mischief of the Five Shillings Tax upon Coal*, published in 1699, 'since the war there is a vast increase of manufactures made with coal in the north'. He also drew attention to the advertisement placed in London by Ambrose Crowley seeking to encourage ironworkers to migrate to his works at Winlaton, near Newcastle.[62] Ambrose Crowley's works at Winlaton consumed about 1,600 tons a year in the early eighteenth century, and he had other ironworks nearby at Winlaton Mill and Swalwell.[63] Lime-burning, glass-making, and alum manufacture were among other significant consumers of coal in the north-east, but most important of all was the anciently established salt industry, which was burning around 100,000 tons of pancoal annually at the turn of the century.[64]

[62] Moller thesis 1933, 26–7.
[63] Flinn 1984, 245.   [64] See below, Ch. 12 (ii).

Rising industrial consumption undoubtedly offered some compensation for a stagnant sea trade, but none the less so impressive was the achievement of the Northumberland and Durham coal industry, that its ability to raise coal frequently threatened to overtake its ability to dispose of it, even at prices which had not increased in money terms for decades.[65] The potential supply of coal at reasonable prices was far in excess of the demand for it, and so it was to remain for decades into the eighteenth century. The seventeenth century closed with the coal-owners receiving 8–10s for each chaldron of coal, which is almost exactly what their predecessors had received when the century opened. When J. C. published his *Compleat Collier* in 1708, he lamented that noble Main Coal was being sold for a mere 8s. a chaldron, whereas in the past it had fetched 11s. 6d. or 12s.[66] In such circumstances it was inevitable that coal-owners should devote considerable time and ingenuity to generating sales, including advertising in London and granting discounts to dealers there. It was also perhaps inevitable that they should resort once again to combinations and cartels. Our period closes with the resurrection of Limitation Agreements, last used in 1637, by which the major proprietors shared agreed levels of output among themselves.[67]

Finally, we must collate the wealth of evidence available at the turn of the seventeenth and eighteenth centuries and chart the productivity and distribution of the leading north-eastern collieries. In Map 5.2 the location and estimated outputs of the leading Tyneside collieries, and also the majority of the second-rank, are given. On the basis of this evidence it is possible to hazard a plausible estimate of the total output of Tyneside. The outputs of these leading identifiable collieries at the close of the seventeenth century total some 750,000 tons, to which must be added the yield of those collieries which have not come to notice, including many small-scale undertakings. By this method the annual output of Tyneside alone would perhaps be estimated at 900,000 to 1,000,000 tons in a good year. Tackling the same task by an alternative route, we know that customs accounts record that an average of 560,000 tons were shipped out of Newcastle each year between 1698 and 1700.

[65] See App. B (i).

[66] *Compleat Collier*, 17–19.

[67] In 1700 proposals were made for several of the great coal-owners of the Tyne to reach agreement with 'several considerable coal traders living in and about London'. One such agreement was reached between John Clavering and the Oldner family, lightermen of Southwark, by which Clavering paid the Oldners 4d per London chaldron for all Stella Main coals which they caused to be loaded by shipmasters on the Tyne (HRO Cowper D/EPT 4854). For 18th-cent. Limitations of the Vend see Flinn 1984, 256 ff.

The incentive to evade duties and the practices and conventions of the coal trade, including the granting of overmeasure and gift-coal to the shippers, meant that customs records inevitably understated actual shipments, and due allowance must also be made for sales by landsale collieries and for landsales by seasale collieries, including salt-pans. If we opt for Michael Flinn's percentage additions to seasales for these omissions, then the 560,000 tons would become 800,000 tons[68] Leaving the relative security of the excellent Tyneside sources, an attempt must be made to estimate the output of the many substantial seasale collieries on Wearside and the north Northumberland coast.[69] Customs accounts suggest that 150,000 tons were shipped from non-Tyneside collieries at the turn of the century, which indicates that they may well have produced in excess of 200,000 tons. Finally, account must be taken of the output of landsale collieries, of which there were many in south Durham. All in all, therefore, it would seem likely that the greatest coalfield in Britain was producing for sale 1.1 to 1.3 million tons a year at the close of the seventeenth century.

ii. Scotland

The coalfields of Scotland lie in a belt across the central lowlands from the Firth of Forth to the Ayrshire coast. It is possible to divide and categorize them in a variety of ways, but for the purposes of studying their development before the eighteenth century a threefold division based upon both geology and local economy has much to commend it.[1] The prime region was the Firth of Forth where the accessibility of rich seams of top-quality coal neatly complemented the benefits of dense population and good water communications. By the close of the seventeenth century productive collieries lined the northern shores of the Firth and clustered around Bo'ness in West Lothian and Lasswade in Midlothian on the southern shores. In Lanarkshire a focus for mining was provided by Glasgow, but elsewhere despite great potential for

[68] Flinn 1984, 29–33. Unlike the methods of estimating output adopted by Professer Flinn, in this volume estimates of output are of saleable coal and, following the practice of 16th- and 17th-cent. sources, take no account of unsaleable waste brought to the surface, nor of colliers' free coal or of coal burnt on the site.

[69] Lists of Wearside collieries are contained in DuCL Sharp 167, 172–6; Nef 1932, ii. 413–16; Wilcock 1979, map on 22.

[1] The division adopted here is based more upon economic than geological factors, and follows Nef rather than Flinn.

expansion the sale of coal was handicapped by the shallowness of the Clyde, which was navigable only by tiny boats of a few tons capacity. The Ayrshire coalfield had ready access to water, and the ports of the west coast were able to berth large ships, but, with a sparse population and scant industry, production depended critically upon shipments to Ireland, and the Irish trade was highly competitive.

There can be no doubt that Scotland was one of the leading British coal-producing regions before the eighteenth century, but there are good reasons for believing that its output has been substantially over-estimated by its historians. In important respects the environment within which the Scottish coal industry had to operate was decidedly inferior to that prevailing in many English coalfields. The Scottish economy was more primitive, and population was sparser and poorer. There were few towns of any size, industrial development was stunted, and commercial and financial structure retarded. Even in the later sixteenth century, a leading historian of the economic history of Scotland has maintained, 'while the cultural life of the nation was break-ing ancient fetters, the economic remained essentially medieval, indeed it is arguable that economic life reached its medieval apogée in the reign of Queen Mary'.[2] Such an environment created towering obstacles to the growth and development of coalmining. Yet it did not delay the start of the coal industry. The sources for the early history of mining in Scot-land are extremely poor, but we can be confident that before the mid-fourteenth century coal was dug in very many places where it outcropped on the exposed coalfields.

The earliest references to mining, perhaps distorted by the dispro-portionate survival of ecclesiastical records, relate exclusively to monastic estates. Among the first of all may have been the pits on the estates of Holyrood and Newbattle abbeys at Carriden and Preston on the south shore of the Firth of Forth. Other thirteenth-century pits, or heughs as they were known in Scotland, occur in a number of monastic cartularies. At Pittencrief in Dumfermline in 1291, for example, William de Oberwill granted the right to the abbot and convent to open up a coal-mine anywhere on the estate, excepting arable land, to take fuel for the needs of the house. Coal-carrying services to be performed by tenants of agricultural holdings are also mentioned in cartularies. Docu-mentation generated during the Scots Wars reveals that small quantities of coal were purchased in Edinburgh, Glasgow, Linlithgow, and

---

[2] Lythe 1973, 57. For further general discussions of the early modern Scottish economy see Lythe 1960; Grant 1930; Lythe and Butt 1975.

Dunipace (Stirlingshire) by the English armies, often for the use of their smiths.[3] These towns were probably the focus of the medieval coal trade, such as it was.

Coal was almost certainly dug in small quantities in many places where surface outcrops demanded scant effort, but the heavier concentration of mining activity which can be identified in the Lothians around Bo'ness, Linlithgow, Lasswade, and Loanhead is likely to represent the centre of the medieval industry. Although total output could not have been high, Scottish coal was supplying overseas markets from at least as early as the mid-fifteenth century. Customs accounts reveal regular but tiny shipments from Leith and a number of lesser ports along the Firth of Forth.[4] Coastwise traffic can also be observed from the fourteenth century, with shipments destined for a multitude of ports as far north as Aberdeen.[5] By the mid-sixteenth century coal was also being exported from Dumbarton, Ayr and Irvine on the west coast to Ireland, and from the Firth of Forth down the east coast to Hull.[6]

By the mid-sixteenth century domestic coal consumption was on a significant scale. According to Estienne Perlin, who visited Scotland in 1552, 'in this country the people warm themselves with coals'.[7] Certainly the appointment at Dundee of a 'deacon of the coal trade' to keep a register of the coal boats unloading there suggests that the inhabitants in this burgh conformed to Perlin's stereotype.[8] Scotland had never been well provided with trees, and rising population soon led to fears of fuel shortages, especially in the vicinity of towns. As early as 1555 the Scottish Parliament legislated to curtail severely the felling of trees and the destruction of woodland, while at the same time care was taken to nurture the timber trade with Norway.[9] By 1563 so intense had the phobia of fuel famine become that all exports of coal were prohibited, because coal reserves were thought to be 'decayed and growing scant daily'.[10] In reality, of course, the enhanced demand for coal swiftly led to enhanced supply, and the later sixteenth and early seventeenth centuries in Scotland, as well as in England and Wales, was an era of sustained rapid growth for the coal industry.

---

[3] Lythe and Butt 1975, 39; Galloway 1898, i. 18; Grant 1930, 116; Guy thesis 1982, 146.

[4] Guy thesis 1982, figs. 6.1–6.4; Nef 1932, i. 44 n.

[5] Exchequer Rolls of Scotland, *passim*.

[6] Guy thesis 1982, 146; R. Davis, *The Trade and Shipping of Hull, 1500-1700*, East Yorkshire Local History Society (1964), 13–14.

[7] Quoted in Lythe 1960, 46.   [8] Grant 1930, 317.

[9] *APS* ii. 499. The legislation was reiterated in 1567 (*APS* iii. 39);

[10] *APS* ii. 543.

Emblematic of the surge in production which flowed through the Scottish coal industry, though far too prodigious to be typical, was the 'unfellowed and unmatchable work' undertaken at Culross colliery. The digging of coal at Culross for the monks of the nearby abbey had a lengthy history, but in 1575 when the estates of the abbey were seized the coalworkings were said to have 'long been in desuetude'. George Bruce was chosen as the new lessee 'for his great knowledge and skill in machinery such like as no other man has in these days, and for his being the likeliest person to re-establish again the colliery of Culross'. The choice was inspired, for Bruce went on not just to restart production but to create a technologically advanced colliery, part of it deep under the sea and drained by an impressive battery of dams, channels, and machines, and to establish a flourishing saltworks. Sadly no management accounts survive, but there can be no doubt of the success of Culross, it was even accorded the twin accolades of a royal visit and an epic poem. The town of Culross soon throve to burgh status, and a necklace of coal-using industries ringed the colliery, including salt-boiling, glass-making, and ironworking. The colliery itself was soon exporting coal, and it was for long to remain among the most productive on the Firth of Forth despite intermittent flooding.[11]

There are no surviving accounts for any Scottish colliery from this time, but although we can discover little detail about the coalworkings which proliferated, an impressionistic trawl among the none too comprehensive sources reveals the names of well over fifty which were active before 1650.[12] By no means all of these should be dignified with the title of colliery rather than mine or pit, and many were undoubtedly temporary rather than permanent features of the industrial landscape. Yet there were some sizeable operations among them. Airth colliery, for example, was exporting before 1596 and its owner reported 'the death of the number of three or four score of horses' at his pits, and the disbursement of 'great sums of money in casting and winning of his coals'. There was some substance in his bluster, for in 1614 his grandson concluded an agreement with London coal-dealers to supply them with first 4,000 and then 8,000 tons of 'great pit coals of Scotland' each year.[13] We are also led to believe that, as time passed, the numbers of large collieries increased, along with the overall growth of output. In 1615, for example, a commission of inquiry deemed it permissible for the collieries of Bonhard,

---

[11] Bowman 1970; Beveridge 1885.   [12] Their distribution is given on Map 5.3.

[13] W. B. Armstrong, 'Two Papers Relating to the Export of Coals from Scotland, 1596 and 1614', *Proceedings of the Society of Antiquaries of Scotland*, NS 12 (1889–90), 474–7.

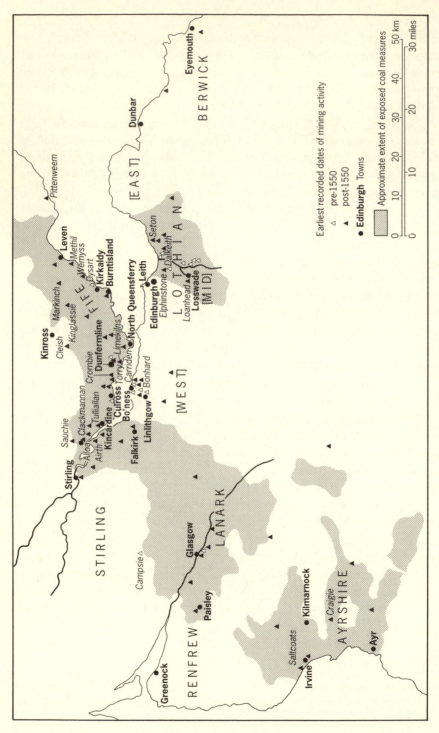

Pittenweem

Leven
Methil
Markinch
Kinglassie
FIFE
Wemyss
Dysart
Kirkaldy
Burntisland

Kinross
Cleish
Crombie
Dunfermline
Limekilns
North Queensferry

Clackmannan
Sauchie
Tulliallan
Culross
Torry
Carriden
Stirling
Alloa
Airth
Kincardine
Bo'ness
Bonhard

STIRLING

Campsie

RENFREW
Greenock
Paisley
Glasgow
LANARK

Saltcoats
Irvine
Kilmarnock
Craigie
AYRSHIRE
Ayr

Falkirk
Linlithgow
[WEST]

Edinburgh
Elphinstone
Leith
Loanhead
Lasswade
[MID]

Seton
Dalkeith
LOTHIAN

[EAST]

Dunbar

Eyemouth
BERWICK

Earliest recorded dates of mining activity
△ pre-1550
▲ post-1550
● **Edinburgh** Towns
▨ Approximate extent of exposed coal measures

0   10   20   30   40   50 km
0   10   20   30 miles

Map 5.3. The Scottish coalfields

Carriden, Airth, Alloa, Sauchie, Kincardine, Culross, Torry, and Crombie to gain exemption from the export prohibition then in force, and send some of their output overseas, because of their 'great and daily charges and expenses'. By 1627 the list of legitimate exporting collieries had grown to at least fifteen, and in 1643 no less than twenty-five coalmasters faced accusations of serving strangers in preference to natives.[14] For some of these collieries we can discover supplementary confirmation of their size and importance. Little Fawside was said by its owner to have cost more than £10,000 Scots to save after a fire, while a new pit was costing more than £4,000 Scots to sink. The master of Elphinstone claimed to have spent over 20,000 marks Scots on his colliery 'which [sum] is not able to be recovered in many years', while the master of Smeton testified that he had spent over £20,000 Scots on his coal-heughs over the previous seven years with scant return.[15]

The major protagonists in the struggle to manipulate the coal trade were the burghs and the coal-masters. The former, who exercised some of their power through the Convention of the Royal Burghs, wished for coal to be kept for the home market, while the latter, who exerted considerable influence over the Privy Council, wished for free trade.[16] Despite rising production, complaints about the shortage and high price of supplies on the home market continued to be voiced, and export restrictions continued to be reiterated.[17] Inevitably price controls were added to the armoury of weapons used in attempts to protect the consumer, and regulation of the coal trade also extended to the forcible direction of coal supplies into favoured local markets. In 1642 the magistrates of Edinburgh and other towns in East and Mid Lothian complained:

without coal they cannot live, wanting all other fuel [but] some tacksmen have of late defrauded them of coal, for they cause waste and ryve up the ground to get great quantities of coal which they sell to strangers in such sort that not only are our lieges postponed to these strangers and forced to pay exorbitant prices, for also the said coal heughs in short time will be consumed and spent.

---

[14] *RPCS* x. 372, 374, 382–3; 2nd ser., ii. 146–7; 2nd ser., viii. 14–17.

[15] Ibid., xii. 434; xiii. 207–8. The Scots pound was worth one-twelfth of an English pound.

[16] The regulation of the coal trade was a major theme of policy, and consequently there are a multitude of references in Scottish public records; see in particular *Records of the Convention of Royal Boroughs*, ed. J. D. Marwick (1866–80) and *RPCS*.

[17] See e.g. *RPCS* viii. 232; x. 277–8, 280, 291, 292; xii. 387–8, 418–9, 433–5, 466–7, 482, 605–6, 645–6, 668, 752–3; xiii. 207–9, 240, 305, 555, 570–1, 844–5; 2nd ser., i. 156, 169–70, 276–80, 301; ii. 72–3, 146–7, 162, 176; iv. 156, 255–6; v. 190–1, 217, 219, 223–4, 258–60, 341–2; vi. 94; vii. 160–1; viii. 8–10, 12, 14–17, 341; 3rd ser., i. 258–9.

The coal-owners they complained against were duly cautioned by the Privy Council and required to amend their behaviour and henceforth to favour native buyers.[18] Later evidence concerning Linlithgow suggests that justices of the peace of the shires had power to direct that the production of particular collieries should be used to supply one parish rather than another.[19]

Such fears, and consequential legislation, are reminiscent of the early stages of the English coal boom and of the protection sought by London authorities for their citizens. Yet beyond the confidence with which fears for the exhaustion of supplies or excessive price rises were expressed, there is little to suggest that they had any substance. Price rises were erroneously blamed upon insufficiency of supply or excessive foreign sales rather than on modestly increasing costs in an inflationary era, and there was, of course, no possibility of exports leading to the exhaustion of collieries. None the less, the sympathy of the monarchy and the constitutional authority of the boroughs, who were the major consumers of coal, combined to impose export restrictions for far longer than south of the border. Exports of salt, malt, sheep, and tallow were also prohibited in order to satisfy the consumers' lobby. Yet Scotland had need of imports, most notably grain and timber, and without export earnings she lacked the money to pay for them. As the coal-owners correctly argued, by the export of their coal 'a great deal of treasure ... is yearly brought within the country'.[20] In the event, ambition far outran achievement and export restrictions were unable to be enforced effectively with the rudimentary machinery available to the government, nor was it difficult for coal-owners to obtain lawful exemption from them.[21] Thus the realities of economic triumphed over the primitive instincts of narrow self-interest.

The scale of the Scottish coal industry is a matter of some dispute. Nef believed that the Scottish coalfields were second in importance only to the north-east, and that production soared to almost half a million tons by the close of the seventeenth century, and many historians have followed him.[22] Estimations of output on this scale have to be predicated upon a flourishing of both export trade and home industrial

---

[18] *RPCS* 2nd ser., vii. lvi–lvii, 579.

[19] Ibid. 3rd ser., iii. 98, 118–19.

[20] Ibid., viii. 568–9.

[21] See the general discussion in Lythe 1960, ch. 3.

[22] Nef's original estimate, though criticized, has been broadly accepted by successive writers, including B. F. Duckham (1970, 19–20) and M. W. Flinn (1984, 26). C. A. Whatley, however, has recently argued that it is far too high (1984, 146 n. 22; *Scottish Historical Review* 64 (1985)).

consumption. It is probable, however, that the dimensions of both have been substantially overestimated. Before the later seventeenth century, customs accounts provide almost the sole quantitative index of the progress of the Scottish coal industry, and consequently much reliance must be placed upon them. Recent work and new discoveries have enabled a fair series of figures to be amassed, beginning as early as 1460, when exports amounted to a few tens of tons. Starting from this minuscule base, growth in the first half of the sixteenth century was slow and undramatic, but thereafter the pace quickened and at times in the 1570s and 1580s exports exceeded 2,000 chaldrons, or approximately 5,000 tons. The bulk of this coal was shipped out of ports in the vicinity of Edinburgh.[23] A chance mention reveals exports of 6,308 chaldrons (c.15,000 tons) in 1614,[24] and for a decade from 1621 there is a continuous record of shipments from the Forth, whether of coastal and export shipments or just exports we do not know, in which an average of just 10,000 chaldrons (c.25,000 tons) a year were transported.[25] These exports took place, as we have noted, in times of hostility towards shipping coal to overseas markets, and there can be no doubt that such an environment encouraged evasion. Nevertheless, although there are few grounds for confidence in the efficiency of customs administration in Scotland at this time, these are modest shipments by any standards.

Nor, to judge by later customs account, does there appear to have been any sustained growth in exports during the remainder of the century. The customs books of the 1680s record exports of only 20,000 tons annually at best.[26] There had been a brief period in the early 1660s when Scottish exports soared above 70,000 tons but it was a short-lived boom occasioned by the collapse of the English export trade under the weight of new massive duties.[27] According to English merchants in 1663, the Scottish coal industry was 'not heard of' before high duties had been placed on English exports, and had consisted merely of 'several coal-mines for smiths'. Typical of the furore which followed was an effective lobby of coal-owners and shipmasters from the north of England who petitioned the king in 1663 claiming that the trade supplying brewers, sugar-bakers, smiths, soap-boilers, glass-makers, lime-, and brick-burners in Holland, Flanders, France, Hamburg, and 'other more

---

[23] Guy thesis 1982, 143–62, figs. 6.1–6.4. The Scottish customs chaldron weighed approximately 2.5 English tons (Smout 1963, 256).

[24] Nef 1932, i. 45.

[25] NLS MS 2263; ScRO Cardross GD 15/896.

[26] Smout 1963, 226–7.

[27] PRO 30/24/7/594. Exports in 1658–9 had been only just over 20,000 tons.

eastern countries and cities' was now largely supplied from Scotland with foreigners carrying the coal.[28]

The surge in exports to the Continent in the early 1660s demonstrates the ability of the Scottish coal industry to respond almost instantaneously to enhanced demand for coal, but conditions in overseas markets at the close of the seventeenth century had ceased to be propitious. One by one the countries traditionally served by Scottish coal raised their tariffs, sometimes prohibitively, and competition from Liège collieries became ever fiercer.[29] Nor did Ireland offer much relief for western collieries. Competition from Welsh and Cumbrian mines was strong, and the adventurous and costly project undertaken by Robert Cunninghame in the 1680s at Saltcoats (Ayrshire), involving a colliery, salt-pans, and a harbour, also had to face rivalry from the newly discovered fine-quality rock salt of Cheshire.[30]

Exports to England rose dramatically during the blockade of Newcastle in the Civil War, but the market for Scottish coal south of the border during normal years was insubstantial. The exceptional quality of the 'great burn coal' did, however, ensure some place for it on the hearths of the rich, especially in London. Thus, when Lionel Cranfield reluctantly sanctioned the use of coal in his household it was at first exclusively of the Scottish variety.[31] However, although well established by the opening decades of the seventeenth century, the trade with the capital did not live up to its early promise. Price was strongly against Scottish coal, and weight for weight it also burned more quickly. It was not an 'oeconomical' fuel, and one eighteenth-century reckoning suggested that it took 3 tons of Scottish coal on the hearth to match only 2 tons from Newcastle or Sunderland[32] Thus, although Scottish coal was at first the only coal which proved suitable for use in the newly invented coal-fired glasshouses, they were soon adapted to burn cheap Newcastle coal.[33] Despite the high hopes enshrined in contracts made between Scottish coal-masters and London coal-dealers, imports into London rarely exceeded a few thousand tons and showed no tendency to increase in the face of soaring shipments from Northumberland and Durham.[34] Things had changed little by the 1720s, when Defoe saw a

[28] PRO 30/24/7/594, 595.
[29] Smout 1963, 227–8; Nef 1932, ii. 229–32.
[30] Nef 1932, i. 51.　　　　　　　　　　　　　　　　[31] See above, p. 40.
[32] Whatley 1987, 33 n.　　　　　　　　　　　　　　[33] Godfrey 1975, 83.
[34] Nef 1932, i. 117–19. Recorded imports of Scottish coal into London may well be understatements, for in 1680–1 Sir John Halkett alone sold 1,500 chaldrons (c.3,750 tons) to Charles Charteris, a London coal-broker, from his Pittfirrane colliery (NLS MS 6432, fo. 34).

proposal by the York-Buildings Company of Clackmannan to send 20,000 tons a year to London as a 'boast, or rather a pretence to persuade the world they have demand for such a quantity, whereas while the freight from Scotland is, as we know, so dear, and the tax in England continues so heavy, the price of Scottish coals will always be so high at London, as will not fail to restrain the consumption'.[35]

Coal was never throughout this period, therefore, one of the leading Scottish exports. In the later Middle Ages the value of coal sent overseas was less than half that of wool exports and scarcely more than one-seventh of that of skin and hides, and even as late as 1615 coal was reckoned to constitute only some 3 per cent of exports by value.[36] By the later seventeenth century coal had become more important but it was still not 'right in the forefront' of Scottish exports. It did, however, employ a disproportionate share of shipping, and by the 1680s one in every two vessels leaving Scottish ports carried coal.[37]

This judgement on the export trade is confirmed by the archive created by the outcry against the sharp increase at the Restoration in the level of duties on English exports, which includes two surveys of leading Forthside seasale collieries.[38] English coal-owners and traders feared that the new duties would allow the Scots to seize their markets, and the intention of the first survey, conducted during Anthony Ashley Cooper's tenure of the Exchequer in the 1660s, was to calculate the price advantage which Scottish coal could expect to enjoy in foreign markets.[39] It revealed that the coal of ten of the twelve collieries surveyed started out free-on-board in the Forth as more expensive than the equivalent coal on Tyneside, but ended up transformed into a sub-stantially cheaper commodity by the excessive duties which Tyneside coal had to bear. The second survey, made in 1670, listed fifteen Forth-side seasale collieries, most but not all of which appear in the earlier document. Quantities of coal are given against each colliery in both documents, and these quantities are described in that of 1670 as 'what the respective coal-masters can put forth in a year'.[40] The most satis-factory interpretation, therefore, is that they are estimates of the

[35] *Tour*, ii. 801.

[36] HMC *Mar and Kellie*, 72.

[37] Smout 1963, 225–7.

[38] The Shaftesbury Papers (PRO 30) contain a clutch of documents displaying concern with 'unfair' duties on Newcastle coal, dating from the early 1660s.

[39] PRO 30/24/7. This document was drawn up in the form of a table and headed 'Calculation of Scotch Coales'.

[40] Printed in Nef 1932, ii. 409.

amounts of coal that could be made available for export, rather than estimates of actual exports or of potential or actual total capacity. In the 1660s survey the total quantity given for all twelve collieries is 71,300 tons, while that for the fifteen of 1670 is around 50,000 tons. If we compile one list from the two we have nineteen collieries and a total of around 95,000 tons, but of course not all the collieries would have been in production at any one time. Both surveys are therefore compatible with the highest recorded exports of around 70,000 tons, which had apparently been achieved in 1662–3.

These are not particularly large quantities of coal, especially as they relate to a period when Scottish exports were enjoying substantial advantages over English. We must therefore conclude that the great bulk of Scottish coal was burnt within Scotland. Scotland, of course, had a range of coal-using industries similar to those found in England—lime-burning, ironworking, brewing, sugar-refining, soap-boiling, glass-making, pottery manufacture, and so on—though they were much smaller in scale than those of her southern neighbour.[41] Far and away the leading industrial consumer was the salt industry. The relationship in Scotland between the coal and salt industries was extremely close, far closer even than on Tyneside.[42] From early times it had been customary for coal-owners to engage in salt distillation, and at the close of the seventeenth century few of the leading coal-owners did not operate salt-pans. The reasons were simple but powerful. Most Scottish collieries in their normal course of operations produced substantial quantities of small coal, also called pancoal, waste, or trash, which though well suited to boiling salt-pans was otherwise virtually unsaleable. In the absence of conveniently proximate salt-pans this coal was frequently not worth bringing to the surface, and was instead stowed underground. It thus made good economic sense for coal-owners to operate salt-pans. Indeed, when the seasale market weakened many collieries could find themselves producing primarily for salt-pans, and in some instances they were almost wholly sustained by them. For example, when Tulliallan colliery was helping to ease the fuel famine in eastern England during the blockade of Newcastle and Sunderland in the Civil War, approximately 50 per cent of its output was 'great coal', which was loaded on to waiting ships for immediate shipment south. But in 1679–80 over 90 per cent of its output was small coal led direct to the salt-pans.[43] A collapse

[41] Smout 1963, 6–7.
[42] For the Scottish salt industry see in particular Whatley 1984 and 1987.
[43] ScRO Register House, RH9/1/31; RH9/1/33.

in the demand for sea coal also seems to have lain behind the dramatic shift in the relative proportions of the types of coal produced at Grange colliery at the end of the seventeenth century. In the last eight months of 1695 sea coal accounted for 60 per cent of output, but over the next five years the proportion slumped. In 1701–2 sea coal constituted less than 1 per cent of output, while the salt-pans took over 90 per cent, the balance being accounted for by local sales. Pancoal accounted for a similar proportion of the output of nearby Bonhard colliery in the same year, while at Elphinstone from 1694–7 all the production revealed in surviving accounts was destined for the pans. When Bo'ness colliery was closed down in 1702 the single pit which produced pancoal was kept open[44]

Clearly the proportion of Scottish coal output utilized in native salt-pans was substantial, and had been so for many centuries. But Nef's estimate that it amounted to 150,000 tons a year at the close of the seventeenth century is pitched far too high, probably by at least a factor of two. New evidence demonstrates conclusively that Scotland's salt industry was not larger than that of Tyneside but far smaller, and that in the late seventeenth and early eighteenth centuries its output was unlikely to have consistently exceeded 6,000 to 8,000 tons. To produce this quantity of salt would have required no more than 50,000 to 70,000 tons of coal, and probably less.[45]

There can be no doubt that demand for coal for domestic heating and for fuelling local industries increased in the sixteenth and seventeenth centuries, but levels of coal consumption varied widely throughout the country. The chief Scottish cities and towns lay conveniently across the major coalfields. Edinburgh, Glasgow, Haddington, Linlithgow, Falkirk, Stirling, Dunfermline, Kirkcaldy, Renfrew, Paisley, Ayr, and many others could all be supplied by packhorse or boat from pits located no more than a few miles away. Glasgow and Edinburgh burnt little but coal. Coal consumption was highest in the densely settled counties bordering the Firth of Forth, where collieries were rarely far away. Glasgow, with a population of perhaps 15,000 in 1700, was surrounded by small coalworkings which derived their existence from fuelling the workshops of its artisans and the domestic hearths of its inhabitants. The city authorities ran some of the mines, and an important landsale colliery was located in the Gorbals. Edinburgh, with a population in excess of 30,000 by 1700, provided a major stimulus to

---

[44] Whatley 1987, 34; ScRO Elphinstone GD 156/11/5.

[45] Whatley (1984, 146 n. 22) puts the probable coal consumption at 40–60,000 tons.

Scotland's most productive mining region.[46] The city, which already possessed the smoggy disposition which earned the nickname of 'Auld Reekie', was supplied by a dozen or so inland collieries on the western side of the Esk valley as well as through the port of Leith.[47] Additionally, a number of attempts were made by Edinburgh city authorities to discover and operate its own pits, though with only moderate success.[48]

Water facilitated the coastwise shipment of Forthside coal, as it had for centuries, and some went northwards to Aberdeen, Inverness, Banff, Montrose, Arbroath, Perth, and Dundee. The small boats which plied southwards with oats, barley, textiles, timber, and fish often returned with coal, salt, and 'general merchant goods' from the ports of the Forth. Yet we must be careful not to exaggerate the scale of this coastal trade, for even the largest towns of northern Scotland rarely had more than a few thousand inhabitants, and only those close to the coast could be reached economically. The state of Scottish roads throughout the kingdom was so appalling that wheeled vehicles were prodigies rarely to be encountered, and there were scarcely any stretches of navigable inland waterway.[49] Although there may well have been a million persons in Scotland by 1700, a high proportion of them lay far out of reach of coal. Instead many relied on local peat, and peat-burning was for many thousands the only source of heat available through the long cold winters experienced by this northerly kingdom. For these reasons it is not likely that the quantities of coal shipped coastwise from Forthside to other parts of the realm much exceeded a few thousand tons. Moreover, we should be careful not to overestimate the consumption by domestic households even in coal-producing regions, for the bulk of the population may have been too poor to provide adequate heating for their dwellings. If we are to believe the constant protestations made to the Privy Council, native merchants seeking coal at Forthside ports were regularly outbid by foreigners willing to pay prices far higher than Scotsmen could afford.[50]

Further support for the downgrading of the output of the Scottish coalfields is forthcoming from evidence of the capacities of individual

[46] B. Lenman, *An Economic History of Modern Scotland, 1660-1976* (1977), 33–4; Nef 1932, i. 49–50.

[47] Some of these are listed in Nef 1932, i. 47.

[48] e.g. in 1609 Thomas Hunter was given permission to search for coal in the town grounds 'to the welfare and benefit of the burgh and whole country' (M. Wood (ed.), *Extracts from the Records of the Burgh of Edinburgh, 1604-26* (Edinburgh, 1931), 56–7).

[49] Smout 1963, 9–15, gives a concise summary of internal communications in the 17th cent.

[50] Ibid. 12–13.

collieries. A number, of course, were truly substantial enterprises. In the surveys noted above the export potential of the undertakings of the earl of Wemyss, presumably at Wemyss and Methil, was given as 9,000 tons, that of Clackmannan colliery as 11,250 tons, and Sir Walter Seaton's colliery at Seton was said to be capable of sending 17,500 tons of 'small brewer's coal' overseas each year. Moreover, although the export capacities of most of the collieries listed were below 5,000 tons, a large part of the production of the majority went straight into adjacent salt-works. We can have no doubt that Clackmannan, Seton, Tulliallan/Kincardine, and the earl of Wemyss's collieries ranked among the larger British collieries, with capacities of perhaps 20,000 tons or even more. We also learn that in the seven years before 1667 Wemyss had sunk over £8,000 sterling into an ambitious venture, which included a new mine with drainage work, salt-pans, and a harbour. The earl of Winton's workings at Cockenzie and Methil must also have had excellent prospects, for in 1679 he constructed a new harbour at Easter Cockenzie to enable ships of 300 tons to berth there.[51] But such undertakings should not be seen as typical, even of the more famous Scottish collieries. Many of the renowned Forthside coalworks are revealed by their surviving accounts to have been of modest size.

Loanhead has become famous for the management regime instituted by its owner, Sir John Clerk, rather than for the scale of its output; none the less the annual revenues of less than £300 sterling obtained from the sales of coal from 1695–9 indicate an annual output of less than 2,000 tons. Production at Elphinstone in 1663–4 and 1694–5 was little, if any, greater. Alloa colliery was more productive, but it had lain idle and unworked for seven years before the earl of Mar asked a viewer to assess its prospects. The anonymous expert reported that with a work-force of ten hewers and their bearers it should be capable of producing 3,000 chaldrons a year, some 3,750 tons, and a profit of some £500 sterling for the earl. An account of actual proceeds in the three years after Lammas 1689 shows average production of approximately 3,000 tons a year and profits of under £200 sterling. Similar profits of just over £200 per annum were obtained by the owners of Sheriffhall from 1679–81, but only £100 a year from Cassingrey colliery in Fife.[52]

Thus from many quarters there are firm indications that the widely accepted and frequently repeated estimate of an annual output of

[51] Nef 1932, i. 46.

[52] ScRO Clerk of Penicuik GD 18/990/1; Elphinstone 156/11/5; Mar and Kellie GD 124/17/516, 525; Buccleugh GD 68/1–7; Leven and Melville GD 26/5/319.

around half a million tons from the Scottish coalfields at the close of the seventeenth century is far too high. The joint consumption of salt manufacturing and exports is unlikely to have averaged more than 150,000 tons annually, and in most years was probably appreciably lower. As for the domestic market, excluding the salt-pans, constrained as it was by wretched communications, a relatively small and poor population, and the availability in many regions of peat fuel, it would be unwise to postulate an annual consumption of more than 200,000 tons. Accordingly, it may well be that the total output of coal in Scotland at this time lay nearer to a quarter of a million tons than a half-million.

What is more, the closing years of the seventeenth century and the opening years of the eighteenth was a period of crisis and retrenchment for the whole Scottish economy, which created a particularly unpropitious environment for the coal industry. Wars, liquidity crises, rising tariffs, trade barriers, and devastating harvest failures combined to produce what one historian has described as a 'decade of indescribable anguish'.[53] Having been forced inwards towards the home market by increasing international competition, the coal and salt industries found that the demand for their products slumped during the second half of the 1690s, as a long succession of famines sent food prices spiralling and produced widespread destitution among an already impoverished population. Moreover, the excessive rain which caused the harvest failures also exacerbated the drainage problems of many collieries and some, like Bo'ness, were forced to close by an excess of water.[54]

The prognosis for the Scottish coal industry made at the close of the seventeenth century by contemporary observers was therefore justifiably gloomy. In 1702 John Callendar reported that on Forthside the 'whole coals on both sides of the water are at present in an ill condition', and there would have been few experts in these crisis years who would have disagreed with him. Yet the primary problem of the industry was a long-standing one, namely surplus capacity. Although some rich and favourably located seams had undoubtedly been exhausted, the Scottish industry was neither at the limits of technology nor facing spiralling costs. We need look no further than the price stability and output growth of the first half of the eighteenth century, before the adoption of steam engines, to disprove such a hypothesis.[55] As contemporaries readily appreciated, there was simply not enough demand. This was not a new problem. Many of the leading collieries seem to have led a hand to

---

[53] Lenman, *Economic History of Modern Scotland*, 44.
[54] Whatley 1987, 32.   [55] Duckham 1970, 17–18.

mouth existence for much of our period. Production in general in Scottish collieries seems to have been even less smooth than in English ones, future demand was not anticipated, and the stockpiling of coal was far less common. Even in the larger collieries working was often geared directly to the arrival of a ship to be filled with coal or the needs of the salt-pans.[56]

In recognition of the urgent need to create new markets for Scottish coal and conserve those that already existed, marketing trips abroad were undertaken and imaginative projects to foster the interests of coal-masters were proposed. In 1680 William Brown, an Edinburgh merchant, returned after 'having been through most part of the seventeen provinces of the Low Countries designing to settle a constant coal trade to best advantage'. He reported that although at first sight the ruling price of coal in Bruges and other cities offered the prospect of good profits, in practice he found himself unable to break even. The reason was, he maintained, that the duty on Scots coal was excessive compared with that from Newcastle, and 'coal being a gross commodity none of this can be concealed'. In consequence 'even though the coal is desired, men cannot afford it'.[57] An anonymous memorandum dating from Queen Anne's reign proposed, harking back to the sixteenth century, the establishment of a staple for Scottish coal at Campveere. To do so, it was maintained, would extend the use of coal and stimulate production, it would also 'draw down strangers money [for] the greatest part of the commodity which otherwise must lie still buried underground to be altogether useless and unprofitable to the nation to the value of at least 300,000 marks Scots per annum'.[58] We may conclude, with this memorandum, that for much of the seventeenth century the Scottish coal industry possessed vast untapped capacity but moderate trade.

iii. Cumberland

The development of the Cumberland coalfield was a late process, which began in earnest only in the second half of the seventeenth century. The potentially workable coal lay almost exclusively in the small west Cumberland coalfield, in a band of no more than five miles width. The band ran for about sixteen miles northwards along the Solway Firth from just south of Whitehaven to Maryport, whence it turned inland to form a narrow east–west strip. Apart from the digging of a few widely

---

[56] See below, Ch. 10(v).
[57] ScRO Mar and Kellie GD 124/17/522.   [58] Ibid. 124/17/509.

scattered outcrops of limited significance, some over the border in Westmorland, mining during the period covered in this volume was confined to this coastal strip.

A combination of sparse documentation and limited exploitation has left remarkably few traces of coalmining in Cumberland before the seventeenth century. From the archive of the Percys, earls of Northumberland, we learn that a small mine at Great Broughton, to the east of Workington, was worked fairly continuously in the fifteenth century, and that licences were granted for digging coal at Dean and Loweswater. In the latter part of the same century mines at 'Tynyelfell', near Tindale Tarn to the east of Carlisle, were rendered valueless by the pillaging of the Scots.[1] It seems certain, however, that by the mid-sixteenth century mining was well established in the manor of St Bees on the southern edge of the exposed coalfield. Some time around 1560 Sir Thomas Chaloner, the lord of the manor, reserved his right to dig coals when he granted leases to farmlands, although he did permit the tenants to take coal for their own use, as long as they paid for it and continued to 'labour from time to time in the lord's coalpits according as they ought to do by the custom of the lordship'.[2] Also suggestive of the antiquity of coalmining is the custom of carrying coal to the manor house at Gilcrux performed by tenants of Warthall manor.[3] But these are mere scraps, and there is nothing to suggest mining on a substantial scale within Cumberland at this time. The establishment of copper works near Keswick in 1567 by the Society of Mines Royal did create some demand, and we learn that it was being supplied from a pit at Bolton, four miles north-west of Appleby. But it could not have been productive, for a year later the operators were complaining of the great difficulty in obtaining coal.[4]

With a sparse and scattered population, and poor communications, local demand for coal in Cumberland was bound to be limited. Pack-horses rather than wains and carts continued to be the most efficient method of moving goods until well into the eighteenth century, and there were scarcely any stretches of navigable inland waterway. Of equal significance in limiting the scale of mining was the abundance of turves, which for the majority of the population were far more easily and

---

[1] J. M. W. Bean, *The Estates of the Percy Family, 1416-1537* (Oxford, 1958), 24, 27–8, 51; *CIPM Henry VII*, i. 69 (157).

[2] *VCH Cumberland*, ii. 358–9; Galloway 1898, i. 118–19; Wood 1988, 3.

[3] C. E. Searle, 'The Cumbrian Customary Economy in the Eighteenth Century', *P. & P.* 110 (1986), 113.

[4] *VCH Cumberland*, ii. 359.

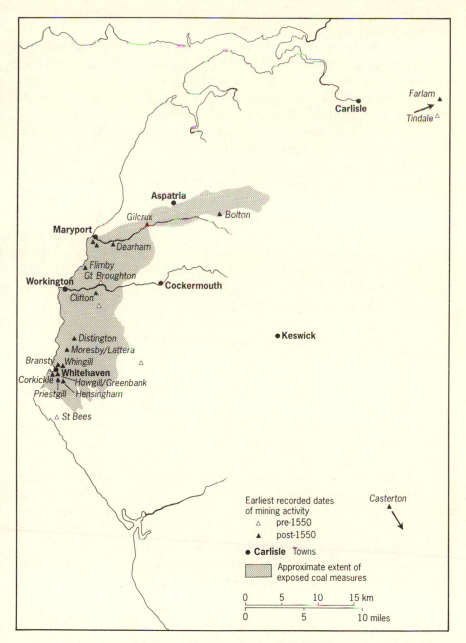

Map 5.4. The Cumberland coalfield

cheaply obtainable than coal. Even by the early seventeenth century, therefore, the Cumberland coal industry consisted almost exclusively of scattered small pits serving their immediate hinterlands.

During the seventeenth century, and for long after, the scale of production in Cumberland was to be critically dependent upon just two elements: the Irish trade and the Lowther family. Farlam colliery, owned by the Howards of Naworth Castle, located on an outcrop to the east of Carlisle, produced profits which before 1650 sometimes rose higher than £50.[5] But even a colliery of these modest dimensions was a rarity away from the coast. Nor did the sea at first provide much stimulus, for scattered customs accounts reveal exports of only 2,000 to 3,000 tons annually in the first quarter of the century, largely from Workington and Parton.[6] It was Sir Christopher Lowther of Whitehaven (1611–44), who first embarked with vigour upon supplying Dublin with coal. As a young man, apprenticed by his father to commerce, he enthused from Dublin in 1632 that 'coals I think would be our best trade, for as much stock as they would require'. But he also astutely noted that the trade required larger ships, like the Flemish, for 'our own country barks are so little they carry nothing at a time' and the manning of them ate up all the profit. A further restraint on exports was the poor facilities at Whitehaven harbour, which in 1633 was deemed to be 'decayed and dangerous [and] the cause of the wreck of many good ships'. Christopher set about building up trade with Ireland, selling salt refined in Lowther pans and coal that was produced in the family collieries as well as purchased for shipment; he also constructed a new pier at Whitehaven.[7] At Clifton, Sir Patricius Curwen was also mining coal and exporting it to Ireland and elsewhere through Workington, as were a number of his tenants. A petitioner in 1635 claimed that at Clifton 'coals there gotten have been usually carried, and from thence transported . . . for Ireland [and] divers parts both of England and Scotland'. Mining was also taking place in Distington manor, owned by the Fletcher family.[8]

But it seems that trade prospered only modestly. Mining at Clifton subsequently lapsed, while at Distington the ambitions of the Fletchers were hindered by the rights of their freeholders. Output at Whitehaven

---

[5] Ornsby (ed.), *Lord Howard of Naworth*. pp. xliv–xlv, 5–8, 68, 119, 155–6, 212, 224, 233–4, 255, 282–3; Hudlestone (ed.), *Naworth Estate*, 10, 67.

[6] Nef 1932, ii. 380–1.

[7] Hainsworth (ed.), *Sir Christopher Lowther*, pp. x, 3, 7, 43–4, 64, 75, 132, 152–3; Wood 1988, 5–6.

[8] Nef 1932, i. 70; Wood 1988, 1–3.

and St Bees, the latter newly acquired by the Lowthers, was no more than a few thousand tons in the 1630s. In 1636 Charles Lowther sold 2,400 tons, and his total profits from coal between 1631 and 1637 were just £220. Moreover, the development of Whitehaven and the coal of its hinterland was halted by his untimely death in 1644.[9] If we are to believe the testimony of his son, Sir John Lowther (1642–1706), writing in about 1705, coal production in the Whitehaven region at this time was seriously inhibited by the pattern of land ownership and occupation, as well as by inadequate port facilities. For although 'The country adjacent afforded coals sufficient for a staple export . . . a great part of them were in the hands of small freeholders, and could not be wrought without great and expensive levels'. Yet these drainage levels would have had to be driven through the lands of several people and consequently the driving of them 'could enable such as have none of the charge to under sell and ruin those who did, so that the working of them under these circumstances was impracticable and they were lost as well to the owners as to the country'.[10]

Sir John shared the ambitions and talents of his father, and his solution was to set about engrossing the coal deposits along the western slopes of the St Bees valley into his own hands and draining them. So numerous and remarkable were the drainage machines he installed that the area acquired the name of Ginns. Among his many other improvements was a network of cartways begun in 1682 and finished by 1714, and the development of the port of Whitehaven, where he built a new pier and deepened the harbour. Between 1668 and 1700 there is evidence of at least nine collieries worked by Lowther, although not all were kept in production at the same time.[11] Lowther's entrepreneurial spirit was amply rewarded. From 1668–74 the average annual profit from his collieries had been just £400, whereas from 1684–8, during the last five years of peace before the Irish War, it averaged £1,400.[12]

Despite his acquisitions Lowther still faced some competition. On Moresby manor, two and a half miles north-east of Whitehaven, there were collieries owned by William Fletcher, and Lowther was frustrated in all his efforts to gain control of them. They were clearly of some size, since the lessee, Thomas Lamplugh, alarmed Lowther's agent with his plans to build a staithe at Parton, and freight his coal direct to Dublin.

[9] Beckett 1981, 43–4; Wood 1988, 2.
[10] 'The Case of Sir John Lowther, Bart. c1705', printed in Fletcher 1878, 271–2.
[11] Wood 1988, 6–17; Hainsworth (ed.), *Sir John Lowther*, pp. xix–xxi; Nef 1932, i. 71 n.
[12] Wood 1988, 305.

Henry Curwen was also working a number of pits on and around Clifton manor and exporting coal from Workington. This port was described in 1676 as 'a fair haven, but not so much frequented by ships, the colliery being decayed', but plans were entertained to improve it, and in 1688 a salt-pan and colliery at Clifton were valued at £20 per annum.[13] In the 1680s several collieries in the vicinity of Whitehaven were leased by William Christian, a Newcastle Hostman, and in 1693 he was mining at Priestgill, Corkickle, Hensingham, and Distington. There are few indications of output, but Corkikle in the mid-1680s produced 10 tons daily, perhaps 3,000 tons in a year. There were also, of course, many tiny, primitive operations where small quantities of coal were mined on an intermittent basis by the agricultural tenants who held them or by solitary labourers or working partners.[14]

It is only at the very close of the century that substantial output data become available, and then only for the Lowther collieries of Howgill, Greenbank, and Lattera. The dominance of Howgill is immediately clear, and it is revealed as a large colliery by any standards, with outputs between 1695 and 1700 ranging from 15,000 to 20,000 tons. Both Greenbank and Lattera were small, producing on average less than 2,000 tons each. Lowther's colliery profits over the same period averaged £634. It is probable therefore that output had been very substantially higher in the later 1680s, just prior to the Irish War, when Lowther's annual colliery profits had ranged between £1,268 and £1,531. In those times, according to Sir Walter Harris's computations, Whitehaven and Workington had sixty ships continually employed in the coal trade to Ireland, to which they carried almost 40,000 tons in a year.[15]

The capacity of Howgill colliery was to rise sharply in the opening years of the eighteenth century, to reach 40,000 tons by 1710, but trading conditions in the late seventeenth were not smooth. Whereas Cumberland came to dominate the Irish trade, eclipsing in scale the shipments from South Wales, Flintshire, Lancashire, and Ayrshire, so the Irish trade dominated the Cumberland industry. In 1695 and 1705 respectively, 93 per cent and 87 per cent of Lowther's total output was sent across the Irish Sea. Consequently the war with Ireland from 1689–91 brought serious problems. In 1689 Lowther's pits actually made a small loss, and in 1690 the profit was a mere £145. Nor was recovery swift

[13] Hainsworth (ed.), *Sir John Lowther*, 29, 131; Fletcher 1878, 218–19.

[14] Beckett 1981, 44; *VCH Cumberland*, ii. 360; Hainsworth (ed.), *Sir John Lowther*, 23.

[15] Wood 1988, 299, 305–6; Harris, *Trade of England and Ireland*, 19–20. Output calculated at 22 cwt. for each contemporary ton, following Fletcher 1878, 276.

when the war ended. Indeed, Cumberland in the closing years of the century displayed the familiar signs of a glut of coal. Lowther not only had great difficulty disposing of the coal that he produced, all concerned with the management of his collieries were convinced that production could have been maintained at a far higher level if only there had been sufficient demand. Lowther was counselled not to attempt to raise prices, for fear of losing the trade that he had, and a variety of schemes to sell into new markets or consume coal in local industries were entertained, including shipping it to different parts of Ireland and to Cornwall, building a glassworks, and praying for the successful smelting of iron with coal. A further ploy, at which the Lowthers had long been adept, was to buy up the collieries of competitors. In the dismal economic climate which then prevailed, most acquisitions were closed down, and other competitors simply went out of business.[16]

We know the output of Lowther's collieries at the close of the century, and if we estimate that of his major competitors and add a few thousand tons at most for the produce of small independent pits in the coastal region as well as in scattered sites in east Cumberland and over the border in Westmorland, we may postulate that the total output of the coalfield ranged between 30,000 and 50,000 tons. The consumption of coal in Cumberland remained slight away from the pits. It was in the 1720s, for example, that the Kendal textile and tanning industries were first forced to turn to coal by the exhaustion of turf supplies, 'hitherto their usual fuel', and peat as well as coal was apparently burned in the hearths of superior Carlisle households throughout the eighteenth century.[17] In Cumberland, as in very many British coalfields, the latent capacity of the coal industry was severely restrained by intense competition for external markets and the high costs of transport incurred in reaching inland ones. On the west coast of Britain, as on the east, there was simply too much capacity.

iv. Lancashire

The Lancashire coalfield before the eighteenth century was broad in area but small in output. Although mining was widely scattered, there were just two centres of major activity: in the north-east, where a concentration of mining sites to the north of Burnley lay in a band stretching from Colne and Trawden to Padiham, and in the south-west,

---

[16] e.g. Hainsworth (ed.), *Sir John Lowther*, 131, 138, 466, 471–2, 662–5.
[17] Hughes 1965, ii. 133–4.

where there was a pronounced clustering of mines within a ten-mile radius of Wigan. In the south-east mining extended beyond Manchester as far as Oldham and Stockport, but was much more thinly scattered. Geologically the Lancashire coalfield is notable for the great depth and thinness of its seams, as well as for their steep inclinations. But it is also notable for the profusion of seams, and for the abundance of folds, fractures, and faults which occur in them. These geological features ensured that there were many sites where coal could be relatively easily extracted from surface outcrops, but they also determined that within our period the great majority of mines tended to be both small in scale and short in duration. Underground flooding was a particular problem.[1] To the geological features which helped to mould the pace and character of development within the coalfield should be added the poverty of Lancashire gentry and the shortages of capital which this produced, the lack of large towns within the coalfield, and the difficulties of transporting coal owing to the distance from the sea and a lack of navigable rivers.

The innumerable surface deposits of coal encouraged early mining, and although Lancashire is not well endowed with thirteenth- and fourteenth-century records, references to pits are far from rare. It can be seen from Map 5.5 that medieval mining sites were quite widely scattered in the north-east and the south-west, but none that have been identified were other than inconsequential undertakings requiring the labour of no more than a handful of persons. The rents and profits of such scratchings were counted in shillings rather than pounds. The abundance of free or cheap turf and wood throughout the region restricted domestic demand. As James Roberts, aged 79, long-time resident of Burnley parish, stated in 1527, nobody had 'any need in time past to get coals for their fuel, by reason they had plenty of wood from the forests and turves at their liberty'.[2] It seems that much of the coal that was dug for sale was for industrial use, particularly in smithies. Thus in 1294 Bolton priory purchased coal for its forge, possibly from Colne as it did in the fourteenth century. Colne coal was obviously well suited to the forge, for it was preferred by the monks of Bolton to the coal produced on their own lands closer to the priory, and thought worth the extra cost.[3]

There are few if any signs of major advances in the Lancashire

---

[1] *VCH Lancashire*, ii. 356; Langton 1979a, 61–4.
[2] PRO DL 3/19/T3 (quoted in Swain 1986, 163).
[3] Galloway 1898, i. 28, 61; *VCH Lancashire*, ii. 356.

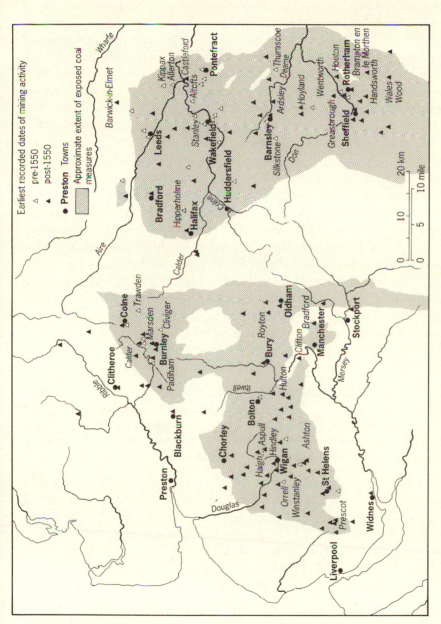

Map 5.5. The coalfields of Yorkshire and Lancashire

Earliest recorded dates of mining activity
△ pre-1550
▲ post-1550
● Preston Towns
▨ Approximate extent of exposed coal measures

coalfield in the later Middle Ages, and even during the course of the sixteenth century progress was slight. One of the more important developments was the discovery and working of cannel, a coal formed from the spores of plants rather than from woody plant tissues, which is light in weight, has a very high calorific value, and a low sulphur content. The first mining of cannel took place at Haigh, a few miles to the north-east of Wigan, some time prior to John Leland's visit in 1540, for he reported that a Mr Bradshaw there 'hath found much cannel like sea coal in his ground, very profitable to him', and had established 'a great mine'.[4]

The abundance of mining sites on the Lancashire coal measures did not result in high levels of output for the coalfield, because they were generally small in scale and so few were in production at any one time. John Langton has identified no less than fifty-six collieries in south-west Lancashire which were worked in the century after 1590, but he has also found that never more than sixteen of them were working at any given time, eighteen if one includes small urban diggings. Individual operations opened and closed with great frequency, and 70 per cent of collieries had recorded durations of less than ten years.[5] As a consequence the coal output of south-west Lancashire was paltry. After a detailed study of all available evidence Langton has estimated production in 1590 at less than 15,000 tons a year, and he would envisage no more than 20,000 to 30,000 tons by 1690. We can do no better than repeat the reasons he gave for this low output and slow development:

The coal industry of south-west Lancashire was in a primitive state throughout the century before 1690. A large portion of the coalfield in the West was almost completely unexploited. Elsewhere, mining was usually intermittent, and when collieries were worked their outputs fluctuated randomly from week to week, from month to month and from year to year'.

There were very few collieries in south-west Lancashire whose outputs exceeded 2,000 tons, and none which regularly exceeded 5,000 tons. The highest concentrations and consistency of activity were to be found within a ten-mile radius of Wigan and close to Liverpool, where coal was in regular use from at least the mid-sixteenth century and from whence it was shipped. Haigh colliery, already in production by 1540, was worked throughout the seventeenth century without interruption, and was yielding around 4,000 tons in the late 1680s. Located close by were collieries such as Aspull, Winstanley, and Orrell which yielded less than Haigh but which also remained in production for long periods.[6]

⁴ Leland, *Itinerary*, v. 41, 43.   ⁵ Langton 1979a, 35–9.   ⁶ Ibid, 40–4.

Prescot too, less than ten miles from Liverpool, was continuously worked, or nearly so. We are poorly informed about production levels at Prescot, but it was claimed in a court case that 7,000 to 8,000 tons had been raised there in the three years from 1594–6, and that in 1637 certain tenants of the manor were said to be digging coals on their holdings and sending them to Ireland, Cheshire, and 'other remote places'.[7]

A similar predominance of small collieries with short or discontinuous working lives was evident in north-east Lancashire. The surveys carried out by parliamentary commissioners in 1650 and 1654 identified a few significant collieries, by drawing attention to the discrepancies between the rents which their proprietors paid and the profits which they drew. At Trawden, for example, Mr Hammond paid just 11s. for a coal-mine which was said to be worth £60 annually, while coal-mines at Padiham rented by Mr Braddill for 53s. 4d. were valued at £40 yearly 'upon improvement', and those at Briercliffe rented by Nicholas Townley for 6s. were valued at £20. 6s. 0d. For the 'full liberty to dig and carry away coal and make watercourses for draining mines' for a period of twenty-one years in his copyhold lands on the manors of Ightenhill and Colne, Nicholas Whiteacre paid a fine of £20 and agreed to an annual rent of 40s.; just two years later his rights were valued at £30 each year over and above the rent. Such operations may have produced up to 1,000 tons, but not much more.[8] Perhaps somewhat larger were the ventures of Nicholas Mitchell at Castercliff and Dryhurst in the township of Great Marsden, for which he agreed in 1629 to pay a rent of £46. 10s. 0d. annually, which was huge by the standards of the region, or the mine in Henry Barcroft's hands at Great Marsden at the close of the sixteenth century which it was claimed was producing between 160 and 200 horse-loads, perhaps 16–20 tons, a day.[9] Further west at Clayton-le-Moors, near Blackburn, a colliery was alleged in 1669 to have been producing a yearly profit of £200. On the other hand, failure is also encountered in the parliamentary surveys. On Colne manor, for example, mines which had been leased to Henry Walmesley for 15s. a year were reported 'drowned with water and for the present no benefit is made', those of two other tenants were declared unproductive, and a further leaseholder had yet to begin digging.[10]

There is thus no cause to challenge the judgment that the landlocked Lancashire coalfield was among the least productive and least dynamic of British coalfields during this period. The total output of north-east

---

[7] Bailey, 1947, 1–20.
[8] PRO E. 317/8, 9.
[9] Swain 1986, 170–2.
[10] Nef 1932, i. 63.

Lancashire is impossible to estimate with any confidence, but we would be unwise to place it any higher than the 20,000 tons or so suggested by Dr Langton for the south-west of the country at the end of the seventeenth century. We must also take account of developments in the far south-east of Lancashire where the growth of Manchester may well have stimulated some adjacent collieries. Astley Bradford, for example, was valued at £150 in 1662, and witnesses claimed during a legal dispute that Clifton colliery produced profits of perhaps £100–200 in 1687–8.[11] Notwithstanding that there are signs that both domestic and industrial consumption were rising in the late seventeenth century, and that Lancashire coal was also shipped overseas and coastwise, Nef's assertion that the total output of the coalfield 'may easily have exceeded 150,000 tons' is obviously far too high. Output is more likely to have been sustained at little more than a third of that figure. The capacity of the coalfield to expand rapidly when demand existed was, however, to be admirably demonstrated in the first half of the eighteenth century. Under the incentives which were then provided by the growth of the region's towns and cities and the fuel requirements of its burgeoning industry, and aided by canals and other major improvements in transport, the rate of growth of the Lancashire coalfield was to be exceeded only by the seasale collieries of Cumberland.[12]

v. Yorkshire

The Yorkshire coalfield is an artificial entity, created for the convenience of the managers and the students of the industry. In geological terms the exposed coal measures which lie within Yorkshire are simply the northern section of a vast oval deposit which covers some 900 square miles and stretches more than sixty miles from Leeds in the north to Nottingham and Derby in the south. Yet the sparsity of mining activity along the south Yorkshire border before 1700 adds a certain justification to this adopted county division, as do the advantages of making this work comparable with that of previous historians. In Yorkshire the coalfield broadens out to a width of twenty miles or more, from Halifax to Pontefract at its extremes. The western boundary of the exposed coalfield, which separates it from that of Lancashire, is formed where the

---

[11] Blackwood 1978, 16; Crofton 1889, 63–6. Nef was in error in claiming that the cannel and coal-mines of Clifton were 'worth to be sold' £4,000 and upwards in 1689; this figure was a valuation of the whole manor (1932, i. 64).

[12] Flinn 1984, 8–9, 26.

millstone grit crops out from beneath the basal coal measures to form the flank of the Pennines, while on the eastern limits the measures plunge downwards beneath magnesian limestone.[1]

Even the patchy coverage provided by the study of surviving sources reveals a remarkable diffusion of mining throughout the Yorkshire coalfield before the sixteenth century.[2] Not only was coal dug in the later Middle Ages in the majority of localities where mining was to take place up to the eighteenth century, the pattern of intensity of medieval mining was essentially similar to that followed in later centuries. There were two regions of notable activity throughout our period. In the south it was the triangle formed by the Don and Dearne rivers, which contained a profusion of coal-seams and, most importantly, outcrops of the Barnsley, Silkstone, and Parkgate seams. In the Don valley, around Sheffield and Rotherham, early mining was greatly facilitated by faulting and subsequent erosion, which raised coal close to the surface. In the north the triangle bounded by Leeds, Wakefield, and Pontefract, along the Aire and Calder valleys, was equally pronounced. As usual, the simple mapping of early references can give a misleading impression of the relative importance of coalmining over time, for the great majority of medieval sources reveal part-time digging on an occasional basis in small holes by farmers and artisans to satisfy their own household or workshop needs. This was the case with Richard le Nailer who paid 6 d. in 1274 for the right to dig 'sea-coals' during the year for his smithy at Hipperholme.[3] Rents were generally low, but not all were exiguous, and in some parts there are indications of commercial mining. At Kippax in 1357, for example, there were a number of new pits which realized £16. 13 s. 4 d. in rent, and it may be assumed that at least some of the peasant lessees sold the coal which they raised.[4] We know that lessees did so on the great manor of Wakefield, for the court rolls contain notices of licences for the right to sell coal as well as of fines for doing so without licence, and for debts contracted by not paying for coal received or not delivering coal which had been paid for.[5]

Beyond demonstrating the widespread digging of coal, extant sources

<hr />

[1] A. Trueman (ed.), *The Coalfields of Great Britain* (1954), 167–70.

[2] Reviews of medieval evidence are contained in *VCH Yorkshire*, ii. 338–41; Cox thesis 1960, ch. 2.

[3] W. P. Baildon (ed.), *Court Rolls of the Manor of Wakefield*, i, Yorkshire Archaeological Society Record Series, xxix (1901), 96.

[4] *VCH Yorkshire*, ii. 339.

[5] See e.g. H. M. Jewel (ed.), *Wakefield Court Rolls, 1348–50*, Yorkshire Archaeological Society Record Series, 2nd ser., ii (1981), 21, 26, 36, 39, 48, 63, 164.

are not sufficient to allow us to chart the progress of the industry in Yorkshire during the fourteenth and fifteenth centuries, but the observations of John Leland on his travels through the county in the late 1530s provide a touchstone of sorts:

Though betwixt Cawood and Rotherham be good plenty of wood, yet the people burn much earth coal, because it is plentifully found there, and sold good cheap. A mile from Rotherham be very good pits of coal . . . Hallamshire hath plenty of wood, and yet there is burned much sea coal . . . there be plenty of veins of sea coal in the quarters about Wakefield . . . the easterly parts of Richmondshire burn much sea coals brought out of Durhamshire.

Continuing his discourse on the fuelling habits of Yorkshiremen, Leland went on to note that in the north of the county, beyond the exposed coalfield, ling, peat, and turves were burnt. He also further elaborated upon the situation in the north of the county:

There be some veins of coal found in the upper part of the west mountains of Richmondshire, but they be not used for the incommodity of carriage to the lower part. Most of the coal that be occupied about the quarters of Richmond town be fetched from Railey pits towards the quarters of Auckland.[6]

In the absence of good transport facilities collieries of necessity had to depend upon strictly local consumers for their livelihoods. Nowhere were such constraints more in evidence than in the Yorkshire coalfield. For although traversed by many major rivers and their tributaries, none was navigable. Moreover, as Leland noted, the region was not lacking in alternative fuels. South Yorkshire and the West Riding before the seventeenth century were well wooded in comparison with many lowland regions of Britain, and the moorlands produced an abundance of turves. Nor, with the exception of York, were there cities within easy reach of collieries. Yet even York was late coming to a dependence upon coal, for, although wood ran scarce, Inclesmoor with its expansive turbaries lay only a short river journey away.[7] Moreover, such coal as was consumed in the city came down the coast from Northumberland and Durham, and indeed occasionally from Scotland also, as well as overland from the collieries of the West Riding. In 1527–8 the Fabric Roll of York Minster records the disbursement of £5. 5s. 8d. for divers sacks of

---

[6] Leland, *Itinerary*, v. 14, 32. Ling is a species of heath.

[7] As early as 1553 the citizens instructed their MPs to obtain an act forbidding the destruction of woods within a 16-mile radius of the city (Smith 1970, 23). For the turbaries of Inclesmoor see R. A. Skelton and P. D. A. Harvey (eds), *Local Maps and Plans from Medieval England* (Oxford, 1986), 147–61.

coal from Wakefield as well as chaldrons of coals from Newcastle, for use in building works.[8] None the less, despite the proclamation of the citizens in 1579 that turves are 'now the greatest part of our fuel', the consumption of coal continued to rise. Increasing supplies were brought by water from north-eastern collieries, via Hull and the Ouse, but so many wains carrying West Riding coal made the journey overland into York that the causey leading to Micklegate Bar was damaged by them.[9]

Total dependence on land transport, combined with competition from Northumberland and Durham coal to the north and east, Lancashire coal to the west, and Derbyshire and Nottinghamshire coal to the south, determined that the markets for Yorkshire coal had to be found within the boundaries of the coalfield itself. Although there were many bustling towns and industrial villages on the coalfield to be supplied with fuel, before the later seventeenth century only Leeds and possibly Sheffield among them had populations of more than 5,000. It was inevitable therefore that the Yorkshire coalfield was distinguished by the numbers rather than the scale of its collieries. Indeed, there do not appear to have been any genuinely large mining enterprises in early modern Yorkshire. Geography, geology, and local economy combined to generate a multitude of small mines, with outputs of less than 1,500 tons, topped with a thin tier of medium-sized undertakings whose outputs scarcely if ever rose above 5,000 tons. A survey of surviving documentation, inevitably less than comprehensive, has revealed well over one hundred separate locations in which coal was mined before 1700, and we can be certain that there are very many more to be discovered, while in most locations there was a cluster of pits, and in some more than one colliery.

The leitmotiv of multitudes of small units of production likewise runs through analyses of owners and operators. In his study of the Yorkshire gentry, Dr Cliffe found at least eighty families with coalmining interests between 1558 and 1642, although the profits that they drew from them might be only £50 or £100 a year, and were not infrequently a mere £20 or £30.[10] Handsworth colliery, located about four miles south-east of Sheffield, for which there is a splendid series of virtually continuous accounts between 1652 and 1684, as well as rich complementary documentation, fell into the latter category. In a number of respects it

[8] Galloway 1898, i. 112.

[9] Hey 1986, 156; B. F. Duckham, *The Yorkshire Ouse: The History of a River Navigation* (Newton Abbot, 1967), 57.

[10] Cliffe 1969, 57, 62.

may have claims to typicality, although it was, unusually, run as a profit-sharing partnership by Sir John Bright and his estate bailiff, Thomas Stacey. Over the thirty-two years covered by the series, profits averaged just under £24 a year and output around 1,000 loads, probably 1,000 tons or a little more.[11]

Even the aristocracy, however, could find it worth while to operate small enterprises, and the colliery accounts of the mines of the earls of Shrewsbury in Sheffield Park in the 1580s reveal average annual profits of just over £40 and output of around 1,250 loads. The subsequent history of Sheffield Park colliery reveals expansion. Production in 1599–1600 was 2,823 loads, and it commanded rentals of £76 in 1619 and £200 on the eve of the Civil War. In a survey of 1650 the 'casual yearly profits of the coalpits' of Sheffield Park were stated to be £140, and in 1692 they were leased to Richard Richmond, a London merchant for twenty-one years for £140 per annum, an arrangement which left him scope to sublet them to Richard Bagshawe, a leading local lead-mine owner.[12]

The rents and profits achieved by Sheffield Park in the seventeenth century place it firmly in the front rank of Yorkshire collieries. There were a small number of comparable undertakings in the Don valley around Sheffield, a region in which commercial mining dates back to at least the fourteenth century. Kimberworth, to the north-east of Sheffield, was rented for £100 in the Commonwealth, and nearby Whiston for £55. Both were owned by the Effingham family and operated by Lionel Copley, the leading south Yorkshire ironmaster of his day. On Crooks Moor, west of Sheffield, a colliery was leased by its owner, the duke of Norfolk, for £40 and a fifth share of the profits. Some seven miles or so to the south-east lay Wales Wood colliery which was said to have produced about 2,000 tons in 1598. For Hooton, located four miles to the north-east of Rotherham, there is a set of accounts which run from 1668 to 1675 which detail a colliery producing between 1,600 and 2,700 loads a year at handsome profits of between £100 and £200.[13]

The clustering of collieries in the Don valley was an integral part of the industrial development of the region.[14] In the vanguard of this development was the working of the iron dug from prolific local ironstone mines, on forges fired with local coal. The reputation of the Don

---

[11] SCL Bright 55/1–31. See also below, Ch. 10 (App.)

[12] See below, Ch. 10 (App.); Hopkinson 1976, 3–4, 8; BoL Selden Supra 115, f. 12ᵛ.

[13] Hopkinson 1976, 4; *APC 1598–9* 657; LCA Mexborough, MX 295, 296.

[14] See in particular Hey 1972.

valley for cutlery and ironwares stretches back far into the fourteenth century, and in the 1540s Leland reported that 'There be many smiths and cutlers in Hallamshire [and] in Rotherham be very good smiths for all cutlery tools'. By the 1630s, according to a survey made for the duke of Norfolk, on the great manor of Sheffield alone there were four or five hundred master workmen using the lord's 'cutler wheels', as well as quarries for clay, stone, and lime.[15] Using parish registers, it can be learnt that between 1655 and 1659 almost 27 per cent of Sheffield bridegrooms were cutlers, a proportion which was to rise to almost 40 per cent by 1700–4. While Sheffield itself specialized in high-quality cutlery, the rural districts around it produced a wide range of metal wares, as well as inferior cutlery.[16] Norton parish specialized in scythes and sickles; Shiregreen in table forks; and while Sheffield had relatively few nailers, in rural south Yorkshire and north Derbyshire, beyond the cutlery area, there were many villages where the production of nails was a major occupation.

Further confirmation of thriving industrialization is offered by the hearth-tax returns of 1672, which dramatically illuminate a region where agriculture often took second place to the working of iron and steel. Sheffield is shown to have had a population at this time of some 5,000, and within a ten-mile radius of the town there were nearly 600 smithies.[17] Much coal was consumed in these smithies, and the interdependence of coal and ironworking is further stressed by the prominence of ironmasters among the lessees of leading collieries. But perhaps of even greater significance for the consumption of coal, is that industrialization and a buoyant local economy stimulated the growth of the population of the region, thereby providing more domestic hearths to be fuelled as well as a range of coal-using industries serving local needs, of which tanning, textiles, glass-making, and brewing were just a few. As the banksman of Sheffield Park colliery reported in 1631, the major outlets for his coal were the town and country of Sheffield, the cutler trade, and the brewsters' trade. But demand has a tendency to call forth supply, and he also mournfully reported that the 'great sort of coals got at Totley pits and Whitley Wood pits' had hindered his sales.[18]

---

[15] Leland, *Itinerary*, iv. 14; J. G. Ronksley (ed.), *An Exact and Perfect Survey and View of the Manor of Sheffield by John Harrison, 1637* (1908).

[16] E. J. Buckatzsch, 'Occupations in the Parish Registers of Sheffield, 1655–1719', *EcHR* 2nd ser. 1 (1948–9), 145–6.

[17] Hey 1972, 9–12.

[18] SCL Bright 50/1.

In the West Riding collieries were more numerous still, and their combined output may well have exceeded that of south Yorkshire. The focus of activity here was the Aire and Calder valleys, and the 'great towns' of Halifax, Leeds, and Wakefield. By the close of the seventeenth century Leeds had around 10,000 inhabitants, and was understood by Celia Fiennes to be 'the wealthiest town of its bigness in the country'. Tax returns reveal that the town indeed had few paupers and that over half of the inhabitants had two or more hearths upon which to burn coal.[19] The main industry of the region was cloth production, which although it used only modest amounts of coal in its manufacturing processes helped to support relatively high densities of population. As early as the mid-sixteenth century York clothiers complaining of mounting competition from the West Riding drew attention to the advantages which the clothworkers there enjoyed by having cheap household fuel supplied from local collieries.[20] Wakefield supported a local colliery which commanded £80 a year rent in 1620, and £140 in the mid-seventeenth century, and when water hindered production the construction of a sough costing up to £1,000 was considered.[21] At Baildon, just north of Bradford, a colliery was said to have made profits of £80 a year between 1620 and 1640, and in 1658 accounts show an output of 40 tons and profits of 13s. each weak. The largest and most profitable colliery of all may have been Kippax, some seven miles south-east of Leeds and three miles from Pontefract. In 1623 it was claimed that Sir William Slingsby had made £6,000 from his pits there over a twenty-year period, and that in some of those years profits had risen as high as £600. Since this claim was made in a legal dispute we must treat it with caution. However, an account survives for 1650 which reveals sales of coal worth £877. 16s. 1d., indicating an output perhaps in excess of 4,000 tons.[22] Further evidence of mining on a significant scale comes from the manor of Leeds itself; in 1588 Christopher Anderson of Lostock, Lancashire, paid £613. 6s. 8d. for a thirty-four year lease of coal-mines there and in the waste of Whinmore in the honour of Pontefract.[23] Sir Thomas Gascoigne claimed to have spent £800 soughing a colliery at Seacroft in Whinmore between 1665 and 1667.[24]

Sadly it is largely upon such scraps of information that an understanding of the development of the Yorkshire coalfield in the medieval

[19] Defoe (1728), quoted in Corfield 1982, 23; Fiennes, *Journeys*, 182; Hey 1986, 234.
[20] Smith 1970, 23.   [21] Nef 1932, i. 59; Moller thesis 1933, 131.
[22] Cliffe 1969, 57–8, 62.   [23] Nef 1932, i. 58–9.
[24] LCA Gascoigne GC/C.

and early modern eras must be based. Hosts of small and poorly documented collieries provide a flimsy foundation for measuring output, and
any estimate must rest more upon intuition derived from working
through surviving records than scientific quantification. But it is
necessary to review the divergent estimates made by previous historians. Direct comparison with Nef is rendered difficult, for he dealt
with what he termed the Yorkshire–Midland field, which included
Nottinghamshire and Derbyshire. Although Nef admitted that it was
'out of the question to make a satisfactory estimate of the output from
the hundreds of small pits scattered through Derbyshire, northern
Nottinghamshire and Yorkshire', he went on to suggest, by a circuitous
route, that the output of Yorkshire was some 150,000 to 200,000 tons in
1700.[25] This is considerably at variance with the estimate of 300,000 tons
made by Michael Flinn.[26] There were hosts of Yorkshire collieries, they
do seem to have been worked more continuously than those to the west
of the Pennines, and the numbers attaining middling size were probably
greater, but frankly it is difficult to imagine how 300,000 tons of coal
could either have been produced or consumed within the county. From
what is known of the scale and numbers of Yorkshire collieries and their
markets even 200,000 tons would seem to be too high. A figure of
around 150,000 tons at the close of the seventeenth century is therefore
more plausible. It was only after the long-delayed improvements in the
waterways of the county, including the navigability of the Don and the
Aire and Calder, which were under way at the very close of our period,
that coal could at last be moved any distance in Yorkshire without
adding prohibitively to its price. Transport improvements, combined
with a continuing surge in the populations of Yorkshire's industrial
towns and villages, ensured a sharp increase in coal production in the
opening decades of the eighteenth century well before the impact of
steam.

vi. North Wales

The seams of the North Wales coalfield are heavily fractured and
faulted, but it was precisely this feature which facilitated a widespread
early start to mining, including some evidence of digging in Roman
times.[1] As can be seen from Map 5.6, coal-seams were tapped in a

---

[25] Nef 1932, i. 57–60.   [26] Flinn 1984, 26.

[1] A useful account of the Flintshire coalfield is contained in Gruffyd thesis 1981.

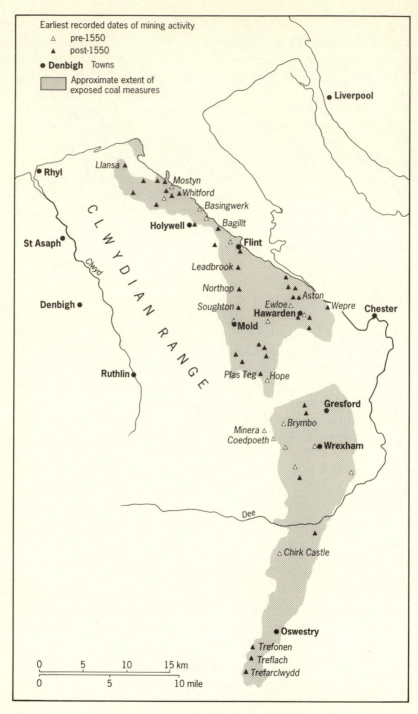

Liverpool

Rhyl

Llansa ▲

Mostyn

Whitford

Basingwerk

Holywell

Bagillt

St Asaph

Flint

Clwyd

Leadbrook

C L W Y D I A N   R A N G E

Northop

Aston

Soughton

Ewloe

Wepre

Denbigh

Hawarden

Chester

Mold

Ruthlin

Plas Teg ▲ Hope

Gresford

Brymbo

Minera △

Coedpoeth △

Wrexham

Dee

Chirk Castle

0   5   10   15 km

0   5   10 mile

Oswestry

Trefonen

Treflach

Trefarclwydd

Map 5.6. The North Wales coalfield

multitude of places where they had been thrust up to the surface, but it was in the northern section, alongside or close to the Dee estuary, that the most intense activity took place. Indeed, the earliest details we have throw a spotlight on a surge in output in coastal collieries generated by Edward I's massive castle-building programme. The amounts of coal dug from a number of Flintshire collieries in the 1280s and 1290s must have soared to levels which were not matched thereafter until the seventeenth century. The construction of Flint, Beaumaris, Conway, and Caernavon castles required much iron to be worked and huge quantities of lime to be burnt to make the mortar which cemented the blocks of stone and the plaster and wash which decorated the interior walls. Both processes consumed much coal. Only partial building accounts survive, but in just five months in 1283 over 500 tons were carried to Conway, and in a comparable period in 1295 a minimum of 2,500 tons were carried to Beaumaris. A fleet of thirty boats was based at 'Holston', between Basingwerk and Bagilt, to carry to Beaumaris the coal and stone produced by neighbouring collieries and quarries.[2]

The building of castles, however, was an exceptional interlude in the development of Flintshire mining; the enduring demand for coal was more prosaic and substantially lower. In just a few instances can some indications of its scale be gained. Coal-mines at Mostyn were worth, together with a stone quarry, only 5 s. annually in 1294, and £3. 6 s. 8 d. on their own in 1423. At Hope, lead- and coal-mines were rented for £3 a year in 1353, and mines of coal and limestone rented for £2. 6 s. 8 d. in the early fifteenth century. At Ewloe coalmining appears to have been both more continuous and more substantial. Coal is first mentioned there in 1312–13 when the farm of the manor was in arrears. In 1350–1 the rent of mines situated on the demesne and in the freehold lands of Blethin ap Ithel was £5. 6 s. 8 d., and by 1393 the rent of mines on the manor had risen to £9. 13 s. 4 d. War in the early fifteenth century reduced their value, but in 1461 the Stanleys of Hawarden agreed to pay for them £12. 10 s. 4 d. a year plus a share of the output.[3] Such rents indicate modest but not insignificant mining operations. Whereas ample supplies of wood and turf and high overland transport costs generally restricted the demand for coal, Chester provided a ready market. The Chamberlain's Accounts show coal being brought to the city by water

[2] H. M. Colvin (ed.), *The History of the King's Works: The Middle Ages* (2 vols., 1963), i. 349, 399; J. G. Edwards, *Edward I's Castle-Building in Wales*, Proceedings of the British Academy, xxxii (1944); Gruffyd thesis 1981, 20–4.

[3] Gruffyd thesis 1981, 25–34; Lewis 1903, 146–77; Hewitt 1929, 84–5; Rees 1968, i. 34–5, 70–2.

from at least as early as 1326–7, and a toll of ½d. levied on every cart carrying 'stoune cole' into Chester, which was said in 1534 to be 'used time out of mind', may well date from at least as early as 1279. On the other hand the absence of mentions of coal in Chester customs accounts, or of its importation into any port on the North Wales coast, makes it most unlikely that there was at this time a coastal trade from Flintshire mines of any significant dimensions.[4]

In the landlocked portion of the North Wales coalfield to the south of the Bala fault there are no indications of mining on anything but a desultory scale. The earl of Arundel granted the burgesses of Holt permission in 1414 to dig coal for their own consumption in the wastes of Brymbo and Coedpoeth, but in 1501–2 the coal-mines of Brymbo were leased for a mere 3s. 4d., and as late as 1547 those on the manor of Esclusham near Wrexham realized only £1. 3s. 4d. in a year.[5]

As far as can be gauged from imperfect records, there was no more than a gentle expansion in the North Wales coalfield for much of the sixteenth century. Although shipments of coal from Chester rose four- or fivefold in the second half of the century, they were still less than 1,000 tons in 1602–3.[6] In the early decades of the seventeenth century, however, there was a quickening of activity. The best information concerns developments at Mostyn, and it seems likely that this colliery was the largest and most profitable in the coalfield for much of the century. Indeed for much of the time Mostyn may well have been the largest colliery on the whole western seaboard. In 1602 Roger Mostyn purchased the remaining thirteen years of the lease of the 'mines and veins of coals, called *petticoale or stone coale*' of Mostyn for £70. That the colliery was already of importance is suggested by the identity of the vendors of the residual lease, namely Thomas Cowper and Richard Mason of London. Roger Mostyn embarked upon an ambitious programme of expansion, and by 1616 he had three pits in operation, and was said to be selling 1,200 Flintshire tons (c.14 cwt. each) for shipment, and four times as much for local consumption. By 1619 the colliery was reported to be worth around £700 a year to the family, which suggests an output of possibly as much as 7,000 to 10,000 standard tons. Roger's successor, Sir Roger Mostyn, sank three new deep pits around 1639, and two undated estate records of this period reveal revenues of £200 and £800 from the

[4] Hewitt 1929, 66, 84, 189; *CPR 1272-81*, 311; Gruffyd thesis 1981, 38.

[5] G. G. Lerry, 'The Industries of Denbighshire from Tudor Times to the Present Day', *Transactions of the Denbigh Historical Society*, 7 (1958), 41; Lewis, 1903, 146; *CPR 1547-8*, 28.

[6] Gruffyd thesis 1981, 119.

colliery. As further testimony to its prominence, coal exported from Chester was almost invariably entered in the city Port Books as 'Mostyn coal'.[7]

By contrast, and perhaps consequentially, the ancient colliery at Ewloe had ceased working some time before 1594. A survey of that year reported that the coal-mines of the manor had 'been in decay for many years past . . . because of the great store in other places most convenient and nearer to the sea, where they are digged with less charge'. The most important of the 'other places' were listed by commissioners in 1616 investigating the weights and measures used in shipping coal, as Bagilt, Leadbrook, Wepre, Englefield, 'Uphfytton', and, of course, Mostyn. But the spatial distribution of production was fluid. At the close of the century Edward Llwyd concluded that the leading mines of Flintshire were Mostyn, Llansa, and Whitford on the north of the coal measures, and Holywell, Bagilt, Hawarden, Flint, Soughton, Northop, Aston, and 'Whichdein' further south.[8]

A modest stimulus to production came from the export trade. By the 1630s shipments from Chester had reached 4,000 tons, and they had doubled again by the last quarter of the century. Exports from Liverpool, also probably consisting largely of Flintshire coal, followed a similar upward path, from around 750 tons a year in the first quarter of the century, to around 2,000 tons in the 1630s, and 3,000 to 3,500 tons in the 1660s, before they dipped sharply in the closing decades. Whereas the scale of overseas trade was thus at best small, the coasting trade was exiguous. Shipments coastwise from Chester rarely exceeded 1,500 tons a year before 1690, while those from Liverpool were, if anything, lower still. We must make some allowance for inefficient monitoring by customs officials, but the main reason for these slight water-borne trades was the intense competition which Flintshire coal faced from other coalfields.[9] The location of Flintshire meant that it could not serve continental consumers, and although Dublin throve to become the second largest city with a population of around 60,000 by the close of the century, it drew its coal from Cumberland, Lancashire, and Glamorgan, as well as from Flintshire. Moreover, Flintshire was losing the battle, for whereas Chester ships had about half of the Dublin market in 1640, by 1685 Cumberland had captured around 70 per cent, aided by the silting of the Dee estuary. Similarly, in the coastal trade

---

[7] UCNW Mostyn, 6935; Gruffyd thesis 1981, 45–6, 53, 65; Evans thesis 1928, 9.

[8] Gruffyd thesis 1981, 53; Rees 1968, i. 74–6; Nef 1932, i. 55.

[9] Gruffyd thesis 1981, 116, 196–7, 199; Evans thesis 1928, app. A.

with south-west England, coal from South Wales eclipsed that from Flintshire.

A witness to a special commission held at Mostyn in 1616 deposed that landsales from the colliery were four times as high as seasales. But given that Mostyn was probably the leading seasale colliery at the time, and that the commission was investigating possible customs frauds, the accuracy of this testimony may be doubtful. There were no large centres of population within easy carting distance, but local demand for the product of Flintshire collieries was enhanced as rising population and fuel consumption reduced the abundance of turf and wood to something more resembling adequacy, and in some few parts even scarcity. Moreover, advances in the use of coal in local brick-making and pottery manufacture can be seen, and lime-burning for agricultural use was expanding. Before the close of the century coal was probably being used to smelt lead at Mr Pennant's coalworks at Flint, though the major breakthrough in smelting this metal took place in 1704 when the London Lead Company began operating a reverbaratory furnace at Gladlys by Bagilt.[10] In addition to a modest seasale enjoyed by most of the bigger collieries on the Dee, those near Chester also supplied the city. Aston and Hawarden collieries sent their coal by land, however, and at the close of the century Andrew Yarranton with characteristic exuberance argued in favour of the Dee navigation project by claiming that at least £1,000 would be saved in carriage, 'if the Dee were made navigable to Chester [and] coals could be brought from Aston to the City of Chester by water, which are now brought by land'.[11]

In Denbighshire the total absence of water communications restricted overall growth to even more humble levels than in the northern portion of the coalfield. Yet, in the right circumstances even landlocked collieries could thrive to modest proportions. Those in the vicinity of Wrexham benefited from the market it provided. John Norden in his survey of 1620 found Esclusham colliery worthy of notice, and Richard Grosvenor held no less than six mines on Brymbo common. The Grosvenors of Easton were long-standing coal-owners around Wrexham, for Richard's father had held a mine there, and Sir Thomas Grosvenor entered into an agreement with Roger Mostyn of Brymbo which allowed the latter to mine for coal at Coedpoeth.[12] North Wales is abysmally served by colliery accounts, and they survive

[10] Gruffyd thesis 1981, 65, 106–13.
[11] Yarranton, *England's Improvement*, i. 192.
[12] Lerry, 'Industries of Denbighshire', 41–2.

for only Plas Teg and Chirk Castle collieries. For Plas Teg, near Caergwrle on the southern tip of the northern portion of the coalfield, just ten months accounting from 3 April 1630 survives, during which a mere 280.5 tons was raised. So exiguous is this output that it may be correct to infer that the fuel needs of the Plas Teg estate may have been the major reason for the operation of the pit. Not so with Chirk Castle colliery, which lay some nine miles south of Wrexham and about the same distance north of Oswestry. Here a series of accounts which cover the years from 1681 to 1694 reveal average annual outputs of 3,500 wagon-loads, of perhaps a ton each, worth around £450. The colliery was owned and worked by the Myddeltons of Chirk Castle, a wealthy gentry family who played a leading role in the opening up of the metal-liferous reserves of Wales, as well as Denbighshire's coal. In the vicinity of Chirk, coal was used in at least four forges, and it was coked to make it suitable for drying malt on the estate.[13]

It is upon such impressions that a quantitative assessment of the performance of the North Wales coalfield must be based. It is certain that there was substantial expansion in the seventeenth century, but it seems unlikely that output before the mid-sixteenth century comprised more than a few thousand tons. By the close of the seventeenth century, a maximum output in excess of 50,000 tons seems unlikely in any but the most exceptional of years. It is possible to deal only in the roughest of orders of magnitude, but in average years the collieries of Flintshire may well have yielded 30,000 tons, or perhaps a little more, while the combined output of those of Denbighshire was probably rarely more than 10,000 to 15,000 tons.

vii. South Wales

The bulk of the bountiful reserves of coal in the extensive South Wales coalfield were to lie undisturbed until well into the nineteenth century.[1] The state of prospecting and mining technology during the period covered in this volume meant that only the upper seams and the surface outcrops on the periphery of the coal basin were able to be tapped, while distance from the sea and navigable rivers severely constrained the exploitation of even the geologically accessible seams on the northern fringes and to the east of Neath. The map of mining sites on the South

---

[13] ClRO Glynde D/G/3311–12; NLW Chirk Castle, 12548–60.

---

[1] Flinn 1984, 11; Church 1986, 7.

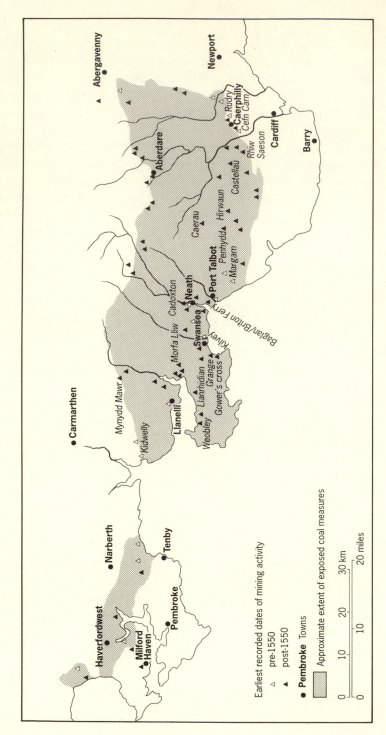

Map 5.7. The South Wales coalfield

Wales coalfield is in some ways even more misleading than most, since in the vast majority of identifiable mining sites digging was confined to small easily won surface deposits and geared exclusively to the modest needs of a handful of consumers in the immediate vicinity. The exceptions lay close to the sea on either side of the neck of the Gower peninsula, around Neath and Llanelli, where the coalfield bordered the sea and heavy faulting threw coal strata up close to the surface, and in Pembrokeshire to the west, where the reserves consisted of easily won high-quality anthracite. By contrast the abundant but landlocked seams in the Rhondda and to the north of Cardiff were scarcely scratched.

After the well-verified archaeological evidence of coal-burning in the Roman villas at Ely, Gelligaer, and Llantwit major, records are silent until the abbey of Margam leased in 1250 the right to mine coal on the land of Owen ab Alaythur at Penhydd near Margam, together with a right of way for two-wheeled and four-wheeled carts.[2] With the exception of an almost total lack of records of mining in the Llanelli region, which may or may not denote an actual lack of coal working, the development of the industry in the Middle Ages was predictable, with concentrations of pits around Neath, Swansea, and Port Talbot, as well as in Pembrokeshire. Far away in the north-east near Abergavenny, at Cefn Carn and Rudry to the north of Cardiff, and in the extreme north-west of the Glamorgan portion of the coalfield, sporadic activity was doubtless due to the presence of irresistible surface outcrops.[3]

There is little direct evidence of the scale of mining enterprises in the Middle Ages, although in Pembrokeshire we can observe that the rent of pits in Coedraeth forest to the south-east of Narberth generally ranged between £2 and £3 in the first half of the fifteenth century, and those at Roch and Pulle in the north-west were rented for £3. 6s. 8d.[4] These rent levels are indicative of modest rather than significant mining operations, but it is unlikely there were many in South Wales which rendered much more. One exception that we can observe in rare and satisfying detail is the colliery of Kilvey, located adjacent to Swansea. The escheating of the lordship of Kilvey to the Crown, on the death of its owner the duke of Norfolk, has resulted in the survival of two colliery accounts, one for a full year from Michaelmas 1399, and the other a partial and undated but obviously contemporary record.[5] These accounts reveal Kilvey to have been a large colliery, exceptionally so for the times. Production is given

---

[2] *Glamorgan County History*, ii. 301–4; iv. 48; Rees 1963, i. 34.
[3] Rees 1963, i. 34–5, 102.   [4] Lewis 1903, 146–7.
[5] PRO SC6 1202/15. The accounts have been edited in Rees, 1949, 180–92.

in lasts and weys which, if we are right in assuming that they were of similar proportions to the same measures in the same county in the seventeenth century, suggests an output of the order of 5,000 to 6,000 tons a year.[6] The ratios between the numbers of hewers and total output, and between hewers and putters, are suggestive of a rich and easily worked coal-face located a long distance from the surface, while the high costs of carriage from the bankside indicate that it was also some distance from the sea.

Customs accounts suggest that the coasting and export trades of South Wales were tiny before the seventeenth century, and modest up to the Civil War. Of all the ports on the Glamorgan and Pembrokeshire coasts, Swansea alone appears to have shipped more than 1,000 tons a year before 1600. Although shipments increased thereafter even as late as the 1630s and 1640s the combined coal trade of Swansea, Llanelli, Burry, Neath, Milford, and Tenby seems rarely to have exceeded 20,000 tons, and scarcely any coal at all was shipped from either Cardiff or Carmarthen before the eighteenth century.[7]

Yet these low recorded shipments should not be taken to reflect an equivalent lack of development of the industry of the region. The possibility of customs evasion on a significant scale must be entertained, but more importantly there is also evidence of considerable local demand. Consumption in Pembrokeshire was stimulated by both the shortage of wood and the excellence of the anthracite. When John Leland visited the county in the later 1530s he remarked that the inhabitants commonly made their fires of coal rather than of wood, and George Owen's delightfully informative *Description of Pembrokeshire*, first published in 1603, reported that coal 'serveth most people especially the chief towns'. Owen also went on to remark that 'those gentlemen of the shire [who] dwell near the coal or that may have it carried by water with ease, use most coal fires in their kitchens and some in their halls'; consequently 'this coal may be numbered as one of the chief commodities of this country and is so necessary as without it the

---

[6] The accounts show that there were 4 weys to a last. In Glamorgan in the 17th cent. a wey of coal weighed 5 tons (Rees 1963, i. 80; Flinn 1984, 462). A last would thus weigh 20 tons. According to Malynes in the 1620s a last of coal passing through the Sound was equivalent to 7½ Newcastle chaldrons; at 53 cwt. per chaldron this would have resulted in a last of 19.875 tons. A 20-ton last is quite plausible for the late 14th cent., given that it could be sold for 17s. 4d. to the shippers at Kilvey at a time when in Newcastle a ton of coal was being sold to shipmasters for around 1s.

[7] Coasting and export figures are given in tabular form in Evans thesis 1928, app. A, and Nef 1932, ii. app. D(iii). Evans is unreliable, and he mistakenly takes a wey of coal to be equivalent to 7 cwt.

country would be in great distress'. Most interestingly, with respect to the evidence of the customs accounts, he informs us that although 'the lower parts as the hundreds of Narbeth and Rowse make some gain by selling of seacoal by sea to Ireland and France . . . generally the country people dislike with the selling of the commodity, least in time it grow so scarce that the country shall want it, being the greatest fuel, as it hath already enhanced the price'. Owen's judgements find broad confirmation in contemporaneous assessments emanating from government sources. A lobbyist in favour of restricting coal exports in the 1590s asserted that the 'veins and pits growing in Wales . . . are no more than needful for that country, so that all the coasts are and must be served from Newcastle and those parts'.[8]

Confirmation of high levels of local consumption is also forthcoming from the production side, which was underpinned by gentry finance and enterprise. George Owen noted the existence in Pembrokeshire of mines at Talbeny, Johnston, Freystrop, Picton, Jeffreston, and Begelly, and from other sources we may add Roch and Saundersfoot. Furthermore, these mines were commonly twelve, fifteen, or twenty fathoms deep, and therefore likely to have been capable of sizeable outputs.[9] Nor should we underestimate the aggregate scale of output in east Glamorgan and Monmouthshire, where recent local research suggests that pits were more numerous than has hitherto been thought. The region around Neath and Llanelli was rapidly developing into the most productive on the South Wales coalfield, and the Evans family of Gnoll rose to prominence within it. In the 1620s they took over the mines in Neath town from the burgesses, and we can observe also their allies, the Prices of Briton-Ferry, who had coal interests in their home town as well as in Neath and Kilvey. As indications of the scale of some of the ventures of the Evans family, the port book for 1643–4 records that Edward Evans shipped over 4,000 tons from Neath, while a single surviving account reveals that a colliery leased by him produced nearly 800 weys (c.4,000 tons) in 1654. There is also a record of David Evans taking a lease of coal concessions at Melin Crydden and Llantwit for five years, and agreeing to pay the handsome sum of £300 a year; though his ambitions were soon thwarted by flooding, despite the installation of 'water-commanding engines'.[10]

[8] Leland, *Itinerary in Wales*, 115; Owen, *Pembrokeshire*, 57, 87–8, 92; PRO SP 15/41/85.

[9] Owen, *Pembrokeshire*, 88–90; Rees 1963, i. 35, 82; Nef 1932, i. 54.

[10] *Glamorgan County History*, iv. 49–50; 365; Rees 1963, i. 85, 87, 109; Jenkins 1983, 57–8; G. D. Owen, *Elizabethan Wales: The Social Scene* (Cardiff, 1964), 150; Trott 1969, 50–5.

Leland noted the digging of coal at Llanelli when he passed through the area between 1536 and 1539, but further mentions are scarce until the opening of the seventeenth century, when a surge of activity occurred. Evidence of fierce competition for coalmining leases, of the importation of skilled viewers to advise on the location of coal-seams and of the sinking of new pits, together with testimony that in 1613 an adventurer sank more than £1,000 into a colliery, all point to expansion, as does the advent of a succession of coalmining dynasties. Among these were the Vaughans of Golden Grove, and the Jenkins and Grundy families of Llanelli.[11]

Thus, growth and development can be identified in the South Wales coalfield in the decades before the Civil War, but it was in the latter half of the century that a much more substantial surge in output took place, and this time it was led by seasales, both coastwise and overseas. Surviving accounts are too scattered, and the trade too volatile, to permit any but the most impressionistic of quantification, but it does seem likely that over the first seventy-five years or so of the seventeenth century shipments from the South Wales coalfield probably increased at least fifteenfold, from some 5,000 tons to 75,000 tons or more each year. Swansea and Milford were the leading coal ports with shipments regularly reaching 20,000 tons or more, followed by Neath and Llanelli with 10,000 to 15,000 tons each, while even the coal trade of Tenby emerged from the obscurity of a few hundred tons to attain more than 7,000 tons. Such was the relative paucity of the trade in other commodities, that coal dominated the commerce of Glamorgan and Pembrokeshire.[12] The great bulk of this increase was accounted for by the coasting trade and by shipments to Ireland and the Channel Islands. Coastwise almost all coal went south-westwards, not only to the nearby ports of Bridgwater, Minehead, Ilfracombe, and Barnstaple, from whence it was distributed inland, but also around the Cornish peninsular to Falmouth, Exeter, and Plymouth. Somewhat surprisingly small amounts of Welsh coal occasionally found their way to London, or even Yarmouth, but despite the fine quality of Pembrokeshire anthracite the costs of carriage were stacked heavily against it. Foreign trade too was greatly hampered by distance, as well as by competition from the north-east, and it remained small by comparison. The best markets overseas for the coal of South Wales

---

[11] Leland, *Itinerary in Wales*, 60; Symons 1979, i. 30–5.

[12] This overview of the coal trade of South Wales is based upon a reworking of data given in Nef 1932, ii, app. D(ii) and Evans thesis 1928, app. A.

were said in 1706 to be 'Brittany, Normandy and downwards as far as Bordeaux'.[13]

Progress was not secure, however, and the trade of most ports peaked before the mid-1680s. Not only did the Whitehaven collieries succeed in capturing much of the Irish trade, wars with Holland and France harmed overseas trade, and sharply increased duties on coastal shipments damaged the market for coal throughout the coastal regions of Britain. Both industry and trade were in recession at Llanelli at the close of the century, while the coal trade of Neath, according to Sir Humphrey Mackworth in 1695, 'had been almost totally lost', and Neath itself 'became very poor for want of trade'. Mackworth, who was to perform wonders at his Neath collieries and ironworks, no doubt exaggerated the extent of the slump and thereby his own subsequent achievements, but confirmatory evidence of recession can be found in the customs records.[14] Whereas at its peak the South Wales coalfield may have yielded 150,000 tons a year, it is probable that the recession of the 1690s may have cut this figure by a third or even more.

viii. The West Midlands

Shropshire

The Shropshire coalfield was one of the most productive in Britain in the early modern era. Yet the coal measures, though widely scattered, were in the main deep and difficult to exploit, and before the nineteenth century most parts of the coalfield were scarcely touched. Despite frequent prospecting around Shrewsbury, for example, mining failed to flourish, for the seams that could be reached there were thin and easily exhausted. To the south of Bridgnorth mining came late and was restricted to small, scattered outcrops. Still further south in the Forest of Wyre, later sometimes known as the Bewdley coalfield, sporadic attempts were made to extract coal, but the accessible seams were thin and often of poor quality. Mining in the Clee Hills, in the western segment, had a far longer history and was somewhat more widespread, but it was constrained by remoteness as well as the depth of the coal.

It was only in the precociously industrialized region in the north-east, centred on the Severn Gorge around Coalbrookdale, that coalmining thrived. Here the east Shropshire coal measures are heavily faulted, and

[13] Hoskins 1935, 103; Jenkins 1983, 60. See NorRO C.26/8 for a shipment of 60 tons of Welsh coal arriving in Yarmouth.

[14] Symons 1979. 36; Trott 1969, 56–7.

several major outcrops lay astride the Severn which were able to be tapped from the sides of the steep gorge itself or from neighbouring hill-sides, by way of shafts which were often more horizontal than vertical. It was these outcrops, centred on the parishes of Madeley, Broseley, Benthall, and Willey, which came to dominate production.[1] 'From Benthall the seams of coal are continuous through Broseley, where they lie so near the surface in places that the inhabitants not infrequently meet with it in their gardens and cellars, and here on the upper side of the Broseley fault their depth seldom exceeds twenty yards.'[2] Here was a lesser Tyneside. Through the efficient communications provided by the Severn and its tributaries, the easily mined coal of the Coalbrookdale region was able to flow both upstream and downstream into the ready markets of an expansive hinterland.

Surviving records reveal a scattering of mining sites in medieval Shropshire. There is mention of pits in the Clee Hills as early as 1260, nearby on the Ludlow outcrop at Caynham and Whitton in 1291, as well as in and around Coalbrookdale at Madeley, Benthall, and Little Wenlock. From 1326, at Benthall where a right of way for the carriage of coal owned by the abbot of Buildwas had existed since at least 1250, Adam Peyeson of Buildwas held all the coal-pits for a rent of £2 yearly, with the right to employ four men to dig the coal, and as many as he wished to carry it to the Severn for shipment.[3] By the 1530s we learn from Leland that 'coals be digged hard by Wombridge, where the priory was'. At its dissolution, Wombridge priory was receiving £5 yearly for the lease of its colliery. Leland also visited the Clee Hills and remarked that there was plenty of coal, much of which was used to burn lime, which served the neighbouring country.[4]

Concern over fuel supplies was increasingly displayed by the larger towns of the Severn valley as the sixteenth century progressed, and it frequently took the form of attempts to control through legislation the supply, consumption, and price of wood.[5] It also found more positive expression in a search for coal. In 1565 the corporation of Worcester took over the running of a coal-mine at Pensax in the Wyre forest, and in 1571 the corporation of Shrewsbury proposed the raising of £100 to fund coal-prospecting. When Richard Gardiner, a dyer and freeman of

---

[1] Brief descriptions of the Shropshire coalfield can be found in *VCH Shropshire*, i. 31–4, 450–2; Trinder 1973, 5–6. For the Forest of Wyre see *VCH Worcestershire*, ii. 265. See Map 5.8 p. 150 below.

[2] *VCH Shropshire*, i. 454–5.

[3] *Ibid.* 449; xi. 47–8, 87; Trinder 1973, 9–10; Galloway 1898, i. 61.

[4] Leland, *Itinerary*, v. 18, 189; *Valor Ecclesiasticus*, iii. 194.   [5] See above Ch. 3.

the drapers' company, duly discovered a 'great store of seacoal' at Emstry, close by the city, the corporation professed him 'worthy of commendation and maintenance, but also to be had in remembrance for ever'. The coal reserves he discovered, however, proved merely mortal and soon failed. Similarly, Worcester's mine swiftly disappeared, and no record of it exists after 1574.[6] The lasting solution lay in the Severn Gorge, and Worcester and Shrewsbury, along with numerous other towns and villages along the Severn valley, soon came to rely for their heat upon coal shipped from the parishes around Coalbrookdale. Coal barges had plied the Severn since at least the early fourteenth century, and by the opening years of the sixteenth century craft from the Gorge can be traced passing through Bridgnorth.[7] As population multiplied, and the scarcity of wood and other fuels heightened, coal became the most common freight on the river. Aided by improvements in the navigability of the Severn, coal by the 1590s was regularly shipped downstream as far as Tewkesbury and Gloucester, and from at least as early a date Madeley and Broseley coal was on sale in Worcester at prices which undercut that produced by closer but landlocked Black Country collieries. The dependence of Shrewsbury upon the same source of supply is evidenced by the building of Mardol Quay in 1607.[8]

The experience of the north-east Shropshire coalfield provides abundant testimony to the virtual universality of the late sixteenth-century boom in the British coal trade. Stimulated by the demands of the Severn valley region, rapid expansion of production was well under way by 1600, although details are hard to find in the sparse records which survive. Debts incurred by Severn bargemen, who bought coal on credit from mine operators, suggest that John Brooke, lord of the manor of Madeley, was heavily engaged in coalmining. To the north of Madeley there was a 'Coalpit Way' in Donnington by 1592, and just a little earlier Camden described Oakengates as a 'small village of some note for pit coal'.[9] It is likely, however, that Broseley was the leading centre of production, and that the lord of the manor, James Clifford, was in the vanguard. In 1575 we find him presented by the Commissioners of Sewers 'because he made a coaldelf or coalpit in his lordship of Broseley at a place called the Tuckeyes, and cast all the rubbish, stone

[6] Moller thesis 1933, 152–3; Dyer 1973, 54–5.

[7] T. S. Willan, 'The River Navigation and Trade of the Severn Valley (1600–1750)', *EcHR* 8 (1937–8), 68–79.

[8] Wanklyn 1982, 3; Trinder 1973, 9, 12; *VCH Shropshire*, xi. 25.

[9] Wanklyn 1982, 3; Trinder 1973, 10.

and earth into the deepest part of the Severn'. Despite soaring demand, so great was the potential capacity of the Severn Gorge collieries that in the early years of the seventeenth century there was fierce competition between Clifford and his freeholders over the right to exploit the abundant mineral reserves of the manor. The feud culminated in a series of violent raids carried out by both parties on the mines and equipment of their rivals. From the extensive litigation which ensued, and from the existence of the early waggonway from the pits to the riverside which it reveals, there can be no doubt as to the large scale of mining in several parts of the manor, nor of the imperative of access to the Severn. Competition among producers for markets probably also lay behind the financial problems which beset a number of over-ambitious producers, including the Cliffords, Wilcoxes, and Lacons.[10]

Yet demand continued its upward course, receiving a major boost in the 1630s when the Avon was made navigable as far as Stratford, thereby enabling Shropshire coal to compete in the Vale of Evesham.[11] Such was the commerce of the Severnside collieries that control of them was a matter of priority in the Civil War. But even war, and the inept leasing policies of the county committee which followed immediately afterwards, brought only a temporary lull in the development of the industry.[12] By the early 1660s, when a scheme was proposed to render the Stour and Salwarpe navigable, it was claimed that almost 100,000 tons of Shropshire coal was carried on the Severn each year.[13] By 1670 Shropshire coal had arrived on the quays of Bristol and was selling for less than 6s. a ton in Tewkesbury, fifty miles from the collieries which produced it. This was a third of the London price and less than that which the citizens of Nottingham had to pay despite having collieries almost on their doorstep. In 1676 when Madeley coal arrived in far off Bideford it was greeted as a great bargain compared with the price of normal supplies from South Wales.[14]

There was thus a vast market for coal in the Severn valley, the Bristol Channel, and beyond to the north coast of Devon, but there was an abundance of producers anxious to meet its demands. Soon after passing Bridgnorth, coal from the Gorge faced possible competition from collieries around Stourbridge, but this was stifled by the failure of the

[10] PRO STAC 8/310/16; Wanklyn 1982, 3.
[11] Willan, 'River Navigation', 69–70.
[12] VCH Shropshire, i. 454; xi. 48.
[13] Willan, 'River Navigation', 71–2; Wanklyn 1982, 3.
[14] Nef 1932, i. 96–7; Moller thesis 1933, 617–18.

Stour and Salwarpe navigation projects to come to fruition. By the time
that Shropshire coal reached Tewkesbury and Gloucester, however,
that produced in the Forest of Dean and Kingswood Chase was close at
hand and, as has been noted, there was a large trade in coal between
Glamorgan and Pembrokeshire ports and south-west England. That
coal from the north-east of the Shropshire coalfield was able to
penetrate these distant markets and, in many cases, to undercut local
producers, says much for the cheapness with which it was able to be
produced and transported, aided by the absence of tolls or duties.

To this thriving commerce we must add the consumption of coal in
the vicinity of Shropshire collieries. As the collieries grew, so did the
townships in which they were based, and the cheapness of fuel fostered
the establishment of a wide range of coal-burning industries. Large
numbers of households needed to keep themselves warm in winter and,
as Yarranton asserted, 'pit-coal in all these places is not so chargeable to
the owner of the woods as cutting and carrying the woods home to his
house'.[15] Ironstone was often found in conjunction with coal, and the
production of iron and steel flourished around Coalbrookdale for
generations before Abraham Darby. Although coal was not successfully
used for the smelting of iron ore before the close of the seventeenth
century, large quantities were consumed in roasting and purifying the
ore before it was smelted with charcoal. Unlike the neighbouring Staffordshire coalfield, metalworking does not appear to have developed
much beyond local needs, but there was a substantial trade in lime burnt
in stacks using low-grade coal. Once again the Severn provided the
conduit, and lime from the Gorge was shipped to customers as far away
as Worcester. Low-grade coal was also used for producing salt from
brine springs, and tobacco pipes and bricks were manufactured, but
little pottery. In the last quarter of the seventeenth century at least one
glass-making plant was established, and the production of tar, pitch, and
oil from coal was pursued under patent at Jackfield in Broseley.
Attempts to establish soap-boiling, however, do not appear to have been
successful.[16]

The records of the great riverside coal-producing parishes and
manors of the Severn Gorge provide some insights into how this soaring
demand was met, although scarcely any documentation of the internal
operation of Shropshire collieries has survived. When Edward Cludde
in 1649 secured an adequate lease from the committee charged with the

[15] Yarranton, *England's Improvement*, 61.
[16] Trinder 1973, 14–18; Wanklyn 1982, 3–6.

disposal of assets sequestered from delinquent Royalists, he set about developing the colliery and improving both the scale and the efficiency of production. By 1651 he had invested £2,000 and the colliery was reported to have prospects of twenty years of profitable life and to be in better condition than it had been earlier when in the hands of Sir Basil Brooke. It was said that there were four 'insets' of prodigious proportions driven into the hillside of Madeley Wood, two of 1,000 yards in length, one of 700 yards, and one of 500 yards. The coal they gave access to varied in thickness from a yard to eighteen inches. Even allowing for some exaggeration, the scale of these workings suggests high levels of production, well in excess of 10,000 tons a year. On Cludde's death later the same year, his successor immediately set about raising more capital, and when the colliery subsequently passed to young Basil Brooke he too ventured large sums of money 'in digging and winning coal'. But mining at Madeley was by no means limited to the pits worked by Cludde and Brooke. There were also small operations undertaken by individual master colliers working on their own behalf or with a few partners or hired labourers, and in 1692 we learn of a substantial lease of prospects in the north of the manor to two London adventurers with rights to lay 1,500 yards of wooden rails from their pits to the Severn.[17]

In Little Wenlock the coal-pits lay in three main groups: one just east and south of the village, another further to the east in Coalmoor, and a third, called the new works, to the north-east of Huntington extending into Wellington parish.[18] The sole surviving colliery accounts from the whole of the Shropshire coalfield before 1700 relate to the Forester family's mines at Warham's Work and Old Master's Work in the Coal Meadow at Little Wenlock between 1681 and 1691. Production, which took place in conjunction with ironstone and a little limestone mining, averaged around 3,000 stacks (c.5,000 tons) annually.[19] Output thereafter rose, however, for in 1705 Sir William Forester contracted to supply Thomas Sprout with 4,000 stacks of coal annually for twenty-one years for shipment on the Severn.[20]

The papers of the Weld family, including the remarkable memorandum composed by John Weld in 1631 when he thought he was at death's door, throw considerable light on the contentious hurly-burly of gentry fortune-building in this rapidly industrializing region.[21] Weld, the son of

---

[17] *VCH Shropshire*, xi. 48–9.   [18] Ibid. 87.
[19] ShRO Forester 1224, box 296.   [20] *VCH Shropshire*, xi. 87.
[21] For John Weld see in particular Wanklyn 1969 and 1970–1. The memorandum is contained in ShRO Forester 1224, Box 163.

a London haberdasher, nephew of a Lord Mayor and son-in-law of an alderman, was trained in the law but decided to set himself up as a country gentleman. His background and the financial resources upon which he could call gave him a head start, and he capitalized upon these advantages by employing good business judgement and pursuing consistent policies. East Shropshire was his chosen hunting-ground, and he paid especial attention to the acquisition and exploitation of minerals. His first purchase was the manor of Willey, just south of Broseley, upon which there was a coal-mine worth £50 per annum, as well as ironstone, timber, limestone, and a forge and a furnace. He resolved to develop and sell all the natural resources, and 'to except out of the leases to my tenants timber, common rights, coals, ironstone and lime'. One further attraction of Willey, for which Weld paid £7,000, was the claim it gave him over neighbouring Benthall Marsh, where more coal was to be found. Four years later, after first acquiring major freeholds, he purchased the manor of Marsh, just to the east of Willey, which contained coal and ironstone mines and 'iron mills'. In 1620 Weld acquired a third part of Broseley manor itself, and finally eight years later he added the manor of Chelmarsh, on the Severn just south of Bridgnorth, where he hoped he would also find 'a great store of coals'. After having expended considerable sums prospecting, sinking pits, and building waggonways, Weld estimated that the coal, together with the much less valuable limestone, of Willey was worth £5,000, possibly as much as £7,000 if he could 'procure a constant way to the Severn' from Francis Langley, the owner of the waterside. In a systematic fashion Weld set about acquiring rights of way for the transportation of the coal which he dug, while denying such rights to rivals whenever he could. Limestone proved unprofitable, but in order to take advantage of cheap fuel Weld considered the possibility of manufacturing glass and soap.

The energetic investment policies of John Weld were replicated in the region by both greater coal-masters, like Laurence Benthall, and a multitude of lesser men, the freeholders and master colliers. Opportunities for investment abounded, for the hills surrounding the Severn Gorge were 'full of coalpits'.[22] The wealth generated in the region translated itself into the construction of large numbers of fine timber-framed houses and some splendid mansions along the banks of the Severn.[23] The scale of the boom is evidenced by the exceptional rates of population growth in these industrial parishes. Between 1570 and 1700 the population of Broseley is estimated to have grown at least eighteenfold to reach

[22] The phrase is that of Celia Fiennes (*Journeys*, 186).   [23] Trinder 1973, 12.

almost 2,000. Of these inhabitants, over 40 per cent of adult males may have been colliers, and a further 20 per cent trowmen or watermen who spent most of their time transporting coal. So great was the expansion of Broseley that in the early 1680s it was claimed that the ancient commons were 'in greatest measure built up and enclosed by poor people', and that the village 'has become a country town'. Certainly, the size of its population made it the fourth largest settlement in the county, and there can be no doubt that its collieries and the trades associated with them had provided the prime stimulus. In neighbouring Benthall the rate of population growth though less was still spectacular, from around eighty in 1570 to over 500 in 1700. At Madeley population leapt in the first half of the seventeenth century, but unlike Broseley and Benthall it grew little more in the ensuing half-century.[24] Perhaps the capacity for further expansion here was curtailed by the increasing difficulty of mining north of the Severn. When a proposal was made by customs commissioners to tax the lucrative Severn coal trade in 1695 they proclaimed, no doubt with zealous exaggeration, that collection should prove easy because almost all of the coal on the river came from 'the three great collieries' of Broseley, Benthall, and Barr on the south bank.[25]

There can be no doubt that Shropshire was in the very front rank of coalfields, after Northumberland and Durham. But putting figures to the scale of its output must still be an exercise in inspired guesswork, for we lack the output of any of the major collieries and cannot measure the trade upon the Severn. Nef's estimated 150,000 tons does, however, appear to be too low.[26] The total output of the whole coalfield, including sporadic and largely small-scale workings in the west around Shrewsbury, in the Clee Hills,[27] on the Ludlow outcrop, and to the south of Bridgnorth, was more likely to have been in excess of 200,000 tons in most years in the closing decades of the seventeenth century.

Staffordshire

Mining on the coal measures of Staffordshire and Worcestershire before 1700 had three distinct centres of activity, primarily determined by geology. The most important of the three by far lay in the south and

---

[24] Wanklyn 1982, 4.

[25] Nef 1932, i. 360. Barr is difficult to locate with confidence but was probably adjacent to Broseley, or part of the manor.

[26] Nef 1932, i. 65.

[27] For mining in the Clee Hills see Goodman thesis 1979.

extended from the River Stour northwards as far as the Bentley Faults, which ran east-west from the vicinity of Wolverhampton to that of Walsall. Between the Stour and these towns the magnificent Ten Yard Seam or Thick Coal was located, and it frequently outcropped or rose close to the surface, where it could be tapped by a profusion of pits and in some places gathered from opencast workings. The seams were thrown precipitously downward by the Bentley Faults, and to the north they became both thinner and deeper, and it was not until Cannock Chase that coal could be mined profitably again. The third centre of mining activity lay twenty or so miles further north again, where there was a scattering of accessible deposits around Newcastle under Lyme and Stoke.[28] Although well endowed with large reserves of procurable coal, Staffordshire had no navigable rivers and few large towns. Moreover, it was closely bounded to the west by the Shropshire coalfield and to the east by the Leicestershire and Warwickshire coalfields. None the less, these disadvantages did not impose a strait jacket upon development since, to an extent greater than almost anywhere else, central Staffordshire was an industrializing region where a wide range of coal-burning industries flourished close to the mines.

Medieval Staffordshire was a relatively well-wooded county, and in most parts population densities, even by the later thirteenth century, were not high. The distribution of medieval mining was remarkably wide and, as Map 5.8 clearly shows, a very high proportion of all pre-1700 mining sites were active before 1550, although the amounts they produced were usually tiny. In the north, for example, the iron-mines of Tunstall were worth 40s. a year in 1282 and £30 by 1316, whereas an adjacent coal-mine fell in value over the same period from 14s. 8d. to a mere 40d. Indeed, excavations have revealed that thirteenth-century ironstone miners sometimes had so little regard for coal that they sank straight through seams and tipped it back with the rubbish when refilling exhausted pits. At the same time, there were a few more sizeable operations, which produced pounds rather than shillings and pence for their owners and venturers. At Coombs Wood in Halesowen manor, for example, there was a coal-mine worth £4 per annum in 1307, £4. 13s. 4d. two years later, and £6. 13s. 4d. in 1310. Coal-pits at Sedgley in 1273 were accorded a similar value. Mining at Longdon was undertaken by freelance workmen who obtained weekly licences costing 6d. 'per pick'

[28] For a concise account of the geology of the Staffordshire coalfield see *VCH Staffordshire*, ii. 68–71.

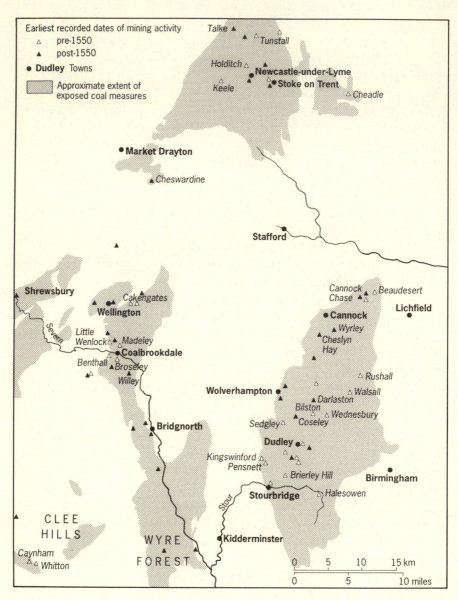

Map 5.8. The West Midlands coalfields

from the bishop of Coventry and Lichfield, which was as much as the annual rent on an acre of moderate land. The bishop's receipts from 'picks' totalled more than £5 in 1312 and 1313.[29]

Inevitably, outcrops of the Ten Yard Seam provided a focus for mining activity in the Middle Ages and later. Coal production was well established around Dudley by the fourteenth century, and in 1490 the coal-mines of Knowle Hill on Pensnett Chase were leased for £8. We can also find references to pits at Kingswinford, Amblecote, Brierly Hill, Netherton, Sedgley, Bilston, Bradley, and Wednesbury before 1500. Wednesbury appears to have been especially active, to judge from the plethora of disputes about pits and coal in the manor court rolls. Most of the disputes centred on rights to mine coal, particularly on the common lands, and they raged between tenants and between the lord and his tenants. Claims also arose over damage to land and crops caused by the carting of coal as well as by the mining itself.[30] We have some information on where and how the coal produced in south Staffordshire at this time was consumed. In addition to the demand for domestic heating, it is known that the smiths of the region were major consumers, for by the later Middle Ages commercial metalworking was already well established in Birmingham, Wolverhampton, and Walsall. More surprising, perhaps, is the purchase of coal at Pensnett by the monks of Westwood priory for use in their saltworks near Droitwich, some fifteen miles or more distant.[31]

It is difficult to establish a detailed chronology of the expansion of the Staffordshire coalfield, because the production side is ill-documented. With the notable exception of the Paget collieries in Cannock and Beaudesert, scarcely a colliery account has survived. That the reputation of Staffordshire coal was well authenticated by the sixteenth century is not in doubt, and there are sound reasons for believing that the region was making good use of its resources. When John Leland visited in the 1540s he remarked on the dearness and scarcity of timber and the importance of the coal supplied by Wednesbury and Walsall. The smiths of Birmingham, he tells us, depended upon local coal supplies to work

[29] VCH Staffordshire, ii. 72; Galloway 1898, i. 33; *Court Rolls of the Manor of Hales, 1270-1307*, ed. J. Amphlett and S. G. Hamilton, Worcestershire History Society, xxx (1910-12), 566; Z. Razi, *Life, Marriage and Death in a Medieval Parish: Halesowen, 1270-1400* (Cambridge, 1980), 8; StRO Anglesey D(W) 1734/J2057.

[30] Court 1938, 92; R. H. Hilton, *A Medieval Society: The West Midlands at the End of the Thirteenth Century* (1966), 216; StRO Anglesey D. 593/0/3/3; Rowlands 1987, 83-4.

[31] Birmingham Reference Library, MS 473426; Hereford and Worcester County Record Office BA 3835/10/10. I am indebted to Dr C. C. Dyer for these references.

their iron.[32] Camden in 1586 wrote of the 'profusion of pits' in the region, and coal flowed from them into the hearths of the 'mysteries or manual occupations of nailers, bucklemaking, spurriers, locksmiths, lorimers, stirrupmakers and such like services'.[33] Yet, as is found time and again in British coalfields, so great was the potential capacity that output threatened to outrun even a spiralling demand. In a dispute concerning the deliberate blocking of a sough nearby at Darlaston and Wednesbury in 1614, it emerged that payments had been made 'to forbear getting coal' and that coal-mines in the area had been engrossed in order to close many down.[34]

Yet the rampant industrial development of south Staffordshire and west Worcestershire continued to accelerate, and it provided the springboard for a truly prodigious surge in coal production after the Civil War, which continued to gain ever greater momentum in the closing decades of the century. Around 1624 we hear the parishioners of Over Arley complaining that 'within the space of 16 years ... by reason of certain coal works' the parish had been flooded with an extraordinary number of poor people.[35] In the industrialization of the region, the villages which developed most rapidly were those located on the coalfields close to thriving collieries.[36] From Kingswinford to Walsall artisans and tradesmen multiplied and the relative importance of agricultural employment plummeted. Between 1578 and 1679, if parish registers provide an accurate guide, the proportion of the population of Sedgley engaged in farming and agricultural labouring fell from 40 per cent to 5 per cent, while the proportion engaged in metalworking and mining rose from just under a half to almost 90 per cent. In Wednesbury in 1666, a parish of only 2,000 acres, there were 200 households, a third of whom gained their livelihoods from the collieries; a proportion which was exceeded only by nailers.[37] The oft-quoted assertion made by Dud Dudley in the mid-seventeenth century that there were as many as 20,000 smiths 'of all sorts' at work within a ten-mile radius of Dudley Castle, must be taken with a pinch of salt, for Dudley is not renowned for the consistent verisimilitude of his writings on industrial matters.

---

[32] Leland, *Itinerary*, ii. 97.

[33] Camden, *Britannia*, ii. 343. The list of industries comes from a petition presented to the Staffordshire justices in 1603 (Rowlands 1967–8, 37).

[34] PRO C. 78/322/2.

[35] Frost thesis 1973, 383.

[36] For the industrial development of south Staffordshire see Court 1938; Frost thesis 1973; Rowlands 1967–8; 1975; 1977.

[37] Frost thesis 1973, 435; Rowlands 1967–8, 39–40.

But we can find ample support for his claims that coal usage was spreading from metalworking into the 'making of steel, brewings ... copperas, alum, salt, casting of brass and copper, dyeings and many other works' including glass- and brick-making.[38] Likewise Dudley's report that there were twelve or fourteen active collieries within a ten-mile radius of Dudley Castle, and twice as many lying idle, has a ring of plausibility about it. Nor does he appear to be exaggerating when he wrote that some of the collieries 'afford 2,000 tons of coal yearly, others three, four, or five thousand'.[39] Some at least of the disused collieries noted by Dudley must have lain idle for want of a market.

That the demand for coal in south Staffordshire continued to soar in the closing decades of the century cannot be in doubt, nor can the increase in the numbers of colliers or the wealth of the region. Yarranton, the enthusiastic projector of waterway improvements, had his own axe to grind, yet his assertion in 1677 that within ten miles of Dudley there were 'more people inhabiting and more money returned in a year than in those four rich fat counties' of Warwickshire, Leicestershire, Northamptonshire, and Oxfordshire, does not have to be taken at face value to offer resonant support.[40] Plot (1686) also writes persuasively of the increase in the numbers of deep, productive mines in south Staffordshire. He tells us of land, under which there lay seams many yards thick, selling for £100 or even £150 an acre: 'And well indeed it might be so ... since out of one single shaft there have sometimes been drawn £500 worth of coal'. Such must have been the case at Moorfields near Sedgley, where a Mr Persehouse boasted he had a bed of coal fourteen yards thick. The want of colliery accounts forces us to rely upon such indirect and undoubtedly overcoloured accounts, but a rare survival of a contract with a London engineer for the construction of a pump at Bilston in 1692, which would require up to four men at a time to operate, indicates the considerable scale and depth of mining there.[41]

It is the mines of Dudley which provide the most immediate evidence of scale, and very substantial they were too. A single rent roll compiled in 1701 on the death of Edward, Lord Dudley and Ward, put an annual value on the collieries of Knowle Hill, the Paddock, and New Park of

---

[38] *Metallum Martis* (1666) repr. in J. Thirsk and J. P. Cooper (eds), *Seventeenth-Century Economic Documents* (Oxford, 1972), 277–84. Dudley's claim to have invented a process for smelting iron using coal in 1621 is, for example, now widely discounted.

[39] See also Plot, *Staffordshire*, 127–8.

[40] Quoted in Frost thesis 1973, 427.

[41] Plot, *Staffordshire*, 128; WSL Hand Morgan (Robins), uncatalogued, 34/6/1.

£858. 1s. 9½d., £443. 0s. 3d., and £540. 14s. 10d. respectively.[42] These were grand sums by any standards and suggest outputs of many thousands of tons in the year. We cannot hope to quantify the output of south Staffordshire with any confidence. For although there may well have been other collieries as large as those of Lord Dudley's, the majority were smaller and worked by a legion of independent coal-masters who have left scarcely any records.[43] Undoubtedly, some of these coal-masters were rich and powerful; John Bate of Gornal, for example, ventured for coal and ironstone in Pensnett Chase, Coseley, Sedgley, Gornalwood, and Coneygre, and his grandson felt confident enough to call himself a gentleman. But most, like Miles Cook of Wednesbury, who left at his death in 1684 mining equipment and a store of coal worth a little more than £32,[44] were more modest men. Yet their numbers were very great. The extensive rights of tenants, even base copyholders, to dig coal wherever they wished under the lands they occupied, turned the fields of outcropping areas into patchworks of pits and cultivated plots, and their farmers into colliers.

The scale and pace of development along the outcrops of the Ten Yard Coal were not replicated elsewhere on the Staffordshire coalfield. The seams of the Cannock Chase field to the north of the Bentley Faults provided fine quality coals which were more suited to the domestic consumer, including some prized cannel, but they dipped sharply away to the north-west, and were for the most part overlain by deep glacial drifts of boulder clay. Mining was therefore strictly curtailed before modern times, and the field was renowned more for the quality than for the quantity of the coal which it yielded. The pits of Beaudesert and Cannock, owned by the Pagets, earls of Shrewsbury, were only inter-mittently worked in the fifteenth century, and as late as 1543 were leased for only £4 a year. However, Sir Rafe Sadler felt able to reply in 1584 to enquiries regarding the availability of fuel at Tutbury Castle, where plans were being made to imprison Mary, that sea coal was much used in the area and counted their best fuel.[45] In the event the castle was warmed by coal from Beaudesert, where the pits were yielding around 1,000 tons annually. From scattered references output at Beaudesert does not seem to have risen much higher before the Civil War, but additional pits were

[42] Court 1938, 151–8.
[43] For the persistence of small-scale mining see, for example, Frost thesis 1973, 430–1; Jenkins 1927–8, 108; Rowlands 1987, 147.
[44] Frost thesis 1973, 434–5
[45] Galloway 1898, i. 115–16.

opened in Cannock Wood and in 1641 they produced around 4,000 tons. When records become available again on the resumption of direct management by the Pagets in the closing years of the seventeenth century, the combined outputs of Beaudesert and Cannock Wood collieries averaged around 6,000 tons. There were a few other pits and collieries in this part of the coalfield, but none appears to have been worked on a substantial scale.[46] Thus, even as late as 1700 the total output of this part of the Staffordshire coalfield was most unlikely to have exceeded 25,000 tons.

The exploitation of the segment in the far north of the Staffordshire coalfield was eventually to outstrip the Cannock Chase region and, like south Staffordshire, its expansion was closely tied to sales to industry. In the latter decades of the seventeenth century coal was burnt in ever increasing quantities to heat the pans of the Cheshire salt industry, to dry and fire the clay of the burgeoning pottery industry around Burslem, Stoke, and Newcastle under Lyme, to fuel the hearths of iron-workers, and to heat the vats and boilers of the Newcastle hatters. Thus stimulated, a few local collieries grew appreciably in size. We hear, for example, of a colliery at Talke which, though previously unsuccessful, yielded a clear profit of £800 in the years 1674 and 1675, and of a colliery at Cheadle which was reputed to be worth £1,000 per annum.[47]

Nef guessed that the output of the whole of the Staffordshire coalfield in 1700 lay somewhere between 100,000 and 150,000 tons, and Michael Flinn placed it as high as 170,000 tons.[48] The higher ranges of these estimates have a certain plausibility about them, for although the failure of the project to render the Stour navigable to the Severn deprived Black Country mines of any distant outlets, industrial development on the south Staffordshire coalfield, and ultimately in the north also, provided a massive internal stimulus to coalmining.

ix. The East Midlands

Warwickshire

The exposed, and therefore potentially mineable, portion of the Warwickshire coalfield consisted of a thin belt stretching from Tamworth in the north through Nuneaton to Coventry in the south. This belt had a

[46] Nef 1932, i. 66; *VCH Staffordshire*, ii. 73–4.
[47] Galloway 1898, i. 193; H. A. Chester, *Cheadle Coal Town* (1981).
[48] Nef 1932, i. 67; *VCH Staffordshire*, ii. 73; Flinn 1984, 27.

maximum width of just four miles at its northern limit, and in the southern half where most mining was concentrated it was rarely more than a mile from east to west. The cause of this narrowness was an extremely steep dip in the principal coal-seams, mostly of thirty degrees or even more, away from the outcrop towards the south-east, which soon rendered even the topmost coal unreachable by the miners of the day. A further vital geological feature of the southern portion of the coalfield was that the coal measures were overlain by water-bearing Lower Keuper sandstone, which was to plague those who attempted to raise coal with formidable and, on repeated occasions, insurmountable problems.[1]

It is possible that coal was dug in Warwickshire during Roman times but, in keeping with most coalfields, documentary evidence of the industry commences in the later thirteenth century. The hinterland of Nuneaton features prominently in medieval sources, which probably reflects the survival of the records of Nuneaton priory rather than the absence of mining elsewhere. The earliest reference comes from Chilvers Coton in 1275, and later references in priory records suggest a lively interest in surface deposits, which revealed itself in numerous fines levied on villagers for unlicensed diggings and for failing to fill in abandoned pits. Nuneaton priory also ran its own pits, and annual receipts from them in the later fourteenth century ranged as high as £10. 13s. 4d. and averaged around 50s., which indicates a minor but not insignificant level of operations. After a lengthy break in documentation lasting until just after the dissolution of the priory, we learn that the new owner, Sir Marmaduke Constable, was deriving a profit of only 53s. 4d. annually from the colliery, and although profits increased thereafter they stood at a mere £4 in 1564.[2]

From the later sixteenth century the Warwickshire coalfield was dominated by the collieries of Bedworth, Griff, and Hawkesbury, which all lay in the half a dozen miles between Nuneaton and Coventry. Each had a chequered history, with fitful working punctuated by floods of water and gluts of coal. Bedworth was the most productive, and probably also the most consistently worked. When Sir William Dugdale compiled his *Antiquities of Warwickshire* in the mid-seventeenth century, he deemed it to be the only colliery worthy of note in the county.[3] Bedworth was developed at a relatively late date, if we are to believe a survey of the manor made in 1570, in which the jurors were distinctly

[1] *VCH Warwickshire*, ii. 217–19; Flinn 1984, 14–15.
[2] *VCH Warwickshire*, ii. 219–20.
[3] *Antiquities of Warwickshire*, 83a, 84a.

unimpressed by 'mines called stonecoal or seacoal' there, professing ignorance of their extent and assessing them to be worth just '20s. yearly if it be let'.[4] Yet less than a decade later Sir Francis Willoughby and Nicholas Beaumont received more than £400 profit from an output of almost 8,000 tons.[5] At the turn of the sixteenth and seventeenth centuries Bedworth was being operated by Thomas Beaumont who, despite paying no more than the old rent of 20s., was said to be making profits of at least £300 a year.[6] But the peak of production came under the management of John Bugges and Anthony Robinson who, in partnership with Robinson's brother Thomas, took over the colliery after it had flooded and been abandoned by Beaumont. Massive expenditure by the partners on drainage, said to have amounted at first to £2,500 a year on equipment and labour, reducing to £1,000 annually after £4,000 had been spent on two drainage machines and a sough, succeeded not only in drying the pits but raising output to record levels. It was claimed that 20,000 loads, or some 20,000 to 25,000 tons, were raised annually in the 1620s before very heavy rain in the early 1630s brought a recurrence of flooding.[7] Such levels of production made Bedworth a large colliery by any standards, and one of the very largest landsale collieries in Britain.

If Bugges and Robinson are to be believed, the greater part of the counties of Warwickshire, Leicestershire, Northamptonshire, and Oxfordshire were supplied from Bedworth. Certainly, there is independent evidence of the transportation and sale of Warwickshire coal in all of these counties, including locations well over the twelve to fifteen miles which normally constituted the maximum economic overland carriage. It does seem likely, however, that Celia Fiennes was mistaken in identifying the coal unloaded from vessels on the Severn at Gloucester as 'the great Warwickshire coal'.[8] The Warwickshire coalfield was centrally located in a region otherwise bereft of coal, and despite the great handicap of the absence of navigable waterways much use was made of the ancient but still serviceable Watling Street and Fosse Way, and the marketing facilities of Coventry and, to a lesser degree, Nuneaton. Yet there were limits to the amounts of coal that the hinterland could absorb, and these limits may well not have been much higher than the upper reaches of output produced at times by Bedworth alone. For

[4] *VCH Warwickshire*, ii. 220.
[5] NoUL Middleton Mi. Ac. 124-6.　　　　　　　　　　　[6] PRO C.2 James I, F4/53.
[7] PRO SP 16/204/83; Grant thesis 1977, 86-9; Moller thesis 1933, 186-9; Hughes thesis 1979, 20-1.
[8] White thesis 1969, 6-8; Grant thesis 1977, 153-4; Nef 1932, i. 101-2; Stocks (ed.), *Records of Borough of Leicester*, 239-41; Fiennes, *Journeys*, 189.

when either Griff or one of the Hawkesbury collieries opened up, the proprietors of Bedworth frequently found themselves with coal left on their hands. Bugges and Robinson, like the Beaumonts before them, were accused of attempting to engross 'all the coalmines thereabouts [and] within the liberties of the city of Coventry', and of 'endeavouring to buy off all who attempted to dig for coal in the neighbourhood'. Under conditions of such intense rivalry it was scarcely surprising that resort was occasionally made to sabotage, although the partners denied the charges which were made against them of deliberately flooding competitors' pits and poisoning the horses which they used to transport their coal.[9]

Despite its obvious potential, and the large sums of money which were invested in it, Bedworth frequently went out of production. We have noted its abandonment in 1610 and the difficulties experienced by its proprietors in the 1630s, and in 1662 Fuller lamented of Bedworth 'that those Black Indies, both in quantity and quality fall short of their former fruitfulness', and uttered a prayer that 'they may recover their lost credit'. His prayer was eventually answered and Bedworth was flourishing once more by the end of the century.[10]

Mining at Griff was even more intermittent. Between 1603 and 1709 it is possible to discern at least seven distinct forays, five of which were made by the owners, the Newdigates of Arbury Hall. Two of these ventures, in 1603–5 and 1701–9 are exceptionally well documented and are the subject of extended discussions elsewhere in this volume.[11] The scale of operations varied widely as did the degree of success which accompanied them. Although at its peak Griff may have yielded more than 10,000 tons, 5,000 tons is a more likely average of those years when it was in production.[12] If mining at Griff occasionally proved rewarding, the experiences of those who sought to profit by leasing the mines of Coventry corporation at Hawkesbury, Foleshill, and Wyken were unremittingly chastening. The bait was a corporation anxious to encourage investment, and offering privileged access to a ready market for coal in the city. The requital seems invariably to have been heavy losses and forced closures, 'with the great charge proving many times too nimble for a present supply of money'. Time and again water washed away all chances of profit or even of sustained production.[13]

[9] PRO C.2 James I, F4/53; *VCH Warwickshire*, ii. 222–3; Moller thesis 1933, 186–9.
[10] Fuller, *Worthies*, ii. 403; Grant thesis 1977, 91–2.   [11] See Ch. 10(ii) below.
[12] Grant thesis 1977, 93–105; Grant 1979; White thesis, 1969; Larminie thesis 1980.
[13] *CSPD 1671-2*, 181; Grant thesis 1977, 79–85; Hughes thesis 1979, 21–4.

The contribution made by collieries other than these three to the output of the Warwickshire coalfield was relatively slight. Mining continued on the outcrops in the immediate vicinity of Nuneaton, on lands owned by the Stratfords, Pagets, and Newdigates, but there are no indications that the scale was more than modest. In the north of the coalfield we learn of a lease of pits at Dordon in 1590, of colliers from nearby Polesworth being enticed to Griff in 1603, and of colliers appearing in the parish registers of Tamworth, but the region is too poorly documented to yield more than such scraps of information.[14] Nef concluded that the output of the small Warwickshire coalfield increased 23–35 fold between 1550 and 1700, 'a rate not exceeded in any other coalfield', to reach 70,000 tons. But, as Dr Grant has pointed out, such a total 'has to be seen as potential output rather than a constantly maintained figure'.[15] When Bedworth, Griff, and Hawkesbury were simultaneously in peak production the capacity of the coalfield may well have exceeded 70,000 tons, but this could have occurred only fleetingly. The output of the coalfield fluctuated wildly as these major collieries went in and out of production, and an average of 40,000 to 50,000 tons seems far more plausible.

Leicestershire

The Leicestershire coalfield was a small, roughly circular deposit some ten to twelve miles in diameter, situated in the north-west of the county and the extreme southern tip of Derbyshire. Although the coalfield had limited potential it was exploited early. As Map 5.9 indicates, a clustering of outcrops led to a proliferation of mining sites along its eastern border, most of which can be dated from the Middle Ages. It is possible that coal was being mined at Swannington as early as 1204, and in the late thirteenth century we have conclusive evidence of mining at Donnington, Worthington, and Breedon, as well as at Swannington. Every freeholder in Swannington had the right to dig for coal in the common manorial wastes, while at the other end of the spectrum we can observe mining undertaken by landlords. Sir William de Staunton and Isabel de Hastings both dug coal in conjunction with their iron-mines at Staunton Harold and near Worthington respectively. Similarly, when John de Findon, lord of the manor of Swadlincote, granted a messuage and a virgate of land to Thomas Kateson and his wife, he carefully reserved the right to 'take profits from sea-coals and other minerals

[14] Grant thesis 1977, 106–9, 111.
[15] Nef 1932, i. 67–8; Grant 1979, 2.

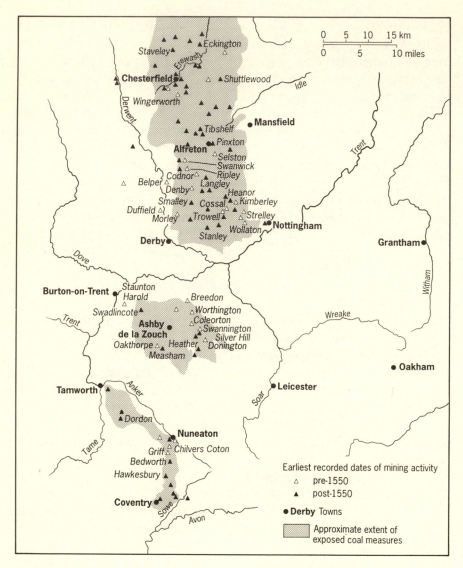

Map 5.9. The East Midlands coalfields

found underground in the said tenements'. We first hear of Leicester abbey's colliery at Oakthorpe in 1477, and the earliest indisputable documentary reference to mining at Coleorton is the mention of 'collyers' in 1498, though there is reason to believe that coal was dug there on a substantial scale well before this date.[16]

The market for the coal of Leicestershire and south Derbyshire was constrained not only by the lack of navigable waterways common to the heart of England, but the band of highly productive collieries by which it was ringed: Wollaton, Strelley, and Trowell to the north; Bedworth, Griff, and Hawkesbury to the south, and the mines of the Black Country to the west. Moreover, to the east strict limits on the sale of Leicestershire coal were set by the penetration of the product of Northumberland and Durham mines far inland along an extensive network of navigable rivers. In the seventeenth century the city of Leicester drew its coal supplies from Derbyshire, Warwickshire, and Staffordshire, as well as from the Leicestershire coalfield, and in the mid-fourteenth century Leicester abbey was reported to have bought cart-loads of coal at Nottingham.[17] The production and marketing of coal in the Midlands was thus often a fiercely competitive business, but opportunities did exist for the enterprising Leicestershire coal-owner. By the later sixteenth century the poor of Leicester were heavily dependent upon coal,[18] and even in the smaller towns and villages there are signs of early usage and later dependency as the complaint of the local woodland being 'very much wasted and decayed' echoed round the county.[19] For example, coal was transported to Wigston Magna, lying to the south of Leicester, as early as the later thirteenth century, and we can trace the more affluent farmers of this village at a later date fetching coal in their own carts from pits at Swannington and Coleorton, some eighteen miles distant.[20]

The earliest indications of large-scale mining on the Leicestershire coalfield come from Coleorton, where recent archaeological discoveries have revealed extensive systematic pillar-and-stall workings which,

[16] Griffin thesis 1969, 1–2; *VCH Leicestershire*, ii. 31. Unfortunately the charter which supports the pre-1204 date for mining at Swannington cannot now be traced. For a notice of recent archaeological evidence of large-scale mining at Coleorton in the mid-15th cent. see the *Daily Telegraph* (21 Feb. 1991).

[17] Stocks (ed.), *Records of Borough of Leicester*, 241; *VCH Derbyshire*, ii. 353; R. H. Hilton, *The Economic Development of some Leicestershire Estates in the Fourteenth and Fifteenth Centuries* (Oxford, 1947), 137.

[18] Bateson (ed.), *Records of Borough of Leicester*, iii. 149, 152, 160, 172–3, 178, 278, 414, 441, 448.

[19] Stocks (ed.), *Records of Borough of Leicester*, 239–41.

[20] Hoskins 1965, 192.

according to the tree rings of the oak pit props, date from the mid-
fifteenth century. Analysis of the site is still in its early stages, but it is
possible that as much as 6,000 tons a year could have been produced at
this time. Even in prime locations, however, mining was apt to be discontinuous. The Coleorton pits were subsequently reported as having
burnt underground for many years in the first half of Henry VIII's reign,
and a Parliamentary survey of 1652 revealed that no mining had taken
place at either Oakthorpe or Swadlincote since the Civil War.[21] The setback at Coleorton appears to have been substantial, for in 1566–7 all the
rights to mine for coal there owned by Sir Walter Ashton were sold to
Nicholas Beaumont for the niggardly sum of £9. 15s. 0d.[22] Within a few
years, however, in partnership with Sir Francis Willoughby, Beaumont
was making handsome profits raising 6,000–8,000 tons annually.[23] At the
turn of the century Camden remarked that Coleorton coals 'yield much
profit to the lords of the manor, and supply all the neighbourhood far
and near with firing',[24] and in 1631 the colliery was said to be worth at
least £300 per annum.[25]

It may have been the steady profits from Coleorton which seduced
Thomas Beaumont into offering in 1611 the absurdly inflated rent of
£500 annually for Measham colliery, in the south-west of the coalfield.
The Beaumonts were aggressive entrepreneurs, and Thomas's plan was
to gather into his hands a dominant share of the total capacity of the
region, which would enable him, in collaboration with the Willoughby
family, to achieve a mastery over supply. There is little doubt that
Measham was at this time a sizeable operation with a capacity of several
thousand tons, but the profits it generated for its new master fell far
short of meeting the rent. Beaumont claimed that over the course of a
decade he had lost almost £5,000 on the undertaking.[26]

The Hastings, earls of Huntingdon, were one of a small number of
entrepreneurial aristocratic coal-owning families, and they were very
active on the Leicestershire coalfield. In 1618 Henry, the fifth earl,
approached Sir John Beaumont requesting permission to drive a sough
across his land and to prospect for coal, which was duly granted. In 1621
Henry bought a colliery at Heather, and four years later we learn that
the town professed itself incapable of supplying three able men for

[21] Griffin thesis 1969, 3, 11; PRO E. 317, Derbyshire 26, m. 1–2.
[22] PRO C. 3/2/105.
[23] As detailed in a short series of colliery accounts: NoUL Middleton Mi. Ac. 125, 126, 140.
[24] Camden, *Britannia*, ii. 194.
[25] Stone 1965, 340.
[26] Nef 1932, ii. 16–17.

military service, because 'the greater part of our labouring men are turned colliers, so that we are much destitute of labouring men for husbandly occasions'.[27] In the same year Bardon Park, near Charnwood Forest, was said to contain 'coalmines whereby a great part of the county are relieved with fuel which otherwise would suffer great want thereof'.[28] At the time of the Civil War the Hastings family were also operating a colliery at Newhall, near Swadlincote, and sometime prior to 1652 they also worked Oakthorpe colliery. In 1662 Oakthorpe was sold by Lord Loughborough, another member of the family, to William Bale for the handsome sum of £800. Bale probably lacked sufficient resources to conquer the drainage problems which afflicted the colliery, and five years later after spending £415 he sold it to Lord Hastings and Sir Edward Kirk of Middlesex for £840.[29]

The most notable Leicestershire coalmining entrepreneur in the later seventeenth century was, however, John Wilkins. In 1682 his father-in-law was leasing Swannington colliery for £140, and a few years later Wilkins had taken it over to run in conjunction with Silver Hill. Subsequently Wilkins obtained Coleorton on lease from the Beaumonts. Since Wilkins was said to have employed 300 colliers working double shifts at Silver Hill, and to have produced twenty-four loads daily from the pits of Coleorton, the combined capacities of these three collieries must have exceeded 30,000 tons. But it is doubtful whether sufficient demand existed for them to have operated for long together, and Wilkins soon ceased production at Coleorton. The Beaumonts, whose lease must have included a provision requiring the colliery to be worked, responded to the closure by sabotaging the sough by which Silver Hill was drained, thereby causing it to be drowned. In the litigation which followed the Beaumonts accused Wilkins of deliberately closing down Coleorton in order to work Silver Hill and Swannington at full capacity. Wilkins denied the charge by maintaining that Coleorton was unable to be worked because of water, and that he had expanded production at his other two collieries in order to supply the urgent demand for fuel in the surrounding area occasioned by the closing of Coleorton.[30] It is impossible to get at the truth from this distance in time, but it is clear that once again we have a coalfield where supply threatened to outstrip demand.

In the later seventeenth century there is confirmation that both

---

[27] HL Hastings HA 672, box 7; box 11 no. 2884; *VCH Leicestershire*, iii. 33.

[28] HL Hastings HA 672, legal box 2(3).

[29] Griffin thesis 1969, 11–12; *VCH Leicestershire*, iii. 33.

[30] Griffin thesis 1969, 12–14.

Oakthorpe and Measham were in production,[31] and although no direct evidence survives of collieries such as Swadlincote, Heather, Newhall, and Newbold it is likely that one or more would have been in operation at any given time. To the tonnage flowing from major collieries must be added the multitude of trickles emanating from petty pits, and occasional quaint occurrences reveal that the spirit of enterprise was not breathed by coal-owners and mining adventurers alone. When seeking the removal of an unacceptable parson during the Commonwealth, the parishioners of Netherseal, close by Measham, compiled a list of complaints against him, including that he had 'high church ways', that he quarelled with his betters 'objecting to the excessive height of the squire's pew, that he frequented alehouses and often departed them shouting "God live the King!"', and that he leased coal-pits on church lands and settled his accounts with the colliers every Saturday night in the alehouse. No less individualistic was the inhabitant of Belton, a few miles east of Leicester, who sought to capitalize on a chance outcrop of coal by sinking bell-pits in the village road. When prosecuted he claimed that he believed it to be the right of every Englishman to do with the King's Highway as he pleased![32]

There can be no doubt that the total output of the Leicestershire coal-field at the close of the seventeenth century was many times greater than the 10,000 tons or so hazarded by Nef. But it was always overshadowed by the Nottinghamshire and Derbyshire coalfield a few miles to the north. Even the construction of canals and sustained population increase in the eighteenth century failed to permit the output of the coalfield to grow more than modestly.[33]

Nottinghamshire and Derbyshire

The vast coal deposit that stretches southwards for more than sixty miles from Leeds to Derby and Nottingham has been segmented in a variety of fashions by those who have administered the coal industry or written about its history. For our purposes the virtual absence of mining activity before 1700 along the south Yorkshire border provides us with a convenient dividing-line. To the south of this line lay a high density of outcrops, situated broadly along the valley of the River Erewash, which for much of its course forms the boundary between Derbyshire and

---

[31] *VCH Leicestershire*, iii. 34.

[32] Griffin thesis 1969, 29.

[33] Nef 1932, i. 69. Flinn (1984, 27) suggests that even by 1775 the output of the Leicestershire coalfield was only 50,000 tons.

Nottinghamshire. Here a multitude of small pits were sunk to win good coal from rich seams lying just below the surface. South of a line between Clay Cross and Mansfield the intensity of mining rose again, and in the southern tip of the exposed coalfield, which projected eastwards towards the city of Nottingham and the River Trent, there arose a cluster of major collieries, many of which have been blessed with an outstanding range of surviving accounts.

In addition to the plentiful but unremarkable references to the small-scale mining of coal throughout the outcropping regions of Derbyshire in the thirteenth and fourteenth centuries, in the south-east corner around Nottingham something of greater moment was taking place, despite the seemingly plentiful supplies of wood available nearby in Sherwood Forest. In the records of the borough court of Nottingham frequent presentments were made of 'common forestallers and gatherers of coal', and no less than nineteen city coal-dealers were fined in 1395.[34] Commensurately, we find that mining in the region at an early date had passed beyond the simple quarrying stage. A lease made in 1316 at Cossall, half a dozen miles to the north-west of the city, refers to the possibility of encountering 'damp' in the workings, and the existence of a sough ('le sowe'). Although the sough may have been a surface drain, damp could only have arisen at depth, and the rent of 12d. per pick per week employed also points to productive workings. Similarly, the lease of a mine at Trowell, bordering on Cossall, drawn up in 1390, deals with the occurrence of damp, and mentions 'watergates and heddryftes'.[35] The prevalence of deep mining in the vicinity of Nottingham is further evidenced by the terms of the lease of Selston colliery in 1457, which granted to the lessees the power to sink shafts, construct underground drains ('fossae'), and take timber for underground punches and props. A few years later the colliery had a sough, and simultaneously we learn of mining at Newfield and Kimberley, both within reach of the city.[36]

It was the ready market provided by Nottingham and beyond via the Trent as well as overland, which provided the prime stimulus to the precocious development of coalmining in south Nottinghamshire. This favourable environment duly fostered the rise of the famous Wollaton colliery, which was soon destined to become one of the greatest in

---

[34] Stevenson and Baker (eds.), *Records of Borough of Nottingham* i. 275.
[35] HMC *Middleton*, 88, 100.
[36] *VCH Nottinghamshire*, ii. 325.

sixteenth-century Britain.[37] Wollaton colliery, in the Old Park less than three miles from Nottingham Bridges, was ideally located to supply the city and boats on the Trent. It was probable that the colliery was not developed until the Willoughbys moved their family seat to Wollaton around 1460. The first mention of mining there occurs in a will of Sir Henry Willoughby dated 1489, and in a subsequent will made some four years later he ordered his executors to keep 'going yearly five coalpits besides the level pit in the lordship of Wollaton during the nonage of my son and heir'. The extraordinary scale of production is confirmed by the series of bailiffs' accounts commencing in 1497–8, which reveal annual profits averaging more than £200 between 1498 and 1503, suggestive of an output of around 5,000 tons yearly.[38] Both output and profits continued to increase thereafter. In the 1520s Wollaton produced profits of £350 per annum, and in 1526 around 9,000 tons of coal were raised and sold. If profits are a reliable guide, output must have averaged 10,000 tons in the 1530s and 1540s, before the construction of a vast new sough facilitated yet higher production.

Such levels of production were seldom to be met with outside of the north-east at so early a date, and they depended upon the existence of an exceptional market area within reach of the collieries of south Nottinghamshire. Even from the patchy coverage of coroners' inquests into the deaths of carriers we can discern an active overland trade in the first half of the sixteenth century. In June 1545 two carters were killed carrying coal: one was swept away while attempting to ford the Trent from Chilwell to Barton-in-Fabis, and another tumbled while asleep under the wheels of his waggon at Skegby, near Tuxford, to the north-east of Nottingham. In 1548 another carter fell under the wheels of his vehicle at 11 p.m. while passing through Cotgrave a few miles south-east of Nottingham.[39] In 1560 the entire output of Wollaton of the week ending 8 June was 'kept for my lord of Rutland', to be burnt on the fires of Belvoir Castle twenty miles away.[40] It is likely, of course, that even more coal went by water, and so vital was the Trent for the disposal of

[37] Although original sources in the Middleton Collection have been consulted where appropriate, and there are some differences of interpretation, the following discussions of Wollaton, the Willoughbys, and Huntington Beaumont, have relied heavily upon Smith MS; Smith 1957; Smith 1960; and Smith 1989.

[38] See also A. Cameron, 'Sir Henry Willoughby of Wollaton', *Transactions of the Thoroton Society*, 74 (1970).

[39] R. F. Hunnisett, 'Calendar of Nottinghamshire Coroners' Inquests, 1485–1558', *Thoroton Society Record Series*, 25 (1966).

[40] Smith MS, 32.

Wollaton's ample output that Sir Francis Willoughby not only took action against weirs and other obstructions on the river, but invested heavily in the improvement of its navigability.

The success of Wollaton inevitably encouraged competitors; the most serious of whom were the Strelleys, neighbours of the Willoughbys, who owned the coal-seams in the adjoining parishes of Strelley and Bilborough. Nicholas Strelley professed himself to be altruistically bearing in mind the needs not only of the city and county of Nottingham, but 'the shires of Leicester and Lincoln, being very barren and scarce countries of all manner of fuel', when he attempted to start mining in Strelley Field abutting the Wollaton pits. Squabbles inevitably ensued, not least because the Wollaton sough was essential for the drainage of all pits in the area, and litigation remorselessly proceeded to Star Chamber, with claims and counter-claims of trespass and sabotage. An agreement was finally entered into which entitled Willoughby to the lion's share of the output of Strelley's collieries in return for allowing the use of his sough.

The prize which competing coal-owners struggled to win, as Nicholas Strelley indicated, was not only the Nottingham market, but extensive trades overland with Leicestershire and the Vale of Belvoir and waterborne through the Trent valley to Newark and Gainsborough. The market for the coal of south Nottinghamshire was substantial and growing, but it was not infinitely extensible. The more coal-owners were encouraged to raise their output, and the more prospectors were driven to search for new mining sites, so the more the capacity of the industry pulled ahead of its ability to sell coal. In this respect, the situation in the Vale of Trent resembled those in the hinterlands of Coleorton colliery in Leicestershire and Bedworth colliery in Warwickshire, where the Willoughbys also operated.

In the bumper years of the later sixteenth century output at Wollaton soared close to 15,000 tons, which made it by far the largest colliery on the coalfield. But at the turn of the century, as Wollaton began to encounter severe production problems, the threat from Strelley began to loom ever more formidably. Fortunately for Sir Percival Willoughby the extreme indebtedness of the Strelleys had landed their collieries in the hands of creditors, so the threat was temporarily curbed, but there were fears that coal might also be found in Lenton, just to the south of Wollaton and still closer to the river and the city. The prospector there was one Huntingdon Beaumont, son of Nicholas Beaumont of Coleorton, whose pits at Coleorton and Bedworth had been worked by Sir

Francis Willoughby in the 1570s. Huntingdon Beaumont already enjoyed a reputation as a man of great knowledge and skill in mining, and in 1601 he concluded a bargain with Sir Percival, who, beset by debts, was happy to lease his pits at Wollaton to him. Beaumont's response to mounting competition was to marshall ever more audacious strategies to control the output of the entire region. His prime target was naturally Strelley, but he had to pay dearly to secure a lease of only three and a half years. When, at the renewal of the lease in 1603, Beaumont also acquired a lease of nearby Bilborough colliery, he must have controlled a potential capacity of at least 30,000 tons, and quite possibly far more. But the problems posed by attempting to produce this quantity of coal were small compared with those of successfully selling it. Collieries, actual and potential, lay all around, and Beaumont was soon casting covetous eyes on Annesley, Ilkeston, Awsworth, Heath, and Blackwell. He was also justifiably fearful of coal being found in Trowell Moor, adjoining Wollaton to the west, and when the pressure to dispose of his bloated output mounted he lamented, 'behind us they set up their pits as fast as ever they set them down ... for the country is cloyed with coal'.

Acquiring collieries in order to shut them down was an expensive and risky business, so once again Beaumont's solution was adventurous and innovative. Strelley was situated farther from the Trent than fading Wollaton, but much of the distance was conveniently uphill. So, correctly diagnosing transport costs as a major impediment to higher sales, Beaumont set about building a waggonway from the Strelley pits to the end of Wollaton Lane, where the coal could be stacked ready for carting to the Trent and elsewhere. This railed-way has strong claims to being the first ever constructed in Britain, but, as if this were not innovative enough, Beaumont drew up plans to divert the course of the river Leen, via a man-made channel, so that it flowed direct to the Trent. In other words, Beaumont proposed the building of a canal to avoid costly overland transport. The canal was never built, but Beaumont's final ploy to dispose of burgeoning mounds of coal was even more breath-taking: namely, to supply London. It was extremely fanciful to imagine that south Nottinghamshire coal could compete with sea coal from Tyneside in the streets of the capital; none the less Beaumont did manage to persuade Percival Willoughby, Hugh Lenton, a Lincolnshire merchant, and John Bate, a London grocer, to enter into partnership with him. Lenton and Bate undertook to ferry the coal down the Trent, to which end they acquired a fleet of small boats, although there is no evidence that they actually moved any coal. The market for coal could neither be cornered, nor infinitely inflated. On the one side there were simply far too many collieries in Derbyshire and Nottinghamshire capable of producing far too much coal if given the incentive to do so, while on the other even heroic efforts to transport to distant markets were doomed since they inevitably encountered competition from the coal of other fields. As Beaumont reflected mournfully when staring ruin in the face, 'we may see most plainly that which I ever feared, that the country would never take away so great a proportion'.

How great a proportion we may gauge with accuracy from the output and sales figures of Beaumont's and Willoughby's collieries. In 1603 Strelley and Wollaton together produced almost 20,000 rooks (c.25,000 tons), but managed to sell only 14,500 rooks. In the following year, in an effort to clear stocks, production was reduced to 12,000 rooks, but sales rose only marginally to 15,500 rooks. Wollaton was forthwith closed down, but Strelley working double shifts had no difficulty filling the gap. Between 1605 and 1611 output at Strelley averaged almost 16,000 rooks a year, with any excess production doomed to lie on the bank at the end of the account.[41] There is no information on Bilborough colliery at this time, but in the 1580s it had averaged less than 1,500 rooks a year.[42] We may thus be assured that Beaumont's total sale was no more than 25,000 tons, although it is equally clear that he could have boosted production substantially at short notice. In the agreement with Bate and Lenton, for example, while the delivery of 7,000 loads annually from Strelley and Wollaton to the Bridges was specified, it was acknowledged that the quantity delivered could be raised as high as 14,000 loads if notice were given 'in the twelve days after Christmas at the mansion house at Wollaton'. Sadly little is known of the scale of other collieries in the Nottingham region at this time, but from their number and the fear which Beaumont had of them, their combined output could not have been less than 10,000 tons. For northern Derbyshire we know little more than the names of a fraction of the profusion of the pits which peppered the landscape, beyond the certain fact that the outputs of the vast majority could be counted in hundreds rather than thousands of tons.

The Civil War and its aftermath produced a crop of records which throw new light on the industry. For example, parliamentary requisitions for coal in the Nottingham district in 1646 were addressed to

[41] Figures for Strelley extracted from NoUL Middleton.
[42] Ibid., Mi. Ac. 1–7.

constables at Selston, Greasley, Trowell, Bulwell, Bramcote, Eastwood, Strelley, Toton, Wollaton, Chilwell, and Nuthall.[43] An anonymous native of Nottingham, writing in the year before the outbreak of the Civil War, stated that the main sources of the city's coal were Strelley, Wollaton, and Bramcote.[44] Wollaton had been reopened soon after the demise of Huntington Beaumont, though with limited success, and mining was also commenced at Shortwood, by Trowell, where 2,700 loads were dug in 1619–20.[45] Strelley appears to have remained very productive.[46]

Commissions of Committees of Compounding dealing with royalist properties after the war reveal the existence of significant collieries at Alfreton and Eckington, and in Duffield Frith, some four miles to the north of Derby, which doubtless was a major source of that town's fuel.[47] Another source of Derby's coal was Stanley, where a colliery was leased in James I's reign for £80 per annum.[48] From a variety of sources it is possible to identify the region to the east of Chesterfield, including Scarsedale hundred, as the major production centre of north Derbyshire. When Celia Fiennes visited Chesterfield at the close of the seventeenth century she found that 'coalpits and quarries of stone are all about, even just at the town end'. Near Bolsover, at Shuttlewood Common, a mine had produced a profit of £83 in 1586, at Barlborough coal worth £500 was sold by Dame Martha Rodes in several years before 1677, and the earls of Devonshire received about £100 a year from collieries at Heath and Hardstoft in the 1630s.[49] Blackwell colliery, just north of Alfreton, was said in 1673 by the vicar of Tibshelf to be 'a coalmine treble to mine'. Chatsworth, where the earls of Devonshire spent more than £100 on a mine in 1623–5, may have been operated solely to serve the family's domestic needs.[50]

There can be no doubt that the aggregate demand for the coal of Nottinghamshire's and Derbyshire's pits continued to expand during the seventeenth century. The population of Nottingham, which was

[43] NoUL Middleton Mi. X. 5/3.

[44] Anonymous, *Transactions of the Thoroton Society*, 2 (1898), suppl., 48.

[45] NoUL Middleton Mi. Ac. 12.

[46] In the 7 weeks before 3 Oct. 1656 Strelley produced 1,320 loads and sold 1,163 loads. The 'clear profits' for the whole year were £581. 16s. 9d. (NoRO Edge of Strelley, DDE 5/34, 5/50).

[47] PRO E. 317/9, Derbyshire, no. 10a, 16, 18, 19. See also *VCH Derbyshire*, ii. 352.

[48] PRO C.2 James I G1/76.

[49] *Journeys*, 113; Hopkinson 1976, 3, 5; Stone 1965, 342.

[50] C. E. B. Bowles, 'Coal Raising in the Seventeenth Century', *Journal of the Derbyshire Archaeological and Natural History Society*, 31 (1909), 223; Stone 1965, 341–2.

heavily dependent upon coal from an early date,[51] was rising fast and probably totalled 7,000 by 1700.[52] In addition to the normal range of urban industries, the city's metalworkers served not only Nottinghamshire 'but divers bordering shires as Leicestershire, Rutland and Lincoln, the reason of which number I suppose to be the great plenty of coals got and the great plenty of iron made'.[53] Furthermore, advances in the coking of coal led to a rising consumption in the thriving brewing industries of the region, especially in the city of Derby, which was itself expanding. The trade in coal with neighbouring counties continued to flourish, and on a scale which assured a plentiful supply of grain in the region, even in times of scarcity. In the food crisis of 1630, for example, the justices of Nottingham expressed every hope that 'in summer time when coal carriages do come into our country for coals, that they will bring corn with them as formerly divers countries have done'.[54] Likewise the flat-bottomed barges which plied the Trent taking coal downstream as far as Gainsborough, where they met with vessels with 'deeper bottoms', returned with grain as well as a wide range of other necessities and luxuries, some of which had been imported through Hull.[55]

Yet the rate of increase in the Nottinghamshire and Derbyshire coal trade in the later seventeenth century may well have been less than that experienced by the majority of British coalfields. Coal output had reached high levels in south Nottinghamshire in the later sixteenth and early seventeenth centuries, buoyed by a precocious use of coal and an already extensive network of trade. Thereafter, as Huntington Beaumont found to his cost, the market for coal grew at a rate which was relatively modest by the standards of the age. Although the water-borne trade with Newark and Gainsborough and their hinterlands was substantial, it fell far short of that carried on the Severn from the mines of north Staffordshire, for the towns along the Trent's course were far less populous than those of the Severn valley. Newark itself was a modest market town with no more than a couple of thousand inhabitants. A project to improve the coal trade between Nottingham

---

[51] The citizens of Nottingham preferred coal even when wood was available (Anonymous, *Thoroton Society*, 2 (1898), suppl., 49–50). Camden was perplexed that although Sherwood Forest supplied a great store of wood for fires 'many prefer pit coal notwithstanding its offensive smell' (*Britannia*, ii. 283).

[52] Corfield 1982, 109; L. Clarkson, *The Pre-Industrial Economy in England, 1500-1750* (1971), 47.

[53] Anonymous, *Thoroton Society*, 2 (1898), suppl., 34.

[54] PRO SP 16/187 no. 28; see also *VCH Nottinghamshire*, ii. 283–4, 327.

[55] Anonymous, *Thoroton Society*, 2 (1898), suppl., 26; J. D. Chambers, *The Vale of Trent, 1670-1800*, Economic History Society Supplements, 3 (1957), 10–11; Green 1935, 63–4.

and Newark, drawn up in 1655, postulated the carrying of no more than 8,000 loads each year, despite necessarily viewing matters in an optimistic light.[56]

Nor were the collieries of south Nottinghamshire alone in attempting to supply coal to these markets. Although the mines of northern Derbyshire were too far distant and too comprehensively landlocked, those in the south-east of the county were gearing up to compete. Moreover, to the north of Newark, Nottinghamshire coal was likely to find itself in competition with both the product of south Yorkshire collieries and north-eastern sea coal shipped down from Hull. The market for coal was not merely well supplied; in many locations it was potentially glutted. For Heanor, just within reach of Nottingham, there is a good series of accounts which span the 1640s and 1650s.[57] They reveal a small colliery struggling to make a profit, with unpredictable sales and an output which scarcely rose above 1,500 loads. Doubtless many mines on this scale, or even larger, have left scant trace in the records, but there can be no doubt that the vast majority of all country collieries relied upon such demand as existed in the immediate vicinity for their sustenance. Most proprietors could have greatly expanded their output if given the incentive to do so but, like the vicar of Tibshelf who lamented that 'in the last 16 years my bank has been bared but 3 times', they found themselves having to compete fiercely with neighbouring enterprises for such local markets as did exist.[58] According to a correspondent who wrote to John Houghton concerning Derby in 1693, 'the chiefest mines thereabout are at Smalley, four miles, at Heanor, six miles, and at Denby, five miles from Derby; through which abundance in summer are carried as far as Northamptonshire, from whence is brought back barley'. Houghton goes on to tell us that Heanor and Smalley were in the hands of Mr Samuel Richardson 'who finding that Derby consumed annually about 3,000 loads, besides what was fetched into Leicestershire and Northamptonshire, designed to sell his coal for 3d. the hundred' at the pits. However, John Lowe of Denby, who had spent between £900 and £1,000 'in perfecting a sough to lay his delf dry, the last spring accomplished the same, and has laid as many coals dry as will be got these forty years'. The end result was that 'this year we bought coals delivered for 3½d. the hundred'.[59] No

---

[56] Smith MS, 170.
[57] NoRO Charlton of Chilwell DDCH 35/34–46.   [58] Bowles, 'Coal Raising', 222.
[59] Houghton, Newsheets (20 Apr. and 16 June 1693). Denby was already a substantial colliery in 1631, when it was leased for 21 years at £50 p.a. (NoRO Foljambe DD FJ/X/12/i/1527).

doubt falling prices stimulated consumption somewhat, but with output able to be raised with such ease inefficient producers were bound to face closure.

As for the aggregate output of this coalfield around 1700, it would be wise to discount heavily Nef's estimated 100,000 to 150,000 tons for Trent valley collieries alone. Whereas the potential capacity of the multitude of collieries and pits of the region was probably far in excess of such figures, the demand was simply not there to sustain it. On the other hand, Flinn's suggestion of just 50,000 tons for the whole of Nottinghamshire and Derbyshire seems far too low.[60] The 50,000 tons level was probably breached well before the Civil War, and consistently exceeded by a wide margin thereafter. By 1700 output is likely to have averaged perhaps 75,000 tons, with peaks in good years possibly approaching 100,000 tons.

x. The south-west

The Forest of Dean

The coal measures of the Forest of Dean lay, encircled by belts of carboniferous limestone and millstone grit, broadly within the triangle bounded by Coleford, Cinderford, and Lydney. The forest itself nestles between the Wye and the Severn Estuary. It is one of the smallest coal-fields, less than forty square miles in area, and few of the workable seams in our period were more than two feet thick. Its output was duly modest.

The location of the coalfield within a royal forest bestowed a distinctive character upon its development. Among its most singular features were the customary rights and privileges of the free miners of Dean, by which they claimed and exercised the ability to dig for coal, iron ore, and ochre wherever they pleased within the bounds of the forest, on the lands of the Crown or of private persons, subject only to the approval of the king's local officer, called a gaveller, and the payment of appropriate dues. Additionally, the free miners claimed free timber for their mining, rights of way to and from their pits, the power to exclude 'foreigners', and an independent Mine Law Court run by themselves. Comparable rights elsewhere were possessed by tinners and frequently by lead-miners, but no other colliers were set apart in this

[60] Nef 1932, i. 60; Flinn 1984, 27. With typical exuberance Nef writes: 'The whole district to the west and north of Nottingham was given over to coalmining. It must have resembled in appearance the Tyne valley about Gateshead, or the Wear valley about Lumley Castle.'

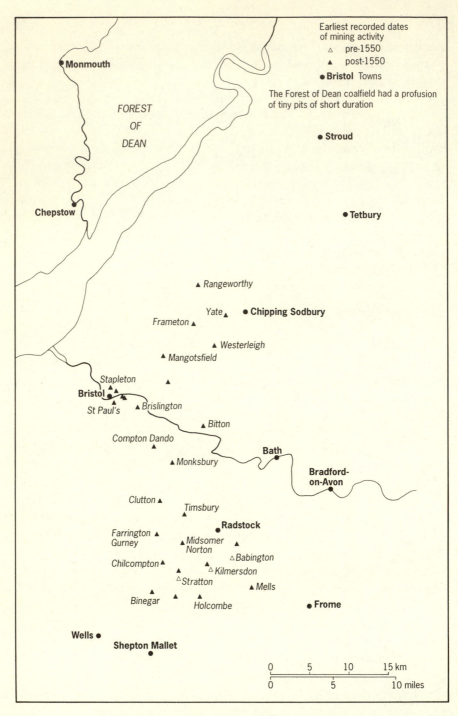

Map 5.10. Coalmining in south-west England

way.[1] To qualify as a free miner it was necessary to have been born in the Forest of Dean and the hundred of St Briavels, to be living there, and to have worked for at least a year and a day in a coal-mine or an iron-ore mine. When a free miner wished to open up a new mine it seems that he had only to find a suitable spot and begin digging. When he had 'digged the pit three steps deep' he was required to inform the gaveller and pay him 1 d. for himself and 1 d. each for additional workmen 'for entering his name and the name of the pit'. The origins and legal foundations of these valuable privileges are obscure, but evidence from as early as 1244 confirms that men were allowed to dig coal at will 'when it is found' upon payment of the requisite dues.[2]

As with the neighbouring Somerset coalfield, there is evidence that coal was worked during the Roman occupation.[3] Evidence is also forthcoming of widespread mining from the thirteenth century onwards in virtually every bailiwick in the forest, and some coal was carried beyond the Severn.[4] But total output appears to have been no more than negligible, even through to the sixteenth century. Iron was of far greater significance, and it is likely that much of the coal was raised as a by-product of mining for iron ore. The ready availability of wood doubtless severely restrained demand for coal despite the proximity of navigable waterways. The seventeenth century, however, in the Forest of Dean as elsewhere, brought enhanced activity although progress remained slow. We learn, for example, that in 1628 Sir John Winter of Lydney surveyed the forest for coal, using a specialist prospector and borer sent by his father-in-law, Lord Howard of Naworth.[5] Seven years later Edward Terringham, one of the gentlemen of the bedchamber, petitioned Charles I to be granted a monopoly to mine Dean's coal, claiming that such a grant would not prejudice the king's profits from woods and ironworks. In response the Surveyor-General duly reported that 'the coalmines have yielded small or no benefit to His Majesty or the Crown at any time', and in the following year Terringham was granted 'all the mines of coal and quarries of grindstone' in the forest for thirty-one years for a mere £30 a year.[6]

---

[1] The customs of the free miners are dealt with by Hart 1953. See also Moller thesis 1933, 268–84.

[2] Hart 1953, 12.   [3] Hart 1971, 253; Webster 1955, 211.

[4] *VCH Gloucestershire*, ii. 218–19; Hart 1953, 14–15, 158–9.

[5] For Sir John Winter's coalmining adventures elsewhere see below, Ch. 7(i); for his experiments with purifying coal for domestic fires and smelting iron with coal see below, Ch. 12(i) and (ii). Lord Howard had a colliery at Farlam in Cumberland (Ornsby (ed.), *Household Books)*.

[6] Hart 1971, 254–5.

The Forest of Dean was a sadly neglected Crown asset, and the privileges of the free miners flourished under the disregard of successive monarchs. In the seventeenth century the stage was set for protracted and often violent struggles between a forest community fiercely defending its ancient customs and a financially pressed Crown, constantly seeking to establish its legal rights and enhance its revenues.[7] In 1631 and 1632 there was widespread disorder following upon the enclosure of forest land. Terringham's monopoly was a grave infringement of the free miners' rights, and was accordingly met by both legal and illegal opposition. Not only did the miners continue to dig coal in defiance of the lease, Terringham claimed that his mines had been attacked and his colliers 'outrageously beaten and drawn out thence for dead, and their works smothered and fired'. Not for the first time the miners' ancient claims were found to have no standing in law, but the effective halting of their mining was quite another matter. That we are still dealing with small amounts of coal is indicated by Terringham's assertion in late 1636 that 1,000 tons of coal had been mined illegally since the granting of his lease more than a year earlier.[8]

It was claimed that Terringham had taken many steps to boost coal output in the forest, including the importing of 'Staffordshire men and other strangers' to work in his pits, the construction of a sough which, unusually for the region, had permitted year-round mining, and the opening of at least eight mines.[9] None the less, the opposition of the free miners and the enticement of a £300 annuity persuaded him to abandon his lease in 1640. But the threat to the free miners was not lifted, for the withdrawal of Terringham allowed the Crown to negotiate a comprehensive disafforestation of the Dean with Sir John Winter. In return for £106,000 paid in instalments, a loan of £20,000 at 8 per cent, and an annual rent of almost £2,000 the Forest of Dean was effectively made over to Winter. Coal, of course, formed only a small part of the resources granted to Winter, but the free miners were also affected by the loss of many other perquisites and sources of income from the forest, and in a series of riots Winter's enclosures were thrown down. Respite for the community came when Winter, an ardent royalist, was deprived of his title to the forest by the Protectorate in 1642. The Restoration eventually brought Winter's return to favour, and he

[7] For the decay of Crown administration over Dean see Hammersley 1957. For the unruly relations between the Crown and the forest community see Sharp 1980, esp. 175–219.

[8] Sharp 1980, 212–14; Hart 1971, 255.

[9] Moller thesis 1933, 270–1.

sought to resume his sovereignty of the Dean, but once again the free
miners and the commoners helped to prevent his successful exploitation
of the forest's resources, and he finally relinquished his claims in the
following years.[10]

The data simply do not exist upon which to base a plausible estimate
of the output of the coalfield. That it remained small throughout our
period is beyond doubt, but there are signs of some advancement in the
latter decades of the seventeenth century. The interest of Terringham
and Winter in the coal reserves bears witness to their potential, as do the
efforts in 1675 of 'several gentlemen and freeholders of the parish of
Newland, not free miners [who] associated themselves together for the
purpose of working and selling coal'. Indirect indications of rising
output appear in the proceedings of the Mine Law Court, with concern
expressed in 1680 about the 'many young men and boys that, contrary
to former usage, have of late times set up for themselves to work and
carry ... coal', and with the decree passed five years later that one-half
of the jury of the court should henceforth consist of colliers.[11] There are
also indications that soughing was becoming more common, which
heralded an increase in the scale of some mines as well as an ability to
work them throughout the year. Yet the constant flow of small-scale
independent miners and the strength of their privileges militated against
the growth of larger collieries, especially those operated by outsiders,
while the greater part of the free miners themselves were poor, even
when incomes from iron were combined with those from coal. Such
powerful constraints upon expansion were to curtail growth severely
even in the eighteenth century.[12]

Although conveniently placed for the Severn, scarcely any Dean coal
found its way to the extensive markets served by this river; instead the
major outlet was the Wye, which provided much less scope. The coal
was normally loaded between Huntsham and Wilton Bridge, above
Monmouth.[13] The exclusion of Dean coal from the Severn denoted its
failure to compete with the produce of the Shropshire and South Wales
coalfields, and while some coal was used within the forest, notably in the
iron industry, the amounts were not substantial. Although it is likely
that Nef's guess of 25,000 tons in the 1680s was pitched too low,[14] the

---

[10] *VCH Gloucestershire*, ii. 225–6; Sharp 1980, 216–19, 242.
[11] Moller thesis 1933, 274, 276–7, 279–80.
[12] Flinn 1984, 12–13, 27; Sharp 1980, 180–2.
[13] Hart 1953, 73–115; *VCH Gloucestershire*, ii. 226–8; Moller thesis 1933, 277–8.
[14] Nef 1932, i. 20.

output of the whole coalfield probably failed to match that achieved by one of the larger collieries on Tyneside.

The Bristol coalfield

The Bristol coalfield lay in a pear-shaped basin, bounded by millstone grit and carboniferous limestone, just to the east of the city. It was a small coalfield, but the accessible coal measures were easily exploited and widely scattered, although generally modest in size.[15] In this there was great similarity with the neighbouring Forest of Dean. A further similarity was that the major part of the coalfield lay within a heavily wooded area, Kingswood Chase, over which the Crown had claims of ownership and jurisdiction as royal forest. Yet again, these claims were resisted by the forest dwellers, 'a community without government or conformity',[16] but unlike the Forest of Dean the Crown also faced the opposition of powerful local landlords.

Early references to mining in this coalfield, dating from the second half of the thirteenth century, derive from receipts by the Crown of payments from individual miners for the digging of coal in Kingswood Chase, probably reflecting the purchase of licences or the value of royalties. The sums were not great and indicate the desultory nature of mining in the Middle Ages. For example, the crown received a total of 29 s. 8 d. in 1284–5 and at the close of the thirteenth century the number of persons making payments seems rarely to have exceeded ten.[17] Naturally, the lax administration of the Crown failed to register all those who dug for coal, and there may well have been mining for coal outside of Kingswood, but it has left no trace. Bristol was one of the most populous cities in England, but its hinterland was well-supplied with wood. Some coal was exported from Bristol to France, but the quantities were exceedingly small.[18] The conclusion must be that the output of the coalfield was very low in the Middle Ages, despite the abundance of outcrops, perhaps amounting to only a few thousand tons.

Bristol had the enviable reputation of enjoying abundant cheap fuel of all sorts. In 1566, for example, a correspondent wrote to Cecil informing him that 'at Bristol all manner of fuel is good cheap', and almost 200

---

[15] *VCH Gloucestershire*, ii. 236.

[16] The description is contained in representations made to the Crown in 1675 (Malcolmson 1980, 91).

[17] *VCH Gloucestershire*, ii. 236.

[18] N. D. Harding (ed.), *Bristol Charters, 1153-1375*, Bristol Record Society, i (1930), 103, 113; E. M. Carus-Wilson (ed.), *The Overseas Trade of Bristol in the Later Middle Ages* (1967 edn.), 222, 237, 247, 286.

years later Daniel Defoe marvelled at the low price of coal there.[19] Yet even in Bristol the pressure on fuel supplies on occasion made itself felt, and in the harsh winter of 1570 the corporation ordered several hundred horse-loads of 'stone coal' in order to augment wood supplies. There are increasing signs thereafter that coal soon came often to enjoy a price advantage over wood. For although it was only in the direst of emergencies that the city Council Chamber was heated by anything except charcoal before 1700, we learn that the children of the poor, who were being taught to knit worsted hose at a school over Froom Gate in 1598, were warmed by a coal fire.[20] For the poor, and indeed for most of those who had to buy their fuel, the prejudice against coal was vanquished by necessity.

Bristol was supplied with coal by sea from South Wales and down the Severn from Shropshire, but the city was also well served from local pits. The correspondent of 1566 drew attention to a coal-mine four miles from the walls and a little later reference is made to a mine within a mile of the city. In 1615 it was claimed that 'the poorer sort of the inhabitants of Bristol do use to burn stone coal alias sea coal in their houses, which coal they have had from Kingswood and other places adjoining the said city . . . not being able to buy wood which is very dear and scarce to be had'.[21] The population of Bristol may have risen to more than 20,000 by the end of the century, and coal consumption there was further enhanced by the range of coal-burning industries which flourished within its walls, including copper- and brass-founding, sugar-refining, brewing, distilling and glass-making. In addition modest quantities of coal were shipped with regularity through Bristol to overseas destinations as well as up the Severn to Gloucester.[22]

The straitened finances of the early Stuarts, and the paltry returns which they obtained from the mineral resources of Kingswood, inevitably attracted the attention of speculators. And, as with the Forest of Dean, the route to riches was seen to lie in the securing of a royal monopoly. But, as also with the Forest of Dean, a royal grant could fall far short of constituting an effective monopoly. In 1609 James I granted Captain Edward Fitzgerald a lease of all the coal-mines and stone and slate quarries in Kingswood, but he appears to have had little success in

---

[19] Galloway 1898, i. 118; Defoe, *Tour* (1769 edn.), ii. 313.

[20] J. Latimer, *Sixteenth-Century Bristol* (Bristol, 1908), 55, 96.

[21] Galloway 1898, i. 118, 212–13; J. Latimer, *Annals of Bristol in the Seventeenth Century* (Bristol, 1900), 29, 84.

[22] Corfield 1982, 15; LCA Customs A/Cs TN/PO 6 VI(4)–(10); GRO Bledisloe D421/E62.

establishing his claims. Unlike the Forest of Dean, Fitzgerald's main opponents were the local landlords. The next lessee, Arthur Player, was one of the landlords who had opposed Fitzgerald, and he enjoyed a greater measure of success. Indeed the mayor and commonality soon began to express concern over the city's coal supplies. It was claimed that Player had taken not just the coal-pits of Kingswood into his own hands, but others near to the city, and that he was restricting production by paying rents simply in order to close them down. In this way, it was claimed by the Mayor and Aldermen, Player had been able to force up prices and reduce the size of the sacks in which the coal was retailed.[23] Monopolists were not the only force with whom the city had to contend; in 1625 there was a concerted refusal by the colliers of Kingswood to supply coal to Bristol, with the result that recourse had to be made to Swansea 'to relieve the sufferings of the poor'.[24]

Concern by the Crown with the numbers of unruly squatters in Kingswood, and the damage they caused by illegally erecting multitudes of cottages, cutting wood and killing deer, led to the compiling of a series of surveys which provide rare insights into the occupational structure of the forest and the extent of mining there. In an age of land scarcity and labour surplus, Kingswood proved an extremely attractive haven for migrants. The dilatoriness of royal lordship meant that land could often be encroached, buildings erected, animals pastured, and employment found in a wide range of activities, including most notably the mining and carrying of coal. The population of Kingswood grew rapidly: in 1629 Crown surveyors claimed that there were forty-six newly erected cottages whose occupants were paying rent to neighbouring lords but not to the king; in 1652 parliamentary surveyors found 152 cottages on what they believed was Crown property; and by 1691 it was claimed that there were no less than 500 colliers in the forest. This latter figure is doubtless an exaggeration, but an incomplete survey of the same year lists over one hundred colliers' households, and more than fifty households which gained their living from driving pack-horses laden with coal.

The abundance of colliers in Kingswood would have come as little surprise to the surveyors, for in 1608 John Smith had found that around a quarter of the male inhabitants of the manor of Bitton and Hanham, which bordered on Kingswood to the south, were colliers, and that

---

[23] *CSPD 1603-10*, 499, 606; Sharp 1980, 188–9; Galloway 1898, i. 212–13; *VCH Gloucestershire*, ii. 236.

[24] Latimer, *Annals of Bristol*, 94.

nearby in Estor the proportions of colliers rose higher still. Yet another survey of Kingswood, carried out in 1686, lists seventy-four active pits in the liberties of the local gentry families, and many more which were 'wrought out', 'unworked', or 'lying open dangerously'. Small wonder that a visitor should report that the forest contained a 'multitude of coalpits, and was stuffed with cottagers and alehouses, and was overlaid with horses for carrying coals'.[25] What is more, many productive pits lay outside the bounds of Kingswood, including those at Brislington, Bitton, Hanham, Estor, Frameton, Yate, and Rangeworthy. Sadly, however, not a single colliery account survives for any operation within the coalfield.[26]

Celia Fiennes on her visit in 1698 remarked on 'the great many horses passing and returning loaden with coals' on their way between Bristol and Kingswood, and also of Bristol harbour being 'full of ships carrying coals and all sorts of commodities to other parts'.[27] Her enthusiasm for coal may well have encouraged overstatement, and it must be remembered that each packhorse carried only a couple of hundredweight of coals; none the less unlike the Forest of Dean, there were major outlets for the coal of the Bristol coalfield. In consequence its output might well have attained more significant proportions. Most pits were tiny, and most miners were part-time, but there were scores of them, and aggregate production may well have exceeded 50,000 tons.

Somerset

In an inquisition into the bounds of Somerset coalmining in 1678-9 an expert local witness testified that 'the forest of Mendip where coalpits are or have been wrought, do extend in length between four and five miles and about one mile in breadth, and the manors of Ashwick, Kilmersdon, Holcombe, Mells, Babington, Luckington and Stratton are manors bordering upon and adjoining to the forest of Mendip'. A subsequent witness testified more succinctly that the part of the forest where coal was worked extended 'from Mells or near to Binegar', a distance of no more than eight miles.[28] The early mining of Somerset coal was concentrated in a compact section in the south of the coalfield. Although by the opening of the seventeenth century some inroads had

[25] Many of the surveys and related documents are to be found in BrRL Ellacombe, e.g. vi. 103, 123, 173-4; vii. 15, 57; x; xvi. 23, 25.

[26] Nef 1932, i. 73 n. Gibson in 1695 considered that Brislington abounded with the same sorts of coals as Newcastle (Galloway 1898, i. 214).

[27] *Journeys*, 191-2, 193.

[28] *VCH Somerset*, ii. 381.

been made into the reserves of the northern sector, very little mining had taken place in what was potentially the most fruitful region of all, the central area around Radstock and Midsummer Norton. The reason for the chronology of exploitation was, of course, primarily geological. In the Radstock basin the coal measures were concealed between Triassic and Jurassic overlays, there were few outcrops and the bulk of seams were deep as well as faulted and steeply dipping. By contrast, much of the coal to the south was exposed and therefore accessible.[29]

It is possible that the Mendips were the source of the coal used in the cluster of Roman sites found in south-west England where this fuel was burnt, and it seems to have been coal which kept the perpetual fires burning in the temple of the goddess Sul-Minerva in third-century Bath.[30] What is possibly the earliest medieval notice occurs in an inquisition at Kilmersdon manor in the mid-1270s, which reported *proficium carbonum* of 2s. 4d. While unqualified *carbonum* at this time should normally be read as charcoal, the form of this phrase and the fact that Kilmersdon was soon to emerge as a leading centre of coalmining, raises the possibility that in this instance it refers to mineral coal. Subsequent references to coal are confined to the southern portion of the coalfield, and, although quite plentiful by the close of the Middle Ages, contain nothing to indicate mining on a substantial scale. At Babington, near Kilmersdon, for example, Richard de St John was accused in 1353–4 of unlawfully 'digging, carrying away and selling coals'. At Stratton-on-the-Fosse in 1443 the lord of the manor sold coal worth £2. 16s. 1d., and in 1456–7 he leased the mine for £1. 6s. 8d. per annum. By 1477 another mine had been opened up at Stratton, and it too was leased for £1. 6s. 8d., and an identical rent was being paid when Henry VIII reigned.[31]

The Mendips continued to be famous for their lead rather than their coal through the sixteenth century. Mines proliferated in the south of the coalfield but there is nothing to suggest any leap forward in scale. Leland showed his awareness of mining in the region, when he wrote of a brook which flows 'from the coalpits in Mendip and striketh by south into the bottom of Mells and then runneth into Frome River', but neither he nor Camden a couple of generations later found coal worthy of extended notice.[32] It was not until the early seventeenth century that

---

[29] Bulley thesis 1952, 10–13; Bulley 1953, 52; Flinn 1984, 13–14.
[30] Webster 1955; *VCH Somerset*, i. 220.
[31] *VCH Somerset*, ii. 379–80; Bulley thesis 1952, 10–11.
[32] Leland, *Itinerary*, i. 168; Camden, *Britannia*, i. 82, 87.

a substantial increase in the scale and extent of mining took place, and it is in the 1600s that we first learn of coal being raised to the north of Radstock, as mines at Clutton, Timsbury, and Farrington Gurney come into view. Although the coal reserves at Timsbury were in 1610 erroneously thought to be almost exhausted, mining operations 'newly entered into' at Clutton, within easy distance of Bristol and Bath, were on a sizeable scale, with weekly output estimated at 600 horse-loads, perhaps amounting to 3,000 to 3,500 tons in a year. A fine of £300, paid for a lease of a colliery called 'Les Holmes' at Stratton, some time before 1624, is also indicative of significant scale.[33]

The parliamentary surveys of 1650–1 paint a dismal picture of coal-mining in the two Somerset manors surveyed, reflecting the adverse effect on the local economy of the Civil War and the subsequent seques-tration of property. Of Farrington Gurney the surveyors reported that 'no one undertakes to sink any new pits, not conceiving it would quit the charges of working, in consideration whereof and that there hath been no profit made there so long time, we know not how to put any value on the same'. Stratton too was sorely depressed, and we are told that 'All those coalpits and coalmines or drifts of coal commonly called the Barrow' were judged to be worth only 40s. a year, while 'the coal-mine commonly called the Holmes' was assessed to be worth a mere 20s. above the ancient rent of 55s. 1d. because it is 'almost wrought out, having been twice wrought already, and also because of the excessive charge in drawing the coals by reason of six water mills with their pumps, pump pits, fence pits, water courses and other materials requisite for carrying away the excessive flux of water from the mine, besides the fines, yearly rents and compositions with other lords for watercourses upon their grounds'.[34] But the impact of the war was rela-tively short lived and the essential quality of Stratton, evidenced by the extensive capital equipment installed there, soon reasserted itself. In the 1690s a pit no less than 140 yards deep was said to be in use, and on one occasion around 70 tons were raised from Stratton Common colliery in a twenty-four-hour period.[35] Such a depth of working was rare in Somerset and, from the context in which it was reported, such a level of output was undoubtedly exceptional even for Stratton.

Sadly there are no true colliery accounts for our period, and the

[33] Bulley thesis 1952, 12–13; Nef 1932, i. 73–4; *VCH Somerset*, ii. 382–3. For the size of horse-loads in Somerset see Bulley 1952, 51.

[34] PRO E. 317/19, m. 14–16; E. 317/39, m. 1–8.

[35] Bulley 1952, 48, 63.

prevalence of royalties, called free-share, rather than rents means that there are relatively few indications of the values of mines. We are best informed about Kilmersdon, for which we have a series of rather confusing free-share and partnership accounts running from 1680 to 1691, an excellent plan of the coal-mines on the manor, and James Twyford's mining notebook. Twyford estimated that the total value of the coal raised from Kilmersdon between 1694 to 1700, when the pits were 'in great perfection', at not less than £4,000, perhaps amounting to around 3,000 tons a year. In fact, if the accounts are studied it is obvious that Twyford is referring to Sheere's Close alone, the colliery formerly worked by his master. The output of all the pits on the manor may well have reached 7,000 tons or thereabouts.[36]

Collieries of such scale were undoubtedly rare in Somerset, and we must conclude with the historian of the coalfield, J. A. Bulley, that the 'typical unit of production in mid-seventeent century Somerset was responsible for an output that could best be measured in tens or hundreds, rather than thousands of tons'.[37] The Somerset coalfield was landlocked, and the market for its output was severely circumscribed. The nearest navigable rivers lay six or seven miles from the major mining areas, and the road system was poor, necessitating packhorse carriage. The bulk of production was sold locally in the market towns of Bath, Bradford-on-Avon, Frome, Shepton Mallet, Wells, Glastonbury, and Warminster.[38] Further afield, Mendip coal ran into stiff competition, from Welsh, Shropshire, Forest of Dean, and Kingswood coal. During the period covered in this volume no Mendip coal seems to have been sold in Bristol. Nor was the hinterland to the south a captive market. An expert correspondent in 1709 reported that Welsh coal, which in his view was more durable and stronger for furnaces and lime-burning, was cheaper than Mendip coal in Yeovil and Ilchester, and that when the 5 s. a chaldron coasting duty expired it would be cheaper at Sherborne also.[39] We may agree with Bulley, and conclude that although in peak years output may have reached 50,000 tons, in an average year it is not likely to have exceeded 30,000 tons.

[36] SoRO Hylton DD/HY boxes 12, 13, 14, 45.
[37] Bulley 1952, 47.
[38] Ibid. 53–4, 59–60; Fiennes, *Journeys*, 37.
[39] SoRO Phelips of Montacute DD/PH 212/29, John Speke to William Pittard 15/9/1709.

PART III

THE PRODUCTION OF COAL

CHAPTER 6

Mines and the Techniques of Mining

Were it not for water, a colliery in these parts might be termed a Golden Mine to purpose.

J.C., *The Compleat Collier* (1708)

i. Types of mine

Mining was a curious activity, much remarked upon by travellers and antiquaries, so there are a number of excellent contemporary descriptions of how coal was dug, as well as a multitude of colliery accounts and a rich store of contextual documentation to enlighten the historian. Sadly, there is little to be gained from the physical remains of early mining sites, for they have rarely survived the depredations of later workings and even when discovered are normally extremely difficult to date. *The Compleat Collier* (1708), contains an incomparable account of the great collieries of the north-east and of the technology of coalmining at the close of our period. But it is important to realize that J.C. depicts coalmining technology at its peak; the skills and techniques that he describes are derived from best practice in the great collieries of the most advanced coalfield in the world. In earlier periods and other places less elaborate and less expensive methods were usually employed in winning coal on a far smaller scale. It would be a mistake, however, to believe that there was a simple cumulative progression in the history of the working of coal, from the easy digging of surface deposits to the difficult and costly exploitation of deep seams. Indeed, shaft mining using systematic pillar-and-stall methods of working was used in favoured locations in the Middle Ages. None the less, for the purposes of explaining the various systems and techniques, it is appropriate to begin with the most rudimentary forms, while always bearing in mind that these were by no means confined solely to the earliest centuries of coalmining, nor was practice reducible to a set of neat exclusive categories.

Simplest of all, when the coal not only lay within a few feet of the surface but in a virtually horizontal seam, was opencast mining. According to Robert Plot, writing in 1686:

The open works at Wednesbury [Staffs] seem to be of this kind, where there being but little earth lying over the measures of coal, the workmen rid off the earth, and dig the coal under their feet and carry it out in wheel-barrows, there being no need for these, of windlass, rope or corfe, whence these sort of coal-works are commonly called foot-ridds or footrills.[1]

Where the coal lay further, but not very far, under the surface, there were other cheap and rudimentary, but effective, methods of extracting it. Prominent among these were the ubiquitous beehive or bell-pits, used also by ironstone miners, which derived their name from their shape. It was pits of this sort that Celia Fiennes observed around Chesterfield (Derby.) just before the eighteenth century, where the miners 'make their mines at the entrance like a well, and so till they come to the coal, then they dig all the ground about where there is coal and set pillars to support it and so bring it to the well, where by a basket like a hand-barrow by cords they pull it up, so they let down and up the miners with a cord'.[2] Cruder still were the shallowest of bell-pits mined without supports, in which the coal was cut from around the foot of the shaft until the sides and roof were in danger of collapse, at which point a new adjacent shaft would be sunk. The old shaft would be filled in with the debris obtained from the excavation of the new. When the seam was merely a few feet below the surface it might be less expensive to sink new shafts than to support the roofs of existing pits. Aerial photography has revealed a cluster of early bell-pits near Denby (Derby.), to the south of those viewed by Celia Fiennes. At the surface they are circular, ranging from six to twelve feet in diameter, with one somewhat exceptionally being oval, and they average twenty feet in depth.[3] In areas of prolonged mining activity the surface became literally honeycombed with a multitude of small shafts.[4]

   Bell-pits were not, however, the province of impecunious, small-scale miners alone. They have been discovered by aerial photography in a field between the notable collieries of Trowell Moor and Wollaton, in an area mined by the Willoughbys.[5] The earl of Shrewsbury's colliery in Beaudesert Park followed essentially the same methods in the later

---

[1] *Staffordshire* (1686), 129. For an opencast working, said to be 50 yds. broad and 10 yds. deep in Dronfield (Derby.) in Charles I's reign, see Benson and Neville (eds.) 1976, 6.

[2] *Journeys*, 103.   [3] Griffin 1969, 392–3.

[4] Anderson 1982, 25; Singleton 1969, 428–9. See also pl. 2*a*.

[5] Henson and Smith 1955, 256–8.

sixteenth century. An excellent series of accounts reveals that some 2,000 tons a year were raised there from a succession of short-lived shallow pits, usually no more than twenty feet deep and costing only 10s. or so to sink.[6] In the course of a year as many as a dozen or so might be sunk. They were of a necessarily rudimentary character, and utilized the crudest of winding gear, perhaps not that much different to the 'little wheel or windlass like a well', which Celia Fiennes found on her visit to the colliery a century later.[7] Yet Beaudesert colliery was very long lived, and the work-force had a core of full-time specialist colliers, sinkers, and timbermen. So labour intensive was the propping of roofs that in some years it required a timberman to keep two or three hewers at work. Drainage arrangements at Beaudesert also went beyond the winding up of buckets full of water. Even with shallow pits a drainage channel, called a sough in Staffordshire, might be necessary, and in the 1570s and 1580s frequent and occasionally heavy charges for soughing appear in the accounts.

Mining temporarily ceased at Beaudesert in the mid-1580s. When it was restarted in 1600 it was on a grander scale. It cost £57. 9s. 3d. to set four pits at work, excluding one which had to be given over before it was sunk to the coal 'by means of the great abundance of water'. The new pits went as deep as ninety-five feet, and a new sough was constructed and the old one 'scoured'. In addition a head was driven between the two deepest pits, a distance of twenty-six yards, with the intention of working the coal along its length. Moreover, such depths brought ventilation problems, and devices were purchased to rid the workings of 'earth damp'. Within two years a water pit, to act as a sump, had been added 'which is and must be kept with drawing of water continually day and night'. There had been a marked change in the character of mining in the park, and bell-pits had been superseded.[8]

Where the terrain was hilly and the seam outcropped on or near the side of a valley, coal would be worked first by simply extracting as much as could be obtained before the hillside collapsed. Once all the coal which could be safely got in this way had been won, or if a larger-scale operation was intended from the outset, a tunnel would be driven into the side of the hill more or less horizontally, either following the seam or driven to intercept it. Such mines were known by a variety of names in different areas; the most common being 'day-hole' or 'drift'. In Scotland they were known as 'in-gaun-e' en' ('ingoing eyes'), and in

[6] StRO Anglesey D(W) 1734.
[7] *Journeys*, 148.   [8] StRo Anglesey D (W) 1734/3/3/254-5.

Cumberland 'bearmouths'. If the seam was on the rise then the workings would be self-draining, the colliers could walk in and the coal could be carried or pushed out. Even when the seam dipped it was often possible to drain the coal-face cheaply by cutting open trenches or short tunnels to it from lower down the hillside, thereby enabling the coal to be worked back upwards to the outcrop. The maximum amount of coal could be obtained by cutting the drainage channel as near as possible to the bottom of the valley, and thus intercepting the seam at the greatest possible distance from the outcrop.

Day-holes were ubiquitous in hilly terrain with outcropping seams. In sixteenth-century Pembrokeshire we learn from George Owen, writing in 1603, how 'in former time they used no engine for lifting up of the coals out of the pit but made their entrance slope, so as the people carried the coals upon their backs along stairs which they called landways'.[9] Like bell-pits, such methods were well suited to small-scale workings supplying limited markets. But it was with disdain that Sir John Lowther's steward, John Spedding, looked back upon the activities of the petty colliers around Whitehaven (Cumberland) in the 1630s, before Sir Charles Lowther's entrepreneurial endeavours had begun. As he wrote in his notebook in 1705:

People were very ignorant in the manner of working their coals and only got some small quantities in the outburn of such of their collieries as were most easy to come at, which were all wrought at bearmouths and left roof full of water . . . as not knowing the use of pits whereby they might with more facility have taken out their coals, nor the use of levels to drain their collieries.[10]

Day-holes could of course be adapted to serve enterprises of far larger scale, as John Spedding intimated, but by so doing their character changed decisively. A report to the Royal Society in 1697, for example, stated that in Llanelli 'their coal works were not pits sunk like draw wells, but great inroads made into the side of the hill, so that three or four horsemen might ride in abreast. The top is supported with pillars left at certain distance, and they make their by-lanes (as in other pits) as the vein requires'.[11] Drift-mining on a prodigious scale was in evidence in the Severn Gorge. At Madeley in 1651 the colliery was said to consist of four insets driven horizontally into the hillside; two of the insets were said to be 1,000 yards long, and the other two 700 and 500 yards respectively. We are also told that water had to be forced out of the insets by

⁹ *Pembrokeshire*, 89.
¹⁰ CuRO Lonsdale D/L/W John Spedding's notebook.   ¹¹ *PTRS* 38. 338.

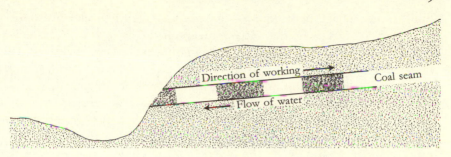

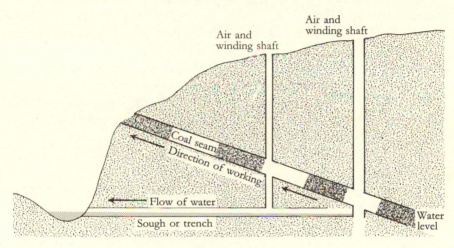

Fig. 6.1. Drift-mining (*a*) On the rise; (*b*) On the dip

drainage engines, in addition, no doubt, to extensive soughing.[12] It is also certain that ventilation shafts would be required to keep the air fresh enough for the colliers to work drift mines of this scale. Once again we are far from the primitive. In turning to consider the circumstances when coal outcrops were less easy to discover, and the techniques of exploiting them somewhat less simple and straightforward, it is necessary to deal separately with the various elements involved in the discovery of deposits and the mining of the coal.

ii. Exploration, boring and sinking

The study of the earth before the late eighteenth century has been described as 'an incoherent jumble of cosmogony, fossil-collecting,

---

[12] *VCH Shropshire*, xi. 48.

Biblical theorising, topography and so on, lacking even the name "geology"'.[13] Those who chose to write about the natural world understandably concentrated upon those elements which were visible above the ground, and stressed physical relief, flora and fauna, and antique remains, as well as finding ample space for the romance of genealogy and history. When at last the earth was subjected to scrutiny it was frequently imbued with living qualities, or with a philosophical or religious aura. It was thus with some justification that the early nineteenth-century founders of the science of geology considered their predecessors to have been 'in the thrall of Moses'. It is a simple matter to augment their torrents of scorn by referring to the profusion of quack recipes for the finding of coal, such as those published in 1639 by Gabriel Plattes entitled *A Discovery of subterraneall Treasure... from the Gold to the Coale*, or to the beliefs that seams of coal could be made to grow by manuring, or by nourishing them with water or sulphur.[14] However, it would be falling into a trap to follow the embryonic geologists of the nineteenth century into seeing the early modern world as irredeemably ignorant. Even before 1700 significant strivings towards a more systematic and scientific approach by men of letters can be discerned. The founding of the Royal Society in 1660 was undoubtedly a landmark in the evolution of geology, for the Society displayed a particular interest in the Earth and in mining, and it facilitated the collection and study of data. Coal-mines, especially underground gases and explosions, featured in the first generation of topics reported and discussed by members, and the same topics featured prominently in Professor George Sinclair's *Hydrostaticks* (1672) and Dr Robert Plot's *Natural History of Staffordshire* (1686), two notable works in the early development of Earth Science.

But of far more importance in these times was the practical knowledge of working men. It would be absurd to measure the knowledge of geology by sole reference to the published works of men of letters. The collier, the viewer, the borer, and the sinker acquired an intimate acquaintance with aspects of the strata of the Earth's crust. They were men who worked underground, and who cut through the superincumbent strata in search of coal. Moreover, there were among them some whose expertise rose far above the generality of practitioners, who

[13] R. Porter, 'The Industrial Revolution and the Rise of the Science of Geology', in M. Teich and R. Young (eds.), *Changing Perspectives in the History of Science* (1973), 320. For the history of geology see also R. Porter, *The Making of Geology* (Cambridge, 1977).

[14] See e.g. the anonymous early 17th-cent. 'Rule to know how to find coals', BoL Rawlinson 868, fo. 98.

emerged as men renowned for their exceptional knowledge and skill in finding coal, in efficiently estimating and exploiting the deposits that they discovered, and in maximizing the yield from existing collieries. These were the 'viewers' and men 'skilled in coalery', whose services were much in demand and highly rewarded. Landowners in increasing numbers also sought to acquaint themselves with the mineral reserves of their estates, and some did so in a highly effective manner.[15] The accumulated experience of those working in the industry, despite usually being based on the experience of a single coalfield, geared primarily to the practicalities of mining, and most often lacking any formal or theoretical framework, constituted a fund of rule-of-thumb knowledge which during our period far exceeded in value that which was picked up by the gentlemen–amateur naturalists and topographers who became interested in such matters. Before the eighteenth century it was the science of geology which learnt from those in the industry, rather than vice versa. The detailed accounts of Staffordshire coalmining methods in Plot's *Natural History* were undoubtedly largely based upon information gleaned from colliers and mine-owners, while Sinclair relied upon correspondents from within the coal industry for the most useful sections of his *Hydrostaticks*.

It is not possible to appreciate the true extent of the expertise of those in the industry, for the incomes and careers of its leading practitioners depended upon the mysteries of the art remaining secret. Wisdom was for passing down within families or for the training of assistants, not for broadcasting. Thus even such well-informed accounts as *The Compleat Collier*, though in large measure emanating from within the industry, cannot be taken to constitute the state of the art when it was published. Instead we must rely upon the direct testimony of colliery records, which reveal much about how the coal was mined, and upon general and indirect indicators of progress, of which the positive achievements of the industry in massively increasing output through the discovery of new deposits and improvements in the methods of extraction are the most eloquent.

The location of deposits was the first requirement of mining, and the rapid expansion of output during the later sixteenth and the seventeenth

---

[15] See e.g. the extensive geological surveys commissioned in the 1630s by Sir Thomas Gascoigne of his estate near Barwick-in-Elmet, Yorks. (LCA Gascoigne MSS, uncatalogued vol. fos. 27ʳ–29ʳ); of Roger Bradshaigh's coal reserves at Haigh, 1670 (WiRO Haigh Colliery Orders, D/DZ A13/34, fos. 8ᵛ–13ʳ); and of Sir John Lowther's estates (CuRO Lonsdale, 6 notebooks 1687–1705 containing information on collieries, direction, and thickness of seams, etc.).

centuries rested critically upon the discovery of a multitude of new sites for mining. In weighing the reasons for this success, there can be no doubt that the evident profusion of outcrops on almost all British coalfields was paramount, for the art of prospecting fell far short of perfection. As for the ability to discover new deposits, a sharp distinction must be drawn between the search for coal in areas where mining was already prevalent and prospecting in virgin territories, even those which were subsequently to prove richly endowed. In the era before 1700 the former was overwhelmingly the most significant. This is not to deny, of course, that it was natural for men to yearn for abundant supplies of coal to be forthcoming from collieries where none existed, simply that the augmentations forthcoming from new collieries set up in long-established mining areas far outweighed those which followed from the expansion of the boundaries of mining regions.

It has already been noted that repeated attempts were made to discover coal closer to the walls of towns already served by local collieries, in order to save the inhabitants transport costs.[16] But the lure of black gold sometimes drove men to prospect far away from any known coal reserves; the risks of the venture in their eyes being outweighed by the chances of enormous rewards. A group of Southampton merchants dug extensively and expensively for coal in the New Forest, while prospectors explored the East Riding of Yorkshire and south Worcestershire as well as, less sensibly, Wiltshire and Dorset. Between the 1690s and the 1750s at least eight separate attempts to discover coal in the vicinity of Sherbourne have come to light. Sometimes dreadful shortages led to desperate quests. When Newcastle and Sunderland were blockaded in 1643 the Corporation of London sought for coal in Blackheath, and later, when the Dutch Wars dislocated the collier fleet, the focus of prospecting turned to Windsor forest. In 1665 a consortium of high-ranking venturers in the forest reported that 'a knowing and very skilful person, who is come from Newcastle ... doth assure us that with less than £100 charge he will lay us above ground 100 chaldrons of coals, and afterwards will work them for 3s. 6d. per chaldron'.[17]

A long succession of entirely spurious recipes for discovering coal were published in the course of the seventeenth century, as well as many more which were at best of only limited value. Prospectors were advised to look at plant life on the surface for clues as to the possible presence of

---

[16] See above, Ch. 5.

[17] Nef 1932, ii. 72–3; H. S. Torrens, 'The History and Technology of Coal Prospecting', lecture given in the Engineering Faculty, Cambridge University, 27 Jan. 1986.

carboniferous strata below. Holly with oak was thought to indicate coal
in Wiltshire, as it did around Newcastle. Coal might also be indicated by
surface covers, in particular shales, limestones and freestones, but they
were of course far too frequent in occurrence to be of any real use. In
areas of established mining, however, new outcrops and seams of coal
were relatively easy to discover 'by the judgment of those that are skilful
in choosing the ground for that purpose'.[18] By observing the location of
coalworkings in the vicinity, and the depth and direction, rising and
dipping, of their seams, much could be learnt. As J.C. would have it, the
prime reason for hoping that coal might be found on one's land was that
the ground bordered that on which there were working collieries.[19] As
Plot wrote, perhaps with excessive confidence:

where coal is already known to be, either by their appearing to the day
anywhere, as by riversides, or having been dug not far off: the ranges of the
metals already known, and their distances, with their dipping, and the rise of
ground above them, giving directions almost infallibly where they shalt let
down their pit. For these being known, 'tis no great difficulty to judge where-
about they'll crop out; that which lies lowest, coming forth furthest; and that
which uppermost, nighest to the place foreknown.[20]

   In practice there was, of course, much more to successful prospecting
than this. But many further fruitful indications could be revealed by the
scrutiny of surfaces in river valleys and watercourses, especially on hill-
sides after downpours of rain had washed away the topsoil. Hunting for
traces of coal, and also for the distinctive yellow clay that had the taste
of rusted iron, was highly recommended.[21] Within heavily worked coalfields it must be expected that knowledge would be gained of the order
of rocks in the strata, and that in the right hands it could prove a fair
predictor of the presence of coal. Indubitably, there were quacks as well
as unscrupulous colliers who, working either for a daily wage or for so
much per yard sunk or bored, were willing to indulge over-eager
adventurers or recklessly hopeful landowners in their willingness to
spend large sums of money in prolonged searches for coal where none
existed. But, in the broad run, the employment prospects and earning
power of the professional prospector depended upon his success rate.
Unscrupulously optimistic, or just plain bad, advisers could always be
found, but the men at the top of their profession had services of great

[18] PRO Duchy of Lancashire Pleadings, 185/T/12 (quoted in Nef 1932, i. 352).
[19] *Compleat Collier*, 10.   [20] *Staffordshire*, 47.
[21] As Sir John Clerk advocated (Duckham 1970, 41).

value to offer. This is not to say that, even in their hands, prospecting for coal was not apt to prove an uncertain and risky undertaking; rather, that, with the exercise of due prudence and skilled judgement, the risks were normally worth taking. For the landowner who had some knowledge of the mineral resources of his estate, and perhaps also some awareness of basic geology, the risks were lessened still further.

When a promising site had been identified, the surface had then to be broken to determine the accuracy of the prediction. In searching for outcrops this might take little more than the lifting of the topsoil or the digging of shallow trenches. But for deeper seams there was from the early decades of the seventeenth century, at least in the technically advanced coalfields, a choice between sinking an exploratory shaft and boring. It was the high cost of digging down to find coal which undoubtedly inspired the invention of boring rods[22] They are first mentioned in the north-east, but William Gray, the historian of Newcastle (1649) attributed the introduction there of 'the art to bore with iron rods to try the deepness and thickness of the coal' to Huntingdon Beaumont, and some credence is leant to their earlier usage in Nottinghamshire by the occurrence in the Wollaton accounts of the 1570s of 'a wimbell' and a 'great ager [auger] and a little ager'.[23] In 1616 when the earl of Northumberland's steward wished to discover whether one of the collieries being worked for pancoal possessed 'London coal' at a lower level, he sought the services of a borer, though he was unable to obtain him despite offering double pay.[24] Awareness of boring appears to have spread quite rapidly for an invention at this date. In 1618 Lord William Howard purchased a set of boring rods in Newcastle for £6. 15s. 9d., for use on his coal-bearing estates in Cumberland, and in 1628 he sent a similar set, along with an expert to operate them, to his son-in-law, Sir John Winter, in the Forest of Dean.[25] By this latter date we know that boring was being undertaken in Warwickshire, and soon afterwards in the vicinity of Halifax. In 1639, near Leeds, depths down to 126 feet were plumbed by rods.[26]

The techniques of boring and the tools of the borer were described at length by contemporaries.[27] Basically it was a percussive/rotative

---

[22] An informative account of the history of boring is contained in Nef 1932, ii, app. N, 446–8.

[23] Smith MS, 97–8.

[24] DN Syon Q. II, 111. The steward maintained that Hostmen hostile to the earl working his own collieries were keeping the borer from him.

[25] Ornsby (ed.), *Household Books*, 94, 249.

[26] Galloway 1898, i. 184.

[27] For the fullest accounts see *Compleat Collier*, 11–14, and Brand 1789, ii. 678–9.

process, during which wrought iron rods were bounced on a beam supported on a timber tripod. At each stroke the handle gripped by the borers was twisted a quarter turn. A chisel of a type appropriate to the substance being cut through was attached to the end of the bottom rod and, as the hole deepened, further rods were attached. Every four to six inches the rods were lifted up, to enable the chisel to be sharpened and for samples to be taken in a device called a wimble, which collected fragments of rock. Hopefully the motion of the rods caused the dust to rise, but when the hole was choked the chisel had to be replaced by a boring implement to cleanse it. Progress was relatively slow; Waller put it at a yard a day through hard rock in Cardiganshire.[28]

By the later seventeenth century boring provided an alternative to sinking in most parts of the country, but its success depended crucially upon the skill and experience of the borer, not just in propelling the bit downwards but in interpreting accurately the samples which were periodically drawn up. Doubtless the expertise of the borers and the technology of boring continued to improve as time passed, and experience accumulated, but Robert Plot and George Sinclair remained sceptical of its superiority over sinking. Both felt that boring was best suited to shallow seams, 'but if it lie deep, it becomes almost as expensive as sinking a pit [because] the drawing of the rods consuming so much time, in regard it must be frequently done', and whereas the evidence resulting from sinking was usually clear-cut and relatively easy to interpret correctly, the samples brought up by the wimble were often far from conclusive. Even when a borer struck a seam of coal, Plot and Sinclair feared lest he should not be able accurately to discover its thickness or quality, still less the declivity of the vein, how wet it was, or whether it could be drained.[29]

J.C. by contrast was much in favour of boring, even to the extent of completely ignoring exploratory sinking, and he maintained that it cost only a third as much. That J.C. exhibits none of the reservations or scepticism highlighted by Plot and Sinclair may be explained, at least in part, by the fact that he was writing some twenty to thirty years later, and from the north-east rather than from Staffordshire or Midlothian. There is reason to believe that the efficiency of boring improved over the intervening period, and we know that borers from the north-east had long enjoyed a national reputation.

Sinking, at least until rock was encountered, was a pick and shovel job. It was labour intensive, utilizing little in the way of equipment or

---

[28] Rees 1968, i. 116 n. 119.   [29] *Staffordshire*, 146; *Hydrostaticks*, 295.

raw materials, and wages invariably comprised more than 90 per cent of the total costs of a new shaft.[30] A simple windlass would be installed across the top of the hole to wind up the waste, and perhaps a rudimentary roof to shelter the sinkers and keep the shaft as dry as possible. Sinkers necessarily operated in small teams because of the confined spaces in which they had to work, for only rarely were shafts as wide as six feet across, unless they were gin pits. Their two major adversaries were water and stone, with quicksand much rarer but even more formidable. The increasing difficulty of the task as the depth grew was often reflected in a rising scale of payments, or by enhanced payments for sinking through stone or other difficult material. Contracts attempted to cope with the unpredictability of the undertakings, but it was impossible to plan for every eventuality and flexibility was the key.[31]

The lining of shafts with timber, to strengthen the sides and stop the earth from falling in, was common at an early date.[32] A series of timber-lined shafts, ascribed to the mid-fifteenth century, have recently been discovered near Coleorton in Leicestershire.[33] Timbering was essential to prolong the life of the shaft. After two untimbered shafts at Tynemouth had collapsed because of water seepage in midsummer 1616, Nicholas Hardwick wrote to the earl of Northumberland to inform him that they were now timbering new shafts at a cost of 16s. each in timber; he assured his master that a timbered pit was worth more and would last longer than three untimbered.[34] Timbering also improved the safety of the sinkers and colliers who worked in the shaft. As Adam Martindale remarked of an old pit near Prescot (Lancs.) in the early years of the seventeenth century: 'It was timbered near the top to keep the earth from falling in, as is usual, for the security of the workmen.'[35] *The Compleat Collier* stresses the necessity of laying in a good stock of timber prior to commencing work: oak spars or more commonly cheaper fir balks, deal boards, and a supply of nails. The oak or fir balks

[30] The statement is based upon the analysis of large numbers of accounts of the cost of sinking new pits, which was of course a frequent occurrence in working collieries.

[31] The methods of remunerating sinkers are discussed in Ch. 11(iii).

[32] Hence the common purchases of timber and employment of carpenters included in sinking costs or the granting to lessees of free access to timber expressly for use in the sinking of shafts. Imports of Norwegian timber were held by the mayor, aldermen, and burgesses of Newcastle to be essential for coalmining (Moller thesis 1933, 74–5).

[33] *Daily Telegraph* (21 Feb. 1991).

[34] DN Syon Q. XI. 59.

[35] Bailey 1947, 15.

would be let into the sides of the shaft, three or four feet apart, and the boards nailed to them.[36]

When water was encountered, as it frequently was from underground streams, or feeders as they were known in the north-east, the sinkers attempted to make the timber lining watertight. To do this they utilized a number of skills learnt by experience or picked up from other crafts. The lining could be constructed in the style used by coopers in making barrels, hence the name of 'tubbing' which was sometimes given to it. The term 'cribbing' was also used. Fir was the best wood to use for it swelled when wet. Clay or hemp caulking would be driven into the joints to seal them. When the water flowed from a small parting in stone, even greater skill was required on the part of the leader of the sinkers, for the stopping of just the one leak might well force the water to find another way out. The stone would be smoothed off as far as possible, and a wooden frame constructed of an appropriate size. The frame would then be fixed, and backed with earth and clay, and if it still leaked then 'sheep-skins with the wool on help to provide a durable seal.'[37]

Clearly a balance had to be struck between the cost of staunching the water and the ease of sinking a new shaft elsewhere. The shallower the shafts and the shorter their projected lives the more likely they were to be given over when an appreciable volume of water was encountered. Such occurrences were by no means rare. With shallow shafts and bell-pits abandonment might not be of great moment, but when a new shaft was being sunk at a precise spot to maximize the coal that could be won, and to link up with existing shafts, headings, and adits, in a well-established and profitable colliery, it could prove far more damaging. It was in such circumstances that the more extreme and costly of the timbering and tubbing expedients enumerated above would be resorted to. If, however, these proved unsuccessful then a further shaft might be sunk, adjacent to the flooded one, to a level below the feeder, into which the excess water would be drained via a channel, 'to be drawn there by horses or water wheels, as there is a conveniency for it, that so the water may not follow or descend, with sinking'.[38] For J.C. this was a far more effective method of dealing with a substantial flow of water than attempting to staunch it by timber lining or tubbing. But it was expensive, not only in the sinking but in the continual drawing of the

---

[36] A detailed contemporary account of 'tubbing and cribbing' in mid-18th-cent. Cumberland is contained in Flinn 1985, 76.

[37] *Compleat Collier*, 24–8.

[38] Ibid. 20–1.

water thereafter, and if the water could be caulked or staunched by a frame this was normally the chosen solution. Once the shaft had been sunk there were, of course, other methods of drainage, and these are dealt with in the next section.

Water, being both frequently encountered and unpredictable in scale, was perhaps the greatest threat to thrifty sinking. But though the odds of encountering quicksand were far longer, when it was struck it was little short of disastrous. Even in the late nineteenth century, and in major collieries, quicksand could force the abandonment of sinking.[39] Yet there were methods of successfully overcoming it in the seventeenth century. If the stratum of sand was not thick, then with 'extreme quick vigilancy and care' it could be sunk through, using piles to which walls made of planks, reinforced by stiff clay, were nailed. At Harraton, J.C. reports, 'I have heard of iron frames that have been used (made square and deeper than the thickness of the quicksand) to put back these quick-sands, which may be of good use, though they must be dear to be so cast or wrought'. Although J.C. went on to remark that iron tubbing was not much used, it is strange that John Buddle senior should have been credited with pioneering its use in Wallsend colliery almost a century later.[40]

When the sinkers came to stone, as they normally did at a depth which could vary from a few feet to many yards, further excavation was often painfully slow. Commonly the sinkers would rely solely upon picks, wedges, and hammers to work through stone, taking care to have facilities for the sharpening and repair of their tools on hand. But it sometimes proved necessary to try other methods. One was the stock and feathers. A hole would be drilled in the rock, and the feathers, which were two thin plates of iron thickened towards the lower ends, were placed in it. Then a wedge was placed between the feathers and driven home until the rock was split or a fragment torn off.[41] Cutting through rock was a dangerous as well as an arduous task, with the workmen liable to be struck and seriously injured by flying fragments of stone.[42] Once again a high premium was placed upon the experience and skill of the gang-leader, and left-handed gang members were highly prized. Prior to attacking the rock, it might be weakened or softened by lighting fires in it. Otherwise the sinkers might not 'work away so much in a day, as will fill a hat'.[43] The hardest stone of all was igneous intrusions called

[39] Galloway 1898, i. 451–2.   [40] *Compleat Collier*, 21–2; Flinn 1985, 76–7.
[41] Taylor 1858, 190.   [42] *Compleat Collier*, 22–3.
[43] Smith MS, 61; NLS Niddrie MS Acc. 5253/MS 17952; Plot, *Staffordshire*, 134.

'whin', and colliers delighted in telling stories of how much time and money had, on occasion, been expended inching through it.

A major advance in sinking through stone came with the use of gunpowder. Blasting had been introduced into England by German metal miners, and there is some evidence that it was used in lead-, copper-, and tin-mining before the late seventeenth century, though not commonly. The consensus of historians has been that gunpowder was not used in the coal industry before the eighteenth century.[44] However a number of references to its use in sinking for coal in the closing years of the seventeenth century can be found; for example, in Warwickshire in 1687, in Lancashire in 1699, and in Yorkshire in 1700.[45] But these mentions are too few to claim that blasting had a significant impact on sinking before the end of the seventeenth century, and it is salutary that none of the treatises on coalmining thought fit to mention it.

iii. Methods of working

When the shaft struck the coal to be worked the sinkers' job was over, unless they were required to sink additional shafts elsewhere on the site. The way in which the coal was then worked often appears to have been both simple and expedient. George Owen described mining in a Pembrokeshire colliery in 1600 thus: 'the coal being found the workmen follow the vein every way until it end or be letted by water or rock . . . they work sundry holes, one for every digger, some two, some three or four as the number of diggers are; each man working by candle light and sitting while he worketh.'[46] Yet if the maximum amount of coal was to be won, and the safety of the colliery was to be preserved, it had to be worked systematically. At the risk of pruning the rich variety of experience, it has become customary to divide methods of working into either 'longwall' or 'pillar-and-stall', also known locally as 'bord and pillar' and 'stoop and room'. In practice, however, there was no clear division into just two types; instead there was a vast range of variants adapted to suit the precise geological conditions which were encountered, as well as the resources of those who worked the collieries, and the size of the markets which existed for their coal. Even in the most systematically worked collieries idealized versions of the two contrasting methods were rarely reproduced. Pure pillar-and-stall and pure longwall were therefore at the two extremes of a spectrum. None the

[44] Galloway 1898, ii. 226–7; Nef 1932, i. 352.
[45] White thesis 1969, 59; BoRO Bradford ZBR/1/8; Hopkinson 1976, 25.
[46] *Pembrokeshire*, 90.

less, this broad division has some explanatory value. It was variants of
pillar-and-stall which were by far the most common method of winning
coal before the eighteenth century, and systematic pillar-and-stall
workings, partly backfilled with slack, have been found in archaeological excavations of workings dated to the mid-fifteenth century at
Lounge, near Coleorton (Leics.). This method of working coal was to
predominate not only up to 1700 but for long after, and it is here that we
shall begin.[47]

If it were more than a simple bell-pit that was being opened up, when
the shaft struck coal a heading, also called a level or road, would be
driven into the seam to provide access to greater reserves, sometimes
using a specialist team but more often using colliers. As with the
location of the shaft itself, the direction of the heading would be determined after the most skilled advice available had been sought and surveys had been made of the direction and dip of the seam, in order to
ensure gravity drainage and maximum yields. When additional shafts
were to be sunk, as they often were, great skill was required to ensure
that the horizontal level or heading actually joined up with the vertical
shaft. Little of a precise nature is known of the methods and instruments
used by viewers and mine surveyors to plot the layout of collieries, for
colliery accounts and contracts of employment yield scarcely a trace.
These were 'mysteries' to be jealously guarded and the publication of
any but the most obvious was discouraged. But the *Pantometria*,
published by Thomas Digges in 1571, deals in chapter 36 with underground surveying using a compass, and Thomas Houghton's *Rara Avis
in Terris, or the Compleat Miner*, published in 1681, details the square-
point dialling or co-ordinate method, which involved plotting to full
scale on the surface.[48]

Very often, perhaps in the generality of collieries above the very
small, pairs of shafts would be sunk, one in the outcrop or shallower
part of the seam, usually called the basset pit, and the other some
distance away down the dip, usually called the deep pit. Then a heading
would be driven between the two, which not only opened up the coal to
the hewers, it often improved ventilation and also lessened the costs of
underground haulage. While headings were being driven some coal was
won, and its sale helped to defray the costs of the work.

---

[47] 'In 1830 most coal was got by one of several variants of pillar-and-stall working, while longwall was mainly confined to Shropshire, the South-west, and to certain thin seams elsewhere'
(Church 1986, 329). See pl. 1.
[48] The history of mine surveying has been neglected, but see *HRCM* 219–38.

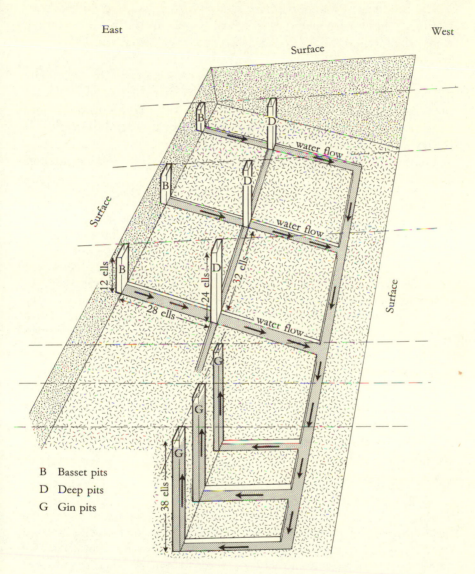

East Surface West

Surface

Surface

water flow

water flow

water flow

12 ells

24 ells

32 ells

28 ells

38 ells

B Basset pits
D Deep pits
G Gin pits

Fig. 6.2. Idealized reconstruction of Griff colliery, 1701

The coal-seam at Griff had a dip of approximately 30°. The coal was worked up the dip, from the deep shafts to the basset shafts, so that the coal-face was drained. Sketch based upon information and drawing in White thesis 1969.

The heading, or an appropriate stretch of it, would be divided into sections. These were given a variety of names; in the north-east they were called 'winnings', in Staffordshire 'wallings'. Each winning would accommodate a single hewer, who would cut coal from the centre, and leave pillars intact on both sides in order to support the roof. The dimensions of the winnings, and more particularly the size and shape of the pillars which had to be left, were a matter of careful judgement, and were determined largely by the depth of the workings and the nature of the roof. Robert Plot, in the late seventeenth century, described mining in a Staffordshire colliery at Hardingswood owned by a Mr Poole thus:

He shewed me a level of 35 yards . . . in this level he had five wallings or stalls, out of which they dug the coal in great blocks; between the wallings there were ribs left, and passages through them called thurlings, which give convenience of air . . . they mind not so much the [substance] of the coal as the roof, the wallings or stalls being made narrower or wider, according as that it is found better or worse, which sometimes being nothing but a bass, full of joint; and perhaps soluble in the air, they are forced then to leave a yard of coal that lies next under it for a roof, and make their walling narrow: whereas on the contrary where there is a strong rock next the coal, and no bass, they will then venture their roof so far sometimes as to make their wallings 8 or 9 yards wide.[49]

So vital is this method of winning to the fortunes of the whole industry that a further description of pillar-and-stall working, this time from the north-east at the turn of the seventeenth century, is warranted. The account given in *The Compleat Collier* is extremely informative, and describes a technically advanced industry, in which the coal is mined methodically and efficiently, to maximize output.

After we have carried our head-ways drift, about eight or ten yards from the pit-shaft, then we consider of a winning, how much to allow for a winning, which is about seven yards in these parts, or otherwise, according to the quality, or tenderness of it, more or less, as by judgment is thought safest and best; out of this winning of seven yards, perhaps we dare not venture to take above three yards breadth of coal for a bord; so that then there is but three yards for one man to work by himself, and therefore would be dangerous for two persons to work together, least they strike their coal-picks into one another, or at least hinder one another; then the remainder of four yards is left for a pillar to support the roof and weight of the earth above; which makes it out so, that there is not quite half of the coals taken out of the ground which lies there.[50]

[49] *Staffordshire*, 147–8.   [50] *Compleat Collier*, 42–3.

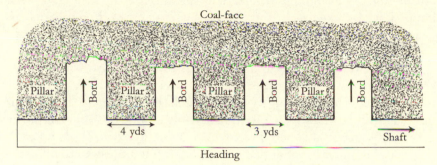

Fig. 6.3. Bord-and-pillar or pillar-and-stall mining in early stages
Source: dimensions specified in J.C., *The Compleat Collier*.

The great depth of many of the larger north-eastern collieries, and the consequent high cost of sinking new shafts, meant that headings were frequently long. J.C. envisages a heading of about 150 yards, to provide bords for twenty hewers, who would work out one side first.

When that side is wrought out we begin *de novo* to work on the other side, the same headways serving us again as before . . . and after this south headways is thus wrought out to the east and west hand of it; then it follows to turn the workings to the north headways, or other side of the shaft, which we go on with after the same method, as in the south, till we have wrought by these same rules, all the coal we can with safety venture to work or take away; and so by chance have wrought, or wasted the colliery 8 score or 200 yards to the east, west, north, and south of the pit-shaft, then it is time to have another shaft at that distance sunk for another new pit, which if happily done by the daily care, prudence, and orders of the viewer, and his drift to the new pit, carried on exactly so as to hit the new shaft, and supply her with air.[51]

If pillars were too small the lives of the colliers could be threatened by roof falls. Moreover, the colliery could be seriously harmed or even destroyed by 'creep' or by 'crush or thrust'. Creep was the heaving up of the floor, often first detected by a curvature in the bottom of the gallery. The next stages saw the cracking of the floor, compression of the pillars, sometimes detected by the noise it made as the pressures increased, and finally the crushing of the seam. Crush or thrust resulted from insufficient pillars when both the floor and the roof of a seam of coal were composed of hard materials. The weight of the superincumbent strata

[51] Ibid. 43–4.

crushes the pillars and the coal. Both distortions rendered the coal either impossible, or expensive and dangerous, to mine, though crush is generally thought to have caused the greatest damage. Extensive damage could also be caused to the surface through subsidence.

The attractions to unscrupulous lessees of mining with small pillars are too obvious to need stressing, and hewers working on piece-rates might likewise be tempted to 'rob' the pillars in order to attain their target output more easily. Consequently, the leaving of sufficient pillars was always a central concern of owners and employers. From an early date leases frequently contained clauses requiring the lessees to mine the colliery in a workmanlike manner.[52] One contract made in 1424 between the bishop of Durham and William de Eure required the latter to 'govern the same mines well and properly in all points according to that which the custom of mines of coals demands', and to make amends for any damage. By the seventeenth century leases contained the specific injunction to 'leave sufficient pillars standing . . . for bearing up of the ground'.[53] Likewise, we find comparable injunctions upon hewers in many of the sets of surviving colliery orders. At Haigh the precise dimensions of the hewers' rooms were laid down, with pillars to be not less than 'a yard and sixteen inches on the side. Nor under a yard and a half and sixteen inches on the ends.' Though fines of a few pence were levied for most breaches of the rules, that for hewing coal from the pillars or for any other action which weakened them was 40s., with further punishment at the discretion of the justices of the peace at the next session.[54]

On the other hand the leaving of excessive pillars could severely diminish the amount of coal which could be won. Whereas one witness in a trial concerning the competence with which lessees had worked Harraton colliery on the Wear maintained that it 'has been well and carefully wrought and sufficient pillars left', another proclaimed that walls and pillars had been left 'such as have never been left in any colliery in Durham so that a thousand chalders of coal might be wrought out of the walls and pillars and yet sufficient be left to support the roof thereof'.[55] It is not possible to date the introduction of the

---

[52] See below, Ch. 7(iv).

[53] DUDP Church Commission box 204, 244139; DUPK, register 14(N), fo. 121ᵛ.

[54] WiRO Haigh Colliery Orders, D/DZ A13/34, fos. 4ᵛ-5ᵛ. Roger Bradshaigh recorded that 'a little below the middle Halecroft there is about 30 drifts of cannel standing which was long since left (as is supposed) when that pit was overthrown by reason of the slenderness of the pillars, about the pit eye, which caused afterwards these strict Articles which are now in force in this book' (fo. 10ᵛ).   [55] PRO E. 134, 14 Charles II, Trinity no. 6.

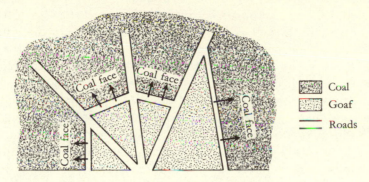

Fig. 6.4. Longwall working

practice of systematically thinning the pillars and walls when a heading had been worked out. This was done by teams which retreated to the eye of the shaft, leaving the roof to collapse in a controlled fashion after they had departed and the workings had been abandoned.

The deeper the workings, other things being equal, the thicker the pillars that were needed to support the weight of the superincumbent strata. Thus in the deep collieries of the north-east we have the massive pillars reported by J.C., comprising four of the seven yards of every winning, which resulted in more than half of the coal being left underground. The dimensions of the pillars were clearly one of the prime determinants of the amount of coal which could be raised from each colliery, and were thus a major ingredient in the productivity of the whole industry. Sadly, technological improvements in this vital area are largely hidden from our view. Yet it would be mistaken to assume that they did not occur. On the contrary, it is plausible to assume a substantial accretion of knowledge and expertise in the methods of winning coal as the industry expanded, and this is lent ample support by the existence of highly valued viewers and mining experts, and the widespread recognition that hewers acquired considerable skill and expertise which could be passed on from region to region.

In some senses longwall mining marked a technical advance over pillar-and-stall, and it was eventually to supersede the latter almost everywhere, because it normally resulted in far less coal being left underground.[56] In the pure longwall method a broad length of seam was

---

[56] Concise descriptions of the longwall system are contained in *HRCM* 44–8 and Galloway 1898, i. 203–4.

worked by a number of hewers simultaneously, and all the coal extracted, with no coal pillars left behind to support the roof. Yet there were limitations, as well as disadvantages, in this system which help to explain the dominance of pillar-and-stall and its variants into the nineteenth century. For instance, the amount of auxiliary labour required underground was considerably increased, because the roof still needed to be supported as the coal-face advanced. First it was propped with timber, and then by walls of small coal waste and stone, called 'gob' or 'goaf', which were built in the space left by the retreating seam. Large quantities of sturdy punchwood were consumed, and a ready supply of cheap timber was therefore essential. Moreover, such propping was not as effective as the sturdy pillars and walls of coal left by the pillar-and-stall process, and longwall was best suited to locations where the coal was roofed by solid rock. As it was practised before the end of the seventeenth century, longwall was also better suited to relatively shallow seams, but even then it caused more damage to the surface through subsidence than pillar-and-stall.

The longwall method was previously known as the 'Shropshire system', and it is reasonable to assume that it was widely practised in the great drift collieries of the Severn Gorge. There are signs that it was also used in the seventeenth century in parts of the south-west and in the West Midlands. But it is not always easy to tell which system was in use in any particular colliery. For example, the two historians who have studied the abundant records of Griff colliery in Warwickshire are undecided whether it was mined in the seventeenth century using pillar-and-stall or longwall. Perhaps a further clue is offered by the fact that in 1703 Sir John Newdigate went to considerable lengths to attract colliers from Shropshire to Griff.[57]

As we have stressed before, in the majority of collieries practice may not have conformed closely to theory. In Derbyshire and Yorkshire by the later seventeenth century a type of small-scale longwall, or large-scale pillar-and-stall, had begun to be practised.[58] It was called 'narrow work', later to be known also as the 'Yorkshire system', within which the coal was cut by a small group of hewers at short faces. The growth of 'narrow work' was a technical improvement, in that in certain conditions it enabled more coal to be won than under conventional pillar-and-

[57] White thesis 1969, 120, 123–4; Grant 1979, 14–15.

[58] Benson and Neville (eds.) 1976, 25. During the 18th cent., where the condition of the roof permitted, longwall working, or variants of it, advanced in Yorkshire at the expense of pillar-and-stall (Flinn, 1984, 86–7).

stall working. It may not fit easily into the hard and fast divisions frequently applied to early mining methods, but narrow work fits easily into the more pragmatic and workmanlike context of flexible methods adopted by skilled men to suit a miscellany of working environments.

iv. Hewing and hauling

In collieries all over Britain the first stage in the production of coal consisted of a single hewer hacking and hammering at the face, in the cramped and dusty confines of his room, stall, or board. He used a small range of tools—picks, hammers, and wedges—specially adapted to suit his task.[59] The pick or mattock was commonly short-shafted and with a small head, for working in confined spaces, as was the hammer or maul used for driving in the wedges. The hewer would begin by making cuts in the seam using his pick. Often his first assault would be to undercut the seam by hacking out a space running parallel to the floor. This was a job requiring skill, athleticism, and stamina, for the hewer had to work lying on his side. When this had been done over an appropriate distance and depth, he would then make a series of vertical cuts along the face of the coal, thereby cutting the coal on three sides. Then the hewer drove his wedges into the coal and, sometimes with the assistance of a crowbar, brought it down in as large pieces as he could. He would then proceed to take slice after slice of the coal until he reached the top of the seam. In thick seams he might have to stand upon piles of small coal and waste to reach up to the roof. Wherever possible headings were driven in such a direction as to position the hewer's room across the cleats and cleavages of the coal-seam, so as to facilitate the splitting action of his wedges. With soft coal much of his work might be accomplished by pick alone.[60]

Great coal was far more valuable than small coal, which was sometimes scarcely worth the trouble of hauling to the surface. Accordingly, hewers were paid at different rates for getting great and small coals, and

---

[59] For contemporary lists of hewers' tools see *inter alia*: J. S. Moore (ed.), *Goods and Chattels of Our Forefathers: Frampton Cotterell and District Probate Inventories, 1539-1804* (1976), 55 n. 32; Grant 1979, 18; GRO, inventory goods of Anthony Andrewes of Littledean, 17/14/1702; J. Lister, 'Coal Mining in Halifax', in W. Wheater (ed.), *Old Yorkshire* (1885), 279–80; *HRCM*, app., pl. 5, fig. 1. Owen (*Pembrokeshire*, 90–1) remarked 'their tools about this work is pickaxes with a round poll, wedges and fledges to batter the rocks that cross their work'.

[60] The details of the hewers' task did not much excite contemporaries, but see e.g. James Twyford, 'Observations on Cole works' (quoted in Bulley 1952, 66); Dudley, *Metallum Martis* (1665), quoted in Galloway 1898, i. 192.

the differential could be very wide indeed.[61] Great skill was required to maximize the production of coal in large lumps, and this was one of the elements which placed good hewers at a premium. The productivity of hewers and, since they were normally paid on a piece-rate basis, their earnings also, were closely tied to the ease with which the coal could be worked. Some differences in the hardness of cutting coal were common to all hewers in a colliery, and were taken into account when fixing the rate for getting a given quantity. Others stemmed from the location of the particular stall, for some places were inevitably more difficult to work than others. In larger collieries it became common for hewers to be allocated to their places by overmen, while sometimes greater fairness was assured by the systematic rotation of places or the drawing of lots.

The efficiency with which coal was moved from the face to the surface was a crucial component of the productive capacity of a colliery, and of its profitability. The hauling of coal underground often absorbed more labour than any other activity.[62] It did so primarily because hauling relied exclusively upon human muscle-power; no horses were used. In some respects the methods of transportation employed underground barely qualify for inclusion in a section devoted to technology. With scarcely an exception coal was either carried or pushed in baskets; wheeled carts or trolleys were very rarely employed, and it is at the very end of the seventeenth century that the first mention of underground rails occurs. The major reason for the extremely primitive modes of transport was quite simply the migratory nature of almost all mining and the short duration of the roads and levels. When mining relatively shallow seams, it was usually less costly to sink new shafts than to permit long hauls from the face to the eye. It was only when roads had a long life that it was economic to smooth or board their floors, or to lay rails to facilitate the movement of coal.

Most primitive of all was the humping of coal in baskets on the back. For this we have Owen's description of boys stumbling stooped along the passageways of Pembrokeshire pits,[63] and the many poignant eighteenth- and nineteenth-century accounts of the age old drudgery endured by women and girls, usually the wives and daughters of hewers, in the drift or 'edge-mines' of east Scotland.[64] Here the coals, weighing

[61] See below, Ch. 11(iii).
[62] For the ratios of hewers to putters see below, Ch. 11(i).
[63] *Pembrokeshire*, 90.
[64] Duckham 1970, 94–101; Ashton and Sykes 1964 edn., 24–5.

perhaps 70–100 lb. were carried on their backs in baskets called creels, along the underground roadways and then out of the pit by means of a series of ladders. The carrying of baskets was unavoidable when the coal had to be transported from the pit by means of ladders or stairs, but when the coal was wound up a pit shaft a somewhat more efficient means of transport could be used. This consisted of loading the coal at the face into corves, which were then pushed or pulled, or propelled by a combination of both, to the eye of the shaft. This process went under a variety of names, 'putting' in the north-east, 'trailing' in the north-west, 'hurrying' in Yorkshire, and was frequently undertaken by boys and young men.

The precise structure of the corf, and the means of propelling it, were adapted to suit the conditions of each colliery. The best description, almost inevitably, comes from the large north-eastern collieries around 1700. Here the corves were made of young rods of hazel, with saplings of oak, ash, or alder, some three inches thick, providing the corf-bow. They were loaded on to a sled, and then filled with coal; the sled was then propelled by two or three putters, one or two behind and one in front.[65] In many other collieries there is reason to believe that the corves themselves were pushed or dragged from the coal-face to the eye, and would thus have needed to have been appropriately sturdy. Some were more like boxes than baskets, although there is no indication that, before the eighteenth century, they were commonly shod with iron. While on a sled, corves were spared the heavy pounding given out by the floor and sides of the roadways, but even so they were 'subject to clash and beat against the shaft sides' as they were wound up. The manufacture of corves was clearly a skilled business, for since the corf was the usual unit of measurement of output it was essential that they were made and maintained to a consistent dimension, as well as able to endure their daily pounding. In larger collieries a highly paid full-time corver would be employed for making and repairing, while in smaller collieries corves would be purchased and the services of a corver used when necessary.

With the exception of the introduction of railed-ways in the Neath mines of Sir Humphrey Mackworth around 1700, the movement of coal underground does not appear to have experienced any spectacular improvements in technology. Yet, once again it would be unwise to ignore the possibility of piecemeal, pragmatic advances in such humble areas as the design of corves and the use of sleds. Local weights and measures are a minefield even for the wary, but there does seem to be a

[65] J.C., *Compleat Collier*, 35, 36.

clear relationship between the size of the corf and the means by which it was transported. When the loaded corf had to be handled by a single man or boy its dimensions and weight were strictly limited, but larger sleds and teamwork allowed them to rise. In the mid-sixteenth century at Carterthorne corves contained a mere five or six pecks, though a number of the bishop of Durham's mines at the turn of the fifteenth and sixteenth centuries had corves of ten pecks, amounting perhaps to more than two hundredweight of coal. The corf used in the same county in J.C's time had a capacity of fourteen or fifteen pecks.[66] When technology is at such a primitive level even the most rudimentary improvements can lead to significant increases in labour productivity.

v. Drainage

There were precious few pits, even among the very shallowest, which did not have water to contend with, and the draining of workings was frequently among the most costly and taxing tasks which the producer had to face. It is estimated that around a third of all rainfall percolates through the surface soil to the strata below, and this water seepage mingled with underground springs and feeders and found its way around impermeable strata and through permeable strata into shafts and workings. The amounts of water that had to be coped with were variable and their incidence unpredictable, and flooding was one of the major causes of the failure of collieries and of the bankruptcy of their owners and operators.[67] The technology available for dealing with water in mines often proved excessively expensive, and more than occasionally also proved inadequate for the task. The ingenuity of generations of miners and inventors produced a miscellany of devices for draining pits, but they all had to follow one of two basic procedures. Water could be drained off via a downwards sloping channel, using simple gravity, or it could be lifted out.

   Both sets of procedures rested upon ancient principles, and both were early employed in British coal-mines. When a mine at Cossall (Notts.) was leased in 1316, the lease specified that the lessees were to repair the gutter called 'le sowe' at their own expense, and the accounts kept of the productive Glamorgan mine at Kilvey around 1400 reveal an elaborate network of conduits, gutters, and sluices.[68] Both Kilvey and Cossall were substantial undertakings for the fourteenth century, but

---

[66] Nef 1932, ii. 374; DUDP Church Commission box 79; Flinn 1984, 461.
[67] See below, Ch. 10(i).   [68] HMC *Middleton*, 88; Rees 1949.

soughs, adits, and gutters were by no means confined to the largest of medieval mines; they were often essential even to small-scale scratchings close to the surface. From a multitude of references it is apparent that modest diggings often depended upon the construction of extensive soughs and gutters for their continued existence. Doubtless a good proportion of the 'aqueducts', 'adits', 'gutters', and suchlike referred to in medieval and sixteenth-century documents were surface trenches and ditches rather than underground tunnels, but we may be certain that true underground soughing was also widely practised. The fifteenth-century leases of the bishop of Durham, for example, make frequent reference to 'watergates', the north-eastern word for an underground sough. As a priority, lessees were enjoined 'to keep, maintain and sustain' watergates, and to leave them 'well and properly made and repaired' at the end of the term. William de Eure was assured that if he incurred 'any great and considerable costs in making any new watergate' the bishop would allow him half the expense.[69]

Simple man-powered windlasses were the main mechanical means of drainage in early times, but in 1486-7 the monks of Finchale priory (Durham) spent £9. 15s. 6d. on the construction of a horse-driven pump at a pit in Moorhouseclose.[70] Machines and soughs both had their particular advantages as well as limitations, and it was common in the larger mines of the later sixteenth and seventeenth centuries to drain water by a medley of pumping engines and soughs and gutters. Soughs and engines were both costly, but in different ways. The sough, if it had to be driven more than a few hundred feet, consumed large quantities of time and money in its construction, but once it was finished it was reliable, cheap to maintain, and durable. Drainage engines, on the other hand, were relatively cheap to build—few in the seventeenth century cost more than £100—but costly to operate unless they could be harnessed to water or wind. Horses were expensive to purchase and feed, and their working lives often proved short. Moreover, all engines were unreliable, and those which depended upon the flow of water or the wind were the least reliable of all.

Much depended upon the volume of water to be drained, and the expected life of the colliery, but few long-term operators chose not to construct a sough when soughing was permitted by the terrain. Whenever possible the sough would be driven to meet the seam at the lowest

[69] A number of these leases are conveniently located together in DUDP Church Commission box 204. For collections of other references see Moller thesis 1933, 47–9 and Simpson 1909–10, 587–8.   [70] Raine (ed.), *Finchale*, pp. ccclxxiv, ccclxxxviii, cccxci.

possible point, in order to render the coal-face dry and to permit the maximum amount of coal to be worked 'up the dip'. If practical, it would drain freely into a stream or river. Success in achieving these objectives depended upon the skill of the soughers to excavate a tunnel from the chosen spot on the surface, to meet up with the coal workings, and permit the free flow of water. In these considerable feats of engineering, which sometimes incorporated extremely fine tolerances, they were usually aided only by a simple water-level and plumb-line, although the quadrant was gaining acceptance by the late seventeenth century.[71]

Soughing could not always provide a cheap and universal remedy, for it depended upon an ability to break the surface a reasonable distance from, and at a level below, the place where coal was to be worked. It was therefore most easily and successfully undertaken in hilly districts. Most British coalfields had hilly districts within them, and undulating terrain abounded in the coalfields of the north-east, Cumberland, Derbyshire, Somerset, South Wales, and Forthside. Many collieries could hope, therefore, to be drained by a sough of a few hundred feet in length, and the ability to sough cheaply and conveniently was a major factor in location and profitability. Though, as George Owen testified, even relatively short distances underground could prove costly: 'a level as they call it, which is by a way digged underground, somewhat lower than the work, to bring a passage for the water, this is very chargeable and may cost sometimes £20 and oftentimes more.'[72] Even in hilly districts far more substantial excavations were often unavoidable. The sough could not always be permitted to discharge its water at the point where it first broke the surface. The volume of water draining from a series of pits might be such as to threaten to flood adjacent farmlands, unless it were channelled into a suitable watercourse. The compliance of neighbouring landowners might not be forthcoming, especially if they owned rival collieries.[73] Moreover, the deeper the working the greater the distance the sough had to be driven to break the surface. The combination of deeper mining and rich but inconveniently sited coal-seams could result in soughs of prodigious length and cost even in hilly locations, while in flatter terrain soughs, if they were feasible at all, were inevitably often of great length.

---

[71] HRCM 237–8.

[72] Pembrokeshire (1603), 90. See pl. 2b.

[73] The outflow from soughs was a common source of dispute between landowners and colliery operators.

Wollaton colliery was not well sited for ease of gravity drainage, but a sough was indispensable and there is the first confirmation of the existence of one there in the late fifteenth century. A new sough was constructed in 1509, but as the colliery expanded and the location of mining shifted this too eventually proved inadequate. Such were the drainage requirements of the colliery that Henry Willoughby in his will, proved in 1549, envisaged spending £1,000, more or less, on soughing. In the event when a new sough was built a few years later it cost far in excess of this figure, and ran for a distance of about a mile. Its length was greatly enhanced by the need, when it finally broke surface, to extend it over meadows and fields, under the River Leen, and over the Beston to Nottingham highway, before it was permitted to flow into the River Leen at Alwell Close, where apparently it could at last discharge without fear of flooding.[74] Soughs of comparable dimensions, while by no means common, can sometimes be found serving other large collieries. Indeed a single sough could sometimes be made to serve a number of collieries. Sir John Lowther began in 1663 to drive a water-course from Pow Beck westwards along the St Bees valley past Green-bank to Howgill and the Burnt (or Bannock) Band seam. By the time it was completed it ran for over 1,800 yards, and the Bannock Band surface water level remained in use until the present century. Howgill was a massive colliery with an output of around 20,000 tons at the close of the seventeenth century.[75] Not so Aspull (Lancs.), which struggled to exceed 2,000 tons annually in 1624–5. Nevertheless it was claimed, doubtless with exaggeration, that Aspull's sough had cost £3,000 to construct in the early seventeenth century.[76]

There is a detailed and most informative survey of the Main Sough of Haigh colliery (Lancs.).[77] In it Roger Bradshaigh chronicled with loving care its length: 'being in all 7 score roods and one yard, at eight yards to the rood'; the pits sunk to service its construction and maintenance: '10 pits sunken, one with another being three yards wide, and the depth one with another coming to 300 yards and two foot'; and the form of its construction throughout its length: 'from the first to the second pit 14 roods, the pit being 16 yards deep, the sough betwixt being all posted and paved with timber upon the one side and the earth cast below'. He also gave instructions on its maintenance: 'must be often looked at',

[74] Smith MS, 65–70.
[75] Wood 1988, 7; *VCH Cumberland*, ii. 359.
[76] Langton 1979a, 73; Stanning (ed.), *Royalist Composition Papers*, 34–5, 44.
[77] WiRO, Haigh Colliery Orders, D/DZ A13/34, fos. 8ʳ–10ʳ.

'take care often', and 'let there always be care taken to appoint some persons to go quite through the Main Sough every two months at least to prevent decay in time that the benefit of my 16 years labour, charge and patience (which it pleased God to crown with success for me and my posterity) may not be lost by neglect'. In this single document we can observe the pre-eminent position which a sough often occupied in the working of a colliery, the time it took to build, the capital it absorbed, and the absolute necessity of keeping it in a good state of repair.

Basically, soughs were long in construction because only a single man could dig and hack at any one time. The Haigh sough was exceptionally broad being, according to Langton, in some places as much as six feet by four feet. Usually they were cut far smaller to save money and lessen the chances of roof falls. In order to provide ventilation and to facilitate the removal of waste, pits had to be sunk to the sough at intervals, in itself a lengthy and costly exercise. An unusual survival of a document detailing progress in the making of a sough at Farnworth colliery (Yorks.) throws much further light. An agreement had been concluded between the colliery owner and two workmen, and work on the sough was begun on 6 April 1657. By 6 April 1662 the men had driven 540 yards, an average of a little over 100 yards a year. According to the terms of the original contract the men had received £400 in advance, and five years later they had between 400 and 640 yards still to go, depending upon whether they kept to the owner's land or took a short cut across John Dixon's land.[78]

A sough was as close to a permanent piece of fixed capital as anything to be found in coalmining, and it was usually designed to drain a colliery for a very long time. As the location of the coal-face shifted, so additional channels were cut to connect with the sough. Sometimes coal would be worked below the level of the sough, and water would have to be raised to its mouth. Such a necessity lay behind the otherwise obscure references which sometimes occur to hand-bailing underground, and to wooden scoops purchased for this purpose.[79] Moreover, it was not always possible for the sough to be ideally located, such precision took great skill on the part of both the surveyor and the soughers, and the end result was not invariably completely satisfactory. Finally, there were many collieries where soughing was not cost effective, or where it was never likely that a sough by itself could lay a

[78] BoRL Bradford ZBR/5/1/2.
[79] e.g. at Wollaton in 1549 regular payments were made for 'ladyng the leyvell water' (Smith MS, 66).

whole colliery dry. For these and for a multitude of additional reasons, water sometimes needed to be raised from a pit.

In seeking the best means of raising water from his pits the early modern colliery owner had a wide and often perplexing array of choices before him, encompassing combinations of four sources of power—man, horse, wind, and water—and three broad species of machine. One species was the windlass, generally called a gin when it was worked by horses; the second included various types of chain pumps; and the third, much rarer, was the piston-driven vacuum pump, the antecedent of the steam pump. There are instances where, as at Ewloe colliery in Henry VIII's reign, water was carried out of the pit in buckets strapped to the backs of workmen,[80] but in practice this was extremely rare and, though a very great deal of drainage was effected by manpower throughout our period, it was through the medium of hand-driven windlasses rather than pure muscle alone. The windlass and the gin were developed early and persisted in use until recent times. Even the shallowest of shafts benefited from a windlass, the simplest of which would comprise a horizontal axle set across the mouth, to which a handle and rope were attached, and by which baskets full of coal and waste would be wound to the surface. This contraption could easily be adapted to wind up buckets, barrels, or tubs filled with water. When the quantities of water that needed to be removed were small, or the incidence of water intermittent, this method could serve well enough. Moreover, the humble windlass enjoyed substantial technological enhancement as the sixteenth and seventeenth centuries progressed. Iron axles might be substituted for wooden, or broad drums fitted in their stead to allow greater weights to be lifted. Two handles might be fitted to permit two men to work it at a time, while the fitting of a transverse axle allowed it to be wound by rotating a horizontal wheel, which could be pushed by still more men. With a stronger axle and greater motive power, heavier weights could be lifted and two large barrels might be operated at a time, one of which was wound up full while the other descended empty.[81]

Nor, even in the larger collieries before the eighteenth century, were manpowered machines easily superseded, and some were far more sophisticated than the simple windlass. In this connection a contract made in 1692 between Benjamin Wood of the City of London, gent., and

[80] Nef 1932, ii. 449.
[81] Details of the construction of windlasses can be gleaned from the parts purchased to repair and improve them, recorded in colliery accounts. For illustrations of windlasses in use in Germany and countries to the east and south see Agricola, *De Re Metallica* (1556), 171–200.

William Robins, gent., of Bilston (Staff's) is instructive. Wood agreed to make an engine 'which being worked by four men at most (except when flood) shall drain the coal-mine' at Bilston. Wood undertook to keep the engine in good repair at his own cost, though Robins was to provide such pumps and chains as Wood required. Robins also contracted to use the engine for at least one year and to pay Wood £8. 15s. 0d. a quarter from the time the mine began to yield coal. If the engine could be worked by two men only, then Robins was to pay £10 quarterly. For this drudgery the workmen were to be paid the lowly wage of 4s. each per week.[82]

Since horses are capable of generating as much energy as ten men, it was essential that they were able to be harnessed to that most intractable of tasks, the drainage of coal-mines. Horse-driven drainage machinery was in use in mines on Tyneside and Wearside in the late fifteenth century. The 'horse-pompe' at Moorhouseclose has already been noted, and in 1492–3 two iron chains were purchased 'for drawing coals and water out of the coalpit' at Whickham. But it does not seem likely that they were for the construction of a true chain pump; the reference to the chains being used for the lifting of coal makes this highly improbable. It must be presumed that this was an early, doomed, attempt to use chains in a windlass or gin, and there are no further references to chains in subsequent Whickham accounts.[83] Horse-driven machinery was almost certainly rare at this time, and we have to wait until 1544 for a further unequivocal reference in the admittedly scanty surviving records of north-eastern coalmining. In this year Henry Pauxton and William Crosbie were paid £10 for making 'a horse pump for lifting water from Rainton mine'.[84]

The windlass was relatively easy to adapt to the horse. An engine with a horizontal wheel or drum could be turned by horses following a circular path around it. The most common form was the cog-and-rung gin which, like the windlass, had a drum placed across the mouth of the shaft, upon which the rope-roll was wound. One end of the drum had 'rungs' or bars on it which were turned by the cogs or teeth of a larger horizontal wheel, which in turn was rotated by a horse or two. On a pit at Mostyn colliery (Flintshire) in 1675 stood such 'a horse-engine of substantial timber, and strong iron-work, on which lay a trunk or barrel for winding the rope up and down of above a thousand pound of weight,

[82] WSL Hand Morgan (Robins), uncatalogued 34/6/1.

[83] Galloway 1898, i. 66–7; DUDP Church Commission box 79, 189532, 190027.

[84] Fowler (ed.), *Abbey of Durham*, 722.

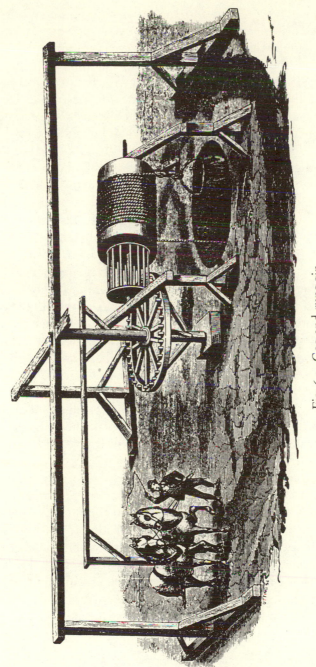

Fig. 6.5. Cog-and-rung gin

... one bucket going down and the other coming up full of water'.[85] Such simple devices were often favoured, even when more powerful but complex machines were available. They were ubiquitous in British coal-mining before the eighteenth century, and continued to be used for centuries afterwards. They were well suited to shallow shafts with short lives, for they were easy to dismantle and to reassemble. They could double as winding gear for coal and colliers, and, perhaps most important of all, they were cheap to build and maintain, and reliable in operation.

The whim-gin was, however, superior in a number of ways to the cog-and-rung gin, providing an easier draught for as many as four horses at a time, but like the steam engine it came too late to have much impact upon the industry within the period covered in this volume.[86] With a whim-gin the drum with its rope-roll was built horizontally on to a vertical axle placed some distance clear of the mouth of the shaft; the ropes being connected to pulleys hung on a frame over the shaft. The mouth of the shaft was thus left clear, and additional horses could be added as desired without fear of obstruction. Although in the course of the eighteenth century many whim-gins were replaced for drainage purposes by steam engines, they continued to be widely used into the nineteenth century for winding coal and colliers, and near Eckington, south-east of Sheffield, one remained in use until the colliery closed in 1943.[87]

The persistence of simple portable machinery, a high proportion of it man-powered, was well-suited to the small-scale and migratory nature of much coalmining throughout our period. Even when pits were planned as longer-term operations, the encountering of an unexpectedly large flow of water might well lead their proprietors to abandon them and sink anew elsewhere. Yet drier mines were not invariably on hand, and some wet collieries offered prospects of high profits by virtue of their proximity to markets. Moreover, as production soared the richer and more favourably sited collieries inevitably employed deeper shafts, and the deeper the workings the wetter they were likely to be. Windlasses and horse-gins had their limitations, most notably in the relatively small quantities of water that they could raise in any given period of time using only two receptacles, even when the horses were

---

[85] *PTRS* xii. 899.

[86] Horse-engines are described in most of the standard works on coalmining, but see in particular Atkinson 1960.

[87] Flinn 1984, 99–100; F. D. Woodall, *Steam Engines and Water Wheels* (Stoke, 1975), pl. 4, p. 10.

kept at a trot.[88] When larger volumes of water had to be dealt with a first option was to sink a separate water pit into which the water from adjacent working pits would drain. The gin could then be devoted exclusively to the raising of water. When there were still larger quantities of water to drain, additional water pits served by gins might be sunk. Well-sited and sufficiently deep water pits were able to keep dry a succession of working pits and the headings driven from them. A further option was to install a pumping-engine.

A dazzling array of pumping-machines confronted the inquisitive coal-owner. Mining was, of course, far from being the only province where drainage machines and pumps were utilized. For centuries they had been used for irrigation and land drainage, for pumping water from rivers for domestic and industrial uses, and for draining ships. Many of these pumps in turn shared the technology of mills, with their wheels, cogs, gears, and transverse axles. The potential benefits of borrowing more advanced technology from other fields, from metalliferous mining, and from overseas was well appreciated by many engaged in British coalmining, and a number of case-studies are described below. Agricola, who had illustrated and described many species of drainage machines, was a prime source of ideas, and Sir Francis Willoughby combed his treatise at the close of the sixteenth century. Such was the importance not only of the coal industry but of the necessity to pump water in a multitude of situations, that a veritable legion of inventors and engineers sought to create better engines, or introduce them from overseas. Inventors and salesmen enthusiastically purveyed their wares, often constructing working models of their engines to persuade potential customers of their efficiency. One such engineer, who sought to solve the problems Sir Francis was encountering at Wollaton, claimed in a document ascribed to 1610 but probably earlier that 'there are models to be seen of all the waterworks that are of any worth or value in Italy, Germany or the Low Countries'.[89]

Chain pumps came in two basic types: the bucket and chain and the rag and chain. The former had wooden or leather buckets fixed to the chain at regular intervals, which filled with water as they hit the sump mouth-down at the pit bottom, and then ascended upright. At the top of

---

[88] The gin at Howgill in 1695 ordinarily raised about 40 tubs an hour, with 50 the maximum (Hainsworth (ed.), *Sir John Lowther*, 219.)

[89] Smith MS, 83–4; HMC *Middleton*, 174–5. For further details of inventors and inventions see, *CSPD 1629-31*, 393, 396, 483, 552, 554; *CSPD 1671*, 380; *CSPD 1691-2*, 14. Nef 1932, i. 243 contains many further references.

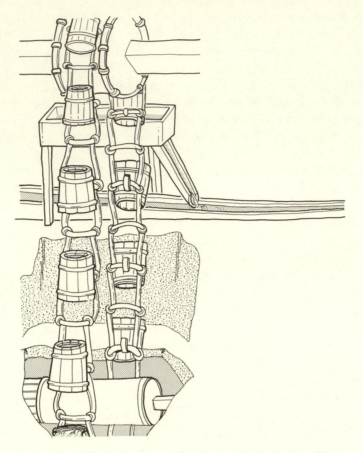

Fig. 6.6. Bucket-and-chain pump (after Agricola, *De Re Metallica* (1556))

the shaft the buckets would be automatically inverted and their contents thrown into a trough, to be run off via a channel to an appropriate spot well clear of the site, so that water would not percolate back through the surface into the workings below. The chain itself often revolved over cogs which slotted into those links which had no buckets attached to them.[90] In the rag-and-chain pump the chain in its ascending section was enclosed in a hollow pipe, which extended from the mouth of the shaft down into the sump at the pit bottom. At intervals along the chain were fixed a series of precisely fashioned attachments, of a size and shape

[90] A later version is illustrated in Galloway 1898, i. 158.

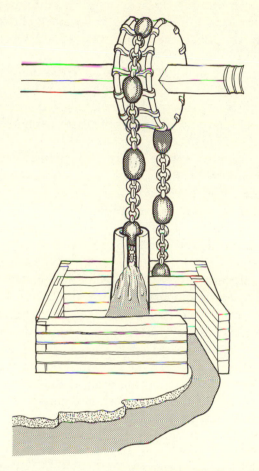

Fig. 6.7. Rag-and-chain pump (after Agricola, *De Re Metallica* (1556))

designed to fit snugly the internal dimensions of the pipe. These discs, or suckers as they were called, could be made of metal or of leather stuffed with horsehair or anything else that would make them watertight yet low in friction. Thus, as the chain ascended, each of the attachments trapped a quantity of water which it forced upwards, until at the top it was discharged into a trough and channel to run away. The vacuum pump, a version of which was patented in 1618 by Robert Crump, consisted of a rod attached to a leather-covered piston, enclosed in a pipe. As the piston was raised water was drawn into the pipe to fill the vacuum. The piston was designed to allow water to flow past it on the downstroke, so that once the pump was primed succeeding strokes forced water out of the top of the pipe.[91]

Robert Plot concluded his section on coalmining in his *Natural History of Staffordshire* with the observation that drainage 'engines being so common, and so easy of apprehension, as not to deserve a cut, or the Reader's view; so I have saved myself the expense and him the trouble, both of the one and the other'.[92] It is not necessary to share fully Plot's sentiments in order to appreciate the abundance of contemporary descriptions of all sorts of engines, machines, and contraptions, real and imagined, working and projected. Moreover, since his day they have formed the subject of many investigations, and there are some excellent accounts.[93] Consequently, we shall concentrate upon the drainage of actual collieries, and the machines that were installed and the ways in which they operated. It is fitting to begin with Wollaton colliery, which was run in a highly innovative fashion by the Willoughbys and Huntingdon Beaumont.[94] It provides an excellent and relatively early case-study of the adoption of new drainage technology. Wollaton's great soughs have already been mentioned, but they soon required supplementing by engines. In 1553 two brass sockets were made to order for 'pumping the water out of the pits', and early in 1573 we can observe two gangs of men, at work day and night, turning windlasses bearing 'hogsheads' in the water pits. Later in the same year new pumping machines were under construction: seven stones of English iron were purchased 'for the pumps', followed by payments to labourers and 'pump-makers', including at least six Cornishmen and a pump-maker from Derbyshire. A party of Cornishmen remained at Wollaton until the following June, no doubt to ensure that the pumps were working efficiently and to train the local work-force in their operation and maintenance. The clear inference must be that Wollaton's pumps were based upon those already in use in Cornwall, probably in the tin mines, and in Derbyshire, probably in the lead-mines. The scale of mining at Wollaton, however, soon rendered these new pumps inadequate for the flow of water, and the account books of 1578–9 reveal yet more pumps. This time the technology was drawn from mills, and skilled millwrights were

[91] Nef 1932, ii. 450–1.

[92] Plot, *Staffordshire*, 148–9.

[93] In particular, Galloway 1898, i. 157–8, 168, 178–9; Nef 1932, ii, app. O, 449–51; Griffin 1971, 90–3.   [94] Much of the rest of the paragraph is drawn from Smith MS, 72–81.

employed to make a 'windmill' and a 'watermill'. Close scrutiny of the accounts reveals that the 'windmill' powered a chain of buckets, and that the 'watermill' was actually a horse-driven rag-and-chain pump. A true water-driven mill was, however, soon installed. Despite all this experimental equipment, it is chastening to learn that frequent heavy use was still made of gangs of men turning water by hand, and that in 1610 an observer was able to remark that drainage 'is now found to rest and rely upon the old and usual chain pump, such as are now used in London to force the Thames water to serve their houses'.[95]

Thus all of the major types of drainage engine had been used in Wollaton before the close of the sixteenth century, and what is more they had been driven by all of the forms of power available before the invention of the steam engine. We also see the benefits that were derived from borrowing techniques developed in other branches of mining. So too the advances made at Wollaton were disseminated, although Geoffrey Foxe, a former employee of Sir Francis Willoughby at Wollaton, claimed that the machines installed by him at Griff (War.) around 1600 were unique. Foxe claimed that he 'made a pool or dam to hold water for the continual drawing or draining of the coalmines, and did force a spring forth of his course to maintain the pool with water, and built a gin-house and made both a water mill and a horse mill with engines thereunto belonging which before were never invented'. The owners of the colliery, the Giffords, who were seeking to minimize Fox's expenditure, however, denied their novelty and counter-claimed that the engines did not differ from the 'usual and common works'.[96] Yet, according to Gray, when Huntingdon Beaumont ventured from Wollaton into the north-east he built 'rare engines not known in these parts', which were almost certainly rag-and-chain pumps.[97]

The Willoughbys were undoubtedly innovators, but further evidence of advanced drainage machinery is also forthcoming from large collieries in other coalfields. From Fife, for example, we have John Taylor's detailed description of the 'Egyptian wheel' at Culross:

The sea at certain places doth leak or soak into the mine, which, by the industry of Sir George Bruce is all conveyed to one well near the land, where he hath a device like a horse-mill, that with three horses and a great chain of iron, going downward many fathoms, with thirty-six buckets fastened to the chain, of which eighteen go down still to be filled, and eighteen ascend up to be

[95] HMC *Middleton*, 174-5.
[96] PRO C.2 James I F4/53; Nef 1933, i. 355 n. 3.
[97] *Chorographia*, 20.

emptied, which do empty themselves (without any man's labour) into a trough that conveys the water into the sea again.

Taylor claimed at the time of his visit in 1618 that the wheel had been in operation for around twenty-eight years. In 1590 it had probably been one of the first bucket-and-chain pumps to be installed in a Scottish coal-mine.[98]

A number of proposals were made in Scotland at this time for advanced drainage machines, including a 'pumping machine' invented by John Napier, of logarithm fame, in 1595, and 'an artificial engine or pump' which could be operated by wind, water, horse, or man, invented by Gavin Smith and James Aitchison in 1598.[99] If proof were needed that not all such contraptions were able to make the transition from drawing-board to coal-mine, it is forthcoming from the dispute between Sir James Lundy and James Crawfurd in 1618. According to Lundy, Crawfurd had fled after failing to build a 'horse-mill' for Lundy's coal-heughs 'with forty buckets well dressed and wrought in all things necessary for the drawing of water', which would render the coal-heughs 'dry and empty of water for ganging work'.[100]

It will be obvious by now that, before the invention of the steam engine, technological advance in drainage machines was largely a matter of improving the performance of traditional forms. At the same time, just because the basic designs were already in use, it would be unwise to assume that few significant advances were made. Indeed as the demand for coal continued to grow, so ever greater attempts were made to drain those wet collieries which had high potential for profit. Inevitably this meant an innovative use of drainage machines as well as soughing wherever possible. At Bedworth, seductively close to fuel-starved Coventry, it was claimed in the 1620s that £4,000 had been spent on a new sough and two engines, and that prior to this expenditure, draining the colliery had cost as much as £2,500 a year.[101] One solution to the limited depths at which machines could work, applied later in the century, was to link them in storeys. Lord Lambton's collieries at Lumley Park 'had but one drain of water drawn by two engines, one of three stories, the other of two'.[102] George Sinclair's *Hydrostaticks* details how these multi-storeyed

---

[98] Quoted and discussed in Bowman 1970, 359–62. It would be unwise to accept Lord Dundonald's opinion that the wheel drained to a depth of 'forty perpendicular fathoms'.

[99] Ibid. 360; *RPCS* v. 490; *APS* iv. 176; J. McKechnie and M. MacGregor, *A Short History of Scottish Coal Industry* (Edinburgh, 1958), 42.   [100] *RPC* xi. 301.

[101] *VCH Warwickshire*, ii. 222; Grant thesis 1977, 88.

[102] North, *Life of Francis North*, 134–5.

drainage machines worked in the bishopric of Durham by the sinking of three pits. The first was sunk to the full depth from which the water needed to be drawn, another was sunk close by to about two-thirds of the depth, and a third close by that to a third of the depth. The engine in the first and deepest pit would then raise the water up to the level of the second pit, to which it would be conveyed by a short channel; from the second pit it would be raised and conveyed to the level of the final shaft by another engine and channel. Finally the engine in the third shaft would raise the water to the surface.[103]

Sinclair also marvelled at Sir Thomas Liddell's Ravensworth colliery, where the steep fall of the land, a convenient stream, and an underground river combined to provide the means of an efficient drainage system. Sir Thomas 'procuring a fall of water which may serve the wheels of all the three sinks, hath erected the first upon pillars like a windmill, pretty high above the ground, from which the water falling makes the second go close above ground. And to make the water fall to the third, the whole wheel is made go within the surface of the ground'. Each wheel operated its own chain pump and raised water into a sump from whence it was raised by the next.[104] When the value of a colliery justified it, therefore, prodigious feats of drainage could be accomplished before the advent of steam. It cost Sir Ralph Delaval £2,300, largely 'spent upon engines', to recover his colliery at Seaton Delaval, when it flooded in 1676, but within six weeks of the flood he was raising coal again and a happy man to be doing so.[105]

Expenses like these were, of course, wholly exceptional, but even operating a typical horse-drawn engine was costly. At least four shifts of horses, with a spare or two, were needed to keep each pump in continuous operation, and they ate heartily and had short working lives. Fifty-six pump horses were required to keep the drainage machines of Wollaton turning, while at Bedworth in 1612 sixty horses were employed in draining water out of the pits.[106] Suitable horses cost at least £6 or £7 each in north-east England around 1700, and to pay any less was a false economy, for 'old weak horses (though cheap bought) are soon wrought out or spoiled by such labour'.[107] Even though the rates of pay of 'watermen' or 'wallowers' were low by general colliery standards, the sheer numbers required to keep a windlass going day and

---

[103] *Hydrostaticks*, 298–9.   [104] Ibid.

[105] North, *Life of Francis North*, 138.   [106] *VCH Warwickshire*, ii. 222.

[107] *Compleat Collier*, 32–4; Flinn 1984, 113–14. Unfortunately the expenses of horses were frequently omitted from colliery accounts.

night soon forced up the costs of manual drainage. In the words of Stephen Primatt:

In most collieries in the North they make use of chain-pumps, and do force the same either by horse wheels, tread wheels, or by water wheels; and this they find the surest way for the drawing their water, although the charge of such wheels, for timber, leathers, chains, pumps, and other materials about the same, is very great, and often requires repairing, besides the great charge of men and horses they are daily at.[108]

It was common also to retain the services of an engineer on an annual contract to maintain pumping machinery. Thomas Bowyer of Ravenfield was paid £4 per annum plus materials to maintain the rag-and-chain pump at Hooton (Yorks.), and between 1668 and 1675 the annual cost of pump maintenance at this modest colliery averaged just under £30.[109]

Not surprisingly, therefore, cost-cutting was a priority for coal-owners, and every effort was made to drive pumps by wind or water rather than by horses or men, if at all possible. Drawing water with water doubtless gave great satisfaction, but it depended upon the presence of suitable streams or rivers, or the ability to divert water from them. When suitable water was freely available, however, water-powered pumps did not need to be restricted to large collieries. They were particularly common in Somerset, though even here they could not be universally applied. In 1610 a mine at Stratton was drained by pumps driven by 'the fall of a stream conducted to the same', but a nearby pit flooded by underground springs could not be so drained, because of its height and position.[110] Moreover, surface streams might dry up during drought, while those underground seeped with greater persistence. Attempts to harness the wind posed similar risks, for although potentially available everywhere it could not be relied upon even in the more exposed parts of the country. 'Want of wind, which one would not readily suspect in a country like Scotland', led Sir John Clerk to shun windmills in his own collieries, and J.C. concurred that even in the north-east "tis sure the wind blows not to purpose at all times.'[111] It was a mistake, therefore, to rely exclusively upon wind-driven machinery, and this was rarely done. But the wind was free, and windpumps using up-to-date Dutch engineering were relatively cheap to construct, and so they were often installed as supplements.

---

[108] *City and Countrey Purchaser*, 28–31.   [109] LCA Mexborough MX 295, 296.
[110] Bulley 1952, 70.   [111] Duckham 1970, 77; *Compleat Collier*, 28.

In the great wet collieries it was common to rely upon a profusion of drainage engines, driven by a variety of forces. At Harraton in 1662 there were 'divers engines to wit a tread wheel made by one Matthew Corner, a wind mill made by one Booker, another mill to draw water made by one Mr Sherewen . . . but none of those proved effectual . . . yet . . . there was divers other engines as chain gins and tub gins which are very useful and without which the said colliery could not be wrought'.[112] In 1685 when Lowther finally introduced drainage engines to the Whitehaven pits, he built a cog-and-rung horse-driven gin and a six-sailed windmill pump. Advice given to the earl of Eglinton for expanding his colliery at Montrose in 1664, included plans for a bucket-and-chain pump which could be driven by water or horses, or both at the same time, and between 1686 and 1709 the Newdigates persisted with experiments at Griff colliery to harness both water and wind.[113]

Yet the very profusion of contraptions and the variety of energy sources used to drive them bespeaks a certain desperation. The temptation to share uncritically in the enthusiasm displayed by many academic contemporaries and historians alike for the more imaginative examples of innovative technology must be resisted. Quite simply very many theoretically ingenious contraptions failed to make the transition from paper to pit, while many others failed to perform as promised when they were installed. 'Small models often fail and soon prove defective when they come to work upon heavy and continual weights in greater proportions.'[114] As a consequence those within the industry retained a healthy scepticism. In Primatt's advice to would-be investors in collieries, he counselled them to consider

what engines they use to draw their water with for the convenience of their working; whether they make use of water in any river, and so draw water with water, or whether they draw water with buckets, or hand-pumps, or chain pumps, or whether they make use of tread wheels, or horse wheels, or what other device they have, there being very many devices for that purpose, but very few good for anything.[115]

It was the intention of Primatt's treatise to urge caution upon would-be speculators, but his scepticism finds confirmation in J.C.'s expert report on the north-eastern industry, in which he concluded that the 'engine being wrought with two horses at a time . . . though it be of plain

---

[112] PRO E. 134, 14 Charles II, Trinity no. 6, deposition of William Wilkinson, 'oversman'.
[113] VCH Cumberland, ii. 360; SoRO Whitehill GD 3/11/8; White thesis 1969, 186.
[114] HMC Middleton, 174.   [115] City and Countrey Purchaser, 28–31.

fashion, yet is found by experience to be more serviceable and expeditious, to draw both water and coal, than any other engine we have seen in these parts yet, notwithstanding we have had many pretenders, in many kinds and methods'.[116]

J.C. was referring, of course, to the common cog-and-rung horse-gin which drained by virtue of barrels attached to lengths of rope, and it is a sobering conclusion to a century of frenetic invention. Clearly, all of the drainage machines available to seventeenth-century coal producers had serious limitations. With the variants on the windlass, horsedriven as well as manpowered, the greatest deficiency was the relatively small volumes of water that they could lift, since only two buckets or tubs could be employed, even allowing for the fact that the tubs could be made to carry 60 gallons apiece, and the horses which worked them could be kept at a trot. Chain engines of both major types, with a whole series of buckets or suckers, could lift far greater quantities of water, but when working at any depth the great weight of the laden chain frequently caused it to fracture. When the gin pit at Thomas Gascoigne's colliery near Barwick-in-Elmet (Yorks.) was sunk a further ten feet to a total depth just in excess of sixty feet the water-driven pump 'went with much more difficulty in respect of the great weight of the chain, which if it be not well attended and the hooks and rings made very round and artificially and of the toughest iron will often break'.[117] According to a somewhat later account, 'when a bolt gave way the whole set of chains and buckets fell to the bottom with a most tremendous crash, and every bucket was splintered into a thousand pieces'.[118] Forty yards of necessarily thick iron chain, with half the buckets attached to it full of water, comprised a tremendous weight, but it is clear that pumps with even longer chains were successfully operated before the close of our period. James Twyford reported in his 'Observations' on Somerset coalmining in the 1690s, on a water-driven pump at Paulton which drew about seventeen fathoms (about 100 feet), and another at Stowey which drew twenty-six fathoms (over 150 feet). The mill wheel at Stowey was apparently thirty feet in diameter.[119]

Drainage technology had made substantial progress in the later Middle Ages and the early modern centuries, and most collieries were

[116] *Compleat Collier*, 28.

[117] LCA Gascoigne unlisted vol., fo. 27ᵛ.

[118] Duckham 1970, 79, quoting Robert Bald, *A General View of the Coal Trade of Scotland* (Edinburgh, 1808).

[119] SoRO Hylton DD/HY Kilmersden. The MS contains many technically accomplished diagrams of drainage engines, some based on those used in Holland.

adequately served by a combination of sough and simple engine. Yet the great collieries usually required more, and although relatively inexpensive engines capable of lifting larger quantities of water existed, they were unreliable and, unless they were able to be powered by water, extremely costly to operate. Here if anywhere we have a significant technological restraint upon our industry. As J.C. put it in 1708, standing as he was on the very edge of 'the Steam Age':

> If it would be made apparent, that as we have it noised abroad, there is this and that invention found out to draw out all great old wastes, or drowned collieries, of what depth soever; I dare assure such artists may have such encouragement as would keep them their coach and six, for we cannot do it by our engines, and there are several good collieries which lie unwrought or drowned for want of such noble engines or methods as are talked of or pretended to, yet there is one invention of drawing water by fire, which we hear of, and perhaps doth to purpose in many places and circumstances, but in these collieries here a way, I am afraid, there are not many dare venture of it.[120]

vi. Winding

The raising to the surface of the coal which had been cut was a crucial stage in the production process. In large collieries with extensive headings, accommodating a host of hewers, it was possible for a ceiling to be imposed upon output by the amounts of coal which could be lifted to the surface by a basic winding engine. Yet the great majority of collieries were well enough served by simple devices which were, none the less, relatively efficient in the conditions within which they normally operated. Winding and drainage, as we have already noted, were often performed by the same machine, working alternately at the two tasks, and most of the technology of the two functions was inevitably shared. In the ubiquitous small collieries where production amounted to at most a few tons per day, the winding gear would be flattered to be termed machinery. Celia Fiennes recorded that at Beaudesert (Staffs.), they 'draw up the coals in baskets with a little wheel or windlass like a well'; at pits near Chesterfield she tells us, 'by cords they pull it up'; and in Flintshire she saw 'engines that draw up their coals in sort of baskets like hand barrows which they wind up like a bucket in a well.'[121] For relatively shallow pits where water did not have to be lifted, as at Sheffield Park, a basic pulley and rope worked by a man might serve well

---

[120] *Compleat Collier*, 29.
[121] *Journeys*, 103, 148, 159.

enough. Greater draught was obtained with the same device by harness-
ing a horse to the rope and driving it off in a straight line for a distance
equal to the depth of the shaft; this simple but effective method of lifting
was both widespread and persistent.[122]

Horse-driven gins, mainly of the cog-and-rung type, were essential in
deeper collieries, both to provide the force necessary to lift heavy
baskets from the bottom, and to wind at sufficient speed to raise all that
was produced. For J.C. a good day's work in a north-eastern pit working
at a depth of 60 fathoms was twenty-one scores of corves (perhaps
amounting to some 70 tons), and he estimated that it required at least
eight horses, working two at a time, to draw it to the surface.[123] Some
finely detailed calculations for a cog-and-rung gin to work at thirty-five
fathoms at Dundas in the 1740s is in broad accord with J.C.'s surmises. It
was a handsome machine, very expensive to build at an estimated 120
guineas, which could lift 600 lb. of coal at a time, in addition to the 300
lb. which the rope and the corf weighed. With two horses harnessed to it
and driven 'at the trot', this gin could hoist some 120 tons in a twelve-
hour shift.[124] In order to save the time and expense of unloading, it was
usual, as Celia Fiennes noted, to hook the corves or baskets in which the
coal had been hauled from the face on to the rope. At the surface the corf
would be unhooked and placed on a sledge, to be drawn by a horse to an
appropriate heap of coal, and an empty corf sent down the shaft.

Colliers as well as coal had to be wound up and down the shafts, and
there was little in the way of special equipment to enable them to ride
with safety or comfort. In the shallower pits they simply rode upon the
rope with the aid of a crossbar made by inserting the shaft of their picks
through the strands of the cable.[125] Sometimes they used a noose at the
end of the rope or the corves in which the coal was carried. In the scene
described in 1691 by Guy Meige, the collier attempted to make himself
as secure as possible by getting into the noose 'a leg and knee . . . as far as
the very hip. Thus hugging the rope with one arm, his life wrapped up
with it' he signalled to the driver of the team of horses working the gin
and plunged spiralling downwards, with only his free arm to save him
from being buffeted and scraped against the sides of the narrow shaft.[126]
The journey was little safer in practice than would appear from the

---

[122] Stone 1950–1, 99; Griffin 1971a, 32.
[123] *Compleat Collier*, 32–3.   [124] Duckham 1970, 105–6.
[125] e.g. in 1694 2 colliers were killed at Stretton (Derby.) when they fell off pick shafts inserted
in the haulage ropes while descending (Benson and Neville (eds.) 1976, 7).
[126] *New State of England*, pt. 1. 165.

descriptions we have of it, and the coroners' rolls and colliery records are peppered with fatal accidents caused by men losing their grips, ropes breaking, and rocks or other objects falling down the shafts. In 1673 an elderly collier returning to work in the pit after retirement was killed while being lowered when a piece of wood set above the 'scoop' on which he was riding, in order 'to poise it', slipped out of the rope and struck him.[127]

vii. Ventilation and lighting

Although problems of ventilation tended to increase with the depth of workings, it is mistaken to believe that relatively shallow pits were rarely troubled. From the earliest days of recorded coalmining foul and dangerous air was recognized as a hazard to life and to profits. Tunnelling underground could result, after a sufficient distance had been dug from the eye of the shaft, in a simple lack of fresh air. In primitive undertakings this by itself could bring a cessation to working, but there might also be 'chokedamp' or 'styth' to contend with. One of the earliest mentions of these hazards occurs in a lease of a coal-mine at Cossall (Notts.), dating from 1316, which recognized that work might be interrupted by flooding or by 'le dampe', and when this occurred the lessees were to be excused their rent.[128] Similar clauses were to become standard in north-eastern coalmining leases in the later Middle Ages.[129] Often, as the leases indicate, damp could be a short-lived and intermittent problem, but on occasion it could persist and the mine might have to be abandoned altogether.[130]

Chokedamp is a mixture of carbon dioxide and nitrogen, and it is produced by the slow oxidation of carbonaceous matter, which deprives the air of its oxygen. It must often have been present in relatively low concentrations in poorly ventilated pits, and the colliers working there would have been forced to increase their breathing in compensation, with potential long-term risks to their health. Its presence could often be indicated to the observant collier by the manner in which his candle burned. The lack of oxygen would cause the flame to falter, and when chokedamp was present in substantial concentrations the flame would

---

[127] Trigg 1930–2, pt. 1. 124.

[128] HMC *Middleton*, 88.

[129] e.g., those entered into by bishops of Durham (e.g. DUDP Church Commission box 204, 244148, 244185, 244242, 244244) and earls of Northumberland (e.g. *NCH* ii. 453–4).

[130] Abandonment was not common, but see Moller thesis 1933, 84.

be extinguished, but by the time this occurred the colliers themselves might have lost consciousness.[131]

The solution to the problems posed by stale air and chokedamp was, of course, to improve the circulation of air in the workings. At Railey (Durham) in 1460 a great screen was erected at the mouth of the pit, 'ad removendum ventum ab eodem'.[132] The sinking of additional shafts and connecting headings often had a salutary effect. As we have seen, it became common even in collieries of modest size to sink both a deep and a basset shaft and to work the coal by driving a heading between them. Likewise, the cutting of soughs, normally the preferred method of draining mines, also improved the supply of air, as did the operation of drainage engines and the flow of water. With additional shafts and soughs a measure of natural ventilation could then ensue, occasioned by differences in the temperature between the air in the mine and that outside on the surface. Underground temperatures are normally higher than surface, and during winter months especially the warmer air would be drawn up the deeper of the shafts and the colder air from the surface drawn down the shallower. In summer the temperature in the shallow shaft would usually be higher than in the deeper, so the flow of the current would be reversed. When there was little difference in the temperature of the air above and below ground, however, the current could slow or even cease. Which is why, as was well known at the time, damps were much more likely to occur in warm weather than in cold.[133]

Knowledge of damps and how to combat them was far more advanced in the industry in pre-modern times than has customarily been acknowledged. Most coal-owners and operators were well aware of the beneficial effects upon ventilation of additional shafts, soughs, water pits, and the operation of drainage engines. As Randolph, farmer of Cannock Wood colliery (Staffs.) wrote in about 1602: 'then is there a head to be driven betwixt these two pits being the one distant from the other 60 yards; and this is to be done with some speed least when hot weather commeth the work be hindered by the earth damp.' Almost contemporaneously, when Sir Richard Leveson and Francis Fitton reopened Griff colliery (War.) they sank an 'air pit' in addition to seven

---

[131] A good account of subterranean gases is contained in *HRCM* 270–80. Dr Caius in the mid-18th cent. provided one of the earliest analytical notices of 'unwholesome vapours' in coal-mines (Galloway 1898, i. 108–9).

[132] *VCH Durham*, ii. 325.

[133] Hinsley 1970, 29–30; *HRCM* 126–7. In Pembrokeshire according to Owen 'all times of the year is indifferent for working but the hot weather is worst by reason of sudden damps that happen' (*Pembrokeshire*, i. 91).

coaling pits and a water pit.[134] Natural ventilation could also be assisted by the layout of the workings, with longwall mining allowing freer circulation than pillar-and-stall. Even so the latter could be designed to offer as little restriction as possible to the flow of air. Doubtless the acquisition of expertise was a cumulative process, and in the early eighteenth century J.C. was able to recommend a number of procedures which were taken in north-eastern mines to 'guide' the air underground. Although each hewer carried his own work forwards 'a pretty long way' on his own, he would frequently 'hole, or cut through from one board to another, to carry their air forwards with their works, and to the end or face of their boards'. As for the air, 'the brisker it ranges in the works, the sweeter and safer it is for the miners'.[135]

Other specific measures could also be taken to deal with 'earth damp', and two were introduced at Beaudesert (Staffs.). When the colliery was reopened in 1600 at a greater depth, 6s. 4d. was spent on 'a lamp to keep fire in the pit for assuaging of the earth damp', and 21s. 11d. spent on 'making a device with older [?alder] poles to put away the earth damp'.[136] The lamp was almost certainly a cradle or brazier designed to induce a draught by warming the air, and it is an early mention of a procedure which later was to be widely practised. According to Twyford it was usual in the Newcastle area in the late seventeenth century to lower a grate of cinders into the pits each morning before work began, and Plot maintained that in Staffordshire 'they let down [a fire in] an iron cradle, they call their lamp, into the shaft or bye-pit next to that they intend to work'.[137] At Heanor (Derby.) a colliery inventory of 1647 reveals a 'fire pan', and a 'lamp' was in use at Heath colliery (Derby.) fifty years later. A stronger current still could be generated by building a chimney on top of a special air shaft and making a furnace in it, as was done at Beightonfield (Derby.) in 1700.[138]

An alternative or, as we have seen at Beaudesert, additional ploy, was to invest in a set of hollow wooden tubes, called 'poles', 'pipes', or 'trunks'. At Heanor (Derby.) in March 1655 pipes were borrowed to be hung in the 'wind pit', and at Trowell (Notts.) in May 1653 a bye-pit was sunk 'to set pipes to draw damp'.[139] In order to be effective, pipes would have to be connected to bellows, with the intention of forcing fresh air

[134] StRO Anglesey, D(W) 1734/3/3/254; Grant 1979, 9–15.
[135] Compleat Collier, 44–6.
[136] StRO Anglesey, D(W) 1734/3/3/255.
[137] SoRO Hylton DD/HY, Kilmersden fo. 161; Plot, Staffordshire, 138.
[138] NoRO Charlton of Chilwell, DDCH 35/34–46; Hopkins 1976, 9, 25.
[139] NoRO Charlton of Chilwell, DDCH 35/34–46; NoUL Middleton Mi. Ac.

down into the workings or drawing stale air out. According to Twysden, blowing with a great pair of bellows was carried on for three or four days at a time. Twyford, drawing on Hungarian practices, also suggested that if a board were made to go round the pipes, of a size to block off the shaft, then impure air might be forced out by raising and lowering the device in the shaft.[140]

By the later seventeenth century even men of letters were becoming better informed about subterranean gases, and the Royal Society began to display considerable interest in explosions in mines.[141] Though Robert Plot fancifully divided 'damp' into seven species, including 'peas blossom' and 'smoky', there is much in his lengthy passages on the subject which reveals a sound grasp of the practicalities.[142] A special concern was evolving with firedamp, a gas largely composed of methane which burns readily in air and explosively when in the 4–15 per cent range, particularly with coal-dust. It was produced by the decay of vegetation when the coal-seams were formed, and it is released when the coal is cut as the seams are being worked. The presence of firedamp in excess of about 1.5 per cent could be detected by a blue cap above the flame of the collier's candle, but such timely indications may not have been appreciated at this time and explosions often occurred without warning. Although the incidence of firedamp may increase with the depth of the workings, and it is most frequently encountered below 100 or even 150 feet, fires and explosions afflicted many collieries in our period. The first major explosion is thought to have occurred at Gateshead in 1621, but the underground fire which raged at Coleorton for many years in Henry VIII's reign was probably the result of spontaneous combustion, for which the region is notorious.[143]

The incidence of fires and explosions increased as the seventeenth century progressed, and some were of major proportions. In the fire and flood at Harraton (Durham) in 1647 more than fifty persons were slain.[144] Although few fires and explosions were serious enough to close pits or cause a major loss of life in a single incident, in some 'fiery' collieries there was a constant succession of casualties. Benwell was greatly affected by firedamp in the late seventeenth century, and its owner, Sir Charles Montagu, confessed himself troubled by the frequent

---

[140] SoRO Hylton DD/HY Kilmersden.
[141] See, *inter alia*, *PTRS* i. 44; ix. 391–3, 450–4; xi. 762–6; xii. 895–9.
[142] Plot, *Staffordshire*, 133–46.
[143] Galloway 1898, i. 132; Camden, *Britannia*, ii. 201.
[144] Welford (ed.), *Committees for Compounding*, 389.

accounts which he received 'of scorching the poor men'. Sir John Lowther's Whitehaven collieries were also notoriously fiery; the major cause of Lowther's concern was, however, the frequency with which he was 'put to charges either in the cure or burial' of the victims.[145] Clearly as collieries became ever deeper, major explosions became ever more likely, despite the precautions which were taken to prevent them, and thirty colliers were killed at Gateshead (1705) and sixty-nine at Fatfield, near Chester-le-Street (1708).[146]

With firedamp the naked flames of the colliers' candles posed the greatest danger, but there was little that could be done to make them safer. As pits sank deeper and workings proceeded far from the eye of the shaft all natural light failed, just as the air became fouler. The distance from the shaft to the coal-face in collieries can often be gauged in an approximate fashion from the consumption of candles, which in some accounts was recorded weekly. At Winstanley (Lancs.) in 1678 it was felt necessary to explain that the high expenditure on candles, over £3. 15s., was partly due to the prolonged working of an old pit. When a new pit was sunk soon after, the candle bill fell to £1. 11s. 6½d., 'because near the eye and less occasion for light of candles'. In Somerset, it was reported that in fiery mines the colliers use smaller candles with a single wick, 'and they always place them behind them and never present them to the breast of their work'.[147] Edward Llwyd (1696) recounted how on one occasion colliers at Baglan, near Aberavon, when troubled with firedamp, had enclosed their candles in a lantern, with every crevice stopped with clay and an old garment about it, but had still set off an explosion.[148] The solution had to await the invention of the safety lamp.

Lethal concentrations of chokedamp could often be detected by sending small animals ahead. We hear nothing of the use of birds in our period but in Durham mines, we are told by Roger North, it was 'an infallible trial' to lower a dog down the shaft each morning.[149] For firedamp, failing a good current of air, the most expeditious procedure was to send a 'fireman' into the workings each morning in advance of the colliers, to set off any gas that was there in as safe a manner as possible. Sometimes the damp would gather in the form of a globe which, being lighter than air, would hang from the roof. The fireman with great care

---

[145] NeUL Montagu, 27/12/98 Montagu to Baker; Hainsworth (ed.), *Sir John Lowther*, 418.
[146] *Compleat Collier*, 44; Galloway 1898, i. 232; *PTRS* xxvi. 215.
[147] Bankes 1939, 40–1; Bulley 1952, 69.
[148] Rees 1968, i. 127.
[149] *Life of Francis North*, 135.

would break the globe from a distance using a pole, and sometimes also ropes and pulleys, to disperse the gas. In bad cases the workings would then be purified by draughts engendered by the lighting of fires. The fireman, we are told, should be 'a man of purpose', who would put on rags and soak himself in water. When sensing firedamp he would grovel forward on his belly, holding in one hand a long wand or pole, to which lighted candles were tied. No doubt firemen acquired expertise to combine with their 'resolution', but it was a desperately dangerous way of earning a few extra coppers.[150] The intractability of the task of providing adequate ventilation ensured that firemen continued to be employed throughout the eighteenth century.[151]

[150] See the descriptions in *PTRS* xii. 897–9; Plot, *Staffordshire*, 139; Sinclair, *Hydrostaticks*, 294.
[151] Flinn 1984, 136–7.

CHAPTER 7

Ownership and Enterprise

> I estimate that there is coal in Chelmarsh which I doubt not that I
> will find, which will be worth at least £2,000.
>
> Sir John Weld of Willey (Shropshire), 1631

Throughout the medieval and early modern centuries landed wealth far
surpassed all other forms of wealth, and since the initiative in the exploitation of minerals resided first of all with the owners of the land under
which they lay, it was destined that landowners and the patterns of landownership should be fundamental to the history of coalmining. With
the notable exception of Tyneside, the overwhelming bulk of the enterprise which accomplished the expansion of coalmining, and the capital
which financed it, was provided by rural landowners. But upon close
examination major contrasts are revealed between the attitudes and
responses of the various strata of the landowning hierarchy. How the
land was distributed was therefore of crucial significance, and massive
changes occurred in the course of our period. All statistics must have the
character of very rough estimates, but it is believed that in the mid-
fifteenth century the aristocracy held around 15–20 per cent of all the
land of England, the Church and the Crown between 25 and 35 per cent,
the gentry around 25 per cent, and yeomen and husbandmen the
remainder, amounting perhaps to 20 per cent. By the late seventeenth
century, although little if any change had taken place in the extent of
aristocratic landholdings, those held by the gentry had doubled to
around a half of the whole realm, and the share of yeomen and husbandmen had risen to between a quarter and a third. The gains of the gentry
and yeomen were primarily at the expense of the Church and the
Crown, whose share of the land of England had dwindled to a mere 5–10
per cent.[1] The dissolution of the monasteries, and the expropriation of
the estates of many other religious institutions by the Crown during the
English Reformation played a central role in this redistribution. So too

---

[1] J. P. Cooper, 'The Social Distribution of Land and Men in England, 1436–1700', *EcHR* 2nd
ser., 20 (1967); G. Mingay, *The Gentry: The Rise and Fall of a Ruling Class* (1976), 59.

did the interminable financial difficulties of the Crown which lay behind a perpetual haemorrhaging of royal property on to the market, where it was devoured by the gentry.

The precise determination of the sources of the enterprise and capital which propagated and nourished the booming coal production of the later sixteenth and seventeenth centuries would require both a large and constant sample of collieries, able to be kept continuously in observation in each of the coalfields, and a sufficiently detailed knowledge of local families to enable the hoards of coal-owners, managers, and investors to be placed with confidence into their appropriate socio-economic categories. Such a task, and such knowledge, is sadly far beyond the feasible goals of a national study. None the less, upon such evidence as it has been possible to gather and interpret, we can be certain that landowners provided the overwhelming share of the finance and enterprise which launched and developed the British coal industry, and that from within the landowning classes the initiative and the resources came primarily from the gentry.

The gentry, when opportunities arose, frequently committed themselves wholeheartedly to all forms of industrial activity on their estates, including the mining and smelting of iron and lead. It was not simply that the gentry held a greater share of coal-bearing lands, though that was undoubtedly true, it was that they tended to respond in a far more positive and direct manner than their social superiors to the possibility of mining coal on their estates. Here we touch upon attitudes and behavioural patterns which embrace far more than coal. The degree to which the greater landlords either leased the range of assets which comprised their estates or sought to manage them directly is one of the grand themes of the economic and social history of medieval and early modern Britain. Overall, despite the achievements of the era of high farming in the central Middle Ages, the great landlords were reluctant entrepreneurs, preferring the life of a rentier to that of a farmer. Even though their incomes were threatened by rampant price inflation under the later Tudors and early Stuarts, the aristocracy displayed little desire to run their farms. Innate conservatism, fostered by extreme wealth, combined with distrust of the honesty and efficiency of estate managers and a preference for a predictable income, to encourage them to remain rentiers. By contrast the gentry, especially those of middling and lesser status, were active investors and managers, choosing to live from the sale of the produce of their estates. Thus, when faced with a choice of whether and how to profit from coal reserves upon their lands, the aristocracy and the gentry were likely to pursue different courses.

i. Proprietors and entrepreneurs

The aristocracy and the Church

The long thirteenth century was a golden age of seigneurial enterprise, when the lay and ecclesiastical aristocracies cultivated their demesnes, raised increasing numbers of cattle and sheep, and supplied the market with the produce of their farms. It was also in this era that the mining of coal began in earnest, but the initiatives for this process usually lay elsewhere. It is not possible to discover who was responsible for the opening up and development of the great collieries owned by the bishopric of Durham, but they were in the hands of tenants when our first unequivocal references to them occur in the thirteenth century. Leasing persisted into the later fourteenth century, and it was in 1372 that we first learn of a change in policy, when Nicholas Coke of Newcastle was appointed keeper of the bishop's coals, with responsibility for sales. For some time afterwards the bishop seems to have kept his leading collieries in his own hands, and through the fifteenth century into the early sixteenth direct management was interspersed with leasing. Likewise, both Durham and Finchale priories operated coal-mines in the later Middle Ages. Such direct management should not be viewed in too positive a light, however, for it was generally part of a defensive rather than an entrepreneurial strategy, precipitated by falling rents and a dearth of satisfactory tenants. Moreover, many mines were not run commercially, but as the source of cheap fuel for religious households.[2]

It is not only in the north-east that ecclesiastical estates feature prominently in the formative years of the coal industry, and time and again throughout British coalfields they provide either the first or very early evidence of mining. As, for example, with Nuneaton priory in Warwickshire, the priories of Much Wenlock, Wombridge, and Wigmore, and the abbey of Buildwas in Shropshire, the bishopric of Coventry and Lichfield in Staffordshire, Bolton abbey in Yorkshire, Beauchief abbey in Derbyshire, and Holyrood and Newbattle abbeys in

---

[2] DUDP Church Commission box 204, 244134, 244136, 244182–3; box 79, coal-mine accounts; DUPK Dean and Chapter, *Rotuli de Mineris Carbonum*, 1409–53; Terrar's coal-mine receipts, 1446–53; Bursar's rental and coal-mine account 1437–42; Raine (ed.), *Durham Household Book*, 56–283; Fowler (ed.), *Abbey of Durham*, 708–13; Raine (ed.), *Finchale*, *passim*; Lomas thesis 1973, 134–7.

Scotland. Yet these references, and a multitude more drawn from lay as well as from Church estates, stem overwhelmingly from the activities of the agricultural tenants, from the lessees and licensees of mining rights, and from landlords seeking to supply their own hearths rather than the market.[3] Mining in the Middle Ages was, with few exceptions, a small-scale affair, concerned largely with self-supply or the servicing of the fuel needs of the immediate neighbourhood. The initiative to mine in the early centuries of the industry seems to have come largely from below, from tenants paying small fines to their lords for licence to scratch a few tons from outcrops on the agricultural lands they rented, from freelance labourers seeking to rent a 'pick' to work by the day or week in a mine located on demesne or common land, or, more rarely, from mining adventurers seeking to lease an established mine, or set one up for themselves.

Yet landlords, even if playing the role of rentiers, did not entirely have to lack enterprise. The monks of Durham priory, for example, took great care to reserve the rights to any coal which might be found on the new agricultural tenements that were being created on reclamations at Spennymoor and Hett in the later thirteenth and early fourteenth centuries.[4] Steps were also taken by them to ensure that adequate returns were made from existing coal reserves, and leases were developed with clauses which sought to protect their interests as well as the long-term future of the leased property. On rare occasions great landlords can be found playing the role of industrialist. One of the few large commercial collieries of the Middle Ages, Kilvey in Glamorgan, was being operated by the duke of Norfolk when it escheated into the hands of the king in 1399.[5]

In the succeeding era of booming production from 1550–1700, direct participation by the greater landlords shrank still further. Although from time to time small and medium-sized mines were operated by their aristocratic owners, as in Beaudesert Park by the Pagets, Sheffield Park by the Talbots, and Heather and Oakthorpe in Leicestershire by the Hastings, it was rare for larger collieries to be run by great landlords. In the north-east, where the greatest collieries lay, the bishops of Durham, the greatest coal-owners of all were perpetual rentiers from the mid-sixteenth century, and so were the Dean and Chapter of Durham, while

---

[3] Further details and references are given in the historical surveys of British coalfields in Ch. 5.

[4] By contrast the bishop of Durham made composition in 1303 with his great freeholders confirming their right to take minerals from their lands (*VCH Durham*; ii. 321).

[5] Rees 1949.

the earls of Northumberland and Scarborough dabbled only occasionally in the mining of the rich seams which lay under their estates.

Mining on a grand scale required capital, and men of substance and
ability to provide and apply it. They were not invariably forthcoming,
and faced with such a dearth aristocrats might reluctantly be tempted
into mining themselves rather than see their assets go entirely to waste.
Such considerations may well play a part in explaining the prominence
of the Scottish aristocracy in the financing and running of that country's
industry. For we find the earls and dukes of Wemyss, Kincardine,
Winton, Mar, Linlithgow, and Hamilton, and many others of the higher
nobility, in the forefront of the production of coal. But Scottish aristocrats were poorer than their English counterparts, and few lairds were
so rich that they could afford to neglect their coal, or the possibility of
making salt with it. Moreover, Scotland in the seventeenth century
lacked a capital market worthy of the name, and there were few apart
from the great landowners who had the resources to develop sizeable
collieries and salt-pans.[6] Outside of Scotland, however, the contribution
of the aristocracy to the rise of the coal industry was minimal.

The gentry

In drawing a distinction between the aristocracy and the gentry there is
a danger of placing too much emphasis on the possession of titles rather
than on the possession of wealth, for some of the greater gentry were
wealthier than some of the lesser aristocracy. Indeed, in terms of wealth
the Scottish nobility were comparable more with the upper gentry of
England than with its nobility. That great landed wealth and the social
pretensions of high status provided a strong disincentive to venture into
industry and commerce is further suggested by the behaviour of
baronets, if evidence from Yorkshire is at all typical. Baronets required
incomes in excess of £1,000 a year to qualify for the title, and, possessed
of such ample levels of wealth, they accordingly displayed far less
inclination than the mere gentry to work the mines on their lands.[7]

None the less, even for the gentry the relative importance of coal
must be kept in perspective. Although the reserves of Britain were
widely scattered, the concentration of rich seams in compact areas, for
reasons of geology, transport, and marketability, provided relatively

[6] Lists of leading coal producers are contained in the *Registers of the Privy Council of Scotland*;
see e.g. *RPCS* 1st ser., xii. 433–5; 2nd ser., ii. 146–7. See also PRO 30/24/7; Duckham 1970, 141–8;
Whatley 1987; Nef 1932, ii. 6–7.
[7] Roebuck 1980, 324–5.

few families with the opportunity to thrive to prosperity on fortunes made from coal. Although many more gentle families were able to derive substantial benefit from coal, and most strove actively to do so, for the greater part of that minority fortunate enough to have coal under their lands its exploitation provided an income which was subsidiary to that which they derived from agriculture. The vast majority of collieries, outside of the north-east, were modest ventures, often comparable in terms of capital invested and numbers employed with thriving artisans' workshops.

A high degree of direct participation in exploiting the coal on their lands was a natural response for the gentry. They owned the land, were accustomed to overseeing its management, and often had sufficient resources to begin mining on a modest scale without borrowing. If they desired to raise money for the investment of larger sums, they possessed in their agricultural estates the prime asset to offer as security for loans. In short, if a gentleman owned a manor where coal could be mined he was likely to try his hand at mining, and if he lacked the conviction or resources to dig coal himself there were likely to be neighbours who would want to lease the right from him. Thus, in Yorkshire between 1558 and 1642 at least eighty gentry families out of the 679 in the county had interests in coal, while in Lancashire in the early seventeenth century the proportion has been conservatively estimated at forty-three out of 774 gentry families. Studies of the local gentry of the coal-bearing counties of England and Wales invariably stress the pre-eminent contribution which they made to the development of the industry. Dr Cliffe has concluded that 'To a large extent the rapid growth of the Yorkshire coal industry was due to the efforts of the gentry who owned the coalbearing land', while Dr Jenkins has found that in Glamorgan 'most of the gentry from the Neath and Swansea valleys, both elite and lesser families . . . were prospecting for coal, and were anxious to expand their production'. Moreover in Glamorgan participation in industry bore no relation to political affiliations, and there is no evidence of stereotype progressive puritans to contrast with backward royalists, 'members of all factions were equally prepared to exploit their opportunities to the full'. In Lancashire too, the political stereotype breaks down, for gentry coalmining entrepreneurs there were if anything more commonly royalist than parliamentarian.[8]

At the same time, in addition to the majority of coal-owning gentry who simply exploited the resources of estates which they already

[8] Cliffe 1969, 5, 57–8; Blackwood 1978, 16, 62; Jenkins 1983, 57–60.

owned, a significant minority systematically leased or purchased mines or land with mines or mining potential. Having made a success of mining coal on their own estates they sought to repeat the process elsewhere. Opportunities were not only seized, they were created, and the examples that can be found are legion, and span the spectrum from the leasing of small mines on adjacent manors, through specialist coal-masters whose activities extended beyond the boundaries of their native counties, and culminating with those who sought to monopolize the output of whole regions. If the incomes which the majority derived from coal were significant rather than substantial, and if the majority chose to concentrate their energies upon mines which they already owned, the ranks of the gentry also contained many who engaged with persistence in mining on a wider and grander scale. As our survey of the coalfields of Britain has indicated, most regions had their groups of landowning coal entrepreneurs who ran the major coal-mines. Numbered among them in South Wales we find the Evanses, Vaughans, Mansells, Jenkins, and Grundys; in North Wales, the Myddletons, Grosvenors, and Mostyns; in Cumberland, the Curwens, Fletchers, and Lowthers; in Lancashire the Bradshaighs, Winstanleys, Gerards, and Charnocks; in Shropshire, the Cliffords, Brookes, Foresters, Benthalls, and Welds; in Warwickshire, the Newdigates; in Nottinghamshire, the Strelleys, Beaumonts, and Willoughbys; in Yorkshire, the Slingsbys and the Gascoignes; and in Scotland there were the Clerks, Blackadders, Setons, Bruces, Johnstons, Prestons, and many more. The role of the gentry in the financing and operation of the greater collieries was also substantial. Outside of the north-east, where the Hostmen flourished and businessmen's partnerships were the normal means of financing, it appears that over half of all the collieries which at any time between 1550 and 1700 produced in excess of 10,000 tons annually were in the hands of the gentry.

It would be tedious to elaborate upon these examples of gentry coal entrepreneurs, but a few details might help to convey the spirit of enterprise that enthused these men. Most common, of course, were those who speculated modestly in the leasing, or occasionally the purchase, of an additional mine or two in an attempt to repeat a success they had enjoyed upon their own estates. Thus, we find Sir William Gascoigne of Sedbury (Yorks.) operating pits in Durham as well as in his native West Riding. Gascoigne's colliery at Ravensworth close to the Tyne was said in 1607 to be worth £400 a year, and he also entered into partnership with a local landlord, two Newcastle merchants, and Richard

Gascoigne, to dig coal near Chester-le-Street. In addition to mining at Kippax, and it was claimed making £600 per year 'for divers years together', Sir William Slingsby of Scriven near Halifax leased a colliery at Seaton Delaval from Sir Ralph Delaval in 1611.[9] Gentlemen from outside Yorkshire also ventured into that county for coal. For example, both Christopher Anderson from Lostock in Lancashire and Thomas Lowther from Cumberland can be found investing in mines near Ponte-fract.[10] Sometimes investment by new proprietors occurred on a truly spectacular scale, as when Sir George Bruce was granted possession of Culross in 1575, and immediately set about turning it into the largest and most technically advanced colliery in the whole of Scotland, and when Sir Humphrey Mackworth, second son of a Shropshire gentle-man, married into the Evans family and transformed the flagging Neath coalworks into the greatest and most technically advanced colliery in Wales. Naturally, investment more normally took place closer to home, and no less ambitious were the plans of Sir John Lowther (1642–1706) to acquire all the significant collieries and coal-bearing lands in the most productive and accessible parts of his native Cumberland coalfield. Of course, ambition that was not harnessed to good judgement could result in failure. Success bred confidence, and occasionally recklessness, as spirited entrepreneurs strove to capitalize on the abundant oppor-tunities for profit offered by this flourishing and potentially lucrative industry. No schemes were more ambitious than those hatched by Huntington Beaumont and his partners, and no failures were more catastrophic.[11] But it is important to remember that the cautionary tale of Huntington Beaumont has been told so many times not because it was typical, but because it was exceptional.

The ability to succeed, as well as to fail, depended upon the availabil-ity of opportunities for investment, and here entrepreneurs were well served. The Tudor and Stuart land market was characterized by its energy and fluidity, and the market in coal-mines and mining leases was no exception. While the Civil War doubtless accelerated the dispersal of assets, it should not be allowed to overshadow the persistence of an active land market throughout these centuries. Thus, when John Weld received his inheritance in 1610 on the death of his father, a member of the Haberdasher's Company of London, he was soon able to fulfil his ambition of setting up as a country gentleman with a special interest in coal. Although the family appear to have had no previous connection

---

[9] Nef 1932, ii. 10–11, 147; Cliffe 1969, 62.
[10] Nef 1932, i. 58–9; ii. 11.   [11] See above Ch. 5 (i) and (ix).

with the county, deriving rather from Cheshire gentry stock, Weld was able to acquire manors on the Shropshire coalfield with excellent mining potential.[12] The land market was fed by those families which by dint of misfortune or ineptitude failed to manage their affairs well. Just as there were coal-owning families which throve and accumulated property, so there were coal-owning families which declined, and devolved their mines or the rights to work them along with the rest of their landed estates. Nor did the activity of the market depend upon economic factors alone. Few families, however enterprising their spirit and successful their ventures, were in a position to run their mines continuously for long periods of time without interruption. In the course of any century, for personal as well as for demographic reasons, such as premature death or a surfeit of daughters, it was not uncommon for the same coal-owning family to act as both lessee and lessor. It was the ready availability of such development opportunities which enabled the flow of entrepreneurial spirit and investment capital to find a profitable home.

Yeomen, husbandmen, and colliers

A substantial portion of the land of Britain was occupied by tenants, and in coalmining districts the occupiers of what had hitherto been solely agricultural tenancies could find themselves in possession of mineral reserves worthy of exploitation. This is no place to delve deeply into the complexities of medieval and early modern land and mining law, but although in the broadest terms the ownership of coal and the right to mine it lay with the owners of the surface, the respective rights of owner and occupier were often in practice a complex matter to unravel.[13] Much depended upon the precise status of the land and the tenancy in question. There were three main categories of land: demesne, tenanted, and common. Demesne was the simplest, for it was the landowner's own, to do with as he wished. The uses to which common land could be put, by contrast, were severely hedged with communal rights, customs, and by-laws. The terms upon which leaseholders held their land were specified in the terms of their leases, but the greater part of the tenanted land was held by freeholders and copyholders with ancient title. Unless they occupied land from which mineral rights had been specifically excluded, such tenants could find themselves with some ability to profit from coal. Freeholders in general had wide and inalienable rights of

[12] Wanklyn 1969, 88–99.
[13] There is a valuable discussion in Nef 1932, i. 266–318.

exploitation, and landlords could not gain access to their land without agreement, while customary and copyhold land was occupied by tenants on terms which derived from the customs of the manor upon which the land was situated, and these often also severely limited the rights of the owners. Since such tenures were steeped in local custom the right of access which copyholders enjoyed to the coal under the lands which they occupied was highly variable. Whereas in some parts copyholders could mine coal and sell it, in others these rights were reserved solely to the lord, and in yet others, perhaps the majority, tenants had the right to dig coal for their own consumption but not for sale.[14]

At any one time there was a multitude of farmers digging coal on their lands, as there had been since the thirteenth century. Some yeomen and a few peasant farmers were fortunate to have tracts of coal-bearing land rich enough and large enough to allow mining on a significant scale, but the majority can each have raised no more than a few hundred tons a year. The operators of tiny pits and mines were likely to be commensurately modest in wealth and status, whether they were agricultural tenants engaged in digging coal on their farmland, or labouring lessees. In both instances men could work full-time or part-time and, if their own resources and those of the coal permitted, they could form partnerships or hire additional labour in order to boost production. Such domestic undertakings proliferated in all coalfields and were dominant in Kingsfield Chase and the Forest of Dean. Similarly, in the far south-western section of the Lancashire coalfield absentee landlords, a concentration of coal-bearing manors in the hands of disinterested nobility, and a poor gentry weakened further by forced sales by papist royalists, resulted in a preponderance of modest lessees, yeomen, husbandmen, colliers, skinners, and suchlike, who sometimes banded together in large partnerships to raise sufficient capital and labour to run modest collieries.[15]

Few peasants throve upon mining coal, for setting up pits capable of producing more than a few hundred tons of coal a year usually lay beyond the resources of peasant farmers. Moreover, as the industry

---

[14] e.g. it was claimed that the copyholders of Cannock and Rugeley (Staffs.) had no right to mine for either coal or iron, except under manorial licence (Harrison thesis 1974, 19). On the south Staffordshire manors of Sedgeley and Darlaston 'free copyholders' had the absolute right to mine coal, but 'base copyholders' had to pay a small fine to do so (Rowlands 1987, 84). According to the customs of Sheffield manor all copyholders were entitled to dig for coal without licence from their lord (Cox thesis 1960, 26).

[15] Langton 1979*b*, 130.

grew so did the awareness of the value of coal-bearing land. Land which had hitherto been valued solely according to its agricultural worth began to derive far greater value from the mineral which lay beneath it. Land adjacent to large collieries was especially prized, as was that over which colliery traffic had to pass. It was inevitable that in the course of time much passed from the hands of small men into those possessed of greater resources.

Merchant adventurers

From what we have already stated it is clear that entrepreneurs drawn from outside either the landowning classes or the industry itself played only a subsidiary role in the rise of the British coal industry before 1700. There was also an element of speculative froth. In the early stages of the coal boom, when former monastic lands and Crown estates were being disposed of by Henry VIII and Elizabeth, a flood of outsiders, including many courtiers and royal favourites, acquired mining lands and rights. But, whereas the gentry were avid buyers and exploiters, few courtiers had serious pretensions to mine coal, and fewer still had the judgement and expertise to do so with much chance of success. Leasing was the obvious route to follow, and thereby quick profits were often made, for those who held court office were often rewarded by Crown assets at huge discounts.[16]

London money-lenders and speculators made a more substantial contribution to the development of the industry, and it is possible to glean examples from almost all coalfields of merchants and lawyers from the capital taking mining leases, advancing money to be invested in mining, or even running collieries, either by themselves or in partnership with others. Thus, we find in the North Wales coalfield Thomas Cowper and Richard Mason of London leasing Mostyn colliery in 1594, and a London Haberdasher, John Wich, leasing all the coal-mines, lead-mines, and stone quarries in the lordship of Bromfield and Yale in 1633.[17] In 1580 another Londoner, John Osbaston, purchased mines at Oakthorpe and Swadlincote in Leicestershire; and in 1692 Richard Richmond, a London merchant, leased a colliery at Sheffield.[18] Such examples could be multiplied, and in the north-east under Elizabeth and James I Londoners occur with even greater frequency. Yet the size of the list that we can compile reflects the large number of collieries in operation

---

[16] Nef 1932, ii. 9–10, 36–8.
[17] UCNW Mostyn 6935; Nef 1932, ii. 31–2.
[18] Griffin thesis 1969, 9; Hopkinson 1976, 4.

at any time and the length of the period we are surveying rather than the disproportionate influence of the metropolis. Moreover, the over-whelming majority of examples relate to trading in leases or the lending of money to coal-masters rather than any direct engagement in the production of coal. When Londoners actually ran collieries, which was not often, it was usually as a result of a foreclosure for debt. The capital provided few examples of genuine mining entrepreneurs.

The picture is not radically different with respect to the burgesses of provincial cities. Capital was often forthcoming from urban sources, but direct involvement in mining was rare. Apart from Newcastle, the most notable exceptions to this rule were the attempts which many boroughs on or close to coalfields made to develop local collieries to supply the fuel needs of their inhabitants. When necessary such ventures included the investment of corporation funds in the search for coal and in the raising of it when found.[19] The most spectacular ventures of all were those undertaken in the seventeenth century to supply Coventry from collieries at Bedworth, Hawkesbury, and Griff by a succession of lessees, which included many Coventry burgesses as well as the earl of Dover, Sir John Winter, and John Pym, the parliamentarian. Between 1609 and 1682, of the more than forty-five adventurers who leased the mines of Hawkesbury, Foleshill, Lowe, and Wyken from the city of Coventry, fifteen have been positively identified as London merchants, and among the remainder were many citizens of Coventry. In these aquatic pits many fortunes were lost, and Coventry Corporation 'lent round sums freely' to the venturers which it never saw again.[20]

The coal-masters of north-east England

The distinctiveness of the north-east coalfield is one of the major themes of this volume, and both the structure of the ownership of coal-bearing lands and the nature of those who exploited them differs markedly from patterns observable elsewhere. In particular, coal output soon came to be dominated by burgesses rather than gentry, especially in the most productive areas around the Tyne and the Wear. As has been noted many times, a disproportionate share of the richest mining areas were owned by Church institutions, most notably the bishopric and the priory of Durham, and there was also a strong aristocratic presence in the form of the earls of Northumberland. By contrast the gentry of both

[19] See above p. 48.
[20] The story is told in Ch. 5(ix). For the identification of the adventurers see White thesis 1969, 30–1.

counties were few and generally lacking in wealth. Northumberland and Durham were poor agricultural counties, with moderate soils and a harsh climate. While the lowlands were capable of improvement much of the counties consisted of infertile moorland, and communications inland were bad. When in 1615 heralds from the College of Arms visited Northumberland, they recorded less than eighty gentle families, a tiny class, with only one gentle family for every 900 or so inhabitants, compared to 1 to 400 in Yorkshire. Moreover, the majority of gentry were poor, even by the standards of the north. According to Thomas Wilson 'Northward and far off a gentleman of good reputation may be content with £300 and £400 yearly'. In Northumberland it would appear that almost three-quarters of the rural gentry must have been malcontent, for their incomes fell below this level. However, at the same time in the city of Newcastle, there were twenty-three armigerous families, the great majority of whom were engaged in the coal trade and far wealthier than their rural counterparts.[21]

The poverty of the Northumberland gentry, and the lack of rich coal-bearing lands in gentry hands around the Tyne, clearly played a major part in restricting the role of middling landlords in the development of the coal industry of the region. Complementary to this, and perhaps of even greater influence, was the pivotal role of Newcastle in the shipping of coal, and the extensive rights over the trade claimed by its citizens since the thirteenth century. Newcastle burgesses had been prominent in the production of coal since the first stirrings of the Tyneside industry, but dominance was a product of the late sixteenth and early seventeenth centuries. Until the close of the sixteenth century the lessees of the bishops' Tyneside collieries continued to comprise a mixture of household and estate officials, local gentry, townsmen, and merchants. A detailed local knowledge is required to place all the lessees firmly into one category or another, but, renting mines at Whickham in the 1550s, 1560s, and 1570s, we find, in addition to Newcastle men such as Bertram and Henry Anderson, Anthony Bird, Robert Barker, and Andrew Goston, a large number of rural gentlemen. Also prominent were Thomas and Anthony Thomlinson, members of a gentry family which had risen to this status by serving the bishops.[22] A similar mix had been in evidence in the mid-fourteenth century. The first grand lease of Whickham and Gateshead collieries had been granted in 1356 to Sir

---

[21] Watts 1975, 59–63; James 1974, 70.

[22] Based upon a study of the Receiver-Generals' Accounts (DUDP Church Commission boxes 1–12, 188686–221233 F).

Thomas Gray and John Pulhore, rector of Whickham, though we are unable to discover whether they mined coal themselves or sublet rights to others, and in 1364 the lessees of Gateshead colliery were John Plummer, a Newcastle burgess, and Walter Hasilden, a burgess of Gateshead.[23]

Under the twin stimuli of the passing of the Grand Lease into the hands of Newcastle merchants in 1583 on the one hand, and the incorporation of the Hostmen's Company in 1600 on the other, an oligarchy of merchant-producers burgeoned, and the numbers of non-Hostmen engaged in production dwindled. Londoners complained that their coal supply had been seized by a 'few person, being men of great wealth' who held not only Whickham and Gateshead but all the major seasale collieries in the environs of Newcastle. The Hostmen countered by claiming that above thirty persons had interests in the Lease, though they went on to undermine their case by stating that some of the thirty possessed only a 144th part.[24] Further credence is lent to the fears of Londoners by the first attempt of the Hostmen's Company to regulate the sale of coal in 1603, which not only threatened the operation of a free market but revealed that just twenty-four Hostmen and family partnerships were assumed by the company to control an output of over 225,000 tons, amounting to 75 per cent of the annual seasale. Henry Chapman was at the head with almost 25,000 tons to his name, followed by Mrs Barbara and Mr Peter Riddell with 20,000 tons, Lionel and Henry Maddison with 20,000 tons, and Sir William Selby with 16,000 tons.[25] To put these figures in context we should note that the 225,000 tons controlled by just twenty-four Hostmen was higher than the estimated pre-1700 output of any British coalfield, excluding only Scotland and possibly Shropshire.

In 1647 the Grand Lease was held by just nine owners, with Ralph Maddison holding a quarter share and Thomas Bewick a sixth.[26] By the close of the century, although the monopoly of the Hostmen's Company over the sale of coal from the Tyne had begun to wane, the control over production exercised by a small clique of coal-masters had been enhanced. A series of vend agreements and listings and estimates of production at this time reveals that collieries in the possession of fewer than a dozen men were together capable of raising half a million tons of coal each year, which was almost as much as the total seasale from the Tyne. Sir Henry Liddell through his collieries of Ravensworth and

[23] Galloway 1898, i. 44–6.   [24] Dendy (ed.), *Hostmen.*, 2–3, 6.
[25] Ibid. 43–7.   [26] Kirby (ed.), *Bishopric of Durham*, 87.

Bensham may well have been producing an average of 80,000 tons annually, followed by Sir William Blackett and Sir John Clavering with around 40,000 to 45,000 tons each, and Sir Lionel Vane, Sir Ralph Carr, and Matthew White with 25,000 to 35,000 tons each. All the afore-mentioned were Hostmen, but the largest producer of all, Sir Charles Montagu, whose soaring output had probably reached 100,000 tons by 1700, was not.[27]

The distinctions between urban and rural status and wealth were in practice far less clear-cut than mere membership of the Hostmen's Company might imply. The industrial and commercial élites of New-castle had similar social ambitions to rich industrialists and merchants elsewhere in England, namely to acquire land, titles, and social standing. The gentry of Durham and, to a lesser extent, of Northumberland also, were augmented by a flood of entrants from rich Newcastle families with coal-producing and coal-trading backgrounds. We can find most of the leading coal producers in the Herald's Visitation of 1615, and by the 1630s around a dozen leading Hostmen had settled on country estates within Durham. The quest for arms, status, and land, especially if that land also overlay rich coal-seams, was a powerful force among the Newcastle oligarchy throughout our period. Assimilation into the ranks of the gentry was assisted by the great wealth of many Newcastle coal-owners, even at an early date in the coal boom. Sir George Selby, for example, became sheriff of the Palatinate of Durham in 1608. One of his colleagues in the ruling élite in the early years of the Hostmen's Company was Henry Anderson, who had also been instrumental in the securing of the Grand Lease. Anderson's father, Bertram, had left on his death in 1571 an estate comprising, *inter alia*, three houses in Newcastle, half-shares in two ships, two keels, three farms, extensive colliery interests, around 20,000 tons of coal worth more than £1,000, and move-able goods worth over £2,500. In 1580 Henry built a prodigious mansion with parkland and gardens within the walls of Newcastle, which was the equal of many a fine country seat.[28]

Just as burgesses strove to become gentlemen so the distinctions between rural-agricultural and urban-industrial wealth and status were also blurred by the gradual admission of some of the coal-owning members of the upper gentry into the ranks of Newcastle burgesses and

---

[27] HRO Cowper D/EPT 4858; GPL Colesworth CK/3/135; Hughes 1952, 167–8; Cromar thesis 1977, 66; NEI Buddle 14/212; NuRO Cookson ZCO/iv/47.

[28] James 1974, 69–70; Raine (ed.), *Wills and Inventories*, 335; Hodgson (ed.), *Wills and Inventories*, 58. See Pl.8 infra.

Hostmen, and by the inter-marriage of the two élites. Sir William Gascoigne, the head of an ancient and powerful Yorkshire family with mining interests in Ravensworth as well as the West Riding, married the daughter of Henry Anderson, and eventually sold his Ravensworth estate to his wife's brother-in-law, the leading Hostman Thomas Liddell in 1607. Of the three children of Sir William Selby, who was a mayor of Newcastle, Grand Lessee, and founder-member of the Hostmen's Company, George married Margaret, daughter of Sir John Selby of Twizel, William married Elizabeth, daughter of William Widdrington, and Margaret married Sir William Fenwick of Wallington.[29] Further blurring between landed wealth and industrial and commercial money occurred through the increasingly exorbitant sums which could be exacted from the granting of wayleaves, whereby a landowner sold or leased permission for the transport of coal across his land by horses and carts or a newfangled waggonway. The running of a colliery demanded investment and enterprise, but even the most slothful of conservative landowners could derive a handsome income from the coal trade without dirtying his hands if his lands were strategically placed.[30]

Away from the Tyne and the Hostmen's monopoly, conditions allowed for far more diversity among leading coal-owners. Newcastle men played little part in the development of the Wearside coal industry. Instead it was driven by a combination of local landowners, Sunderland burgesses, and outsiders. Notable among local landowning coal-masters were the Lambtons, Lumleys, Bellasises, and Boweses, although the first two families produced no genuine entrepreneurs and moved into mining from leasing slowly and somewhat reluctantly. The Bowes had no such inhibitions, and were heavily involved in both coal- and lead-mining. Robert Bowes of Biddick developed Offerton colliery on the Wear, claiming to have invested more than £2,000 in the process, and he owned salt-pans at Sunderland. His elder brother, George, opened up mines on the Biddick estate and also held a share in a lease at Lumley. Members of the Bellasis family leased Morton colliery from the bishop of Durham and were in partnership in Lambton colliery.[31]

The great seasale collieries of the Wear attracted some interest from London investors and money-lenders. Harraton, for example, was leased in 1603 for £300 per annum by Robert Bromley, a London merchant, and three years later it was leased by Sir John Bourchier for

[29] Nef 1932, ii. 10–11; Watts 1975, 262–3.
[30] Stone and Fawtier Stone 1984, 285; Nef 1932, i. 329–35.
[31] James 1974, 71; Stone 1965, 341–2; Beastall 1975, 14–15; Nef 1932, i. 29–30.

£500 per annum on behalf of a group of London businessmen who planned to manufacture alum near Guisborough and Whitby and needed large supplies of coal for the purpose. London merchants who advanced money on the security of this colliery were also on occasion drawn in to work it by defaulting debtors, as Thomas Jones, a dyer, and Roger his brother were obliged to do when Sir John Hedworth failed to pay a debt of £520. Josiah Primatt likewise found himself obliged to turn coal-master at Harraton when a consortium of adventurers led by Robert Conyers, of the great gentry family from Sockburn, got into grave financial difficulties.[32] More rarely, Londoners assumed the role of investor rather than money-lender from the outset. The noted historian John Rushworth of Lincoln's Inn, for example, was a partner of Thomas Davison of Blakiston and Thomas Delaval of Hutton in 1649, in leasing the right to mine in Stub Close and North and East Lumley Park, at the impressive rent of £100 a year for every pit which they sank.[33]

Harraton had become a great colliery long before the Civil War. In 1603 it was said that there were 6,000 chaldrons of coal lying on its banks, and in the 1630s it was claimed that it was contributing 6,000 to 10,000 tons annually to shipments from the Wear. Yet, successive consortia of primarily local adventurers provided the driving force behind its development. A partnership involving John Shepardson and his family was running Harraton before that led by Conyers, and Conyers was succeeded by a partnership which included George Grey of Southwick and George Lilburne of Sunderland. Grey and Lilburne were successful Wearside coal-masters, and in 1651 they managed Lambton colliery in partnership with two members of the greater gentry, Ralph Lambton and Sir William Bellasis. The seasale coal trade of the Wear valley was capable of producing entrepreneurs of considerable wealth and enterprise, and while many came from landowning gentry stock many also came from Sunderland, with a background in the coal trade and salt production. When Sunderland was incorporated as a borough in 1634 it is said to have had 'a list of aldermen that was a roll-call of the Wear coal-owning families'.[34]

Away from the great seasale collieries of Tyneside and Wearside the control and influence of townsmen waned and the complexion of coal-mining entrepreneurs resembled far more closely that to be found in most other British coalfields. In the management of the substantial but

[32] PRO C.2, James I B23/71; Gough 1969, 184–5; PRO E. 134, 14 Charles II, Trinity no. 6 (1662).
[33] Beastall 1975, 14.
[34] Welford (ed.), *Committees for Compounding*, 388–96; James 1974, 87 n. 3; Nef 1932, i. 437.

landlocked south Durham collieries of the bishopric and priory of Durham, urban involvement was slight. Instead the gentry came to the fore, sometimes supplemented by their peers from south of the border in Yorkshire. Most notable in the fifteenth century were the Eures of Witton, who leased for long periods the productive mines around Railey in Evenwood to the north-east of Barnard Castle, paying for them rents in excess of £100 a year. In the succeeding centuries the lessees of these and other landlocked mines of the bishop and the Dean and Chapter of Durham included a broad range of gentry, and the names of Bellasis, Conyers, James, Blakiston, and Mallory occur among many others, including the mayor and burgesses of the city of Durham and the occasional Yorkshire gentleman.[35]

On the coast to the north of the Tyne the attractions of collieries close to water and free of the grip of the Hostmen flattered to deceive, and seduced many adventurers into parting with fortunes. But few achieved much success before the close of the seventeenth century, despite their enterprise and ingenuity. Spectacularly disastrous attempts were made by Huntingdon Beaumont and his London and Midlands associates to establish great collieries at Bebside and Cowpen and at Bedlington. After Cowpen and Bebside had lain vacant and decaying for some thirty years following this débâcle, David Errington took up a lease from Charles I, though he appears to have invested little money and neglected to pay any rent.[36] Eventually the Delavals' endeavours at Hartley and Seaton Delaval were to prove far more successful, and a thriving colliery and harbour with salt-pans and other coal-using industries were established there by Sir Ralph by the close of the century.[37] Between 1688 and 1692 the first mining joint-stock company was formed in London under the name of the Blyth Coal Company, with the object of opening up collieries around the River Blyth and shipping their produce to the Thames. But it made little progress before 1700.[38]

[35] DUDP Church Commission, Receiver-Generals' Accounts, boxes 1–12, 111–112; Lease Register 184958, Renewals Books 235423, 235424; DUPK Dean and Chapter Audit Book A1; Registers 1(A), 6(F), 14(N). Softley, to the north-east of Barnard Castle, was granted in 1632 for 21 years at a rent of £20 p.a. to Humphrey Wharton of Gillinwood, Yorks., gent. (PRO E. 317 Durham no. 6, m. 1–2).

[36] Smith 1957; PRO E. 317 Northumberland no. 2, m. 1–2.

[37] *NCH* viii. 22–3, 281–3; ix. 225–7.

[38] Nef 1932, ii. 46.

ii. The sources of mining capital

An ample supply of capital at moderate cost is a prerequisite of rapid
industrial growth, and a twelvefold increase in output between 1550 and
1700 would suggest that coalmining did not suffer from a shortage of
capital during this period. But, as we discuss elsewhere, it is important
to resist the temptation to overstate the appetite of the industry for
capital. The capital that the industry required for the expansion of
output was provided from a variety of sources, including the income
and savings of the proprietors and venturers, the loans that they raised,
the partners that they took on, and, occasionally, the landlords who
were leasing their mines. J. U. Nef approached the financing of colliery
ventures largely through the distorting mirror of litigation, which
produced a bias towards both excessive borrowing and large-scale
highly speculative and ultimately unsuccessful ventures. The use of a
broader and more representative range of sources reveals that a very
substantial proportion of the capital that was invested did not have to be
borrowed, and that the bulk of all investment capital was obtained from
within the industry itself. A prime source of funds was the ploughing
back of the profits of existing coal-mines.

It is essential not to exaggerate the size of the average individual
investments which were made. Most collieries were not large, and it
generally cost only around £100 to set up an annual capacity of around a
thousand tons. As for the investment of new capital, since the majority
of mining entrepreneurs emerged from the ranks of the landowning
classes, the land provided the bulk of new mining finance. It did so by
direct and by indirect methods. For the landowner desirous of exploiting the minerals on his lands, the first recourse would be to the income
which he received from his estate, or to the savings which had been
accumulated from past income. Such capital was likely to be overwhelmingly derived from agriculture, in the form of rents paid by
tenants and profits from the sale of produce. There was considerable
wealth among the knights and squires, and many must have been able to
embark upon modest ventures without recourse to money-lenders. For
those who needed to borrow, either because they were short of cash, or
because the venture they planned was large in scale, loans were in
general not difficult to arrange, as long as the borrower was credit
worthy and had assets to put up as security. The aristocracy and gentry
were no strangers to borrowing, they did so to finance the purchase of
land, settlements for daughters, the building of houses, or mere

thriftlessness. The purchase of a manor absorbed resources far beyond those required by all but the largest collieries, and manors worth a few thousand pounds apiece were constantly changing hands among the gentry. It has also been noted above that the great coal-masters of the north-east, though having urban and commercial roots, were enthusiastic purchasers of land, and therefore also normally possessed the best form of security for any loans which they might wish to raise. Most of the funding required to finance coalmining, or other industrial ventures, thus fell into accustomed patterns and well-tried procedures.

Capital seeking a safe but rewarding haven resided in both country and town. In rural communities of prosperous landowners and thriving farmers there were many who had cash to lend and were attracted by the distant prospect of foreclosing on a bond for up to double the amount of the original loan, or on a mortgage secured against a desirable manor. Most provincial towns had inhabitants with funds to lend to landowners, and the larger ones also had attorneys, trustees, and scriveners who acted as financial intermediaries, loaning the funds of others on mortgage or bond. For larger advances recourse had naturally to be made to larger towns, but many coalfields were well enough served. In Yorkshire, mercantile communities in Hull, Wakefield, and York provided a ready supply of credit to the county's gentry, in the north-east Newcastle was of national importance, as was Bristol in the south-west. London, of course, remained the major source of loans running to thousands of pounds rather than hundreds.[39]

Moreover, the supply of credit and the terms on which it could be obtained improved appreciably over time. In the sixteenth century long-term credit was difficult to obtain and interest rates on secure loans were in excess of 10 per cent, but thereafter conditions for borrowers inproved materially. In the seventeenth century there was a sustained and substantial fall in interest rates, suggesting an ample supply of credit. Following market rates downward, the statutory maximum rate was reduced to 8 per cent in 1625, and to 6 per cent in 1651. By the later seventeenth century around 5 per cent was the maximum that most lenders could obtain without taking undue risks. The amount of time that loans could be outstanding without threat to the underlying security also lengthened appreciably over the same period. Credit instruments before about 1620 normally had lives numbered in months or at most a year or two, with the threat of forfeiture if repayment were not

[39] This paragraph and that which follows owe much to the discussions in Stone 1965, ch. 9; AHEW iv. 299–300; and Cliffe 1969, 145–52.

made in full on the appointed day. The high level of risk involved in such transactions inevitably acted as a powerful deterrent to embarking on any venture with borrowed funds, and landowners before the early seventeenth century seem rarely to have financed improvements on their estates by means of loans. When they did so they tended to prefer the bond to the mortgage, by which means loans were advanced against the security of bonds for up to twice the amount of the loan, and which were forfeited if interest was not paid promptly and the capital repaid on the due date. In the course of the early decades of the seventeenth century, however, the Court of Chancery encouraged the prolongation of loans, and increasingly protected the defaulting debtor against foreclosure, even allowing him to remain in possession of the land beyond the expiry of the term of the mortgage as long as he continued to pay the interest due and undertook to repay the principal with costs within a reasonable time. The Court of Chancery also fostered the evolution of the principle of the equity of redemption, which meant that mortgages could remain outstanding indefinitely and were able to be assigned from creditor to creditor. Such favourable developments in the terms of loans and the level of interest rates undoubtedly made it more attractive for landowners to borrow the money that was available to them, and thereby facilitated the opening up of coal reserves.

Moreover, the nature of the coalmining industry emphasized short- and medium-term rather than long-term loans. Most capital expenditure took the form of digging pits and soughs and the payment of wages rather than lump sum purchases of costly pieces of capital equipment, and the potential returns of successful ventures were high enough to hold out the promise of early repayment. At the same time, this is not to say that cheap credit was always readily available to everyone who wanted it, or that coalmining suffered not at all from a shortage of capital. The price of money in the seventeenth century, as now, was heavily dependent on the level of risk. Poor risks had to pay dearly for their borrowings, if they could borrow at all. Nor was capital equally available in all coalfields and in all periods. In south-west Lancashire, for example, capital and enterprise was only forthcoming from the gentry, yet most of them were Catholic royalists who were sorely troubled by debts, exacerbated after the Civil War by recusancy and sequestration. When Philip Langton found it 'costly and chargeable' to reopen his mines at Hindley he was forced to borrow £50 from a spinster and his tenants. When subsequently he was unable to repay, they dragged their lord through the courts. Thus, while the Bradshaighs and Bankes were able to finance their collieries at Haigh and Winstanley and maintain continuous production by ploughing back a part of the ample profits that they yielded, in the mines of their papist neighbours 'it was usual for profits to be pillaged quickly from under-financed workings'. Dr Langton has concluded that coalmining in this underdeveloped region 'showed strong signs of chronic undercapitalization in most places'.[40] Yet, while it is probable that a shortage of capital contributed to the slow growth rate of this coalfield, underdevelopment had additional causes including the absence of water transport and the scarcity of large centres of population. To some extent therefore the low level of investment in Lancashire coalmining may have reflected the poor investment prospects to be found there.

In addition to self-financing and borrowing, capital could be raised by the taking on of partners. Instances of gentry taking on partners in small and medium-sized collieries are not often encountered, but in south-west Lancashire the straitened Sir William Gerard even entered into partnership with colliers when he took on a colliery at Parr, and John Rigby formed partnerships for each of a series of modest ventures.[41] Partnerships of working miners, sometimes supplemented by sleeping partners contributing only money, were common in the south-western coalfields, which were typified by small, freelance enterprises.[42] But partnerships were also much in evidence at the other end of the spectrum, where they provided the means of raising the fortunes required for the financing of many of the greater collieries. Although in Scotland the single owner-proprietor dominated, along the Tyne and the Wear the larger collieries were almost invariably run by groups of investors who shared the risks, costs, and profits. Partnerships were less ubiquitous in the greatest collieries in other English coalfields but still relatively common. In the Midlands, Bedworth and Hawkesbury were run by partnerships, but Strelley and Wollaton alternated between sole proprietors and partnerships. Howgill near Whitehaven was the sole property of the Lowthers. In Scotland partnerships, like leases, were scarcely in evidence, and the greatest collieries, like the lesser collieries, were almost invariably operated and financed by their owners. The Scottish coal industry may well have suffered as a consequence, for few lairds were rich.[43]

---

[40] Langton 1979b, 128–30.
[41] Ibid.
[42] e.g. Bulley 1953, 17–26.
[43] Duckham 1970, 141–2, 146–8; Whatley 1987; Nef 1932, ii. 6.

It was in the north-east that the largest amounts of capital needed to be raised, and here that the partnership reached its most advanced stage of development, and came in some respects to resemble the joint-stock company. Joint-stock companies themselves, however, were virtually unknown in coalmining. The only attempt to establish one, the Blyth Coal Company, took place at the very end of our period and the company itself did not become active until the early years of the eighteenth century. The asset of a partnership, commonly a lease of a colliery, was divisible into many parts, and we find them broken down to 110ths and 144ths. The partners could hold any combination of the parts, according to their resources and desires. There were six chief partners in a venture to open up a new colliery in Benwell in 1617: Sir Peter Riddell held a quarter share, Robert Shafto, one-sixth, Thomas Surtees and Henry Chapman, one-ninth each, Thomas Crome, one-twelfth, and William Jennison, one-eighteenth.[44] Joint ventures were early in evidence, and leases of the larger bishopric collieries in the opening years of the sixteenth century were often held by groups. In 1509–10, for example, the Evenwood collieries were demised to Robert Simpson *et sociis suis*, and two years later Robert Hedworth, Nicholas Harrison, and Alan Harding jointly leased the mines of Whickham and Gateshead.[45] Sometimes a sole leaseholder took on partners in order to share the costs and risks, or contribute management skills. James Cole, a Newcastle Hostman, when 'lawfully possessed for divers years yet enduring in divers coalmines in Newburn, Northumberland, of the demise of earl Henry of Northumberland', some time before 1613 granted a half-interest to Timothy Elkes, one of the earl's officers, in return for £200. The moiety subsequently passed to Robert Clarke and then to Henry Taylor of London, gentleman. Because he was living in London, and because Cole 'had knowledge and experience in said coal-works', Taylor agreed to let Cole have a quarter of his profit (one-eight of the whole) in return for Cole managing the mines for them both. But, significantly, Taylor revealed himself in subsequent litigation, not to be a genuine adventurer at all. For he claimed to have advanced money to Cole towards the running costs of the colliery in the form of loans secured by bonds, which did not affect his entitlement to a proportionate share of profits.[46]

The ease with which the half-share of Benwell was passed from

[44] Nef 1932, ii. 55.
[45] DUDP Church Commission, 189832, 189833.
[46] PRO C.2, James I 20/74.

partner to partner, and the arrangements entered into by Taylor and
Cole, might seem to suggest that it was an uncommon type of partnership. In fact, colliery partnerships frequently differed greatly from conventional contemporary partnerships and the current law of partnership
in more respects than the numbers of partners or the divisibility of their
shares.[47] Colliery partnerships normally drew up articles of association
to suit their needs. The transfer of shares in colliery partnerships
normally did not need the assent of the partners, and the death of a
partner did not automatically lead to reorganization. Partnerships
endured for the length of the lease upon which they were based, and
shares were able to be sold, leased, assigned, used as security, or
bequeathed at the will of the partners. Nor was this just the case in the
north-east or in large partnerships. For when a partnership was formed
to operate a small colliery in Colne (Lancs.) it was stipulated at the
outset that each partner had the right to sell, will, or otherwise assign his
part or fractional part. In this way the partnership was adapted to meet
the needs of the coal industry, especially with regard to capital-raising.
Capital could be raised in line with the resources and inclinations of
interested parties, and shares could be distributed accordingly, with
subsequent changes in circumstances able to be accommodated by a
redistribution of the shares. The everchanging lists of partners of the
Grand Lease, with constant mobility of the shares, exemplifies the
flexibility of the system. The major drawback of the partnership was
that it frequently became the vehicle for disputes between its members
centring on contributions to costs and shares of outputs, but, in an age
of miscellaneous and unstable local weights and measures, imperfect
accounting procedures, and inadequate management controls, it is difficult to envisage how any major industrial enterprise could have been
run without considerable scope for contention.

There is every indication that north-eastern partnerships usually
succeeded in supplying the capital requirements of a large and
exceptionally fast-growing industry, and that they were an efficient
method of raising the very large sums needed to finance collieries
capable of producing 20,000 tons and more each year. Indeed it was rare
for any of the major collieries of the north-east not to be operated by a
partnership, and Ravensworth owned and managed by the Liddells as a
private venture was a conspicuous exception. Coal-masters also
benefited from being able to spread their investments across a range of
collieries, which was a great advantage in such a fluctuating and risky

[47] Moller thesis 1933, 146–8; Nef 1932, ii. 54–65.

industry. The spreading of investments was in evidence at a very early date, and it is rare to find a great Tyneside coal-master who did not have interests in a range of collieries. When William Jennison of Newcastle died in 1587 he had shares in seven collieries and an estate valued at £4,259. 1s. 10d.[48] Although the scale of Jennison's investments was exceptional at this time the principles he followed were not, and very few of the leading Hostmen coal-masters had interests in less than three collieries. Finally, the system allowed for the granting of shares to working managers as an incentive to effort, in much the same way as present-day company directors are often granted share options.

While risk-spreading and diversity of investments remained the hall-mark of north-eastern coal-masters throughout the seventeenth century, some signs of change are discernible by the close of our period. The numbers of partners in many partnerships were beginning to contract, as were the numbers of investments made by leading coal-masters, perhaps encouraged by greater stability in the industry. We have noted above how the hold of the leading coal-owners over production tightened in the course of the seventeenth century. It is also evident that although their investments were on average larger than they had been earlier, they were less likely to be spread quite so widely, and more likely to consist of the major, often the majority, shares of leading collieries. In the opening years of the eighteenth century Charles Montagu, the greatest coal-owner of his time, produced in excess of 100,000 tons from just two collieries in which he held the overwhelming majority of shares. Montagu was based in London, and had ready access to its peerless capital market, but he also borrowed in Newcastle, and from the bishop of Durham.[49] In 1709 a Newcastle goldsmith, and prominent coalmining financier, had £5,000 out on loan to the Montagus. William Cotesworth's business dealings reveal that it was possible for him and for men of his standing to raise several thousand pounds locally without much difficulty. In addition to resorting success-fully to conventional local and London money-lenders, leading Tyne-side and Wearside coal-masters sometimes borrowed from the capital's coal-dealers. Dr Ellis's conclusion, based on a study of Cotesworth's papers, that there is 'little evidence of any major short-fall in either long or short-term capital for commercial or industrial investment' can be amply supported from a wider range of evidence.[50] The supply of risk

[48] Greenwell (ed.), *Wills and Inventories*, 152.
[49] NeUL Montagu, Montagu to Baker 5/10/97. The bishop agreed to lend £600.
[50] Ellis 1981, 179–96.

and loan capital to the industry in the later seventeenth century, as in all previous periods, seems on the whole to have been adequate for most prudent investment.[51] Indeed we know that finance for unsound ventures was often also forthcoming, since the most spectacular failures of all occurred in partnerships and on borrowed money.

iii. Executive decision-making

Few decisions to start up, enlarge, reduce, or close a colliery, or to engage in large-scale expenditure on equipment, were taken without an attempt to estimate the potential costs, profits, or losses that such action would entail. Sometimes the estimates would be prepared by the proprietor alone or in consultation with employees, but often outside advice would be called upon from those expert in the matters under consideration. While the majority of such estimates may well have been made informally, and many more have left no record, a significant number have survived and they show that determined efforts were made to calculate costs, outputs, and returns. The quality of the assumptions made was, of course, far higher when they were based on what had actually happened in the past or what was happening at the present in an established colliery, than when they were trying to predict what might happen on a green-field site. None the less, the tools of executive decision-making in the coal industry well before the eighteenth century were far from primitive.

A good insight into the sort of information to which a leading owner or proprietor might have access in the early seventeenth century is provided by correspondence sent to the earl of Northumberland between 1616 and 1620 concerning Newburn colliery and a dispute with Nicholas Cole, the lessee.[52] A letter sent by Hugh Bird to Northumberland in September 1617 purported to give each item in the current and former costs of working every ten (ten chaldrons) of coal in the colliery. These were broken down into the daily wages of the various employees—hewers, barrowers, drawers, overmen, and the 'keeper of the heap'—and placed against the daily output. Then Northumberland was given the estimated average costs of each ten 'for waterwork' and

---

[51] Many of the optimistic conclusions on the adequacy of the supply of credit and the availability of investment funds reached by Peter Mathias with regard to the later 18th cent. (Mathias 1979, 88–115) could be applied, with limited modifications, to the experience of the coal industry a century and more before.

[52] DN Syon QVI 80, 93. For a series of calculations made around 1608 see ibid., PV 2(a)–(d).

for leading, and the weekly costs of corving, candles, and 'odlowes', and smith's charges. The calculations finish with the total weekly costs and output, namely £11. 3s. 2d. for seven and a half tens, which are finally placed against the projected selling price, namely £26. 5s. 0d.; 'so profit is £14. 11s. 10d.' Bird then goes on to remind Northumberland that the water charge is constant, and so will be reduced the more pits that are working, and to give him further figures including definitions of the weights and measures that he has been using. Some months later Bird wrote again to update his master, this time projecting a year's output, costs, and profits for each pit. Having fully and precisely put his calculations into context by stipulating the number of gallons in a bowl, the number of bowl-corves in a ten, and the number of corves required to load a keel over the eleven-chaldron nail, with overmeasure for the shipmasters, Bird offers his estimate of the number of tens that can be produced in a year and the price they would be sold for. From this projected sum he takes away the likely costs of production (working, leading, watering), sinking charges, and fitters' salaries, and is left with £555 per annum per pit clear.

Although the figures quoted by Bird may well have been somewhat wide of the mark, for despite being experienced and knowledgeable he was not unbiased, his methods were methodical and soundly cast. It is possible that Bird may have been a little ahead of his time in his addiction to computations, for arithmetic peppered his repeated attempts to persuade Northumberland to run his own collieries or at the least obtain a realistic rent from them, but he was far from unique. The earl's other officers, not noted for their expertise in 'matters of collery', also offered advice and information which were frequently backed up by estimates of costs, output, and prices.[53] Although there are no suviving records, it is safe to assume that Hostmen coal-masters at this time made similar computations when seeking to assess the worth and prospects of their collieries, as we know that they did later in the century.

Nor was the north-east alone in adopting a systematic approach by the early seventeenth century. An estimate of the value of coal-pits in Cannock Wood, on the edge of Beaudesert Park (Staffs), was made around 1602, which clearly sets out in a detailed and precise form most of the data necessary for decision-making.[54] It is worth reproducing the

[53] See e.g. letter from Whitehead and Robert Delaval to Northumberland detailing recent costs at Newburn, QVI 109, 7/3/1620.
[54] StRO Anglesey D(W) 1734/3/3/254.

report in full, for it demonstrates the range and quality of information that could be available to those who were deciding the fates of small collieries at the start of the seventeenth century. The procedures thus in evidence provided a sound base upon which to build. Progress in business planning, and in accounting and estimating techniques, continued to be made in the course of the next hundred years, but as elsewhere in coalmining it tended to be a cumulative rather than a revolutionary process.

Estimates of the Coalpits in Cannock Wood, as is estimated by Randolph, now farmer of the same coalpits:

First there is four coalpits and one water pit which is and must be kept with draining of water continually day and night.

Two of these coalpits hath been wrought in, the other two are not yet wrought through the coal, but one to the coal and the other wanteth a yard and a half.

The charges of working these two pits through to the coal with the drawing of water is rated to—20s.

Then there is a head to be driven betwixt these two pits being the one distant from the other 60 yards, and this to be done with some speed least when hot weather commeth the work be not hindered by the earth damp. But coals gotten by the way will defray the charges.

These four pits set in order and furnished with workmen, there may be gotten out of them every week four score loads of coals, which rated 2s. 6d. a load comes to—£10.

Out of this the getting of these four score loads will cost—£4. 9s. or thereabouts. Rating as is now paid for the getting of every 12 horse-loads 16d., and of every 12 wain-loads 13s. 4d.

The repair of tools and other like charges, besides timber is rated at—13s. 4d. weekly.

And the weekly charges at the water pit at—10 s.

It is hoped that these four pits, or the most of them, will hold this rate until Candlemas next, but after that these pits are wrought out, there is no hope of getting any more coals at all in this mine.

Decision-making in the late seventeenth century in the north-east is illuminated by some fine collections of records. Most informative of all, perhaps, is the Montagu correspondence, which contains intimate details of the management style of the largest coal producer in Britain.[55] Charles Montagu believed in deep reflection before he made decisions, and in approaching major issues from a variety of perspectives. His

[55] NeUL Montagu MSS *passim.*

letters are so stuffed full of calculations, projections, and 'suppositions' that it is possible to mention only a few of the most interesting. One of the first to occur in the collection is a projected cash-flow account or, as Montagu put it, 'an account by supposition of the money required to manage Gibside colliery from May until Martinmas 1696'. On the out-flow side he noted rent for three quarters at £122. 10s. 0d. per quarter, sinking and drifting costs at £3 a week, working costs for eleven tens a week at £1. 5s. 0d. a ten, leading costs for twenty tens weekly at 40s. a ten, and various salaries, staithe charges, wayleave, keelrooms, and incidentals amounting to £5 per week, resulting in a grand total of £2,175. Montagu affirmed that he had taken high estimates of costs, particularly of the amounts of coal that would be led, and the inflow of cash which he projected at £2,100 came satisfyingly close to matching the outflow.

As an example of Montagu's thoroughness we have his extensive calculations and ruminations on the prospects for reopening Benwell colliery after a flood. Warner, the colliery manager, was optimistic that the source of the inundation could be staunched and the water drained without excessive cost. According to Montagu, Warner was also being optimistic about operating costs when he estimated sinking costs at 6s. per ten, working costs at 36s., leading costs at 10s., and rent at 12s. 6d., giving a total production cost of £3. 4s. 6d. a ten. With 'making out' at 30 per cent (i.e. converting land measures to sea) and a selling price of 8s. a sea chaldron, Montagu calculated that there would be a gross profit of almost £2,000 on a production of 10,000 tens. Which after deducting £1,100 for the costs of drainage, left '£900 for management'. But what, Montagu postulated, if sinking were to cost 15s. per ten, working 50s., leading 15s., and rent 13s.? Then the scheme would be barely profitable at an annual vend of 3,000 tens. After confirming Warner as colliery manager, Montagu ordered that Benwell should be surveyed by three or four of the best Newcastle viewers, in order to resolve the question and to help in determining how the colliery should best be worked.

Montagu was well aware of the importance of the London end of his trade, and he analysed in fine detail the potential profits which might arise from selling his coal in London at 23s. a London chaldron. He did this by itemizing all outgoings down to the salaries of the bookkeepers and the cost of sacks. Then he embarked upon a detailed and highly critical review of the performance of his fitter, Charles Anderson, over the last year, and followed it with projections of his vend in the coming year. Next he reflected on the price and quality of coal from Benwell and

Hutton (Gibside) collieries, and the frequency of explosions at Benwell, and concluded the letter by instructing his cousin George Baker to hire two underfitters, one at each colliery, in case Atkinson should prove troublesome.

Montagu returned to these and related matters many times, but the theme *sans pareil* running through his correspondence is the construction of a waggonway from Gibside to the Tyne, a distance of more than four miles. When the surviving correspondence begins in earnest in May 1696 its construction had already been under consideration for some time, and Montagu expressed the hope that the vend would go a long way towards paying the cost of building it, should they decide to go ahead that year. But the following spring he was still undecided as to which route it should follow, or perhaps indeed whether it should be built at all. The ensuing months produced a long succession of investigations and projections: should it proceed to Smallwell, Dunston, or Derwent staithes, what were the respective distances and the ease of transport and construction of these alternatives, which route posed the fewest problems in securing wayleaves, in which destination were the staithes likely to prove the most suitable from the points of view of access, keelrooms, depth of water, and vend, what economies could be made on current production and leading costs, and perhaps most important of all, what would be the carrying capacity of the wagonway, and could all the coal be sold? On 10 July Montagu determined that the waggonway must be laid to Derwent. In addition to saving £30 per annum on wayleaves and 3 d. per waggon led, the Derwent staithes would be capable of taking great quantities of coals, and he was already postulating that it might be possible to raise production at Gibside to 4,000 or 5,000 tens a year, approximately 100,000 tons. If sales were at this level it might be worth building an additional waggonway, Montagu mused. The problems now to be dealt with were wayleaves, a dispute with the landlord over the measures to be used to calculate his royalty, and the exact measurement of the coal which would be delivered to the shipmasters. Montagu hoped that much of the waggonway would be laid by Christmas 1697. In fact it was not completed until 20 May 1699, with much of the intervening period being filled with fresh investigations and calculations, as well as with tense negotiations over leave to cross the lands of others. In a letter of 11 April 1698, for example, Montagu embarked upon yet another estimate of the savings which would be enjoyed when using the proposed waggonway, yet he finishes the letter by reflecting that the most that he could lose in the project would be £900 and that, should he fail, the wood, waggons, and 'trunk' could be sold to another colliery.

He need not have agonized; after the waggonway had been constructed, to Dunston rather than Derwent, his 'ridiculous' dreams were soon surpassed by real achievements. In the year May 1700–May 1701 he led 1,721 tens, almost two and a half times as much coal as the annual average from 1693–1700, and in 1701–2 more than 2,500 tens were led. Perhaps it was the meticulousness with which Montagu sought to acquaint himself with all relevant factors combined with the vision and boldness of the decisions which he eventually took that led to his meteoric rise to the summit of British coal-masters. He prided himself that he had first obtained the lease of Gibside in the face of competition by offering a shilling per ten more in royalty than was usual at the time.

It is a pity that, for the most part, only Montagu's side of the correspondence exists, and in particular that we do not have access to most of the undoubtedly voluminous data that he received from his advisers and employees. However, a projection made of the likely production, costs and profits of new pits to be sunk at Stumplewood pits at Benwell in the twelve months from October 1699 to November 1700, does survive, and it can serve as an exemplar of the reports which viewers were making of the future prospects of working collieries in the north-east at the close of the seventeenth century.[56] Estimated production was put at 13,000 chaldrons (c.35,000 tons) and valued at the likely sale price of 8s. 6d. per chaldron, amounting to £5,525; from this sum were then deducted working and leading costs, rent, staithe charges, repair of roads, salaries, and 'petty charges', amounting in all to £4,070. 16s. 8d. The projection closes with the following statement, 'Then there rests towards defraying water charge, sinkings, driftings and accidents £1,464. 3s. 4d.'. All these estimates were able to be based on the current experience in the colliery. The sharp distinction drawn in this document as well as in many others, between the expenses of working, transporting, and selling the coal, and expenditure on colliery maintenance is most significant. It drew a distinction between those costs that were reasonably predictable and geared to the amount of coal that was produced, and those costs which were either less predictable, such as drainage, or at the discretion of the proprietor, such as sinking and drifting. The proprietor could thus see how much gross profit he might make on every unit of coal he produced, and how much was left over to maintain or expand output in the future.

[56] NuRO Benwell MBE/VI/16.

A briefer and, it must be confessed, much cruder estimate was made in 1656 of what the earl of Mar might make if he 'had ane owt beare set down upon the mean coal and put in 10 colliers and bearers'.[57] It was postulated that each collier (hewer) would produce a chalder a week, which would result in an output of 3,000 chalders in a year, which would in turn result in an income of 18,000 Scottish marks. On the cost side, each collier would be paid one mark per chalder, leading would cost another mark, and the projector estimated that repairs and on-cost would absorb yet another mark. 'So there will remain 9,000 marks, and all charges paid.' If Mar decided to lease the coalwork, it was suggested that he should ask for a rent of 6,000 marks and 500 more for small coal. The roundness and symmetry of the estimates raise suspicions, but to be fair the venture was small and unlikely to require large investment, and the projected returns on capital were so spectacularly high that they left ample room for error.

Larger and more costly ventures naturally demanded deeper and more thorough investigations. When Sir Richard Newdigate fancied that reopening Griff colliery might lead to a recovery in his family's fortunes, a staged estimate was made on 1 October 1700 of the likely investment that might be required and the rate of return that could be expected.[58] Three working pits were to be sunk in the first year and another two in the second. Three months later the estimates were revised in the light of work already undertaken, and Newdigate rejoiced that he had 'sunk near the coal at an easier charge than anyone did expect'. Total costs of opening up the colliery were put at £2,700, but these included the costs of working 12,000 loads worth 6s. 8d. each, and £500 worth of small coal. As a result a clear profit of £1,200 was in prospect. But even this magnificent rate of return might be bettered, Newdigate mused, and that 'by the Grace of God twill prove much more'.

The projections undertaken by proprietors and their consultants in the seventeenth century may well appear at first sight to be rudimentary, and without doubt very many of them must have proved in the event to be seriously inaccurate. But this did not mean that they were without value, or that they were able to be substantially improved upon. The fact that so many were wide of the mark is not surprising, for projecting into the future is no less hazardous in business than it is in other fields, and projectors in such an unpredictable activity as coalmin-

[57] ScRO Mar and Kellie GD 124/17/516.
[58] WaRO Newdigate CR136/V/147, fos. 55–7 (detailed in White thesis 1969, 205–8).

ing had very many potential hazards to overcome. Even today, with all the experience and skills at our disposal, estimating the costs and profits of new ventures, or the patterns of trade and rate of return of start-up businesses is a notoriously uncertain science as the experience of any venture capital fund will testify. When compared with the relationship which the average business plan written for a new venture today bears to actual experience, the better efforts of the seventeenth century cease to look irredeemably poor. As has been noted above, there was a body of viewers and consultants available in most coalfields, and some attained high degrees of expertise. The greatest hostages to fortune were the over-speculative adventurer and the self-seeking expert. Sound advice allied with the good judgement of proprietors could do much to eliminate flaws, lessen risks, and promote success in this period as in any other.

iv. Mining leases

Since coalmining was a risky as well as a potentially profitable under-taking, rents offered a more certain return to the owner, and, although defaults and arrears could often occur, the losses which landlords could suffer were strictly limited. There were, of course, a multitude of additional reasons, cultural as well as economic and managerial, why land-lords might choose to lease rather than work their collieries, and one of the major influences upon their decision-making was the sort of agreements which they could reach with putative operators. The form of the lease, as well as the level of compensation it offered, was of prime significance.

With so great a proportion of the coal reserves of Britain in the hands of those who did not wish to exploit them, the mining lease was clearly a major influence on the level of mining activity and the shaping of entrepreneurial decisions. Nef has argued that the terms included in many early mining leases acted as a deterrent to enterprise and growth, and that the subsequent weakening in these terms, together with a substantial decline in the share of the selling price of coal taken by landlords, was instrumental in unleashing the coalmining boom which characterized the later sixteenth and early seventeenth centuries. Landlords in the Middle Ages, especially religious institutions, Nef maintained, behaved in a highly restrictive manner, imposing leases prejudicial to the tenants, with severe limitations on output, oppressive rents, and very short lives. However, a transformation occurred consequent upon Henry VIII's expropriation of the estates of the monasteries and other religious institutions, during which the terms of leases were relaxed and their duration extended, rents plummeted, and restrictions on output were abandoned. If the coal-mines remained in Crown hands they were leased on the easiest of terms, while if they passed into the hands of gentry they tended to be either sold on, leased on realistic terms, or exploited directly. The scale of this transformation was made all the greater by the subsequent attainder of a series of lay estates rich in coal, which were then sold or let on easy terms. These monumental changes in landownership in the reigns of Henry and Elizabeth, and in the attitudes of the new owners to the leasing of their coal-mines, according to Nef, propelled the industry forwards. In the course of the seventeenth century, however, the share of the profits of the industry enjoyed by rentier coal-owners once again began to rise and after the Restoration royalties and rents amounted to more than a quarter of the pithead price in highly productive mines in many of the major coalfields. These were heights which were never subsequently to be exceeded.[59]

An investigation of the leases of coal-mines, based upon a far wider range of local evidence than that available to Nef, whose sources were strongly biased towards central records and litigation, does indeed reveal substantial changes over time. But the changes were more complex and less clear-cut than Nef envisaged. Moreover, it would seem that his exposition relies too heavily on the supposition that the determination of the terms of leases and the levels of rents was primarily a matter of landlords' preferences rather than market conditions. It is true, of course, that in the half-millennium from 1200 to 1700 the market was often far from free, that mines were not a homogeneous commodity, and that knowledge was far from perfect, and it is also demonstrably false to assume that landlords invariably behaved in an economically rational manner, ceaselessly seeking to maximize their returns. None the less, it is equally false to assume that the terms of leases did not reflect in some powerful measure prevailing market conditions for mines and for coal, and the interests of lessees as well as lessors.

There was much more to the making of a lease than a landlord passing the right to mine coal to tenants for a period of years in return for a rent. Having regard to the respective, and at times conflictive, interests of landlords and tenants, it is possible to construct a series of heads of

[59] Nef 1932, i. 133–56, 319–29.

agreement that a comprehensive lease would contain. The most basic of these were the rent payable and the right of the tenant to mine coal. But both were capable of extensive refinement and adaptation. The rent could be flat; it could vary with output, taking the form of a royalty payable at so much per unit produced; or it could be a combination of both rent and royalty. Compensation might also take the form of a share of production, a fifth or an eighth and so on. The right to mine could be completely unrestricted; or it could have a maximum, specified in units of output, numbers of pits that could be sunk or worked, numbers of colliers that could be employed, hours and days of work, and so on. Additionally, safeguards might be inserted to protect either the landlord's or the tenant's interests. If the landlord's income was to come primarily from royalties, he might insert a requirement to mine. For the tenant's part, he might wish for abatement of rent if he were stopped from mining for reasons outside his control, such as chokedamp or flooding. The landlord, desirous of protecting his asset, might require that the tenant mine in a prudent manner. The tenant for his part would require wayleaves to transport coal over the landlord's property; he might also seek to obtain concessions from the landlord to facilitate his mining, such as access to timber or even a financial contribution should major drainage works become necessary. The tenant might even secure a covenant prohibiting the landlord from granting any further coalmining leases in the neighbourhood. Finally the landlord might seek to secure adequate rights of access for his officials to supervise methods of working and to audit production.

Generalization about the forms of mining leases across five centuries and fifteen coalfields inevitably leads to oversimplification and is prone to lead to manifest error. For it is scarcely ever possible to compare like with like, since the fortunes of collieries rose and fell, along with the competence of their owners and occupiers. Yet some broad patterns do emerge from the multitudes of surviving leases. In the Middle Ages, most strikingly, there was no provision for the financial return to landlords to vary in accordance with output or profits. Rents were flat. Doubtless landlords and prospective tenants had likely outputs in mind, having regard both to the capacity of the colliery and the market for its coal, when rents were fixed. But the landlord stood to lose if production soared above this projection. Consequently a very high proportion of leases of sizeable collieries throughout the country made between the early fourteenth century and the mid-sixteenth imposed restrictions on output, including almost all of those drawn up by the bishopric and the priory of Durham. Thus, in 1326 when Adam Peyeson leased 'all the "quarries" of seacoal' at Benthall (Salop) from Hugh, lord of Scheynton, it was agreed between them that Adam could use no more than four labourers to dig coal, although he was allowed as many as he wished to carry it to the Severn. Similarly, when in 1486 a 'new thyrled' mine at Cortworth (Yorks.) was leased for five years by Sir Thomas Fitzwilliam, the lessees were permitted to use no more than three pickmen, one barrowman, and one banksman, except in the first year when two barrowmen might be employed. When the earl of Northumberland granted a lease of his Bilton mines three years later for a six-year term, the lessees were restricted to sinking only two pits, one in the first three years and another thereafter; a maximum output of sixteen chaldrons a day was also stipulated.[60] Such examples would appear to be typical of the Middle Ages, and in the first half of the sixteenth century output restrictions were also ubiqitous.[61] Three pits and sixteen chaldrons per pit per day were specified at Gateshead in 1513; twenty chaldrons per day at Elswick in 1530, and a maximum of two pits and a total of forty chaldrons per day at Elswick eight years later. At Nuneaton (War.) leases in 1583 permitted no more than six colliers to be employed.[62] In addition to output and man limits, leases sometimes limited the use of the coal which was dug to the personal consumption of the lessee, and in 1306 the lord of Gower leased the pit-coal of 'Byllywasta' to the burgesses of Swansea with the proviso that the coal was not to be sold in trade.[63]

To Nef such restrictions were a severe restraint on the growth of coal output, but it would appear to be turning logic on its head to see them as a cause rather than as a consequence. There is little reason to believe that the first priority of landlords was the preservation of their coal reserves rather than the maximization of their incomes, even though in these times they were likely to believe that coal-seams could be exhausted. The rents that were set were thus more likely to reflect the sales that lessees felt they were able to achieve. If a market for more coal existed, higher output limits could be negotiated in return for higher rents. When the facility for unlimited output was sought by a lessee, it could sometimes be bought, as in 1525 when Thomas Wolsey, in his capacity

---

[60] *VCH Salop*, i. 454; Clayton 1966, 75; *NCH*, ii. 453–4.
[61] e.g. Galloway 1898, i. 45–6, 61; *VCH Notts.*, ii. 325; DUDP Church Commission, 244138, 244148, 244185, 244242, 244244; Gruffyd thesis 1981, 34.
[62] DUDP Church Commission, 244246; Galloway 1898, i. 86–7; Grant thesis 1977, 71.
[63] Evans thesis 1928, 8. For other examples see Trigg 1930, 130–1; Guy thesis 1982, 146.

as bishop of Durham, leased the collieries of Grewburn and Railey to the widow of Richard Bellassis and Bartholomew Harwode for thirty years at the hefty rent of £180. The only provision relating to output was that an additional £10 was to be paid when the colliery was producing sufficient to 'serve the country'.[64]

There are indications that coalmining leases were being granted for far longer terms in the later fifteenth and early sixteenth centuries than formerly, in keeping with trends in the general run of estate leases at this time. As the experience of the bishopric of Durham over the Grand Lease was to demonstrate, long leases were apt to provide poor compensation for the loss of productive collieries in an era of soaring coal output and sustained price inflation. Yet short leases at high rents offered no solution to an equitable sharing of risks and rewards between landlord and tenant, for in order to make investment worthwhile tenants required the security bestowed by lengthy leases. Rents linked to the number of pits that were sunk offered some advance, but the best solution lay in the provision of royalties linked to output. The earliest true royalty leases, containing provision for a specified payment for each unit of output, seem to have been in use in South Wales from at least 1530, when the earl of Pembroke leased the right to work and sell all coal found in the manors of Llandimore and Weobley to William Herbert of Swansea for a royalty of 6d. per weigh.[65] In addition, we should note the occasional existence of the practice, commonly found in metalliferous mining areas, whereby the landlord took in kind a prescribed share of output, as at Ewloe colliery (Flints.) in 1461. A mine at Richmond (Yorks.) was leased in 1544 for a ninth share of the coal produced, and George Owen claimed at the turn of the sixteenth and seventeenth centuries that in Pembrokeshire landlords took either a rent 'or the third barrel after all charges of the work deducted'.[66]

The leases by which the collieries of the earl of Northumberland were demised in the 1610s provide an excellent example of variety of practice, including a certain (flat) rent with restrictions on output, a certain rent with no restrictions on output, and a royalty linked to output. That no one method was ideal for the earl, is suggested by a letter from Hugh Bird in which he argues that Newburn colliery, which was let in return for a royalty of 6s. 8d. for every twenty-one score corves of coal produced, should instead be let for £200 per annum for unlimited

[64] DUDP Church Commission, 244247.
[65] Rees 1968, 97. It is possible that royalties were of even earlier date in North Wales: Gruffyd thesis 1981, 33.   [66] Moller thesis 1933, 120; Owen, *Pembrokeshire*, 89–90.

production at two pits, with production from additional pits, if any, paying the aforesaid royalty.[67] Leases made for a certain rent were still common on Tyneside at this time,[68] but royalty leases, based upon the ten and called tentale, soon came to predominate for larger collieries, sometimes in conjunction with a relatively low flat rent. Variants continued to persist, however, including restrictions on output. In 1661, for example, when Jane Shafto was granted all the coal-mines in Wallsend and Hoods Moors, Jarrow, for £10 per annum by the Dean and Chapter of Durham cathedral, she had to warrant that she would not get more than twenty score of corves daily from any of them.[69]

Contrary to the prognostications of Nef, restrictions upon output were to continue in many of the leases enacted through to the eighteenth century.[70] Practice varied not only over time but from coal-field to coalfield. It is held by one historian of the Yorkshire coalfield, for example, that the typical local coal lease of the seventeenth century 'contained both a fixed annual rent and restrictive covenants drawn up in the interests of the landowner to prevent more than the customary output of coal'. In the last years of the seventeenth century, the lease of the duke of Norfolk's Sheffield Park colliery stipulated that no more than two pits should be worked at a time and no more than ten getters should be employed, thereby replicating the methods which were used to restrain output over 400 years before.[71] The most common form of lease, however, outside of the north-east, was a flat rent without restrictions on output.

The scale of the consideration which the landlord received from the tenant was, of course, one of the most crucial elements in any lease, not just for individual tenants but for the health of the industry as a whole. Rents which were too high could inflate the risks of mining, even to the extent of completely undermining the incentive to produce coal or the ability of the lessees to remain solvent. In one sense all rent and royalties can be seen as detrimental to the production of coal, for they diverted money out of the industry and sliced into profits which in themselves were often far less predictable than those derived from farming the land. Although the yields and prices of agricultural produce could vary widely from year to year, crops never failed entirely to grow nor animals

---

[67] DN Syon PV 2(a).

[68] Bird provided extensive surveys of the leases prevailing on Tyneside in 1608, which consisted overwhelmingly of flat rents (DN Syon PV 3(c), 3(f)).

[69] DUPK Dean and Chapter, Register 14(N), fo. 121ᵛ.

[70] Flinn 1984, 43–4.

[71] Hopkinson 1976, 8.

to produce young or meat, milk or wool, and in the medium term bad years tended to be balanced by good. The costs of farming were also infinitely more predictable than those of mining.

It is an easy task to find many examples of rents plunging coalmining operations which might otherwise have been profitable into losses. Sometimes, as with Thomas Beaumont at Measham, for which he willingly agreed to pay £500 annually, the rent was recklessly high. Sometimes, as with the partners who leased Cannock Chase colliery from the Pagets at the close of the seventeenth century for £350, the agreed rent was a fine misjudgement of the level of profits which the colliery was capable of making. Certainly, there was little margin for error if landlords received advice similar to that given to the earl of Mar in 1656, who was told to ask 6,500 marks a year for a projected coalwork which was estimated to produce profits of just 9,000 marks.[72] Rent was an integral part of the costs of production, and estimating what could be afforded was one of the essential skills of entrepreneurs. On occasion there were tenants who undoubtedly paid far more than a colliery was worth, just as there were landlords who failed to secure tenants because their demands were too high. Yet Nef would appear to be in error in maintaining that rents were sustained at excessive levels for much of the seventeenth century across many coalfields. Indeed, it would be difficult to imagine circumstances in which this could have been possible in any but the shortest of terms or the most particular of circumstances.

In fact by far the most significant and sustained deviations from market levels arose from rents which were too low rather than too high, and the most striking of all were to be found on the coal-rich estates of the bishops of Durham. After the Reformation the higher clergy were in a weak political position and felt themselves under pressure to grant their possessions cheaply in order to buy protection. But in addition there is abundant evidence of favouritism, nepotism, corruption, and straightforward incompetence in the granting of coalmining leases by both the bishopric and the Dean and Chapter of Durham.[73] Although

[72] See above Ch. 7 (iii).

[73] For an account of the administration of the Dean and Chapter in the later 16th cent. see Marcombe thesis 1973, ch. 3. For a particularly blatant act of nepotism see the lease granted by Richard Barnes, bishop of Durham, in 1582 only a few years after the bishopric had lost the right to a fair return for the Grand Lease collieries, to his three sons. By the terms of the lease they were granted full rights for their lives of all coal-mines, opened and unopened, in Ryton parish, together with full wayleave, timber, and staithe rights, and the liberty to sink as many pits as shall please them, paying just 26s. 8d. p.a. for each pit (DUDP Church Commission, 184958, 782–5). See also C. Clay, '"The Greed of Whig Bishops,"?: Church Landlords and their Lessees', P.&P. 87 (1980).

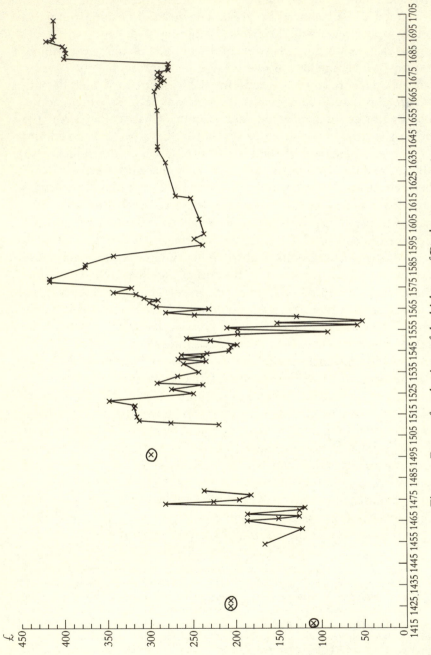

Fig. 7.1. Rents of coal-mines of the bishops of Durham, 1415–1695

Sources: DUDP Church Commission Receiver-General's Accounts.

Fig. 7.1, which illustrates the total rents received from all bishopric coal-mines, does not include substantial fines payable on renewals of leases, since they are not often revealed in surviving records, it dramatically exemplifies the scale of the losses suffered by the bishopric in an era of soaring values, and the benefits enjoyed by its tenants. Losses were by no means restricted to the Grand Lease collieries, they extended to all of their possessions. Nor were the bishops acting in ignorance, for successive surveys stressed the massive disparities between rentals and values. In Bishop Cosin's survey of 1663 the Grand Lease collieries were said to be worth £2,000 a year to the lessees against a rent of £117. 5s. 8d.; Ryton, granted in 1635 for three lives, was said to be worth £2,400 above the rent; and Blackburn leased for three lives in 1637, worth £300 above the rent. The bishopric granted long leases with rents based upon the number of pits in operation, rather than leases of moderate length with royalties upon output, and suffered mightily for it. Few lessons were learnt, however, for in 1662 a whole series of new leases were granted for twenty-one years on similar terms to the old. Doubtless the bishop enjoyed substantial fines from the new tenants, but in the longer run these were yet again to prove scant compensation for the loss of a realistic rent year in and year out.[74]

The tenants of the bishopric of Durham were far from alone in enjoying advantageous terms, for Crown tenants prior to the Civil War were likewise favoured throughout the country. As output soared in the later sixteenth and early seventeenth centuries, the gap between rents and values grew ever wider. Eventually the scale of the windfall gains enjoyed by tenants paying virtually fixed rents led to royal inquisitions in 1610–11. In Northumberland and Durham the commissioners found around a score of royal collieries with a combined annual value to their tenants of more than £1,400 but a rental of less than £200.[75] Rents for coal-mines on royal manors in North Wales were frequently 'ridiculously low', and the Exchequer received only 10s. a year from Mostyn, although the colliery was worth perhaps as much as £700 annually.[76]

Such inquisitions provide some means of assessing the reasonableness of colliery rents, but ideally one would wish to be able to express rents as a percentage of either selling prices, costs of production, or profits. This is rarely possible, but fortunately the prevalence of royalties and some sound information on prices, provides a good basis for assessing

[74] DuCL Sharp 167, fos. 170–6.
[75] Nef 1932, i. 145–8.
[76] Gruffyd thesis 1981, 51–3.

the landlord's share in the larger north-eastern collieries in the late seventeenth century. At this time tentale, that is, the royalty payable on each ten production chaldrons, amounting to around thirteen Newcastle sea chaldrons or some thirty-five tons, ranged from 6s. 8d. to as much as 18s. As the colliery proprietor received 8–9s. a chaldron for his coal, royalties therefore ranged from 7–17 per cent of the selling price, though 10 per cent may have been the norm. The market for leases was becoming efficient, and high royalties generally indicated a very profitable colliery. Prime leases were often open to bidding, and Montagu lived to bless the day that he was bold enough to offer a shilling more per ten than was usual to secure the lease of Gibside.[77]

[77] Based upon royalties at the collieries of Whitley, Earsdon, Whorlton Moor, Hewarth, Tynemouth, Butterlaw, Gibside, Benwell, and Hedley Fell (DN Syon CX 2a(1), CX 2b, CX 4a(1–3), CX 4b(1–2), CX 4c; DUPK Church Commission, Post Dissolution Loose Papers, box 10 provisional (mines); NeUL Montagu, Montagu to Baker 21/6/97, Montagu to Baker 22/9/98; HRO Cowper D/EPT 4877, 4878).

CHAPTER 8

Management

In colliery you will find more lying and tricking than in any dealings you have ever had yet, but at the same time I hope by this first
trial you will find it will neither require very much time to attend
nor any great difficulty in it when attended, except keeping
accounts.

Charles Montagu to his cousin George Baker, 16 May 1696

i. The priorities of colliery management

A venturer, having decided to mine coal, was presented with a number
of choices of how to manage his enterprise. Basically, the alternatives lay
between managing directly, with a high degree of personal involvement,
or indirectly, by delegating managerial functions to subcontractors and
agents. At any time before 1700 there was great variety in the structures
of colliery management, and one should not expect to be able to
chronicle any irresistible drift, either from leasing to operating, or from
indirect to direct management. Yet there are some patterns and progres-
sions to be discerned, and the responses of owners and managers to the
changing scale and fortunes of the industry were far from random.

The nature and structure of management was, of course, closely
related to size. Smaller collieries could be turned into profitable,
smooth-running enterprises by the supervision of the owner, the
establishment of a routine, and the employment of a trustworthy officer
or two. According to Captain Langdale Sutherland, a cavalier whose
mineral estates at Featherstone had done much to salvage a fortune
wrecked in the service of the king, success could be assured by following
a few simple rules. He wrote in 1671 to his sons:

The coalmines on Featherstone Moor, if discreetly managed, with a true
banksman, bottom-man, and four rolls upon the coal wall, will not be much
short of a yearly rent of £200 ... Whether Abram or Brian be master of it,
observe these following directions ... Let the bottom-man come to him every
week, to give an account of every man's work, and confide in no other collier

belonging to the work ... The whole trust lies in the bottom-man and the banksman, and only them and none but them.[1]

Larger undertakings required more complex arrangements, of course, and in an age when industry was dominated by outwork and small workshop production, the management required for collieries producing more than a thousand tons or so was inevitably precocious. Well before the eighteenth century, the greater collieries possessed many of the characteristics commonly used to distinguish the classic new industrial enterprises of the industrial revolution from their predecessors. Production was concentrated upon a single site, or a cluster of proximate sites; substantial amounts of capital were sunk into fixed assets; and they were operated by sizeable specialist, full-time workforces. Moreover, even collieries of more modest size were multidimensional enterprises, the efficient management of which necessitated a combination of detailed monitoring and creative policy-making. The work-force had to be recruited, trained, controlled, and rewarded, output and sales monitored and recorded, and the fabric of the colliery and its machinery and equipment maintained. Production had to be geared to what was often a highly volatile market, dependent not only upon the vagaries of the demand for coal within the hinterland, but upon the cost and availability of transport and the presence of competition. Moreover, the production process was not simply a matter of ensuring the efficient working of muscles or machines. The cutting of coal was rarely a matter of routine, and managers had to react to the geology of the seam as it revealed itself, and to the incidence of water or foul air. Finally, the assets of the colliery needed constant renewal, and continuous production demanded not only the undertaking of new sinkings and headings, but the provision of an ample flow of cash to pay for them. In comparison with the managerial challenges posed by a nineteenth-century cotton mill, where structures and organization lent themselves to easy copying, where machinery was standardized and factory layout predictable, those faced by colliery owners of the later sixteenth and the seventeenth centuries could appear very formidable indeed.[2]

There was little tradition of industrial management for coal-owners to build upon, and the supply of trained and experienced managers must have fallen far short of the burgeoning demand for them as coal pro-

---

[1] Trigg 1930–2, 128.

[2] On cotton mills see F. Crouzet, *The First Industrialists: The Problem of Origins* (Cambridge, 1985), 13–14.

duction soared. Moreover, a distrust of the honesty and diligence of the common run of officers, which at times could border on despair, prevailed in all fields of management. One obvious solution was for the coal-owner himself to assume a major role in the management of his colliery. Indeed, owner-managers were dominant in manufacturing throughout the early stages of the industrial revolution. Sidney Pollard, echoing the sentiments of Adam Smith, wrote in his classic text on the *Genesis of Modern Management*, that 'up to the end of the eighteenth century at least . . . management was a function of direct involvement by ownership, and if it had to be delegated either because of the absence of principals or because of the size of the concern, then the business was courting trouble'.[3] None the less, although many of the most successful collieries were closely supervised by owners, sheer size and the variety of processes undertaken within them often placed the task beyond the energies of a single proprietor. Extraordinary challenges, however, could be met by pragmatic advances founded upon customary practices as well as by naked innovation. The greater collieries inevitably demanded advanced managerial systems which placed them in the vanguard of pre-industrial enterprises, but they also often relied heavily for their efficient operation upon the improvement and refinement of the best of traditional methods. Many also relied upon a thoroughgoing delegation of duties and responsibilities, which involved the extensive use of independent or semi-independent subcontractors, agents, and consultants, rather than direct employees. Once again we find the evidence of evolution is stronger than that of revolution.

The focus of this chapter is day-to-day management, as distinct from the exercise of entrepreneurial functions, which were discussed in the preceding chapter. Although the distinction is not always easy to draw, the study of colliery management can be facilitated by separating the strategic from the tactical, and policy-making and risk-taking from organization and day-to-day routine. The routine management of a colliery can be grouped into three major sectors: the precise monitoring and accounting of output and sales, expenditure, and income; the supervision and control of the work-force; and the maintenance of the colliery and its equipment. All three areas readily gave rise to formidable problems. Literate men with skill in casting accounts were not easy to find in the countryside of sixteenth- and seventeenth-century England, especially among those who chose to work in collieries.[4] The lower tier

---

[3] Pollard 1965, 12.
[4] Literacy was rare among colliers (see below, Ch. 11 (iv)).

of colliery management was not well paid, and when pay was inadequate honesty was at a premium. As for the precise measurement of coal, it was a perennial problem which defied all attempts at a solution. The predicament of the coal-owner seeking to monitor the production of his hewers in order to calculate their wages, or that of the landlord seeking to monitor the output of the mines he had leased in order to calculate the royalty which was due to him, mirrored that of the customs officer seeking to measure the coal which was shipped. Coal simply does not lend itself to exact measurement, except by weighing, which would of course have been uneconomic for such a cheap and bulky commodity, even if it had been technically feasible. When gauged by volume, as is discussed in Appendix A below, the measurement of coal was a task which relied far more upon upon estimation than upon precision.

The correct maintenance and working of a colliery demanded the highest skills in disciplines still in their infancy. As for the management of colliers, it was almost universally held to be a notoriously arduous and unpleasant task unbefitting any gentleman. For Captain George Whitehead, who supervised the earl of Northumberland's collieries in the early seventeenth century, it was 'a great misery for a man of any good condition to be troubled with such a company of rascals as these colliers are'.[5] The overriding concern of every owner was to minimize dishonesty and fraud among his work-force, for which opportunities abounded in coalmining. Since hewers were paid according to their output it was a great temptation to pack the corves so that they appeared full when they were not, or conceal inferior coal or slate in them. Partially filled corves, or the mixing of cheap small coal with expensive great coal, could cause the mine proprietor substantial losses in the course of a year through the overpayment of his work-force on the one hand and the erosion of goodwill by the defrauding of purchasers on the other. Colliers might also resort to robbing the pillars which supported the roofs of their mines in an effort to boost their productivity. Collusion between colliers and managers could result in part of the output not being accounted for, or allowing it to be sold for personal profit. Coal could also be stolen from the banks. More serious still, accounts could be falsified, money could be embezzled, and accountants could abscond. In such an environment the maximization of output and sales often had to take second place to the eradication of petty fraud.

[5] DN Syon QII 123.

ii. The management of small collieries

In the ubiquitous smaller collieries heavy responsibility for the bulk of managerial functions fell upon the shoulders of the banksman. The office of banksman, however, was not normally an elevated position. Having much in common with the medieval manorial reeve, the banksman was usually a humble man, and more often than not illiterate. Banksmen often seem to have formerly been colliers, notably hewers, for the post required knowledge of mining. But it was not normally a true promotion, for banksmen were generally paid less than hewers and most received scarcely more than the average labourer's wage. Yet knowledge of the role of the manorial reeve shows that illiteracy is not of itself a bar to the keeping of accounts and the exercise of managerial functions. Memory, assisted by tallies, enabled more formal accounts to be dictated by the banksman to a senior official or the owner. It was the banksman's responsibility to monitor production, keeping tallies of the output of each hewer, and ensuring that each measure sent up the shaft consisted of the correct quantity and quality. He had also to pay the colliers, to provide them with sharp tools and candles, and to hire outside workmen as necessary to maintain the colliery and its buildings and equipment. The banksman was further responsible for selling the coal on a daily basis, judging the credit-worthiness of the customers, and again taking care to monitor quantity and quality. In addition, in the smaller collieries, he normally had to wind up the coal and stack it on the bank, as well as no doubt assist with the loading of coal on to the horses and carts of customers. Finally, he had to account for every penny of the money that he received and disbursed, as well as for every measure of coal that was produced, sold, or banked.

The office of banksman thus demanded considerable managerial and accounting competence, but combined these requirements with those of arduous manual labour. While most banksmen seem to have performed their manifold duties at least adequately, the owners of small collieries not infrequently faced difficulties in filling this post to their satisfaction. Men with sufficient expertise were hard to find for the wages that were paid, while the requirement to wind, stack, and load coal was doubtless a further deterrent. There were frequent difficulties with the keeping of satisfactory accounts. Handsworth (Yorks.), although presumably closely supervised by Thomas Stacey, agricultural steward of Sir John Bright and equal partner in the colliery, was plagued by incompetent and fraudulent banksmen during the thirty-two years covered by surviving accounts, including two who absconded and one who was accused of fraud. As Stacey explained to Sir John Bright, it was inevitable that banksmen were going to be of poor quality because persons of 'estate' would require a higher salary than the mine could afford, and he commented of the fugitive of 1674, 'He is, as most colliers, but a beggar'.[6]

At the same time, although responsible for the day-to-day running of the ubiquitous small colliery, banksmen rarely stood alone. Coal-owners frequently kept a close eye on their pits, while many small collieries were part of a larger estate, sometimes of the vast estate of a nobleman. Sheffield Park (Yorks.), for example, was owned and operated by the earl of Shrewsbury in the later sixteenth century, and it had its allotted position in the elaborate administrative system of the earldom. Weekly accounts, with a balance struck each quarter, were inscribed in large books along with the accounts of other local posses-sions of the earl. They were written there under the supervision of the earl's bailiff, Richard Roberts, from information supplied by the banks-men, Randle followed by Gilbert Haberiam. We may suppose that it was part of the bailiff's duties to supervise operations at the colliery, and that he in turn was overseen by estate stewards, receivers, and auditors.[7] Exceptionally, Beaudesert colliery (Staffs.), owned and operated in the later sixteenth century by the Pagets, in the park adjacent to their main residence, was so intimately intertwined with the local estate manage-ment that a banksman was felt to be unnecessary; the work-force of the colliery was composed entirely of labourers. But, also exceptionally, the colliers were paid a flat day wage rather than by piece-rate and thus one of the banksman's major tasks did not exist. Within Beaudesert colliery the gang leaders in each of the pits assumed some of the responsibilities normally borne by a banksman, while the earl's bailiffs and stewards were also on hand to compile weekly accounts and exercise manage-ment control whenever it was needed.[8]

iii. The management of larger collieries

The nature and structure of management was closely correlated with size, and as we progress up the scale of colliery dimensions specializa-tion of function increases and the numbers of men performing essentially supervisory and management functions inevitably multiply.

---

[6] SCL Wentworth Woodhouse (Bright) Br. 55/1–31; 56/4, 6, 11.
[7] BL Add. MSS 27532, fos. 83–97, 207–11ᵛ, 241ᵛ–3, 245ᵛ–62; LPL Shrewsbury 704, fo. 135.
[8] StRO Anglesey D(W) 1734.

Quite simply larger collieries, with higher outputs and more numerous work-forces required more management than a single lowly banksman carrying out a wide range of other duties was able to provide. The scope for the appointment of more highly skilled and rewarded managers was also enhanced. Turney Fell colliery in the small north Yorkshire coal-field, although producing little more than 1,000 tons annually in the 1680s, had as its banksman a former yeoman farmer called Ewen Waller, who was paid a bonus related to sales as well as a salary of 6s. a week.[9] As a first stage the banksman might be relieved of the winding and stacking of coal by the appointment of an assistant, thus leaving him more time to monitor production and sell coal. Next, where a colliery consisted of · a number of productive pits, separate banksmen would serve at each pit, perhaps assisted by manual helpers, with a supervisor above them. This supervisor would have overall responsibility for the day-to-day running of the colliery and the production of its accounts. In some larger collieries, there might be a further division of function, with an overall manager having immediately beneath him two officers, one responsible for the monitoring of output and wages and the other responsible for the maintenance of the underground workings and for on-cost operations and other deadwork.

The abundant records of the Fife collieries of Tulliallan and Torry provide some details of the hierarchy of management there in the mid-seventeenth century.[10] At Tulliallan in 1646 seven permanent grieves and one temporary were employed in the course of the year to supervise a work-force of just over 100 colliers and bearers. Although their individual functions are not described, it is clear from the weekly stipend of £6 (Scots) that John Bruce received that he was considerably senior to the others, since they received between 40s. and 53s. 4d. (Scots). We are given more details of the management structure of the same colliery in 1679, when the total colliery work-force was somewhat higher. There were then two 'hill clerks', who attended to the 'receipt and sale' of coal; an oversman and an assistant, who supervised the working of coal underground; an on-costman; and a 'compter'. The 'compter' must have acted as senior manager as well as accountant, for he received a stipend of £5, which was almost twice as much as the next most highly paid officer, the oversman, and also 6s. a week for paper and ink. At Torry in the same year a total colliery work-force of around 100 was supervised by two men on the bank, an oversman, and an overseer.

[9] PRO C. 5/195/15. For a further instance of a 'yeoman' becoming a banksman see Nef 1932, i. 425.   [10] ScRO Register House RH9/1/31-5.

Almost all of the coal produced at Torry went to the salt-pans and in addition a man was employed 'directing coals to pans' and another, called a salt-grieve, with a helper, 'taking in salt fra' pans'. The salt-grieve's helper also doubled as the night-grieve on Westerhill when that pit was working double shifts.

Owner-managers

Within such simple pragmatic managerial frameworks it was possible for medium-sized and larger directly operated collieries to function adequately, but in practice oversight by a higher authority was normally conducive to increasing the level of efficiency. Oversight could be exercised by owners or by agents or employees acting on behalf of owners, or by a combination of both. There is no doubt that as a counterweight to inefficiency and dishonesty, collieries benefited in true medieval fashion from having many tiers of overlapping management. While close supervision by an owner was almost invariably beneficial, under some enterprising owner-managers basic managerial procedures were transformed into models of systematic routine. Haigh colliery owned and worked by the Bradshaighs was just such a model. It remained in continuous production through the seventeenth century, averaging perhaps 2,500 to 5,000 tons a year, and employing upwards of twelve hewers. The Haigh Orders, drawn up by Sir Roger Bradshaigh and his heirs from the 1630s onwards, reveal a small team of auditors and overseers acting under the supervision of the estate steward.[11] In this south-west Lancashire colliery the banksmen were simply manual workers who stacked the coal on the bank. However, the duties of the auditors, who were illiterate, mirrored the managerial and clerical functions of banksmen in small collieries, and included supervising the hewers, recording their output, keeping them up to their daily production quotas of full-measure baskets, ensuring that they worked complete weeks, and fining them for any defaults. Auditors were also kept under scrutiny themselves, and if one should fail to dock the pay of a defaulting hewer he was to be deemed a 'wrong reckoner, and shall suffer and pay as such'. Similarly if any auditor should 'tally false with the aforesaid Roger Bradshaigh ... or shall *compaxate, confederate, coinbynde* or agree with any hewer or other person or persons whatsoever to tally false' then for each offence he was to be fined 5 d. The auditors were also at risk if they falsely claimed that baskets wound up were short measure; and if the offending baskets were weighed and

11 WiRO D/DZ A13/34.

proved to be 'convenient measure and so seen and known by the said Roger Bradshaigh', the guilty auditor was to be fined 6 d. Close attention also had to be paid to the size of the free baskets of coal which were allowed to the colliers when they had fulfilled their contractual quotas; and the fraud by which the auditors would only buy these free baskets if they were of extravagant size was to be stamped out, because it 'was a most horrid cheat and shame'. The supervision of the underground workings also fell within the remit of the auditors. Furthermore, they seem to have had the daily responsibility for selling coal, and were under instructions to use full measures and to treat the customers with civility. Finally, every Saturday afternoon between four and five o'clock the auditors had to repair to Haigh Hall to render account, and it was then that the weekly colliery accounts were drawn up.

In order to ensure that as far as possible Haigh colliery was 'truly wrought' and that the Great Sough was maintained there was a threefold strategy. Each hewer was strictly bound to cut his coal according to precisely specified methods and dimensions, under pain of severe penalties. Secondly, according to the 1687 Orders, 'the auditors and the overseer(s) of all the pits shall see that the pillars and works be truly wrought and left at their due bigness and that they do duly see into their own pits each week that this be done to prevent in time the overthrow of the works; and also that they go into each other's pits and through the works once a month at the least', fining hewers for defaults and informing the bailiff, Thomas Winstanley. Finally, it was decreed in the 1687 Orders that the sough had to be inspected by persons nominated by Winstanley every two months at least, and 'viewed and cleaned from the bottom upwards and not from the top downwards, and the least decay thereof in any place speedily and substantially repaired'.

Perhaps enough of the flavour of the Orders has been imparted to demonstrate the special quality of the management at Haigh. Haigh would thus appear to have been an exemplar for good colliery management in the seventeenth century. It had a series of expert and involved owners; it was located at the centre of the Bradshaigh estate, and thus enjoyed the full support of its administration; and, most importantly, it had a clear hierarchy of management and managerial tasks and followed a precise regimen of routine. Hewers had daily targets to meet, tallies had to be reported and reconciled weekly, the coal-faces and workings had to be inspected weekly by pit auditors and monthly by the auditors of other pits, and the Great Sough had to be inspected regularly. Sadly, no colliery accounts have survived so it is impossible to compare managerial theory with practice, but we are able to glean enough from the fame and longevity of Haigh to know that it was at least broadly successful.

So too was the colliery of the Clerks of Penicuik at Loanhead, near Edinburgh. The regime instituted by Sir John Clerk I when he acquired the colliery in the 1690s, had much in common with that of the Bradshaighs at Haigh, and indeed with that imposed by other pioneers of modern management, including Ambrose Crowley in his Durham ironworks.[12] Sir John, like the Bradshaighs, laid emphasis on written orders, bonds, and terms of employment, and the extensive surviving Loanhead Memoranda reveal the running of his colliery in extra-ordinary detail. For it was primarily by attention to detail, and by the laying down of meticulous management and working practices, that Sir John strove to create exemplary standards of efficiency and, con-sequently, satisfying levels of profit. Sir John I, as his sons and grandsons after him, made himself a renowned expert in many aspects of coalmining, and stood firmly at the head of the management of Loanhead. Beneath him was the grieve, and beneath the grieve the oversman and the check-grieve.[13] The grieve had overall day-to-day control of the colliery and its work-force, and was to supervise the oversman and the check-grieve, but his special responsibilities were the sales of coal, the regulation of measures and prices, and the payment of wages and other expenses. Much of his time had to be spent on the coal hill, where sales took place, to avoid any opportunity for the bearers to practise deceits, even if it meant being present 'in the midst of the night'. The grieve had to be literate, for he was required to keep a written account book, and to lay it before Sir John every third (*recte* second) Saturday, 'wherein two weeks debits and credits shall be recorded, and to pay punctually what he owes'. He was given fourteen days at the end of the accounting year to deliver his annual account to Sir John, together with his acquittance for all money due.

The primary responsibility of the oversman was to supervise the correct working of the coal, ensuring that the level was advanced at right angles straight forward, guarding against the 'sitting' of the ground and the falling of the roof, and keeping the workings free of rubbish. He was also required to supervise all on-cost work, to agree rates for the work, and to keep a book to cross-check the payments made by the grieve. The check-grieve, as his name suggests, was responsible for the recording of

---

[12] The account in Marshall 1980, 235–47, is excellent.
[13] Their duties are prescribed in ScRO Clerk of Penicuik, GD 18/995(1), 18/1011.

output by inscribing each hewer's production upon the check-rolls, which were then sent to Sir John to provide a cross-check to the grieve's account book. A vital ingredient in the Loanhead administration was the literacy of all its officers, and to ensure this Sir John placed great weight upon education, not just for his managers but for all colliers who wished to take advantage.

A major priority for Sir John Clerk was continuity of production, and high levels of output. This was encouraged by emphasis on good time-keeping and the working of full days and full weeks. A twelve-hour day and a six-day week were prescribed, and it was the responsibility of the management to see that each hewer and bearer conformed. Supplementary measures were also taken to standardize procedures and enhance output, for example, by the allotting of the hewers to their rooms at the end of each working week rather than at the beginning of the next, and by paying the whole work-force on the same evening rather than in 'dribs and drabs' over the course of the week. Continuous production was also facilitated by a battery of measures designed to ensure that the colliery was properly worked and well maintained, that repairs were speedily undertaken, and that future requirements, such as raw materials, tools, drainage, new shafts, and levels, were anticipated so that time, sales, and hence potential profit, were not lost. The maximization of profits, within the standards of honesty and fair dealing which Sir John set himself, was to be further facilitated by having stockpiles of coal always on hand to serve any customers who wished to purchase, by stamping out theft and the taking of excessive coal allowances by colliers, and by stopping them trading in coal on their own behalf. To preserve Sir John's good repute, and customer loyalty, buyers were to be given 'as good pennyworth as is given in any part of Lothian and rather a greater than less'.

Sir John paid meticulous attention to proper accounting, not only in the monitoring of coal from coal-face to customer, but by instituting routine and standardization into the payment of all moneys, and the frequent and regular compiling of full written accounts. Moreover, the system he instituted relied as little upon the honesty of his officials as possible. None of them was permitted to fraternize with the colliers, lest they be 'tempted to corruption'. On the evening set aside for the grieve to settle his dues and debts and pay the colliers, the presence of the master or at the least the oversman and check-grieve was mandatory. And further, to avoid any fraud or connivance between the officers, the grieve was to accept the on-cost book from the oversman and the check roll from the check-grieve only at an appointed meeting-place and time.

It was by methods such as these, allied to good judgement in strategic decision-making, that executive coal-owners could thrive. Sir Humphrey Mackworth excelled in a range of enterprises, and was patently an entre-preneur of exceptional talent and flair, yet he too owed much of his success to the establishment of meticulous accounting procedures and to a routine designed to lessen waste and uncertainty, as well as to maximize profits. William Waller, who found much to praise in Mackworth's coal and copper works, and 'observed his new con-trivances in the management thereof', drew specific attention to the 'prudent methods, for reducing all his undertakings to a certainty, free from hazard; his copper-men working by the tun, and his colliers by the weigh, at a certain price, which is constantly and punctually paid; whereby no fraud can happen to himself, without a combination of all, so good encouragement is given to the workmen, to be careful and industrious, for their own interest as well as their masters'.[14] In a sentence or two Waller thus highlighted many of the major themes in the genesis of efficient colliery management, themes which recur again and again in the history of coalmining in this period, the heroic as well as the prosaic: good industrial relations and labour productivity, the centrality of accurate weights and measures, and the indispensability of sound accounting practice.

Stewards, colliery managers, and viewers

There can be no doubt that the well-documented collieries run by Mackworth, and the Bradshaigh and Clerk families, lay towards the summit of efficient management, but this efficiency was not achieved by the owners' personal efforts alone, however efficacious they might have been. Owner-managers also relied upon the competence of the managers beneath them, and especially upon the head manager. At Haigh this role was filled by Thomas Winstanley, while Sir Humphrey Mackworth's works at Neath were all managed by Thomas Hawkins, the 'Pay Steward', who must have been a man of exceptional ability. At Loanhead, which was not a large undertaking, despite the close personal involvement in day-to-day colliery affairs exhibited by Sir John Clerk, much depended upon the grieves. But Sir John had difficulty recruiting men of sufficient quality locally, and frequently found himself compelled to dismiss incompetent or corrupt grieves and oversmen. One of his most successful appoint-

---

[14] Waller, *An Essay on the Value of Mines* (1698).

ments was a Newcastle man, but another grieve proved so disastrous Clerk lamented that profits fell by half, the coal works caught fire, colliers deserted, and 'all my business went wrong'.[15]

While the presence of the owner was usually beneficial, it was not indispensable to success. Absence, however, made the services of loyal men 'skilled in collery' even more indispensable; men who were capable of representing their master's interests in a businesslike manner. And if absolute honesty was not invariably the prime requisite, skill and judgement were. With a colliery manager of the right quality, especially if the collieries were part of a larger estate with its own tiers of management, a coal-owner could restrict himself to deciding matters of broad policy. Sir John Lowther was able to direct the management of his Cumberland estates, and mastermind a phenomenal expansion of output from his Whitehaven collieries, while living in London and visiting Cumberland but rarely.[16] Between 1667 and 1688 the rental income from his St Bees–Whitehaven estate increased by about a third, while the profits of his collieries increased fourfold. The secret of Lowther's success lay in trusted stewards and voluminous correspondence. Lowther was extremely well served by Thomas Tickell, who was his principal estate steward from 1666 to 1692, and by Thomas Jackson, who served as colliery manager from 1666 to 1675. Men of Jackson's calibre, reporting locally to Tickell, could adequately deputize for an absentee coal-owner, by receiving and interpreting on a day-to-day basis the broad policies which were communicated. How vital Jackson was to the success of the Whitehaven collieries is demonstrated by the rapid turnover of unsatisfactory colliery managers after his departure, which drove Lowther to attempt to lease the Whitehaven collieries in 1682. However, the potential lessee, John Gale, accepted the post of colliery steward, and remained in that office for more than twenty years.[17] Although Gale was ultimately dismissed following allegations of corruption, his tenure must be viewed as a success overall. By the date of his departure Lowther's collieries were capable of producing well over 35,000 tons and of yielding profits in excess of £1,000 each year, yet the structure of management under Jackson and Gale was broadly conventional. At Howgill in 1699, when over 18,000 tons were produced, there were five banksmen and three overseers in a total work-force of eighty-one. The

[15] Duckham 1970, 121.

[16] Details of the management structure of Lowther's collieries can be obtained from Hainsworth (ed.), *Sir John Lowther*; Beckett 1981; and Wood 1988.

[17] CuRO Lonsdale D/Lons/W, Collieries 18.

banksmen were to scrutinize and account for the quantity and quality of coal sent up the shaft and led from the pit, 'to go underground to prevent irregular workings, and to visit other pits as well as what they have in charge, the better to gain experience'.[18]

An owner searching for utter probity among his managers was likely to have to search in vain. Experience and expertise had to be balanced against the probability of a measure of dishonesty. The higher the skills a manager possessed, the greater the transgressions that might have to be tolerated. Even a man of such notoriously unsavoury reputation as John Hill, variously accused of theft, extortion, and manslaughter, remained in the employ of Sir Francis Willoughby because of his exceptional 'skill in searching forth and finding coalmines and getting coal', and the fear that if he were not retained he would set up in competition.[19] Charles Montagu likewise nursed deep suspicions of the honesty of Thomas Fenwick who managed his interests in Benwell colliery, fearing that as much as £200 of his money might be going into Fenwick's pocket each year, but he too hesitated to dispense with his services fearing that he might not be able to replace him with a manager as capable or more trustworthy.[20]

Montagu provides a further example of the success which could be achieved by an absentee owner. He was the dominant shareholder in the leases of Benwell and Gibside collieries in the Tyne valley, whose combined output exceeded 100,000 tons a year at the turn of the seventeenth and eighteenth centuries. But despite his extensive business interests in the north–east, and serving as MP for Durham, chancellor of the diocese of Durham, and High Sheriff of Durham, Montagu spent almost all of his time living in Jermyn Street, London. Montagu did not come from a mining background, but worked hard to acquire knowledge when he became a coal-owner; like Lowther he also kept in constant touch through correspondence. Lacking a local estate management, Montagu relied upon members of his family to act as his agents. He administered his collieries through his cousin, George Baker of Crook, a substantial landowner in his own right, but a man who also initially lacked direct experience of mining. Further assistance was provided by another cousin, Francis Baker. To cement the family connection Montagu allowed Baker to take a significant share in the leases; he held a third of Benwell. For the day-to-day management of

[18] CuRO Lonsdale D/Lons/W, Collieries 16.
[19] Smith MS, 86–90.
[20] NeUL Montagu, Montagu to Baker 8/3/97.

Benwell colliery and the sale of its output, Montagu and Baker relied upon two experienced Hostmen, both expert in running collieries and the coal trade, Thomas Rawlins and Thomas Fenwick. Both were also shareholders in the lease, Rawlins with a quarter and Fenwick with a twenty-fourth, though neither was liked or trusted by Montagu or Baker.

None the less, while such arrangements were sometimes conducive to success, the key role played by personalities is further illustrated by the failure of the ninth earl of Northumberland to extract adequate returns from his collieries while he languished in the Tower between 1605 and 1622. A major part in his disastrous attempt to run some of his collieries himself was undoubtedly played by the implacable opposition of the Hostmen to an outsider meddling in the coal trade, but by no means an inconsiderable part was played by the incompetence of his local estate officers, most notably Captain Whitehead. As an outsider Whitehead found himself constantly outwitted by Hostmen, lessees, fitters, and overmen, taking refuge in frequent protestations that 'I am not skilled in collery' and 'I find them all false knaves'. Despite the richness of the earl's collieries his venture into coal production was an unmitigated disaster.[21]

Subcontracting and delegation

The successful operation of a large colliery was a herculean task. The acquisition by the coal-owner of a knowledge of such diverse skills as accounting, marketing, and the geology and technology of mining was most valuable, as was the devotion of his time and energy. But even with such resources at his command he might be well advised to subcontract some functions, rather than attempt to retain all the diverse and complex spheres of production, maintenance, renewal, and sales under the direct management of salaried employees. In coalmining managerial expertise was often available from independent contractors, who shouldered some of the risks of the enterprise and drew their rewards from the contracts which they negotiated with the owners or lessees of collieries. The potential profits of mining a rich and conveniently located seam were generally high enough to permit a share to remain with such subcontractors, and in a great many cases the subcontractors may well have contributed more to the enterprise than they took out.

In collieries with sizeable work-forces the recruitment, training,

[21] The story of Northumberland's failure as a coal producer is told in greater detail below, Ch. 15(i).

remuneration, and monitoring of labour were among the most taxing of all managerial tasks. Inevitably, therefore, these responsibilities were very often subcontracted. For the owner there was much attraction in being able to engage a subcontractor who would agree to deliver on the bank a certain quantity of coal at a certain price. Contractors, called chartermasters in the midlands or overmen in the north–east, with gangs of colliers at their disposal, would then supply, supervise and remunerate the production workers. The precise mix of services offered by contractors and sought by owners and lessees were negotiable, but with this system in place the day-to-day responsibilities of owners could largely be limited to checking that the contractor was delivering the correct quantity and quality of coal, and that he was working the colliery in an acceptable fashion.

Such a charter system can be observed in operation at the renowned Wollaton colliery in the later sixteenth century. Here the charter-masters, known locally as 'stevers' or 'stovers', not only contracted to produce coal for the Willoughbys for an agreed price, they were also responsible for the sale of what they produced. A list of colliery rules specifies that 'all you stovers of the field shall make your just account unto your undermen every noon and every night what you have get and what you have sold'. Clearly the stover occupied the role of the banks-man with respect to his pit, supervising his colliers, calculating their earnings and paying them, and accounting for output and sales.[22] Indeed, by the later sixteenth century the charter system was prevalent not only throughout the Willoughby collieries but the whole region, and it continued to be the preferred method of very many coal-owners through to the nineteenth century.[23]

The subcontracting of production has often been seen as especially suited to longwall mining methods, and therefore more a feature of the midlands coalfields than elsewhere. But it was far more widespread than this, and far older in its origins than has often been appreciated, though forms varied to suit local conditions. A series of accounts for the collieries of the bishop of Durham in the later fifteenth and early sixteenth centuries, for example, contains many indications of subcon-tracting. At Railey in the opening years of the sixteenth century every thousand corves cost exactly 13s. 4d. in wages to stack on the pit bank, and a half-century earlier there was a fixed daily production quota for the colliery of precisely twenty-three chaldrons one quarter and six

[22] Smith MS, 43–5; HMC *Middleton*, 169–70.
[23] Ashton and Sykes 1964 edn., ch. 7.

bushels, for which each collier in the work-force, whatever his skills, was paid a flat 5 d. Such specifications suggest a contract between the bishop and the colliery work-force, which relieved his bailiffs of the chore of monitoring the performance of individual colliers.[24]

In the early seventeenth century, around the Tyne, the great coal-owning Hostmen bargained with overmen for the production of coal from their pits. The essence of the bargain was an agreed rate of pay for every ten chaldrons that were produced and an agreed level of daily or weekly output. Hugh Bird counselled the earl of Northumberland in 1608 that the best course for coal-owners was to appoint an overman to have sole charge of workmen, and he promised that he could obtain an agreement with Christopher Bowmar, a 'workman' in Newburn, to produce six tens a week at 26 s. 8 d. a ten. If the pits had no water Bird claimed he could get them worked for 20–24s a ten, and the only extra charge to Northumberland would be for 'roules', ropes, barrows, corves, 'trammes', and shovels. The overman would maintain this equipment and deliver such quantities of coal to the pithead as he had agreed to, at the rate of forty fothers to the ten, and eight bowls to the fother. Bird in a further letter provided a long list of Hostmen who, he claimed, did not work coal for themselves but contracted with over-men at the rate of 16–22s. a ten. The Hostmen, according to Bird, merely needed to employ a man who every Friday and Saturday 'pays out and totals the coal won'. Negotiations over rates between the coal-owners and the overmen depended upon working conditions in the collieries, and the ease with which the coal could be won, and both would need to be well informed about their history and projected productivity. In this the overman would probably be guided by his own judgement, and that of his colleagues, while the coal-owner would rely heavily upon advice from an expert viewer. Bird claimed to be such an expert, and if Northumberland had decided to operate his collieries himself he would doubtless have been prepared to supervise the manner in which the overmen were working them to ensure that his master's interests were not being harmed.[25]

It was in the great collieries of the Tyne valley that the fragmenting of responsibility and the delegation of function went furthest. In addition to producing the coal and maintaining the colliery, owners had to lead the coal to navigable water, provide staithes and storage facilities, and sell it to shipmasters. Faced with managing such mammoth and

[24] DUDP Church Commission box 79, 190024, 25, 28; 189700.
[25] DN Syon, PV 2(d), PV 3(f).

diversified undertakings it was sensible that they should depend heavily upon the division of responsibilities, upon subcontractors and agents, and upon successive tiers of overlapping management. The employment of independent overmen was not, however, entirely risk free, either for the owner or the overman. The sheer scale of operations sometimes placed independent contractors in great jeopardy, as they had to meet production targets and large wage bills. Owners often demanded bonds and sureties for the delivery of the contracted amounts of coal, and since unpredictability of output is inherent in the nature of mining, legal proceedings were frequently brought by partners against contractors who had failed to meet their agreed quotas. Nef has argued that the independent contracting overman, heavily burdened by debt, disappeared from the collieries of the Tyne valley early in the seventeenth century.[26] But his obituary was premature. The complete substitution of these entrepreneurs by a class of professional wage-earning managers was not feasible within our period. Managers with requisite skills willing to work for others for wages alone were simply not available in sufficient numbers, and contemporaries were unshakeable in their belief that wage earners were untrustworthy and poorly motivated. The independent contractor, on the other hand, was profit motivated; he took sizeable risks and reaped substantial rewards for success.

The independent overman is not hard to find in the late seventeenth century, and he was to enjoy a role throughout the eighteenth century.[27] As always in the coal industry there was a great variety of experience. In the collieries on the Wear in the early eighteenth century, according to J.C., owners rather than overmen appear to have played the primary role in the setting of the wages of hewers and barrowmen, and their output quotas. Here the major responsibilities of the overmen are said to have been 'to place the miners in their workings, or boards, or headways; and every hewer gives him an account of what quantity he will work daily, or give; so that he every day taking the account of the work, finds what number of men will complete the intended day's work or quantity'.[28] Likewise Fenwick felt that he could run Benwell colliery on the Tyne without independent overmen, and he set the colliers' wages and paid them himself.[29] By contrast, around the same time at Chopwell a fully fledged contracting system was in operation, with overmen

[26] Nef 1932, i. 426-7.
[27] For the 18th cent. see Flinn 1984, 56-7.
[28] J.C., *Compleat Collier*, 35-6.
[29] NeUL Montagu, Montagu to Baker 1/2/98.

responsible for the employment and management of the colliers, paying their wages, and supervising their performance. Each pit at Chopwell, of which there were up to eight working at any moment, had an overman at its head, who received payment in arrears from the Claverings based upon the numbers of corves which had been worked. The accounts of the overmen were settled quarterly in arrears, although cash was often advanced to them from time to time in the intervening periods.[30] Thus there was at the close of our period a wide spectrum of arrangements for the management of colliers and the production of coal which embraced the truly independent contractor, the working partner, and the mere employee.

Specialization of management functions as well as subcontracting also prevailed elsewhere in the organization of a great seasale colliery. Viewers and engineers, often employed on a consultancy basis, were required to advise on and oversee the technical side of the colliery: how it should be worked, the sinking of new pits, and the driving of new headings and soughs and so on. Drainage machinery was often sufficiently complex and important to justify a separate sphere of responsibility. Specialist managers for leading, waggonways, and staithes were often essential, and the fitters who sold the coal to the shipmasters were normally independent in earlier years, though increasingly salaried in later. All these sectors and their personnel needed to be supervised and co-ordinated by a tier of higher management.

A significant element in this co-ordination was often supplied by the partners of major collieries who acted in a fashion similar to boards of directors, holding meetings to review progress in the colliery, to instruct the viewers and managers, to supervise the keeping of accounts, and to take decisions on major issues of policy. For the part to be played by the enterprising partner in the running of a great colliery we have the list of 'Things to be considered of in order to the well managing of the affairs in the colliery' tendered to Sir Lionel Vane. First, 'your worship would be pleased to come over to Newcastle one day or two before the first Wednesday of every month; to inform yourself what is most fit to be done; using the day appointed by the owners to meet on to order the concerns of Stella colliery'. At this meeting the viewer should be given his instructions, after having had him read over what was asked of him at the previous meeting, and nothing should be done by any owner in the setting on or laying in of pits except at this monthly meeting. 'Next

---

[30] HRO Cowper, D/EPT 4877, 4878.

your worship would order all the overmen to present their bills . . . that
yourself may see their reckoning, and their moneys paid them where
most need is.' The cash for such disbursements would be made available
by Vane's fitter. The fitter would also be required to pay the staithe-
men's bills, which were expected to be presented weekly. Finally the
fitter was required to render an account monthly of all the sales which
he had made.[31]

Sir Lionel Vane's putative duties spanned both the oversight of
partnership business, namely the running of Stella colliery, and his
personal business. Vane had to ensure both that the colliery as a whole
was being efficiently run and that his shares of the costs and of the
output were being honestly computed. In most north-eastern collieries,
when the coal had been raised to the surface it ceased to be partnership
property and was divided among the partners in proportion to their
shares. Thenceforth it was the personal property of each partner, whose
responsibility it was to lead it to water and sell it. As we have noted elsewhere, while the transporting of coal by wain was almost exclusively
accomplished by hiring the services of freelance carters, waggonways
were owned by coal-owners, though lesser partners were able to pay for
the use of them.

In the last quarter of the seventeenth century there are many indications of a quickening of the pace of change in the management of north-
eastern collieries. Under the stimuli of difficult trading conditions on
the one hand and the growing expertise and professionalism of the
managers available to coal-owners on the other, colliery management
was becoming distinctly more centralized. The tendency for independent contractors to give way to employees is seen even in the enterprises of an absentee outsider like Charles Montagu. With growing
confidence and experience Montagu began to resent the loss of revenue
and peace of mind that he suffered from dependence upon the services
of independent profit-sharing Hostmen, and when he gained a new lease
of Benwell he appointed Mr Warner as colliery manager, who with the
assistance of his cousins left Montagu able to dispense with Milbourne
and Fenwick. Montagu also made plans to dispense with the services of
his fitter, Tom Rawlins, and replace him with another over whom he
could exercise greater control.[32] The transformation of the independent
fitter from a merchant who purchased coal from producers into a
salesman acting on commission or even an employee has been traced

[31] NoRO Cookson, ZCO/VIII/1/10.
[32] NeUL Montagu, *passim*, esp. Montagu to Baker 8/10/98, 8/11/98.

below.[33] The draft heads of agreement proposed as the basis upon which Lionel Vane sought to employ a fitter exemplifies the role envisaged at the close of the century. Under them the fitter was to be bound to vend the coals of Vane alone and to devote his whole time to the task. He had to promise to render a full account of ships loaded and money received monthly, or oftener if so requested, and to pay over such money promptly. The fitter was also to observe such orders and directions touching the price of coals or gifts to the masters, or any other matters, given to him by Lionel Vane; nor was he allowed to sell on credit without Vane's permission. Finally, the heads provided that Vane should pay the fitter a salary and furnish him with the keels and boats required for the vending of his coals.[34]

iv. Accounting procedures

'I must beg we may use (tho' at expense) <u>A good Accountant</u>.' It was by underlining his sentiments thus that Charles Montagu impressed upon his cousin the indispensability of keeping accurate and informative colliery accounts.[35] The first priority of every coal-owner was to know how much coal he had produced, how much it had cost to produce, and how much he had received from selling it. His second priority was to ensure that he had paid out only what he should, and had received everything that was due to him. If Montagu's sentiments are symptomatic of the increasing interest in systematic accounting which was being displayed in the later seventeenth century by coal-masters influenced by the rise of 'political arithmetic' in many fields from population studies to tax-collecting, they were scarcely novel. The keeping of accurate accounts and the elimination of fraud had always been recognized as priorities.

There are many ways of keeping an account of the operation of collieries, however, and variety had always burgeoned in luxuriant profusion. There was little standardization, particularly among those accounts drawn up on the site by mining employees, who often had little or no training in accounting, or even in communicating in writing, and who also had a host of other tasks to perform. Clearly the requirements of owner-managers of small collieries also differed both from those of large partnerships sharing costs and profits, and from those of

[33] See below, Ch. 15(i).
[34] NoRO Cookson, ZCO/VIII/1/6.
[35] NeUL Montagu, Montagu to Baker 16/5/96.

the nobility or greater gentry for whom a coal-mine was a small part of a vast estate, and this produced yet further variety. Other differences stemmed directly from the way in which collieries were managed; obviously subcontracting led to the keeping of briefer and simpler accounts than did direct management, while yet other types of account were kept by lessors checking whether they were being paid the correct amount of royalties. Finally, especially in the larger collieries, a proliferation of accounts stemmed logically from the proliferation of managers and the numbers of different activities which they sought to monitor. Production, leading, sales, and on-cost work were essentially separate operations, as was the receipt and disbursement of money, and increasingly they resulted in the keeping of separate accounts. Not all of these accounts were necessarily kept in written form. In the Lowther collieries at the close of the seventeenth century, for example, the banksmen were required to bring in tokens at the end of each month which exactly matched the quantities of coal which the written accounts recorded as having been sold.

It is best to begin with the summary accounts, drawn up for owners or higher management, for not only are they the most numerous of surviving accounts they are also the most comprehensive. For all their variety of form, they sought to record a common core of data on output, sales, and costs. Most frequently output is given weekly in the measures by which the coal was to be sold, such as wain-loads, horse-loads, rooks, chaldrons, etc., though it is sometimes given in the measures by which it was produced, such as corves and baskets, and occasionally only the value of output is given, or even the net value after the getting costs have been met. The costs of getting were then normally recorded, with hewing, putting, timbering, candles, and so on inscribed separately. Drainage, whether manual or by machine, usually had its own section. On-costs or deadwork frequently pose difficulties for the historian, for it is not always easy to discern whether they have been recorded in the summary accounts in their entirety. Sometimes separate on-cost accounts were kept because the sinking of new pits, headings, or soughs was considered a distinct operation, or fell under the supervision of a different officer.

Naturally, the form used for the earliest surviving accounts, which were of collieries run as demesne operations within the estates of the nobility, retained a close similarity with classic medieval manorial ministers' accounts. They were essentially constructed in keeping with the charge and discharge system, with income including any arrears

1. Remains of regular late fifteenth-century pillar and stall workings at a depth of 10–30 metres, revealed recently during open-cast mining operations at Coleorton (Leics.). The pillars average a metre in width, and the stalls 2 metres; the galleries have an average height of 1.2–1.5 metres.

2a. An abundance of early bell pits near Hopton Wafers (Salop), clearly revealed by aerial photography.

2b. A small drainage sough, with wooden prop, revealed during open-cast working at Newman Spinney (Derbyshire).

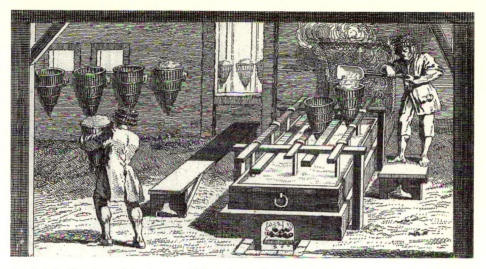

3a. Salt-boiling in coal-fired pans. Although the illustration dates from 1748 it is closely based upon a mid-sixteenth-century engraving by Agricola.

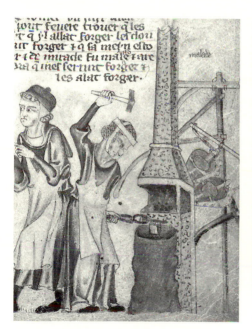

3b. A smith's forge with bellows and anvil illustrated in the Holkham bible, 1325–30. The fuel in the forge appears to be coal.

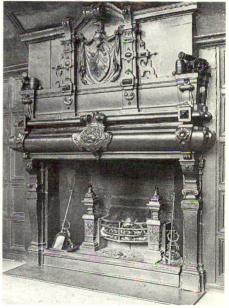

3c. The fireplace in the great dining hall of old Charterhouse, London, c.1610, with a cast-iron grate designed for coal-burning. It is decorated with the arms of Thomas Sutton, founder of Charterhouse and first holder of the Grand Lease of Whickham and Gateshead collieries.

4 and 5. Changes in the format of accounts of Trowell Moor colliery (Notts)

a) account for 1655.

March 28:1657	Pitts	Yett	Chalder	Sale	Moneys	Rem
Beginning of y yet load and upon y last accompt 2Booggs pitt Remaind: 298 load Burke: yett 311 load	Booggs	72. load: 2 Qd at: 3s 2d y load	6 — 1 — 2	28: load: 2 Qd at: ms y y load	6 — 16 — 6	342: load
Burke: yett 311 load	Burke	0	0	8	0	311: load
Annes pitt: 237: load	Annes	34: load & 2 galb at: 3s 2d y load	2 — 17 — 6	30: load & 2 galb at: 14 y 8: 2 load	19 — 2 — 5	191: load
Rem: tott: 846: load	Tott	106: load: 2 Qd & galb y load	8 — 18 — 8	188: load 2 Qd & galb y load	25 — 18 — 11	844: load

Aprill: 4:1657	Pitt	Yett	Chalder	Sale	Moneys	Rem
	Booggs	30: load 2 Qd & galb load	2 — 12 — 0	24 load: 2 Qd 2 galb load	5 — 19 — 10	348
	Burke	0	0	2: load 2 Qd	0 — 13 — 0	308: 2 Qd
	Annes	20: load & 2 galb	1 — 14 — 6	6: load & 2 galb	1 — 10 — 11	205:
	Tott	51: load: 2 Qd:	4 — 6 — 6	34: load & 2 galb	8 — 3 — 9	861: 2 Qd

Aprill: 11: 1657:	Pitt	Yett	Chalder	Sale	Moneys	Rem
	Booggs	79: load & 2 galb	6 — 12 — 6	71: load & 2 galb	16 — 19 — 7	356:
	Burke	41: load: 2 Qd	3 — 8 — 10	36: load 2 Qd	8 — 14 — 6	313:
	Annes	62: load & 2 galb	5 — 4 — 2	41: load & 2 galb	9 — 17 — 2	226
	Tott	183: load 1 Qd	15 — 5 — 6	149: load: 2 Qd:	35 — 11 — 3	895: —
				Rem tott	69 — 13 — 11	

b) account for 1657.

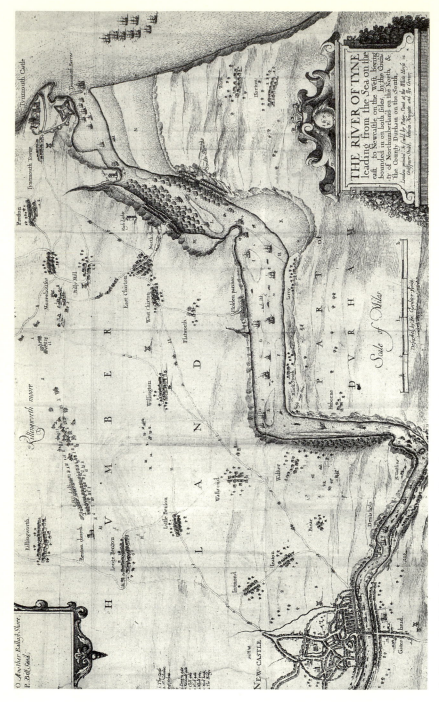

6. Wenceslas Hollar's map showing colliers clustering in the Tyne, waiting to be loaded by keels, 1655.

7. Coal barges on the Cam by Magdalene College, Cambridge, 1675.

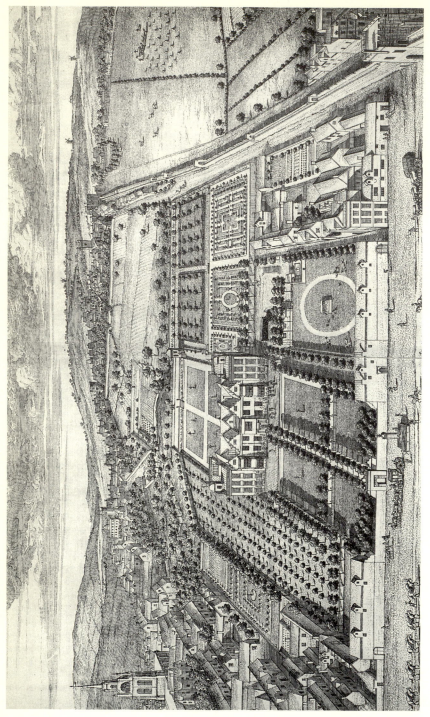

8. The Seat of the Honourable Sir William Blackett, Newcastle upon Tyne, 1708. The house lay within the city walls, which can be seen on the right. It was built in 1580 by Henry Anderson, a leading Hostman and Grand Lessee. In 1675 it was purchased by Sir William Blackett, one of the richest coalowners of his day, and he subsequently added the two wings.

recorded in the first half of the account, and costs, deductions, and allowances made in the second half against the total recorded in the first half. A balance was then struck of the money due to the owner. Such accounting was employed at Kilvey, in the Gower peninsula, at the close of the fourteenth century, and for the mines of the bishop of Durham at Whickham, Railey, Grewburn, and Hargill in the later fifteenth and early sixteenth centuries.[36] But echoes of this system persisted long after the end of the Middle Ages in very many collieries. The accounts of the modest colliery of Sheffield Park (Yorks.) retained strong redolences of the charge—discharge method not only into the 1570s but into the 1670s.

On the Willoughby estate from the later fifteenth century until the 1570s, the proceeds and expenses of the great colliery of Wollaton appeared in three separate accounts. There were two sets of colliery accounts, the Coal-pit Books which recorded output, sales, and getting costs, and the Sinking Books which recorded the costs of sinking new pits and other deadwork, the purchase of raw materials, and the salaries and wages of colliery officials and temporary labourers. The third set of accounts was contained in the estate Bailiffs' Accounts, in which alongside other estate accounts the material from the Coal-pit and the Sinking Books was presented and reconciled in the form of charge and discharge. In the course of the 1570s a single colliery account book took the place of the separate Coal-pit and Sinking Books, in which weekly entries struck a net balance after the deduction of sinking costs.[37]

Beaudesert colliery was, like the bishop of Durham's collieries, part of a vast estate. Yet the surviving summary accounts drawn up in the later sixteenth century took a quite different and far simpler form.[38] Weekly entries record in a few lines the number of days worked by each of the colliers and the wages due to them, the wages of the timbermen, the cost of candles, and the sum of money 'left clear'. The value of the coal sold or dug has therefore to be derived from adding all the amounts together. At the end of the year we are given a 'total of all clear of wages of the coal-mine'. From this total a deduction is then made for the costs of 'sinking, soughing, sawing timber etc.' and a final balance is struck. It will be noted that the production and sales of coal are not directly recorded in these accounts, but a single surviving document proves that separate sales accounts were kept. It consists of weekly entries of the cash received from sales. Also included in this document are occasional

---

[36] Rees 1949, 189–92; DUDP Church Commission box 79.
[37] Smith MS, 13–17.
[38] StRO Anglesey D(W)1734/3/3–3/4.

small sums for odd estate expenses, such as repairing the paling in Beaudesert Park, or carrying muck to the garden.[39] It is also clear that separate detailed lists of expenditure on deadwork were kept, though few have survived. Beaudesert colliery was run without a banksman and the form taken by the accounts reflects that fact, and the consequent necessity for estate officials to play an active role in the day-to-day sales of coal and the supervision of sinking and soughing operations.

The clarity of the Beaudesert accounts doubtless owed much to the fact that they were drawn up by professional clerks and accountants. The accounts kept of collieries outside of the central accounting systems of the great estates of the later sixteenth and early seventeenth centuries consisted far more typically of dense paragraphs of undifferentiated receipts and expenses. The account book of Trowell (Notts.) for 1619, for example, contains weekly entries in a jumbled form, in which output is hidden among miscellaneous payments to labourers and equipment suppliers, and no attempt is made to isolate production costs from other costs, or even from payments in cash made to the owner.[40]

Colliery accounting methods may well appear eccentric and inefficient to the modern eye, but it would be wrong to see them as irredeemably uninformative. They reflected the priorities of the owners and operators rather than the needs of historians or the requirements of modern chartered accountants. Almost all accounts contained within them a core of vital data on costs, output, and sales, even if it was presented in a form which made it laborious to extract. In Chapter 10 it is demonstrated that few accounts cannot be made to yield insights into the profitability of enterprises, even if they do lack formal capital accounting. Moreover, it must not be forgotten that a major determinant of the profits which the owner received was his ability to keep track of output and cash, and to limit fraud and impose efficiency. Consequently, the form of the accounts was often driven by these preoccupations, and as such they generally performed adequately. The control of fraud undoubtedly absorbed a disproportionate amount of an owner's or operator's energy and ingenuity. Such preoccupations were, of course, centuries old and by no means confined to mining. They were a major force in determining the approach of the medieval nobility to demesne farming, and the system of charge and discharge accounting which evolved to monitor it was primarily designed to cope with

---

[39] StRO Anglesey D(W)1734/3/3/246.
[40] NoUL Middleton Mi. Ac. 16. See also Pl. 4 and 5.

potentially dishonest officials.[41] It would appear that the energies of coal-masters were not wasted, and the indication is that the steps which they took were ordinarily successful in keeping the problem within acceptable bounds. Nor could the owner of coal-bearing lands necessarily avoid exercising a close supervisory role simply by choosing to lease them. Many leases by the seventeenth century required the payment of a royalty geared to the amounts of coal which were dug or sold, and lessees were accordingly required to present to the landlord accounts of output and/or of quantities led to the staithe, and many of these have survived. At the same time, because of the scope for dishonesty and the large sums of money which were often involved, many landlords felt the need for independent monitoring, which resulted in the compilation of yet another set of accounts.[42]

For all their deficiencies colliery accounts were among the most advanced of all forms of contemporary business accounts. The very nature of mining enterprises, with their periodicity and their flow of output and sales, and the need to record the productivity of the workforce and pay them wages, encouraged the keeping of records in a more regular and systematic fashion than was normally found elsewhere. Moreover, significant improvements were made during the course of the seventeenth century, most notably in layout. Data began to be grouped into appropriate categories and presented in tables and in headed columns which ran vertically and horizontally across the pages of account books. By the close of the seventeenth century it is rare to find an account that was not tabulated. Moreover, such changes were far from being merely a matter of style. Behind the improvements in format lay a more systematic approach to the running of collieries, and a management which was demanding a system of record-keeping which enabled many aspects of the business to be conveyed almost at a glance.

Though few if any colliery accounts drawn up before 1700 were designed to produce reckonings of profits acceptable by present-day standards, and there was no true profit and loss or capital accounting, and scarcely any signs of genuine double-entry bookkeeping, it cannot be held that their absence severely inhibited the rise of the coal industry. Such methods and data would unquestionably have proved useful to

[41] e.g. N. Denholm-Young, *Seignorial Administration in England* (1963 edn.), 120–61. For early bookkeeping procedures in general see B. S. Yamey, 'Scientific Bookkeeping and the Rise of Capitalism', *EcHR* 2nd ser., (1949).

[42] See e.g. the accounts of royalties payable to the earl of Northumberland: DN Syon CX 2*a*(1), 2*b*, 2*c*, 4*a*(1–3), 4*b*(1–2), 4*c*; to the bishop of Durham: DUPK Dean and Chapter, post Dissolution loose papers, box 10 provisional (mines); to Sir William Bowes: DuRO Strathmore vol. 36.

sixteenth- and seventeenth-century coal-owners, but prosperity often
came readily enough without them. The experience of the early modern
coal industry lends no support whatsoever to the hypothesis that
scientific (double-entry) bookkeeping was essential to the formulation
of rational business policies or the systematic organization of industrial
ventures. In an age when selling prices were often far above total costs of
production, and in an industry where most fixed capital was renewed
every three to five years at most, other methods could suffice. As will be
demonstrated in Chapter 10, few colliery accounts did not permit
output, sales, costs, and revenues to be calculated and mapped, albeit
with the expenditure of some effort, and it has been shown in Chapter 7
that information extracted from accounts could provide a serviceable
basis for weighing the prospects of future ventures. Of the higher order
of data, cash flow was also normally discernible, and so too was the
balance between output and sales, the average cost of producing each
unit of coal, and the average profit obtained from its sale. Bookkeeping
as practised by very many collieries, in all its eccentricity and lush
profusion of styles, was a serviceable tool of management and did not
put a significant brake on enterprise.

CHAPTER 9

Labour Relations and Work Discipline

colliers hate truth or true dealings as much as the devil hates a saint
or a religious person . . . and how to know a true bottom-man and
banksman, you must observe, if the colliers love them you may
swear safely they are knaves.

Langdale Sutherland of Featherstone, 1671

In contrast to conditions prevailing elsewhere, coal-owners and
managers had frequently to deal with workmen who were aware of their
scarcity value. Colliers fully justified their reputation as hardy and
independent men, and many of their customs and work habits were
inimical to the standards of efficiency which employers sought to
impose in their collieries. A priority of management was that labour
should work when required, and in many collieries regular working was
demanded. Coal had to be available when customers sought it, or sales
could be lost; bare banksides or large stocks of unsold coal were potentially costly. Yet colliers, especially well-paid hewers, had their own
preferred patterns of working, which often included broken weeks.
Moreover, underground labour was inherently difficult to supervise.
Seams had to be cut correctly or future profits and lives could be put in
jeopardy, and while piece-rate remuneration stimulated output it also
tempted hewers to increase their production at the expense of safety or
the ultimate viability of the pit. Fraud had also to be combated, as had
straightforward theft. Not only did owners feel that colliers were likely
to overstate the size and quality of their output, but also to steal coal,
candles, ropes, tools, and other pieces of equipment.

In addition to the normal conflicts of interest between employers and
employees, there was in coalmining a deeper clash of cultures, which
was heightened by the boom conditions which often prevailed, and
during which the bargaining strength of coal-owners was often severely
diminished. Winlaton colliery had a seemingly limitless market for its
coal in the later 1580s, and doubtless Winlaton colliers were well paid
and enjoyed benefits that in other circumstances would not have been

forthcoming. But the partners who ran it were plagued by a shortage of labour. In desperation they sought to recruit from Scotland and even resorted to the unusual expedient of employing women, but still 'many coalpits [were] laid in within the said coalmines for lack of workmen [and] in default, sickness and sloth of workmen'. Yet even here there was behaviour that they would not tolerate. Sometimes colliers were placed in the stocks for negligence in their work, and on a number of occasions men were sacked, the partners saying that 'they would rather have their pits lie than any such persons as did neglect their work should have their wills'.[1]

The larger collieries posed tasks of work-force supervision and discipline the like of which were rarely encountered elsewhere in industry, commerce, or agriculture at this time. Consequently, whereas in the smaller collieries discipline and conformity could be an *ad hoc* or informal matter, in the larger collieries labour was often subcontracted or elaborate codes of rules and practice instituted. One of the earliest examples of such a code, from Wollaton (Notts.) in the late sixteenth century, laid down rules for the 'stevers' or gang-leaders to enforce and obey. Fines were specified for the theft of coal or wood from the site, or candles, ropes, or tools from the pit. Penalties were high: if candles or tools were found in any collier's house he was to pay 3s. 4d., and if he were found cutting pit ropes, or with any rope in his house, the fine was a massive 6s. 8d., probably in excess of a week's wages. Sabotage was deemed to be a felony.[2] Doubtless because Wollaton colliers were under the authority of the stevers rather than directly under the governance of Sir Francis Willoughby, there is little in these rules concerning working practices and labour discipline, but in the orders of Haigh colliery (Lancs.), which was directly managed by its owner, such matters received close attention.[3] Large sections of the orders are devoted to the prescribed manner in which the coal should be worked. The precise dimensions of each hewer's room are specified, and it is laid down that pillars should not be made or shaped 'under a yard and sixteen inches on the side. Nor under a yard and a half and sixteen inches on the ends.' Hewers should get the cannel clean and not leave it 'growing to the bottom or the top' to the loss of the owner and the hindrance of the drawers, and every hewer should keep 'his drift or gates open according to the custom of the work'. Small fines of a few pence were to be levied for each breach of these rules, but for the hewing of coal from pillars or

---

[1] PRO E.134, 29 Elizabeth, Easter 4.
[2] HMC *Middleton*, 169–70.   [3] WiRO D/DZ A13/34.

any other action which weakened them and thereby threatened the whole pit, the fine was to be 40s. with further punishment at the discretion of the justices of the peace at the next session. Much attention is also directed to ensuring that the permitted allowances of free coal were not exceeded, and that they should not be received by those who had not worked a full week. As we shall see, the working habits of colliers, especially when they were relatively well paid, tended to fall far short of the commitment sought by management and owners. At Haigh no less than five clauses in the orders of 1687 were devoted to the 'sham practice' of voluntary absenteeism.

It is of particular note that the orders of 1636 and 1664 were drawn up in the form of a contract between Sir Roger Bradshaigh, his heirs, executors, administrators, or assigns on the one part, and the 'auditors, hewers, drawers, winders, treaders, takers of cannel at the pit eye and all other officers and work folks belonging to the pit and pits, mine and mines, of cannel for coal' on the other. The contracting colliers, men and women, 'in testimony of the free consents and agreements of all the other parties beforementioned ... set their hands' by making their marks before witnesses at the foot of the contract. Other agreements or bonds also survive in the Haigh archive. On 22 September 1662, for example, Richard Low of Whelley, near Haigh, signed a new agreement with Sir Roger in which in return for 12s. he pledged 'to bind myself and continue to be his faithful hired servant for the getting and hewing of cannel' in accordance with the orders and articles contained in the book, and 'upon such conditions as I have formerly wrought upon'. No term was specified. On 2 February 1669 James Glassbrooke, alias Wood, alias Anns-sone, bound himself for life as a hewer at the accustomed wages and according to the terms of the Article Book dated 23 April 1632. James also undertook to provide 'a sufficient drawer of cannel to draw from himself', and Bradshaigh agreed in return to pay him 4s. annually and to loan him 10s., 'which he is to pay again when he begins to hew by 6d. per week'. The payment of 4s. for the renewal of hewer's bonds dates back at least to 1636. While such bonds indicate a shortage of skilled labour and the desire of employers to secure colliers on annual contracts by offering them inducements, at Haigh we can also see them being used as a means of securing obedience to colliery rules. Such twin aims were not unique to Haigh and in 1676 a collier promised to well and truly serve in coal-mines within the manors of Hulton and Denton (Lancs.), according to the customs and orders there established.[4]

[4] Nef 1932, ii. 156.

None the less, despite the widespread scarcity of experienced colliers in periods of expanding output, bonds do not appear to have been common in England and Wales, outside of Lancashire, before the eighteenth century. But they were not completely unknown.[5] Sir Humphrey Mackworth, for example, was said to have used 'covenant servants bound to serve ... for the term of one or more years' in his collieries and mineral works at Neath after 1695, although his rival, Sir Edward Mansell, claimed that these bonds were only a means of evading forcible enlistment in the king's service. Mackworth's perennial difficulties in filling vacancies also led him to employ condemned felons, who were pardoned and released from jail on condition that they served in his works for a minimum of five years.[6] The earliest known bond in the north-east was made between Charles Montagu and the miners of Benwell in 1703. It was a simple document which bound the colliers to work for Montagu for twelve months and set out their wages and allowances.[7] An instance survives of a collier in 1681 being committed to Bridewell for breaking the terms of his bond, but there is no reason to believe that imprisonment was a common penalty for such a misdemeanor.[8]

Too much should not be made of the bonds found in English and Welsh coalfields, for in many respects they had their origins in the ubiquitous annual contracts entered into by labourers and servants of all kinds throughout the country. In Scottish coal-mines, however, there existed a system of bondage of a quite different order.[9] Here the politically powerful coal-owners mounted a remorseless and comprehensive assault upon the freedom of colliers and saltworkers, which resulted in the evolution of a species of industrial serfdom sustained by the common law. The scarcity of skilled labour and the acknowledged value of coal and salt to a primitive economy were instrumental, when supported by the might of the coal barons, many of whom either sat on the Privy Council or had kin who did, in the passing of a series of acts through the Scottish Parliament which effectively secured, in law at least, an unfree work-force of colliers bound for life to their employers.

---

[5] We should be careful not to confuse those 'bonds' which are in essence contracts between the lessors and lessees of pits and collieries and those which are genuine bonds between hired labourers and their employers.

[6] Trott 1969, 63–5.

[7] Flinn 1984, 352.

[8] R. K. Kelsall, *Wage Regulation under the Statute of Artificers* (1938), 35.

[9] The following passages owe much to the material contained in Barrowman 1897–8; Ashton and Sykes 1964 edn., 70–84; and the excellent studies by Duckham 1969 and 1970, 240–4.

Although it would be erroneous to seek the origins of collier serfdom in Scotland in direct survivals from rural serfdom, there can be no doubt that in important respects it antedated the Act of 1606, which has commonly been deemed to mark its inception. Scottish coal-owners, for example, made use of the Poor Laws of 1579 and 1597, which allowed for the binding of vagrants and their children for life, and the distinguished eighteenth-century lawyer, James Erskine, argued that the Act of 1606 'ought not to be so interpreted as to cut off or weaken any right which they [coal-masters] had been entitled by our former custom'. It was prescribed in this Act that no coal-hewers or bearers were to be employed without testimonials from their previous owner freeing them from their service; that fugitive colliers might be recovered by their lawful masters if challenged within a year and a day; and that offending colliers were liable 'to be esteemed, repute and holden as thieves and punished in their bodies'. An employer who failed to deliver a fugitive back within twenty-four hours was to be under pain of £100 (Scots), to be paid to the rightful master for each workman and for each occasion he was not duly released.

Subsequent legislation further extended the rights of coal-masters over their work-forces. By an Act of 1641 'watermen, windsmen and gatesmen' were brought under the law, because they were found to be 'as necessary to the owners and masters ... as the coal-hewers and bearers', and colliers were required to work six days each week and the number of their permitted holidays was reduced. In 1661 attention was turned to the leisure pursuits of colliers, and 'drinking and debauchery to the great offence of God and prejudice to their masters' was roundly condemned. The rights of coal-masters to impound 'vagabonds or beggars, wherever they can find them and put them to work in their coal-heughs' were ratified in a Poor Law amendment of 1672, and in 1701 the primacy of the interests of coal-masters and salt-masters was expressly recognized when colliers and salters were exempted from the protection of laws passed to prevent unlawful imprisonment and undue delays to trials.

Yet, as we learn from the history of serfdom elsewhere and at other times, the provisions of the law could be quite different from the relations which actually existed between masters and their men. According to the law, one might expect to find in the collieries of seventeenth-century Scotland a wretched subservient work-force, cowed into docility by chains of bondage and the subsistence wages set by their masters in defiance of the forces of supply and demand. In practice, however, the scarcity of skilled and experienced workmen endowed colliers with a sturdy wilfulness and an appreciation of their own value, and competition between employers mitigated the oppressions of the law. Recourse to the law seems most often to have been made by employers against each other, alleging enticement and unjust detention. The years of the English Civil War, when the Scottish industry had the English east coast trade to supply, produced a spate of labour cases as coal-masters fought with each other to secure sufficient manpower.[10] The Privy Council duly sought to apply the full force of the law to offending coal-masters. Some were charged with prodigious fines like the £2,000 (Scots) levied on John Henderson, the laird of Fardel in Fife, who wrongfully employed a fugitive collier of the earl of Dunfermline and refused on twenty separate occasions to return him. Colliers could be punished with severity for running away from their masters; they were beaten and liable to be held 'in torture in the irons provided only for colliers and witches and notorious malefactors'. But most masters realized that crude coercion alone was rarely effective, and sought to induce their colliers to remain at work with high wages and tolerable working conditions.[11]

There is little security in generalizations, and greater insight can be furnished by the experience of well-documented collieries. Tulliallan and Kincardine are two such enterprises.[12] Here the earnings of colliers, especially hewers, were high; on occasion exceptionally so. Yet flight and labour shortages could still be a major problem. At Tulliallan in April and June 1644, men were paid for tracking down and fetching home hewers and bearers who had absconded, while £8. 2s. (Scots) was the bounty paid for bringing a new bearer to the colliery. At Kincardine in 1679–80 labour scarcity revealed itself in recruiting drives as well as in unremitting efforts to retain the existing work-force by incentives and coercion. In May men were paid on a number of occasions to go to Clackmannan and elsewhere 'to speak some of those coalhewers to come to Kincardine works', and when six did come to see the works they were given £1. 10s. (Scots) expenses. Colliers were paid bonuses on completing every six months of service, but the blandishments of other employers seeking to entice Kincardine employees to work for them kept the numbers of fugitives high. Sometimes they fled to Bathgate, sometimes to Edinburgh, and on occasion they ran off to join the

[10] See e.g. *RPCS* 2nd ser., vii. 389–90; viii. 22–5. See also Nef 1932, ii. 158–61.
[11] ScRO Biel GD 6/999(3); Duckham 1969, 186 n.
[12] ScRO Register House, 9/1/31–5.

munition and oil works at Wolmit. On occasion recourse was had to imprisonment in the tollbooth at Culross to break the spirit of resistance. In November William Summer was incarcerated 'until he be engaged not to do the like', and three months later John Anderson, hewer, found himself in the same predicament. It is also possible to discover fugitives suffering the withholding of bonuses. John Thomson and Thomas Drysdale, for example, received reduced half-year fees in 1679–80 because they had both absconded together twice during the period, once in early July and again in September.

Recapture, imprisonment, beatings, and fines certainly formed part of the armoury of Scottish coal-masters, but it would be simplistic to view these as effective in themselves. The maintenance of a work-force of adequate proportions and acceptable efficiency could not be achieved by coercion alone. The high wages and bonuses paid to the hewers and bearers of Tulliallan and Kincardine have been noted, and the bearers also received small sums for 'shoe silver'. Drinking money was frequently allowed when work became especially arduous or unpleasant, or when there was need for urgent progress. In June 1646, for example, £2. 15 s. (Scots) was paid to the hewers of Tulliallan 'at Witsonday to entice them to work off drink'. Nor is there reason to believe that industrial relations at Tulliallan and Kincardine were in any way exceptional. In September 1662, just months after legislation had further confirmed and extended their legal powers, the masters of the coalworks of the barony of Glasgow made supplication to the Privy Council complaining that 'the prices of coalhewers are exorbitant and far beyond those allowed by the acts of parliament and paid in other parts of the kingdom'. They also complained of the great damage caused to them 'by the coal hewers not working but four complete days of six, and by their exacting their full prices in said time, harvest and every week', and that 'the workers at the petitioners coal pits spend all in drinking, having so many vacant days, contrary to the acts of parliament'. In response the Privy Council appointed yet another commission to establish rules for reforming these 'enormities'.[13]

The regime which the ardent Calvinist, Sir John Clerk, attempted to establish at his colliery at Loanhead, near Edinburgh, when he acquired it in the 1690s, has justly been made famous by the writings of a succession of historians.[14] What makes this magnificent archive of especial

[13] *RPCS*, 3rd ser., i. 258–9.
[14] In particular Duckham 1968; Marshall 1980, 235–47; Houston 1983. The Clerk of Penicuik archive (GD 18) in the Scottish Record Office has also been consulted.

interest is that the endeavours of Sir John, and his sons after him, extended far beyond the securing of the efficient management and high profitability that has already been dwelt upon, into reforming the morals of his work-force, educating them and their children in reading and writing, and instilling in them the true Christian principles of the Calvinist rule as he interpreted it. The magisterial study of G. D. Marshall has taught us that it would be mistaken to doubt the authenticity of Clerk's religious convictions,[15] but it is also manifest that the twin goals he set himself and his colliers engendered financial as well as spiritual returns. Idleness cost money in lost output, while leisure provided opportunities for intemperate and immoral behaviour. Like most coalmasters, Clerk struggled unceasingly to cajole his hewers into working full weeks, and he enjoined the grieve to 'banish the base practice of half and quarter days, which is so destructive to the master'. Fines of 26 s. (Scots) were to be levied on every collier for every day which he lay idle without such excuse as Sir John or his grieve would accept as reasonable. The absentee had to prove genuine sickness,

and as sure evidence thereof either keep his house or if he go to walk abroad to take the air for his health that he make it appear he hath abstained from drinking and tippling. Because for the most part it hath been found that such as lay idle did nothing but go up and down seeking people to drink and tipple with them, to make them that which they pretended to be, to wit, sick indeed, not with too much work but with too much drink.

Likewise, when Clerk sought to stamp out dishonesty he aimed to enhance both Christian morality and the profitability of his colliery. Consequently, he paid close attention to preventing excessive allowances of free coal, bearers from 'bringing up pieces of coal on their necks, in their hands, or otherways for their own account', and his employees from conducting private sales with his customers.[16]

Under Sir John the grieve's duties were in large measure religious and moral. He was enjoined to discourage 'all immoralities, flyting, fighting, cursing, swearing or stealing', to prevail upon the colliers and their families 'to wait on divine ordinances and Diets of Catechising', and to censure all who wilfully absented themselves from church. In the latter task he was aided by the Lasswade Baron Court which he also controlled and which in 1695 had ordered all tenants, cottars, colliers, and

---

[15] In particular Marshall 1980, 225 n. 23.
[16] See in particular ScRO Clerk of Penicuik GD 18/995(i), 'Coal Grieve's Obligation', 1702–3; and similar orders in GD 18/1003, 1023, 1033.

their dependants to attend church.[17] Clerk wrote personally to 'immoral' employees in letters to be read 'over and over again', how they might be saved from a 'sad and lamentable' end, and how by hard work and adherence to the faith they might secure a return to grace. From the written confession of John Kirkwood it may be learnt that Clerk even on occasion took colliers into his own house. Kirkwood recounts how he was 'kept in his [Clerk's] family and recommended to the care of his chaplain to instruct me and examined daily with his own children of my knowledge and catechism'. Nor was Clerk simply interested in the religious education of his work-force and their families, and in 1696 a request was made that 'all colliers and coal bearers who are not able to educate their children at schools give up their names to the said Sir John, who is content to cause to educate them at schools to read and write upon his own expenses'. Further evidence of his genuine concern with literacy is found in his offer to pay for anyone 'who is willing and desirous to learn to read the Scriptures'; with a reward of twenty Scots marks going to 'each old person who shall learn to read distinctly'.[18]

Clerk saw himself as an eminently fair man. In his dealings with colliers he contrasted himself with those coal-masters 'who bubble them up with a few fair words and a little beef and some pints of ale till first they gets them, and get the ton brought over their neck. Then their next step will be to diminish their allowance and last of all to force them to serve upon harder terms than ever I required.'[19] He was also determined to establish honest dealings with his customers, and the grieve was required to subscribe 'that the country be not oppressed by insufficient loads and exorbitant prices, I oblige myself to regulate both the measures and the prices according to the said Sir John his orders, that none may have reason to complain'.[20]

Yet for all his energy and authority Clerk found himself engaged in a relentless struggle for the minds and muscles of his colliers. Bondsmen and bondswomen they may have been, and subject also to the jurisdiction of their employer's private baron court in addition to a thoroughgoing regimen of by-laws, bribes, and blandishments, but they managed to retain a formidable degree of free will. Their obduracy led Sir John in June 1703 to stage a lock-out and to proclaim a further and yet more comprehensive set of 'Articles of Agreement with the Colliers'. But in these articles Sir John was careful to stress that 'if any of

[17] Houston 1983, 13.
[18] Ibid. 7.
[19] Quoted in Duckham 1968, 118.
[20] ScRO Clerk of Penicuik GD 18/995(i).

my servants, or tacksmen or servants shall do anything [that] is unjust or cruel to any of my colliers, wives or bearers, I'll take care to see a sufficient and speedy amends to be made to them with as great tenderness as if they were my brethren and sisters'.[21] Nor was he able to hand a docile work-force over to his son and heir. Sir John Clerk II proudly boasted in 1723 'that the colliers are not so uneasy as they used to be in my father's time, since I have calmly let them understand that I was indifferent whether they left me or not'. 'Till this secret was out', he maintained, 'they were a plague to all about them.' The records of John Clerk II's period of management tell us that his optimism was misplaced, however, and they impart little of his confidence that he had been able to resolve the labour problems which had plagued his father.[22] The colliers had their own sets of priorities and the confidence to practise them.

The regime which the Clerks attempted to impose at Loanhead was, of course, exceptionally dour and thoroughgoing. The nature of the industry, its working conditions, and the character of its work-force frequently meant that labour relations were rough and ready. The Clerks of Penicuik were by any standards exceptional men, but coalmining appears to have produced more than its fair share of extraordinary personalities, and John Wilkins, though cast from a very different mould, was certainly one.[23] Rising from lowly stock through 'his knowledge of coal delphs and by marriage to an heiress of the Wollastons of Shenton', Wilkins became mayor of Leicester in 1692 and acquired Ravenstone manor and 1,000 acres in the neighbourhood. But his main interests lay in coalmining, and he was one of the leading adventurers in the Leicestershire coalfield. Testimony given in a lawsuit brought by Wilkins against Lord Beaumont concerning a lease at Silver Hill, where Wilkins was said to employ nearly 300 colliers, paints a vivid picture of labour relations at his pits. Witnesses hostile to Wilkins testified that he had repeatedly beaten and ill-treated his colliers; to which the reply was given that he had only struck his men after great provocation, and that heavy drinking and other 'miscarriages and bad habits' made severe treatment necessary. Other hostile witnesses deposed that the pits were worked both night and day, and one claimed that his day's work ended around 11 p.m. On Wilkins's behalf it was testified that 'double turns'

<hr />

[21] ScRo Clerk of Penicuik GD 18/1017.

[22] Duckham 1968, 113.

[23] This paragraph is based on Griffin 1969 thesis, 12–19, 58–60; *VCH Leicestershire*, iii. 34–5; PRO E. 134, 5 William and Mary 17.

were worked only in emergencies or when new shafts were sunk. Friendly witnesses also deposed that Wilkins lavished attention on the families of colliers who were disabled and unable to work, or who had been killed in pit accidents, providing them with food, blankets, and medical care. Such benevolence, it was claimed, cost him £30 a year. In addition miners who were unable to work were sometimes paid 4s. a week. The charter system appears to have operated at Silver Hill, and Wilkins drove hard bargains with gang-leaders. But it was said in his favour that if men made bad bargains with him 'he frequently made amends with them by paying the diligent with rewards above their wages', and that hard-working colliers earned more than they would have done at another colliery. Some testimony was yet more specific: one man who had spent eight years in Wilkins's employ asserted that colliers would rather work for him than for any other master, but another no longer in Wilkins's pay recalled how he had been thrashed with a stick, which caused him to bleed for several hours from his injuries. Another testified how he was also beaten, for theft, and how after apologizing was told by Wilkins to report to the surgeon to have his wounds attended. Through the conflicting testimony there emerges a picture of a headstrong and violent, but compassionate employer, locked in a struggle with a sturdy and sometimes wilful work-force. There are thus some points of similarity between conditions at Loanhead and at Silver Hill.

For some rare glimpses of the attitudes of a leading north-eastern coal magnate towards his workmen, expressed in his own words, we may turn to the correspondence of Sir Charles Montagu, who operated Benwell and Gibside collieries. Immediately we do so, however, layers of ambivalence are encountered. Colliers do not feature prominently, primarily because Montagu subcontracted the management of production and the labour force to his partner, Thomas Fenwick, a Hostman. Yet Montagu was concerned both about their welfare and Fenwick's honesty when he wrote from London in March 1697 to his cousin, George Baker: 'I know of no reason my colliers should not take the same pay others do. I am sure if cousin Francis paid them they would. But I must doubt whether Tom Fenwick pays the same money he receives of you or pays the poor people in corn or some other of his master Sir James Clavering's methods.' Behind Montagu's misgivings lay the fear that he was paying too much for the working of his pits, with perhaps £200 a year going into Fenwick's pocket. In 1698 Montagu faced a strike of colliers for higher rates of pay. A letter written by him

in May reports that he had successfully resisted their demands, and that
Fenwick had quieted them and put them on work again. Yet he also
muses, with sentiments worthy of David Hume, whether raising his
colliers' wages might lead to increases in their productivity. In
December 1698 Benwell colliery was drowned during a widespread
flood of the area, and in a mournful letter lamenting the loss of the
colliery and making arrangements for the sale of coal, tools, horses, and
engines, and the transfer of salvageable equipment to Gibside, Montagu
finds time to reflect that 'the poor people are the objects most afflicting,
being without a retreat'. In the event Benwell was saved, but it continued to pose problems, and at the turn of the year, amidst a mass of
projections on its future profitability, Montagu wrote 'I confess the
frequent accounts of scorching the poor men makes it less comfortable
getting money by that colliery'. Finally, Montagu in December 1700
addressed himself to the opportunities for raising output and profits at
Benwell. He thought that thinner pillars might be left, though not at the
expense of safety, 'that we lose not a sheep for a half pennyworth of tar'.
As for their introduction,

no doubt the workmen will be against all improvement. But it is the part of a
manager to persuade and convince them; at the same time I desire no barbarity
nor hardship be put upon the poor men, but let them live as well as any
labourers in their condition do. It is my design and desire to give as good wages
for everything as any Gent. does, who pays well and has work well done.[24]

Actions speak louder than words, of course, but Montagu's private
correspondence with his cousin has the hint of compassion about it. The
same cannot be said of the estate correspondence of Sir John Lowther of
Whitehaven. Lowther's Cumberland colliers were poorly paid and their
allowances were niggardly. When in November 1696 the price of coal
sold to the country was raised from 3d. to 4d. the corf, John Gale the
colliery steward wrote to William Gilpin the estate steward pleading
that the colliers might continue to pay but 3d. and promising to 'take
especial care they do not abuse the favour by extending it any further
than to the coals they themselves do burn in their own houses'. But
Gilpin refused, asserting that 'they will only supply their friends', and
offered them a little free coal at Christmas instead. Gale knew the sort of
man he was dealing with, and when in August 1697 he mentioned at the
end of a letter that of late several colliers had been burnt in Greenbank

---

[24] NeUL Montagu, Montagu to Baker 8/3/97; Montagu to Baker 20/5/98; Montagu to Baker
16/12/98; Montagu to Baker 27/12/98; Montagu to Baker 3/12/1700.

and Howgill pits, and that one had died of his injuries, he was careful to excuse the intrusion by adding 'I only acquaint you herewith because we are frequently put to charges either in the cure, or burial of such'.[25]

The peculiar circumstances of mining encouraged experimentation in labour relations, and could spawn progressive attitudes. Some remarkable sentiments are expressed by William Waller in an essay expounding the potential of the great Cardiganshire copper-mines and smelting works, which in 1698 were lying idle following a dispute between the partners.[26] Waller had been steward of the mines, and at the time of writing he had recently spent time with Sir Humphrey Mackworth studying his coal-mines and copper works at Neath. He was clearly greatly impressed by both the man and his works, and his essay contains an 'Epistle Dedicatory' to Sir Humphrey, praising his generosity to his partners, charity to the poor, and conducing to the public good. Waller concluded that good success at Neath 'will be a means to encourage others to do the like, and to follow such a precedent as may in time extend to make a provision for all the poor in England'. Sadly, we can learn little in detail of the regime which was followed in Mackworth's mines, although there is independent evidence that he had the reputation of a philanthropist and it was claimed that his colliers were so well remunerated that none was ever likely to be chargeable to the town and parish.[27]

Waller concluded his epistle with the resounding statement 'labour now for the poor who will hereafter labour for you', and then went on to suggest in the body of his essay that a contented and prosperous work-force, enjoying among other things the benefits of sick pay and pensions, would lead in the end to higher profits:

That the poor may have some small share with you in so rich a treasure, especially the poor miners and labourers. That when they have spent their lives to make you rich and grown impotent and are unable to work, either through age or accident, they may have a comfortable subsistence provided for them.

This will bring you a blessing from heaven on your undertakings and encourage the most skilfull miners (and at the lower rates) to resort to that work, where they shall be provided for in their old age, and against all accidents. And this will tend to no small advantage to all the partners concerned, who will every year save more by cheap bargains than the charity will amount unto; and in this case, every miner will have an interest in the works,

---

[25] Hainsworth (ed.), *Sir John Lowther* 327–8, 332, 418.
[26] Waller, *An Essay on the Value of Mines*.
[27] Trott 1969, 57–8; Moller thesis 1933, 262.

and will be careful thereof, as if they were his own. Your works will never be in want of able miners or in danger of being lost either by neglect or treachery; you may then be truly called the Friendly Society of Miners and fear no combination to destroy your works.

The need to convince hard-headed, and perhaps hard-hearted, investors doubtless made Waller stress the ultimate financial benefits that would flow from enlightened management, but elsewhere he leaves us in no doubt as to where his true feelings lay: 'Who can admire that mines are sometimes unsuccessful when men presume to ship out the very bowels of the earth, enter into the secrets of the deep, and rifle the choicest cabinet of nature, without so much as consecrating the least part thereof to pious and charitable uses.'

Whereas nowhere in coalmining records can we find the visions of Waller put into practice, *ad hoc* welfare payments to sick colliers, or the widows of deceased colliers, are frequently encountered. At Trowell colliery (Notts.), for example, when Daniel Tylor was 'damped in the gin pit to death' in 1657 his widow was paid 1s. a week for a time, and in the same year Henry Cassell was given coal when he was sick and unable to work; in 1665, 2s. 6d. each was given to Robert Burton and Francis Beaton 'being hurt in the work', and 4s. 6d. to widow Stillington 'her son being hurt in the pits'. At Trowell, as elsewhere, it was customary for the owner to pay the costs of medical treatment for injuries received while working.[28] At Handsworth (Yorks.) we have notices of payments of corn and 5s. to sick workmen in 1660–1, and 2s. to a hewer named Firth in 1669 during a long illness. Compensation paid to a Handsworth widow in 1663–4, however, amounted to only 1s. 6d., while at Haigh Mrs Lowe received only 2s. for the loss of her husband. At Winstanley (Lancs.) we learn of a payment of 4s. to Lawrence Fareclough when he was hurt in a fall, and 3s. 6d. to Bill Birchall 'for the like'. Common though such compensation was it was entirely at the discretion of the coal-owner, and was not universal. Two Whiston (Lancs.) colliers claimed that they had been forced into an unsafe pit by their overseer. Their candles had ignited firedamp, and they told how the resulting explosion had thrown '[us] from one side of the drift to another and left [us] at the coal pit eye with our flesh torn off our arms, and arms and bodies so ill burnt that to look upon we were thought to be mortally wounded in so much that the pains made us mad'. They were unable to work as a consequence, and because they had received no compensation

[28] NoUL Middleton Mi. Ac. 16–33.

from their employer they were left owing money to a doctor and an apothecary, and forced to seek parish poor relief.[29]

Even in the collieries of the most sympathetic owners and managers such concessionary payments as there are record of could have provided only partial compensation for the financial hardship occasioned by incapacitating accidents or sickness, or the loss of the main family breadwinner. Yet, inadequate as they may appear, the very existence of these welfare payments attests to the special value placed upon colliers, as also do other perquisites, such as the financial contribution made by the owner of Hooton colliery to the wedding celebrations when any of his men married.[30] On occasion such considerations prompted corporate as well as personal action. On 15 August 1662 in the depths of a trade depression, a petition addressed to the king, 'in the name of at least 2,000 workmen in the coal pits', was read in the Hostmen's court. It complained that coal-owners and their overmen had not paid wages due to them or had forced them to take corn or other commodities in lieu of wages at rates far above their true market prices. The court responded by declaring that all arrears of wages should be paid forthwith and that in future all wages should be paid promptly and in ready money. Moreover, the court warned that if any coal-owners persisted in 'oppressing the workmen as aforesaid . . . they may be punished according to their demerits'. Likewise, when a complete cessation of production was orchestrated by the Hostmen in 1665, to cope with surplus stocks and trade curtailed by war, it was recognized that colliers were likely to suffer extreme deprivation. Accordingly, it was ordered that any member who managed to sell and ship coals should pay 1 d. per chaldron to the stewards of the company, who would then pay it to the owners of the collieries from whence the coal had come, so that it could be distributed by them to the workers of those collieries 'towards the relief of their present necessity'.[31] Even in desperate times the coal-owners recognized the need to retain a contented work-force.

The nature of coalmining and the rapid expansion of the industry demanded new approaches to relations between masters and servants. None the less, the mores and value-systems which prevailed outside mining necessarily influenced those who operated within it. New industrial entrepreneurs aplenty there may have been, but there were also aristocratic coal-owners who viewed their colliers as their own

---

[29] SCL Wentworth Woodhouse (Bright) Br/P/55/1–31; Langton 1979a, 71.
[30] LCA Mexborough MX 295, 296.
[31] Dendy (ed.), Hostmen, 127, 131.

men, and expected a loyalty and obedience from them which trans-
cended the mere performance of their labour in coal-mines, even to the
extent of rising to arms at their behest. When in 1648 Sir Robert Shirley
(Earl Ferrers) was arrested in connection with the alleged murder of
parliamentary soldiers at Ashby, he claimed that if he were not released
his colliers would plunder the town using muskets and pistols which
had been hidden in his coal-mine at Lount. His threat was ignored, and
we may perhaps dismiss it as the scaremongering of a distraught man.
Yet when Lord Hastings was ordered by Parliament to be taken, he
resisted with a force which was said to have included about a hundred of
his colliers, armed with muskets and pikes. When Hastings was
eventually captured at Leicester along with a number of his followers,
several colliers were brought before the mayor. They claimed that they
had been ordered by their lord to come to Leicester to aid the king.[32]

In some situations, then, the bond between master and collier
extended far beyond the paying and receiving of wages and the performance of labour. But such instances must have been rare, the product of
the potency of civil strife. It cannot be that there were many who hired
themselves out to toil underground with motives beyond the need to
earn a living, though there were some in authority who believed that
such motives were narrow and selfish and lacked nobility. In concluding
this chapter on labour relations in coalmining we cannot do better than
recount the exasperation of one Ralph Hope of Coventry, who wrote to
Sir Joseph Williamson of the valiant efforts of the city corporation to
keep the Hawkesbury pits open in the face not only of torrents of water
and the inconstancy of bankrupted undertakers, but the selfishness of
the colliers, who insisted upon being paid for their labours: 'Yet as the
money came in, it went to pay off the many debts contracted, which
caused a want of a full and ready pay, without which those damned
fiends, the colliers, will not budge.'[33]

[32] Griffin 1969 thesis, 57–8.
[33] CSPD 1672-3, 112.

CHAPTER 10

The Economics of Mining

If no profit can be raised, I see no reason why any man should
adventure his money.

J. C., *The Compleat Collier* (1708)

i. Risks and rewards

A paradox lies at the heart of the conventional view of the economics of
coalmining in the sixteenth and seventeenth centuries. On the one hand
we are presented with a matchless record of soaring output which was,
we are told, facilitated by massive capital investments made by
hundreds of eager adventurers; while on the other, both contemporary
observers and historians have painted for us a gloomy picture of an
industry plagued by inordinate risk, wildly fluctuating fortunes, and
frequent crippling losses.

J. U. Nef, despite being the most exuberant of champions of the rise of
the British coal industry, was profoundly pessimistic about its profitability.[1] Peering through a lens distorted by dependence on the
records of litigation in the central courts, he concluded:

after we have discounted the stories of failures, and have made the most of
such evidence of profitable enterprises as can be found, the impression remains
that coalmining was a venture subject in the normal course of events to
peculiarly serious risks, and we may apply to it the same words which Adam
Smith used in describing the quest for precious metals—'a lottery, in which the
prizes do not compensate the blanks, though the greatness of some tempts the
many adventurers to throw away their fortunes in such unprosperous
projects'.

However strenuous the attempts to spread risk might be, Nef continued, 'to judge from the accounts left us by the early investors in coal-
mines ... the losses nevertheless were great'. While maintaining that
many of these losses were sustained by 'landowners' who sought
inexpertly to exploit single-handedly the mineral resources of their own

[1] Nef 1932, esp. ii. 65–78.

estates, or were drawn into taking leases of mines in other men's estates, Nef also believed that 'the enterprises belonging to partnerships seem to have been hardly more successful'. Of course, he admitted that there were good profits to be made at certain times and in certain circumstances, but even in the booming Tyne valley the experiences of coal-mining adventurers did not make cheerful reading. Writing almost contemporaneously but independently, Aster Moller characterized the sixteenth century, from the perspective of the investor, as the 'decay of mining', and the seventeenth century as the 'risk of mining'. For Moller, it was only in the eighteenth century that profits became more certain and more substantial.[2]

Succeeding writers have found themselves swayed in a similar fashion by spectacular bankruptcies sustained by the likes of Huntington Beaumont, Sir John Ashburnham, and Sir John Winter, and the vast losses sustained by coal adventurers such as the Strelleys, the earl of Dover, Sir Percival Willoughby, the second earl of Wemyss, and Robert Cunningham. Those who have acquainted themselves with the proliferous jeremiads of apparently well-intentioned independent contemporary observers have found scant reason to stray far from this path. Lawrence Stone determined that 'the truth of these gloomy prognostications can easily be demonstrated from the history of the coal industry, in which many of the greater gentry of the north and midlands ... plunged heavily and often disastrously'. As Bevis Bulmer put it so succinctly, 'whosoever is a mineral man must of force be a hazard adventurer ... as if he were a gamester playing at dice or such unlawful games', while the musing of James, Lord Mountjoy, that 'a wise man would not hazard certain things for uncertain, neither would seek his living under the ground if it might be gotten above ground', has a folksy persuasiveness.[3] These homilies were uttered with respect to gold- and alum-mining respectively, but Stephen Primatt had coalmining very much in mind when he concluded his sober account of investment opportunities underground with the warning that 'mines of whatever nature or kind soever in England, are for the most part, very great casualties, and the profit of them very uncertain', and that the generality of unwrought collieries were 'worth little or nothing'.[4] William Gray, the historian of Newcastle who did much to publicize the undoing of Huntington Beaumont, cautioned that he could 'remember one, of many, that raised

[2] Moller thesis 1933, 162.
[3] Stone 1965, 339–40.
[4] Primatt, *City and Countrey Purchaser* (1680), 28–31.

his estate by the coal trade [but] many of them, hath consumed and spent great estates and died beggars'. Especially notable, he tells us with northern relish, was the high failure rate of ventures by southerners into the mines of Northumberland and Durham.[5] Gray's eloquence does little to conceal his pleasure at Beaumont's journey southwards 'upon his light horse' having wasted £30,000, and Primatt a generation later concurred 'that it hath often been observed that South-country men do very seldom get anything but trouble by undertakings in collieries; it being the nature of many North-country men to have a kind of anti-pathy against the thriving of any but themselves'.

It is only in recent years that systematic studies have been made of the records generated by the owners and managers of collieries, and they have perforce concentrated upon individual collieries, the collieries of a single coal-owner, or at most a single coalfield.[6] Hitherto our knowledge of the economics of British coalmining in the medieval and early modern eras has been drawn largely from a range of individual instances and random notices, often culled from biased evidence presented in liti-gation and the comments of contemporary observers who were more attracted to the extraordinary than to the typical. J. U. Nef relied very heavily for his impressions of risks and rewards upon litigation con-ducted in the central courts between colliery partners, or between part-ners and their creditors or landlords. Contentious proceedings between interested parties frequently produce distortion: mine operators plead-ing in such circumstances have an understandable tendency to exagger-ate the sums which they have invested, to inflate the costs or losses which they have incurred, and to minimize the profits which they have pocketed. Moreover, in the nature of things, litigation is likely to con-tain more than its fair share of failures, while those collieries which featured in the lofty proceedings of Star Chamber, Chancery, Exche-quer, and the Duchy of Lancaster, upon which Nef relied so heavily, are likely to have been exceptional in many further ways.

Mining was without doubt one of the most 'venturesome' of all industrial activities. Compared to the sedate occupation of landowner or gentleman farmer, it was positively fraught with danger. Unlike most forms of industrial production, the success of a coal-mine did not depend solely upon the efficiency with which it was operated and the health of the market for its product. The profitability of coalmining was

---

[5] Gray, *Chorographia*, 86–7.

[6] Most notably, Langton 1979a (south-west Lancs.); White thesis 1969 and Grant thesis 1977 (Newdigates and War.); Beckett 1981 and Wood 1988 (Lowther and west Cumberland).

additionally dependent upon such unpredictable factors as the richness of the seam being mined, its accessibility and durability; ventilation; the presence of water and the scale and direction of its flow. Luck inevitably played a major part. Skill and caution, as well as ample supplies of cash, could greatly lessen the risks of mining, but they could not eliminate them, or even in most instances reduce them to modest proportions. Sir Ralph Delaval, an astute and highly successful coal-owner, received a note one evening in 1676 while at dinner, which informed him that Seaton Delaval, his best colliery, had flooded. Pessimistically he put the loss at not less than £7,000. When learning that the colliery had been flooded by a spring and not the sea, Delaval rejoiced, and he finally drained it at a cost of £2,300. The importance of a deep pocket was, however, in this instance crucial. For after the expenditure of £1,700 no progress had been made towards lowering the water level. Many a colliery failed because its proprietor ran out of money. At the same time, ample resources by themselves provided no guarantee of eventual success. Sir William Blackett, one of the greatest coal-owners of his day, related how he had 'cut into an hill, in order to drain the water, and conquered all difficulties of stone, and the like, 'till he came to clay, and that was too hard for him; for no means of timber, or walls, would resist, but all was crowded together; and this was by the weight of the hill bearing upon a clay that yielded'. In attempting to construct this sough Blackett claimed to have lost £20,000.[7]

There was a multitude of ways of losing money in coalmining, but water was perhaps the most potent of all. Richard Knightley and Isaac Bromwich, while struggling to drain Bedworth colliery in 1640, complained to the mayor of Coventry that they were 'compelled to run upon two desperate conclusions, either proceed at a vast charge and hazard, or else give over and lose all'.[8] Fire too could overwhelm a colliery, and its proprietor's fortune. It was claimed that the fire at Little Fawside colliery had cost the Master of Elphinstone £10,000 (Scots) by 1621, and that it 'undid the late laird's estate, made him sell a part of his old heritage, and to contract great debts, which are not yet paid, and the daily charges of that coal occasioned by the fire on the one side and the water on the other exhausts the whole profit of that coal'.[9] If geological problems could make it impossible to mine coal at an economic price, even an efficient colliery could suffer the loss of its market. Sales might slump because of war and the consequent disruption of shipping,

[7] North, *Life of Francis North*, 136–8.
[8] Hughes thesis 1979, 23.   [9] *RPCS* xii. 434.

harvest failure and trade depression could force down demand, or customers might be better served by a newly-opened colliery with yet lower costs of production or a more favourable location. Thus the Dutch War was said in 1653 to have caused great damage to the hitherto highly profitable Winlaton colliery, where the proprietors claimed they faced a loss of 3 *d.* on each chaldron without taking account of rent, since the coal, which was considered too small for the English market could no longer be sent to Holland.[10] The manifold reasons put forward for the poor performance of Sheffield Park coal-pits in 1630–1 were by contrast wholly domestic, but none the less compelling. Namely the mild winter, the high price of corn so 'people was constrained to sit with small fires rather than want bread', the depression in the local cutlery and brewing trades, increased competition from other pits in the vicinity, the faulting of the seam, and the poor quality of the coal which was dug.[11]

Nor was the financial health of a colliery dependent solely on good fortune, efficient production, and buoyant demand. An excessively high rent payable to a landlord might substantially reduce the profits of the proprietor or even turn them into losses. To take an extreme example, Measham colliery made an operating profit between 1611 and 1623, but it came nowhere near meeting the inflated rent of £500 which Thomas Beaumont had agreed to pay, with the result that he claimed to have lost over £4,890 in the course of the twelve years that he worked the colliery.[12] In a similar, though less dramatic vein, we find that the mines of Beaudesert and Cannock Chase when worked by their owner the earl of Shrewsbury between 1697 and 1701 produced a profit which ranged between £368 and £485, giving him a return of 25 per cent on turnover. Yet if profits had been at the same level in the preceding nine years, when the collieries had been worked by lessees, they would have been virtually eliminated by the annual rent of £350 which they had to pay to the earl. Small wonder then that the leseees quarrelled and the earl was forced to repossess.[13] Landlords could often make a profit when lessees could not.

Clearly then, there were so many potential pitfalls in this industry that even the successful entrepreneur was likely to advise those dear to him against prospecting for coal and investing in mining. When John

[10] Welford (ed.), *Committees for Compounding*, 287.
[11] SCL Wentworth Woodhouse (Bright) BR (50)1.
[12] *VCH Leicestershire*, iii. 33.
[13] StRO Anglesey D(W)603/F/3/1/17; PRO C. 5/133/57.

Weld mistakenly thought he was close to death, he cautioned his son 'not to be busy in building, nor in suits in law, nor in searching for coals, nor in ironworks, nor in much hospitality or expense etc.; for these will be means to waste his estate; and let him not be led away by colliers, or miners, or proprietors, whose fair speech is but to get themselves money'. Yet Weld himself had engaged in all of these activities, and with a considerable measure of success.[14] Likewise, William Cotesworth could freely proclaim that coalmining 'cannot be undertaken without the hazard of an excessive loss', while appreciating that it lay at the very heart of his rise to prosperity.[15] And if coalmining was apt to prove hazardous to the prudent and skilful how much more so was it for the foolhardy or ignorant? It is difficult to improve upon Stephen Primatt's warnings:

There are many projectors (who have more of fancy and imagination in their designs than of any real operation) that do undertake even impossibilities in the draining these and other sorts of mines; being many times such as the owners value at little or nothing . . . until at length by sad experience they find that instead of draining the water, their pockets are drained.[16]

Instances of pockets being drained rather than water abound in the annals of early modern coalmining, but does this mean that the industry as a whole was unprofitable? Could an industry which failed to generate profits succeed in attracting sufficient capital investment to underpin a massive long-term surge in output? If investment in coalmining was so much more likely to result in losses than gains, why did generations of adventurers and investors devote ever increasing amounts of time and money to raising ever greater quantities of coal? Was the rapid and sustained growth of one of Britain's leading industries founded more upon a fever of misguided speculation than upon a rational assessment of risk and reward? Common sense, the laws of economics, and a mass of evidence ranging from the circumstantial to the hard statistical tell us that the conventional wisdom is most unlikely to have been true. We know from the wealth accumulated by scores of coal-owners that the gloomiest reflections of contemporaries and historians cannot be true. Sir William Blackett may have wasted £20,000 on a single sough, and a fortuitous underground spring may have cost Sir Ralph Delaval £2,300 to staunch, but they both died rich men and coalmining was the main source of their wealth. As the anonymous author of the *Compleat Collier*

---

[14] ShRO Forester box 163.   [15] Ellis 1981, 67.
[16] Primatt, *City and Countrey Purchaser*, 31.

drily remarked, 'if no profit can be raised, I see no reason why any man should adventure his money'.[17]

Good history can rarely be written from anecdote alone, and the following sections on profitability, capital investment, productivity and patterns of production, instead draw heavily on analyses of surviving colliery accounts, as well as upon a wide range of ancillary management records. Well over thirty series of colliery accounts have been studied, most of them for the first time. The core of the new statistical material which will be presented comes from fourteen collieries which, in terms of the numbers, quality, and continuity of their accounts provide the firmest foundations that can be obtained for the period before 1700. These collieries are: Handsworth and Sheffield Park in Yorkshire; Heanor in Derbyshire; Trowell Moor, Cossall Moor, and Wollaton in Nottinghamshire; Beaudesert and Cannock Chase in Staffordshire; Farnworth in Lancashire; Railey in south Durham and Chopwell on Tyneside; Niddrie and Tulliallan in Scotland; and Chirk Castle in Denbighshire. To these may be added a host of less informative series, as well as individual or small clusters of colliery accounts, and the mass of information that may be drawn from a wide variety of sources including estate surveys, correspondence, projections and business plans, litigation, and the mining literature and commentaries which emanated from both inside and outside the industry.

Colliery accounts burgeoned in a bewildering variety of forms. The skills of the accountant, who might be a lowly man indeed, and the needs of the colliery proprietor, largely determined their shape. Consequently they are frequently ill-suited to the convenience of the historian. Before 1700 there was no true profit and loss accounting, and precious few signs of any genuine double-entry bookkeeping. Indeed, strong redolences of the medieval system of charge and discharge accounting persisted through to 1700 in most of the smaller collieries. It should not come as a surprise, therefore, that the enticing of acceptable and accurate investment or profit figures from such documents poses some formidable problems. We should not complain too stridently, however, for colliery accounts were superior to the majority of comparable records kept in other sectors of industry or by merchants. Despite the variety of their constructions, the accounts kept by owners and managers of collieries sought to record a common core of facts on output, sales, and costs, and with persistence they can be made to disgorge them in a useful form. It is by the analysis of such data that the

[17] J.C., *Compleat Collier*, 19.

paradox surrounding the risks and rewards of coalmining can be best resolved.

ii. Capital investment

There can be no doubt that coalmining was among the most highly capitalized of the industries of later sixteenth- and seventeenth-century Britain, but it did not have an insatiable appetite for investment funds. Although by the close of the seventeenth century the amount of capital sunk into one of the greatest seasale collieries of Tyneside may have exceeded £10,000, such collieries were few and far outnumbered by multitudes of lesser undertakings. Moreover, only a small proportion of working collieries were established on green-field sites in any given period, and growth was normally a cumulative process. Research into the records of mining enterprises of all sizes reveals the remarkable extent to which the industry was able to be self-financing. By far the greater part of capital requirements, even during periods of rapid growth, were met from ploughed-back or retained profits, rather than by funds attracted from outside the industry. The nature of coalmining and the manner in which it was operated, both necessitated and facilitated a constant flow of capital from within.

Mining is unique in its demands for the constant replacement and renewal of its capital stock, and before 1700 this characteristic was especially prominent. Mining in this period was a shifting process. The relatively low costs of sinking and the fact that the majority of pits were normally not deep, meant that it was frequently less costly to sink new pits than to suffer the enhanced costs and technical problems of working coal-faces long distances from the eye of the shaft.[18] Shallow pits were worked for a matter of months, and few of the the deeper ones had lives longer than a couple of years. Moreover, such machinery as existed was largely constructed on-site from wood, leather, and hemp, with only a little iron, and consequently it too lacked durability. Even at the most capital-intensive end of the industry, the annual maintenance and repair bill of a waggonway seems often to have amounted to upwards of 30 per cent of its original construction cost. The consequence was that the fixed capital of the larger coal-mines was effectively replaced completely in cash terms, if not necessarily in all respects physically, every three to five years at the most, while in the majority of smaller mines the longevity of capital was briefer still. Thus

[18] See above Ch. 6(i).

investment in capital was continuous even in stable working collieries, and largely took the form of running investment rather than true capital investment. In other words the overwhelming bulk of investment in the medieval and early modern coal industry took the form of capital expenditure devoted to the maintenance of output rather than true net capital investment designed to increase output.

A further and related characteristic was that the capital value of even heavily capitalized mines was not large in comparison with the value of the coal they produced each year or even with the costs of producing it. Thus a colliery capitalized at £10,000 might produce coal worth at least half this sum each year, and the annual turnover of smaller collieries might frequently exceed their capital value. In this respect coal-mines shared similarities with other forms of contemporary industrial enterprise. In the iron industry, for example, a furnace and forge might cost £400 or £500 to build in the mid-seventeenth century, but this was small in comparison with the costs of the fuel and raw materials required to operate it for a year.[19] Furthermore, since by far the greater part of any large-scale capital project in coalmining was contributed by labour and, with the exception of the wood required for the construction of waggonways, few items costing more than a few pounds were ever purchased outright, capital expenditure largely took the form of wages and was spread over many months and sometimes, in the case of soughs, over many years. Therefore, capital expenditure could often be geared closely to income, and major new investment which was undertaken in response to rising profits could often be largely financed out of them, without undue strain upon the cash flow of the business.

Detailed costings of the starting up of production from scratch are not plentiful, for the documents on which this extraordinary expenditure was recorded have rarely survived. Generalizations are never easy to make for an industry which ran the gamut from mere holes in the ground sporadically scratched by a single man to enterprises employing hundreds, and consisting of multiple deep shafts, soughs, drainage and winding machinery, buildings, horses, waggonways and their rolling stock, staithes, and keels. Moreover, among the surviving records of start-ups, medium-sized collieries are overrepresented. The handful of cases we can call upon, therefore, are more in the nature of instances than illustrative examples, but they do throw light on the fixed capital cost of providing each additional ton of output in the later sixteenth and seventeenth centuries.

[19] L. A. Clarkson, *The Pre-Industrial Economy in England, 1500-1750* (1971), 98-9.

We begin with the opening of three collieries in the first years of the seventeenth century. Beaudesert, after a lengthy and generally highly profitable phase of exploitation, ceased working sometime between September 1585 and 1588, when a survey made of Rugeley manor described the workings as decayed and of no profit to the lord. Between spring and autumn 1600 'Wilkins and his company . . . set the coalpits anew'. In all, four pits of between 70 and 95 feet in depth were successfully sunk and timbered, and one sinking 'was given over before it was sunk to the coal by means of the great abundance of water'. A head 26 yards in length was then driven between two of the new pits, an old sough was scoured and a new one constructed, a smithy was built, a device was made with poles 'to put away the earth damp out of the coal-pits', and a lamp was purchased with the same intention. The total cost of setting up the colliery was £58. 2s. 6d., which included all necessary tools for winning coal, and fees of £3 to Mr Wilkins who had supervised the work. Just two years later the four coal-pits and one water pit then existing at Beaudesert were said by the retiring lessee, Randolph, to be capable of yielding eighty wain-loads (c.100 to 125 tons) weekly, which could be sold at 2s. 6d. per load. He may well have exaggerated, but it does seem likely that a capital investment of under £60 had established a colliery with a capacity well in excess of 2,000 tons. Precision is elusive, but it would not seem overly generous to view each shillingsworth of capital investment at Beaudesert as capable of supporting output worth 4s. In a cautionary note, however, Randolph added that 'it is hoped that these four pits or the most of them will hold this rate until Candlemas next, but after that these pits are wrought out'.[20] Such levels of investment in fixed capital were comparable with those at Halesowen and Wolverhampton in the mid-1570s, where expenditures of less than £100 may well have been sufficient to establish collieries capable of producing 1,500 to 2,500 tons.[21]

Almost contemporaneously with the reopening of Beaudesert, Sir Richard Leveson and Francis Fitton proceeded to start production from scratch on the Seven Foot Coal-seam at Griff. After a series of trials, sinking began in earnest just before Christmas 1603. The plans were to sink a row of three main pits some 80–86 feet deep, running parallel with a row of three shallow pits, plus another shallow pit, an air pit, and a water pit, and numerous interconnecting heads. All were duly successfully completed at a recorded cost of £181. 17s. 10d., with the deep pits

[20] WaRO Landor of Rugeley C. 931/173; StRO Anglesey D(W)1734/3/3/254, 5.
[21] NoUL Middleton Mi. Ac. 130, 138, 139.

costing £22–26 each, the shallow pits in total £15, a sough £13, an air pit £2, and the water pit and drainage equipment £39. The balance was made up of miscellaneous surface costs amounting to £2 and tools, ropes, barrels, etc., costing £12. We should perhaps allow additionally for the transfer of some equipment from the adjacent Slate Coal-pits and for the value of the wood which was granted free under the terms of the lease. Even so the total investment could scarcely have exceeded £250, yet approximately 3,500 tons worth £535 were raised in the first six months of full working. Thereafter production slowed dramatically, but this was probably due to difficulties in selling the coal rather than producing it, since production costs did not rise. Within a matter of months Leveson and Fitton had ceased working, as had Sir Thomas Beaumont in his neighbouring collieries.[22] Though this episode of mining was short lived, it seems likely that, if a market could have been found for the coal, Griff like Beaudesert could have sustained output worth 4s. per annum for every shilling of capital invested.

Our third contemporaneous example comes from Chilvers Coton in Warwickshire. In a legal dispute in 1602, Geoffrey Fox, the plaintiff, claimed that he had spent £600 reopening the colliery which hitherto 'lay desolate and drowned with water' despite many attempts to drain it. He had done this by sinking a number of pits, for drainage as well as coaling, making a sough and constructing a water mill and a horse mill. The circumstances of the case mean that we may take £600 as the maximum expended by Fox in opening what was evidently a troublesome but sizeable colliery, and the defendant disputed that he had spent so much.[23]

Handsworth colliery had a markedly less favourable capital—output ratio than Beaudesert and Griff, and probably Chilvers Coton also. It had been leased for a rent of £66 annually in 1635, and had ceased production some time between 1645 and 1650. When Sir John Bright took up a lease for £30 per annum he set about restoring it to working condition. The prime necessity was the drainage of the workings, and between August 1650 and March 1652 a sough was constructed, and then three pits were sunk. An account book entitled 'A particular of all disbursements about the setting of the cole mine agate' records total expenditure of £265. 12s. 3d., of which well over £200 was absorbed by the sough. In addition Bright had to pay for mining tools and equipment, and perhaps also for repairs to the smithy and bellows, and for houses for workmen. According to a former tenant, Bright hazarded

[22] Grant 1979.   [23] PRO C.2, James I F4/53.

somewhat more than £400 in all. In the ensuing two decades production averaged around 1,000 loads (1,000 to 1,500 tons) a year. Even allowing for the fall in the value of money which occurred between the 1600s and 1650, by reason of its extensive sough Handsworth was a far more costly colliery to set up than Beaudesert or Griff. It also produced far lower profits each year, but it did enjoy a virtually continuous working life of thirty years.[24]

The reopening of Griff colliery in 1700–1 by its owner, Sir Richard Newdigate, after an eleven-year closure, was a more substantial venture. It was planned that, by the end of the first year after the ground had been broken, there would be three deep 'coalpits', each approximately 90 feet in depth, connected to three shallow or 'basset pits', together with three gin pits. It was also expected that in the following year two new coal-pits would be added.[25] Unfortunately for our purposes Newdigate, who was desperate to recoup his outlay as soon as possible in order to repay his debts, quite understandably viewed the venture in terms of the total amount of money he would have to spend and the amount of money he could hope to receive in the near future. He was also anxious that production should begin as soon as possible, and his estimates of costs and income over the first twelve months intermingle fixed capital investment with operating costs on the one side, while on the other side of his account he included the sums which he hoped to derive from the sale of coal. Accordingly, it is impossible to isolate capital expenditure with any confidence, but we can make some progress. Newdigate's first estimates of outlay were soon proved pessimistic, and on 1 December 1700 he rejoiced, 'having now I thank God sunk near the coal at an easier charge than anyone did expect'. Using his revised estimate, we can deduce that he expected to spend around £600 sinking and heading, with a further £120 for 'making a pond, wheelpit, and fixing the wheel', to which we must add a further £300 to £400 for the costs of timber and drawing water during the construction phase, and the costs of tools and other surface equipment and buildings. On the other hand, Newdigate expected to offset a significant part of the costs from the sale of the coal which was won as a by-product of opening up the workings. When completed, Newdigate expected to have a colliery capable of producing 12,900 loads, perhaps as much as 20,000 tons, from its three coaling pits each year. In the event, Griff in 1701–2 produced just over 7,000 loads (10,000 to 11,000 tons), to be sold at

[24] SCL Wentworth Woodhouse (Bright) BR P52/10, 54, 55/1–31.
[25] See Fig. 6.5 and the discussion in Ch. 7(iii) above.

6s. 8d. per load, which was still a very creditable performance for an out-lay unlikely to have been more than £1,500.[26]

The fixed capital investment in Griff does not seem out of line with the £654 estimated as the cost of establishing a colliery 'from the grass' at Strelley (Notts.) in 1660, which was to consist of three coaling pits, two water pits, a sough 400 yards long with ten sough pits, and horse-and water-wheel gins for draining and winding up coal. It was estimated that the machinery would need thirty-two horses daily to work it, but the costs of the horses were not included.[27]

Sadly, we have no details of the costs of setting up a great seasale colliery within our period, but obviously fixed capital investment rose with scale. Shafts were apt to be deeper, often 200 feet or more, and being deep and expensive to sink they were invariably lined with timber to prolong their lives, in itself an expensive process. Deeper shafts, with commensurately longer headings, often necessitated a greater invest-ment in drainage and ventilation, as well as in winding gear. Buildings were needed on the surface: offices, sheds, shelters, houses for the colliers, and so on. Since getting coal to the water as cheaply as possible was a high priority, especially in the competitive market conditions of the later seventeenth century, coal-owners often had to invest directly in transport. Despite their great cost, waggonways were built in a number of coalfields, and they proliferated on the Tyne. At the turn of the seventeenth and eighteenth centuries it cost around £200 a mile to build a waggonway, and furnishing it with rolling stock and horses could easily double the outlay. The investment of the coal-owner frequently extended still further, for at the water's edge it was necessary to build staithes from which the keels or other river boats could be loaded efficiently and, in order to offer a saleable product in good condi-tion, shelters over the staithes became ever more popular. Coal-owners on the Tyne frequently owned keels and, if not well served with harbour facilities, ambitious owners in seaside coalfields sometimes invested in these too. Thus the great coal-owner's investment finally ceased a long way from the banks of his collieries.

In no sense, therefore, can the handful of examples we have gleaned be considered a satisfactory sample. None the less, we can learn some-thing from them. At the medium-sized collieries of Beaudesert and Griff in the early 1600s it took less than one shilling's worth of fixed capital to establish each ton of new capacity, at a time when coal was selling for

[26] White thesis 1969, 62–4, 205–8; Grant thesis 1977, 101–5.
[27] Smith MS, 186–7.

approximately 4s. a ton. At Griff in 1700–1 it took somewhat less than 3s. of capital investment for every new ton of output, worth approximately 5s. Michael Flinn has calculated from a sample of twenty-eight collieries between 1730 and 1789, mainly on Tyneside, that each ton of capacity required the investment of 2.6s. of fixed capital.[28] Such capital–output ratios were enticingly low, yet it should be borne in mind that they were only beneficial as long as variable costs were not forced higher by the lack of adequate capital stock.

It is necessary to place these examples of the costs of setting up new collieries in a broader context. The sixteenth and seventeenth centuries were in general characterized by low capital investment. In an age when the greater part of industrial production was carried on in rooms or small workshops using rudimentary and relatively cheap equipment and tools, the investment required to open up even a modest colliery was apt to appear substantial. A large shearing shop complete with clothes press was acquired and equipped in 1683 for under £100, and £120 was the valuation placed on the largest production unit to be destroyed in the London weavers' riots of 1675, a workshop with ten looms. In mid-seventeenth-century England the erection of a furnace and forge for iron production, together with all necessary equipment and buildings, might cost £400 to £500, and there were perhaps 70–80 such installations in the country. For a similar outlay one might obtain a sophisticated over-shot water mill or a new ship of 100 tons. Such figures, sparse and random though they are, help to place the costs of establishing small to medium-sized collieries in perspective. If we move upwards to the great collieries, where fixed capital was measured in thousands of pounds, the comparators become scarcer still. Certainly, the largest breweries might cost as much or even more, but even a first-class London-built vessel fit for the Atlantic trade cost no more than £2,000 in the later seventeenth century.[29]

On the other hand, and perhaps to a greater degree than most other forms of industrial plant, collieries could be added to and developed piecemeal over time as funds permitted. Most substantial collieries had long histories, and growth was usually an incremental process. We have described elsewhere the lengthy deliberations, punctuated with frequent misgivings, with which the entrepreneurial Charles Montagu viewed the expansion of production at Gibside and the construction of a

---

[28] Flinn 1984, 201–3.
[29] Clay 1984, ii. 66–7; Clarkson, *Pre-Industrial Economy in England*, 98–9; Davis 1962, 373; Mathias 1979, 217–19.

waggonway to the Tyne.[30] Even lengthier deliberations attended the
construction of a new sough by the Willoughbys at Wollaton, 'because
the old sough was much decayed and they were compelled to sink new
pits in places where it would not serve'. That a new sough had been
under consideration for some time before 1549 is evidenced by the will
of Henry Willoughby, who died at the hands of Kett's rebels. In it
Henry's executors were enjoined to cause the sough to be made within
eight years of his death, spending 'the sum of £1,000, more or less as
need shall require'. In 1552 when permission was being sought to run it
across the lands of neighbouring landowners, the sough was projected
to be over a mile in length. The final cost when it was completed some
years later was undoubtedly far in excess of £1,000, but it provided
yeoman service to the colliery and the family for many decades thereafter. The cost of this sough should also be seen against the surplus revenues of between £350 and £500 which the Willoughbys were drawing
each year at this time from their coalmining.[31]

So far attention has been devoted largely to net or true capital investment designed to increase output. Yet the accounts of working collieries
very rarely consistently made a distinction between true capital investment on the one hand and running investment, the repair and renewal of
existing capital equipment in order to maintain levels of output, often
termed on-cost work, on the other. Nevertheless, from the examination
of scores of surviving accounts it is clear that, as we should expect, the
industry demanded far greater sums to be expended year in and year out
on running investment than on capital investment. Moreover, some of
the best sets of accounts enable expenditure on working costs, that is,
the costs incurred directly in the production of coal, to be accurately
distinguished from other costs over lengthy periods. Some of the data
that can be extracted from these accounts are given in Table 10.1.

The data that has been presented on the fixed capital cost of collieries
and the scale of running capital investment required to keep them in
operation is a slender foundation upon which to build generalizations of
the capital requirements of early modern coalmining, but it may be
rendered considerably more robust by the far greater bulk of less precise
but none the less cogent evidence of the scale of capital inputs and the
working life of capital that can be amassed from the hundreds of
surviving mine records. In aggregate this evidence is of value in supporting broad orders of magnitude. Moreover, since there is obvious value in
the formulation of rough approximations of the capital invested in the

[30] See above, Ch. 7(iii).   [31] Smith MS, 68–72.

Table 10.1 *Running investment in selected collieries, 1549-1668*

Colliery	Running investment s.	Selling price s.	%
Beaudesert (1577–82)	0.67 per load	2.67 per load	25
Sheffield Park (1579–1600)	0.39 per load	1.5 per load	26
Wollaton (1549–80)	0.75 per rook	2–3 per rook	25–37
Bedworth (1578–81)	1.02 per rook	3.33–3.78 per rook	27–30
Trowell (1647–68)	1.5 per load	4.32–5.08 per load	30–5
Heanor (1642–59)	1.1 per load	3.27–4.12 per load	27–33

Note: Running investment sometimes includes the running costs of drainage machinery and horses and the wages of watermen, but even in the wettest collieries such expenditure is invariably the minor constituent.

British coal industry before the eighteenth century, it is possible to reach the following tentative suppositions. Reassuringly, estimates proceeding from different perspectives are in approximate agreement.

It is perhaps least difficult to focus upon the close of the seventeenth century, when British output may have been of the order of 2.5 to 3 million tons. Taking 2–3 s. as the fixed capital required to produce each ton, this results in a fixed capital stock for the whole industry at this time of £250,000 to £450,000. Since there are reasons to believe that the running investment needed to maintain this output was of the order of 1–1.5 s. per ton per annum, an aggregate annual investment in running capital of some £125,000 to £225,000 would have been required. The fact that such estimates of total capital stock and running investment are in broad conformity with the independent conclusion that the life of fixed capital in coalmining was of the order of no more than two to three years, is comforting. To speculate further: on the premises that on average through the seventeenth century it took some 2–3 s. of new capital investment to produce an additional ton of output, and that annual output rose by as much as 2 million tons in Britain between 1600 and 1700, a mean net capital formation of only £2,000 to £3,000 per annum would have sufficed to facilitate this remarkable achievement.

Finally, by hypothesizing still further, we may attempt to place these capital requirements in the context of the revenues which might have been generated by the industry for colliery operators. Around 1700 the 2.5–3 million tons of coal produced annually would have resulted in sales revenues of some £375,000 to £600,000, assuming an average pithead price of 3–4s. per ton. On the basis of the profit data presented below, such sales would have produced a surplus of revenues over expenses of, at the very least, £100,000 annually. Thus, net new capital investment each year would have absorbed only 2–3 per cent of profits.

This is, of course, only a partial computation of the capital absorbed by the industry. For inevitably it fails to take any account of the capital that was sunk into unproductive ventures. Unfortunately, it is impossible to make any sensible quantitative estimate of the costs of failure, and there are no means of knowing what the success rate was.

iii. Profitability

There are many ways in which the financial health and profitability of businesses may be expressed. The ideal would be to seek to assess sixteenth- and seventeenth-century collieries in terms of current accounting practice, by producing standardized profit and loss accounts and balance sheets, and calculating rates of return on sales and assets. But the extent to which any ideal may be accomplished is obviously governed by the quality of the information which early managers sought to record in the accounts which they kept, and the manner in which they recorded it. Handsworth, for example, possesses a virtually continuous series of accounts covering a period of more than thirty years. Yet the Byzantine complexity of its accounting system poses special problems for the investigator. When Sir John Bright leased the colliery from the dowager countess of Arundel, he ran it as a partnership with his estate steward, Thomas Stacey, and whereas the weekly accounts record in a neat and unexceptional manner details of production, sales, and some expenses, the periodic summaries are full of pitfalls. For they attempted to detail not only the banksman's disbursements and receipts, including those paid to Stacey, but the sums disbursed separately by Stacey, including cash paid to the banksman, money owed by coal purchasers 'in the country', the value of 'old coal stocks', and 'profits' paid over to Bright. It is not surprising, therefore, that each of the attempts historians have made to calculate the profitability of Handsworth colliery should have produced markedly different results.[32]

If the maximum amount of information is to be gleaned from surviving colliery accounts it is essential not to be ruled by their form or

[32] Cf. the results in Cox thesis 1960, 88 ff., and Roebuck 1980, 217, with those given in Table 10A. 8 below.

dominated by their idiosyncrasies. In order to analyse efficiently the profusion of variant forms thrown up by colliery managements a specific methodology has to be devised. The one adopted here consists in the main of asking a series of questions of the accounts; namely, how much coal was produced, what was this production worth, how much coal was sold, what was it sold for, what stocks of coal were held at the beginning and at the end of the year under scrutiny, how much was spent in total on the colliery during the course of the account, and how much was spent in each of the major sectors of activity? In this way most of the surviving accounts can be made to disgorge much of the required information, and that information is then able to be presented in a standardized form. It should be noted, however, that the process of extraction is neither straightforward nor speedy. Apart from the hap-hazard manner in which data were sometimes recorded, many accounts lack periodic summaries, so that daily or weekly records have to be broken down into their constituent elements grouped into data sets and then aggregated into annual totals.

Even when this has been accomplished certain deficiencies often remain. First, there are some common omissions from the expenses side of colliery accounts. Perhaps most consistently neglected are the stipends of managers and estate officials. Also of significance in a number of cases is the frequent failure to cost the copious supplies of wood which were used in mining. This could be either because the mine was being operated by its landlord, and it made sense to supply wood free from his estate woodlands, normally using estate carts, or because the lessees had been granted free wood under the terms of their lease. In a similar vein, the costs of feeding horses were often omitted or under-stated, because they were fed from estate supplies or allowed free pasture. Secondly, to arrive at a true profit, it is necessary to take account of the depreciation of assets, which sum should then be deducted from income. The lack of formal capital accounting is an undoubted defect. At best the costs of major new work were included only in the years in which they were carried out and paid for, with the result that it is possible for 'trading profits' to oscillate wildly from year to year as total expenditure rises and falls in a manner only distantly related to current levels of production and sales. Ideally one would wish to amortize net investment over an appropriate period, and also to smooth out expenditure on running investment, but it would be foolish at this distance to attempt to do so. Thus a set of accounts which commences just after a colliery has been established, or after a period of heavy investment, will tend initially to have inflated 'profit' levels, while large-scale expenditure within a series of accounts geared to expanding production in the future will unduly depress 'profits' in the years in which it is undertaken. This problem is potentially of significance in those collieries with expensive soughs. For soughs were frequently the most costly as well as the most durable items of capital. Finally, the manner in which stocks of unsold coal were usually recorded has not enabled them to be incorporated into the calculations of profit and loss. Such stock data as the accounts contain have been reproduced in the tables in order to allow their significance to be assessed, but there are many inconsistencies.

Yet we must be realistic. The calculation of the profitability of mining enterprises has always been a less than scientific matter, and depreciation accounting did not achieve widespread acceptance in the coal industry before 1900.[33] Whereas information derived from single observations and from short runs of accounts must be treated with appropriate caution, when longer series of accounts survive the absence of depreciation accounting is by no means as serious an omission as it would be in most other industries, because of the exceptionally short life of most capital. Even in the twentieth century capital investment has often been treated as part of current costs.[34]

The results of this labour-intensive analysis of the best surviving series of colliery accounts is presented in Tables 10A.1–13 below, and despite the idiosyncrasies of the sources it can be read with a considerable degree of confidence. The records generally allow a fair approximation of standard profit and loss accounts to be constructed, and income (sales revenue or gross profit) can be placed against expenditure (net operating expenses) over given time periods, with the former minus the latter providing a reasonable guide to trading profits. In the first set of tables the complete economic performance as revealed by the colliery accounts is presented, and the final two columns contain profit calculated first as a percentage of the total costs expended during the period of the account, and secondly as a percentage of sales revenues or turnover.

In the nineteenth century the concept of profit per ton was widely employed by owners and managers, while the rate of return on assets was the ultimate test applied by proprietors. Since there is scarcely any data on the total capital invested in collieries within our period, or on their asset values, the latter measure is unattainable, but the former can

---

[33] Pollard 1965, 238–9; Church 1986, 513–16.   [34] Supple 1987, 387–8.

be calculated with some reliability. In the second set of tables (Tables 10A.14–24), the performance of the collieries is approached from this perspective, namely the average cost of producing each unit of output, and the average price at which sales were made. When the former is sub-tracted from the latter we have a close approximation to profit per unit of output. In the final columns this profit is expressed as a proportion of costs and of selling price. The profit calculations in the first set of tables therefore reflect actual sales over the period of account, which could be greater or lesser than the output, whereas the second set of tables are constructed strictly from output-related data, and take no account of whether that output was actually sold.

In no sense can our sample of collieries be taken as representative of sixteenth- and seventeenth-century British collieries as a whole, but it does contain a broad range of experience. At one extreme we have the collieries of Sheffield Park, Wollaton, Beaudesert, and Railey, where for lengthy periods profits constituted half or even more of each pound received from the sale of coal. At the other extreme lay Cossall, where the colliery lost money in three out of the five years we are able to analyse, and Heanor where high costs and a chronic inability fully to dispose of output frequently plunged the colliery from moderate profits into substantial losses. In the middle lay a clutch of collieries—Farnworth, Niddrie, Chirk Castle, Trowell, and seventeenth-century Beaudesert and Cannock—which during the periods covered by accounts were consistently profitable at a rewarding level, showing returns in the range of 20–40 per cent of sales revenues. To these examples we may also add the Lancashire collieries of Aspull, Sheving-ton, and Winstanley analysed by Dr Langton, which reveal returns rang-ing from 33 to nearly 80 per cent of sales revenue.[35] In addition, we have in Chopwell an example of a very substantial colliery which in the saturated market of the north-east at the turn of the seventeenth and eighteenth centuries made profits of less than 20 per cent on each ton it sold, yet, by vending in excess of 30,000 tons, produced a surplus for the Claverings of more than £1,000 per annum from 1702–4. If start-up costs in excess of £250, and the investment income this sum could have realized, are taken into consideration the financial performance of Handsworth colliery over the more than thirty years of its continuous existence was dismal. But the persistence with which coal was mined, for returns which overall were niggardly, as they were for the decade or

[35] Langton 1979a, 72–3.

so that mining lasted at Heanor, demonstrates that not all relatively unsuccessful enterprises were transitory affairs.

The inadequacy of most of the data which are available on returns in other forms of economic activity or investment in later sixteenth- and seventeenth-century Britain highlights the quality of those which can be derived from colliery accounts, but it does make comparisons difficult. There was, of course, no single rate of interest, but those lending at low risk seem rarely to have been able to enjoy more than 6–7 per cent between the late fifteenth century and the close of the seventeenth. Farmland in the seventeenth century is thought to have yielded only 5 per cent gross, 3–3.5 per cent net, with urban property returns somewhat higher at 8 per cent gross. Even when an allowance is made for capital growth, real estate produced steady rather than spectacular returns. Trade was more speculative, but as far as it is possible to judge at present, it would seem that returns of more than 15 per cent on commercial investments were difficult to obtain in any but exceptional periods between 1500 and 1700. It has been concluded by those who have studied the field that in the first half of the seventeenth century the general run of experienced and fortunate merchants in commodity trades could expect to make no more than a 10–15 per cent return on capital, and only 6–12 per cent in the second half of the century.[36] Higher risks quite naturally could bring higher rewards. So too could the manipulation of markets, and luck or expertise, and a combination of the two could create vast fortunes even in the most humdrum of fields, like ironmongery or grocery.[37] Spectacular gains, but also spectacular losses could be made in exotic lands and trades, such as the West Indies or the Levant. Even when sugar prices were low the net return on an efficiently run plantation could be over 10 per cent, 12.5 per cent if capital appreciation is taken into account.[38] This latter return was significantly higher than that which could be expected on rentier investment in England, but life in Jamaica and the fearful mortality rates it entailed must be counted as costs. The especial hazards involved in indulging in the illicit West Indian trades based on plunder and contraband need no emphasizing.

Colliery accounts can thus be seen to reveal the widespread existence of encouraging levels of profitability, as well as profits which were fat

---

[36] Grassby 1969.

[37] Stone and Fawtier Stone 1984, 240.

[38] N. Zahedieh, 'Trade, Plunder, and Economic Development in Early English Jamaica', *EcHR* 2nd ser. 39 (1986), 208–9, 222.

enough to attract the inputs of capital and enterprise which flowed into the industry. Much more importantly, the levels of profitability which prevailed in coalmining appear to have been more than sufficient to generate the substantial and continuous flow of running investment from within required to sustain and enhance production. Coalmining was a venturesome business, and it may well have attracted rather more than its fair share of fools and gamblers, many of whom 'wholly buried their estate in the said coalmines' rather than raised riches from them.[39] There were undoubtedly many more venturers who were simply unlucky and were wracked upon the wheel of fortune. But when considering the overall experience of the industry, it is as well to bear in mind the fortunes of start-up businesses and the venture capital industry in the relatively favourable environment of the later 1970s and the 1980s. Although firm statistics are elusive even in our own times, it is authoritively held that only two out of every ten new ventures could be deemed successful, and that four out of every ten failed to survive for more than five years.[40] As far as it is possible to judge, there is no reason to doubt that the rise of the British coal industry was securely founded upon an acceptable balance between risk and reward.

iv. Productivity of labour

The data which can be compiled on the productivity of labour in late medieval and early modern coal-mines are entirely consonant with the rewarding levels of profitability and capital productivity indicated above. Figures are sparse even for later centuries, but Michael Flinn has suggested, using estimates of the total output of the north-eastern coal-field and the numbers employed there, that in the opening decades of the nineteenth century output per man year across the whole force of mineworkers may have ranged from 269 to 315 tons. For the country as a whole he believed that it may have stood at about 200 to 250 tons, which amounted to no more than a ton per working day, and probably less. Figures for the productivity of hewers are scarcely more plentiful, but range from a high estimate of 6 to 7 tons a shift for a north-eastern hewer, made by Jars in 1765, down to 1.5 to 2.5 tons a day for his counterpart in Scotland and south Staffordshire. Exceptionally low

[39] The phrase is Lady Elizabeth Ashburnam's, whose husband, Sir John, died in 1620 in the Fleet.

[40] T. Lorenz, *Venture Capital Today: A Guide to the Venture Capital Market in the U.K.* (Cambridge, 1985), 49.

levels of productivity are revealed in the Bristol and Somerset coalfields of from 65 to 75 tons per man year in 1800, and at a small colliery at Cluny in Fife in 1751–2, where hewers seem to have produced less than one ton per day, but in both instances we are almost certainly dealing with part-time employment and discontinuous working.[41]

There is no doubt that colliery accounts of all periods can be made to yield far more information on the productivity of colliery work-forces than has hitherto been extracted, although the prevalence of gang working and the employment of part-time and seasonal labour restricts the value of most series. Some extremely detailed insights into labour productivity are obtainable from the collieries of the bishop of Durham as early as the late fifteenth and early sixteenth centuries, where gangs of workmen were paid daily wages for meeting daily production quotas. The numbers of hewers, barrowmen, and drawers in each gang are given and, on the conservative assumption that the land chaldron of four quarters capacity weighed no more than 18 cwt., and with the inclusion of a banksman when appropriate, we find that the productivity of these production workers ranged between 1.2 tons per man day at Whickham in 1500 and 2 tons at Railey in 1460. These are high rates, even though they include no on-cost work. The productivity of the hewers was also high, and ranged from more than 6 tons per day at Railey in 1460 and Whickham in 1465 down to just under 4 tons at the Moyr' pit at Whickham in 1500.[42] At Beaudesert in the late 1570s and early 1580s, before the colliery ran into difficulties and closed, the output per man day of the whole work-force, including timbermen, soughers, and sinkers, was probably around one ton. Since the permanent labourers there usually worked more than 200 days in a year, and sometimes in excess of 250 days, both annual and daily productivity once again bears comparison with later centuries. The productivity at Beaudesert of hewers is impossible to calculate because in the small bell-pits the functions of hewer, putter, drawer, and sinker were often combined.[43] At the small colliery of Gatherick in the 1680s hewers produced 15 bowls per day, perhaps amounting to between 2 and 2.5 tons of coal. For an overview of the productivity of hewers in the north-east at the beginning of the eighteenth century, we have J. C.'s warning that if hewers were paid a flat rate per day or shift 'perhaps you will not have above thirteen or fifteen corves a man per shift'. If we take a corf to hold 3.5 cwt., this

[41] Flinn 1984, 363–5.
[42] DUDP Church Commission box 79.
[43] StRO Anglesey D(W) 1734/3/3.

'unsatisfactory' productivity would have amounted to between 45.5 and 52.5 cwt a shift.[44]

Finally, it is occasionally possible to gain some insights into the total annual productivity of a whole colliery work-force by comparing output with total numbers employed. We can do this for the Lowther collieries of Howgill and Greenbank at the close of the seventeenth century. Howgill in 1698–9 produced 16,000 tons with a total work-force of 81, and 15,580 tons in 1701 with a work-force of 93, resulting in output per man year of 170 to 200 tons. In the same years Greenbank produced 1,002 and 2,993 tons respectively, with a total work-force of 11, resulting in output per man year as high as 272 tons in a year of continuous working. Moreover, a significant portion of these Cumberland workers were not full-time.[45] From 1842 to 1913 average output per man year in the British coal industry ranged between 260 and 330 tons.[46]

v. Patterns of production and sales

The profitability of collieries was also dependent upon the patterns of production and sales experienced through the year. Uneven patterns of sales meant uneven cash flows, and the consequent accumulation of stocks had to be financed. The typical early modern colliery has often been portrayed as working on an intermittent basis, with the sales of coal concentrated in the dry summer months when roads and tracks were likely to be in their best shape. For Nef it was common for coal-getting to be voluntarily abandoned for some weeks or months during every year, and although the season for closure varied from coalfield to coalfield nowhere, he felt, were hewers kept in steady employment.[47] The gearing of production to sales was, in theory at least, an economical way of running a colliery, since the stockpiling of coal was expensive. During 1643–7 at Tulliallan (Fife) output and sales went hand in hand throughout the year, and coal was hewn directly to order. As a consequence output fluctuated wildly, depending largely upon the arrivals of ships.[48] But such hand-to-mouth operations are very rare outside Scotland, or where coal was produced not for general sale but to serve particular needs, such as a household, a forge, or salt-pans. Also rare

---

[44] NuRO Society of Antiquaries ZAN B/18/1/19.
[45] Wood 1988, 15.
[46] Church 1986, 473.
[47] Nef 1932, i. 136–7. See also Griffin thesis 1969, 53.
[48] ScRO Register House RH9/1/31.

were collieries which, like Gatherick (Northumb.), enjoyed consistent sales throughout the year, with the December to February quarter as busy as any other. In 1683–4 receipts from the sale of coal from the bankside of Gatherick averaged just under £6 per week, but in only one week did they exceed £10 and in only seven weeks did they fall below £3.[49]

If Nef had studied colliery accounts he would have found very little support for his contentions of ubiquitous discontinuous working. As always in coalmining there was a wealth of differing experience, but very few commercial collieries normally closed down for part of the year on a regular basis, and although it was sometimes considered economical to cease production for brief periods in order to carry out maintenance and establish new workings, the production labour force would be utilized in these tasks as far as possible. What the colliery accounts reveal is that owners and managers sought to maintain as steady working through the year as possible, and that seasonal fluctuations, if they existed at all, were normally gentle rather than sharp. The most common distortions to the annual production cycle were Christmas holidays and a slackening of intensity in August and September when harvest called, but these were by no means universal. The production records of the great Tyneside colliery of Whorlton Moor, for example, reveal that in the late 1680s and early 1690s coal was produced for fifty-two weeks each year, and that output dipped only modestly during the weeks in which Christmas and the new year fell.[50] Even in small collieries, like Hooton, Beaudesert, Gatherick, and Handsworth, continuity was the norm. At Handsworth although the mean average monthly production from 1653 to 1683 ranged from a trough in August of 65 loads to a peak in June of just under 97 loads, production during nine months of the year exceeded 81 loads. At Hooton between 1668 and 1675 the least productive months were January and February, when output averaged 155 loads, but in the other ten months it ranged narrowly between 175 and 208 loads. At Beaudesert, which has left a long series of exceptionally detailed employment records from the later sixteenth century, a core permanent work-force laboured year in and year out as steadily as geological conditions permitted, with temporary labour drafted in to meet exceptional demands.[51]

[49] NuRO Society of Antiquaries ZAN B18/1/19.
[50] DN Syon CX 2a(i).
[51] SCL Wentworth Woodhouse (Bright) BR P55/1–31; LCA Mexborough MX 295, 296; StRO Anglesey D(W)174/3/3.

This pattern of regular working meant that most collieries had to carry sizeable stocks, not just to be able to satisfy immediate current demands without the loss of custom, but to cope with seasonal surges in demand, when sales far exceeded output. In contrast to the production of coal, sales from most collieries were decidedly uneven, while from many they surged massively over short periods in the late spring and summer. The experience of Hooton, illustrated in Fig, 10.1, lay at one extreme of the spectrum for landsale collieries. Here reasonably steady year-round production resulted in the accumulation of large stocks of coal on the colliery banks in the winter months when little coal was sold. Between late April and early October, however, sales exceeded production by a considerable margin so that a progressive fall in stocks occurred. It has often been held that sales from inland collieries were rendered negligible in the winter months because roads and tracks were normally impassable, but few inland collieries sold such a high proportion of annual output in such a short period as did Hooton.

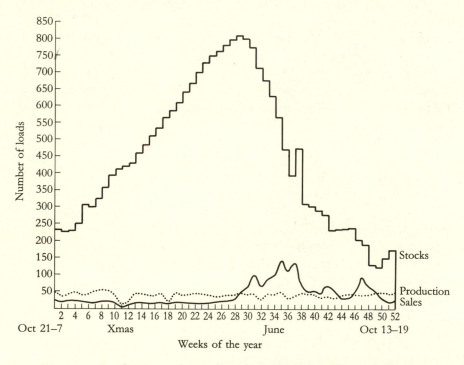

Fig. 10.1. Production, sales, and stocks at Hooton colliery, 1668–1675

Note: Graph represents the mean weekly production, sales, and stocks held during the seven years covered by the accounts.

The pattern of sales from seasale collieries were also distinctly seasonal, being determined by conditions for sailing as well as the ability to lead coal from the bankside of collieries to the water. In normal years a mere handful of ships left the Tyne and the Wear in November, December, and January, and few left in February or late October. Three-quarters or more of all sailings took place in just six summer and spring months.[52] On the west coast, sailings to Ireland were similarly influenced by weather and season. Lowther's 'ships' sales', which far exceeded sales to salt-pans or the country, were almost entirely concentrated within the period from April to August.[53] This pattern of sales fitted well with the best times for leading coal to the water. Although waggonways were eventually to permit year-round overland transportation, heavy traffic of wains and carts in wet weather soon made roads and tracks impassable. If a Tyneside colliery lacked a waggonway it was unable to lead much coal to the Tyne between November and early March.[54]

Appendix. The economic performance of British collieries, 1460–1704

i. Overall performance

Output and sales   Output was most frequently recorded weekly in the accounts in the measures in which coal was to be sold, such as wain-loads, horse-loads, rooks, chaldrons, etc. The measures used for sale and production were rarely the same, but in those accounts in which output is given in production measures—corves, bowls, baskets, etc.—the relationship between the two is often stated or possible to deduce. Some accounts, however, record only the value of output at current prices, or even the surplus value after the costs of producing it have been met.

Stocks   As explained in the notes appended to each of the tables, stocks were not systematically recorded in all collieries. Even in those collieries where stocks were regularly recorded there are discrepancies, due in part no doubt to the difficulties of exact measurement of production, sales, and heaps on the bank, and the incidence of petty theft.

Costs   The most informative accounts allow the various costs to be confidently allocated into broad categories. The majority distinguished

[52] See below, pp. 476–8.
[53] e.g. CuRO Lonsdale D/Lons/W Account books of Greenbank and Three Quarters Band Collieries, 1675–6.
[54] As for example with Gibside, DuRO Strathmore D/St/V36.

between working costs and capital costs. Working costs, or getting costs as they were often termed, were sometimes also broken down into the costs of hewing, putting, timbering, and so on; they were then followed by on-costs and deadwork, and expenditure on maintenance and repair and new investment. Sometimes colliery managers kept another set of accounts because the sinking of new shafts or soughs was considered a distinct operation from the production process, while at some collieries large-scale on-costs were met by a different branch of the estate management, since the colliery banksman was not expected to fund extraordinary expenditure from the running balances of his weekly or monthly budget. Such arrangements can give rise to the understatement of costs, and some otherwise excellent series of accounts have had to be discarded for this reason, including Hooton, Sir George Vane's Stella, Bilborough Hollows, and Strelley.

Profit The measure of profit that has been used is the simple one of revenues less costs. For further discussion of the calculation of profits see above, pp. 339–44.

Note — indicates that there are no data; [Nil] indicates that nothing was produced, received, spent, etc.; ( ) indicates loss.

Table 10.A.1 *Railey*

Period	Output (chaldrons)	Sales (chaldrons)	Stocks (chaldrons)	Value of output (£)	Sales revenue (£)	Getting costs (£)	Other costs (£)	Total costs (£)	Profit (£)	Profit/Loss As a % of total costs	As a % of sales revenue
2 April 1460–25 December 1460	3,769	3,123	2,374	116.5	96.5	36.5	19.8	56.3	40.2	71.4	41.7
9 November 1502–6 November 1503	8,816	8,816	[nil]	225.2	225.7	75	18.5	93.5	132.2	141.3	58.6
6 November 1503–11 November 1504	8,031	8,031	[nil]	205.6	205.6	68.5	18.2	86.7	118.9	137.1	57.8
2 January 1509–6 January 1510	4,578	4,578	[nil]	146.5	146.5	39	23.1	62.2	84.3	135.5	57.5

Notes: Railey colliery was situated some 7 miles north-east of Barnard Castle (Durham); in later times it was frequently known as Carterthorne. It was owned and, in the years covered by this table, also worked by the bishop of Durham. The accounts take the form of annual reckonings, based upon a charge and discharge system similar to that used in contemporary manorial accounts. The accountant in 1502–3, 1503–4, and 1509–10 was charged with the value of all the coal that was produced, and since there were no stocks and no arrears or allowances we must assume that all production was sold. There is some indication that profits may be overstated owing to the under-recording of costs. The chaldron at Railey was probably between 18 and 20 cwt. in weight.

Sources: DUDP Church Commission box 79, 190024–6, 190028, 189700.

Table 10.A.2 *Wollaton*

Period	Output (rooks)	Sales (rooks)	Stocks (rooks)	Value of output (£)	Sales revenue (£)	Getting costs (£)	Other costs (£)	Total costs (£)	Profit (£)	Profit/Loss As a % of total costs	As a % of sales revenue
1549	6,069	5,960	150	606.9	596	183.9	81.8	265.7	330.3	124.2	55.4
1551	9,659	10,234	428	965.9	1,023.4	295.8	185.2	481.0	542.4	112.7	53
1561	—	5,973	—	—	689.6	176.9	111.8	288.7	400.9	138.9	58.1
1578	13,234	11,154	2,108	1,764.5	1,488.5	385.7	565.5	951.2	537.3	56.5	36.1
1579	7,997	9,226	698	1,066.3	1,229.6	281.7	526.5	808.2	421.4	52.1	34.4
1580	11,572	10,042	1,175	1,928.7	1,494	402.3	467.1	869.4	624.7	71.9	41.8
1597	—	6,631	—	—	1,105.2	312.9	603.3	916.2	189.0	20.6	17.1
1602	10,064	9,268	1,501	1,849.4	1,703.2	—	—	1,386.7	316.5	22.8	18.6
1603	11,398	10,744	224	1,903.3	1,794.1	—	—	1,305.8	488.3	37.4	27.2
1604	5,484	5,544	—	914	924	—	—	797.9	126.1	15.8	13.6

Notes: Wollaton colliery lay in the Old Park of Wollaton 3 miles west of Nottingham. It was owned and worked by the Willoughbys. The form of accounting used and running of the colliery is discussed in detail in Smith MS. The table has been constructed from data extracted from the Bailiffs' Accounts and Coalpit Books given in Smith MS, ch. 2. The rook at Wollaton probably weighed between 1.2 and 1.3 tons.

Table 10.A.3 *Trowell Moor*

Period	Output (loads)	Sales (loads)	Stocks (loads)	Value of output (£)	Sales revenue (£)	Getting costs (£)	Other costs (£)	Total costs (£)	Profit (£)	Profit/Loss	
										As a % of total costs	As a % of sales revenue
28 June 1619– 29 April 1620	2,702	2,602	101	420.4	390.2	—	—	527.1	(136.9)	(26.0)	(35)
26 January 1647– 19 February 1648	3,657	2,873	—	822.9	643.7	288.5	219.8	508.3	135.4	26.6	21.0
20 February 1648– 30 December 1648	1,348	1,742	—	303.4	392.1	102.6	66.3	168.9	223.2	132.1	56.9
1 January 1649– 8 December 1649	1,581	1,595	—	356.5	359.9	121.1	80.8	201.9	158	78.3	43.9
9 December 1649– 7 December 1650	3,860	3,842	—	869.9	864.7	293.4	238.2	531.6	333.1	62.7	38.5
8 December 1650– 6 December 1651	6,697	6,302	—	1,507	1,418.1	502.9	413.9	916.8	501.3	54.7	35.4
27 March 1652– 5 December 1652	—	1,689	—	—	382.1	—	—	208.9	173.2	82.9	45.3
6 December 1652– 21 January 1654	3,281	2,142	1,274	742	472.4	294	281.2	575.2	(102.8)	(17.4)	(21.8)
1 February 1654– 23 December 1654	4,064	5,207	377	974.1	1,284.6	323.5	333.3	656.8	627.8	95.6	48.9
14 April 1655– 22 December 1655	4,572	4,227	530	1,059.7	979.3	—	—	676.4	302.9	44.8	30.9

Table 10.A.3 (cont.):

Period	Output (loads)	Sales (loads)	Stocks (loads)	Value of output (£)	Sales revenue (£)	Getting costs (£)	Other costs (£)	Total costs (£)	Profit (£)	Profit/Loss As a % of total costs	As a % of sales revenue
23 December 1656–8 January 1658	3,625	3,785	737	843.5	871.5	302.3	269.3	571.6	300.1	52.5	34.4
9 January 1658–16 December 1658	3,339	3,774	262	726.1	820.3	280.8	282.5	563.3	257.0	45.6	31.3
17 December 1658–31 December 1659	1,903	2,076	[nil]	419.2	456.4	172.9	76.4	249.3	207.1	83.1	45.4
19 April 1662–13 December 1662	1,341	823	520	314.8	190.5	—	—	371	(180.5)	(48.7)	(94.8)
14 December 1662–26 December 1663	1,820	2,819	165	413.6	472.8	154.9	150.2	305.1	167.7	54.9	35.5
9 January 1664–17 December 1664	2,247	2,270	165	498.9	504.2	187.7	189.6	377.3	126.9	33.6	25.2
18 December 1664–23 December 1665	3,348	3,317	176	851.1	843.2	303.1	338.8	641.9	201.3	314	23.9

13 January 1666–										
22 December 1666	2,040	1,573	585	518.2	399.5	203.7	193.8	397.6	1.9	0.5	0.5
23 December 1666–										
30 November 1667	1,117	1,348	181	269.5	327.3	134.6	126.7	261.3	66.0	25.3	20.2
31 November 1667–										
24 December 1668	917	958	—	225.3	235.5	97.3	81.9	179.2	56.3	31.4	23.9
25 December 1668–										
10 July 1669	421	464	—	103.4	114.1	—	—	74.6	39.5	53.0	34.6

Notes: Trowell Moor and associated pits were owned by Sir Francis Willoughby, and worked directly by him. They were located to the west of Wollaton, on the edge of the exposed coalfield, some 5 miles west of Nottingham. The accounts on which this table are based include a number of pits in the vicinity of Trowell Moor, among which are Laund Close, 'the close nye Shortwood', Carrington's house, Nixon's Close, etc., but exclude Cossall Moor (see Table 10.A.4). The accounts contain weekly statements of the amount of coal won in loads, the costs of hewing, and a full list of on-costs. The amount of coal sold, the receipts from sales, and the selling price per load are obtainable from weekly accounts, from periodic summaries, and, in the early part of the series, from specific sales accounts. The stocks of coal reported in the accounts as having been left on the bank at the end of the year do not always tally with the amounts recorded as having been produced and sold. The valuations of output have been obtained by combining the number of loads produced with the average selling price per load. In some years small quantities of coal, generally less than 20 loads, were despatched to the estate brewhouse and lime-kiln. In the charge section of the accounts the accountant was charged as if coal used on the estate had been sold, but in the discharge section the notional sale price was deducted. For the purposes of these tables the deductions have not been made, and such deliveries have been treated as sales. The dating of the accounts has been slightly amended to take account of variations in methods used by the accountants, including both 'week commencing' and 'week ending'.

The majority of the gaps in this series appear to derive from the cessation of mining operations. There was a severe fire in June 1668 and production was halted to be restarted in December 1668.

A load of coal may well have weighed a little more than a ton.

Sources: NoUL Middleton Mi. Ac. 16–33.

Table 10.A.4 *Cossall Moor*

Period	Output (loads)	Sales (loads)	Stocks (loads)	Value of output (£)	Sales revenue (£)	Total cost (£)	Profit on sales	Profit/Loss As a % of total costs	As a % of sales revenue
27 January 1649–8 December 1649	552	209	—	142.1	54	85.3	(31.3)	(36.7)	(58.0)
26 June 1653–20 June 1654	387	346	—	96.8	86.6	97.1	(10.5)	(10.8)	(12.1)
23 March 1659–9 June 1660	2,194	1,761	446	581	465.4	440.5	24.9	5.7	5.4
16 June 1660–29 December 1660	1,823	1,282	837	438.1	308.1	252.5	55.6	22.0	18.0
6 February 1669–26 June 1669	258	253	5	69.7	68.4	297.8	(229.4)	(77)	(335.4)

Notes: Cossall Moor colliery was located close to Wollaton and Trowell Moor, about 6 miles north north-west of Nottingham. It was worked by the Willoughbys who held it on a 99-year lease from the priory of Newstead. The accounts of Cossall Moor were often kept alongside those of Trowell Moor (see Table 10.A.3), the form of which they closely resembled. Cossall Moor colliery was not in production between 14 July 1649 and 8 Dec. 1649, or between 4 Feb. 1654 and 20 June 1654. Production between 6 Feb. 1669 and 29 June 1669 was based on 'Oxclose in the liberty of Cossall'. Mining did not cease on 26 June 1669, but the accounts became much less comprehensive and informative thereafter.

Sources: NoUL Middleton Mi. Ac. 8–10, 17–18, 25–6.

Table 10.A.5 *Beaudesert*

Period	Output (loads)	Sales (loads)	Sales revenue (£)	Getting costs (£)	Other costs (£)	Total costs (£)	Profit (£)	Profit/Loss	
								As a % of total costs	As a % of sales revenues
1577	1,169	1,169	155.9	22.7	33.7	56.4	99.5	176.4	63.8
1578	1,189	1,189	158.6	20.8	33.1	53.9	104.7	194.2	66.0
1579	1,023	1,023	136.4	26	31.5	57.5	78.9	137.2	57.8
1580	1,006	1,006	134.1	21.5	25.6	57.1	77	134.8	57.4
1581	1,090	1,090	145.4	23.4	31.9	55.3	90.1	162.9	62.0
1582	921	921	122.8	21.5	27.7	49.2	73.6	149.6	59.9
1583	892	892	118.9	66.8	38	104.8	14.1	13.5	11.9
1584 to 25 September	583	583	77.7	49.8	26.6	76.4	1.3	1.7	1.7

Notes: Beaudesert colliery lay in Beaudesert Park about 4 miles north-west of Lichfield (Staffs.). It was owned and worked by the earls of Shrewsbury. The accounts were usually drawn up weekly, and give the number of days each pit was worked, the value of the coal produced, and the net value of the coal after having costs deducted. Colliers were usually paid by the day and not by the piece. Timbermen's wages, the costs of sinking new pits, and candles, ropes, and miscellaneous equipment are also accounted for. The costs seem to be comprehensive, except that timber was supplied free from the estate woodlands. There is no reference to stocks of coal or arrears of cash, and all coal produced was apparently sold. Production was probably geared to sales. Coal was sold at 32*d.* per wain-load and 2*d.* a horse-load, although it is not necessarily the case that 16 horse-loads weighed the same as a wain-load. Output is calculated from the stated value of coal produced. The accounting year began on 1 January. The Beaudesert wain-load may have weighed as much as 1.5 tons at this time.

Sources: StRO Anglesey D (W) 1734; PRO E.101/63/17, 675/15.

Table 10.A.6 *Beaudesert and Cannock Wood*

Period	Output (dozens)	Sales (dozens)	Stocks (dozens)	Value of output (£)	Sales revenue (£)	Getting costs (£)	Other costs (£)	Total costs (£)	Profit (£)	Profit/Loss As a % of total costs	As a % of sales revenues
Beaudesert											
1612	2,423	2,192	—	484.6	438.4	241.3	89.8	331.1	107.3	32.4	24.5
24 March 1622–24 March 1623	1,313	1,428	31	328.3	357	178	20.6	198.6	159.3	80.2	44.6
1641	824	813	28	206	203.2	112.2	88.5	200.6	3.7	1.8	0.9
Cannock Wood											
1612	1,866	2,032	—	373.2	407.5	149.2	68.4	217.5	189.9	87.3	46.6
24 March 1622–24 March 1623	1,694	1,700	131	338.8	340	166.8	33.5	200.2	139.8	69.8	41.1
1641	5,137	5,191	580	1,027.4	1,038.2	594.4	100	694.5	343.7	49.4	33.1

Beaudesert and Cannock Wood

10 July 1697–10 July 1698	—	8,194	344	—	1,638.8	—	1,153.8	485	42.0	29.6
10 July 1698–10 July 1699	8,147	8,063	428	1,629.4	1,612.6	—	1,244.3	368.4	29.6	22.8
10 July 1699–10 July 1700	7,835	7,900	363	1,567	1,579.9	—	1,207.2	372.7	30.9	23.6
10 July 1700–10 July 1701	8,829	8,873	319	1,765.8	1,774.6	—	1,376.9	397.6	28.9	22.4

Notes: The accounts on which this table are based are not full colliery accounts but contemporary abstracts drawn up for the use of the owners, the earls of Shrewsbury. The abstracts for 1612, 1622–3, and 1641 provide the output and sales of coal in dozens, the income derived from sales, the costs of production (divided into getting costs and on-costs), and the stocks of coal at the beginning and end of the year. Beaudesert and Cannock Wood are contained in the same documents but accounted for separately. The abstracts of 10 July 1698 to 10 July 1701 combine the activities of the two collieries, and for each week give the value of the coal produced and the costs of winning it. At the end of the abstract the stocks of coal at the beginning and end of the period of account are given. Sales can therefore be calculated accurately. Each account contains a list of outstanding debts; the total amount owed to the owner varied between £118. 15s. 1d. and £140. 4s. 8d. Prior to these accounts the collieries had been leased to Samuel Porter, Richard Blackbourne, and Edward Greenwood for £350 p.a., but they had been repossessed by the earl when the lessees quarrelled (PRO C. 5/133/57).

It is probable that the dozen weighed more than a ton.

Sources: StRO D(W) 1734/3/3/259–61; D(W) 603/F/3/1/17.

Table 10.A.7 *Sheffield Park*

Period	Output (loads)	Sales (loads)	Value of stock (£)	Value of output (£)	Sales revenue (£)	Getting costs (£)	Other costs (£)	Total costs (£)	Profit (£)	Profit/Loss As a % of total costs	As a % of sales revenue
5 July 1579– 2 July 1580	1,140	1,181	–	84.2	88.6	18.8	32.0	50.8	37.8	74.2	42.6
3 July 1580– Midsummer 1581	1,546	1,448	5.8	116.9	108.6	25.7	28.3	54.0	54.6	101.3	50.3
Midsummer 1581– Midsummer 1582	1,647	–	10.0	122.7	–	27.2	19.8	47.0	–	–	–
21 December 1582– Christmas 1583	1,058	988	4.0	78.1	74.1	18.6	21.7	40.3	33.8	83.9	45.6
Christmas 1583– 20 December 1584	1,363	1,160	18.3	101.2	87.0	24.0	19.2	43.2	43.8	96.5	50.3
2 December 1559– 14 December 1600	2,823	–	41.1	231.4	–	52.8	49.3	102.1	–	–	–

Notes: Sheffield Park colliery was owned and worked by the earls of Shrewsbury during the period covered by these accounts. The form of the accounts and the pattern of working is described in some detail in Stone 1950–1. The Sheffield Park load, to judge from the price at which it was sold, may have weighed approximately one ton.

Sources: BL Add. MS 27532; SCL Arundel S115–16, LPL Shrewsbury 706.

Table 10.A.8 *Handsworth*

Period	Output (loads)	Sales (loads)	Stocks (loads)	Value of output (£)	Sales revenue (£)	Total costs (£)	Profit (£)	Profit/Loss As a % of total costs	As a % of sales revenue
28 February 1652–30 October 1652	1,177	—	220	175.2	—	—	—	—	—
1652–3	932	—	135	139.8	—	—	—	—	—
1653–4	1,017	—	—	—	—	—	—	—	—
1654–5	1,043	—	—	—	—	—	—	—	—
1655–6	1,535	—	—	221.3	205.7	141.2	64.5	45.7	31.4
1656–7	1,474	—	150	—	—	—	—	—	—
1657–8	1,306	1,110	225	195.9	166.5	—	—	—	—
1658–9	1,026	1,127	173	153.9	169.1	121.6	47.5	39.1	28.1
1659–60	1,044	1,109	12	155.1	164.8	125.6	39.2	31.2	23.8
1660–1	887	944	[nil]	133	141.6	128.1	13.5	10.5	9.5
1661–2	1,021	911	120	153.2	136.7	129.7	7.0	5.4	5.1
1662–3	1,036	840	290	155.4	126	131	(5.1)	(3.9)	(4.0)
1663–4	1,028	869	474	154.2	130.4	116.7	13.7	11.7	10.5
1664–5	1,107	1,426	—	166	213.9	134.6	79.3	58.9	37.1
1665–6	1,052	1,104	—	157.8	165.5	124	41.5	33.5	25.2
1666–7	1,212	1,181	—	181.8	177.2	125.9	51.3	40.7	30.0
1667–8	1,202	1,290	—	180.3	193.5	132.1	61.4	46.5	31.7
1668–9	1,223	1,173	—	183.4	176	129.6	46.4	35.8	26.4
1669–70	1,001	894	—	151.2	134.2	108.9	25.3	23.2	18.9

Table 10.A.8 (cont.)

Period	Output (loads)	Sales (loads)	Stocks (loads)	Value of output (£)	Sales revenue (£)	Total costs (£)	Profit (£)	Profit/Loss	
								As a % of total costs	As a % of sales revenue
1670–1	1,026	810	414	153.9	121.4	116.8	4.6	3.9	3.8
1671–2	861	983	—	129.1	147.5	107.8	39.7	36.8	26.9
1672–3	819	603	252	122.9	90.5	104.3	(13.8)	(13.2)	(15.2)
1673–4	723	812	72	108.5	121.7	106.7	15.0	14.1	12.3
1674–5	738	804	—	110.7	120.6	104.3	16.3	15.6	13.5
1675–6	1,087	1,112	—	163	166.8	126.2	40.6	32.2	24.3
1676–7	1,099	1,129	—	164.9	169.4	123.7	45.7	36.9	26.9
1677–8	947	996	—	142	149.4	103	46.4	45.0	31.1
1678–9	958	957	—	143.7	143.6	109.4	34.2	31.3	23.8
1679–80	1,042	1,047	—	156.3	157.1	111.3	45.8	41.2	29.2
1680–1	1,045	919	95	156.8	137.8	116.6	21.2	18.2	15.4
1681–2	1,028	945	117	154.2	141.8	101	40.8	40.3	28.8
1682–3	716	832	[nil]	107.4	124.8	121.4	3.4	2.8	2.7
1683– 22 March 1684	209	224	—	31.4	33.5	25.8	7.7	29.8	23.0

Notes: Handsworth colliery was located 4 miles to the south-east of Sheffield. It was leased by Sir William Bright and his bailiff, Thomas Stacey, and run as a partnership between them for a rent of £30 p.a. The accounting year usually ran from 1 Nov. to 31 Oct. The accounts, which were kept weekly, give the amounts of coal won, and the costs of hewing and incidental expenses. Apart from the first few years of the series, annual statements record each year's production and its value, together with a summation of the weekly costs and expenses. In addition, other on-costs, sinking costs, and timber purchases, etc., are given in these statements, as are stocks and banksmen's arrears at the beginning and end of the year. All output was assumed to have been sold unless the banksmen could demonstrate that it had not been. Because sales do not appear on the accounts as such, the figures in col. 3 are estimates derived by subtracting the banksmen's arrears (the amounts of coal represented by arrears have been calculated using the sale price of coal) and the stock at the end of the year, from the sum of the corresponding figures at the start of the year and the year's output. When there was a change of banksman the arrears and coal stocks for which the outgoing officer was responsible might be treated separately and did not necessarily appear on the subsequent accounts. Efforts were eventually made, however, to account for them. Figures for the coal stocks at the end of a year appear only spasmodically, and it is more common to find a single total representing the banksmen's complete obligations. This total might include coal as yet unsold and coal sold on credit where the money had still to be paid to the banksman. In 1672–3 the bank was counted because the arrears of the banksman were worryingly large, but this was an unusual step. Because Bright and Stacey were operating a partnership and pooling expenses and sharing profits the accounts took on an unusual and superficially deceptive form. The differences between the figures in this table and other attempts to analyse Handsworth accounts stem largely from the fact that here we are attempting to monitor the performance of the colliery not the money Bright received from it.

There was great price stability between 1652 and 1684 with hard coal selling, with scant exceptions, for 3s. a load throughout.

The series of accounts is preceded by a sinking book which records expenditure of £265, 12s. 3d. opening up the colliery between 1650 and 1652. The colliery had been leased for £66 p.a. in 1635, and production had obviously ceased some time before 1650. There was a fire in Dec. 1661; the banksman was in difficulties with his accounts in Apr. 1665; and in 1674 and 1682 the banksman absconded in debt. From 1682 increasing difficulties were experienced with water. Mining ceased on 22 Mar. 1684.

Sources: SCL Wentworth Woodhouse (Bright) Br P55/1–31.

Table 10.A.9 *Heanor*

Period	Output (loads)	Sales (loads)	Stocks (loads)	Value of output (£)	Sales revenue (£)	Getting costs (£)	Other costs (£)	Total costs (£)	Profit (£)	Profit/Loss As a % of total costs	As a % of sales revenue
July–September 1642	464	210	254	84.4	38.3	28.5	18.2	46.7	(8.4)	(17.9)	(21.9)
April–October 1646	1,384	888	496	226.1	145.1	98.1	95.3	193.4	(48.3)	(25)	(33.3)
November 1646–October 1647	1,339	1,635	199	268.4	327.8	100.0	125.8	225.8	102	45.1	31.1
October 1647–October 1648	1,290	279	1,205	252.9	54.8	106.6	72.6	179.2	(124.4)	(69.4)	(227)
October 1648–November 1649	961	1,724	411	187.3	313	86	85.2	171.2	141.8	83.0	45.3
November 1649–October 1650	591	671	31	114.6	130.1	54.2	39.7	93.9	36.1	38.4	27.7

November 1651–October 1652	2,130	1,404	789	438.4	288.9	177.5	92.5	267.0	21.9	8.2	7.6
November 1652–November 1653	[nil]	630	108	[nil]	114.6	[nil]	29.6	29.6	85	287.2	74.2
[November 1653]–November 1655	1,292	393	899	239.7	72.8	106.9	135.2	242.1	(169.3)	(69.9)	(232.6)
November 1656–September 1657	2,167	1,500	702	377.8	261.6	172.5	91.1	263.6	(2.0)	(0.76)	(0.76)
October 1657–[August 1659]	1,145	1,698	[nil]	192.7	285.7	90.7	93.2	183.9	101.8	544.4	35.6

Notes: Heanor colliery was situated 3.5 miles north-west of Ilkeston (Derby.), almost equidistant from Derby and Nottingham. It was owned by the Charltons of Chilwell, and during the period of these accounts was managed directly by the family in partnership with a succession of partners. The accounts, which were compiled weekly, give totals of coal won, hewing costs, amounts of coal sold, receipts from sales, and full on-costs. There are also annual summaries which provide stocks. A fire shut the colliery in Feb. 1643. Production was halted in 1652–3 because of a slump in sales. The colliery was closed down in 1658, and existing stocks were sold off by Aug. 1659.

Sources: NoRO Charlton of Chilwell DD/CH/35/34–46.

Table 10.A.10 *Farnworth*

Period	Output (loads)	Sales (loads)	Stock (£)	Value of output (£)	Sales revenue (£)	Getting costs (£)	Other costs (£)	Total costs (£)	Profit (£)	As a % of total costs	As a % of sales revenue
										Profit/Loss	
1683–4	3,524	3,622	12.8	322.4	331.4	—	—	231.4	100	43.2	30.2
1685–6	2,907	2,911	0.2	269.1	269.6	—	—	189.6	80	42.2	29.7
1688–9	3,457	3,428	11.9	320.8	318.1	—	—	223.1	95	42.6	29.9
1699–1700	5,601	5,601	[nil]	559.8	559.8	245.6	140.7	386.3	173.5	44.9	30.9

Notes: Farnworth colliery was located 3 miles south-east of Bolton (Lancs). It was owned and worked by Sir John Bridgeman. The accounts were compiled monthly and give the scale and value of production; every 2 months comprehensive costs were listed. Sales are not given, but stocks at the beginning and end of year are, and the former have been compiled by subtracting stocks from output. The accountancy period shown runs from Michaelmas to Michaelmas. Coal was sold at 30*d.* per load of cannell; 20*d.* per load of 'coal', and 10*d.* per load of small coal. About 4 or 5 times as much coal was sold as cannell, and sales of small coal were trivial. The account for 1699–1700 takes a somewhat different form, and the production of cannell is nearly as high as coal. Sales are not given, but it appears likely that all the production is disposed of.

Sources: BoRO Bradford ZBR/1/5–8.

Table 10.A.11 *Chopwell*

Period	Output (tons)	Sales (tons)	Sales revenue (£)	Production costs (£)	Transport costs (£)	Other costs (£)	Total costs (£)	Profit (£)	Profit/Loss	
									As a % of total costs	As a % of sales revenue
1701–2	48,413	35,325	6,389.6	2,184	2,575.1	1,555.7	6,314.8	74.8	1.2	1.2
1702–3	31,496	34,842	6,474.3	1,494.2	2,442.5	1,378	5,314.7	1,159.6	21.8	17.9
1703–4	35,571	39,830	7,647.6	1,473.5	2,933.5	1,706.3	6,113.3	1,534.3	25.1	20.1

Notes: Chopwell colliery was located some 10 miles south-west of Newcastle, close to the Derwent river. It was owned and worked by the Clavering family. the accounts upon which this table are based are annual abstracts of sales, production, income, and expenditure. The number of Newcastle chaldrons sold within the year is recorded, as well as the money received from the sales. Expenditure is grouped under five heads: working (including sinking and drifting), carriage (including waggonway repairs and equipment), wayleave and staithe rents, keel rents, allowances for skippers, and other expenses and salaries. Output is given in pit tens, which have been assumed to 'make out' at 13 Newcastle chaldrons each. A Newcastle chaldron contained 53 cwt. of coal.

Sources: HRO Cowper D/EPT 4877–8.

Table 10.A.12 *Niddrie*

Period	Output (hill-loads)	Sales (hill-loads)	Stocks	Value of output (£ Scots)	Sales revenue (£ Scots)	Getting costs (£ Scots)	Other costs (£ Scots)	Total costs (£ Scots)	Profit (£ Scots)	Profit/Loss As a % of total costs	As a % of sales revenue
1 June 1696–29 May 1697	42,245	41,149	[nil]	8,891.5	8,662.8	3,521.1	3,198.3	6,719.4	1,943.4	28.9	22.3
29 May 1697–29 May 1698	60,157	58,984	[nil]	12,623.9	12,379.5	5,013.1	2,324.3	7,337.4	5,042.1	68.7	40.7
29 May 1698–27 May 1699	36,127	35,322	[nil]	7,526.5	7,358.8	3,306.2	1,334.7	4,640.9	2,717.9	58.6	36.9
27 May 1699–18 May 1700	19,718	18,931	[nil]	4,425.9	4,095	1,945.4	809.5	2,754.9	1,340.1	48.6	32.7

Notes: Niddrie colliery was located on the south bank of the Forth in Midlothian; it was owned by the laird of Niddrie and worked by him. The accounts provide amounts sold, the value of coal sold after hewing costs have been deducted, and on-costs. However, the on-costs include valuations for relatively small amounts of coal delivered to the laird's dwelling, used in the colliery, used as panwood, or paid for on-cost work. Total output may be calculated by adding these coals to the sales. In accordance with our practice elsewhere, coals consumed by the owner have, for the purposes of calculating profit, been treated as if they had been sold, but coals used in the colliery have been treated as a cost. Such coals were valued by the accountant at 4s. 2d. per hill-load, and this figure has been taken as the price at which sales were made throughout the series. A hill-load was probably equivalent to a horse-load.

Sources: NLS Acc. 5253/MS. 17952.

Table 10.A.13 *Chirk Castle*

Period	Output/Sales (wagon-loads)	Output/Sales value (£)	Total costs (£)	Profit	Profit/Loss	
					As a % of total costs	As a % of sales revenue
February–December 1684	3,776	422	273.4	148.6	54.3	35.2
1685	3,835	479.4	297.5	181.9	61.1	37.9
1686	3,903	487.9	453.1	34.8	7.7	7.1
1687	4,026	503.3	292.9	210.4	71.8	41.8
1688	3,707	463.3	294.7	168.6	57.3	36.4
1689	2,453	306.6	196.8	109.8	55.8	35.8
January–June 1690	1,220	152.5	95.8	56.7	59.2	37.2

Notes: Chirk Castle colliery was located approximately 9 miles south of Wrexham (Denbigh.); it was owned and worked by the Myddleton family. The accounts are rudimentary and give only the value of the coal won and the costs of winning it. Coal was valued at 2 s. 6 d. per wagon-load. The profits are based on the assumption that all output was sold. In the accounts from Jan. 1691 onwards there are indications that the recording of costs may not have been comprehensive, therefore they have not been included in the table.

Sources: NLW Chirk Castle 8588.

ii. Average unit performance

The first column in the following tables gives the average cost of producing each unit of output, which has been calculated by dividing the total expenditure during the period of the account by the total production. The second column gives the average selling price of each unit of output, which has normally been obtained by dividing sales revenues by the numbers of units sold. The average margin per unit sold given in the third column has been obtained by subtracting the figures in column 1 from those in column 2. ( ) indicates that the margin was negative.

Table 10.A.14 *Wollaton*

Date	Costs per rook	Price per rook	Margin per rook	Margin	
	s.	s.	s.	As a % of costs	As a % of selling price
1549	0.88	2.00	1.12	127.3	56.0
1551	1.00	2.00	1.00	100.0	50.0
1578	1.55	2.67	1.12	72.3	37.4
1579	2.02	2.67	0.65	32.2	24.3
1580	1.50	2.98	1.48	98.7	49.7
1602	2.76	3.68	0.92	33.3	25.0
1603	2.29	3.34	1.05	45.9	31.4
1604	2.91	3.33	0.42	14.4	12.6

Table 10.A.15 *Trowell Moor*

Period	Cost per load	Price per load	Margin per load	Margin	
				As a % of costs	As a % of selling price
26 January 1647–					
19 February 1648	2.79	4.48	1.69	60.6	37.7
20 February 1648–					
30 December 1648	2.50	4.50	2.00	80.0	44.4
1 January 1649–					
8 December 1649	2.55	4.51	1.96	76.9	43.5
9 December 1649–					
7 December 1650	2.75	4.50	1.75	63.6	38.9
8 December 1650–					
6 December 1651	2.74	4.50	1.76	64.2	39.1
6 December 1652–					
21 January 1654	3.51	4.41	0.9	25.7	20.4
1 February 1654–					
23 December 1654	3.23	4.93	1.7	52.6	34.5
23 December 1656–					
8 January 1658	3.16	4.60	1.44	45.6	31.3
9 January 1658–					
16 December 1658	3.37	4.35	0.98	29.0	22.5
17 December 1658–					
31 December 1659	2.62	4.40	1.78	67.9	40.3
24 December 1662–					
26 December 1663	3.35	4.32	0.97	28.9	22.5
2 January 1664–					
17 December 1664	3.36	4.44	1.08	32.1	24.4
18 December 1664–					
23 December 1665	3.84	5.09	1.25	32.6	24.6
13 January 1666–					
22 December 1666	3.90	5.08	1.18	30.3	23.2
23 December 1666–					
30 November 1667	4.68	4.86	0.18	3.8	3.7
31 November 1667–					
24 December 1668	3.91	4.92	1.01	25.8	20.5

Table 10.A.16 *Cossall Moor*

Period	Cost per load s.	Price per load s.	Margin per load s.	Margin	
				As a % of costs	As a % of selling price
1649	3.09	5.16	2.07	66.9	40.1
1653–4	5.02	5.00	(0.02)	(0.4)	(0.4)
1659–60	4.02	5.29	1.27	31.6	24.0
1660	2.77	4.81	2.04	73.6	42.4
1669	23.08	5.41	(17.67)	(76.6)	(327.2)

Table 10.A.17 *Beaudesert*

Date	Cost per load s.	Price per load s.	Margin per load s.	Margin	
				As a % of total costs	As a % of sales price
1577	0.97	[2.67]	1.70	175.3	63.6
1578	0.91	[2.67]	1.76	193.4	65.9
1579	1.13	[2.67]	1.54	136.3	57.7
1580	1.14	[2.67]	1.53	134.2	57.3
1581	1.01	[2.67]	1.65	163.4	61.8
1582	1.07	[2.67]	1.60	149.5	59.9
1583	2.35	[2.67]	0.32	13.6	11.9
1584	2.62	[2.67]	0.04	0.15	0.15

Table 10.A.18 *Beaudesert and Cannock Wood*

Period	Costs per dozen s.	Price per dozen s.	Margin per dozen s.	Margin	
				As a % of total costs	As a % of sale price
Beaudesert					
1612	2.73	4	1.27	46.5	31.8
1622–3	3.03	5	1.97	65.0	39.4
1641	4.87	5	0.13	2.7	2.6
Cannock Wood					
1612	2.33	4	1.67	71.7	41.7
1622–3	2.36	4	1.64	69.5	41.0
1641	2.70	4	1.3	48.1	32.5
Beaudesert and Cannock Wood					
1698–9	3.05	4	0.95	31.1	23.8
1699–1700	3.08	4.03	0.95	30.8	23.6
1700–1	3.12	4	0.88	28.2	22.0

Table 10.A.19 *Sheffield Park*

Period	Cost per load s.	Price per load s.	Margin per load s.	Margin	
				As a % of costs	As a % of selling price
1579–80	0.89	1.5	0.61	68.5	40.7
1580–1	0.69	1.5	0.81	117.4	54.0
1582–3	0.76	1.5	0.74	97.4	49.3
1583–4	0.63	1.5	0.87	138.1	58

Table 10.A.20 *Handsworth*

Period	Cost per load s.	Price per load s.	Margin per load s.	Margin	
				As a % of costs	As a % of selling price
1658–9	2.37	3	0.63	26.6	21.0
1659–60	2.41	3	0.56	23.2	18.7
1660–1	2.89	3	0.11	3.8	3.7
1661–2	2.54	3	0.46	18.1	15.3
1662–3	2.53	3	0.47	18.6	15.7
1663–4	2.27	3	0.73	32.2	24.3
1664–5	2.43	3	1.43	58.8	47.7
1665–6	2.36	3	0.64	27.1	33.3
1666–7	2.08	3	0.92	44.2	30.7
1667–8	2.20	3	0.80	36.4	26.7
1668–9	2.12	3	0.88	41.5	29.3
1669–70	2.18	3	0.82	37.6	27.3
1670–1	2.28	3	0.72	31.6	24.0
1671–2	2.50	3	0.50	20.0	16.7
1672–3	2.55	3	0.45	17.6	15.0
1673–4	2.95	3	0.05	1.7	1.7
1674–5	2.83	3	0.17	6.0	5.7
1675–6	2.32	3	0.68	29.3	22.7
1676–7	2.25	3	0.75	33.3	25.0
1677–8	2.17	3	0.83	38.2	27.7
1678–9	2.28	3	0.72	31.6	24
1679–80	2.14	3	0.76	35.5	25.3
1680–1	2.23	3	0.77	34.5	25.7
1681–2	1.96	3	1.04	53.1	35.7
1682–3	3.39	3	(0.39)	(11.5)	(13.0)
1683– 22 March 1684	2.47	3	0.53	21.5	17.7

Table 10.A.21 *Heanor*

Period	Cost per load s.	Price per load s.	Margin per load s.	Margin	
				As a % of costs	As a % of selling price
July–September 1642	2.01	3.64	1.63	81.1	44.8
April–October 1646	2.79	3.27	0.47	16.8	14.4
November 1646– October 1647	3.37	4.01	0.63	18.7	15.7
October 1647– October 1648	2.77	3.92	1.15	41.5	29.3
October 1648– November 1649	3.56	3.63	0.34	9.6	9.4
November 1649– October 1650	3.18	3.88	0.70	22.0	18.0
November 1651– October 1652	2.54	4.12	1.58	62.2	38.3
[November 1653]– October 1655	3.75	3.71	(0.04)	(1.1)	(1.1)
November 1656– September 1657	2.43	3.49	1.05	43.2	30.1
October 1657– [August 1659]	3.27	3.37	0.15	4.7	4.5

Table 10.A.22 *Farnworth*

Period	Cost per load s.	Price per load s.	Margin per load s.	Margin	
				As a % of costs	As a % of selling price
1683–4	1.31	1.83	0.52	39.3	28.4
1685–6	1.30	1.85	0.55	41.9	29.7
1688–9	1.29	1.86	0.57	43.8	30.6
1699–1700	1.38	2.00	0.62	44.9	31.0

Table 10.A.23 *Chopwell*

Period	Cost per ton s.	Price per ton s.	Margin per ton s.	Margin	
				As a % of costs	As a % of sale price
1701–2	3.00	3.62	0.62	20.7	17.1
1702–3	3.23	3.72	0.49	15.2	13.2
1703–4	3.26	3.84	0.58	17.8	18.1

Table 10.A.24 *Niddrie*

Period	Cost per hill-load Scots s.	Price per hill-load Scots s.	Margin per hill-load Scots s.	Margin	
				As a % of costs	As a % of selling price
1696–7	3.18	4.17	0.99	31.0	23.7
1697–8	2.44	4.17	1.73	70.8	41.5
1698–9	2.57	4.17	1.60	62.2	38.4
1699–1700	2.79	4.17	1.37	49.1	32.9

CHAPTER 11

Life and Labour in the Collieries

There young and old, with glim'ring candles burning,
Digge, delve and labour, turning and returning

John Taylor, *On a Visit to Culross* (1618)

It has long been customary to characterize colliers as a race apart; a special breed of industrial workers in an agricultural environment, burrowing in the bowels of the earth instead of labouring on the surface with the rest of mankind. The remoteness of most coalmining areas, it has been said, led to the development of isolated mining communities and reinforced the distinctiveness of colliers. For J. U. Nef, contemporary sources revealed that colliers

had come to be regarded as a peculiarly uncouth race, little better than the savage tribes of Africa and America. Their lives were held scarcely less cheap, the conditions under which those lives were lived were regarded as scarcely more a matter for public concern, than if they had been negro slaves. Their spiritual redemption was thought of as a task to be undertaken only by the most courageous missionaries.[1]

For M. E. James the north-eastern pitworker 'was a member of a despised and suspected group, recruited from the marginal and drop-out elements—the decayed husbandmen and wandering poor, immigrants from Scotland, or from the overpopulated Border dales whose half-savage inhabitants had a reputation for thieving and cattle raiding'.[2] Moreover, Nef went on to develop a thesis of the 'final degradation' of the early modern coalminer, brutalized by low pay and the 'peculiarly revolting and degrading character of work in the collieries', and alienated by a loss of freedom in a new industrial regime and by physical isolation from the rest of society.

These are strong sentiments indeed, but although some do contain elements of truth, others run counter to major themes of this book. In

---

[1] Nef 1932, ii. 135. See also ibid. 136–97.
[2] James 1974, 95.

particular, there is much to suggest the sturdy independence and relatively high earnings of many colliers, and Nef's preoccupation with decline from a status supposedly enjoyed by privileged communities of medieval coalminers is misleading.[3] Further misrepresentation stems from a failure to appreciate that most contemporary views of colliers enunciated by their social superiors, contemptuous as they were, were applied, *mutatis mutandis*, to all the peasant and labouring masses. To genteel observers the common people as a whole were 'confessed to be rough and savage in their dispositions, being of levelling principles, and refractory to government, insolent and tumultuous'.[4] On the other hand colliers did often possess singular characteristics. Underground workers in particular were specialists who followed a lifetime career, and they were often also self-perpetuating, with sons following their fathers into the pits. Moreover, the rapid expansion of the industry fed upon migrations of labour, and strangers frequently encountered the suspicion and hostility of native communities. Yet the majority of pits and collieries were modest in size, and consequently colliers often comprised only a small segment in typical rural communities. There was undoubtedly a distinctiveness about the collier and his life-style, yet even in thriving coalmining regions further research may show that those who worked in coal-mines formed a community within the community rather than a race apart.

In the following sections the emphasis has necessarily fallen most heavily upon the collier in the colliery rather than in the community, and attention has been focused upon working conditions, earnings, and standards of living rather than family life, demography, life-cycle, and culture. The social history of the collier before the industrial revolution is a subject eminently worthy of study, but many of its sources lie beyond those generated by the industry and beyond the competence and scope of this volume.[5]

i. The structure of the colliery work-force

Outsiders indiscriminately lumped together those who laboured to produce coal, describing them simply as 'colliers' or 'miners'. Yet

---

[3] There is no evidence to suggest that medieval coalminers enjoyed privileges commensurate with those of tinners or leadminers.

[4] Nourse, *Campania Foelix* (1700), 15.

[5] The social study of Whickham from the mid-16th to the mid-18th cent. by D. Levine and K. Wrightson was published too late for its findings to be incorporated into this work.

colliers or miners have rarely if ever been a homogeneous body of men. The inherent character of mining inevitably results in broad differentiations of function. Even in the crudest of shallow pits there was work that was carried out underground and that which was done on the surface. Underground work in turn consisted of that directly connected with the production of coal, and that expended on maintenance and preparation. Production in turn involved at least two distinct tasks: the cutting of coal and the hauling of it from the face to the eye of the shaft. Preparation and maintenance in turn involved both the servicing of existing workings and the sinking of new pits. Even in the simple shallow bell-pits of Beaudesert, where the same colliers usually acted as hewers, haulers, winders, and sinkers, there were specialist timbermen and sinkers. With increasing scale and greater complexity the division of labour proceeded apace. At Wollaton in 1549, for example, there were, in addition to colliers and labourers and a trio of managers and clerks, a 'candeler', a smith, and a cooper employed on quarterly retainers. At Howgill (Cumb.) in 1699–1701, working on the surface and draining the pits were winders, bankers, tubmen, dikemen, quarrymen, highwaymen, a slate-picker, a carter, and a corve-maker.[6] The work-forces of the great Tyneside coal-owners often stretched miles from the pits, and were devoted to such divers tasks as maintaining waggonways and guarding the coal on the staithes from the depredations of petty thieves.

Although scratchings manned by a handful of labourers continued to be plentiful throughout the eighteenth century, we do not have to proceed far from a crude hole in the ground to encounter the division of production workers into hewers, haulers/putters, and banksmen. This tripartite structure was ubiquitous in all but the very smallest and the very largest of collieries, and it was duly enscribed as archetypal by justices of the peace when they compiled their assessments of maximum wages in mining regions. As the size of a colliery increased so the banksman might be assisted by a clerk and a winder or two to help in getting the coal to the surface and stacking it on the bank; watermen might be needed to keep the workings from flooding, and timbermen or carpenters to keep them from collapsing, but all such tasks grew naturally out of the fundamental processes of cutting the coal from the seam, carrying it to the surface, selling it, and keeping records. Thus at Railey in south Durham in 1460 the regular work-force consisted of three hewers, three barrowmen, four winders, and one banksman ('appruator carbonum'). In the same year at Whickham, in the north of the county

[6] NoUL Middleton Mi. Ac. 38; Wood 1988, 15.

close to the Tyne, there were four hewers, four barrowmen, four winders, and a banksman.[7] Similar structures can be found as far apart as Plas Teg, north Wales, where the pit was worked in 1630–1 by three hewers, two haulers, and two winders, and Three Quarters Band colliery in Cumberland, where in 1676 the normal shift comprised four haggers (hewers), three trailers (putters), and a banksman.[8] Of course, the precise ratios depended upon the distance from the eye of the shaft to the coal-face, and the depth of the shaft. At Sheffield Park in the 1580s a single barrowman and an occasional helper was sufficient to despatch the coal hewed by an average of three pickmen, and a single banksman was generally able to wind it to the surface, conduct sales, and keep accounts. But in the Pembrokeshire collieries described by George Owen in 1603, it was common to have three pickaxes digging, seven bearers, one filler, four winders, and two riddlers to each pit.[9]

Hewers were the aristocracy of the colliery labour force. Their wages and their status were normally far higher than those enjoyed by other colliers, or by the labouring classes in general. Their work was hard and dangerous, requiring skill and experience in addition to strength, stamina, and courage; not just the skill to wield a hammer and pick in confined spaces, but the ability to judge how to cut a seam in order to maximize output and minimize effort without endangering the safety of the pit or its longer-term viability. Hewers were frequently relied upon to predict and avert the occurrence of explosions from gas or floods from water, thereby saving the lives of their fellows and the money of their masters. The pillar-and-stall method of mining required especial expertise, for if insufficient pillars were left the roof might collapse or the floor rise up, while if the pillars were left too thick profits would be lost. Overmen and viewers, of course, had a responsibility to see that pits were competently worked, but the hewer at the coal-face was instrumental in the achievement. The expert testimony given in mining disputes, and to the surveyors and appraisers of collieries, was dominated by hewers and by overmen who had formerly been hewers. Hewers were at the heart of the colliery work-force, and to a considerable extent the life and prosperity of the colliery depended upon them.

The skills of a good hewer were not easy to acquire, and adult recruitment into the occupation was rarely likely to prove successful.

[7] DUDP Church Commission box 79, 190024, 190025, 190306.
[8] ClRO Glynde D/G/3311–12; CuRO Lonsdale D/Lons/W, Account books of collieries.
[9] SCL Arundel S115; BL Add. MS 27532; LPL Shrewsbury 704 fo. 135; Owen, *Pembrokeshire*, 91–2.

When experienced colliers fled in fear of the press-gang from Sir Humphrey Mackworth's colliery at Neath in 1705, he claimed that those brought in to replace them 'could not attain to or undergo the same work'.[10] The long periods of rapid expansion of the industry which occurred in the later sixteenth and seventeenth centuries inevitably resulted in skill shortages, even though the era was broadly characterized by population growth and a surplus of labour. Such shortages were felt acutely in most of the coalfields at one time or another, and in many places an inadequate supply of skilled workmen persisted. Consequently, employers took positive steps to attract and retain competent hewers, and the prime means they adopted was high wages. The scarcity value of hewers also went hand in hand with indulgent working practices, despite frequent protestations to the contrary. Even in Scotland, where a new form of serfdom was enacted to secure an adequate supply of labour for the coal-mines, there was little sign of docility or deference among hewers. Scarcity also led employers to offer bonuses to any of their colliers who introduced new workmen, and to undertake recruiting campaigns in neighbouring parishes or even in distant counties and countries, seeking to induce colliers, especially hewers, to migrate with offers of money and housing. Hewers were also a prime means of the transfer of technology. When Sir Richard Newdigate expanded operations at Griff (War.) in 1703 he searched for colliers in Shropshire, and offered them 1s. each on recruitment, up to 2s. 6d. travelling expenses, and a lodging allowance of 6d. per week. When William Christian, a Newcastle Hostman, began mining in Cumberland he took Newcastle 'haggers' with him, and the failure of Sir Humphrey Mackworth successfully to reopen his coalworks at Neath 'by the assistance of colliers of that neighbourhood' led him to import miners skilled in the 'manner used in Shropshire and Newcastle'.[11]

The only other manual colliery worker who was sometimes on a par with the hewer, was the expert sinker. For much of the time sinking could be a matter of merely digging a hole in the ground—a pick and shovel job. But stone, water, and gas made the task far more difficult, and sinking the deeper shafts called for considerable expertise, even when the team was led by a viewer. As the anonymous author of the *Compleat Collier* tells us, 'it is not every labourer who has been by chance in a coalpit, or at labour in other sort of digging above ground, that is fit to be employed' working through stone. Similarly, an

---

[10] Trott 1969, 71.
[11] White thesis 1969, 123–4; *VCH Cumberland*, ii. 360; Moller thesis 1933, 232–3.

inexperienced man might cause an explosion and threaten life as well as wrecking the shaft:

Therefore all sinkers should be skilled in these matters for their own security sake, as also for the benefit of the owner or master of the colliery, for if £1,000 or more be spent in carrying down a pit or shaft, almost to the coal expected, and then by an ignorant man should be blasted by a strong blast . . . this would be a dismal accident.[12]

Once again skill and experience warranted a premium, and while much sinking was undertaken at moderate rates, gang leaders earned substantially more.[13]

By contrast the hauling of coal underground was almost invariably sheer drudgery. It is difficult, perhaps impossible, from the perspective of the 1990s to comprehend the working lives of those, young and old, female sometimes as well as male, who performed the backbreaking and soul-quenching toil of carrying baskets or pushing and pulling wooden sleds loaded with coal along the dark, cramped, and uneven tunnels of early coalworkings. Nor was there any compensation in high earnings or enhanced status, for putters and barrowmen received little if any more than the average rural unskilled wage. The description by George Owen in 1603 is evocative of their working conditions in Pembrokeshire mines:

then have they bearers which are boys that bear the coals in fit baskets on their backs, going always stooping by reason of the lowness of the pit, each bearer carrieth this basket six fathoms where, upon a bench of stone he layeth it, where meeteth him another boy with an empty basket, which he giveth him and taketh that which is full of coals and carrieth it as far, where another meeteth him and so till they come under the door where it is lifteth up.[14]

Presumably boys were used because of the low roofs, and some twelve yards was as far as a lad could stagger with a full basket on his back. The return journey with an empty basket gave him a brief respite within which to summon up his strength for the next load.

Conditions for the bearers in these Pembrokeshire pits would seem to have been as bad as any for which we have record. The pushing or dragging of corves or sleds would appear to have been far more common, and very occasionally there were wheeled barrows. Paradoxically, it is also from South Wales that we have the best description

---

[12] *Compleat Collier*, 23.

[13] e.g. gang leaders at Wolverhampton in 1574 received 10–12*d.* per day (NoUL Middleton Mi. Ac. 130, 138, 139).   [14] Owen, *Pembrokeshire*, 90.

of the use of underground rails. In Mackworth's Neath mines the putters were termed waggoners, and we are told that it required 'great skill to keep the waggons upon the rails through the turnings and windings underground which are so intricate'. From this skill came a measure of status, and it was a matter of particular comment that 'a cutter of coal can better be spared in these works than a waggoner that brings it out from under the ground, both with respect to the labour and the skill of the work'. Significantly, however, the writer also added that the work of the waggoner was so arduous that few would undertake it.[15]

Beyond this basic but ubiquitous work-force the range of tasks and occupations to be found was dependent upon the nature of the colliery or pit, and the technology employed in it. Thus, whereas in the small bell-pits of Beaudesert in the later sixteenth century timbermen were kept in full-time employment, elsewhere carpenters were normally used only intermittently, even in large collieries. The wetness of a colliery and the ability to construct an effective sough usually had a major impact on the numbers employed in drainage. Thus at Bedworth in the early 1630s, despite two pumping engines running non-stop, over thirty men were constantly employed winding up buckets of water.[16] Machinery required maintenance, and at Hooton a 'gin-tender' was paid 2s. a week, while at Trowell the man who tended the gin horses was paid 3s. a week.[17] Where horsepower was not employed its place had to be taken by manpower. At the great colliery of Howgill (Cumb.) in 1705 the absence of horse-powered winding engines to raise the coal resulted in winders working fifty shifts a week turning windlasses.[18]

Clear and often fine divisions of labour existed in coalmining before the eighteenth century, but the inherently unstable character of mining meant that these divisions had often to be temporarily abandoned. It was not uncommon, even in well-established collieries, for workmen to engage in a variety tasks. The specialist and highly paid hewers of Gatherick (Northumb.), for example, were transferred to shovelling at much reduced pay when production was brought to a sudden halt in late March 1684, and at Tulliallan (Fife) in 1646 we find even the grieves spending some of the working year as gatemen, on-costmen, wrights, carters, and watermen.[19] Additionally, a sizeable proportion of the men

---

[15] Mackworth, *Case of Sir Humphrey Mackworth*, 5.

[16] Grant thesis 1977, 91.

[17] LCA Mexborough MX 295, 296; NoUL Middleton Mi. Ac. 16–33.

[18] Beckett 1981, 15. There were 50 shifts worked not 50 winders working.

[19] NuRO Society of Antiquaries ZAN B/18/1/19; ScRO Register House RH9/1/131. See also Langton 1979a, 68.

employed in coalworking during the course of a year had neither full-time nor regular employment, and much work was undertaken by free-lance labour on an occasional basis. This was generally the case with sinkers, who were employed as a gang when a new pit or sough was required, although they might be supplemented by unemployed hewers and putters if production had to be halted. Smiths who repaired tools and kept them sharp, and engineers who maintained drainage and winding engines, were usually paid by the job or secured by retainers. At Sheffield Park, for example, George Hinchcliffe was paid 6s. 8d. quarterly for maintaining the 'coalpit gear', while at Plas Teg (Flintshire) the smith received a 'pitch' of coals a week in return for keeping the colliers' tools sharp.[20]

Emma, daughter of William Culhare, was killed by 'le Dampe' while drawing water from a coal-pit at Morley (Derby.) in 1322.[21] But her employment was an exception, and colliery work-forces remained over-whelmingly male up to the eighteenth century. Outside of Scotland and Lancashire women were very rarely to be found working underground in British collieries, and although employment above ground was some-times provided it was normally in menial tasks such as picking out slate and waste from the heaps of coal on the banks. Nowhere did women find employment as hewers. The prevalence of gang-working often makes it difficult to be categoric about the employment of women, but in those collieries where the names of the work-force are given women are rarely encountered, and incidental references to female colliers are also extremely rare. At Gatherick (Northumb.) and the Lowther collieries around Whitehaven (Cumb.) in the late seventeenth century, where the total work-forces are listed by name, there is no trace what-soever of women or girls. In the Lowther collieries this is especially significant in view of the large numbers of females employed there later in the eighteenth century. The records of Griff colliery (War.) in 1701 are also especially detailed, but here numbers of women as well as boys were employed in tasks on the surface including riddling and pumping water.[22]

It appears that only *in extremis* did coal-owners turn to women to satisfy their labour needs underground. Thus when Winlaton (Durham) was booming in the 1580s, and pits had sometimes to be left idle for

---

[20] SCL Arundel S116; BL Add. MS 27532; LPL Shrewsbury 704, fo. 135; ClRO Glynde D/9/311–12.

[21] *VCH Derbyshire*, ii. 351.

[22] NuRO Society of Antiquaries ZAN B/18/1/19; Wood 1988, 15; White thesis 1969, 135–8, 167.

want of workmen, in addition to sending into Scotland and other places for workmen the partners occasionally used women, though this was a matter for special comment.[23] In Scotland and in parts of Lancashire, however, where hewers were expected to provide their own bearers, they often did so by employing their wives and children. Of thirty-nine colliers appending their marks to the Haigh colliery orders in 1636 and 1664, eight were women. Nor did women merely find employment as bearers or putters. Helen Lowe was an auditor at Hallcroft pit. At Tulliallan (Fife) in 1646 many women served as on-cost workers, and women predominated among the winders. Only two out of the sixteen persons listed as leading coal with horses were women, however, and none can be found holding the managerial office of grieve.[24]

The employment of boys, was less uncommon. We find them employed as putters or bearers and as assistants to labourers and craftsmen. Few traces of any training arrangements exist, but it may be safe to assume that the major source of new entrants into hewing was the boys taken into the mines as putters and general helps. In a rare document dated 20 April 1674 Henry Roberts, gang leader at Hooton colliery, agreed to pay Widow Frost 15 s. for the apprenticeship of her two sons for two years, with Roberts also providing their food, drink, and clothing.[25] There is no reliable evidence of the ages at which boys began work, but the testimony given by a small sample of hewers and overmen in litigation and to mine surveyors, which gives their stated ages and the number of years they had been employed in collieries, would suggest that they commonly entered when they were 10–12 years old.[26]

The prevalence of gang-working means that it is normally impossible to follow individual colliers through their working lives. The small sample of the ages of hewers and overmen occurring in litigation and mine surveyors' reports would, however, suggest that contrary to what might be expected the working lives of hewers do not appear to have been unduly short. Indeed significant numbers were in their forties, fifties, and even sixties. Doubtless this sample is skewed, since the most experienced workers were more likely to have been asked to give evidence, none the less their presence confirms that there was far more

[23] PRO E. 134 29 Elizabeth, Easter 4.
[24] WiRO D/DZ A13/34, fos. 8ᵛ–9ʳ; ScRO Register House RH9/1/31.
[25] LCA Mexborough MX 296.
[26] Based upon details of deponents given in the Crown surveys of 1611, the 1587 Winlaton lawsuit, and the 1662 Harraton lawsuit (PRO E. 178/5037; E. 134 29 Elizabeth, Easter 4; E. 134 14 Charles II, Trinity 6).

to hewing than brute strength. Normally paid by piece-rate, the older hewer's earnings no doubt fell as his pace of working slowed, but for the employer he remained good value as his experience and knowledge of mining in general, and of his home pit in particular, continued to grow. Also of considerable interest are the brief statements which witnesses made of their careers, in which the progression from hewer to overman was especially common.

ii. The hours and frequency of work

The length of the working day and the frequency and regularity of employment are crucial to any assessment of the labourer's lot, yet it is rarely possible to amass definitive evidence on these matters. Inevitably in coalmining sources we encounter the recurring problems of random and fragmentary references and local variations in practice and experience, but it is possible to compile a respectable body of information on these elusive topics.

Direct statements on the length of the working day are extremely few, and only three have been traced. But each specifies a day of twelve hours, in keeping with eighteenth-century practice. In the early seventeenth century it was deposed in a Chancery case that the ordinary way of working pits in the East Midlands was by a single shift, 'that is to say from six in the morning until six of the evening'. At about the same time, we are told that Pembrokeshire coalminers work 'from six o'clock to six o'clock and rest an hour at noon'.[27] In Sir John Clerk's colliery at Loanhead (Midlothian) a century later a 'whole day' was defined as 'twelve hours space', and for hewers as 'at least so many hours daily as may furnish to their bearers twelve hours work daily to bear out their masters' wrought coals'. Colliers at Loanhead were enjoined to begin work by 4 a.m.[28] The reference to an alternative to a twelve-hour day for hewers is, of course, pertinent. For once again not only is the central role of hewers in determining the productivity of the colliery highlighted, so also is the failure of piece-rates by themselves to guarantee full-time working. A day's work for a hewer was consequently frequently defined by a specified level of output instead of a specified number of hours. 'Shifts' and 'turns' were also worked as well as 'days', and they were not necessarily of the same duration. For example, at Gatherick in 1683–4 sinkers were paid 8*d.* per shift and 10*d.* per day, while shovelmen were paid 5*d.* a shift and 6*d.* per day until late April,

[27] Smith 1957, 124; Owen, *Pembrokeshire*, 91.   [28] Marshall 1980, 242.

when the rates were changed to 6*d.* and 8*d.* respectively.[29] Unlike surface workers, the colliers' working day was unaffected by daylight hours, and there is no evidence that its length varied with the seasons.

Night work was never the norm during the period covered in this volume, but neither was it rare. When flat rents were payable, lessors, concerned lest their coal reserves should be exhausted, might set limits on the amount of coal that could be raised, the number of miners who could be employed, or the length of time that the colliery could be worked each day or week. Thus, when the bishop of Durham leased a mine in Bearpark in 1457 he specified that the lessees should 'work only on the customary working days and nights', and Sir Philip Strelley was greatly upset when his lessee, Huntingdon Beaumont, worked Strelley contrary to the custom in the area by using double shifts.[30] When demand was healthy and operators were not burdened by restrictions, however, night working could prove a viable means of increasing output and profits, although it was recognized that it also increased the opportunities for fraud by employees.[31] It was deposed by witnesses to a legal dispute at Winlaton colliery in 1587 that double shifts had occasionally been worked at certain pits, but that labour shortage had curtailed the practice. In another lawsuit concerning a Staffordshire mine in 1603 it was claimed that the lessees had got 'coals in great abundance as well by night time as in the day time, and as well upon the Sabbath and Lord's day as upon working days'. At Harraton in the mid-seventeenth century there was twenty-hour working, 'from two of the clock in the morning until ten of the clock in the afternoon'. Even in collieries which were worked only during the day watermen were often called upon to work night shifts, for drainage was frequently a round-the-clock necessity, and we may assume that some maintenance work was, for convenience, carried out when production ceased for the day.[32] Similarly, in times of crisis, extraordinary efforts were required. In April and May 1663 at Handsworth the colliers 'night and day kept the work to strike the pit' without pay, because the 'neglect and fraud' of the banksman had endangered the enterprise.[33]

According to Nef, steady employment in coalmining was the great exception, and he believed it was improbable that between 1550 and

[29] NuRO Society of Antiquaries ZAN B/18/1/19.

[30] DUDP Church Commission, 244185; Smith 1957, 123.

[31] Sir John Clerk believed that night work should be avoided since it provided too much scope for chicanery (ScRO Clerk of Penicuik GD/18/995, 17).

[32] PRO E. 134 29 Elizabeth, Easter 4; Moller thesis 1933, 249–50.

[33] SCL Wentworth Woodhouse (Bright) BR P. 55/10.

1700 many miners could count on working at the pits more than half the days of the year.[34] Nef had little to base his beliefs upon, since he scarcely dipped into the accounts prepared by colliery managers and owners, and his views on this matter were also in conflict with his emphasis on the predominance of large-scale units of production. Certainly, as we have seen, there were pits whose working was almost entirely geared to the fuel requirements of their owners' households or industrial plants, and tiny enterprises which were worked on an occasional basis by men whose main source of subsistence lay elsewhere. There were also, of course, many grander collieries which had chequered fortunes, where working was frequently halted by geological problems, gas, or water, or where profitable working was undermined by competition or insufficient demand. In the early 1530s Durham priory worked one of its collieries solely for its own needs, and although it was kept open throughout the year it was usually worked for just one or two days in each week. Consequently the colliers who worked there gained only seventy to eighty days' employment in a year.[35] Restricted working was also the order at the Fife collieries of Tulliallan, Kincardine, and Torry where, as in so many Scottish collieries, production was geared intimately to immediate demand. At Tulliallan in the 1640s, during the blockade of Tyneside and Wearside, it was the arrival of ships from England which largely determined when coal was dug, and as a consequence the hewers found work at the coal-face for less than half the weeks of the year. While in the 1670s at Torry and Kincardine the fluctuating demands of the salt-pans was the major influence upon employment.[36]

Prevalent though the part-time and discontinuous working of collieries was, however, the evidence of colliery accounts suggests that it was not the norm. There can be no doubt that, other things being equal, the aim of most coal-owners was to achieve as continuous production as possible for the colliery and a six-day working week for each collier. As we have seen above, seasonal production patterns were normally muted if they existed at all, even in small collieries.[37] In the context of the times, when hire for most wage labourers was uncertain and discontinuous, colliers often enjoyed favourable opportunities for regular employment. How far they accepted all the work which they were offered is, however, quite another matter. A major part of our evidence of working practices comes from the order books and injunctions of employers, and

---

[34] Nef 1932, ii. 183.   [35] Raine (ed.), *Durham Household Book.*
[36] ScRO Register House RH9/1/31, 34, 35.   [37] See above, Ch. 10(v).

therefore reflects hopes rather than fulfilment. Indeed, as has been seen, the enactment of rules and orders was usually the direct product of the resistance of colliers, especially hewers, to the adoption of full and regular working. Unfortunately, although we have abundant information on the continuity of production in collieries, the prevalence of gang-working and the subcontracting of labour precludes us from gaining an equivalent overview of the working patterns of individual colliers. But for suggestive examples we can turn to a handful of collieries whose accounts record not only the names of the members of their workforces, but the number of days which each individual worked.

Gatherick colliery during the year 1683–4 was kept as fully operational as possible, and it shut down for only two weeks, although no coal was produced in a further eight-week period while a new shaft and headings were being opened up. Yet the five hewers who were retained throughout the year averaged only 3.6 days work a week while they were hewing, although the extra days they worked each week when they were transferred at lower wages to on-cost work, when the colliery ceased production, raised their annual average labours to just four days a week. In fact a day's hewing at Gatherick was determined not by time but by the production of fifteen bowls of coal, and for this the hewers received on average 13–14*d.* a day. The putters who received just 8*d.* a day worked on average 4.6 days a week, their ability to work, of course, being largely determined by the productivity of the hewers. But the lowest paid, the banksmen (winders and stackers) and watermen, who received only 6*d.* a day, worked an average of 5.5 days a week throughout the year. One among them, Oliver Blaires, worked no less than 307 days in the year, including no less than thirty-four seven-day weeks. In sharp contrast the hewers averaged only 200 days each during the year; no hewer worked a seven-day week, and between them they worked only twelve six-day weeks. None the less, despite the far greater leisure time enjoyed by the hewers, they still earned 40–50 per cent more on average than either the putters or the watermen and banksmen.[38]

Such earnings and work patterns are suggestive of a preference for leisure over work and additional income by the hewers. The probability that we are viewing an example of a supply curve for labour which sloped backwards once a target level of earnings was reached, is strengthened by other facets of the Gatherick hewers' behaviour. Most notable is their tendency to increase work intensity above the annual norm following periods of enforced idleness, and the working of more

[38] NuRO Society of Antiquaries ZAN B/18/1/19.

days each week when serving temporarily as shovelmen at 8 *d.* per day than when hewing at 13–14 *d.* per day. The working of short weeks is a phenomenon which, according to abundant qualitative evidence, was very widespread indeed among the best-paid colliers of seventeenth-century Britain, and it has been discussed elsewhere in this book. Nevertheless, a preference for leisure over work was only likely to be exercised when rates of pay were high; it was not in evidence among the poorly paid watermen and banksmen of Gatherick who worked long hours and many days.

Nor was it in evidence among the relatively poorly paid hewers of Beaudesert (Staffs.) in the later sixteenth century. Here the colliers did not appear to benefit from any special circumstances; on the contrary their wages were no higher than those of common labourers, and it was a time of sharply rising food prices. The colliery was worked virtually continuously from the later 1560s through to the mid-1580s, with around fifty weeks of production in most years for which there are records. There was a core of full-time permanent employees, which was supplemented as necessary by the hiring of occasional labourers as well as by craftsmen brought in to perform specialist tasks. Each year all members of the core labour force consistently worked more than 200 days, and some worked more than 250 days. Most notable of all was the career of Thomas Cooke, who worked as a collier at Beaudesert for at least the nineteen years between 1566 and 1585, eventually attaining the position of pit foreman. Surviving accounts reveal that Cooke worked between 251 and 262 days annually which, allowing for the two weeks when the colliery was shut down each year, meant an average of between 5 and 5.2 days weekly. Nor was such intensity restricted to production workers; in 1583–4 when the names of the timbermen are provided, we learn that Henry Hall and Edward Hinkley each worked a total of 265 days, and in the next account which covers only nine months of 1584–5 Hall is recorded as having worked 200.5 days and Hinkley 194.5 days.[39]

These were prodigious feats of labour, far above those conventionally postulated for sixteenth- and seventeenth-century hired labourers, yet the rewards at £5–6 a year may well have been insufficient to provide their families with a decent subsistence. The colliers and timbermen of Beaudesert, like the watermen and banksmen of Gatherick, could not afford the luxury of leisure.

[39] StRO Anglesey D(W) 1734.

iii. Methods of remuneration

Piece-rates in a variety of forms were prevalent in the coalmining industry. Payments by results were widely seen as both providing colliers with incentives to work hard and relieving owners and managers of much of the burden of close and constant supervision of their underground labour forces. J. C., an anonymous Wearside author, reported that it was usual in the opening years of the eighteenth century to strike a piece-rate agreement with hewers, 'by chance for ten pence or twelve pence for each score [of corves], according to the tenderness or hardness of the coal, or according to what the mine will afford, and not by the day, or shift work'. By contrast, if a flat rate were paid, which he records as commonly 12–14d. per shift, then output would usually amount to only thirteen or fourteen corves per shift.[40] Contracts usually contained provision for payments to vary with the quality of the coal which was produced, and they also often varied according to the difficulty or ease of the work, and the value of the output. Thus, at Gatherick in 1683–4, where hewers had a daily quota of fifteen bowls, they earned 1.6d. for each bowl of 'great coal' which they cut and 0.6d. for each bowl of less valuable 'small coal'. In 1707 a bowl of great coal earned a Gatherick hewer 1d. in June but 1.8d. in July and August, while the payment for a bowl of small coal fell from 0.8d. in June to 0.7d. in October.[41] Colliers, too, may well have found attractions in piece-rates, for they gave them much greater freedom to regulate their own working time, and to intersperse bouts of hard labour with periods of leisure. Piece-rates according to the yard of coal-face cut, rather than the volume of coal delivered, were, however, extremely rare, 'because by the yard they are apt to waste coals by burying them in hollows to spare labour of wheeling'.[42]

Sometimes, especially in Scotland and Lancashire, the rates negotiated with the hewers included the transporting of the coal from the coal-face to the eye of the shaft, or to the surface of drift mines. The hewer was therefore responsible for providing his own putters or bearers, and for remunerating them. This he often did from among members of his own family, including his wife and children. The pace at which the hewers cut coal determined the amount of work available for many other workers, most notably the putters, winders, and banksmen, as well as the output of the colliery. The incentive of piece-rates alone

[40] *Compleat Collier*, 35.
[41] NuRO Society of Antiquaries ZAN B/18/1/19; 650/16/11. [42] Langton 1979a, 70.

was often thought insufficient to provide the required inputs of labour. Given the proclivity of well-paid hewers for irregular working, it was common for production targets to be set, not only of the number of days to be worked but of the output of each of those days. In the north-east it was customary for the overman to get from each of the hewers an account of what quantity he would work daily, so that in turn the over-man would know how many men he would require to meet his production target. At Haigh the hewers, who were paid by the basket, were required to send up thirty baskets a day from Monday to Friday, 'two of which shall be lumps', and twenty baskets on Saturdays.[43]

For these reasons it was rare for hewers to be paid a flat daily wage, or 'day-tale' as it was often termed. Yet it was not unknown. In the Staffordshire colliery of Beaudesert in the late sixteenth century all production workers, timbermen, and sinkers were paid by the day. This may have been because the pits were small and located away from the influence of other collieries, close to the centre of a large estate, and that as a consequence methods of remuneration used on the estate were followed rather than normal coalmining practice. Such an explanation is more difficult to apply to the Whitehaven collieries of Sir John Lowther in the west Cumberland coalfield, where day-tale also prevailed into the eighteenth century, even at Howgill where output exceeded 50,000 tons a year.[44]

Putters and winders were also most often paid by the piece, but it was not as rare for them to be on day-tale as it was for hewers. Since the productivity of the hewers determined the amount of work available for the putters and winders, a daily wage was sometimes seen as a more satisfactory arrangement. Thus at Gatherick only the hewers were on piece-rates, and at Plas Teg (Flintshire), whereas the hewers were paid 13 d. 'the *toone*', putters were paid 5 d. a day and winders 6 d.[45] The setting of equitable piece-rates for putters and winders was not always a simple matter, for account had to be taken of the distance from the coal-face to the eye of the shaft, and from the eye to the surface. Moreover, rates needed frequent adjustment to changing working conditions, and required the constant and accurate measurement of the output of each worker. At the small colliery of Sheffield Park (Yorks.), when composite payments to the whole work-force were not in force we find a multiplicity of rates. In the early months of 1580 hewers ('pickmen') were paid 1 d. for each quarter they cut, the barrowmen 1 d. for every three

[43] *Compleat Collier*, 36; WiRO D/DZ A13/34, fo. 14ᵛ.
[44] Beckett 1981, 64.   [45] ClRO Glynde D/G/3311.

quarters they barrowed to the eye, and the banksman $\frac{1}{2}d$. for every quarter he wound up and stacked. By July 1580, when the length of the barrowman's haul was recognized as excessive, no new shaft having been sunk for more than a year, he was given a flat 6 d. a week in excess of his piece-rates. By October he was also allowed a helper, presumably a boy, who was paid a flat wage of 2 d. per day, and a month later the boy was incorporated into the piece-rate, which now allowed an additional 1 d. for every twenty quarters that were barrowed.[46]

When piece-rates were fixed while the length of journeys increased, as the coal-face retreated, the putters or barrowmen could find themselves working ever harder for the same or even less money. J.C. thought that this was the normal sequence of events in the north-east, 'so that the more and further a pit is wrought, you see the dearer she lies in the charge of the barrow-men, or putting, for they still keep up the first price of a day's work.' He did admit, however, that if a pit had a 'hitch or dipping of the thill or bottom of the way', which necessitated barrow-men pulling their full corves 'up such a sort of rise' then they might gain an increase in pay.[47] Winders too might seek to be compensated for the additional drudgery of winding the corves or baskets up deep shafts. On Tyneside in the early seventeenth century the wage rates of winders, or drawers as they were sometimes called, varied between 8 d. and 10 d. a day according to the depth of the pit.[48]

For obvious reasons piece-rates were often ill-suited to the work of watermen who operated the drainage machinery, and they were commonly paid by the day or the shift; banksmen too were normally paid by the day or the week. Sinking and maintenance work, frequently termed on-costwork or deadwork, however, often demanded flexible forms of remuneration. Sinkers could be either freelance or permanent full-time employees. If freelance they occasionally negotiated a fixed price for a contract. Fixed-price contracts were more common for the construction of soughs, where the length was predetermined, than for the sinking of shafts, where the amount of work depended upon the as yet unknown depth of the coal-seam and the nature of the strata through which the shaft had to be sunk. One unusual contract, between a gang of sinkers and Sir John Bridgeman, involved the advance payment of £400 for driving a sough of around 1,000 yards.[49] Much more commonly payments were agreed for progress by the yard, height, or fathom, and made when that distance had been achieved. Often sinkers

[46] Stone 1950–1, 100.
[47] *Compleat Collier*, 39–40.
[48] DN Syon PV 2(d.).
[49] BoRL Bradford ZBR/5/1/2.

would be paid according to the substances they encountered. Thus
when Beaudesert colliery was being reopened in 1600, William Wilkins's
gang of sinkers was paid 5 s. an ell for progress through earth and 8 s. an
ell through stone.[50] Alternatively, because of the unpredictability of the
speed of progress through stone, some contracts allowed for a flat daily
payment when it was encountered.

When the rate for the whole task was fixed in advance, it would
encompass estimates of the thickness of the various strata which the
gang was expected to encounter, and the differing rate of progress which
they would make through them. It was thus a highly speculative
business. At Bilborough (Notts.) the sinking gang, comprising a leader
and two fellows, was paid a fixed 8 s. 4 d. per height (c.6 feet), but their
progress was extremely variable. In the early stages from late May they
averaged two and a half heights weekly, but by August they were having
problems with firedamp and water, and progress was very slow. Coal
was struck by late October, by which time the gang had sunk twenty-
three and a half heights, at an average rate of just over a height a week.
Upon striking the coal they were given a bonus of half a height's pay.[51]
The custom of providing 'strike ale' when coal was struck was widely
observed.

Such prospective arrangements carried risks for both sides, and a
great deal of good faith and flexibility was required in order to make
them work smoothly. If the work became excessively arduous and
adequate recompense was not offered by the employer, the gang might
break their contract and walk off the job. This happened at Wollaton,
where an entry in the sinking book for 1573 records: 'Paid to William
Smalley and his fellows for sinking one height and a half at the water pit,
which Fallowes began to sink and gave it over for misliking the wages at
7 s. the height . . . 10 s. 6 d.'. Such occurrences were by no means rare. At
Gateshead in the 1540s after sinking twelve fathoms for 6 s. 8 d. per
fathom a gang led by Thomas Walker gave up, complaining that they
'did leave work because they were not able to perform their covenant by
that wage', and at Griff in 1604 Taylor and his partners were reported as
'refusing and giving up their bargain'.[52]

The production of coal and the construction and maintenance of
collieries were occupations which demanded flexible methods of
remuneration and the provision of incentives for the work-force, and we

---

[50] StRO Anglesey D(W) 1734/3/3/255.
[51] NoUL Middleton Mi. Ac. 2(205).
[52] Smith MS, 59; Nef 1932, i. 366 n; Grant 1979, 12.

have already touched upon some of the wide range of additional payments in money and kind which coal-owners were often prepared to
make in order to retain a contented and efficient work-force. Consequently, the basic piece-rates were often only a part, albeit the most
significant part, of the total consideration which colliers might receive.
There was a variety of compensatory payments relating to hard or
unpleasant working conditions, those paid for 'wet-work' being
especially widespread. In dealing with labour relations above, the binding fees or earnest money which colliers might be given upon commencing or continuing a contract of employment were touched upon.[53] In
many collieries evidence of regular bonuses, paid at quarterly, half-
yearly, or annual intervals is also found. At Haigh hewers received 4s. a
year, while at Tulliallan the half-yearly fees paid to hewers in July 1679
ranged from £4. 15s. to £6 (Scots), and the bearers received between
£1. 15s. and £4 (Scots).[54] At Handsworth in 1659 three colliers received
cash bonuses totalling 3s. each, two received 12s., and the barrowmen
shared 12s. between them. A further 15s. was disbursed in 'feasting
money' and ale.[55] Some of these bonuses were clearly related to performance, and there also is evidence of straightforward productivity
deals. At Torry in 1679–80 'drinkmoney' was given to the hewers to get
them to hurry, while at Coleorton in the 1570s, in addition to the set
payment of 1s. a rook to the charter gangs, an additional 2s. 8d. was paid
if the weekly output reached sixty rooks.[56] As has been noted above,
many payments and perquisites were directed towards ensuring that
colliers, especially the hewers, worked 'whole days and all the days', and
it was often specified that bonuses and free coal should be received only
by those whose attendance record and work had been satisfactory.

Free coal was an extremely widespread colliers' perquisite, although
it was not universal.[57] Often it seems the coal which miners were
allowed was produced by them in their own time, and was thus never
part of official production. Accordingly, free coal usually merited
mention in the records only when owners felt that the practice was
being abused by overmeasure or by the colliers reselling what was
intended for their own consumption. Sometimes the colliers were
granted a cash payment in lieu of free coal. At Haigh it was apparently

[53] See above, Ch. 9.
[54] WiRO D/DZ A. 13/34, fo. 5ʳ; ScRO Register House RH9/1/34.
[55] SCL Wentworth Woodhouse (Bright) BR P. 55/6.
[56] Griffin thesis 1969, 47.
[57] Michael Flinn estimated that the free coal allowances to colliers constituted 5.2% of production (Flinn 1984, 32–5).

common for the colliers to sell their free baskets to the auditors, who encouraged them to take baskets of excessive size. It was decreed in 1687 that colliers could take only baskets of due measure or 2 *d.* in money. At the town pits of Newcastle a different problem arose. Here the colliers took their free coal from the bankside, and they were accused of sorting out the best for themselves and leaving the bad, 'which is a great prejudice to the burgesses in their firing'. Within a few months a cash payment had been substituted for the concessionary coal.[58] In some collieries free coal was a concession of less than generous proportions. At Lowther's Whitehaven collieries, for example, free coal was only given at Christmas; at other times of the year it had to be purchased at market rates. At Wollaton in the sixteenth century free coal was dispensed only twice a year.[59]

Also widespread, but less troublesome to administer, was the provision of free ale. It was a practice which dated back at least to the 1380s.[60] Sometimes, as at Hooton, there was a regular and frequent provision of free ale, called in this instance 'Monday pots', perhaps in recognition of the purpose it served in enticing the men back to work on 'Saint Monday'.[61] There is also some evidence of gifts of tobacco.[62] It was rare for colliers to receive free subsistence from their employers, although Owen tells us that in Pembrokeshire it was customary to give a halfpennyworth of bread to each worker and fourpennyworth of drink between a dozen. In keeping with Scottish practice, oatmeal was sold to the work-force of Tulliallan, Torry, and Kincardine in the seventeenth century.[63]

Last, but by no means least, in the total package of remuneration and benefits which a collier might enjoy, came the provision of housing. Again the references to cottages being provided for colliers by the owners and lessees of collieries are legion, and can be found in all parts of Britain. It was a practice which dated back at least to the fifteenth century.[64] Where collieries were remote from centres of population or where their work-forces were composed of migrants, it might well have been essential to erect cottages, and the origins of the facility may well lie here. But in the course of time other considerations also undoubtedly

[58] WiRO D/DZ A. 13/34, fos. 14ʳ, 16ʳ; Nef 1932, ii. 188.
[59] Hainsworth (ed.), *Sir John Lowther*, 327–8, 332; Smith MS, 46.
[60] *VCH Warwickshire*, ii. 220.
[61] LCA Mexborough MX 295, 296.
[62] Bankes 1939, 43.
[63] Owen, *Pembrokeshire*, 91; ScRO Register House RH9/1/31, 34.
[64] *NCH* viii. 453–4.

played a major part in the extension and perpetuation of this perquisite, including of course the desire of producers in an age of expansion to attract and retain colliers. There are scarcely any references to the payment of rent for colliery housing, and it must be presumed that it was normally provided free. Some employers allowed widows to remain in residence after the deaths of their husbands.[65]

iv. Wage rates and earnings

The forms of remuneration prevalent in coalmining, and the wide range of incentives, bonuses, and perquisites which might be given, create formidable problems for the historian seeking to measure the earnings of colliers. The charter and overman system of subcontracting almost invariably presents an impenetrable barrier, for we have no means of identifying individuals within the gang, how much labour was performed by its members for the sums which they were paid, or how these sums were distributed. Moreover, even when individual colliers are identified and their daily or weekly wages recorded, it is essential that we are also able to discover the number of days which they worked. Yet the earnings and standards of living of the labouring and peasant classes in Britain before the eighteenth century are poorly documented and under-researched fields and, by the standards of the exiguous and partial information which is extant on the rewards of workers in most other sectors of the economy, coalmining records are relatively informative. Accordingly, we can be confident about pay differentials within coalmining, calculate the actual annual earnings of the individual members of the work-forces of a small sample of exceptionally well-documented collieries, and make some progress towards placing the pay of colliers in a broader context.

The data which are obtainable on wage relativities are both substantial and unequivocal. Table 11.1 contains a number of examples of the daily wage rates of various categories of colliery labour drawn from colliery accounts over a period of 250 years. These amply display the supremacy of the hewer, and confirm the status attributed to him in so many other records. Across the range of examples from Durham in the fifteenth century to Cumberland at the close of the seventeenth, hewers were consistently paid between 20 and 50 per cent more for a day's work than the next highest paid colliery workers. The exception, not revealed in this table, was the expert sinker, who was sometimes paid at

[65] This was the case at Bedworth (Moller thesis 1933, 257–8).

Table 11.1 *Daily wage rates of colliers*[a]

	Whickham, Tyneside 1460–1501	1600s	Three Quarter Band (Cumberland) 1675–6	Greenbank (Cumberland) 1675–6	Gatherick (Northumberland) 1683–4	Gatherick (Northumberland) 1694	Yorkshire West Riding 1674[c]	Yorkshire West Riding 1671[c]	Preston (Lancs) 1673[c]
Hewers	5–6	12	8½	8½	13–14[b]	12–14[b]	10	12	10
Putters and barrowmen	4	8	7½	7½	8	8	6	6	6
Banksmen	4	—	7	8	6	5–6	8	8	8
Winders and watermen	4	8–10	6	6½	6	5–6	—	—	—

Notes:

[a] Wage rates are given as pence per day without food or drink.

[b] Average daily earnings from piece rates.

[c] Assessments by justices of the peace.

Sources: DUDP Church Commission box 79; DN Syon PV, 2 (*d*); CuRO Lonsdale D/Lons/W, Colliery accounts; NuRO Society of Antiquaries ZAN B/18/1/19, 650/16/11; H. Heaton, 'The Assessment of Wages in the West Riding of Yorkshire in the Seventeenth and Eighteenth Centuries', *EJ* 24 (1914), 218–35; C. Hardwick, *History of the Borough of Preston and its Environs* (Preston 1854), 406.

comparable rates. Further confirmation of these relativities is provided by the assessments of maximum rates of permitted wages drawn up by justices of the peace in Yorkshire, Lancashire, and Derbyshire. In these coalfields where small to medium-sized collieries predominated, the justices set hewers' wages between 25 and 50 per cent above those of banksmen, and between 67 and 100 per cent above those of putters.

The justices assessed the wages of a broad selection of craftsmen and labourers nationwide, but perhaps in recognition of the prevalence of piece-rates in coalmining, or of the special conditions prevailing in its labour-market, even in noted coalmining areas they rarely set the rates for colliers. Our sample is therefore small. None the less we are able to make some comparison between the rates permitted inside and outside mining. The relationship between the assessments made by the justices under the authority of the Statute of Artificers and the wages which were actually paid by employers is, of course, a matter of some obscurity. Yet we may allow that the prescriptions had some internal consistency and that the relativities they established had some validity. If so, the lofty position occupied by the coal-hewer among the 'artificers, handicraftmen, husbandmen, labourers, servants, workmen, and apprentices of husbandry' whose wages the justices attempted to regulate is immediately apparent. The hewer is described as 'skilful in getting of coals', and his maximum permitted wage of 10d. per day was exceeded in the Pontefract assessments of 1647 only by the 12d. allowed to building foremen, 'that taketh charge of a man's building', and by the 12d. allowed to mowers, building foremen, and building craftsmen working long summer days in the Preston assessments of 1673. Mowers of corn, of course, benefited for a short period each year from the urgency created by the need to gather the harvest. In the Pontefract assessments the general run of building craftsmen were allowed only 8d. per day in winter and 9d. in summer and, in what was a notable textile region, the 'very skilful . . . weaver, fuller, clothworker, shearman or dyer' was allowed only 8d. daily. The colliery banksman, with his mix of supervisory, clerical, and manual duties, was therefore seen as being on a par with building and textile craftsmen; while 6d. per day for the putters and barrowmen working underground in the coal-mines was almost identical with the wages of agricultural labourers, who were allowed 5–6d. in winter and 6–8d. in summer.

The actual wages received by colliers depended, of course, upon local factors as well as upon influences pertaining to the industry as a whole. Evidence of wages paid on Tyneside in the early seventeenth century, for example, provides ample confirmation of the validity of the explanation offered by the Newcastle Hostmen to the City of London, that the steeply rising price of coal on Tyneside had been occasioned in large measure by substantial increases in the costs of working pits.[66] According to an informed source in 1608, under conditions when coal 'was never in greater earnest', hewers in 1608 were receiving 12 d. a day, and putters and banksmen/winders 8–10 d. What is more, wage rates continued to rise still higher. In 1617 Bird reported to the earl of Northumberland that hewers at Newburn colliery, who had formerly been paid 4 d. for every score of corves were now paid 5 d. and consequently earned around 18 d. a day, and that the wages of putters, called barrowers or trammers, had risen from 12 d. a day to 14 d., and those of the winders, called drawers, had risen from 8 d. to 9 d.[67] These were extraordinary rates of pay for the times. Donald Woodward's as yet unpublished researches have revealed that in Newcastle in the 1600s building craftsmen were receiving 10–12 d. per day, and common labourers 8 d., and that in the 1610s craftsmen's pay was in the 10–14 d. range and labourers 8–9 d. Thus it would appear that in the acute labour shortage experienced by coal-owners during this period of extraordinary boom, the rate of pay for hewers rose appreciably higher than that of urban craftsmen, and that the pay of putters rose to match that of urban craftsmen. Doubtless the labour-market subsequently settled down somewhat, and evidence from the last quarter of the century demonstrates the sensitivity of north-eastern colliers' pay to market conditions. The coal trade at this time was slack, prices were sagging, and there was considerable pressure on producers to reduce costs. J.C., for example, put hewers on Wearside in the opening years of the eighteenth century on 12–14 d. per shift when paid a flat wage, a level of remuneration broadly confirmed by detailed evidence from Gatherick colliery in north Northumberland in the 1680s and 1690s. Such rates compare very favourably with the 8 d. a day which was the going rate for rural labourers outside the industry, but they were no longer ahead of those paid to urban craftsmen.[68]

Both the relative scarcity of hard data on earnings in coalmining, and the dearth from outside the industry, make precise comparisons difficult, but we may be confident that, almost without exception, the

[66] Dendy (ed.), *Hostmen*, 5–6.   [67] DN Syon PV 2(d.), QVI 80.

[68] *Compleat Collier*, 36. I am grateful to Dr Keith Wrightson for the prevailing rural labourer's wage on Tyneside. J.C. also tells us that putters were paid 20–22 d. a day for each tram and that there were 2 or 3 persons to each tram (36, 39).

pay of hewers stood substantially above that of common labourers. In the bishop of Durham's mines in the later fifteenth century they received 5 d. or even 6 d. a day, compared with the 4 d. per day received by his labourers in the city of Durham;[69] at Kilmersdon (Som.) in 1700 they received 1 s. to 1 s. 6 d. a turn; at Griff (War.) at the same time, where they took home at least 5 s. 3 d. to 6 s. weekly, exclusive of bonuses or payments in kind; and at Winstanley (Lancs.) they may have received 6 s. 8 d. in cash weekly.[70] We may feel for the collier who retired after forty years labouring in the pits, and found himself carding wool for 2 d. a day. On 14 August 1673 he announced, 'Nothing is got with this working. I'll into the coalpit again tomorrow, and I'll never come up again.' He duly went to Mr Rooks's colliery at Rhodes Hall, close to Halifax, and while being let down into the pit in a basket was struck by a piece of wood and killed.[71]

If the hewers seem almost invariably to have received wages which placed them among the aristocracy of British rural labour, there were many other members of colliery work-forces who received substantially less exalted remuneration. In contrast to the lofty status accorded to the hewer, the putter, 'filler or drawer of coals', was seen by the justices of the peace as comparable to a common agricultural labourer, and the banksman as approximating to the status of rural craftsmen and journeymen, and this is broadly confirmed by the evidence available in colliery accounts. Moreover, those whose job it was simply to wind up coal or water on a windlass, without having to keep an account of the production or sale of coal, were often paid less than a common labourer. Evidence for their rate of hire is abundant, for they were commonly paid by the day. Water-drawers, when employed at Beaudesert got only 4 d. for a night's toil, while at Gatherick a century later they received 5–6 d. compared with the putters' 8 d. and the shovelmen's 6–8 d. Even when wages were soaring on Tyneside in 1617 there were some who worked for exiguous pay; the 'keeper of the [coal] heap' at Newburn earned 3 d. per day, and the 'overman of the tree', whose duty it was to see that the corves were correctly filled, just 2 d. Winders and watermen may frequently have been boys, or men past their working prime. At Griff in 1701 boys were paid 3–6 d. a day depending upon age, and the women who worked on the surface earned a flat 4 d. daily, except on the rare occasions when they worked at traditionally male tasks and were

[69] DUDP Church Commission 190048–9. I am grateful to Dr Richard Britnell for these references. [70] Bulley 1953, 38; White thesis 1969, 126; Langton 1979a, 70. [71] Trigg 1930, 124.

paid more.[72] The laws of supply and demand operated in coalmining as they did elsewhere. When a task demanded exceptional stamina, strength, or skill, those who performed it were apt to be well rewarded. But those colliery tasks, however toilsome, which could be performed by most men, even the elderly, or by boys and women, such as riddling or slate-picking, were apt to be ill-rewarded. And the families of better-paid colliers often provided an ample pool of such cheap labour. Lowther's managers became obsessed in the mid-1690s with the costs of draining their collieries and, after a number of trials, the finger of suspicion pointed towards the negligence of the tubmen who drove the horses which wound up tubs of water from the pits. But John Gale hesitated to dismiss them, because they had experience 'and their wages [were] so small none will covet their employment at 6d. a day'.[73]

The daily wage was only a part of the incomes of colliers, and it is essential to take account of the value of the various cash bonuses and payments in kind which most received in the course of the year. Cheap or free housing and abundant quantities of free coal were substantial perquisites enjoyed by many colliers, and they were of a greater value than those commonly accorded to urban workers. On the other hand, account must also be taken of expenses incurred in their employment and of the deductions which were sometimes made from their wages. Hewers had occasionally to provide their own candles and, more commonly, their own tools, and we have also seen that many colliery managers sought to impose fines for poor workmanship or other misdemeanours, though there is little to suggest that they were systematically levied. There can, however, be no doubt that the balance of such receipts and expenditures lay firmly with the colliers.

But this is not all. We need to take into account all sources of family income. In addition to any wages earned by wives and children, the family budget also often benefited from the cultivation of the small plots of land which were so often attached to colliers' cottages, and from any animals which they might have kept on their own plots, pastures which they leased, or neighbouring common land, including a cow or two to provide milk and cheese.[74] While part-time colliers and genuine collier-cottagers like the free miners of Kingswood Chase and the Forest of Dean might possess small farms, even specialist colliers in advanced

---

[72] DN Syon QVI 80; White thesis 1969, 167.
[73] Hainsworth (ed.), *Sir John Lowther*, 353.
[74] According to the Hostmen, colliers on Tyneside commonly kept a cow and rented the pastures upon which it was kept (BL Harleian 6850(39)).

mining regions were rarely without at least a garden plot. In Shropshire
in 1605 a mine-owner took care to allow, when he constructed cottages
for his workmen, 'certain small plots of grounds to make gardens for
their better relief and comfort'.[75] With this amenity colliers could enjoy
some of the benefits enjoyed by agricultural labourers and many rural
artisans, and doubtless hewers spent some of their ample leisure time
tending their smallholdings as well as sitting in the alehouse. Hewers
thus often enjoyed all the perquisites of living in the countryside,
together with wages that matched or approached those received by
urban craftsmen.

But incomes, of course, were also dependent upon the number of
days that were worked in the year, and from our knowledge of working
habits in the industry it would be most unwise to assume that the
majority of hewers voluntarily worked all the full weeks throughout the
year that were open to them. The intriguing evidence from the sole
seventeenth-century colliery for which it is possible to measure the
intensity of work of each collier, suggests that in appropriate circumstances there was a strong inverse relationship between the scale of pay
and the numbers of days worked. At Gatherick in 1683–4 although the
hewers' daily earnings were 75 per cent higher than those of the putters,
and 133 per cent higher than those of the watermen and banksmen, by
working fewer days than the putters and substantially fewer than the
watermen and banksmen, the annual earnings of hewers from the
colliery averaged just 49 and 52 per cent higher respectively. These are
fertile fields for further research, but in the present state of knowledge
of the earnings of the labouring classes of Britain before the eighteenth
century it would be unwise to proceed beyond the broad statements
that colliers in general enjoyed considerable continuity of employment,
and that hewers were among the very best-rewarded labourers in the
land.

Counterbalancing the financial rewards were, of course, the dangers
and rigours of mining. There are strong indications in a range of records
that colliers may have experienced a lower life expectancy than most
other labourers. Added to the heavy incidence of accidents causing
injury and death, there is the likelihood that poor ventilation in many
early mines must have commonly led to respiratory problems. While
high concentrations of 'blackdamp' or 'stythe' would extinguish candles
and cause suffocation, in lower concentrations there would be sufficient
carbon dioxide to increase the breathing rate of underground workers,

---

[75] Moller thesis 1933, 257.

and this in the longer term would lead to bronchitis, known as 'miner's asthma'.[76]

It is not the intention here to investigate how colliers disposed of their incomes, for such matters lie outside the main preoccupations of this present work and warrant their own detailed study. Only a few random remarks can be offered in the place of firm conclusions. In later times colliers were renowned for their conspicuous consumption, but in medieval and early modern times, apart from the habitual complaints that they drank too much, there are few other direct indications in the sources that have been consulted of their consumption patterns. It can be assumed, however, that much of their incomes went on food. Miners would have required a high intake of calories, perhaps of the order of 3,500 a day or even more, in order to work efficiently, and hewers in particular may well have used their relatively large disposable incomes to consume handsome quantities of meat and dairy produce. But it may well also have been the case that even well-paid hewers purchased few durable products. The huge peasant and labouring masses are scarcely represented among those that made wills, and very few colliers amassed sufficient goods in their lives to leave estates worthy of the taking of probate inventories on their deaths. A search has revealed very few inventories of the estates of genuine labouring colliers, as opposed to overmen, viewers, staithmen, coal-dealers, and proprietors, in any part of the country. In the diocese of Durham, for example, a sample of more than 1,000 inventories produced just a single collier.[77] Moreover, those few colliers' inventories that were made in the north Shropshire and Bristol coalfields contain no indication that colliers were acquiring a wider or more expensive range of household possessions than the common run of labourers and poor husbandmen, although they do confirm that colliers often kept a few farm animals.[78] This lack of material possessions is wholly consonant with an emphasis on immediate consumption and also with a preference for leisure rather than the maximization of earnings among the best paid. From Scotland, north-

[76] Wrightson and Levine 1989; *HRCM* 278.

[77] Information kindly supplied by Dr Lorna Weatherall. Care must be taken to exclude the often sizeable estates of overmen, staithmen, and viewers.

[78] e.g. the scattering of colliers' inventories in Telford (B. Trinder and J. Cox (eds), *Yeomen and Colliers in Telford: Probate Inventories for Dawley, Lilleshall, Wellington and Wrockwardine, 1660-1750* (1980), 173, 174, 179, 180, 355, 430, 431) and Frampton Cotterell (J. S. Moore (ed.), *The Goods and Chattels of our Forefathers: Frampton Cotterell and District Probate Inventories, 1539-1804* (1976)). Sizeable numbers of colliers' inventories from the parishes of Bitton, Newland, and Ruardean survive in the Gloucestershire County Record Office, and a few in the Lancashire Record Office. Cattle are well represented in the inventories from Lancashire, Gloucestershire, and Telford.

east England, and Lancashire, there is also evidence which suggests low levels of literacy among coalworkers.[79]

It may thus be imagined that a seventeenth-century coal-owner would have fully concurred with the views expressed by Mrs Elizabeth Montagu in 1766, on the first visit to her collieries at Denton on Tyneside: 'Our pitmen are literally as black as coal, they earn much more than labourers . . . but they are so barbarous they know no use of money but to buy much meat and liquor with it. They eat as well as the substantial tradesmen in great towns.'[80]

[79] None of the colliers covenanting with Sir Roger Bradshaigh could sign his name (WiRO D/DZ A13/34, fo. 9). See also Houston thesis 1981, 227.

[80] J. V. Beckett, 'Elizabeth Montagu: Bluestocking turned Landlady', *Huntington Library Quarterly* (1986), 157.

PART IV

THE CONSUMPTION OF COAL

CHAPTER 12

The Consumption of Coal

Coal is not used only in common fires, but in most mechanic pro-
fessions (except iron-work) that require the greatest expense of
fuel.

(John Houghton, *A Collection of Letters for the Improvement of
Husbandry and Trade* (1682)

i. Domestic heating and cooking

It is probable that more than half of all the coal which was produced in
Britain before 1700 was burnt in the home, to warm the inhabitants and
to cook their meals. Yet the adoption of coal for domestic heating in
place of wood, turf, or any other combustible vegetation, was not
simply a matter of price or even of preference, it was a matter also of the
design and technology of grates, hearths, flues, and chimneys, and the
ventilation of rooms and houses. Fireplaces designed for the burning of
wood were rarely well suited to the burning of coal. The adaptation of
hearths and chimneys for coal, and the provision of adequate ventilation
for coal-burning houses, posed formidable problems for the builders,
architects, and inventors of the sixteenth and seventeenth centuries, and
was of considerable moment in determining the efficiency with which
the fuel was consumed and the salubrity of the rooms in which it was
burnt. The rate of growth in the consumption of coal for domestic
heating and cooking was linked to far-reaching developments in
domestic architecture.

The typical medieval cottage consisted of a single room, with a
central hearth. There was no chimney; the room lay open to the rafters
and the smoke escaped as best it could through a hole in the roof. Even
in the castles, manor houses, and abbeys of the rich the hearth arrangements were for long essentially similar, though naturally on a far
grander scale.[1] Documentary and archaeological evidence shows the

---

[1] For the history of domestic architecture see in particular: M. Wood, *The English Medieval
House* (1981 edn.); M. W. Barley, *The English Farmhouse and Cottage* (1961); *AHEW* iv, chs. 10, 11;
ibid., vii, ch. 20, 21. For the fireplace and chimney see in particular: Bernan 1845; Shuffrey 1912;
Wright 1964.

prevalence of these primitive arrangements before the fifteenth century, with the central hearth confined by a stone or tile surround, or raised upon stone slabs or quarried tiles, and the smoke allowed simply to drift upwards in search of an opening or louvre in the roof or the unglazed panels of high windows. Such a location for the fire was the safest for timber buildings, and it had the important additional advantage of allowing members of the household to gather all around it. The lack of facilities for the smoke was to some extent compensated by the great height of the rooms. Even peasant houses frequently had tall roofs, being constructed from the 'crucks' of trees, though the atmosphere in their cramped interiors could prove objectionably smoggy to discriminating eyes and noses. In the cottage of Chaucer's poor widow, 'Fful sooty was hir bour and eke hir halle.'[2]

As the architecture and domestic arrangements of the homes and living quarters of the upper strata of society evolved, a shift in the location of the fire was encouraged. Greater emphasis came to be placed on comfort and privacy, numbers of rooms proliferated, additional storeys were constructed, and central hearths became both inconvenient and dangerous. Locating fires against or recessed into walls enabled them to be hooded, which often effected a notable improvement in the discharge of smoke. Hoods constructed of brick and stone soon became items of display and adornment and, of course, encouraged the development of the chimney proper. In the great buildings of the later Middle Ages there were many permanent fireplaces in addition to those in the hall and kitchen, and portable iron braziers were also used to heat rooms without fireplaces. Such developments, on a necessarily more modest scale, were followed in the homes of gentry, yeomen, and merchants. As early as 1469, a Romford man wrote to a friend asking him to find a Dutch or Flemish mason who could build him a chimney with a brick mantle.[3]

Changes in the homes of the vast mass of the population came later and were less pervasive. Yet by the second half of the sixteenth century there is clear evidence that standards of domestic comfort and heating were improving in many modest homes, and though it is doubtful that the poorest sections of society shared fully in them, the cumulative effect of such improvements could be dramatic. The seventy years from the accession of Elizabeth to the outbreak of the Civil War have long been

[2] 'Nun's Priest's Tale', 12.
[3] M. McIntosh, *Autonomy and Community: The Royal Manor of Havering, 1200-1500* (Cambridge, 1986), 229-30.

recognized as marking 'the rebuilding of rural England', when a revolution occurred in the housing of a considerable portion of the population. It is now appreciated that the 'Great Rebuilding' spanned a much longer period, running through to the early eighteenth century, and it thus ran parallel to the massive increase in domestic coal consumption. It is not coincidental that this rebuilding incorporated fundamental changes in the numbers, location, and design of fires and chimneys.[4]

John Aubrey (b. 1626) reminisced how 'Anciently, before the Reformation, ordinary men's houses, as copyholders and the like, had no chimneys but flues like louver holes; some of them were in being when I was a boy'.[5] For William Harrison, writing in 1576-7, the 'multitude of chimneys lately erected' was one of 'three things to be marvellously altered in England' within the 'sound remembrance [of] old men yet dwelling in the village where I remain' (Radwinter in north-west Essex).

In their young days there were not above two or three [chimneys], if so many, in most uplandish towns of the realm (the religious houses and manor places of their lords always excepted, and peradventure some great parsonages), but each one made his fire against a reredos in the hall, where he dined and dressed his meat.[6]

In Cheshire also, David King, writing during the Commonwealth, describes how farmers until the early seventeenth century 'had their fire in the midst of the house, against a hob of clay'.[7] The re-siting of the fire, with its attendant chimney-stack was a crucial element in the new developments in domestic architecture which affected buildings in all strata of society. In the homes of yeomen and husbandmen a brick-built chimney-stack was often sited in the centre of the building on the axis, allowing back-to-back fireplaces in the two main downstairs rooms, the parlour and the hall, and perhaps also in the two upstairs rooms. The dwellings of cottagers and labourers could often be improved by building an external free-standing chimney-stack, commonly of wattle and daub on a timber frame, against a side or gable-end wall. Sometimes the primacy of keeping warm led to the hearth becoming a room within a room, the 'down-hearth' of southern England and the 'ingle-nook' of Scotland. In towns the proliferation of chimneys proceeded if anything

---

[4] W. G. Hoskins, 'The Rebuilding of Rural England, 1570-1640', *P. & P.* 4 (1953), 44-59; M. W. Barley, *The House and Home* (1963), 31-47; R. Machin, 'The Great Rebuilding: A Reassessment', *P. & P.* 77 (1977), 33-56.   [5] Quoted in Wright 1964, 36.

[6] Harrison, *Description of England*, 200-1.   [7] *AHEW* iv. 752.

at a faster pace. Doubtless London was ahead of the fashion, but even so the 200 chimney-sweeps who presented a petition to the Lord Mayor and Aldermen in 1618 form a truly prodigious number.[8]

Such improvements enhanced domestic comfort, and in many instances they may have helped to make it possible to burn coal, but huge fireplaces and flues which had been constructed for burning wood were quite unsuited for coal, and so too was the hearth equipment which furnished them. Even in humble cottages wood fires and cooking hearths might be many feet in width, in some cases a whole gable-end might be devoted to the fireplace. Flues also were commensurately large, often a yard or more in span. The fireplace would be furnished with a pair of iron fire-dogs or andirons to support logs and stop them from rolling off the hearth, to carry spits and hooks for hanging pots and meat, and to control the width of the fire. But coal would scarcely burn at all in such a place. Coal needs to be contained in a compact mass for sufficient heat to be generated for its combustion, and provided with a powerful draught to keep it burning brightly. Moreover, while wood smoke has a tendency to drift upwards even with a modest draw on the chimney, coal smoke being denser and heavier will hang unless drawn upwards by an efficient flue. Thus the purveyors of the household of Henry Percy, fifth earl of Northumberland, were charged to purchase twenty quarters of charcoal for use during the earl's stay at Wressell Castle (Yorks.) over Christmas 1512, 'which is because the smoke of the seacoals would hurt mine Arras when it is hung', and sixty-four loads of 'Great Wood', 'which is because coals will not burn without wood'.[9]

Although there were barriers to the efficient and wholesome burning of coal in the household which were to resist the ingenuity of inventors and architects for centuries, the fact that coal was being burnt by an expanding number of households before the reign of Elizabeth encouraged some significant advances in technology at an early date. The monks of Jarrow in 1310 possessed two iron chimneys or grates, designed for burning coal in their hall, and there is a record of the sale of a similar device in Wakefield (Yorks.) to the chaplain of Batley for 10d. in 1317.[10] Perhaps these were adaptations of braziers, which had long been in use for charcoal fires. Early fire-grates for coal-burning also evolved by attaching rectangular baskets fashioned from wrought iron bars to fire-dogs, or even by the addition of a series of horizontal bars to them. In this way coal could be both suspended and heaped, and the

---

[8] Nef 1932, i. 199.   [9] Percy (ed.), *Household of Henry Algernon Percy*, 21.
[10] Raine (ed.), *Jarrow and Monk-Wearmouth*, 3; Cox thesis 1960, 26.

spaces between the bars permitted a through draught to assist combustion and allowed ashes to fall thereby preventing the fire from choking. Yet wrought iron was expensive, and we know that the poor were notable consumers of coal. They must have constructed makeshift grates from piles of stones or bricks, or anything else that came to hand. Even as late as the seventeenth century a treatise was published which contained instructions on how to build a grate from loose bricks by laying them two high an inch apart edgewise on the hearth, with a row of iron shot on top.[11]

Such arrangements might ensure that a coal fire was able to be kept alight, but they did not make it burn 'sweetly'. When coal was burnt in makeshift or ill-designed grates set in vast hearths with prodigious flues it is small wonder that 'stinking and smoky' fumes polluted the halls, parlours, and closets of those who were unfortunate enough to have to use it, filling their eyes and noses with a 'virulent or arsenical vapour', and making their clothes and furnishings reek of 'stinking seacoal smell'.[12] Nor is it surprising that the President of the Council of the Marches should plead with Queen Elizabeth for permission to cut wood in the royal Forest of Deerfold so that he would no longer be 'compelled to burn that noxious mineral pit-coal'.[13] Some varieties of coal, of course, burned more sweetly than others, even in ill-suited locations. George Owen enthused about Pembrokeshire anthracite, which he termed 'stone coal', and claimed that it was 'void of smoke where ill chimneys are' and that it was 'not so noisome for the smoke, nor nothing so loathsome for the smell as "ring" coal is, whose smoke annoyeth all things near it as fire-linen and men's hands that warm themselves by it'. But anthracite was not available to the majority of customers, and Owen chose to ignore the difficulties of keeping it alight even in the 'chimneys and grates of iron' which were used to burn it in Pembrokeshire.[14]

The major technical problems which had to be surmounted before coal could become a wholesome domestic fuel included efficient combustion as well as a means of ensuring that the smoke was conveyed up the flue, and the solution involved the design of suitable grates and a range of equipment for their use, changes in the construction of

[11] H. D. Roberts, *Downhearth to Bar Grate* (Marlborough, 1981), 9–10; Eveleigh 1983, 3–4; Wright 1964, 65–6.
[12] The phrases are contemporary, and taken from Nourse, *Campania Foelix*, 363; Evelyn, *Fumifugium*, 13; *Artificiall Fire, or Coale for Rich and Poore* (1644).
[13] Rees 1968, i. 67.
[14] Owen, *Pembrokeshire*, 87–8.

fireplaces, flues, and chimneys, and the provision of fuel of an acceptable quality. Contemporaries often believed that their coal burnt badly because it was of inferior quality, and it was widely held that 'good and sweet coals, which burn well without ill savour' might be obtainable if only Newcastle coal-owners could be prevented from mixing the product of their collieries with dust and rubbish.[15] It was also recognized, however, that even good coal could have 'noisomeness and unsavoury quality', and much creative energy was devoted to attempting to render it more agreeable by purging it of noxious substances. A licence was sought from Elizabeth I for a method 'to purify pit coal and free it from its offensive smell', and another was received in 1590 by John Thornburgh, Dean of York, to refine coal in order 'to correct the sulphurous nature' by piling it in pyramids and charring it like charcoal, by which process it would be 'cowkefied'.[16] Sir Hugh Platt, the son of a wealthy brewer, was the author of a treatise on the art of preserving the beauty of women, and a serious student of scientific farming and the power of steam; he also wrote a treatise entitled *A New Cheape and Delicate Fire of Cole Balles*, which was published in 1603. In it he describes how to crush coal, mix it with loam pap, and form it into balls, which he promised would make a 'sweet and pleasing fire'. Among the projects and inventions which followed was the patent granted in 1627 to Sir John Hackett and Octavius de Strada for rendering sea coal and pit coal as useful as charcoal for burning in houses without offence from the smell of smoke, and in 1656 Sir John Winter was engaged upon a very similar project, without much impressing John Evelyn with his chances of success.[17] In 1644 a recipe based upon the experiments of an engineer called Richard Gesling was published. It encouraged the 'richer sort' to pound their coal and mix it with red mortar, sawdust, and chopped straw, and then, with the addition of water and coal-dust, cast it into briquettes. When thoroughly dry the briquettes should be burnt with a little Scotch coal or wood. For the 'poorer sort' Gesling claimed that 'cow-dung mingled with saw-dust and small coal, made up into balls, or in a square like a tile . . . [made] a very good fuel, but something noisome'. Some householders, we are told, 'made an oven out of "kennell durt", with a hole at the top for the heat and smoke to ascend up the chimney', and a coal fire kept kindled within. In default of coal

---

[15] For a collection of documents concerning disputes over the quality of coal sent from Tyneside to London see BoL Rawlinson C. 784.

[16] Moller thesis 1933, 7; Wright 1964, 72–3.

[17] Bernan 1845, i. 171; Moller thesis 1933, 8; Wright 1964, 73.

the poor were advised that 'that which comes out of the paunches of beasts killed, it being dried is excellent fire'.[18]

These were desperate remedies, but it was also appreciated that a large part of the problem lay in the hearth, the flue, and the chimney, and in the ventilation of rooms. In facilities built for wood, not only was too little of the coal smoke and too much of the warm air drawn upwards, a coal fire would frequently draw its air supply down the chimney bringing smoke back along with it. Ideally, to produce an efficient and clean coal fire, the size of the hearth would have to be reduced, along with the height of the opening above it, and the flue would also have to be tapered. Not only did these necessary improvements take some time to be recognized and disseminated, in practice they often constituted only a first step towards a solution. For each chimney appeared to have a character of its own, and one which frequently seems to have been exceedingly difficult to reform.

The humble smoky domestic coal fire attracted the enthusiastic attentions of some of the leading inventors and scientists of the day, as well as that of working architects and builders, and a horde of 'smoke doctors' and assorted quacks. It may be noted from contemporary illustrations that bricks were often used in existing over-sized fireplaces to create a hearth within the hearth, while those newly built, or rebuilt, with coal in mind became progressively smaller, even in the finest rooms of the greatest houses.[19] In the dwellings of the less affluent, the fire area could be restricted by the use of cheeks, which were made of iron in regions like the Severn valley where iron was relatively cheap.[20] Fire baskets gradually evolved into well-designed permanent features, when they could be afforded, and were backed by iron fire-backs which served both to protect the chimney and reflect heat into the room. Fire-backs and cheeks were among the very few serious uses of cast iron before the eighteenth century.[21]

Probate inventories throw some light on the dissemination of specialist coal-hearths and their equipment. In Nottinghamshire in the sixteenth century grates were not much in evidence, despite the frequency with which coal was noted in the home, but in the coalmining regions of Gloucester during the seventeenth century they were quite

[18] *Artificiall Fire or Coale for Rich and Poore* (1644).
[19] Cf. for example illustrations given in Shuffrey 1912 of the new hearths designed for coal with those of the hearths which preceded them.
[20] Trinder and Cox (eds.) *Telford*, 103–4.
[21] Information supplied by Professor J. R. Harris.

common. In the Telford region of Shropshire in the later seventeenth century the abundance of local ironworking, as well as good supplies of coal, meant that wrought iron grates were to be found in almost every household, while in those of the richer members of the community there might be a number of grates specifically designed for the burning of coal. So too in Staffordshire, where in 1673 the house of Zachary Kyrke, gentleman of Lichfield, had a little grate in the Great Chamber, an iron grate with 'creepers' in the hall, and another grate in the kitchen. The appraisers noted 'some few coals' in Kyrke's yard.[22] Away from the coalfields and navigable rivers coal-grates were not surprisingly much rarer. In rural mid-Essex, for example, the first 'grate for seacole' is mentioned in an inventory as late as 1672, in the house of a yeoman of Writtle, and the next mention is not until 1725.[23]

At times the presence of grates in inventories as well as in surviving buildings makes it possible to see how widespread the penetration of coal was in social as well as geographical terms. For example, the surviving grates for coal fires in the State Bedroom, Long Gallery, and dining-room at Haddon Hall (Derby.) were installed at a very early date.[24] At Hengrave Hall, close by Bury St Edmunds, the home of Sir Thomas Kytson in 1603, there was 'one cradle of iron for the chimney to burn sea coal with' in the Great Hall. Sir Thomas bought his coal at King's Lynn, and had it shipped down the Ouse almost to his door.[25] In the hall of the Old Charterhouse, London, there is a particularly splendid example of an early iron fire-grate designed to burn coal. It is surrounded by a monumental chimney-piece and overmantel on which are the arms of Sir Thomas Sutton, and has carved cannon and gunpowder kegs to commemorate his appointment as a master-general of the Ordinance. Sutton bought the Tudor hall in 1610, and founded the hospital there. It is fitting that the first holder of the Grand Lease should have so celebrated the use of coal.[26]

Coal fires required special hearth equipment in addition to new-fashioned grates and chimneys. In the Great Hall at Hengrave Sir Thomas Kytson had a pair of tongs and two fire shovels, one of which was 'made like a grate to sift the seacoal with'. From the mid-sixteenth

[22] Kennedy (ed.), *Household Inventories*; Moore (ed.), *Probate Inventories*; Vaisey (ed.), *Inventories of Lichfield*; Trinder and Cox (eds.), *Telford*.

[23] Eveleigh 1983, 3; Steer (ed.), *Farm and Cottage Inventories*, 24.

[24] Shuffrey 1912, 153.

[25] Bernan 1845, i. 158–9.

[26] See Plate 3(c); for Sutton and the Grand Lease, see below, Ch. 15(i).

century in inventories of households in the north-east, there are mentions of pokers and sometimes of little rakes, in addition to tongs and shovels. Almost every house in the Telford region, from 1660 to 1750, possessed a fire shovel or 'slice', and a pair of tongs for stoking the fire, though pokers were less common. The danger of falling cinders also encouraged the emergence and adoption of the fender.[27]

Attempts to invent a more efficient fireplace proceeded in parallel with efforts to produce smokeless coal, fire-grates, and appropriate tools. Sir Hugh Platt's treatise on 'Cole Balles' devoted considerable attention to the fireplace as well as to the fuel to be burnt in it. Platt was among the first to appreciate the advantages of reducing the size of the fireplace, which he did by building a false back and sides; these he extended up into the 'throat', in the hope that this would result in more of the smoke and less of the air from the room being sucked up the chimney. We hear of Captain Thorneff Frank's 'Patent Furnace', which commanded the favour of the king, Louis Savot's convection fire of 1624, and of the busy Sir John Winter's 'fire cage'. One of the most distinguished 'smoke doctors' was Prince Rupert, nephew of Charles I, count palatine of the Rhine and duke of Bavaria, brilliant cavalry commander and admiral, famed mezzotinter, innovator in the fields of guns, gunpowder, and shot, and notable metallurgist. His solution was novel, and it is to be supposed that it constituted a significant improvement on existing practice. In 'Prince Rupert's Fireplace' the flue was small and low, sited just above the fire. Behind the opening an iron baffle-plate was located which forced the smoke down before allowing it to rise up the flue. The baffle was hinged to allow it to be opened fully when the fire was first lit. The fireplace was advertised and offered to the public by a Mr Bingham, bricklayer. That it was not wholly successful in keeping smoke out of rooms, is suggested by Prince Rupert's cautious advice to stoke it sparingly and use charcoal or 'charked coal' whenever possible. The profusion of 'improved' fireplaces which flowed through the succeeding century attests the intractability of this humble but vital matter.[28]

Even well-designed fireplaces required efficient chimneys to provide smoke-free interiors. The cavernous chimneys constructed for wood had to be drastically reduced in width; in later centuries those designed specifically for coal were often no more than a brick and a half ($13\frac{1}{2}$ in.) or even a brick (9 in.) wide. But chimneys were unlikely to prove

---

[27] Wright 1964, 60, 69; Trinder and Cox (eds.), *Telford*, 103–4.
[28] Bernan 1845, i. 150 ff., 171 ff.; Wright 1964, 72–3, 83–5.

satisfactory for coal simply because they were narrow. They had to be built high enough, and very few were. If a chimney is too close to the roof, or to adjoining buildings, winds from certain directions may be drawn down it with disastrous consequences. The misfortunes of the Revd James Woodforde of Weston Longville, Norfolk, who dwelt at length in his diary on the tribulations caused by his chimneys, are instructive as to the intractability of rogue chimneys. Woodforde relied upon coal for his heating, which he obtained via Yarmouth. In 1781 the 'Chimney Place' in his study was altered for the fourth time, but after six further vexatious years, the chimneys for the parlour and study fires were pulled down and rebuilt with narrower dimensions. There was little improvement, and in 1794 both were rebuilt yet again. Still the problem was not solved, and Woodforde was driven from room to room by the smoke, and forced to engage in desperate experiments in ventilation by leaving various combinations of doors open or closed. In 1801 he wrote mournfully that his study chimney still 'smoaked amazingly'.[29]

Woodforde's frustrating and expensive quest for clean air in his home was not, of course, typical of the experience of his social peers. By the eighteenth century considerable expertise had been acquired in the provision of efficient coal fires for domestic heating and cooking. Ample incentive to invent, to build, and rebuild was supplied by the steeply rising cost of wood and charcoal, and each advance broadened the market as coal was transformed into an acceptable fuel for the middling and upper classes. Joievin de Rochford on a visit to London felt confident enough to conclude that 'no fuel is less offensive in a chimney than coal'.[30] If the homes of the poorer classes continued to be smoky and smutty far beyond the endurance of the sensitive eyes, noses, throats, lungs, and complexions of the present day, for those of modest means who were fortunate to have access to supplies of inexpensive coal, warmth was always to be preferred above pure but cold air.

ii. Fuel for industry

Britain before the eighteenth century is commonly categorized as a pre-industrial economy, but this should not lead us to underestimate the importance and scale of the industry, manufacturing, and processing, that she possessed. Agriculture was by far the dominant sector of the

[29] Shuffrey 1912, 176; Wright 1964, 100–5; J. Beresford (ed.), *The Diary of a Country Parson, 1758-81* (Oxford, 1924); *CSPD 1663-4*, 126.
[30] Bernan 1845, i. 207.

economy, and the bulk of the population lived in villages and hamlets rather than towns, but industry was crucial to the well-being of the population. As far back as records can take us, a small range of manufactured, processed, or fashioned articles had always been essential to the running of the farms and households of even the poorest of peasants. At the same time, the gross inequalities of income which characterized these eras, and which exacerbated the poverty and restricted the purchasing power of the many, by the same token furnished the few with large disposable incomes of which no small part was spent on manufactures. Moreover, the long-term trend before the industrial revolution was for the industrial sector to grow, in both absolute and relative terms. Although only rarely dependent upon large-scale investment in fixed capital or elaborate productivity-raising machinery, there can be no doubt that a very substantial increase in both the scale and the diversity of manufacturing and industrial production took place in the course of the sixteenth and seventeenth centuries, and little doubt that by 1700 industrial output accounted for a greater proportion of the national product than ever before. A recent estimate, made with plausibility rather than certainty, would have the industrial and commercial sectors of the English economy at the dawn of the eighteenth century contributing together as much as one-third of the total national product, compared with 40 per cent from agriculture.[31]

Notwithstanding that fuel in these centuries was burnt to provide heat alone, rather than both heat and power as later, manufacturing and processing were very substantial consumers of fuel indeed. In the food and drink trades, for example, high temperatures were required in the brewing of ale and beer, the boiling of salt, the refining of sugar, and in distilling and baking. The production of bricks, tiles, and glass for the building industry depended upon kilns and furnaces, as did the firing of pottery and the burning of lime for use in both building and husbandry. The smelting and working of metals was, of course, very expensive of fuel, as were the elaborate procedures used in the making of basic 'chemicals' such as alum, copperas, saltpetre, and starch. And while fuel was not a major constituent in the costs of manufacturing textiles, dyeing, calendering, and bleaching in the later stages of production were fuel-intensive processes, and the sheer scale of the cloth industry made it a leading consumer.

By the close of the seventeenth century industry and manufacturing

[31] R. Floud and D. N. McCloskey, *The Economic History of Britain since 1700* (2 vols., Cambridge, 1981), 64.

may well have devoured more than a third of all the fuel burnt in Britain. But the energy consumption of industry should be assessed in local as well as national terms, for industry was not uniformly distributed throughout the realm, and its needs could greatly exacerbate, or even cause, severe local or regional scarcity. When conducted on a household basis or geared to serving strictly local needs, brewing, baking, smithing, potting, lime-burning, and suchlike could often survive on whatever fuel was to hand, without placing undue strain on the resources of the neighbourhood. After all, wood, given time, replaces itself. Yet there was a pronounced tendency for many fuel-consuming industries to grow in scale and to become ever more centralized and urbanized as the sixteenth and seventeenth centuries ran their course. Moreover, the appetites of some industries were voracious. Even when located in the heart of extensive woodlands the levels of consumption of iron forges, glasshouses, and lime-kilns could lead to shortages. In 1255 it was reported with alarm that just two of the king's lime-kilns in Wellington Forest had devoured no less than 500 oaks between them.[32]

There are innumerable illustrations of just how finely balanced the fuel needs of communities and the supplies yielded by their hinterlands could be, and how that balance could be disturbed by industrial demands. At Cranbrook, on the edge of the Weald, it was said in 1634 that the Crown commissioner had burnt so much wood in the making of brass, iron ordnance, and shot that prices had been forced so high that it had become cheaper to dye cloth with Newcastle coal brought overland from Maidstone or Newenden.[33] As early as the 1540s the appetite of the furnaces of the Droitwich salt industry had forced the salters to repair far afield for their wood, and had led to shortages in Worcester. The city authorities attempted to alleviate this scarcity in 1548 by forbidding its bakers, brewers, and tile-makers to buy up wood by the boatload, and eleven years later a statute was passed which prohibited the felling of timber for iron-smelting within fourteen miles of the Severn.[34] Towns, consisting as they did of concentrations of consumers, had an inherent tendency to outrun the capacity of their hinterlands to supply fuel, and many were faced at an early date with extended lines of supply and commensurately inflated transport costs. Town authorities were well aware that urban and rural industries could be a major element in the creation of these shortages.

Confronted by the growing scarcity and high price of wood, manufacturers in fuel-intensive industries seeking to restrain their costs and

[32] Salzman 1913, 90.   [33] Nef 1932, i. 214.   [34] Dyer 1973, 53-4.

enhance their profits usually needed little prompting to switch to coal whenever possible. For many the choice of fuel had long since been a simple matter of price and convenience, and in a wide range of industrial processes no substantial technical barriers to coal existed. The boiling of liquids, for example, could be readily accomplished using many types of fuel, and although coal smoke might sometimes pose a threat of con-tamination, this was often easily overcome. Coal, if it was the cheapest and most economical fuel available, had been used whenever possible for centuries. Thus in the fourteenth century in north-east England and in the Firth of Forth it heated the great pans in which sea water was boiled to produce salt, while in London premature fuel shortages at the turn of the thirteenth and fourteenth centuries placed the capital's lime-burners, brewers, and dyers as well as its smiths, among the early regular users of coal.

Away from the immediate environs of coalfields, however, coal was rarely the cheapest fuel in the Middle Ages. Consequently, although, somewhat surprisingly, the monks of Westwood priory can be found using both coal and wood in their Droitwich salt works in the later fourteenth century, for the coal had to be carted overland from Pensnett (Staffs.) more than twenty miles distant, turves were used for heating Lincolnshire salt-pans and those in Cheshire were fired with wood.[35] Yet in these early centuries coal had another role to play, and far from the pits it was preferred by smiths and lime-burners, despite its high cost. It was with pardonable exaggeration that William Gray, writing in 1649, claimed that contrary to the practice of his own day 'coal in former times was used only by smiths and for burning of lime'.[36] The explana-tion is that coal was the best source of heat for the fashioning of iron and the burning of lime.

Thus from the early fourteenth century onwards coal can be proved to have been either readily usable by, or the preferred fuel of, most of the leading fuel-consuming industries, and it was these traditional industries which were to dominate non-domestic coal consumption up to the eighteenth century. In later Tudor and Stuart times salt-boiling, ironworking, and lime-burning boomed, and ever greater proportions of the burgeoning throngs of brewers, dyers, and bakers adopted coal as their customary fuel as wood became ever more scarce and expensive.

[35] Birmingham Reference Library MS. 473426; Hereford and Worcester County Record Office BA 3835/10/10; A. R. Bridbury, *England and the Salt Trade in the Later Middle Ages* (Oxford, 1955), 17–18.

[36] Gray, *Chorographia*, 90.

The establishment of new industries dependent upon mineral fuel, such as soap- and sugar-boiling, and the production of alum, copperas, saltpetre, and paper, further swelled the demand for coal, as did the progressive conquering of technical obstacles to the burning of coal in processes which had hitherto been reserved solely or mainly for wood or charcoal, such as the making of glass, bricks, tiles, and pottery, and the smelting of lead, tin, and copper. But whereas the adoption of cheap coal was of immense importance for new industries and for those older industries which were able to convert to coal, their combined impact on coalmining remained secondary to that exerted by the traditional industrial users.

The traditional coal-consuming industries

Smithing and ironworking   The smith working at his forge keeps a fire going continuously, but intermittently uses bellows to make it burn more fiercely in order to heat the iron which he places in it. Since the iron is repeatedly heated and reheated between beatings, the fire is subjected to constant blowing. A charcoal fire is not satisfactory since the bellows tend to blow it away, making it uneconomical as well as impractical. Coal of the right quality gives out a steadier heat and stands up well to perpetual blowing. It can also be watered to make it cake and bind and thus become even more durable. When Leland visited Carmarthenshire in 1536–9 he remarked, 'there be ii manner of coals. Ring coals for the smiths be blowed and watered. Stone coals be sometime watered but never blown, for blowing extinguisheth them'. George Owen, writing of Pembrokeshire coal some seventy years later, noted that 'stone coal serveth also for smiths to work though not so well as the other kind of coal called the running coal, for that when it first kindleth it melteth and runneth as wax and groweth into one clod'.[37]

Smiths' coal was frequently recognized as a distinct variety. In Scotland it was known as 'smiddy coal', in Wales as ring coal or running coal. It was smaller than good household coal, and frequently more bituminous, and thus smellier and smokier. It was also cheaper. Although 'Great Scots Coal' sold well to most artisans of the Low Countries, the smiths would not buy it, while the coal of Pitfirrane colliery was described as 'only fit for the smith's forge'.[38] The quality of the coal used in the forge was often a crucial element in determining the

[37] *Itinerary in Wales*, 60; Owen, *Pembrokeshire*, 87. See Pl. 3(*b*).
[38] ScRO Mar and Kellie GD 124/17/522; Whatley 1987, 32.

quality of the finished product. As Ambrose Crowley pointed out to the Admiralty in 1703, 'when anchors are not well shutt or wrought sound, it is too oft occasioned by the foulness of coals'.[39]

It was for these reasons that coal was eagerly sought by the smiths of Roman Britain and why, when price was secondary to good workmanship, we encounter in the Middle Ages instances of coal being used by smiths and ironworkers on a regular basis well away from the coalfields or normal coal-trading routes, despite its prodigious cost. For example, it was purchased for use in the lord's smithies on the manors of Clare (Suffolk), Boxley (Kent), and Weston (Herts.). At Weston coal was used for the repair of seigneurial ploughs in the 1290s although it cost from 11d. to 1s. 4d. per quarter, while the cost of charcoal made from the lord's own woodlands cost a mere 1½d. per quarter.[40] Archaeological evidence can provide a welcome supplement to documentary, and inland rural sites often reveal the use of coal in association with ironworking and smithing fifty miles or more away from possible sources.[41] Moreover, its high cost was little deterrent to ironworkers employed by the Crown to fabricate military equipment and ordnance, such as siege-engines, springalds, lances, and anchors, and by the close of the thirteenth century it had become their customary fuel. Other metalworkers also appreciated that coal could sometimes serve a useful purposes in processes such as the founding of guns and bells. Peat, charcoal, and two chaldrons of coal were burnt in the casting of a bell for York Minster in 1371.[42]

Smiths and ironworkers had for centuries been ubiquitous in Britain. Each village had its blacksmith to fabricate and repair the extensive range of ironware crucial to the economic and social life of the community, ranging from horseshoes through agricultural equipment to cooking and heating utensils. It was rare for a village not to possess a smith, and each town had its cluster of ironworkers, producing their wares for distribution to consumers within the walls and in the surrounding countryside. While there is no indication that the use of coal was widespread among these medieval rural smiths, in various parts of Britain, favourably located for both iron and coal, there developed flourishing centres of manufacture, hammering out cutlery, scythes, ploughshares, shovels, axes, spurs, harnesses, horseshoes, locks, bolts,

[39] M. W. Flinn, *Men of Iron: The Crowleys in the Early Iron Industry* (Edinburgh, 1962), 189.

[40] PRO SC6 873/15, 17, 19, 20; 886/2, 8, 11, 22; 992/8, 11, 16, 17, 19, 20, 21, 22, 25. I am grateful to Professor D. Farmer for these references.

[41] *AHEW* ii. 921.   [42] Blake 1967, 4–5.

hinges, andirons, trivets, chains, buckles, and many other wares. But above all they made nails. In a society where the main material for housing, ships, carts, machinery, and tools was wood, vast quantities of nails of all types were consumed. Before the close of the thirteenth century the West Midlands was already displaying specialization in the metallurgical industries. The excellent court rolls of Halesowen manor, near Birmingham, for instance, reveal the presence of smiths in numbers far in excess of the needs of the local community, making them by far the largest occupational group after agriculturalists. Moreover, the abbot of Halesowen actively encouraged smiths to settle on his manor, with grants of land. No doubt part of the attraction of Halesowen for smiths lay in its coal reserves as well as its proximity to iron.[43]

Despite the rising cost of charcoal, the price of wrought iron inflated more gently than prices in general in the sixteenth and seventeenth centuries as ironworkers benefited from a flow of cheap imports from Sweden and a succession of major technological and structural advances in all stages of native iron manufacture. The latter ranged from fuel-saving and economies of scale in the production of pig iron, through the use of water power to forge pig into bars, to the dissemination of rolling and slitting mills to cut the bars into thin rods for fashioning into nails and other small wares.[44] Stimulated further by rising population, the consumption of iron leapt, and with it the consumption of smiths' coal. Moreover, it was not just that the numbers of smiths and ironworkers multiplied, it was that as lines of communication improved and the relative price of coal fell, it became ever more likely to be their sole fuel. William Harrison, writing in the later sixteenth century, marvelled not a little that the smiths of Sussex and Southamptonshire continued to work their iron with charcoal, and believed that 'far carriage' for coal was not a satisfactory excuse.[45] Within the next century, as probate inventories reveal, smiths using charcoal became ever rarer, even in regions where coal was still a scarce commodity.[46] Where coal was

---

[43] Calculations by Dr E. Miller from men with craft surnames appearing in the Halesowen court rolls, 1270–1307 (J. Amphlett and S. G. Hamilton (eds.), *Court Rolls of the Manor of Hales, 1270-1307*, Worcestershire Historical Society (2 vols., 1910–12)).

[44] Rogers 1866–1902, v. 501–4. The price of lath nails, for example, scarcely moved between 1582 and 1702 (ibid. 484). For the technology of the iron industry see Schubert 1957.

[45] Harrison, *Description of England*, 364.

[46] e.g. coal is scarcely in evidence in Banbury inventories, 1621–50, but is recorded in the premises of 2 of the 3 smiths (Brinkworth and Gibson (eds.), *Banbury Wills and Inventories*), and whereas in mid-Essex coal is found in only 5 inventories between 1635 and 1700, 2, possibly 3, of these were of blacksmiths' premises.

generally available metalworkers proliferated. An examination of the occupational structures of early modern towns, for example, reveals a strong positive correlation between coal supplies and the proportions of metalworkers. The anonymous author of a broadside against the tax of 5s. per chaldron on coals (c.1696) maintained that the smiths of London and the east coast towns 'are a numerous, laborious and ingenious people, and use great store of sea coals'. In London, a vast manufacturing city, metalworkers comprised around 10 per cent of the commercial and industrial population throughout the later sixteenth and seventeenth centuries, while York and Norwich also had above average concentrations.[47] But perhaps most significant of all were the developments taking place on the coalfields, where long-standing concentrations of metalworkers and traditional specialization in the production of ironwares were transformed into full-blooded industrialization. Most notable of all were the south Staffordshire coalfield, around Walsall, Birmingham, Wolverhampton, and Dudley, and the south Yorkshire coalfield in Hallamshire around and to the south of Sheffield. But production on a lesser scale also flourished in many more places where coal was cheap—in Nottingham and north Derbyshire, south-west Lancashire, the Forest of Dean, South Wales, and Tyneside—and the pace quickened appreciably towards the close of the seventeenth century.[48]

Lime-burning Lime-burning, like ironworking, could be accomplished with a wide range of fuels, but ideally required a slow and durable fire. Oak brushwood had long been the customary firing for lime-kilns, but a strong preference for coal began to make itself evident in the second half of the thirteenth century. Thus we find that whereas kilns for royal building operations at Westminster were fuelled by oak in 1253, by 1264 oak had been supplanted by coal.[49] Despite its great cost coal soon became the preferred fuel for the production of the best lime. Poor quality coal, including dust, served the kilns well. Oak too was an expensive wood, and the problems many large towns had from the later thirteenth century to secure adequate supplies of wood at reasonable prices further encouraged the adoption of coal.

Lime (calcium oxide) is produced by burning limestone (calcium carbonate), and it was utilized for two distinct purposes: in building,

---

[47] A. L. Beier and R. Finlay (eds.), *The Making of the Metropolis: London 1500-1700* (1986), 148; L. Clarkson, *The Pre-Industrial Economy in England* (1971), 88–9.

[48] These developments are surveyed in the relevant sections of Ch. 5.

[49] Brimblecombe 1987, 7; Salzman 1913, 90–1.

where it was used for mortar and the colouring of walls, and in husbandry where it was used for spreading on acidic soils. Although there is some evidence of the liming of soils before the sixteenth century the practice was not widespread, and large-scale building works provide the most spectacular examples of medieval coal consumption.[50] At times the demand generated by building works for lime was capable of exerting a dominant influence over a local coalfield. The vast quantities of mortar and plaster used in the building of Beaumaris, Conway, and Caernarvon castles in the 1290s sent the production of the small Flintshire collieries soaring to heights which may well not have been surpassed until the later sixteenth century.[51] It was usual to build lime-kilns on the sites of large building operations, and sometimes lime-burning was subcontracted to specialists. At Rochester Castle in 1367–9 John Walsh was paid £15. 9s. 8d. for producing just under 3,000 quarters of mortar.[52] Little is known about the production of plaster, which was made by burning gypsum or inferior deposits of alabaster, but it is probable that this too was often produced on-site using coal. The scale and frequency of coal purchases at a massive structure like the Tower of London or Windsor Castle could give the clerks of works there the appearance of leading coal-dealers, since they had to purchase large consignments in the north-east and arrange their own transport.

The construction of smaller buildings, or minor repairs to edifices, did not justify the erection of on-site lime-kilns. Instead lime would be purchased from specialist lime-burners. Many of these doubtless fired their kilns with local wood but some, especially in large towns, used coal. We know that London lime-burners had become dependent on coal by the close of the thirteenth century, for they were then viewed as the major source of air pollution, and were the objects of the earliest attempts to ban the use of coal on environmental grounds.[53] In 1288 a series of complaints began to be made by the inhabitants of Southwark against the pollution caused by lime-burners who, it was alleged, had formerly burnt their lime by logs but now used sea coal 'so the air is infected and corrupted'. The use of coal was subsequently banned, but apparently to little effect for complaints followed by bans continued to recur. 'Sacoles Lane', in the vicinity of Ludgate Circus, is first mentioned

---

[50] Lime was possibly used in husbandry in late medieval Pembrokeshire, and there is a certain reference to the application of lime to the soil at Doddington (Salop) in 1342 (*AHEW* ii. 440–1).

[51] Gruffyd thesis 1981, 24; H. M. Colvin (ed.), *History of the King's Works: The Middle Ages* (2 vols., 1963), i. 349, 399.

[52] Blake 1967, 3.

[53] For a recent survey see Brimblecombe 1987, 5–21; see also above Ch. 2.

in 1228, and its later designation as Limeburners' Lane gives a strong
intimation of how it acquired its name. In 1253 houses in 'Secole Lane'
are said to have been formerly the property of William de Plessetis, who
may well have come from Plessy, the location of a particularly productive coal-seam on the River Blyth in Northumberland.[54] An even
closer association is suggested by the case of Hugh de Hecham, a
Newcastle burgess, who was prominent among the London lime-
burners. In 1329 Hecham was accused before the Lord Mayor of band-
ing the lime-burners together in order to force up prices, and causing
them to swear not to sell lime at less than $1\frac{1}{2}d$. or $2d$. per sack. The extent
of the extortion, it was claimed, was evidenced by the fact that coal was
then selling at only $16d$. per quarter, whereas in previous years, when it
had cost as much as $40d$. per quarter, lime had sold for only $1d$. per sack.
This Hugh de Hecham may well have been the same Hugh de Hecham
who had leased a colliery at Elswick, just west of Newcastle, prior to
1330.[55] If he was then we have a truly remarkable example of vertical
integration from the early fourteenth century: mine-owner, coal-merchant, and industrial consumer.

The rise in population during the sixteenth and seventeenth centuries
provided a direct and powerful stimulus to the building industry. In
addition, a greater emphasis upon comfort and privacy led to the
rebuilding of a very substantial proportion of the existing housing stock,
from the relatively humble cottages of peasant farmers to the 'prodigy
houses' of the aristocracy. All of which combined to raise massively the
consumption of lime. Moreover, a major additional use for lime
emerged in the sixteenth century, as its application to acidic soils, with
the intention of raising their productivity, became ever more widespread. It was calculated in the 1930s that more than one-third of the
land of Britain was then lime deficient, and we may assume that the proportion was even higher in the sixteenth and seventeenth centuries. The
full extent of liming is only just being appreciated by historians. Scarcely
in evidence before 1500, in the course of the sixteenth century liming
rapidly became widely adopted, and by the mid-seventeenth century it
had become a highly valued and almost universal means of improving
fertility in Britain. Where soil is naturally acidic the growth of plants is
inhibited. Lime helps to neutralize the acidity, and thereby to increase
yields directly; it also enables manure to work more efficiently. As early
as 1523 Fitzherbert referred to the beneficial use of burnt lime by
farmers in his *Boke of Surveying and Improvements*, and he claimed that

[54] Galloway 1898, i. 29–30;   [55] Riley 1868, 174; Galloway 1898, i. 39.

'in many countries [counties] where plenty of limestone is the husbands do burn the limestone with wood and seacoal and make lime thereof; and do set it upon their lands as they do their dung and do spread it in like manner, the which they call much better than dung for lime is hot of itself'.[56] The incentive to lime land increased along with the inexorable climb of the grain market, and the facility to do so was enhanced by the ever greater availability of cheap coal. In consequence, according to Dr Kerridge, 'after 1560, and still more after 1590, liming . . . grew so greatly in extent, frequency and volume, that it became effectually revolutionary'.[57]

By 1652 Walter Blith could put lime first among the substances used to improve fertility, and claim:

it is of excellent use, yea, so great that whole countries, and many counties, that were naturally as barren as any in this nation . . . doth and hath brought their land into such a posture, for bearing all sorts of corn, that upon land not worth above one or two shillings an acre, they will raise (well husbanded with lime) as good wheat, barley and white and grey peas as England yields.[58]

Blith was far from alone in ascribing truly wonderful properties to lime. Gabriel Plattes (1634) was of the opinion that the discoverer of the process 'did a more charitable deed in publishing thereof than if he had built all the capital hospitals in England', while Tristram Risdon (1630) proclaimed that it produced in his native Devon 'a plentiful increase of all sorts of grain where formerly such never grew in any living man's memory'.[59]

With the key requirements for liming comprising an acidic soil and the availability of limestone and cheap fuel, there was at first a pronounced tendency for the practice to be commoner in the north, west, and east, especially where pastures and rough grazing were undergoing conversion to arable. It had a long history in Glamorgan, although in Upper Gwent it was maintained in 1616 that 'the husbandry of liming the ground for corn was first practised within the memory of the fathers or grandfathers of men yet living', and John Norden in 1607 drew attention to the frequency of liming in Shropshire, Denbighshire, Flintshire, and, now lately, in some parts of Sussex. But with the publicity

---

[56] Quoted in Havinden 1974, 112. Havinden makes a strong case for the importance of liming.

[57] E. Kerridge, *The Agricultural Revolution* (1967), 248.

[58] *AHEW* iv. 133–4; J. Thirsk and J. P. Cooper, *Seventeenth-Century Economic Documents* (Oxford, 1972), 112, 127.

[59] G. Plattes, *Practical Husbandry Improved* (1634); T. Risdon, *The Chorographical Description of Devon* (1630).

given by many experts in husbandry it is not surprising that the numbers of farmers who limed multiplied in Northumberland, the Lake District, Lancashire, Cheshire, the Border counties, the south-west peninsula, and much of Wales. By the close of the seventeenth century liming was far more widespread even than this. In a recently published series of studies of agricultural practices in England and Wales after 1640 references to liming abound throughout the east and north-west Midlands, Wharfedale, and east and north Yorkshire, Herefordshire and Gloucestershire, the Derbyshire peaks, and the sterile Surrey lower greensand.[60]

The rate of application should vary according to the pH level of the soil, and current practice would suggest from half a ton per acre for light slightly acid soils up to four and a half tons per acre for extremely acid heavy soils. Evidence of contemporary practice in the seventeenth century suggests that these rates were often exceeded, sometimes by a large margin.[61] Clearly the burning of lime for husbandry consumed very substantial quantities of fuel indeed. With the purchasing farmer confident that he would soon recoup his outlay by enhanced yields, lime was transported over considerable distances when necessary: down the Severn from Ironbridge Gorge as far as Worcester, and from Wales by water and cart to the Lancashire plain.[62] In areas with both limestone and cheap coal kilns abounded: in the 'fringing lowlands of Wales', we are told that nearly every farmer had a limestone quarry and a kiln, while we learn that in the High Peak there were fourteen lime-kilns at work adjacent to quarries at Dove Holes in 1650, and ten more at Broadwell town end close by.[63]

Of course, lime was burnt with whatever combustible material was cheaply at hand. In Surrey in the early seventeenth century, for example, heath was used to fire the kilns.[64] Overall, however, coal was far and away the most important fuel. Every town had a kiln or two to supply its builders, and kilns often proliferated on coasts, estuaries, and river banks, where coal was easy to ship in and lime easy to ship out. In south Devon, which received its coal from the mines of South Wales, the

---

[60] Havinden 1974, 104, 112–13; Swain 1986, 165; Hopkinson 1976, 10; Gruffyd thesis 1981, 65, 96; *AHEW* iv. 117, 118; *AHEW* v(i). 23, 65, 82, 126, 137, 175, 185, 300.

[61] e.g. we learn of applications of 200 bushels per acre in Pembrokeshire (*AHEW* v(i). 395); 40 horse-loads per acre in Wharfedale (Thirsk and Cooper, *Economic Documents*, 151); and about 60 loads elsewhere (Kerridge, *Agricultural Revolution*, 248).

[62] Wanklyn 1982, 4; *AHEW* v(i). 65.

[63] *AHEW* iv. 117; *Ibid.*, v(i). 137.

[64] Ibid. 300.

plotting of early lime-kiln sites reveals a pronounced grouping close to navigable water.[65] The inexhaustible demands of burgeoning south London in the seventeenth century were supplied in large part by clusterings of great kilns around Gravesend and Northfleet on the Thames estuary, some of which cost in excess of £400 to construct. Other notable centres of lime production were on Tyneside, Forthside, and Severnside.[66]

Salt production   The British climate dictated that salt could be produced from sea water only by prolonged boiling, a process which was very expensive of fuel. It was only in the most favoured locations and in good summers that the sun could offer much assistance. Although in the Middle Ages and later salt production was very widespread around the coasts of Britain, significant commercial production was restricted to those places with special advantages in the supply of cheap fuel, suitable salt water, and access to markets; a warm climate was an added bonus. In the mid-fourteenth century England was a major producer and net exporter of salt, with sizeable plants on the east coast in Lincolnshire and Norfolk, and the south coast in Kent, Sussex, and Hampshire. The brine springs of Worcestershire and Cheshire also provided a focus for the industry in the west.[67] Production in Lincolnshire, which had risen to pre-eminence, was fuelled by turf, and its slow burning qualities must have contributed to good quality, large-grained salt. The agitation produced by faster boiling on wood or coal fires resulted in smaller grains but a coarser salt. The Northumberland and Durham coast, from at least the thirteenth century, also had salt-pans, and they were almost certainly fired by local coal.[68] The Scottish industry was at least as ancient. There were salt-pans in the Forth basin in the twelfth century, where they burned wood and caused local shortages. In the thirteenth century the scale of the Forthside industry warranted a Master of the Royal Saltworks, and from the locations of the pans we can be certain that they had been converted to coal.[69]

In the later Middle Ages England's export trade was lost and she became a major importer, as good quality cheap salt from the Bay of Bourgneuf flooded the markets of north-western Europe. For as long as salters on the Atlantic coasts of France and Spain prospered, home

[65] Havinden 1974, 106.   [66] Clay 1984, ii. 64.

[67] A. R. Bridbury, *England and the Salt Trade in the Later Middle Ages* (Oxford, 1955).

[68] Galloway 1898, ii. 64–5.

[69] J. M. Gilbert, *Hunting and Hunting Reserves in Medieval Scotland* (Edinburgh, 1979), 236; Lythe and Butt 1975, 41.

production was confined primarily to serving local needs from small plants. The next major turning-point occurred in the later sixteenth century, and was precipitated by the sharply increasing cost of imports and disruption in their flows, arising from currency debasements and political disorders in France. The response of British producers was so speedy and powerful that it was as if they were waiting for just such a stimulant. Output surged so massively that it must have rivalled the rate of growth of coal itself, and within a short space of time a series of major technical innovations had been adopted. In the scramble to fill the gap left by falling imports so many attempts were made to set up sea-water salt production units around the coasts that this soon led to saturation, and inevitably many ventures failed. Location was paramount, for an assured supply of cheap fuel was more crucial than ever to successful production, while salt, being low in value relative to its bulk, was, like coal, expensive to transport. Waterside locations, for the supply of sea water and ease of shipping, with collieries close by, were most favour-able. Tyneside, Wearside, and Forthside were ideal, and the bulk of the expansion came to be centred there. Lincolnshire, however, sank into decline, squeezed by the growing scarcity of turves and the competition of cheap salt from further up the coast.[70]

The auspicious prospects for British salt producers inevitably attracted a string of patentees, speculators, and would-be monopolists.[71] But much genuine investment was also undertaken, albeit often on an over-optimistic scale. On Wearside salt entrepreneurs gave an early boost to coalmining. Under the auspices of the Wilkes patent of 1586, which bestowed the sole right to make and sell white salt in King's Lynn, Boston, and Hull for the needs of these ports and 'counties there-unto adjacent', Robert Bowes, a member of an old Durham landed family, and John Smith, a King's Lynn merchant, backed by the earl of Huntingdon, constructed a large saltworks at Sunderland and opened a colliery close by at Offerton. The amounts they had to spend were very substantial indeed including, it was claimed, £2,000 on a watergate (sough) and on keels to carry the coals to the pans. The rent of £800 which the pans and pits commanded is a further indication of the scale of the venture as well as the depredations of the patentees.[72] On the

---

[70] *AHEW* iv. 185.

[71] For the early years of the revitalized English salt industry see E. Hughes, 'The English Monopoly of Salt in the years 1563–71', *EHR* 40 (1925); id., *Studies in Administration and Finance 1558-1825* (Manchester, 1934), 31–66; Gough 1969, 197–204; Lipson 1956, ii. 365–6.

[72] Galloway 1878, ii. 103–4; Nef 1932, i. 175–6.

Northumberland coast saltworks were set up at Seaton Delaval, Hartley, Bebside, and Cowpen. Sir Robert Delaval, seduced by the prospect of an outlet for his Hartley colliery unhampered by the Hostmen, built a saltworks. In addition to a high initial capital outlay, he complained that he had to pay a heavy rent to the patentees as well as spend £400 on repairs to the pans. The saltworks and associated coalpits at Bebside and Cowpen were of somewhat greater antiquity. There were two salt-pans and two pits there when a lease was granted to Thomas Bates by the Crown in 1555. Expansion ensued and it soon became Crown policy to subdivide the rights, allotting two salt-pans and a pit to each lessee. In 1595 Sir Robert Delaval's cousin Peter went into partnership with Ambrose Dudley of Newcastle to lease all the pits and pans for £22. 13s. 8d. and two years later he was joined by his brothers, Ralph and Clement. In 1602 Peter retired and received £330 for his share of the lease from Sir Robert, who in turn was followed by the ill-fated band of entrepreneurial investors from London, Sussex, and the Midlands led by Huntingdon Beaumont.[73]

None of these coastal ventures seems to have enjoyed enduring success, hampered as they were by the payment of onerous royalties to patentees and locations which were inconvenient for shipping. It was Tyneside that soon became the leading sea-water salt production area. Fortunately, we have many indications of its scale and, more importantly, of the quantities of coal which it must have burnt. Since relatively little salt was consumed locally, the average annual shipments of around 6,000 tons in the 1650s, 9,000 tons in the 1670s, and 12,000 tons between 1685 and 1703, may well provide sound guidance to total production levels.[74] Sadly, there are no customs accounts which antedate the Civil War, but there are estimates of the numbers of pans and of their output capacities and fuel consumption. In the late sixteenth century, there were 125 pans in the north-east. In 1605 there were 153, and each pan was said to produce fifty weys of salt and consume sixteen tens of coal. Since a wey of salt weighed approximately one ton and a ten of coal weighed 26–7 tons, the Tyneside industry at this time may have yielded just over 7,500 tons of salt and consumed more than 60,000 tons of coal.[75] Within a generation the industry had expanded further. Sir William Brereton, on his visit in 1635, proclaimed the saltworks of

[73] *NCH* ix. 323–5; Watts 1975, 53–4.

[74] Based upon data given in Nef 1932, i. 176n; Ellis 1980, 57. This assumes that a wey was approximately equal to a ton.

[75] DN Syon Y II(7).

Tynemouth and Shields to be the 'vastest salt works I have seen [with] more salt made than in any part of England'. He estimated that in all there were some 250 salt houses and in each house a great iron pan.[76] Brereton's exuberant observations receive some confirmatory support from a sober report on the Shields industry compiled by Sir Lionel Maddison in 1644, in which the number of pans 'within the river' was put at 222 precisely, of which 'in good times some 180 or 190 might be going pans, for there was always some that was amending and some out of repair'. He went on to estimate that 'these pans one with another will cast 80 wey every pan and burn 20 tens of coals yearly each pan, which doth amount to 14,400 weighs of salt and about, 3,600 tens [c.95,000 tons] of coals'. To which must be added a score or so pans on the Northumberland coast, and Maddison also tells us that 'In Sunderland there was some pans which burnt some 300 tens of coals but are at present all out of repair, belonging all lately to Sir William Lambton'.[77]

Iron salt-pans quickly deteriorated when out of use, and the Civil War combined with enhanced imports from Scotland to bring about a substantial contraction in the capacity and output of the north-east. Thereafter, as the customs accounts have shown, the industry recovered, but the number of pans never regained the peaks of the 1630s and early 1640s. It was noted that there were only 121 pans at South Shields in 1667, and 143 in 1696, while in 1713 there were 142 pans at South Shields and 29 at North Shields.[78] Yet the numbers of pans had become a poor guide to changes in capacity, for pans had grown in size. We have already noted that the pans of 1605 were said to consume sixteen tens of coal a year and produce fifty weys of salt, while those of 1644 were said to consume twenty tens and produce eighty weys. Their size continued to grow, and in the mid-eighteenth century Shields pans, with dimensions of around twenty feet by twelve feet, were thought to be the largest in Britain. Moreover, it was claimed that the 170 or so Shields pans of the decades around the turn of the seventeenth and eighteenth centuries were capable of producing as much as 20,000 tons if only there had been a demand for this amount of salt.[79]

Despite abundant supplies of cheap coal, fuel seems to have accounted for well over half of the costs of production. Attempts may have been made to economize on fuel, but achievements were limited. The pans of 1605 used almost eight and a half tons of coal for each ton of salt, while William Cotesworth's careful computations of costs, and the

[76] Brereton, *Travels*, 19–24; see also *CSPD 1636-7*, 304. [77] PRO SP 16/503(i)/39.
[78] Ellis 1981, 139. [79] Ellis 1981, 141, 145 n.

actual operating expenses of his saltworks in the 1720s and 1730s, shows consumption fluctuating between six to eight tons of coal per ton of salt.[80] It would seem that Maddison's 1644 estimate of just over six and a half tons of coal to each ton of salt was too optimistic. Having regard to the most plausible fuel-consumption estimates, it would seem that over 50,000 tons of coal were burnt annually by the north-eastern salt industry in the early years of the seventeenth century, and that just prior to the Civil War consumption may have risen to more than 90,000 tons. Whereas the slump in salt production in the 1650s, and some improvements in fuel economy, may have resulted in coal requirements temporarily retreating, by the close of the century rising production may well have lifted it to between 80,000 to 100,000 tons. At these levels some 7 per cent of all coal produced in the region may well have gone to the pans, whereas a century earlier the proportion could have exceeded 10 per cent.

The Firth of Forth was the principal location for salt production north of the border, and there is every indication that output there surged upwards in an almost identical fashion to that of Tyneside. What is more, it did so over a broadly similar time period.[81] One major difference between the two industries was that for Forthside the prime catalyst was overseas rather than home markets. In the 1550s less than £18 (Scots) was collected in customs on salt exports, but by the 1570s revenue had risen to £1,195 (Scots).[82] Moreover, exports remained buoyant from the 1570s through to the 1630s, or even the 1660s, and complaints from Scottish consumers who felt themselves deprived of home-produced salt, or forced to pay too much for it, flooded into the Privy Council.[83] Sir George Bruce's 'matchless' Culross was in the vanguard of soaring salt production, as it was of coal, and prior to the devastating storm of March 1625 it had as many as forty-four pans. John Taylor, who visited Culross in 1618, proclaimed that Bruce 'makes every week ninety or a hundred tons of salt, which doth serve most part of Scotland, some part he sends into England, and very much into Germany'. Taylor worked hard in his description of Culross to paint a picture of a truly miraculous industrial operation, and his salt output figure is patently absurdly high, even if it only applied to those rare periods when all the pans were in operation. Nevertheless, with over

---

[80] DN Syon Y II(7); Ellis 1981, 147.
[81] For recent surveys see Whatley 1984 and 1987.
[82] Nef 1932, i. 177.
[83] Whatley 1984, 26; Guy thesis 1982, 151–9.

forty pans in a single saltworks, Culross burgh led the ranks of salt
exporters from the 1580s, and in 1663 over fifty pans were working in
Culross alone. A host of saltworks sprang up in the later sixteenth
century along both banks of the Forth, with major plants at Kincardine,
Inverkeithing, Limekilns, Pittenweem, and Wemyss. When Brereton in
1636 compared the south bank of the Forth with Shields, he confessed
that its total output 'cannot be estimated and guessed, because the
works are not easily to [be] numbered' for they spread 'all along the
shore at least thirty English miles from beyond Musselborough almost
to Stirling'.[84]

Recent studies of the Scottish salt industry and trade make it necessary to revise substantially downwards widely held estimates of scale.
Nef, and the historians who followed him, believed that the Scottish
industry was somewhat larger than that on Tyneside.[85] It now appears
indisputable that it was far smaller. Saltworks may have proliferated in
Scotland, but they were almost invariably small in comparison with
those of the north-east. A contemporary estimate for all Scotland made
in 1670 was 83,000 large bolls, or some 8,300 tons. The very highest of
contemporary estimates of the production of the early eighteenth
century is equivalent to some 11,600 tons. Not only were both of these
estimates lower than contemporaneous shipments from Shields, there
are good reasons for suspecting that they were overstatements. In the
second decade of the eighteenth century the actual annual average
recorded output was no more than 6,500 tons, while in the decade after
1716 sales of salt from Fife, the leading salt-making region, ranged
between only 3,250 and 3,500 tons.[86] Scottish salt-masters faced many
challenges in the forty years or so before the Union of 1707. Exports
were suffering increased competition from a revitalized 'Bay' salt
industry and the imposition of tariffs on shipments sent to England,
while the discovery of rock salt in Cheshire posed the prospective threat
of a flood of cheap imports. Yet salt-masters responded positively by
turning their attention increasingly towards their home market. That
the industry was not moribund is evidenced by repeated heavy investment in new plants, as the grand undertakings at Methil and Saltcoats

[84] Whatley 1984, 26; Beveridge 1885, i. 160; Nef 1932, i. 177–8.
[85] Nef estimated that the annual consumption of coal in salt-making within Durham and
Northumberland could harldly have been less than 125,000 tons between 1680 and 1690, while at
the same time the annual consumption of the saltworks of the Forth may have reached 150,000
tons (Nef 1932, i. 208). Succeeding historians, until Dr Whatley (1984, 146–7), have followed Nef,
though sometimes with some scepticism, e.g. Duckham 1970, 16; Flinn 1984, 235–6.
[86] Whatley 1984, 24, 31, 146–7.

(Ayr) testify.[87] Nevertheless, Scottish salt output at the turn of the seventeenth and eighteenth centuries normally ranged between 6,000 and 8,000 tons, and the amounts of coal it required would have been 40,000 to 60,000 tons rather than the 150,000 tons postulated by Nef.

The proportion of total coal output burnt under salt-pans was, however, higher in Scotland than on Tyreside, and the relationship between the salt industries was even closer. In 1713 only a single coal-owner in Northumberland and Durham had a major direct interest in the Shields salt industry, but in Scotland it was rare for seasale coal-owners not to possess salt-pans. Moreover, whereas in Scotland there were very many collieries that were geared mainly or entirely to supplying pans, in the north-east pancoal was rarely other than a by-product of the raising of good quality ship-coal.[88]

Wherever coal was dug close to the sea, salt production was a possibility. The costs of transporting salt, which was a low-value bulky commodity, also helped to scatter salt-pans around the coasts of Britain. Sizeable concentrations were to be found along the Dee estuary in Flint and Denbighshire and in west Cumberland.[89] The pans sometimes provided a welcome outlet for surplus coal production. In Cumberland, especially before the rise of the Irish coal trade, for want of other markets the linkages between collieries and pans could be very close. Christopher Lowther's collieries at Flatfield and Davis Field near Whitehaven in the 1630s, for example, have been viewed as an adjunct to the three salt-pans which they served, while the output of those of Patricius Curwen at Workington was consumed in his household, lime-kilns, and salt-pans.[90] A striking exception to the indispensability of cheap coal, however, was provided at Lymington (Hants), far distant from supplies. But in good years what Lymington salters lost through the high cost of their fuel was compensated for by solar evaporation. Although at neighbouring Southampton coal fetched more than three times as much as it did at Shields, the Lymington salters used very little of it. The sea water was first drawn off into ponds 'for the sun to exhale the watery fresh part of it'.[91] In a hot dry summer on the favoured south coast the salinity of the sea water prior to boiling could rise almost to that of the brine springs of Cheshire and Worcestershire. When bemoaning the competition from Lymington pans, William Cotesworth maintained that salters there used little more than a ton of coal to each

[87] Smout 1963, 229–32; Whatley 1987.　　[88] Ellis 1980, 48; see above, ch. 5(ii).

[89] Nef 1932, i. 178.　　[90] Wood 1988, 5–6.

[91] Fiennes, *Journeys*, 69–70. Prices of coal at Southampton are derived from Houghton.

ton of salt, while his pans used at least six times as much. In a good year the Lymington pans could produce up to 3,000 tons of salt, though in a poor summer production might cease altogether.[92]

The output derived from the brine springs of Cheshire and Worcestershire was far higher and far more consistent than that of Lymington. The high salt content meant that the brine required little boiling to convert it. In 1636 the earl of Huntingdon said that it took only three hours of boiling, and John Collins, in his treatise on *Salt and Fishery* (1682) put coal consumption per ton of salt at 29 cwt at Nantwich, 15 cwt. at Middlewich, and just 12 cwt. at Northwich.[93] Droitwich salters had suffered from a shortage of wood before the sixteenth century, and the adoption of coal throughout the 'wiches' was an inevitable process. In 1636 Nantwich salters used both wood and coal, but by 1669 all the lead pans, which were suitable for wood but not coal, had been replaced by iron pans. By the time that Collins wrote his treatise it would appear that no other fuel but coal was used throughout Cheshire. Collins conveniently estimates the output of each of the Cheshire 'wiches' so that it is possible to calculate the amount of coal which would have been burnt. In good years salt production may have reached 25,000 tons, and the distribution between the 'wiches' given by Collins means that it would have taken only 20,000 tons of coal.[94]

Coal was by no means conveniently at hand for Cheshire salters. It had to be brought from north Staffordshire, or by sea from Lancashire, Flintshire, or Denbighshire to the Cheshire bank of the Mersey near Frodsham Bridge and thence overland. None of the Cheshire 'wiches' was less than twelve miles overland from the nearest colliery. In 1698 it was alleged that coal which cost 5s. 6d. a ton in the Mersey estuary might cost as much as 16s. 8d. in Northwich. At Shields pancoal could be had for less than 2s. 6d. per ton.[95] The key to prosperity in the salt industry was the relationship between the costs of each ton of fuel and the amount required to produce each ton of salt. Thus in the north-east of England and in Scotland long boiling periods were compensated for by extremely cheap fuel, while in Cheshire and Lymington expensive fuel was compensated for by short boilings. In this way, as well as in the costs of transporting the salt itself and the quality of the end product, no one centre was able totally to eclipse the others.

A new internal threat to traditional salters did emerge, however, at the close of the seventeenth century. In 1670, while prospecting for coal

[92] Ellis 1980, 51–2; Ellis 1981, 144–5.   [93] Chaloner 1961, 62–5.
[94] Ibid. 65–6; Nef 1932, i. 175 n.; Barker 1951, 83–6.   [95] Ellis 1980, 49.

in Cheshire, rock salt was discovered. The conversion of rock salt to table salt used very small quantities of fuel indeed, moreover the crystals were concentrated enough to make it possible to transport rock salt to the fuel, rather than vice versa. Rock salt was soon being shipped up the west coast to Lancashire and Cumberland, but although in the longer term it was set to undermine completely the viability of producing salt by the evaporation of sea water, it made little headway before 1700.[96]

The production of salt is perhaps the only industry for which estimates of total coal consumption can be made with any pretence of accuracy, but even so a considerable amount of guesswork is involved. All in all, taking account of the minor as well as the major centres of production, and making allowance for the further refining of salt close to markets, the 'salt on salt' referred to by Brereton,[97] it would seem that as much as 200,000 to 250,000 tons of coal were being burnt annually around 1700. If so the demands of the salt industry would have accounted for some 7 to 10 per cent of total British production.

Brewing   When towns feared for supplies of wood for their domestic hearths because of competition from urban industries, it was almost invariably the brewers who were deemed to be the chief culprits. At Worcester in 1548 bakers, brewers, and tile-makers were forbidden to buy up wood by the boatload in the city, and a similar by-law was enacted at York in the following year. At St Albans brewers were held solely to blame for the town's fuel shortage, and their numbers were forcibly reduced. As wood scarcity became more acute and more widespread in the early seventeenth century we find the town governments of Bury St Edmunds, Exeter, and Sudbury taking steps to compel their brewers to use nothing but coal in order to safeguard what firewood there was for the needs of other consumers.[98]

In London, by sharp contrast, concerns about the quality of the air sometimes triumphed. Since the later thirteenth century London brewers had burned such great quantities of coal that it was believed that they were a major cause of foul air in the city, and a stream of acts and by-laws sought to compel them to use wood instead. Doubtless the proximity of many breweries to Whitehall and Westminster added greatly to their notoriety. In 1578, when concerns began once again to be voiced, a brewer and a dyer were imprisoned for polluting Westminster with coal smoke, and the Company of Brewers, on learning that the

---

[96] Chaloner 1961, 59, 66–7.
[97] Evelyn lists salt-boilers among the greatest coal-burners in London (*Fumifugium*, 6).
[98] Dyer 1976, 602; Dyer 1973, 54.

Queen was 'greatly grieved and annoyed with the taste and smoke of the sea-coals' burned by its members, agreed to ensure that henceforth only wood should fuel breweries in the vicinity of the Palace of Westminster. Inevitably, the dictates of economy in a very competitive industry and the inexorable rise in the price of wood meant that there were innumerable lapses from this code. In 1623 an act prohibiting the use of coal by brewers within a mile of any house within which the court of the king or the prince of Wales was habitually held was passed through the Lords but not the Commons. Archbishop Laud displayed a special concern with air pollution and despite lacking legal authority extracted many fines from Westminster brewers with coal-fired furnaces in the 1630s.[99] That brewers were among the prime industrial consumers of fossil fuel in London is confirmed by their position at the head of Evelyn's list of creators 'of those prodigious clouds of smoke, which so universally and so fatally infest the air' of London in the late 1650s, and of Nourse's blacklist of 'furnace-gentlemen' who polluted London in the 1690s.[100]

It seems certain that this prominence was replicated throughout the towns and cities of seventeenth-century Britain. Overseas, too, brewers were among the leading consumers of British coal.[101] Quite simply brewing consumed much fuel, and it was an exceptionally competitive business in which price-cutting was rife and the minimizing of costs essential. Large quantities of water are heated and cooled at various stages in the production process, to which a variety of substances (malt, hops, etc.) are added from time to time. Despite some passing concern with the possibility of coal smoke impairing the flavour of the finished product, the adoption of coal whenever wood was scarce or expensive was usually a matter of course. The scope for savings was immense. Harrison in the late sixteenth century estimated that wood accounted for a quarter of the cost of brewing beer.[102] In 1578 just three of the twenty-six common brewers in London and Westminster were said to have burnt 2,000 loads of firewood in a year. It was claimed in 1696 by an opponent of a new tax on coal shipments that there were London brewers who burnt 400 or 500 chaldrons of coal each year, which if they were of London measure would have amounted to 600 to 750 tons, and if of Newcastle, 1,000 to 1,300 tons.[103] The latter figure seems the most

[99] Nef 1932, i. 157 and n.; Brimblecombe 1987, 33, 40–2; *CSPD 1547–80*, 612; HMC House of Lords, ns xi. 382–4.

[100] Evelyn, *Fumifigium*, 15; Nourse, *Campania Foelix*, 351 [*sic*].

[101] Nef 1932, i. 119–20, 235–6; above, Ch. 5(ii).

[102] Clark 1983, 101, 160.

[103] Nef 1932, i. 192; ii. 411.

likely, for in 1703 a survey of coal stocks in Thames-side premises in a time of scarcity revealed one brewer with more than 500 tons and two with over 250 tons each.[104]

Brewing is yet another industry for which there is overwhelming evidence of striking expansion in these centuries. Fortunately, a series of governmental surveys and reports, excise returns, and local licensing records provide the means of measuring this expansion, albeit in approximate terms.[105] In 1577 local magistrates were requested by the Privy Council to 'inquire what number of inns, taverns and alehouses are in every shire'. From their returns we may conclude that there were up to 24,000 alehouse keepers in England as a whole. In the 1630s, when the Privy Council on a number of occasions again called on local justices to enumerate the number of licensed and unlicensed houses in their localities, their returns suggest around 50,000 alehouses. By the 1700s excise returns show that there were over 40,000 victuallers in England who brewed their own beer, and possibly around 60,000 public drinking-houses of all sorts. Taking account of movements in the population of England, these figures suggest one drinking-house for every 140 inhabitants in 1577, and one for every eighty or so inhabitants around 1700. Much of this increase took place in towns.

The prodigious numbers of alehouses naturally reflected a very heavy consumption of ale and beer. Late seventeenth-century excise records suggest a *per capita* consumption in alehouses over the whole country of about six pints a week, which must be increased to ten or twelve pints to take account of private and unlicensed brewing. Such levels are by no means out of line with independent evidence of consumption, some of it dating back to the Middle Ages. There may well have been increasing *per capita* consumption, but the rapidly rising numbers of alehouses and taverns owed more to increasing population and the progressive supplanting of home brewing by commercial brewing and victualling.[106] This latter development doubtless further enhanced the use of coal. Whereas the small-scale home or local brewer used whatever fuel was conveniently available, the demands of the commercial brewer were such as could, in all but a minority of locations, have been satisfied by coal alone.

As the seventeenth century wore on, the commercialization of

---

[104] HMC *House of Lords*, NS V. 238.

[105] The following discussion is based upon alehouse data given in Clark 1983, ch. 3, and the population estimates contained in Wrigley and Schofield 1981, 208–9.

[106] Clark 1983, 109, 115.

brewing went far beyond the progressive growth in brewing by publicans at the expense of home-brewing. It saw the triumph in many larger towns of the common brewer, who supplied the publicans with their beer. In London and Westminster in 1578–85 there were twenty-six common brewers, by 1699 there were 194, and their average production was around 5,000 barrels a year each. Centralization of production was facilitated by the addition of hops, which acted as a preservative and helped beer to travel well.[107] By the close of the seventeenth century a number of towns had become renowned for the quality of their beers—Burton, Nottingham, Lichfield, Bridgnorth, Shrewsbury, Dorchester, and Plymouth among them—and the output of their breweries found markets well beyond the confines of their city walls.[108] Burton beers, for example, were highly prized in London. With the exception of Dorchester and Plymouth, these brewing towns all benefited from cheap coal.

As with so many industrial processes, brewers favoured particular grades of coal. Ideally it should be small, but of good quality. The output of certain collieries, such as Montagu's Hutton coals and Sir Walter Seton's Forthside coals, was deemed to be especially suited. The coal should burn freely without much poking or stirring. For, as Montagu stated, 'brewers' fires are so broad and long that they cannot break or stir them'.[109] The increasing size of the operations of many common brewers doubtless led to economies of scale, and to fuel economies in particular. Yet the quantities of beer brewed were so huge, best estimates calculating some 250 million gallons a year in the late sixteenth century, and some 350 million gallons around 1700, that brewers 'collectively, were acknowledged to be among the most important non-domestic users of coal in the land'.[110]

But yet more coal was used in the production of beer. The final stage in malting was the drying of germinated barley in a kiln at a moderate heat. This was a crucial stage in the making of beer or ale, which greatly influenced the flavour of the finished product. The barley was spread over a perforated floor in the kiln, with a fire below. The avoidance of smoke was a high priority for it could taint the malt. The choice of fuel was therefore an important matter, regardless of price. Wood was often held to give the beer a bitter taste, and commonly straw was

---

[107] Mathias 1959, 6; Coleman 1975, 48.
[108] Clark (ed.) 1981, 27; Rowlands 1987, 220–1.
[109] NUL Montagu, Montagu to Baker 31/1/98–99, 16/5/99; PRO 30/24/7.
[110] Mathias 1959, 6.

employed.[111] Raw coal proved unacceptable, apart from the smokeless anthracite of Pembrokeshire. Yet it was correctly conceived that mineral coal which had been purged of its noxious elements might prove the most suitable of all, and there was a stream of applications for malting patents based upon the coking of mineral coal.[112] It was in Derby around the middle of the seventeenth century that coke was first used in malt drying with great success. Within a short time the fame of Derby malt and beer had spread far and wide. Malt and beer from the town were regularly sent to London, and malt as far as Lancashire and Cheshire.[113] Much of the success was due no doubt to the hard, bright coal from pits at Heanor, Smalley, and Denby close by the town from which the coke was made. The use of coke for malting also began to spread elsewhere, including into Edinburgh, Fife, and the Lothians.[114]

The textile and clothing industries   Attempts to combat air pollution by deterring the dyers of fourteenth-century London from using coal met with little long-term success, and in 1578 they and the hat-makers were said to 'have long sithens altered their furnaces and fiery places and turned the same to the use and burning of sea coal'.[115] Thereafter these two sets of craftsmen never fail to be listed among the great consumers of coal in the capital. However, to judge from William Cholmeley's mid-sixteenth-century admonition to England's dyers to switch to coal, as their counterparts in Flanders had long since done, and thereby use native Newcastle coal at home and cease wasting valuable woods,[116] there was as yet insufficient economic incentive to convert to coal in many provincial towns although, as we have noted, the adoption of prohibitions on industrial wood-burning imposed by successive town authorities must have hastened the process.

Dyeing involved the boiling of dyes, mordants, and other agents in large vats, and in 1610 William Slingsby listed it among other 'boilings' in which coal could successfully be substituted for wood. But there are reasons for believing that the adoption of coal for all types of cloth and all forms of dyeing may not always have been entirely a matter of cost. In the mid-sixteenth century when Cholmeley wrote, coal was still a dear fuel in most parts of the country, yet there is evidence of the

[111] Donnachie 1979, 102; Nef 1932, i. 215–16.
[112] Owen, *Pembrokeshire*, 87; Mathias 1959, 412.
[113] Mott and Greenfield (eds.) 1936, 13–16.
[114] Donnachie 1979, 102.
[115] Nef 1932, i. 214–15.
[116] Quoted in Tawney and Power (eds.), *Tudor Economie Documents*, iii. 144.

persistence of dyeing with wood and charcoal at a later date in some places where coal was easily available and cheap. There was doubtless some resistance to change bred of innate conservatism, but it has also been suggested that there were some technical barriers. Although there is no contemporary statement to the effect, Dr Kerridge has concluded that while coal may have been perfect for dyeing cloths, when used for dyeing in the wool the sponginess of the wool allowed coal fumes to be absorbed, thereby spoiling it.[117] Some further light is shed on this issue by the cloth-makers of Cranbrook in the Weald of Kent who dyed in the wool. Not surprisingly, given their proximity to wood and remoteness from coal, they were still dyeing over wood fires in 1637 when they complained to the Privy Council that John Brown, commissioner for the making of brass and iron ordnance and shot, was burning so much wood in his furnaces that its price had been forced up. In reply Brown maintained that whereas he could not manufacture shot without wood, dyeing could be done just as easily, and more cheaply, with Newcastle coal brought overland from Maidstone or Newenden. In support of his contention that there were no technical barriers, he produced certificates from London dyers who professed, after examining samples of Cranbrook dyeing, that 'wool of these several colours' could be dyed as well with coal, and perhaps even better. They added that in London they dyed wool, cloths, silks, and other stuffs perfectly well over coal fires.[118]

Even if we entertain doubts that coal was not universally ideal for dyeing, there were many other uses in the textile and clothing trades. It was utilized early, as we have seen, in hat-making, in which cloth was 'woaded, boiled and maddered' and then pressed. The rising popularity of hats eventually made this a significant usage of coal. Coal was also used to fire kilns for drying flax and yarn, cauldrons for cleaning wool, cotton, linens, and silk, and hot-pressing furnaces. Fuel costs were rarely a major element in the production of cloth, and the quantities used in those stages of production which needed heat were not large in relation to each unit of output, yet the woollen industry was the 'greatest manufacture' in the realm. It grew prodigously in scale over the course of the sixteenth and seventeenth centuries, and its sheer size and universality placed it in the forefront of coal-consuming industries. In centres of production, like Exeter, the manufacture of cloth could consume more coal than any other industry[119]

[117] E. Kerridge, *Textile Manufacture in Early Modern England* (Manchester, 1985), 163–5.
[118] Nef 1932, i. 214.
[119] Hoskins 1935, 103–4.

New industrial demand, 1550-1700

The list of fuel-burning industries which were served by coal at the close of the seventeenth century is very long; indeed there are few industries which burnt anything other than coal when it could be obtained cheaply. Yet the contribution to total coal consumption of new industries and of older industries which were able by technological advances to convert from wood or charcoal has frequently been exaggerated. For the majority of the new industrial users of coal which emerged in the course of the late sixteenth and seventeenth centuries, consumption must be counted in thousands of tons rather than tens or hundreds of thousands. Coal was undoubtedly important for the development and prosperity of these industries, but their impact upon the British coal industry was slight. Moreover, those few non-traditional coal-burners whose demands were to prove more substantial—brick-makers, glass-makers, maltsters, and potters—made their impact relatively late in the period covered by this volume. Perhaps more significant in terms of the quantities of coal which were burnt than any of the technologically advanced industries, was the progressive adoption of coal by village and town bakers, and the proliferation of commercial establishments devoted to the production of salt meats, vinegar, and tallow, as the processing and preserving of food and the consumption of candles expanded along with rising population.

Even in regions where coal was not commonly burnt by the population at large, we find bakers turning to coal-fired ovens, driven by the rising cost of wood and enticed by improvements in oven design.[120] To some extent the rise of commercialized baking went hand in hand with the rise of commercialized brewing as the poor, especially in towns, increasingly lacked the facilities and fuel to cook at home.[121] Food processing in this period has left scant records, but some insight into the quantities of coal that it could require is provided by navy victualling. In preparation for the Dutch War of 1665–7 the 'surveyor of the king's marine victuals' arranged for over 100 tons to be sent to London for 'boiling pickle'.[122] The production of candles has likewise left few records, but the use of coal to heat the tallow is strongly indicated by the prominence of chandlers among the retailers of coal.

---

[120] See e.g. Brinkworth and Gibson (eds.), *Banbury Wills and inventories*, 251, 367.

[121] Clark (ed.) 1981, 27.

[122] Nef 1932, i. 212–13.

In the second half of the sixteenth century many attempts were made to engender new industries, and to nurture infant or stunted projects into adolescence. Elizabeth granted patents for monopolies of the manufacture of soap, alum, glass, paper, brass, and copper, with the intention of cutting imports of these products, increasing employment at home, and, of course, raising revenues. Patentees and licensees with high hopes and deep pockets ventured forth to prosper. Large-scale designs and substantial investments notwithstanding, very few succeeded. A copper mine and smelting works was set up in Keswick (Cumb.) in 1567, and coal as well as wood was burnt in the conversion of the ore into pure metal, but output fell woefully short of targets. In the first seventeen years of operation an average of only 30 tons of copper a year left Keswick, and before the Civil War output never seems to have exceeded 50 tons. At the most the works would have consumed a few hundred tons of coal a year.[123]

England was totally dependent upon imports for its alum, a mordant used to fix dyes in textiles, and searches were undertaken to find native supplies.[124] Promising deposits of ore were finally discovered at Guisborough, on the north–east coast of Yorkshire in 1600, and soon after near Whitby. Alum was made by boiling, in a similar fashion to salt, and at least three tons of coal were required to produce every ton of alum. Expectations rose very high, and in 1606 John Bourchier leased Harraton colliery for £500 a year to supply the nearby alum-pans. It was a false move, for before the 1630s output seems never to have exceeded 600 tons a year, and an attempt to start production in Dorset failed completely. There were numerous production problems, including the presence of impurities in the finished commodity. None the less, technology improved and output thereafter continued to augment modestly. In 1647 Maddison estimated that around 3,000 chaldrons (c.8,000 tons) of Sunderland coal were sent to the alum-pans yearly.

The manufacture of copperas, known as green vitriol, which was also used in dyeing, was technically straightforward and easier to establish.[125] Iron pyrites were mined at Queenborough and Whitstable in the Thames estuary, then piled in heaps and left to be dissolved by weathering. The resultant solution was then boiled with lumps of iron in pans until it crystallized. The need for imports was soon supplanted, but

[123] Rees 1968, ii. 403–24.
[124] The following account is based upon Gough 1969, 176–96; Jack 1977, 84–5; Nef 1932, i. 184–5.
[125] Jack 1977, 84; Nef 1932, i. 210.

scope for expansion was very limited simply because so little was used. The manufacture of copperas was moderately successful, but destined to remain a very minor operation. In 1634 the works at Queenborough consumed about 300 tons of coal in a year. The same might be said of the manufacture of saltpetre, which likewise never came to consume significant quantities of coal. Determined efforts to render England independent of imports, for strategic as well as economic reasons, led to the starting of production in many locations throughout the country. Saltpetre was made from a 'lye' of earth, animal excrement, and the incrustations found on the insides of buildings, especially dovecotes, to which urine was periodically added. The saltpetre eventually crystallized, and it would then be dissolved in water and boiled for days on end before being ready to mix with charcoal and sulphur to make gunpowder. Cheap fuel was essential for profitable manufacture, and saltpetremen changed early to coal, but once again the quantities that were consumed were small. The total output of saltpetre in 1636 was probably no higher than the target of 300 tons which had been set in 1589. Even if very many tons of coal were used to produce a single ton it is difficult to envisage that its manufacture could have had a significant impact on the coal industry, even at a local level. John Foxe, a saltpetreman who located himself adjacent to the great colliery of Wollaton, purchased less than 50 tons of coal in 1596.[126]

The manufacture of soap and the refining of sugar consumed higher levels of fuel, but not much higher until the later seventeenth century. Little soap was manufactured commercially in Elizabeth's reign and sugar imports were scarcely more than a trickle. England at this time relied for finer soaps almost solely on imports, but much of the country's needs for basic cleansers must have been satisfied from within the household using tallow and wood ash. The manufacture of specialist soap within England was developing, however, and commercial production, which required the lengthy boiling of ingredients, seems from an early period to have relied upon coal for its fuel. Together with sugar boiling, soap production was essentially located in a few large towns, most notably London, Westminster, and Bristol, which were themselves, of course, heavily reliant upon coal by the early seventeenth century.[127] It was projected by a group of prospective patentees in 1631, that it was possible to produce up to 10,000 tons of soap, of which some 5,000 tons would be manufactured in London alone. The prospectors

---

[126] Gough 1969, 204–7; Nef 1932, i. 210–11; HMC *Middleton*, 163–4; *CSPD 1637-8*, 45.
[127] Jack 1977, 113; Lipson 1956 edn. iii. 362–5.

were successful in obtaining their patent, but less successful in fostering the progress of the industry. The patentees, whom it was claimed were 'gentlemen soapboilers [never] bred up to the trade', secured prohibitions not only on imports of soap but of imports of whale and fish oil from which English soap had formerly been made. Instead soap was henceforth to be made from native vegetable oil, and all producers were to be licensed. The furore caused by the implementation of these measures indicates an industry of some importance, at least in London and Bristol. The capital's soap-boilers were numbered among that city's leading 'spenders' of coal, and their importance was to continue to wax.[128] In the closing decades of the century, as the consumption of commercially produced soap soared, so soap-boiling in a number of cities developed into a large and profitable, if still barely respectable, business. It was reputed that there were 'many citizens of great worth and esteem ... being soap boilers by trade even and yet accounted gentlemen', and many leading towns were able to support a soapworks. Yet demand was not unlimited, and some attempts to establish soap-works failed, even in places where coal was cheap and at hand.[129]

Sugar-boiling was somewhat slower to take off, and before the Civil War the price of sugar remained so high that only the rich could afford it. The growth of West Indian production, however, led to plummeting prices and soaring imports. Some 7,500 tons a year were brought into England around 1660, by 1700 more than 18,000 tons were imported annually. London's dominant position in the sugar trade extended to processing, and refineries were located in the East End and on the south bank of the Thames. In 1703, when the scarcity of coal in London led to a survey being made of stocks, a Southwark sugar baker was revealed to have one of the largest stocks of all, amounting to 300 London chaldrons, some 400 tons. Importing, refining, and trading in sugar became big business, and was the foundation of some considerable fortunes. One such was made by 'Mr Smith, a great sugar baker of London, a man, as report says, worth £40,000'. As the sugar trade boomed so refineries were established in western ports where sugar was imported and coal could be bought cheaply, most notably Bristol, Liverpool, and Glasgow. In 1665 Mr Smith contracted with Edward Moore to build in Liverpool 'a stately house of good hewn stone, four storeys high, and then to go through the same building with a large entry, and there on the back side, to erect a house for boiling and drying sugar, otherwise called a sugar baker's house'. Moore surmised that

---

[128] e.g. Evelyn, *Fumifugium*, 15.   [129] Wilson 1984 edn., 14.

when this was done the city might gain 'a trade of at least £40,000 a year from the Barbadoes, which formerly this town never knew'.[130]

Glass-making provides a striking example of an industry converting through technical innovation to coal at an early date.[131] But many other influences also combined to effect the complete abandonment of wood-burning glasshouses. At the accession of Elizabeth glass-making was an ancient but essentially small-scale practice. Its roots stretched back to the early Middle Ages, but demand for its products was low; few windows were glazed and glass drinking vessels were a luxury that only the rich could afford. What is more, imports satisfied the greater share of this exiguous market. It is in the 1560s that the first signs of a major increase in the scale of output can be discerned, coinciding with the entry of French, Flemish, and Italian entrepreneurs and craftsmen into English glass production, and the growing affordability of glazed windows. Such expansion inevitably placed severe strains upon supplies of wood in some localities. Glasshouses were widely scattered, owing largely to the difficulties of transporting glass without breakages, so the strains were not felt equally by all manufacturers. But furnaces consumed sizes and grades of wood which were similar to those burnt in domestic hearths and, since they were often located close to sizeable markets, they competed directly with domestic consumers. Moreover, the rates of consumption could be very high indeed. Verzelini bought wood in billets for his London crystal-glass furnaces in the 1570s, and it was said that he burnt 500,000 of them each year. Small wonder that he deemed it prudent to purchase extensive woodlands to secure his future supplies. Another crystal-glass furnace, owned by William Robson, was said to have consumed two or three thousand loads of wood annually in the opening years of the seventeenth century.

Not only did such levels of consumption in an age of spiralling wood prices lead to dramatic increases in costs, Londoners were unlikely to tolerate for long such massive depredations of their precious firewood. In 1611 a patent was issued to Thomas Percival, the inventor, Thomas Hefflyn, the king's glazier, and two courtiers, giving them the exclusive right to manufacture window glass with coal. There are many conflicting claims, but it does appear that Percival was the first successfully to convert furnaces to coal, by using enclosed clay crucibles which prevented the raw materials coming into contact with the fuel and its

[130] Clay 1984, ii. 42; HMC *House of Lords*, NS v. 238; Wilson 1984 edn., 169, 176, 200–1.

[131] The following account is primarily derived from D. W. Crossley, 'The Performance of the Glass Industry in Sixteenth-Century England', *EcHR* 2nd ser. (1972), and Godfrey 1975.

fumes. As such the patent was unobjectionable, since it recognized a striking technical advance and rewarded its discoverer. But in 1614 a further patent was issued with new and sinister provisions: all previous rights to manufacture glass were revoked, the use of any fuel but coal was banned, and imports of glass were prohibited. Within a short time this new patent came into the hands of Sir Robert Mansell.

The compulsion to convert to coal was by no means welcomed by all glass-makers, while even those in London were not immediately rewarded with falling costs. At first only fine Scottish coal at upwards of 14s. a ton was burnt in the patentees' London furnaces, and the result was losses rather than enhanced profits. Operators in well-wooded regions, without competition for supplies, as at the glassworks at Newenton in Gloucestershire, could buy their wood far more cheaply. Others, even where wood was moderately expensive, were not necessarily well placed for obtaining coal. The conversion of most glass producers to coal was thus a matter of coercion rather than choice. This policy suited the Crown because it promised high revenues from the patent, and it helped to appease the vociferous lobby who feared for the destruction of all England's woodlands.

In the longer term, however, economics as well as the law favoured coal. It took little time for Newcastle coal to be successfully substituted for Scottish, and for enterprising manufacturers to migrate to the coal-fields. Mansell himself unsuccessfully built glasshouses at Wollaton and Milford Haven, as well as at Kimmeridge in Dorset, before settling profitably at Newcastle upon Tyne. Licensees established plants at Stourbridge and at Coventry, as well as at seven unidentified locations. Between 1600 and 1650 the price of window glass remained steady during a period of general inflation, and undoubtedly output rose to new heights. But we must be careful not to overestimate its scale. The most recent historian of the industry doubts whether as much as 10,000 cases of window glass a year were produced towards the end of Mansell's regime.[132] If we err on the side of optimism and add a further 10,000 cases for drinking glasses and vessel glass, this gives a total of some 2,000 tons. It took less than six tons of coal to produce each ton of glass. At this time the significance of glass manufacture to the coal industry was therefore symbolic rather than tangible, and although in subsequent decades the production of glass continued to increase, spurred on by improvements in material comfort and the invention of

[132] Godfrey 1975, 212, 256.

flint glass, glass-making did not become a substantial consumer of coal before the eighteenth century.

It will be apparent from these brief surveys of coal-burning industries that the first great boom in coal output, lasting from the 1570s to the Civil War, was founded almost exclusively upon the needs of traditional consumers in industry and the home. In addition to soaring consumption for domestic heating it was the salt-pans, lime-kilns, forges, breweries, and dye-vats of Britain which most stimulated coal production, while the amounts of coal consumed by newly established industries and by those which were enabled by technical advances to convert from wood or charcoal, were small. In the latter half of the seventeenth century, however, sweeping changes occurred in the pattern of industrial coal consumption. While the rate of increase in demand from many of the traditional industries slackened, that from the newer coal-using industries, most notably soap, sugar, and glass, continued to grow. Moreover, coal consumption grew in a range of industries, including the production of bricks, pottery, tiles, and malt, and the smelting of non-ferrous metals, which had previously either not burned coal at all, or had used it selectively.

Whereas technical obstacles to the use of coal in 'boilings' had never been steep, and those that had existed were successfully overcome before the seventeenth century, there remained barriers to 'baking' and 'melting'.[133] With baking in an oven or kiln the problem was not that coal was unusable but that the results were not as satisfactory as when wood or charcoal was used. The grey area of unsatisfactoriness means that technological advances are often very difficult to date, for they frequently took the form of improvements rather than complete solutions. In brick-making it was largely a question of the higher proportion of bricks which were spoiled in firings with coal, while in malt-drying it was the degree of unpleasantness which was imparted to the taste of ale and beer.

Bricks were first used in England in the thirteenth century, most often in the construction of chimneys, and in the later Middle Ages the use of brick for large buildings gradually became more popular. A measure of ostentation sometimes demanded the abandonment of the vernacular style for the construction of grand houses and palaces, and the spread of brick was also dictated by the availability of alternative

---

[133] As Sir William Slingsby correctly diagnosed in 1610 when he petitioned for a patent to protect inventions designed to facilitate the use of coal in various processes (Nef 1932, i. 215).

building materials.[134] Progress was thus most rapid in London, and brickwork also made headway in the east of England and East Anglia, where there were both a lack of good timber and stone, and supplies of soil suitable for brickmaking. In the fourteenth and fifteenth centuries brick houses became ever more common in the capital, and many notable examples of brickwork can be found in the eastern counties. Whereas wood was undoubtedly the best fuel for brick-kilns at this time, it was not plentiful in these parts, and building accounts reveal that turves ignited by wood were used to make bricks for Wisbech Castle and Ely Priory in the mid-fourteenth century, and Caister Castle in the 1430s. If turves could be used, there would appear to be no technical barrier to the use of coal. A fourteenth-century kiln excavated at Boston was indeed fired by coal, and it should be noted that coal as well as firewood was expected to be used by William Vesey when he was appointed royal brick-maker in 1437.

The building and rebuilding booms of the later sixteenth and seventeenth centuries placed great strain on the supply of traditional building materials, but while the price of timber soared the price of bricks fell in real terms.[135] Inevitably the advance of brick gained ever greater momentum. It became the normal material for the construction of even the most humble dwellings in the south-east and East Anglia, and it spread to areas previously dominated by timber-frame construction and where stone was unavailable, such as Nottinghamshire, Warwickshire, Worcestershire, east Lancashire, and Durham. Bricks spread to Yorkshire also, where, at the close of the seventeenth century, it was said of Hatfield:

The manner of building that it formerly had were all of wood, clay and plaster, but now that way of building is quite left off, for every one now from the richest to the poorest, will not build except with bricks: so that now from about 80 years ago (at which time bricks were first seen, used and made in the parish), they have been wholly used, and now there scarce is one house in the town that does not, if not wholly, yet for the most part, consist of that lasting and genteel sort of building.[136]

By the 1660s brick was invading most parts of the country, and in some parts was seriously undermining the vernacular tradition of clay

---

[134] A brief but useful chronological survey is contained in R. J. Brown, *English Farmhouses* (1982), 231 ff. See also N. Lloyd, *A History of English Brickwork* (1983 edn.); J. Schofield, *The Building of London from the Conquest to the Great Fire* (1984), 126–9; J. Blair and N. Ramsay (eds.), *English Medieval Industries* (1991), 211–36.

[135] Rogers 1866–1902, v. 545.

[136] Hey 1986, 196–7.

and wood. Only in regions with ample supplies of stone did brick
houses fail to make much headway before the eighteenth century.

It had been possible to fire brick-kilns with coal for centuries but, as
John Rovenson reported in his *Treatise of Metallica* published in 1613, it
'doth many times spoil much of the brick-clamp by making it run
together in a lump'. Rovenson went on to explain that bricks 'may be
made of pit-coal or stone-coal, or any of the privileged fuels, better than
with Newcastle sea-coal'.[137] Yet in London so high was the price of
wood and so great the demand for bricks that, despite its failings, it was
common to fire them with Newcastle coal, as we learn three years later
from Newcastle coal-owners who, in response to complaints about the
quality of coal shipped to London, pointed out that there was a market
for the meaner sorts of coal among brick-makers, as well as salters, lime-
burners, dyers, and smiths.[138] There is also a detailed description made
by a Venetian ambassador in 1618, of the brick-making process in the
vicinity of London using coal and coal-dust.[139]

Significant advances were undoubtedly made in the performance of
coal-fired kilns in the course of the seventeenth century, probably
including new methods of stacking the bricks using layers of coal and
dust.[140] In 1631 Howe wrote of how they have 'of very late years devised
. . . the burning of brick with sea coal or pit coal', and Sir William Petty
in 1674 felt able to claim that a principal cause of the increase in the coal
trade from Newcastle over the preceding forty years was the firing of so
many bricks.[141] Yet it should not be concluded that the processes had
been perfected; it could still be a matter of trial and error. In 1663
Gerbier claimed that when coal was used 25 per cent of the firing could
be wasted, and at the close of the century Houghton mused that sometimes bricks had been better burnt with two and a half chalders of coals
than at other times with ten chalders.[142] As for the amounts of coal that
were commonly required in the kiln or clamp, Robert Plot felt that
16,000 bricks, which might have built a modest cottage, would take
about seven tons.[143]

Bricks were expensive to transport, so brickworks were widely
scattered throughout the country to serve the needs of local com-

[137] Rovenson, *Metallica*, 13.
[138] Nef 1932, ii. 243.   [139] *CSPV 1617–19*, 320–1.
[140] Houghton, *A Collection for the Improvement* (1727–8), i. 119; Brimblecombe 1987, 33; Nef
1932, i. 217.
[141] Nef 1932, i. 254; W. Petty, *Political Arithmetic* (1690), 99.
[142] Gerbier, *Counsel and Advice to all Builders*, (1663), 52–3; Nef 1932, i. 218 n.
[143] Plot, *Staffordshire*, 128.

munities. Most producers seem to have operated on a modest scale, and many were transient, although for larger building works brick-kilns were often erected on or close to the site. There was thus much in common with lime-burning. Thousands of brick cottages and houses were erected in the course of the later seventeenth century, along with considerable numbers of more substantial dwellings and innumerable miles of boundary walls, and as the production of bricks multiplied and coal increasingly became the cheapest fuel for firing kilns, the consumption of coal in this sector of industry assumed ever more substantial proportions.

Clay roof tiles and pottery were also baked in kilns, and coal was widely used for the firing. Both the tiling of roofs and the consumption of pottery were growing rapidly in popularity in the later seventeenth century. The making of pottery had always been a major industry, though based upon a multitude of small units scattered throughout the country. Woodlands were favoured locations for early potteries, where kindling was cheap and abundant and suitable clay was often also on hand. In the Middle Ages kilns were fired with a variety of fuels; wood was most common, but in eastern England peat was used and archaeological evidence reveals that coal was also used in places where it was plentiful and cheap. Excavation of a sixteenth-century six-flued pottery kiln in the appropriately named village of Potterton in the West Riding, shows it to have been fired with coal.[144] Whereas individuals or small clusters of potters could, if the site were well chosen, subsist adequately on local wood, whenever true commercial production developed fuel supply became a critical issue. For much of our period production was overwhelmingly concentrated upon cheap and functional locally produced wares, with higher quality items imported, first from France and later from China and Japan. In the course of time, however, a number of major centres of country pottery emerged, which served more extensive market areas, among which coal-bearing regions were well represented, notably south and north Staffordshire, Shropshire, Yorkshire, Derbyshire, and Nottinghamshire.[145] Significant advances were also made in the seventeenth century in the manufacture of slipware and delftware with London, Bristol, and Liverpool in the forefront. In the closing decades of the century, the pace quickened appreciably under the stimulus of the fashion for warm beverages, such as coffee, tea, and chocolate, for which pewter mugs were quite unsuitable. Another major

---

[144] *Medieval Archaeology*, 8 (1964), 297; 12 (1968), 117–18.
[145] R. G. Haggar, *English County Pottery* (1950). See also the map in Weatherill 1971, 78.

innovation was stoneware, the making of which spread from London to Nottingham and north Staffordshire.

The expansion of the industry in north Staffordshire was especially rapid, and between the 1660s and the 1700s the number of potteries in the region are thought to have doubled from just under thirty to almost seventy. Additionally, of course, the size of each pottery tended to increase, so that the actual rate of growth in capacity was higher still. The nation's leading pottery district, along with many others, depended solely upon coal for its fuel, using it not only for firing the kilns but for drying the clay beforehand. So commonplace was its use that Dr Plot mentions it only in passing, and although coal was so cheap and close at hand that it scarcely makes an appearance in the probate inventories of potters, it was a vital ingredient in the success of north Staffordshire potteries. None the less, the quantities of coal which the pottery industry consumed do not appear to have been susbtantial. It has been estimated that it took 5–12 tons to dry and fire a ton of clay, and in the early eighteenth century a slipware pottery in Burslem burnt about 6 s. worth of coal a week, perhaps two tons.[146] At these levels of consumption it would have taken exceptional concentrations of potteries to have exerted much of an impact even on local pits.

Of far greater potential significance for the consumption of coal was the ability to smelt metalliferous ores with coal or coke. Yet smelting without using what frequently amounted to vast quantities of wood was to resist the endeavours of generations of inventors and practitioners, and time and again 'experience that great baffler of speculation shewed it would not be'.[147] The prize for success was inestimable, and many were the coal-owners who, sitting on heaps of unsaleable coal, reflected wistfully on how their fortunes would be transformed by this advance. Fuller, writing presciently of Shropshire in the mid-seventeenth century, was driven to exclaim, 'Oh if this coal could be so charked as to make iron melt out of the stone, as it maketh it in smiths' forges to be wrought in the bars'.[148] It was not until the closing decades of the seventeenth century that the barriers to smelting finally began to crumble. First lead and then copper were refined successfully on a commercial

---

[146] Weatherill 1971, 30–1.

[147] A comment made by Robert Plot in 1686 concerning Blewston's attempt to smelt iron with coal in a reverberatory furnace at Wednesbury in 1677 (Plot, *Staffordshire*, 128). A determined effort was made in the 1520s during Wolsey's tenure of the bishopric of Durham to smelt lead with coal, and a large house and furnace was built at Gateshead for this purpose (Galloway 1898, i. 85, 124–5).

[148] Quoted in Galloway 1898, i. 205.

scale using coal, but tin and the most sought after prize of all, iron, were not successfully refined until after the end of the century.

Collectively the production of metals consumed truly prodigious amounts of wood, and output rose steeply throughout the sixteenth and seventeenth centuries. While the production of tin only trebled, from 600 tons to 1,870 tons, between 1500 and 1700 that of lead rose from 600 tons to more than 28,000 tons.[149] The output of iron is a matter of some dispute, but a lower range of estimates would see around 5,000 tons of pig in the 1550s rising to some 25,000 tons around 1700.[150] Account must also be taken of copper smelting, which was restarted in England on a small scale in the 1680s. The reducing of ore to pure metal was in all cases expensive of fuel, but this was particularly evident in the case of iron, and even at the close of the sevententh century more than twelve cords of wood, some 2,000 cubic feet, went into making the charcoal needed to produce just one ton of bar. Not surprisingly, the costs of fuel accounted for at least half and possibly as much as three-quarters of total costs of iron production, depending upon the efficiency of the plant and the prices of local wood.[151]

Much has been learnt from historians of the charcoal iron industry of the economies which were effected in the dressing of ore, in smelting and forging, and in the ability of iron producers to survive by the coppicing of neighbouring woodlands. Yet it would be misleading to conclude that ironmasters were complacent about the cost and sufficiency of their fuel supplies. So fierce and unabated was the desire to smelt non-ferrous and ferrous ores with coal that attempt followed attempt with remorseless determination throughout the seventeenth century.[152] The reason lay not just in the cost of wood, but in the frequent proximity of coal-seams to iron and lead ores. In very many metal-mining regions coal lay close at hand, and supplies were far more reliable as well as far cheaper than those which could be drawn from even the most efficiently husbanded woodlands.

Of the many technical obstacles to the use of coal, the most intractable was the tainting of the metal with the sulphurous fumes which were emitted when coal was burnt. Part of the solution, as had been known

---

[149] The figures are taken from Clay 1984, ii. 58–9.

[150] Hammersley 1973, 593–613; P. Riden, 'The Output of the British Iron Industry before 1870', *EcHR* 2nd ser. 30 (1977).

[151] Hammersley 1973, 610.

[152] An incomplete annotated list of 22 grants of patents for smelting iron ore using coal or peat is given in Rees 1968, i. 294–5. Of course patents themselves provide an incomplete list of all the attempts which were made to smelt iron with coal. See also Schubert 1957, 226–9.

for decades, lay in the 'charking' or coking of the coal. Much inventive-
ness was bestowed upon finding the best method of processing coal, but
success in smelting depended at least as much on the coal which was to
be 'cowkified'. The method described by Houghton, which was used in
Derbyshire at the close of the seventeenth century, closely resembled
that which had been employed by charcoal-burners for centuries.[153] But
also crucial to success was the development of efficient reverberatory
furnaces, in which the fuel and the ore were separated, and the heat of
the fire was reflected or 'reverberated' down from the roof of the
furnace from one section to the other.[154]

It was predictable that lead and copper should succumb first. The low
melting-points of these ores made satisfactory reverberatory furnaces
easier to design and operate. From 1676 onwards a series of patents was
granted for smelting lead with coal in divided, closed, or reverberatory
furnaces, and such furnaces were soon successfully put into operation.[155]
In 1692 a company known as 'The Governor and Company for the
Smelting-down of Lead with Pit-coal and Sea-coal' was chartered, and it
acquired Sir Talbot Clarke's leadworks with five furnaces in Bristol. So
effective had reverberatory furnaces become in Flintshire by the close of
the century that they were known as Flintshire furnaces.[156] We are well
informed about the smelting of lead and copper with coal, previously
'charked', at Sir Humphrey Mackworth's works in Neath at the turn of
the century. According to William Shiers in 1700, 'the smelting and
refining are all done with pit-coal which is much cheaper than wood or
charcoal'.[157] We also learn of copper being smelted with coke in Bristol
from the 1680s.[158]

Sir John Pettus was thus clearly out of date when he wrote in 1686
that sea coal and pit coal 'are not useful to metals', but we must be careful not to equate invention with dissemination.[159] The smelting of non-
ferrous ores was well on the way to being transformed by 1700, but the
technology was new and there were long time-lags in its adoption.
Mackworth felt it worth while to conduct his processes with great

[153] Mott and Greenfield (eds.) 1936, 6–17. See also the earlier attempts to improve the accept-
ability of domestic coal by 'charking' and 'briquettes' (see above, Ch. 12 (i)).
[154] Harris 1988, 38–40; Rees 1968, i. 293–7; ii. 493–7.
[155] Lewis 1965 edn., 24 n; Rees 1968, ii. 496.
[156] Rees 1968, ii. 500–6; Gruffyd thesis 1981, 108.
[157] Trott 1969, 65–6.
[158] R. Jenkins, 'Copper Smelting in England: Revival at the End of the Seventeenth Century',
TNS 24 (1949, for 1944–5), 73–6; Harris 1988, 30–1.
[159] Quoted in Galloway 1898, i. 211.

secrecy to prevent competitors acquiring knowledge of them, and in the Derbyshire Peak District, wood was still the chief fuel as late as 1729 although 'they frequently throw in also some cowke (cinders of pit-coal)'. Tin does not appear to have been smelted with coal on a commercial basis before the opening years of the eighteenth century.[160]

None the less the barriers to the use of coal in the furnace did not preclude it from playing a role in the preparation or dressing of ore prior to smelting. 'Roasting', 'burning' or, as it was later termed, 'calcining', helped to remove impurities, and was carried out either in heaps in the open or in simple kilns. There was little uniformity of practice and a wide variety of fuels were used, including small charcoal, called 'braize', wood, peat, and coal.[161] Presumably this is the reason why coal was sought for the copper works at Keswick in the 1560s, and it may also have been a factor in encouraging joint lead- and coalmining ventures in Derbyshire before it was possible to use coal in smelting. By the close of the seventeenth century we can observe the calcining of iron ore on coal fires in Cheshire, and in Staffordshire the practice had become very common.[162] But perhaps of even greater significance, and certainly antedating its use in calcining, was the use of coal in the forge and the chafery, where the final stages in the manufacture of bar iron were completed.[163] Here the bar was reheated, forged, and drawn out by the power hammer, a process also called 'stringing'. Once again there was no uniformity of practice, and much of the success must have depended upon the qualities of the coal which was used. References to coal sold to forges and slitting-mills abound in colliery accounts, as from Kimberworth (Yorks.) in 1628, Broseley (Shrops) in 1673, and Beaudesert and Cannock (Staffs.) in the 1690s[164] Much earlier still, in 1592 for example, experiments were being conducted in Sir Francis Willoughby's ironworks at Oakamoor in Staffordshire, and at about the same time coal was being successfully employed at Harthey forge in Derbyshire. By the late seventeenth century coal had become the accustomed chafery fuel of the ironmasters of south Wales and Monmouthshire.[165]

Finally, well before the close of the century, coal was being used to produce steel from bars of wrought iron, using the cementation process. Bars of imported Swedish iron of appropriate quality were packed in

[160] Mott and Greenfield (eds.) 1936, 15; Lewis 1964 edn., 25–6.
[161] Schubert 1957, 215–18; Rees 1968, i. 159.
[162] Schubert 1957, 216 n; Plot, *Staffordshire*, 161.
[163] Rees 1968, i. 295–6; Gruffyd thesis 1981, 106.
[164] StRO Anglesey D(W) 603/F/3/1/17; Wanklyn 1982, 5; BoL Selden Supra 116, 23.
[165] Schubert 1957, 226–7; Nef 1932, i. 250.

fireproof chests, sandwiched in charcoal to prevent them from touching each other. The sealed chests were then placed in a furnace of bottle-like dimensions, and then heated for a period of five to nine days. If successful the iron would absorb carbon and become steel, albeit of variable quality and with a blistered surface. By 1700 cementation steelworks were operating in the Forest of Dean, around Stourbridge (Worcs.), Sheffield (Yorks.), London, and on the Derwent and the Tyne in the north-east. Although in aggregate the quantities of coal used were not large, England by the early eighteenth century had become an efficient steel producer and the steel was of considerable importance to a number of industries.[166]

By 1700 coal was the preferred fuel of almost all fuel-consuming industries, and access to coal supplies had already begun to exert a determining influence over industrial location. Yet for all the expansion and innovation, coal at the close of the seventeenth century was still used exclusively for the generation of heat rather than power, and the leading industrial consumer of fuel, iron-smelting, remained chained to costly charcoal. Within a matter of a few years, however, breakthroughs were to occur on both fronts. In 1698 Thomas Savery invented the atmospheric steam engine, in 1712 the first Newcomen steam pump was installed in a coal-mine in Staffordshire, and in 1709 Abraham Darby successfully accomplished the smelting of iron using coke.[167]

[166] Harris 1988, 42–5.
[167] The significance of these events for the coal industry are discussed in Flinn 1984, 239–48.

CHAPTER 13

Sales and Transport

It is the great quantities of Bulksome Commodities that multiplies ships and men.

Thomas Tryon, *England's Grandeur* (1669)

Coal was the most 'bulksome' commodity of all. By the time that Thomas Tryon was writing, the carriage of coal far eclipsed by weight and bulk that of all other commodities. It is probable that more than two million tons each year had to be transported; of which a million tons or so was carried by sea, and a quarter of a million tons by river. The carriage of coal was by far the most important stimulus to the growth of England's merchant marine in the seventeenth century, and it also exerted a prime influence over the size and design of ships. Nor was the necessity of moving coal any less of a stimulus to the improvement of inland water transport and river navigation. As T. S. Willan has written, 'If coal transport were "the dominant factor in the canal movement", it was also the dominant factor in the river movement' in earlier centuries.[1] Relatively little coal was carried long distances overland, but the sheer mass of coal to be carried over short distances from the larger collieries led to the construction of the first railed-ways, for short but habitual journeys from the bankside to the sea or the river.

i. Landsales and transport

Sales at the great majority of landsale collieries almost invariably took place on the pit banks. It was rare for the owners of collieries to engage in distribution. Many customers came to the pits with their own carts, waggons, and pack-horses to collect the coal that they needed, while some carriers acted as coal-merchants, and made a living by distributing coal to distant consumers, or by hawking it in small quantities to the doors of poorer households lacking their own means of transport. The means of transport used to convey coal was naturally dependent upon

[1] Willan 1936, 135–6.

local usage and the state of the roads and tracks, and it is often possible to identify the conveyance from the measures used in the colliery accounts to record sales. To most pits they came with pack-horses and with carts, but to many it was with horses alone. Traffic in remoter parts of the country, most notably Scotland and the south-west and north-west of England, was normally restricted to horses by the poor state of the roads, although yet again the movement of coal encouraged improvements to enable carts to be used where possible. The measurements used for the sale of coal on the bankside were, unremarkably enough, frequently an approximation to the normal carrying capacities of the local means of transport. Only rarely were sales measured in the capacities in which the coal had been raised to the bank. Thus we very frequently encounter sales made by the 'load' and the 'horse-load'. The load carried by a horse is the easiest to determine, around two to two and a half hundredweights, or two bushels, in the two sacks slung across its back. The capacity of carts and waggons was obviously far more variable, although a 'load' seems only rarely to have much exceeded a ton.[2]

With eight or ten horse-loads required to move a single ton of coal a modest trade could seemingly fill the roads, as Celia Fiennes found on the outskirts of Taunton and in the vicinity of Kingswood. Even where carts capable of carrying around a ton were in use a modest colliery producing a few thousand tons generated substantial traffic, while transporting the output of a large colliery necessitated very many thousands of journeys. Landlords naturally guaranteed extensive rights of access to the customers of the collieries which they leased or operated, but rights of way over the land of other landowners had to be negotiated. The carriage of coal on tracks and roads in the vicinity of large collieries could inflict serious damage on the environment and the livelihoods of neighbouring farmers, and was a frequent source of conflict. Sometimes, as with the notorious dispute between the tenants of Whickham manor and the holders of the Grand Lease, local disputes could mushroom into gargantuan legal battles.[3]

Daunting though the costs of transport were, the extent of the market areas served by many inland collieries has often been understated. Carts, horses, and oxen were expensive items but ownership was widespread, especially among rural communities, and they were often not kept fully

[2] See below, App. A.
[3] Detailed in the Palatinate of Durham records in the PRO; see e.g. PRO DuRH 2/14, 2/19, 2/20; 7/18, 7/19.

occupied throughout the year. The larger farmers of Wigston Magna were accustomed to fetch coal in their carts and waggons from the collieries of Swannington and Coleorton, some eighteen miles away, and many provided their services free for the parish coal-stock for the poor. In the same region, the coal from Sparkenhoe and West Goscote hundreds, which fuelled the hearths of Leicester citizens, was brought to the city in carts by husbandmen.[4] Some landlords required their tenants to carry coal for them. The earl of Huntingdon in 1572 covenanted £6 worth of coal a year for seven years to the poor of Leicester, together with free carriage provided by his tenants, and a lease of 1587 specifies that tenants of lands of Wigston Hospital were obliged to go to Coleorton or Newbold each year and take one load of coals to the master's house in Leicester.[5] Nor seemingly were such services invariably ancient or pertaining to coalmining regions. We learn that at the end of the seventeenth century one of the tenants on Sir Basil Dixwell's estate near Folkestone was required to carry two waggon-loads of sea coals annually from Dover to Dixwell's home near Barham, on the way to Canterbury.[6] Such journeys clearly did not have to bear their full economic cost. Nor did the return journeys of carriers who brought merchandise into coalmining regions. Coal was often carried as part of a bilateral trade, by road as well as by water. The magistrates and people of Nottinghamshire and Derbyshire professed themselves to be exceptionally well supplied with food, even in times of dearth, because of the abundance of carriages and barges which came into their counties each summer bearing corn and seeking coal.[7]

Land transport was not a concern for landlocked collieries alone, proprietors of collieries with excellent access to the sea or navigable rivers had to get their coal to water before it could be sold. It was said that the great collieries located on Whickham manor, set conveniently adjacent to the Tyne, required 700 wains to transport their output to water.[8] Such a figure may well have been a pardonable exaggeration, but in the north-east wains carried only a fother, approximately seventeen and a half hundredweights, and there were other coal-carrying vehicles there called 'carts', which were smaller still. Thus, before the construction of waggonways every thousand tons of output necessitated

[4] Hoskins 1965 edn., 192, 206–7; Stocks (ed.), *Leicester*, 168.
[5] Bateson (ed.), *Leicester*, iii. 178; W. G. Hoskins, *The Midland Peasant: The Economic and Social History of a Leicestershire Village* (1957), 128–9.
[6] Chalklin 1965, 63.
[7] PRO SP 16/187 no. 28; *VCH Nottinghamshire*, ii. 283–4, 327.
[8] Lewis 1970, 87.

over 1,100 return journeys from pits to staithes. For some collieries we have detailed records of the leading of coal. For example, between 1682 and 1686 almost 100,000 return journeys were made each year by wains taking coal from Whorlton Moor colliery to staithes on the Tyne at Lementon and Denton. Coal-owners were responsible for the costs of such transport, but they did not invest in its provision. They hired carriers, who provided their own wains and draught animals for an agreed rate per journey. A rare surviving account of coal led from Whitley colliery to Cullercoates in the late 1670s lists the names of the carriers, the number of vehicles they owned, and the number of journeys they made each day.[9]

The organization of cartage on such a scale frequently posed logistical problems which could rival those of the production of coal itself. The Hostmen had claimed as early as 1596 that a major cause of increases in the cost of coal at that time was an increase in freight rates from 4*d.* to 12*d.* a fother, which in turn was due to the rising cost of animals and of the pasture needed to sustain them. They also maintained that in the preceding three or four seasons more coals had been wrought than it was possible to carry to the water because bad weather had made the tracks impassable for much of the year.[10] Sir John Lowther's estate correspondence reveals that in the closing years of the seventeenth century the difficulty in finding sufficient carriage to the sea was a major constraint on the output of his Whitehaven collieries. Lowther was plagued by the shortage and high cost of leaders, and resorted to attempts to compel his tenants to keep more horses after enhanced freight rates and the offer of bounties had failed. Moreover, these troubles occurred after major transport reforms had been introduced by Lowther in the 1680s, which involved building a 'causey' from Wooda-green pit to the harbour, thus enabling carts to carry coal for the first time. Pack-horses, however, remained in service elsewhere in his collieries.[11]

The route to cheaper, speedier, and less troublesome transport lay in the provision of waggonways. But their construction necessitated the coal-owner for the first time becoming involved directly in the transportation of coal, and in making a massive new investment. At the turn of the seventeenth and eighteenth centuries waggonways cost in excess of £200 a mile to build, and the purchase of rolling stock and horses could easily double the outlay. Moreover, waggonways were not at all durable. In 1701–2, for example, the Clavering waggonway from Chop-

[9] DN Syon CX 2*a*(i); 4*b*(i).   [10] BL Harleian 6850(39).   [11] Wood 1988, 11.

well and the waggons used on it cost £1,000 in maintenance alone, excluding the replacement of horses.[12] Yet once the capital had been raised a prudently constructed waggonway could more than pay for itself. In particular, if there were a ready market for coal waggonways facilitated increases in output, for they enabled far more coal to be transported. Waggons could hold on average twice as much coal as wains, they moved it faster, and they could be used in almost all weather conditions. The quantity led by waggons from Gibside colliery in 1701, the very first full year after Montagu had built his waggonway to Dunston staithes, was more than double the annual average of 20,000 tons led by wains and carts over the previous eight years, and in the following year it was over three and a half times as large.[13]

ii. Riversales and transport

In both the sale and transportation of coal, major riverside and seasale collieries had much in common. It was the responsibility of the owners to get their coal to the water, where it was sold to merchants and boatmen. Cutting the costs of the journey from pit bank to river bank was always a high priority, and two of the earliest waggonways were constructed in the opening years of the seventeenth century from Wollaton to the Trent and from Broseley to the Severn. Riverside producers rarely got involved with distribution beyond the river bank. This was left to merchants, some of whom specialized in coal, and to the working proprietors of boats and barges who sometimes dealt in the coal they carried. In the thriving trade on the Severn, the bargemen and boat-owners seem often to have played the same role as the shipmasters of the east coast, buying coal from the colliery owners and selling it at the towns along the river. Its low value and the ease with which it could be sold meant that coal was a safe commodity for relatively small men to deal in, and, what is more, it was sometimes possible for them to buy on credit. When Anthony Bean, a Worcester trowman, died in 1570 he owed £22 to John Brooke, lord of the manor of Madeley and operator of its colliery.[14] In the early sixteenth century the lower reaches of the Severn were supplied with coal from Neath, and Leland reports 'There cometh up *Shippelettes* [for coal] almost onto the town of Neath from the

[12] HRO Cowper D/EPT 4878, fos. 41–3.

[13] DuRO Strathmore D/St/v36.

[14] Wanklyn 1982, 3; Dyer 1973, 62–4. I am grateful to Dr Wanklyn for supplying me with data from the Wolverhampton Polytechnic Portbook Project.

Severn. Boats come to the very bridge of timber that is somewhat lower on the water than the town'.[15]

When traded along English rivers, coal was to a large extent integrated into the prevailing commercial and transport infrastructure of the nation, and was just one of the vast range of commodities which were regularly bought, carried and sold. It formed the whole or a part of the cargoes of these boats of all shapes and sizes that were able to sail on these rivers. On the Severn, which accommodated large vessels, there were barges and frigates with burthens of 20–40 tons and trows which carried up to 80 tons, and the traffic on the lower reaches of the Thames was similarly capacious. In the east river boats usually had a burthen of 20–40 tons. Whenever possible they used their sails, but when the wind failed they were towed by men or horses. Inevitably, the sheer bulk of coal to be transported meant that many boats came to be devoted more or less exclusively to coal, and designed to suit that trade.

iii. Seasale and keels

In many ports ships could be loaded directly from the carts and horses which fetched the coal from the pits; although often loading could only take place at low tide. At Whitehaven before 1675, 'if it be more than half tide, and consequently the ships afloat, the coals are either set down upon the shore, or in the streets of the town, or carried back a quarter of a mile where each coalowner has his winter's provision of coals and there left till the return of the tide'.[16] Accordingly, the construction of piers and improvements to harbours to facilitate continuous loading were often high on the agenda of ambitious coal-owners.

The major collieries of the north-east were not located on the sea, however, but a considerable distance upstream, and this necessitated a further means of transport. The staithes on the Tyne or the Wear were not the end of the journey for the owner of a seasale colliery. His contract of sale with the masters of the sea-going colliers required the coal to be loaded on board ship. But it was possible for very few colliers to dock at any of the staithes to be loaded directly from the bank, even in the later Middle Ages when vessels were smaller. Almost all of the coal that was shipped out of Newcastle and Sunderland had to be ferried from the staithes in river boats called keels. Early records of the north-eastern coal trade, dating from the fourteenth century onwards, contain abundant references to the crucial role played by keels and, despite

[15] Leland, *Itinerary in Wales*, 30.   [16] Wood 1988, 12.

improvements in methods of loading achieved by the use of spouts and drops, they continued to be needed until the coming of the railways and the construction of docks in the mid-nineteenth century.[17]

The Tyne was the first and most vital link in the direct water access which the matchless collieries of the Tyne and Derwent valleys enjoyed with London and a whole host of eastern cities and towns. But it was not without its limitations. Most collieries were located upstream from Newcastle, and the city itself was seven miles from the sea. The Tyne bridge was an impassable barrier to even the smallest of sea-going colliers, and keels had to be built with masts which could be dismantled in order to allow them to pass under its arches. Moreover, the long downstream stretch of water from the bridge to the sea contained many obstacles and hazards, which deterred most vessels from venturing far into the estuary. The passage at the mouth of the Tyne was narrow. In the early eighteenth century it was stated to be no more than forty yards wide at low tide, and it was obstructed by a shelf of sand and rocks which made it especially dangerous to navigate in the persistently prevailing north-east winds.[18] The shallowness of the river in many places and a natural tendency to silt up was gravely worsened by an accumulation of ballast and debris. The extremely heavy traffic on the Tyne inevitably led to a massive dumping of waste, as did the staithes, quays, and salt-pans which lined its banks. Repeated attempts to prohibit the wilful casting of ballast and rubbish into the river, and to limit erosion from wharves, staithes, and quays, involved the Privy Council, Trinity House, the Mayor and Aldermen of Newcastle, the Company of Hostmen and many other pressure groups. But they met with only limited success, and the condition of the river progressively worsened.[19] The prime agent in this deterioration was undoubtedly the coal trade. Many, perhaps most, vessels sailing to Newcastle for coal arrived in ballast, which had to be dumped. Inevitably, some coal fell into the river as it was being loaded into keels or from keels into ships. The sites of staithes had to be moved from time to time as the keels would eventually find it impossible to moor alongside. The waste which accumulated in the bottoms of the keels ought to have been deposited on the designated ballast-shores, but no doubt there was much truth in

---

[17] Flinn 1984, 169–71.

[18] Ellis 1981, 18–20; Moller thesis 1933, 687–9; Flinn 1984, 168–9.

[19] *APC*, 1613-14 276, 579. Ralph Gardiner's *England's Grievance*, 1655, is in large measure a diatribe against the neglect of the Tyne. For attempts by the Hostmen to preserve the river see Dendy (ed.), *Hostmen*, 85, 140.

the claim that the keelmen 'cast it into the river, being more easy and less labour to cast it into the river than upon the top of the ballast shores'.[20]

The consequences of the progressive silting-up of the Tyne were ultimately profound. When combined with a massive growth in the size of colliers, which were deep-keeled vessels, the increased difficulties of navigation drove most ships to anchor further and further down river. Wrecks and groundings were not infrequent, and although masters who knew the river well might, with a high tide and a favourable wind, make their way cautiously some distance up river, there was little incentive to do so since their vessels would still have to be loaded by keels. By the mid-seventeenth century the majority of colliers ventured no further than Shields. It was the coal-owners and fitters who normally supplied the keels, which they owned or hired, and they complained with justification in 1656 of greatly increased costs. The longer journeys into rougher waters in the upper Tyne estuary meant that far more keels were needed, more were sunk, their working lives were shortened, and far more had to be spent on maintenance and repair.[21] The owners' lobby omitted to mention that the opening-up of more collieries further west of Newcastle and Gateshead had also added to the length of many journeys.

The Wear was even less accessible to sea-going ships than the Tyne. It was shallower and loading had to take place at Sunderland, way down river from the major collieries. Even here the harbour was virtually blocked by sand and rubbish, and it could not accommodate colliers of the size which frequented the Tyne. Moreover, Sunderland possessed no pier and vessels venturing there were especially vulnerable to storms. Fortunately, the leading collieries lay conveniently close to the banks of the Wear. At Harraton, it was said, 'the coals may be even from the pit almost put into keels'.[22]

The number of keels on the Tyne soared along with the shipments of coal and the lengthening of journeys to the colliers. It was said that when the masters and skippers of keels formed themselves into a company some time before 1617, they numbered 160.[23] In Charles I's

[20] Gardiner, *England's Grievance*, 42, 43; LCA NCB Swillington Estate, memorandum to Giles Dunstar; Dendy (ed.), *Hostmen*, 89.   [21] Dendy (ed.), *Hostmen*, 75, 89, 107–8.
    [22] J.C., *Compleat Collier*, 52–3; Nef 1932, i. 30–1; for the small size of Sunderland colliers see Table 13.2.
    [23] Gardiner, *England's Grievance*, 43. Nef misinterprets this statement, which clearly refers to the number of masters or skippers of keels rather than the total numbers of keelmen, to arrive at a total of only 40 keels at that time, there being 4 keelmen to a keel.

reign the number of keels was variously estimated at between 200 and 300. In 1707 the keelmen of Newcastle put their number at 1,600, which at four men to a keel would suggest 400 keels, and a document from the next decade counted 338 keels.[24] For the Wear there are not even any contemporary guesses to give guidance, although it was claimed in 1719 that the keelmen of Sunderland were a 'body of 800 men'.[25]

The accounts of the Vanes' Stella operations enables us to approach the matter from a completely different perspective. All the keels they required were hired by the year, and from the numbers hired and the amounts of coal sold and shipped between 1675 and 1683 we find that a keel carried an average of 685 chaldrons a year.[26] The journey from Stella staithes, about one and a half miles west of the Derwent, was somewhat longer than the average, but at these rates just under 300 keels would have been required to carry the average of 200,000 chaldrons shipped each year at this time from the Tyne. In addition a sizeable number of keels were required to supply pancoal to the salt-pans at Shields and elsewhere. Nor must it be forgotten that keels were also used to load other commodities exported from the Tyne, as well as to unload the multitude of commodities which came into the city. Paradoxically, most of the coal consumed in the city came by road, since there were many collieries close by and any advantages of water transport were outweighed by the difficulties of drawing heavy loads up the extremely steep inclines which led down to the river.

It is unlikely that the design of the keel changed much over the centuries. From later seventeenth- and eighteenth-century illustrations and descriptions we know that they were strong, clumsy, oval-shaped, flat-bottomed vessels. The length of a keel would appear to have been no more than thirty feet. They were single masted, with a square sail to utilize any following wind, but for propulsion they were more dependent upon tides and oars. Stukeley reported that 'the manner of rowing their great barges is also very particular and not unworthy of remark, four men manage the whole, three to one great long oar, that push it forward, and one to another such astern, that assists the other motion, but at the same time steers the keel, and corrects the bias the other gives it'.[27] The crew of four appears to have prevailed over the

---

[24] Nef 1932, i. 389; Dendy (ed.), *Hostmen*, 172; Flinn 1984, 168.

[25] Moller thesis 1933, 564.

[26] NuRO Cookson ZCO/IV/47/1–33.

[27] Good descriptions are given by Thomas Pennant (*Tour of Scotland, 1769* (1774), 29), William Stukeley (*Itinerarium Curiosum* (1776), ii. 68), and in a long memorandum presented to Giles Dunstar, general surveyor of customs in the 1670s (LCA NCB Swillington Estate).

latter part of our period, although in 1376 there were five men to each of the keels which carried the king's coal from Winlaton to sea-going vessels in the Tyne estuary.[28]

There are very few indications of the costs of purchasing or hiring keels. In 1618 the earl of Northumberland was advised against purchasing secondhand craft, but his steward was able to obtain only one of the two new vessels he sought. It cost him £60, with a further £5–6 for a sail, oars, anchor, and cable, and £1 to be donated to the poor. In the same year a Sunderland keel was said to be worth £100, but we cannot place the same reliance upon this figure.[29] Charles Montagu in 1696 worked on the assumption that he could hire keels for £10–12 a year in peacetime, although he might have to pay £18 in wartime, and in the 1670s and 1680s hired keels cost the Vanes £11–14 each. In addition the Vanes paid the keelmen a total of 3s. 8d. for each voyage that they made. On average it cost 9–10d. at this time to ferry each chaldron from the Stella staithes to the ships, which was around 9 per cent of the price at which it was sold to the shipmasters.[30]

Very few keelmen owned the keels on which they worked. Employment was highly seasonal, since the vast bulk of all coal was shipped in the spring and summer, and each year a substantial number of 'Scottish men and Borderers' migrated southwards to man the keels, returning northwards as winter approached.[31] The keelmen and their employers provide an interesting chapter in early industrial relations, for both sides were collectively organized. The overwhelming majority of the employers were, of course, members of the Hostmen's Company and, despite being migratory, the keelmen were mentioned among the fellowships and crafts of the city as early as 1516.[32] Inevitably the Hostmen, conscious of the rising costs of ferrying coal from the staithes to the colliers, sought to regulate the wages of the keelmen. This in the main they were able to accomplish because, as the Company records stated, 'they being all coalowners, fitters, or owners of keels etc, are thereby the employers and paymasters of the said keelmen'.[33] But the keelmen displayed considerable solidarity and there were periods of strife. At least three major strikes, termed mutinies by the authorities, occurred between 1654 and 1660, and in September 1676 the keelmen

[28] PRO E. 101/579/18.
[29] DN Syon PV 2(d), QII 126; Nef 1932, i. 388.
[30] NuRO Cookson ZCO/IV/47/1–33; NeUL Montagu, Montagu to Baker, 14/8/97.
[31] Moller thesis 1933, 554–5.
[32] C. Gross, *Gild Merchant* (2 vols., Oxford, 1890), ii. 382.
[33] Green 1865–6, 191; Dendy, (ed.) *Hostmen* 20, 42, 137; DN Syon YII 4.

presented a petition to the Hostmen concerning their rates of pay. Collective action was also taken to further peaceful objectives. In 1630, in order to protect the weak, the keelmen agreed to 'load their keels by turn to make their wages equal', and in 1649 they successfully petitioned the Hostmen 'concerning the providing of a chapel and a minister'. A school, as well as a chapel, was erected, at which the children of keelmen were educated free. In the closing years of the century 'among themselves, without any direction, or influence or compulsion', they agreed to contribute 1 d. per tide for every man, towards a charity which would benefit widows and their children, and aged keelmen. In August 1700 the town of Newcastle granted them a plot of land and the building of a hospital commenced.[34]

The keel was used throughout this period as a means of measuring coal shipped from the Tyne and the Wear. Up to the mid-sixteenth century it was often also used as a means of measuring the quantities produced or sold. Thus, when the bishop of Durham wished to restrict the amount of coal which lessees could extract from Whickham and Gateshead in 1356, he specified a maximum from each mine of one keel-load daily. And when the burgesses of Newcastle purchased coal from the bishop in 1392, and Bishop Fordham made a gift of coal to Richard II, the amounts were computed in keels.[35] But it was as a means of assessing customs duties that the keel enjoyed lasting favour. From 1365 a long succession of local ordinances and acts of Parliament sought to regulate the dimensions of keels, culminating with the famous statutes of 1678 and 1694.[36] The overloading of keels was a simple method of evading customs duty, and in addition when coal was plentiful there was often pressure on coal-owners to grant generous overmeasure, or gift-coal, to the shipmasters. Keels in the sixteenth and seventeenth centuries were frequently built to carry ten or twelve Newcastle sea chaldrons or even more, but there was increasing pressure to conventionalize the keel-load at eight Newcastle sea chaldrons of 53 cwt. each, or just over 21 tons.[37] Although increased surveillance and the perils of taking overloaded keels into the exposed waters of the upper Tyne estuary may well have exerted some restraint on the size of cargoes, the

[34] Dendy (ed.), *Hostmen*, 90, 152; Moller thesis 1933, 555–9; Turner 1915–16; Green 1865–6, 198.

[35] DUDP Church Commission box 204, 244182; Blake 1967, 23–4; *VCH Durham*, ii. 322.

[36] e.g. *CPR 1364-7*, 410, 441; *1381-5*, 499; *1388-92*, 30; *1416-22*, 394; *1452-61*, 608; *Statutes of the Realm*, 9 Hen. V, 1, c. 10; 30 Car. II, c. 8; 6 and 7 Gul. and Mar., c. 10.

[37] Dendy (ed.), *Hostmen*, 109, 121, 135; *CSPD 1655-6*, 280; DN Syon P V 2(c); QII 126; NeUL Montagu, Montagu to Baker 10/7/97; Flinn 1984, 167. The conversion of chaldrons into keel-loads in the Vane accounts is consistently at the ratio of 8:1 (NuRO Cookson ZCO/IV/47/1–33).

pressure on sellers to grant generous overmeasure and gift-coals, along with the perennial desire to evade customs duties, exerted a powerful counterweight. Evasion was sometimes also accomplished by carrying coals for export or coastal shipment in pan-keels, which were larger boats built for carrying customs-free cargoes to the salt-pans.[38] The lax control over Sunderland keels, which was exercised ineffectually by the bishop of Durham, the 'extraordinary measures' used in the port, and the freedom from the 12d. per chaldron duty levied on coastal shipments from Newcastle, were the source of constant complaints and lobbying from Tyneside coal producers and merchants. Eventually, by the statute of 1678, Sunderland and the numerous smaller coal ports of the north-east were brought firmly under royal authority.[39]

iv. Shipping

The carriage of coal far exceeded the shipping requirements of any other commodity, and in terms of tons of cargo and bulk of storage space it had no rivals. In the early stages of the coal boom, in James I's reign, it was described as 'one of the greatest home trades in the Commonwealth of England'.[40] Yet on any list of commodities valued by weight, coal rested firmly at the bottom. Sir William Monson wrote in the 1630s of fish, 'there is no commodity in the world of so great bulk and small value'. He misled his readers, as his example of how 'a mean merchant may freight his ship of 250 tons with fish that will not cost above £1,600' amply demonstrates. For an equivalent bulk of coal would have cost no more than a twentieth of that sum.[41] When the Inspectors-General of customs in 1754 drew up a list of commodities according to their value by weight, red herrings at £11 per ton and pilchards at £7 per ton came very close to the bottom, but they were still very many times more valuable than coal, which was loosely valued at 'less than £1 per ton'. Fish and coal were the prime stimuli to the development of English shipping in the later sixteenth and seventeenth centuries, but the former came a poor second. The incidental expenses of dealing with valuable cargoes

[38] In addition to the preambles of the statutes themselves see, in particular, Dendy (ed.), *Hostmen*, 57, 93–4, 99, 114, 116–17, 128, 136, 137, 138.

[39] Ibid. 111, 118, 120, 123; LCA NCB Swillington Estate, memorandum to Giles Dunbar; PRO 30/24/7/594, 597.

[40] Willan 1938, 55.

[41] M. Oppenheim (ed.), *The Naval Works of Sir William Monson*, Navy Records Society (1913), v. 235. Coal purchased by shipmasters in Newcastle in the 1630s seems rarely to have cost more than 5s. a ton.

were small in relation to the overall costs of a voyage, and affected freight rates hardly at all. 'What mattered to the shipowners was weight and volume, not value. What created the demand for shipping was mass, not price.'[42]

'A meagre coastal traffic, a fishery of moderate scale, a trickle of carrying traffic with the Low Countries, Spain, Portugal, France and the Baltic; this was the maritime basis which Elizabeth I inherited.' Despite the era of modest expansion which preceded her accession, in 1558 the total of all English-owned merchant shipping probably did not exceed 50,000 tons.[43] The transformation which ensued thereafter is quantified in Table 13.1, which is based upon the estimates made by L. A. Harper.

Table 13.1 *The distribution of English shipping by tonnage, 1582-1702*

Period	Total tonnage	Coal trade	% of whole	Other coastal trade	Fisheries	Foreign trade
1582	68,433	7,618	11.1	10,607	17,316	32,892
1609–15	101,566	28,223	27.8	15,743	27,721	29,897
1660	161,619	70,899	43.9	24,051	23,489	42,180
1702	267,444	78,212	29.2	42,454	24,920	122,858

Source: L. A. Harper, *The English Navigation Laws: A Seventeenth-Century Experiment in Social Engineering* (New York, 1939), 339.

Of course, Harper's figures are necessarily based upon conjectures which leave considerable room for error, and they should be taken as no more than broad suggestions of scale and direction.[44] But such is the contribution of the carrying of coal delineated there, it could bear much pruning. By the first decade of the seventeenth century coal consumed more than a quarter of the total tonnage of England's mercantile marine,

[42] Davis 1962, 32–6, 176–7. As Table 13.1 shows, the tonnage devoted to fishing fell far behind that devoted to the coal trade in the course of the 17th cent. Moreover, the bulk of the fishing tonnage was devoted to catching fish not simply to transporting it.

[43] For the pre-Elizabethan expansion see Scammell 1961 and Burwash 1947. For English shipping at the accession of Elizabeth see Davis 1962, 1–3.

[44] Harper's statistics have been criticized and, in part, revised by Davis (1962, 395–406). Harper's estimates of the tonnage of collier fleets may, however, be closer to the mark than Davis's, since Davis may well have overstated the number of east coast voyages which an average collier made each year (Michell thesis 1978, table 4.2 and n.).

and in bulk was equalled only by the whole of England's foreign trade. By 1660 the tonnage devoted to coal had risen to more than 40 per cent of the whole, and was approaching three times the size of all other coastal shipping. The trade boom of the later seventeenth century saw massive expansions of overseas and coastal shipping devoted to commodities other than coal, but even so the collier fleets by 1702 comprised almost 30 per cent of the whole.

The broad trend of these remarkable figures is amply supported by well-informed contemporaries who delighted in the coal trade as 'the special nursery and school of seamen', 'the principal nursery of English seamen', and 'the true parent and support of our Navigation'. As early as 1575, in the first stages of the coal boom, the importance of planning the coal trade so as to give maximum employment to English ships was recognized, and by the opening of the seventeenth century colliers were appreciated as ideal men-of-war. It was calculated in the 1660s that, out of a total of 90,000 English seamen, 20,000 were employed in the coal trade. Special pleading by the coal lobby to resist taxation, impressment, and other forms of state interference certainly coloured many claims, but it was a Royal Proclamation which in 1624 declared that 'the sea-coal trade of Newcastle-upon-Tyne, Sunderland and Blyth is worthy of special encouragement'.[45]

Contemporaries also made estimates of the numbers of vessels engaging in the coal trade. In 1615 a correspondent in the State Papers marvelled at 'what an infinite number of ships and people are now set on work in England by coals, only more than by all other kinds of merchandise, by good report to the number of 400 sail of English ships'. This figure encompassed the whole English coal trade, but in 1624 the navy commissioners estimated that there were 300 sail employed in the Newcastle trade alone. By the end of the seventeenth century the number of ships engaged in the east coast coal trade was put as high as 1,400, but many of these must have made only occasional voyages.[46] We are less well informed about other branches, but according to Sir Walter Harris, who made use of estimates given to the king and council, there were in 1685 a further 180 ships on the west coast engaged in the coal trade with Ireland.[47] To which we must add, of course, those ships engaged in the coasting trade in the west, and Scottish vessels.

[45] Moller thesis 1933, 317, 681–2; Davis 1962, 114–15; BoL Rawlinson a.185.
[46] State Papers Domestic, Charles I, xiv. 9 (quoted by Moller thesis 1933, 321); CSPD 1625-6, 221; Willan 1938, 14.
[47] Harris, Remarks, 19–20.

But it was not merely that the numbers of ships engaging in the coal trade multiplied, their capacities soared, and a core of specialist colliers evolved. Once again the best information relates to the premier trade from Northumberland and Durham. Data from the Middle Ages, sadly of necessity drawn solely from the export trades, reveals that the average coal shipment from Tyneside was of the order of 40–50 medieval chaldrons, or some 50–60 tons.[48] There seems to have been surprisingly little change in the size of shipments before the last quarter of the sixteenth century. As can be seen from Table 13.2, the median shipment both coastwise and overseas hovered between 55 and 65 tons for 200 years. Such averages can be distorted by the presence of a few extremely large ships, or large numbers of small shipments in which coal was only a part of the cargo or even carried primarily as ballast, but this was not the case. Though there were some shipments of over 100 tons in the later fourteenth century, and a handful of over 150 tons, they were a tiny minority of the total. In the Newcastle Chamberlains' Account of 1508–9, covering both coastal and overseas shipments, there was only one instance where over 50 Newcastle chaldrons, around 133 tons, was carried, and only 8 per cent of shipments were of 80 tons or more. Such figures are very much in keeping with what we know of east coast

Table 13.2 *Average cargoes of colliers, 1377-1710*

Period	Leaving Newcastle		Leaving Sunderland	
	Chaldrons	Tons	Chaldrons	Tons
1377–91	(45)	56	—	—
1508–9	21.0	56	—	—
1574–5	21.3	56	—	—
1611–12	—	—	14.6	39
1682–3	65.7	174	24.3	64
1690–1	61.5	163	22.0	58
1702–3	70.4	187	24.5	65
1709–10	80.1	212	29.8	79

Note: For the size of medieval chaldrons see App. B below. All other chaldrons are converted at 53 cwt. each.

Sources: Blake 1967, 17–20; TWRO 543/212, 543/16; Moller thesis 1933, 349, 725–8, 733–6.

[48] Blake 1967, 16–21; Blake thesis 1962, 61–78; Scammell 1961, 333.

shipping as a whole. In 1513 only 36 out of a total of 167 craft at Yarmouth were over 50 tons burthen, and a census of 1544 reveals that 86 per cent of all east coast vessels were of less than 100 tons burthen.

Table 13.2 reveals the striking increase which took place in the size of cargoes from the last quarter of the sixteenth century. Shipments to London, which came overwhelmingly from Tyneside, were the largest of all. As early as 1615 the Lord Mayor reported that colliers were forced to tie up no higher up the river than Tower Wharf because 'they had latterly been built of greater burden than before, and that on account of the shallowness of the water they could not well float at any other place'.[49] According to Nef's calculations based upon imports into London, which may be slight understatements, the average size of a cargo unloaded in the Thames increased from 54 tons in 1592 to 73 tons in 1606, 83 tons in 1615, 139 tons in 1638, and 248 tons in 1701.[50] Sunderland's harbour, and the shallowness of the Wear, would not provide access to large vessels, and throughout the seventeenth century vessels from Sunderland carried on average only a third as much coal as those frequenting the Tyne. As a consequence, Sunderland's ships made a speciality of trading with the smaller harbours and havens of the east coast.[51]

Coal was shipped from Tyneside from at least the beginning of the thirteenth century, but for centuries after very few of the craft which carried it specialized in its trade. Prior to the mid-sixteenth century the demand for coal in the south was insufficient to support a network of coal-dealers and coal-shippers. Instead, coal was usually carried and supplied in an *ad hoc* manner, by shipmasters who having loaded more valuable consignments sought to fill their holds, or by those who were specifically retained by large-scale consumers to transport the purchases they had made in the north. Many of these occasional participants were foreign, and in 1552 Thomas Barnabe wrote that 'you shall see in peace time three or four score ships of Normans' and Bretons' at once, as soon as their fishing is done' resorting to the north-east for coal.[52]

Statistics of the frequency with which particular crafts or merchants participated in the coal trade are laborious to gather, but some suggestive data have been collected from Yarmouth, one of the leading collier ports. Dr Michell's researches have found that, before the trade took off in the last quarter of the sixteenth century, the majority of vessels repairing to Newcastle for coal made no more than a single trip each

[49] Smith 1961, 21.   [50] Nef 1932, i. 390.   [51] See below, Ch. 14(ii).
[52] Tawney and Power (eds.), *Tudor Economic Documents*, ii. 99–100.

year, and there was not a single Yarmouth vessel which devoted itself exclusively to coal.[53] Analysis of the Newcastle Chamberlains' Accounts for 1508–11 reveals that very few of the coal-carrying ships made more than a handful of trips in a year.[54] Before the seventeenth century the coal trade was dominated by the utilization of seasonally or intermittently underemployed shipping, and right up to the eighteenth century casual and part-time participation in the trade by a motley assortment of fishing-smacks, ketches, hoys, doggers, and shallops remained of considerable importance. As late as Charles I's reign, it was observed that 'the ships of Yarmouth and other fishers' towns, as also the ships which export cloths for the east part, do only fetch coals to keep their company together until the times of their several employment'.[55]

Yet there is also clear evidence, especially marked in London, that in the latter part of the seventeenth century an increasing share of the ever expanding traffic was borne in true colliers of great size. As the century progressed vessels of 200, 300, and even 400 tons became ever more common on Tyneside. Typical merchantmen were not well suited to the carrying of so 'gross [a] commodity' as coal, they were too narrow and shallow. Colliers were wide, deep ships, of great strength, designed to carry the maximum cargo with the minimum crew.[56] Illustrations in Gray's *Chorographia* (1649) and Hollar's *View of the Tyne* (1673), portray three-masted, square-rigged, deep craft of considerable bulk. Purpose-built colliers must have borne some resemblance to Dutch fly-boats, which were also appropriate for carrying 'cheap and gross goods'. Between 1,000 and 1,700 Dutch vessels are thought to have been taken as prizes in the First Dutch War (1652–4) and over 500 in each of the Second and Third Dutch Wars of 1664–7 and 1672–4. A great many of these craft went straight into service in the coal trade.[57]

An important chapter in the rise of the English shipping industry was the ousting of foreign-owned vessels from the coal trade, but it was a long process. Up to the close of the sixteenth century foreign vessels made a significant contribution to the coasting trade, and it was not until the later seventeenth century that English ships began to dominate the export trade. In 1594 two out of three ships clearing Newcastle for foreign ports were alien, and in 1615 Kayll complained that 'hither even to the mine's mouth come all our neighbour country nations with their

[53] Michell thesis 1978, 135–8.
[54] Fraser (ed.), *Accounts of Chamberlains*, pp. xix–xx.
[55] State Papers Domestic, Charles I, cxxxiii. 21 (quoted by Moller thesis 1933, 322).
[56] Nef 1932, i. 390; Willan 1938, 11–12.   [57] Davis 1962, 51.

ships, continually employing their own shipping and mariners'. The greater efficiency of Dutch ships in particular ensured continuing supremacy in the export of coal up to the Civil War, but thereafter the imposition of heavy discriminatory duties on exports carried in foreign bottoms, and dramatic improvements in native bulk shipping, progressively eased this branch of the trade also firmly into English hands.[58]

The momentous developments in east coast shipping found echoes in the west, albeit in miniature. Evidence from North and South Wales suggests that cargoes of coal sent coastwise or overseas rarely exceeded 10 tons before the seventeenth century. By the 1620s and 1630s the trade from Mostyn and Whitehaven was conducted in barks, which on the whole were single-masted open boats able to carry no more than 20–30 tons; Christopher Lowther found their capacity wholly inadequate, and longed for 'Flemish bottoms'.[59] In the last quarter of the century as the output of the Whitehaven and Workington collieries multiplied so the ships carrying their coal to Dublin increased in number and size. In 1685 Sir Walter Harris counted sixty ships continuously engaged in the coal trade with Ireland, with capacities ranging from 70 tons to 150 tons. He reckoned the average collier had a burthen of 80 tons, whereas not long before there had been some vessels making the crossing which had carried no more than 10 tons. Some broad confirmation of his computations is provided by the Whitehaven port books which eight years later reveal forty-six specialist colliers, with an average capacity of 60 tons.[60] It was also in the 1680s that Flintshire received its first true colliers, and the average size of shipments bound for Ireland from Chester reached 41 tons in 1682–3 and 52 tons in 1700. Coastal vessels remained small, however, and their average cargo of coal when leaving Chester did not exceed 20 tons in the late seventeenth century.[61]

The emergence of specialist colliers of ample capacity had a favourable impact on freight costs, but, as Table 13.3 demonstrates, the highly seasonal pattern of sailings from the north-east was scarcely affected. Sailing the coastal waters of the North Sea, especially in winter, was no safer mile for mile than many an ocean voyage, and coal was a treacherous cargo, being liable to shift in heavy seas.[62] 'I have heard good sailors say', the anonymous author of the *Compleat Collier* reports, 'they

---

[58] Williams thesis 1952, 164; Nef 1932, i. 172; ii. 23–5; Welford 1884–7, ii. 321; Scammell 1961, 337.

[59] Evans thesis 1928, 64; Gruffyd thesis 1981, 146–7; Hainsworth (ed.), Sir Christopher Lowther, 7.   [60] Harris, *Remarks*, 19–20; Makey thesis 1952, 123.

[61] Gruffyd thesis 1981, 146–8, 186.   [62] See in particular Willan 1938, 21–33.

Table 13.3 *Seasonal patterns of east coast sailings and landings*

Month	Newcastle shipments[a]				Sunderland shipments[a]	London imports[a]	
	1508–11	1612	1634	1655	1676–9	1592	1701
January	0.9	3.0	1.0	0.1	0.3	1.5	1.7
February	4.2	4.2	3.2	3.9	3.2	1.5	1.1
March	11.2	7.2	6.0	10.9	6.2	4.4	3.5
April	9.0	10.9	9.1	8.2	8.6	7.5	7.2
May	12.6	11.1	8.7	11.7	16.1	12.8	14.6
June	18.2	2.0	16.6	14.5	17.8	18.1	15.6
July	22.8	18.8	14.8	14.3	22.2	18.0	12.2
August	11.0	13.4	16.7	13.6	14.1	13.7	16.9
September	4.0	12.5	10.8	10.9	8.2	6.4	15.3
October	3.4	9.4	9.2	10.0	2.3	8.4	6.2
November	1.3	5.2	2.5	1.4	1.0	4.9	5.1
December	1.4	2.2	1.3	0.5	0.4	2.7	1.3

Note:
[a] Given as a percentage of annual shipments.
Sources: TWRO 543/12; Nef 1932, ii. 389.

had rather run the hazard of an East India voyage, than be obliged to sail all the winter between London and Newcastle.'[63] Heavily laden, few colliers could feel secure in high winds. Moreover, although the east coast had many ports, few, it seemed to contemporaries, offered adequate shelter in storms. Whitby, Scarborough, Bridlington, and Hull were good havens, but according to Thoresby there were none between Hull and Yarmouth.[64] Fear of the North Sea led to a virtual cessation of sailings in December and January, and a mere trickle in November and February. Colliers were not insured before the eighteenth century, perhaps because of the low value of the cargo, and owners stood to lose everything if their ship sank or was 'lost upon the shallows or the shore by the violence of the easterly winds ... and left to the mercy of the winds and seas'.[65] Coal prices were consistently higher in winter, and good profits could be made by those shipmasters who were not 'discouraged to adventure ... in the dead of winter'.[66] Yet the vast majority were discouraged, and it was not until the nineteenth century that year-round sailings became accepted practice. Such large-scale winter sailings as did take place during this period were primarily the result of war. During the Third Dutch War a fleet of 400 coal ships left Newcastle on 12 December 1673, and seems to have come to no great harm, but the previous January a similarly delayed fleet had been 'lamentably shattered' by violent tempests. Nor were destructive storms restricted to winter. In the spring of 1667 a storm sank more than thirty colliers, and another the following October was said to have caused the loss of no less than 200. There were good years as well as bad, but the threat of catastrophe was sufficient for most masters and owners to keep considerations of profit secondary to those of safety.[67]

The seventeenth was a war-torn century, and in its latter stages belligerence became an almost perpetual blight on trade in the North Sea, making voyages more dangerous and sailings even less predictable. Wars created urgent demands for ships and seamen, and colliers and their crews presented themselves as an unrivalled source of supply. Despite frequent exemptions granted because of the indispensability of coal, the threat of impressment of both ships and men did considerable harm in the form of reduced sailings and greatly enhanced costs. The wages of seamen rose to unprecedented heights 'not attributable to want of men

---

[63] *Compleat Collier*, 47.   [64] Willan 1938, 23.
[65] Moller thesis 1933, 576; *The Mischief of the Five Shillings Tax upon Coal*.
[66] State Papers Domestic 1638, Charles I, cccciv. 58 (quoted by Moller thesis 1933, 708).
[67] Willan 1938, 23-5.

...but... the fear the men are in of being prest when they come into the river'.[68] The express aims of the government in times of war, namely the provision of adequate supplies of coal to consumers and adequate supplies of ships and crew to the navy, were incompatible, and its actions while under duress were frequently blatantly contradictory. Seamen working on colliers were pressed into service at the same time as proclamations were being issued granting them specific exemption because of the high price of coal, and colliers were forbidden to sail without protection while promised convoys, because of their cost, were often long delayed or failed to materialize. Moreover, the attitude of masters and crew alike to convoys was frequently ambivalent. Sailing in convoy provided protection but mass sailings could cause prices to fall by glutting the market, and the king's navy brought the press-gangs into even greater proximity to the collier crews.

v. The economics of shipping

The prime motivation behind the increasing size of coal ships was economies of scale, especially through reduced manning levels. For the numbers of crew did not increase pro rata with tonnage. Such economies applied, of course, to all types of craft in all trades, and yet simultaneous changes in the design of colliers ensured that particularly dramatic improvements in labour productivity were achieved in the coal trade. The scale of potential savings is clearly revealed in the suggested crew quotas for colliers issued by the Commons in 1667: four seamen to a ship of 100 tons, six to a ship of 200 tons, and eight to one of 300 tons. Almost inevitably figures are hard to come by for the early years of the coal trade, but a list of thirteen ships and their crews owned by Newcastle merchants in 1587 provides welcome guidance. Together these vessels had a total burthen of 1,105 tons and a total crew of 115, which averages out at one seaman to every 9.6 tons of capacity. The scale of productivity increases over the next hundred years is indicated by later seventeenth-century wartime warrants, which permitted colliers to have one seaman to every 25 tons of shipping. That such manning levels were not unrealistically low is confirmed by both Houghton and the masters of Trinity House in London in 1703, who reckoned that in the coal trade there was an average of one seaman to every 28 tons.[69] But

[68] Ibid. 25–33; Davis 1962, 315–37.

[69] *HCJ* viii. 676; Welford 1884–7, iii. 45; Nef 1932, i. 391 n.; Willan 1938, 16–17; Flinn 1984, 180; Houghton, *Collection for the Improvement*, ii. 58; BL Sloane 2902(9), fo. 52.

such manning ratios were exceptionally low in comparison with other trades, and reflected the emphasis placed on carrying a bulky commodity as cheaply rather than as swiftly as possible. Speed through the water required a large sail area, and sail was the main determinant of the size of a crew.[70]

The reduction in manning levels was made all the more desirable by the rapid inflation of seamen's wages. Records of the High Court of Admiralty show that the peacetime wages of seamen rose in the course of the seventeenth century from 17–18 s. a month to 24–25 s. But it was the spiralling of wages in wartime which posed the greatest threat to the price of coal. During the First Dutch War, 1652–4 merchant seamen earned 30–38 s. a month, and during the Second and Third Dutch Wars, 1664–7 and 1672–4, their rates rose to 35–38 s. and 35–40 s. respectively. In the war years of the 1690s monthly rates as high as 55 s. are found. The length of a voyage from Newcastle to London was extremely variable, but it could be expected to average out at a month or a little less.[71]

Historians and contemporaries alike have expended much energy attempting to calculate the costs of carrying coals from Tyneside and Wearside to London and other east coast ports. But in many respects this has been a fruitless quest, not simply because of the wide variations produced by weather and hostilities, and the complexities of tolls and duties, but because the shippers were generally not carriers being paid a rate for the journey but merchants who bought and sold as well as transported. It is not only extremely difficult but artificial to attempt to isolate freight costs from the trading accounts of a voyage. Shipmasters and owners tried to run efficient ships, but their profits were also critically dependent upon the markets for coal ruling in the north-east where they purchased coal and the east coast ports where they sold it. The profitability for shipowners of the east coast coal trade is examined below, but attention can be drawn here to a number of contemporary statements and estimates of shipping costs. There are two examples of the costs paid for shipping large quantities of coal purchased by Londoners in Newcastle in the later fourteenth century. In 1364 the shipmasters were paid £103. 4 s. for carrying 562 chaldrons by London measure from Newcastle to London, amounting to 3.67 s. per chaldron, and in 1377 £320 was allowed for transporting 1,600 chaldrons from Tyneside to London, which was exactly 4 s. per chaldron.[72] In 1601

---

[70] Davis 1962, 49–50, 58–62.
[71] Ibid. 133–58; Willan 1938, 17–20, 212–16.
[72] PRO E. 101/579/18; Blake 1976, 12.

during a fuel famine in London the Lord Mayor reported to the Privy Council that it cost the shipmasters 13s. to freight a Newcastle chaldron to London, perhaps 6s. 6d. to 7s. for a London chaldron, though in similar circumstances in 1606 the Attorney-General plumped for a somewhat lower figure.[73] Five reassuringly close estimates of shipping costs were made between 1628 and 1701, which range between 10s. for a Newcastle chaldron and 6s. 6d. for a London chaldron.[74] Making allowance for inflation, and using a conversion ratio of just under two London chaldrons to a Newcastle chaldron, it would appear that the costs of transport between Newcastle and London fell appreciably in the seventeenth century, despite sharply rising wages for seamen and the increased price of victuals. Indeed, the available data suggest that, in broad terms, shipping costs in the east coast trade almost halved between the later fourteenth century and the 1600s, and fell by a third in the course of the seventeenth century.

Similar economies of scale deriving from reductions in manning during the seventeenth century must be presumed to have taken place in the trade with Ireland from Whitehaven. Christopher Lowther's investigations of the profitability of the trade in the 1630s were not encouraging. The coal was carried in what he contemptuously dismissed as 'country barks [which] are so little they carry nothing at a time, and yet will have dear by reason they are commonly only about 7 or 8 men to one of 30 tons, which eateth up the profit'. The consumption of profits by costs was confirmed when he drew up the detailed balance sheet of a specimen voyage in 1635. For although the 30 tons which cost £3. 10s. in Whitehaven could be sold for £16 in Dublin, when the expenses of the five-week voyage were taken into account, including over £7 in victuals and wages for the six seamen, there was less than £3. 6s. left for 'wear and tear and profit a voyage.'[75]

A final simple calculation can be made of the capital invested in the provision of shipping for the east coast trade. For this it is best to proceed from the amounts of coal that were shipped, and the cost of building the ships which carried it. During the last quarter of the seventeenth century an average of just under 700,000 tons were shipped coastwise and overseas each year, and the cost of building large colliers appears to have been around £4–5 for each ton of capacity.[76] If we allow

[73] Nef 1932, ii. 89–90.
[74] BL Stowe 326, fos. 29–32; Nef 1932, ii. 90–1.
[75] Hainsworth (ed.), *Sir Christopher Lowther*, 7, 151–3.
[76] Willan 1938, 36, 39; Nef 1932, i. 395; Hausman 1981, 241.

a generous ten voyages per vessel per year, then it would have cost around £300,000 to build the ships which carried this coal. Significantly, this is far greater than the amount of fixed capital which was invested in the collieries on Tyneside and Wearside which produced it.[77]

[77] See above, Ch. 10(ii).

CHAPTER 14

Measuring the Coal Trade

It would be interesting to but few to follow minutely, at so distant
a period, the various fluctuations of the Coal Trade.

W. Fordyce, *A History of Coal, Coke and Coal Fields*. (1860), 105.

i. Coal shipments from north-eastern ports

There is a certain irony in the fact that the presentation and interpretation of statistics of the production and trade of coal should have
generated so much more heat than light. Few topics in this period have
remained as controversial for so long, or involved such fundamental dis-
agreements over such mundane data, as the growth of the east coast
trade. Yet measuring the trade is frequently considered indispensable,
and virtually all historians who survey Britain's economic performance
in the early modern period and chart the development of its trade and
industry, are forced to use the results of Nef's discredited attempts at
quantification while simultaneously casting doubt upon their validity.[1]

It would be tiresome to review in detail the historiography of the
debate surrounding the growth of the north-east trade and of imports
into London, but it might be valuable at the outset to note a few of the
reasons why acceptable conclusions have proved so elusive. The most
fundamental source of contention would seem to be the necessity of
producing rates of growth in trades which accelerated at a truly
explosive pace in the first stages of their prolonged booms. There has
also been confusion about the dimensions of the weights and measures
which were used, about how they changed over time, and about which
measures were used when coal was landed in provincial ports. Since
relatively few reliable customs accounts were thought to have survived
from the early years of either the north-east coasting trade or of the

---

[1] See e.g. J. Chartres, *Internal Trade in England, 1500-1700* (1977), 31–3; Clay 1984, ii. 47–8; D.
M. Palliser, *The Age of Elizabeth: England under the later Tudors, 1547-1603* (1983), 274; Wilson 1984
edn., 80. The most stringent criticisms of Nef's 'statistics' are contained in D. C. Coleman, *The
Economy of England, 1450-1750* (Oxford, 1977), 84–5; Coleman 1975, 46–8, 58; and Coleman 1977,
343–5.

London import trade, historians have been forced to choose between constructing a statistical baseline from manifestly inadequate early data or from manifestly inappropriate later data. Neither alternative has proved satisfactory. Yet the coal trade is potentially among the very best documented of all sectors of the early modern economy, and it is to be hoped that the substantial new evidence presented below will enable the charting of the increasing scale of shipments to be less open to dispute.

The following tables contain twice as many observations as those presented by Nef in 1932. We now have complete shipping data, namely coasting and overseas shipments from all north-eastern ports, for a total of 41 years, rather than the 21 years we had previously. There are now 58 years of complete Newcastle shipments in place of 29 previously, and 23 years of complete Sunderland shipments in place of just 11. Moreover, between 1564 and 1700 we now have 80 years of data containing at the very least the preponderant element in the trade, namely coastwise shipments from Newcastle, which rarely comprised less than two-thirds of the total shipments. But perhaps of even greater significance in the light of past contention, there are now 11 years of total north-eastern shipments and a further year of Newcastle coastal shipments prior to the commencement of a more continuous record in 1591–2, and it has proved possible to compile no less than 8 full years of shipments between 1564 and 1575. Thus a firm base now exists from which to calculate the scale of the ensuing boom. Moreover, thanks to the recently discovered clutch of early sixteenth-century Newcastle Borough Chamberlains' accounts, we now have clear evidence of the scale of the coal trade at the close of the Middle Ages.[2]

The fatal flaw in Nef's statistical presentation is not that the figures he amassed were simply too few, but that the edifice he erected had insecure foundations. Nef could find only five years of shipments from Newcastle prior to 1591–2, namely coal sent coastwise in 1549–50 and 1565–6, and both coastwise and overseas in 1561–2, 1563–4, and 1574–5. What is more this base is even flimsier than appears at first sight, for the shipments of 1561–2 and 1563–4 are drawn from accounts which have yawning gaps, while that of 1565–6 runs only from 1 August to 31 January. For the import of coal into London Nef had a base of only two records before 1591–2, one of which covers little more than six months of shipments. It is scarcely surprising that his attempts to calculate rates of growth upon these foundations, *a fortiori* upon the shipments of a

---

[2] These accounts were discovered in 1980, and antedate the earliest previously known accounts by more than 50 years.

single year, have been dismissed as 'statistically meaningless'. Yet it has also to be admitted that attempts by his critics to re-calculate the rates of growth of the north-eastern and London coal trades upon a broader sample of years have not proved much more acceptable. It cannot be denied that taking four- or five-year averages from the well-documented 1590s will have the effect of producing an increase in Newcastle's coastal exports '*not* of nineteen-fold but of rather over three-fold'.[3] But Nef was not attempting to contrast the level of shipments in the 1590s with those in the 1690s, he was contrasting the level of shipments in the 1560s with those in the late seventeenth century. Choosing a baseline which significantly post-dates the commencement of rapid growth, or aggregating shipments scattered over a number of decades during an extended period of explosive expansion, will have the effect of depressing the rates of growth just as surely as Nef's method tended to inflate them.

The size of the Newcastle sea chaldron is a crucial but strangely neglected element in the measurement of the scale and rate of increase in coal shipments from the north-east. Nef believed that there was a substantial and progressive increase in the size of the chaldron over the course of the sixteenth and seventeenth centuries, and his assumptions have found widespread acceptance, even among his critics. But they are disputed here. A full discussion of these matters is contained in Appendix A below, which is devoted to weights and measures. In the following tables, as throughout this book, all post-medieval Newcastle chaldrons have been converted into tons at the rate of 53 cwt. each.

The bulk of the new sixteenth-century figures have been extracted from the Newcastle Borough Chamberlains' accounts, a source almost completely neglected by Nef and subsequent historians of the coal trade. There is no satisfactory explanation of why Nef failed to use this source, but there are clues. In the course of drawing together his quantitative sources, Nef found that the royal customs account covering the six months of coasting trade from 1 February to 31 July 1562 contained entries of 13,033 chaldrons, which was a larger figure than the 11,927 chaldrons recorded in the Chamberlains' account which purported to record overseas as well as coastal shipments for the whole year from Michaelmas 1561 to Michaelmas 1562. He concluded that 'obviously much coal must have escaped entry in the Newcastle account book for this year', and the experience appears to have convinced him that the Chamberlains' accounts as a whole were grossly defective and accordingly he made no use of them.[4] In so doing he was under a serious

---

[3] Coleman 1975, 46–7.   [4] Nef 1932, ii, table D(1) (*a*), n. 3 (opp. 380).

misapprehension, for close inspection of the book of Chamberlains' accounts covering the period 1561–5 reveals that it is in a state of disarray, with a large number of folios missing and many out of order. A careful reconstruction of the entries for 1561–2 discloses that it contains no record of shipments made during the whole of the period from December to April, and that substantial portions of those made during November, May, July, August, and September are also missing. Thus Nef was comparing a partial royal customs account with a partial Chamberlains' account. Comparisons of complete customs accounts and complete Chamberlains' accounts demonstrate, by contrast, the reliability of the latter. For example, in 1591–2 and 1592–3 the coal entered in the royal customs accounts exceeded that in the Chamberlains' accounts by only 3.8 per cent and 4.9 per cent respectively, while in 1593–4 the Chamberlains' account recorded the shipment of 2.6 per cent more coal than the equivalent customs account.

Table 14.1 *Coal shipped from Newcastle, 1505–1700*

Sources and Methods: The intention has been to record only firm and consistent data, and all potential sources have been carefully vetted, and many rejected. The overwhelming majority of figures have been taken directly from surviving accounts of royal customs levied at the ports of embarkation. In addition, from time to time when royal customs accounts have not survived, use has been made of statistics which appear to have been abstracted by contempories from the same accounts. For example, Taylor in 1858 printed in full a series of contemporary manuscripts signed by the customs officials. The figures given in the Cranfield MSS also give every sign of having been abstracted from the customs accounts. The provenances of the Trinity House data has been described by Nef (1932, ii, app. D(i)(a), n. 7) and Hall (thesis 1933, 109). They seem to have been derived from the same sources as Taylor's; and the shipments given by both sources for all ports and categories for the overlapping year of 1621–2 are identical. Nef misdates the accounts, and his doubts on their accuracy derive from making false comparisons with supposedly contemporaneous royal customs accounts. Hall dated the Trinity House accounts correctly, but, fortuitously likewise cast doubt on their accuracy as a result of comparing the figures for 1624–5 with those from the royal customs account for 1626–7, which she incorrectly took to be for 1624–5. The data in the Rawlinson MSS are similarly authenticated; surrounded by contemporary material relating to the coal trade, the figures are described as accounts of coal exported from Newcastle and Sunderland by 'coast coquett' and overseas. The Leeds City Archives figures are taken from the accounts drawn up by the farmers of the first years of collecion of a new tax of 4s. per chaldron on all exports. The data from 1660 to the end of our period have been reproduced many times, from the local historian Hugh Hornsby (d. 1798) onwards, albeit with discrepancies. Copies of the figures survive in the archives of the duke of Northumberland (printed in Dendy (ed.), Hostmen, 260–1), the Wigan Record Office (WiRO D/DZ A/13/35), and the North of England Insitute of Mining and Mechanical Engineers (NEI Buddle, 14. 205–7). The original source of the figures may well have been the MS in the Cotesworth collection, which is headed 'An account of all coals exported for the coast 1661–1710, from the Custom-house books coastwise' (GPL Cotesworth CK/3/47). They may thus be used with confidence.

Previous listings of shipments from north-eastern ports during the 16th and 17th cents. are contained in Nef 1932, ii, app. D(i)(a); Moller thesis 1933; Hall thesis 1933, 108–9; and Dietz 1986.

Table 14.1(a) *Coal shipped from Newcastle, 1505–1700*

Period	Coastal		Overseas		Total		References
	Chaldrons	Tons	Chaldrons	Tons	Chaldrons	Tons	
1505–6[b]			2,846	7,542			PRO E. 122/108/12
1508–9[c]					17,757	47,056	TWRO 543/212
1509–10[c]					14,652	38,828	TWRO 543/212
1510–11[g]					15,471	40,998	TWRO 543/212
1513–14[a]			4,212	11,162			PRO E. 122/109/1
1552–3[a]			16,559	43,881			PRO E. 122/110/11
1555–6[a]			14,137	37,463			PRO E. 122/110/13
1556–7[a]			4,750	12,588			PRO E. 122/110/16, 17
1564–5[d]					21,045	55,769	TWRO 543/14
1566–7[d]					23,152	61,353	TWRO 543/15
1567–8[d]					21,561	57,137	TWRO 543/15
1568–9[d]					25,229	66,857	TWRO 543/15
1569–70[d]					19,456	51,558	TWRO 543/15
1570–1[d]					26,749	70,885	TWRO 543/15
1571–2[d]					33,388	88,478	TWRO 543/15
1574–5[d]					33,065	87,622	TWRO 543/16
1585–6[b]			9,680	25,652			PRO E. 122/111/23–9
1587–8[b]			6,914	18,322			PRO E. 122/111/23–9
1591–2[a]	45,710	121,132	10,354	27,438	56,064	148,570	PRO E. 122/111/40
1592–3[a]	52,160	138,224	12,709	33,679	64,869	171,903	PRO E. 122/111/40
1593–4[a]	53,976	143,036	17,967	47,613	71,943	190,649	PRO E. 122/111/40, E. 190/185/6

Table 14.1(a) (cont.)

Period	Coastal		Overseas		Total		References
	Chaldrons	Tons	Chaldrons	Tons	Chaldrons	Tons	
1594–5[a]	64,150	169,998	16,194	42,914	80,344	212,912	PRO E. 122/111/40
1595–6[a]	61,157	162,066	15,374	40,741	76,531	202,807	PRO E. 122/111/40
1596–7[a]	70,688	187,323	13,045	34,569	83,733	221,892	PRO E. 122/111/40
1597–8[a]	70,360	186,454	9,916	26,277	80,276	212,731	PRO E. 122/111/40
1607–8[d]	105,274	278,976	6,906	18,300	112,180	297,276	TWRO 542/2
1608–9[e]	102,050	279,433	11,884	31,493	113,934	301,925	Taylor 1858, 177–8, 217–18
1611–12[b]	87,550	232,008	10,450	27,693	98,000	259,700	KAO Cranfield prov. no. 6794
1612–13[b]	96,391	255,436	11,860	31,429	108,251	286,865	KAO Cranfield prov. no. 6794
1613–14[b]	101,822	269,828	12,200	32,330	114,022	302,158	KAO Cranfield prov. no. 6794
1614–15[b]	99,550	263,808	12,490	33,099	112,030	296,906	KAO Cranfield prov. no. 6794
1615–16[b]	101,390	268,684	11,780	31,217	113,170	299,901	KAO Cranfield prov. no. 6794
1616–17[b]	93,033	246,537	13,560	35,934	106,593	282,471	KAO Cranfield prov. no. 6794
1617–18[b]	100,540	266,431	13,900	36,835	114,440	302,266	KAO Cranfield prov. no. 6794
1618–19[b]			15,289	40,516			PRO E. 190/188/8
1620–1[b]	118,950	315,218					Trinity House MS (Hall thesis 1933, 109, misdated)
1621–2[b]	143,707	380,824	20,836	55,215	164,543	436,039	Trinity House MS (Taylor 1858, 219)
1622–3[b]	124,455	329,806					Trinity House MS (Hall thesis, 1933, 109 misdated)

Year							Source
1623-4[b]	142,618	377,938					Trinity House MS (Hall thesis, 1933, 109 misdated)
1624-5[b]	82,124	217,629					Trinity House MS (Hall thesis, 1933, 109, misdated)
1625-6[b]	111,192	294,659	14,851	39,355	126,043	334,014	State Papers Domestic, Charles I, xlvii, no. 22 (Nef. 1932, ii, app. D(i)(a))
1629-30[h]	120,657	319,741	17,401	46,113	138,058	365,854	Green 1866, 187
1632-3[b]			15,985	42,360			PRO E. 190/190/5
1633-4[b]	160,500	425,325	17,000	45,050	177,500	470,375	PRO E. 190/190/9
1634-5[f]			14,650	38,323			LCA Customs TN/PO 6VI
1635-6[f]			14,948	39,612			LCA Customs TN/PO 6VI
1636-7			13,954	36,978			PRO E. 190/191/9
1637-8[c]			15,162	40,179			LCA Customs TN/PO 6VI
1638-9[b]			17,794	47,154			PRO E. 190/192/4
1639-40[b]			9,906	26,251			PRO E. 190/192/4, 6
1642-3[a]					20,152	53,403	TWRO 543/27
1643-4[a]					876	2,321	TWRO 543/27
1644-5[a]					126,891	336,261	TWRO 543/27
1654-5[b]	147,078	389,757					PRO E. 190/192/9
1657-8[c]	132,490	351,099	6,247	16,555	138,737	367,653	BoL Rawlinson C. 366, 274-5
1658-9[c]	187,234	496,170	16,379	43,404	203,613	539,574	BoL Rawlinson C. 366, 274-5
1659-60[c]	166,551	441,360	10,966	29,060	177,517	470,420	BoL Rawlinson C. 366, 274-5
1660-1[b]	166,919	442,335	10,294	27,279	177,213	469,614	GPL Cotesworth CK/3/47; PRO E. 190/193/1
1661-2[b]	194,421	515,216					GPL Cotesworth CK/3/47

Table 14.1(a) (cont.)

Period	Coastal		Overseas		Total		References
	Chaldrons	Tons	Chaldrons	Tons	Chaldrons	Tons	
1662–3[b]	178,747	473,680					GPL Cotesworth CK/3/47
1663–4[b]	198,369	525,678					GPL Cotesworth CK/3/47
1664–5[b]	124,124	328,929					GPL Cotesworth CK/3/47
1665–6[b]	84,101	222,868	3,022	8,008	87,123	230,876	GPL Cotesworth CK/3/47; PRO E. 190/193/6
1666–7[b]	106,422	282,018	3,816	10,112	110,238	292,131	GPL Cotesworth CK/3/47; PRO E. 190/194/1
1667–8[b]	188,420	499,313					GPL Cotesworth CK/3/47
1668–9[b]	175,920	466,188					GPL Cotesworth CK/3/47
1669–70[b]	185,100	490,515					GPL Cotesworth CK/3/47
1670–1[b]	189,241	501,489					GPL Cotesworth CK/3/47
1671–2[b]	150,429	398,637					GPL Cotesworth CK/3/47
1672–3[b]	156,053	413,540	12,480	33,072	168,533	446,612	GPL Cotesworth CK/3/47; PRO E. 190/195/11
1673–4[b]	170,268	451,210	13,693	36,286	183,961	487,497	GPL Cotesworth CK/3/47; PRO E. 190/195/13
1674–5[b]	194,268	514,810	15,289	40,516	209,557	555,326	GPL Cotesworth CK/3/47; PRO E. 190/196/2
1675–6[b]	194,946	516,607	10,406	27,576	205,352	544,183	GPL Cotesworth CK/3/47; PRO E. 190/196/7
1676–7[b]	194,405	515,173	14,524	38,489	208,929	553,662	GPL Cotesworth CK/3/47; PRO E. 190/197/2

Year						Source
1677–8[b]	217,782	577,122	11,784	31,228	229,566	608,350	GPL Cotesworth CK/3/47; PRO E. 190/197/7
1678–9[b]	194,948	516,612	19,767	52,383	214,715	568,995	GPL Cotesworth CK/3/47; PRO E. 190/198/5
1679–80[b]	202,262	535,994	15,998	42,395	218,260	578,389	GPL Cotesworth CK/3/47; PRO E. 190/198/13
1680–1[b]	218,942	580,196	18,910	50,112	237,852	630,308	GPL Cotesworth CK/3/47; PRO E. 190/199/14
1681–2[b]	190,380	504,507	16,466	43,635	206,846	548,142	GPL Cotesworth CK/3/47; PRO E. 190/200/8
1682–3[b]	210,972	559,076					GPL Cotesworth CK/3/47
1683–4[b]	204,770	542,641					GPL Cotesworth CK/3/47
1684–5[b]	213,659	566,196	21,014	55,687	234,673	621,883	GPL Cotesworth CK/3/47; PRO E. 190/201/6
1685–6[b]	178,265	472,402					GPL Cotesworth CK/3/47
1686–7[b]	198,528	526,099					GPL Cotesworth CK/3/47
1687–8[b]	231,265	612,852					GPL Cotesworth CK/3/47
1688–9[b]	167,663	444,307					GPL Cotesworth CK/3/47
1689–90[b]	136,847	362,645					GPL Cotesworth CK/3/47
1690–1[b]	177,270	469,766					GPL Cotesworth CK/3/47
1691–2[b]	156,299	414,192					GPL Cotesworth CK/3/47
1692–3[b]	179,650	476,073					GPL Cotesworth CK/3/47
1693–4[b]	160,413	425,094	3,226	8,549	163,639	433,643	GPL Cotesworth CK/3/47; PRO E. 190/204/5
1694–5[b]	170,974	453,081	4,050	10,733	175,024	463,814	GPL Cotesworth CK/3/47; PRO E. 190/204/8
1695–6[b]	151,096	400,404	6,470	17,146	157,566	417,550	GPL Cotesworth CK/3/47; PRO E. 190/205/3

Table 14.1(a) (cont.)

Period	Coastal		Overseas		Total		References
	Chaldrons	Tons	Chaldrons	Tons	Chaldrons	Tons	
1696–7[b]	181,280	480,392	5,443	14,424	186,723	494,816	GPL Cotesworth CK/3/47; PRO E. 190/206/8
1697–8[b]	195,844	518,987	13,944	36,952	209,788	555,939	GPL Cotesworth CK/3/47; E. 190/206/11
1698–9[b]	207,006	548,566	14,530	38,505	221,536	587,070	GPL Cotesworth CK/3/47; PRO E. 190/207/6
1699–1700[b]	190,051	503,635	12,610	33,417	202,661	537,052	GPL Cotesworth CK/3/47; PRO E. 190/207/13

Notes: Only complete years have been included in the tables. All chaldrons have been converted into tons at the rate of 53 cwt. per chaldron.

The accounts are dated as indicated:
a Michaelmas to Michaelmas.
b Christmas to Christmas
c June to June
d October to October
e 21 December to 20 December
f May to May
g August to August
h Period unknown.

Table 14.1(b) *Coal shipped from Sunderland, 1605-1700*

Period	Coastal		Overseas		Total		References
	Chaldrons	Tons	Chaldrons	Tons	Chaldrons	Tons	
1605-6[b]			1,278	3,387			PRO E. 190/186/4B
1608-9[a]	4,412	11,692	1,135	3,008	5,547	14,700	Taylor 1858, 178, 217-18
1611-12[a]	11,509	30,499	1,860	4,929	13,369	35,428[i]	KAO Cranfield prov. no. 6794
1612-13[b]	11,420	30,263	1,926	5,104	13,346	35,367[i]	KAO Cranfield prov. no. 6794
1613-14[b]	10,184	26,988	2,225	5,896	12,409	32,884[i]	KAO Cranfield prov. no. 6794
1614-15[b]	9,332	24,730	2,180	5,777	11,512	30,507[i]	KAO Cranfield prov. no. 6794
1615-16[b]	11,133	29,502	1,649	4,370	12,782	33,872[i]	KAO Cranfield prov. no. 6794
1616-17[b]	13,368	35,425	1,600	4,240	14,968	39,665[i]	KAO Cranfield prov. no. 6794
1617-18[b]	9,238	24,481	1,250	3,313	10,488	27,793[i]	KAO Cranfield prov. no. 6794
1618-19[b]			1,183	3,135			PRO E. 190/188/8
1620-1[b]	10,478	27,767					Trinity House MS (Hall thesis 1933, 109, misdated)
1621-2[b]	11,175	29,614	784	2,078	11,959	31,691	Trinity House MS; Taylor 1858, 219
1622-3[b]	11,423	30,271					Trinity House MS (Hall thesis 1933, 109, misdated)
1623-4[b]	9,942	26,346					Trinity House MS (Hall thesis 1933, 109 misdated)
1624-5[b]	9,216	24,422					Trinity House MS (Hall thesis 1933, 109, misdated)

Table 14.1(b) (cont.)

Period	Coastal		Overseas		Total		References
	Chaldrons	Tons	Chaldrons	Tons	Chaldrons	Tons	
1625–6[b]	13,014	34,487	1,193	3,161	14,207	37,649	State Papers Domestic, Charles I xlvii, no. 22 (Nef. 1932, ii. App. D(i)(a))
1632–3[b]			3,383	8,965			PRO E. 190/190/5
1633–4[b]	24,042	63,711	3,069	8,133	27,111	71,844	PRO E. 190/190/9
1634–5[f]			3,189	8,451			LCA Customs TN/PO 6VI
1635–6[f]			2,061	5,462			LCA Customs TN/PO 6VI
1636–7[b]			2,614	6,927			PRO E. 190/191/9
1637–8[c]			2,336	6,190			LCA Customs TN/PO 6VI
1638–9[b]			4,585	12,150			PRO E. 190/192/4
1639–40[b]			3,559	9,431			PRO E. 190/192/6
1657–8[c]	26,376	69,896	2,147	5,690	28,523	75,586	BoL Rawlinson C. 366, 274–5
1658–9[c]	43,400	115,010	2,849	7,550	46,249	122,560	BoL Rawlinson C. 366, 274–5
1659–60[c]	39,116	103,657	11,044	29,267	50,160	132,924	BoL Rawlinson C. 366, 274–5
1660–1[b]			1,454	3,853			PRO E. 190/193/1
1665–6[b]	20,185	53,490	116	307	20,301	53,798	Moller thesis 1983, 349; PRO E. 190/193/6
1666–7[b]			505	1,338			PRO E. 190/194/1
1672–3[b]	24,684	65,413	636	1,685	25,320	67,098	PRO E. 195/15, 195/11
1673–4[b]	44,194	117,114	3,094	8,199	47,288	125,313	PRO E. 190/196/1

Year							Reference
1674–5[b]			5,291	14,021			PRO E. 190/196/2
1675–6[b]	39,728	105,279	4,227	11,255	43,975	116,534	PRO E. 190/196/8
1676–7[b]			4,956	13,133			PRO E. 190/192/2
1677–8[b]	54,476	144,361	3,046	8,072	57,522	152,433	PRO E. 190/197/10
1678–8[b]	47,455	125,756	8,796	23,309	56,251	149,065	PRO E. 190/198/3, 5
1679–80[b]			5,297	14,037			PRO E. 190/198/13
1680–1[b]			7,281	19,295			PRO E. 190/199/14
1681–2[b]			3,975	10,534			PRO E. 190/200/8
1682–3[b]	49,558	131,329					PRO E. 190/200/15
1684–5[b]	53,821	142,626	8,434	22,350	62,255	164,976	PRO E. 190/201/13
1685–6[b]	46,449	123,090					PRO E. 190/202/3
1690–1[b]	52,188	138,298					PRO E. 190/203/1
1693–4[b]	33,751	89,440	2,861	7,582	36,612	97,022	PRO E. 190/203/7, 204/5
1694–5[b]			2,805	7,433			PRO E. 190/204/8
1695–6[b]	33,638	89,141	3,540	9,381	37,178	98,522	PRO E. 190/205/3, 6
1696–7[b]			1,711	4,535			PRO E. 190/206/8
1697–8[b]			7,549	20,005			PRO E. 190/206/11
1698–9[b]			7,340	19,451			PRO E. 190/207/6
1699–1700[b]			8,988	23,818			PRO E. 190/207/13

Notes: Only complete years have been included in the tables. All chaldrons have been converted into tons at the rate of 53 cwt. per chaldron.

The accounts are dated as indicated:

[a] Michaelmas to Michaelmas.
[b] Christmas to Christmas
[c] June to June
[f] May to May.

The most comprehensive measure of the growth of the north-eastern coalfield is provided by an aggregation of the coastal and overseas shipments of all the ports of the region. Previously attention has been devoted almost exclusively to shipments from Newcastle, and those from Sunderland and minor coal ports have been neglected. Whereas coal before the late sixteenth century was shipped virtually from the Tyne alone, thereafter Sunderland's shipments rose strongly, and those from Blyth and Cullercoats began to assume significant proportions in the last quarter of the seventeenth century. Ideally we would wish to have coasting and overseas shipments for both Newcastle and Sunderland in order to assess the scale of the total trade in any given year. Sadly, although data are prolific, only a patchy record can be constructed from years with complete sets of records from both the Tyne and the Wear, and data of shipments from Blyth and Cullercoats are very sparse. In order to provide as comprehensive a picture as possible Table 14.2 uses all the available records of coal shipped from Newcastle and Sunderland, and attempts to fill the gaps by the use of quinquennial means and estimates.

Only the best-documented quinquennia have been chosen for inclusion. Calculations have been attempted only for quinquennia for which at least two years of Newcastle coasting shipments are available; in over half of the quinquennia included in Table 14.2 a full five years of such shipments are available. Sunderland shipments are less continuously recorded, and averages have frequently had to be struck from one or two years in a five-year period, and occasionally, in the the complete absence of figures within the period, they have had to be estimated on the basis of the nearest proximate data. Had an alternative method of providing estimates of missing years, by averaging the shipments made in the five years preceding and the five years succeeding the missing year, been chosen, it would have produced deviations from the figures used in the table of substantially less than 5 per cent, except for 1690-5, where the deviation would have been 5.3 per cent. Since information concerning the trade of Blyth, Cullercoats, and other lesser coal ports is very patchy indeed, shipments have had to be estimated as best they can from the nearest available records.

Thus Table 14.2 is designed to display the broadest possible picture of changes in the north-eastern coal trade over two centuries. It has no pretensions to absolute accuracy.

Table 14.2 *Total shipments of coal from north-eastern ports, 1508–1700 (annual averages)*

Period	Newcastle		Other ports		Total		Index
	Chaldrons	Tons	Chaldrons	Tons	Chaldrons	Tons	
1508–11	15,960 (3)	42,294	1,000 (e)	2,650	16,950	44,944	100
1564–70	22,089 (5)	58,535	1,500 (e)	3,975	23,589	62,510	139
1570–5	31,067 (3)	82,328	1,750 (e)	4,638	32,817	86,966	193
1591–5	68,305 (4)	181,008	2,500 (e)	6,625	70,805	187,633	417
1595–1600	80,180 (3)	212,477	3,500 (e)	9,275	83,680	221,752	493
1605–10	113,295 (2)	300,232	5,919 (1)	15,685	119,214	315,917	703
1610–15	108,078 (4)	286,407	14,062 (4)	37,264	122,140	323,671	721
1615–20	111,938 (3)	296,636	14,221 (3)	37,686	126,159	334,322	744
1620–5	143,207 (5)	379,499	12,591 (5)	33,366	155,798	412,865	920
1625–30	132,051 (2)	349,935	15,500 (1)	41,075	147,551	391,010	870
1655–60	173,289 (3)	459,216	42,111 (3)	111,594	215,400	570,810	1,350
1660–5	182,810 (5)	484,447	37,190 (e)	98,553	220,000	583,000	1,298
1665–70	151,411 (5)	401,239	21,306 (1)	56,461	172,717	457,700	1,014
1670–5	165,873 (5)	439,563	38,946 (2)	103,207	204,819	542,770	1,208
1675–80	215,365 (5)	570,717	59,987 (3)	158,966	275,352	729,683	1,625
1680–5	226,283 (5)	599,650	69,753 (2)	184,845	296,036	784,495	1,747
1685–90	192,514 (5)	510,162	63,449 (1)	168,140	255,963	678,302	1,509
1690–5	172,559 (5)	457,281	61,322 (2)	162,503	233,881	619,784	1,380
1695–1700	195,654 (5)	518,483	55,817 (1)	147,915	251,471	666,398	1,484

Notes:
( ) Number of observations in quinquennium.
(e) Figures based wholly upon estimates.

ii. Patterns of distribution of the north-eastern trade

Where was all this coal sent and what was the relative importance of the various ports which received it? Answers to these questions are contained in those north-eastern customs accounts and port books which record the destinations of the vessels sailing with coal, and the port books of the receiving ports which reveal the quantities of coal that were unloaded. As can be seen from Tables 14.3, 14.4, and 14.5, substantial changes took place in the patterns of distribution as well as the scale of the east coast trade between the second half of the sixteenth century and 1700. In Table 14.3 records of the shipments of coal outwards from north-eastern ports have been used to provide an overview of the dramatic rise in the share of the east coast trade absorbed by the capital. In Table 14.4 a detailed breakdown is given of the distribution of the trade in terms of the numbers of shipments; in Table 14.5 a detailed breakdown of destinations in terms of quantities of coal is given.

Table 14.3 *Share of the east coast coal trade enjoyed by London*

Period	Coal shipped from Newcastle %	Coal shipped from Sunderland %	Total coal shipped %
1550–1	24.7	—	24.7
1561–2	21.0	—	21.0
1682–3	70.9	21.6	60.1
1690–1	81.6	39.1	71.7
1702–3	81.5	36.3	71.7

Sources: Dietz 1986, 292; Moller thesis 1933, 724-7, 733-5.

Table 14.4 *The east coast trade: destinations of ships, 1561–1691*

Destinations	1561–2		1682–3						1690–1					
			Newcastle		Sunderland		Total		Newcastle		Sunderland		Total	
	(a)	(b)	(a)	(b)	(a)	(b)	(a)	(b)	(a)	(b)	(a)	(b)	(a)	(b)
Northumberland and Durham	6	1.0	10	0.3	73	3.8	83	1.6	9	0.3	4	0.2	13	0.3
Yorkshire	77	13.4	112	3.5	542	28.2	654	12.8	81	2.8	389	16.8	470	9.1
Lincolnshire	40	7.0	46	1.4	309	16.1	355	7.0	37	1.3	240	10.3	277	5.3
Norfolk and Suffolk	261	45.5	977	30.8	353	18.4	1,330	26.1	551	19.3	738	31.8	1,289	24.9
Essex	11	1.9	67	2.1	117	6.1	184	3.6	54	1.9	95	4.1	149	2.9
London	133	23.3	1,340	42.2	310	16.1	1,650	32.4	1,810	63.3	659	27.8	2,469	47.7
Kent	9	1.6	153	4.8	108	5.6	261	5.1	114	4.0	125	5.4	239	4.6
South coast	9	1.6	344	10.8	57	3.0	401	7.9	125	4.4	33	1.4	158	3.0
West country	0	0	59	1.9	3	0.2	62	1.2	3	0.1	0	0	3	0.1
Unknown	27	4.7	64	2.0	39	2.0	103	2.0	75	2.6	37	1.6	112	2.2
Lost at sea and taken	0	0	5	0.2	7	0.4	12	0.2	1	0.0	0	0	1	0.0
Total shipments	573		3,167		1,928		5,095		2,860		2,320		5,180	
Mean size of shipments	24.5 chaldrons (65 tons)		65.7 chaldrons (174 tons)		24.3 chaldrons (64 tons)				61.5 chaldrons (163 tons)		22.0 chaldrons (58 tons)			

Notes:

(a) = number of shipments; (b) = percentage of total shipments.

Sources: Dietz 1986, 292; Moller thesis 1933, 725–6, 733–4.

Table 145 *The east coast trade: destinations of coal, 1550–1683*

Destinations	1550–1		1682–3					
	Newcastle		Newcastle		Sunderland		Total	
	Tons	%	Tons	%	Tons	%	Tons	%
Northumberland and Durham	604	0.9	90	0.0	505	0.3	595	0.1
Yorkshire	9,484	14.8	6,636	1.2	32,712	20.9	39,348	5.5
(Hull)	(6,230)	(9.7)	(5,539)	(1.0)	(16,935)	(10.8)	(22,474)	(3.1)
Lincolnshire	7,190	11.2	2,226	0.3	18,891	12.1	21,117	3.0
Norfolk and Suffolk	26,378	41.1	100,846	18.0	42,747	27.3	143,593	20.0
(King's Lynn)	(13,920)	(21.7)	(43,847)	(7.8)	(8,421)	(5.3)	(52,268)	(7.3)
(Yarmouth)	(5,637)	(8.8)	(37,704)	(6.7)	(9,702)	(6.2)	(47,406)	(6.6)
Essex	2,416	3.8	5,435	1.0	11,251	7.2	16,686	2.3
London	15,821	24.7	396,655	70.9	33,630	21.6	430,285	60.1
South coast	1,739	2.7	39,610	7.1	12,731	8.1	52,341	7.3
West country	122	0.2	8,284	1.5	408	0.3	8,692	1.2
Unknown	373	0.6	451	0.1	3,470	2.2	3,921	0.5
TOTAL	64,128	100.0	560,233	100.0	156,345	100.0	716,578	100.0

Sources: Dietz 1986, 292; PRO E. 190/200/15. Newcastle chaldrons converted at the rate of 53 cwt. each.

iii. Imports of coal into London

Attempts at measuring the long-term growth of London's coal imports have proved no less controversial than those directed towards quantifying shipments from the Tyne and the Wear. Once again the major cause of the uncertainty is the scarcity of early records. In fact Nef based his claims for a nineteenfold increase in London's coal imports in less than a century and a quarter, upon a single customs account which runs for just six and a half months of 1580. Unfortunately, it has not proved possible to augment substantially the later sixteenth-century sources, and only a handful of partial accounts have been found for the period before 1585. The first three entries in Table 14.6 are derived from such accounts. An Exchequer customs account for Newcastle, which identifies the destinations of shipments, exists for Michaelmas 1549 to Michaelmas 1550, but sadly it is illegible from April to July 1550. An artificial year has therefore been created by inserting into this account those shipments which were made in the identical period of another partial account dating from 1551. The figures for 1562 are based upon an

Table 14.6 *Imports of coal into London*

Period		Tons	Source
	Newcastle chaldrons		
(1549–50)	(5,970)	(15,821)	PRO E. 122/110/3, 6
(1561–2)	(4,025)	(10,667)	PRO E. 122/111/4
(1580)	(10,273)	(27,224)	PRO E. 190/6/8
1585–6	17,900	47,435	PRO E. 190/7/6
1587–8	18,454	48,903	PRO E. 163/15/5
1591–2	26,068	68,080	PRO E. 190/9/3
1605–6[a]	54,488	144,393	PRO E. 190/13/14
1614–15[a]	68,699	182,052	PRO E. 190/18/1
1637–8[b]	106,934	283,375	PRO E. 190/41/6
	London chaldrons		
1670–1[b]	245,652	343,913	PRO E. 101/635/37 pt. I
1676–7[b]	224,256	313,958	PRO E. 101/635/38 pt. I
1677–8[b]	290,247	406,346	PRO E. 101/635/39
1679–80[b]	241,184	337,658	PRO E. 101/635/40 pt. I

Table 14.6 (*cont.*)

Period		Tons	Source
	London chaldrons		
1680–1	295,092	413,129	City Chamberlains' books
1683–4[b]	228,383	319,736	PRO E. 101/635/41 pt. II
1684–5	230,380	322,532	City Chamberlains' books
1685–6	282,393	395,350	City Chamberlains' books
1686–7	315,642	441,899	City Chamberlains' books
1687–8	412,306	577,228	GHL Alchin bdl. 31
1688–9	233,135	326,389	GHL Alchin bdl. 31
1689–90	242,575	339,605	GHL Alchin bdl. 31
1690–1	327,631	458,683	GHL Alchin bdl. 31
1691–2	274,084	383,717	GHL Alchin bdl. 31
1692–3	334,764	468,670	GHL Alchin bdl. 31
1693–4	322,264	451,170	GHL Alchin bdl. 31
1694–5	326,907	457,670	BL Lansdowne 846, fo. 252
1695–6	254,269	355,977	BL Lansdowne 846, fo. 252
1696–7	320,274	448,384	HMC House of Lords, v. 228
1697–8	349,979	488,571	HMC House of Lords v. 228
1698–9	361,889	506,645	HMC House of Lords, v. 228
1699–1700	335,114	469,160	HMC House of Lords, v. 228

Notes:

( ) estimated.

Years run from Michaelmas to Michaelmas, except for those marked [a] which run from Christmas to Christmas, and those marked [b] which run from Midsummer to Midsummer.

Newcastle chaldrons have been converted at the rate of 53 cwt. each, and London chaldrons at the rate of 28 cwt. each.

Figures not given in Nef are: 1549–50 (recalculated from data given in Dietz 1986, 292), 1561–2, 1587–8, 1670–80, and 1683–4.

account which runs from 2 February to 31 July, while that for 1580 is based upon an account which runs from 12 March to 28 September. Estimates of total imports into London during the whole of 1562 and 1580 have been based upon the seasonal patterns of shipments obtaining in other years. Such methods are, of course, uncertain, and can impart no more than a suggestion of likely levels of imports.

Since the data in Table 14.6 are drawn from a variety of sources, great care must be taken to determine the dimensions of the chaldrons recorded in them. Shipments from Newcastle and Sunderland (PRO E. 122) were always recorded in Newcastle chaldrons (53 cwt.), as were those listed in port books (PRO E. 190). Nef made the mistake of assuming that coal was recorded in port books in London chaldrons, which he took as weighing 1.33 tons. The data from 1670 onwards are drawn from sources which were compiled to record the receipts from a variety of duties collected in London, and these duties were levied on each chaldron by London measure (c.28 cwt.) unloaded in the Thames. The new figures presented for 1670–84 derive from collections made for the rebuilding of London after the Great Fire.

iv. Imports of coal into provincial ports

A wide range of data is available on imports of coal into east coast ports other than London, much of it printed in Nef. It would be redundant to repeat what is easily obtainable elsewhere, but imports into King's Lynn and Great Yarmouth are given in Tables 14.7 and 14.8, because they were the two leading provincial coal ports and substantial new data are available.

Table 14.7 *Coal landed at King's Lynn*

Period	Newcastle chaldrons	Tons	Source
1561–2	4,955	13,130	PRO E. 101/110/8 (Williams thesis 1952, 163)
1566–7	4,647	12,315	PRO E. 190/425/6 (Williams thesis 1952, 163)
1675–6	2,570	6,811	PRO E. 190/427/9 (Nef 1932, ii. 384)
1586–7	9,582	25,392	PRO E. 190/430/1, 2 (Williams thesis 1952, 164)
1681–2	15,253	40,420	PRO E. 190/439/4

Table 14.8 *Coal landed at Yarmouth*

Period	Newcastle chaldrons	Tons
1558–9	946	2,504
1566–7	1,147	3,040
1580–1	1,932	5,120
1593–4	3,158	8,369
1600–1	4,982	13,202
1613–14	6,017	15,945
1622–3	7,143	18,929
1637–8	11,148	29,542
1638–9	14,503	38,433
1644–5	(7,200)	(19,080)
1645–6	(7,082)	(18,767)
1646–7	9,019	23,900
1661–2	12,354	32,738
1671–2	12,633	33,477
1679–80	16,849	44,650
1681–2	16,858	44,674
1684–5	14,232	37,715
1685–6	13,804	36,581
1687–8	16,416	43,502

Source: Mitchell thesis 1978, table 4.3.
Note:
( ) = estimated.

v. The Irish coal trade

It is unlikely that much more than 50,000 tons of coal were ever exported to Ireland in a single year before 1700. Yet there were five coalfields which participated in this modest trade, and the fortunes of a number of seaboard collieries depended upon it. Dublin, which consumed well over 80 per cent of all exports, was virtually equidistant from Whitehaven, Liverpool, Chester, Milford, Swansea, Saltcoats, and Irvine. Small as the amounts were, coal ranked third in the list of Irish imports from England in 1665.[5]

[5] L. M. Cullen, *Anglo-Irish Trade, 1600-1800* (Manchester, 1968), 31-2.

Scarcely any coal found its way to Ireland before the seventeenth century. The population was low and people dwelt overwhelmingly in the countryside, often close to ample supplies of peat. The rise in coal imports was intimately linked to the growth of Dublin, whose population is thought to have expanded from less than 10,000 in 1600 to 60,000 by 1700, making it the second city in the British Isles. The nearest peat bogs were thirty miles overland and, like London, Dublin soon came to be almost wholly dependent on coal.[6]

Coal was mined in Ireland in a number of locations, including Ballycastle, near the northernmost tip of County Antrim, Drumglass and Drumgannon in County Tyrone, and Kilkenny, in Kilkenny. But nowhere was production significant, and scarcely any Irish coal reached Dublin. Although Ballycastle was on the sea, it lay 180 miles from Dublin, and suffered from a lack of investment in both coalmining and shipping, while the pits in Tyrone and Kilkenny were virtually inaccessible. As late as 1800 the total output of all Irish mines was put at a mere 20,000 tons a year.[7]

Information on the scale of the coal trade to Ireland is available in the customs records of the exporting ports, and Table 14.9 contains the available data collated to provide estimates of total shipments for the best-documented periods. A number of complementary contemporary estimates are also available. In 1684, for example, Sir William Petty put the total export trade at 43,000 tons, but in 1696, after many years of political turmoil, including a temporary ban on imports by the newly elected Irish parliament in 1689, they were estimated by Sir Francis Brewster to be only 25,000 tons. Data from Irish customs ledgers suggest imports of just over 40,000 tons in 1700. Although trade with ports other than Dublin was very slow to develop, by this date they were receiving around 10,000 tons.[8]

vi. The export trade

Despite the ancient origins of the trade in coal with Europe, exports never attained substantial proportions. English coal was being shipped to Bruges in the 1250s,[9] but once fuel had become scarce shipments overseas met with little encouragement. Consumers feared, especially during

---

[6] R. A. Butlin, 'The Population of Dublin in the Late 17th Century', *Irish Geography*, 5/2 (1965); Makey thesis 1952, 48–9.   [7] Nef 1932, i. 75–6; Makey thesis 1952, 160–7.

[8] Makey thesis 1952, 53, 216–17.

[9] E. King, *England 1175-1425* (1979), 71.

Table 14.9 Coal exports to Ireland, 1560–1700 (in tons)

Period	Cumberland	Liverpool	Chester	Milford	Swansea	Ayrshire	Total
1560–70	[nil]	300	50	100	[nil]	[nil]	450
1580–90	[nil]	350	100	220	[nil]	[nil]	670
1590–1600	[nil]	500	180	320	[nil]	[nil]	1,000
1605	1,900	450	600	450	[nil]	[nil]	3,400
1617	1,700	900	1,950	900	800	[nil]	6,250
1625	3,400	—	—	(900)	(600)	[nil]	—
1635–40	1,000	3,000	7,000	1,600	1,300	[nil]	13,900
1660–5	1,800	3,500	(7,000)	1,600	1,500	100	15,500
1684–7	26,900	500	6,500	2,900	[nil]	1,200	38,000
1699–1701	18,500	400	7,300	2,800	[nil]	5,400	34,400

Sources: Makey thesis 1952, 179, 193, 214, 221; D. Woodward, The Trade of Elizabethan Chester (Hull, 1970), 17.

the later sixteenth and early seventeenth centuries, that the loss of such a valuable commodity would drive up prices and possibly lead to the exhaustion of reserves, and export embargoes were enforced in Scotland. In addition to the high costs of transport, English and Welsh coal exports suffered from extremely onerous customs duties. From 1599 duties of 5s. per Newcastle chaldron were levied on exports, and in 1631, when it was learnt that since the end of James I's reign £20, £22, and even £26 had been obtained in Rouen for a hundred barrels of coal (c.15 tons), and that during the late wars with France and Spain coal had been sold along the French and Spanish coasts at prices ranging between £4 and £7 per Newcastle chaldron, the Attorney-General was instructed to impose a further tax of 4s. per chaldron, in addition to the 6s. 8d. and 8s. 4d. which was by then being imposed upon each chaldron exported in English and foreign vessels respectively. A further 1s. 4d. per chaldron was levied upon Tyneside exports by the burgesses of New-castle, together with lesser sums for ancient dues. Moreover, tariffs were progressively erected in foreign ports in the second half of the seven-teenth century, and a general movement may be detected in Holland, Belgian Hainault, and France to restrict imports of British coal.[10]

Not surprisingly, despite substantial potential demand overseas, the high prices at which English and Scottish coal had to be sold abroad severely curtailed the market. Exports from the north-east, which had averaged around 7,000 tons annually in the later fourteenth century, climbed to 40,000 tons in the mid-1550s. But growth thereafter was limited. Exports hovered around 50,000 tons for much of the seven-teenth century, and scarcely ever surpassed 70,000 tons, and their share of the total seasale fell below 10 per cent. Overseas shipments from most other English and Welsh coalfields with easy access to the sea increased sharply in the seventeenth century, but from tiny beginnings, and even when shipments from all other ports are combined they fail to match the modest levels attained by Tyneside and Wearside. The prime potential beneficiary of heavy English duties was Scotland but, despite the importance of overseas markets for Scottish coal-owners, shipments appear to have remained well below 50,000 tons except in the most exceptional of years.[11]

[10] These matters are discussed in detail in Nef 1932, ii. 211–38; Moller thesis 1933, 387–97.

[11] Exports from north-eastern ports are given in Tables 14.1 and 14.2 above. Exports from Welsh ports and a number of ports in north-western England are contained in Nef 1932, ii, app. D (ii). The theses produced in 1928 by B. M. Evans and in 1981 by K. L. Gruffyd also contain tabula-tions of exports from Welsh ports, but the former is unreliable because of its erroneous treatment of measures. For exports from Scotland see above pp. 102–6.

CHAPTER 15

The Organization of the East Coast Trade

A Welch pedigree, doth not descend by more steps, and degrees,
than the property of their coals is varied, while it is derived from
the owner of the colliery, unto him that at last buys the commodity, to spend it.

Ralph Gardiner, England's Grievance (1655), 25

Gardiner's picturesque statement encapsulates the long tortuous route,
with multiple changes of ownership, which coal experienced on its
journey from the coal-face of a Tyneside colliery to the hearth of a
London consumer. The Tyneside coal-owner sold his coal to a Hostman
or fitter, who then sold it to a shipmaster and loaded it on to his collier
anchored in the Tyne. On arrival in the Thames, the shipmaster sold his
cargo to brokers or dealers, by turns woodmongers, lightermen, and
crimps. When the chain was at its most extended, these middlemen
might then sell on to factors or wholesalers, before the retailer who
served the public gained possession. The links between the Tyne and the
Wear and London and other east coast towns might on occasion be
rendered yet more intricate by the ownership of colliers, or shares in
them, by Northumberland and Durham coal-owners and London coal-
dealers. And, in the later seventeenth century, direct links developed
between Northumberland and Durham coal-owners and London coal-
merchants, with the latter being paid commissions by the former for
buying from the shipmasters in the Thames the coal produced by their
collieries.

To contemporaries concerned about the price of an essential commodity, each step in this journey was seen as not merely adding to
genuine costs but multiplying the opportunities for profit, for which a
host of rapacious but superfluous middlemen eagerly jostled. From the
time when coal first became of importance consumers were obsessed
about the manipulation of the trade by all who engaged in its production and distribution. A seemingly endless stream of complaints,
sometimes assuming the proportions of a flood, was made against the

owners and operators of collieries and the Hostmen of Newcastle, who were accused of monopolizing the production and sale of coal on the Tyne, and against the masters of the ships which carried the coal down the east coast, who were accused of colluding to create scarcities and extravagant prices. When the vast tonnage which was shipped to London was finally unloaded it was seen to fall into the clutches of a tiny cabal of unscrupulous dealers, who bought cheaply and sold dear, and when at last retailers were able to set about supplying customers they did so with false measures.

For Londoners coal was 'of like condition with food and victuals',[1] and its trade was scrutinized accordingly. A procession of enquiries, commissions, and committees issued forth from the Lord Mayor and Aldermen of the City, the Privy Council, Parliament, Lords of the Council in the Star Chamber, and the mayor and burgesses of Newcastle. They studied its organization, interrogated its practitioners, and examined its books, searching for restrictions on production, the rigging of prices, deceits in quality and weights and measures, and the manipulation of markets. For historians, too, the conduct of the east coast coal trade has exercised a special fascination, evidenced by the plethora of books and articles which have been devoted to it. The extensive modern literature on the subject makes further detailed descriptions of each and every aspect of the trade redundant. Instead attention will be largely devoted in this chapter to a critical review of current knowledge and interpretations.

i. The Hostmen's Company and the organization of the Newcastle coal trade[2]

The early history of the 'lords of coal'

It has become fashionable to belittle the influence which guilds and monopolists were able to exert over the trades and industries which they purported to control. Yet for a time the Newcastle Hostmen bestrode the coal trade of the north-east like a colossus. The origins and legality of the monopoly which they came to enjoy over the sale of coal are obscure and uncertain but, when combined with a near monopoly of

---

[1] As admitted by the Corporation of London in a dispute with the city of Newcastle, c.1595 (GHL Remembrancia, ii. 134).

[2] Substantial, but not invariably consonant, accounts of the Hostmen's Company and the regulation of the Newcastle coal trade are contained in Dendy (ed.), *Hostmen*; Nef 1932, especially ii. 20–3, 110–34; Sweezy 1938, 3–21; Moller thesis 1933, 529–42.

the production of coal in the Tyne valley, it provided the means whereby the Hostmen exerted a dominant influence over the development of the richest coalfield in the world and its seaborne trade. The abundance and accessibility of the seams in and around the city meant that Newcastle merchants were destined to be intimately involved in the coal trade from its inception, and the earliest surviving records show them buying and selling coal, both as individuals and as members of consortia. A striving after the control and regulation of the trade was also early in evidence, and there are many instances from the thirteenth and fourteenth centuries of the officers and citizens of Newcastle acting corporately in mining as well as trading. In 1393, for example, the mayor, bailiffs, and commonalty of the city purchased thirteen score keel-loads from the bishop of Durham. The citizens also acted corporately in bringing the trade of the whole of the Tyne under the jurisdiction of the city and keeping it there, and in the exercising of control over the navigation of the river.[3]

As with many ancient rights and perquisites, the claims of the citizens of Newcastle to a monopoly over all coal sold from the Tyne have a confusing history, with a large number of complementary but distinct threads to be unravelled. Among these were various rights and privileges conferred on the burgesses by a succession of royal charters, frequently confirmed and occasionally modified; the custom of foreign bought and foreign sold; the Crown's desire to facilitate the collection of customs revenue by restricting the trade of the Tyne to the precincts of Newcastle; legislation which sought to place alien merchants under the supervision of native hosts; and the origins and incorporation of the Hostmen's Company itself. The task of unravelling these threads is made all the more difficult by the actions and writings of the Hostmen, who had everything to gain by vagueness and confusion since, as was eventually to be demonstrated, the extensive privileges which they arrogated were not at all securely founded in law.

The original liberties of the city of Newcastle were granted by Henry II and, when confirmed in 1214 by John, gave the burgesses jurisdiction over the Tyne 'from the Sparhawk in the sea to Hedwin Streams', which was from the mouth of the estuary to a point some ten miles upstream of the city beyond which the river was not navigable to sea-going vessels.[4] Royal charters, of course, carried no guarantee that the rights they bestowed were to be enjoyed peaceably and in perpetuity. The will

---

[3] Blake 1967, 22–5; Fraser 1962, 217–18; Galloway 1898, i. 41; Simpson 1909–10, 576.
[4] Brand 1789, ii. 132–6; Welford 1884–7, i. 316–18.

of monarchs was notoriously inconstant, and the very span of these rights made them an inevitable focus of discontent. Naturally the burgesses felt justified in attempting to channel all the trade of the Tyne through the city, and they duly sought to negate any attempt to load or unload merchandise elsewhere. Moreover, they strove to enforce their rights with a combination of tenacity and ferocity. In 1267, for example, the mayor himself led a band of burgesses on a raid to a wharf at North Shields belonging to the prior of Tynemouth, and there seized a ship laden with coal and other merchandise and, it was claimed, set fire to buildings and assaulted the monks and prior's men they found. Such precipitate action did not, of course, produce a permanent settlement, and in 1290 we find the burgesses taking legal issue with the prior to prevent him from making Shields a rival port. They won their case, and in 1292 Parliament ordered the prior to destroy all his wharves below high-water mark, and forbade vessels to load or unload there.[5]

The liberties of Newcastle faced even greater threat from the south bank of the Tyne, where the bishop of Durham held sway. The bishop was a far more formidable adversary than the prior, and the coal reserves at his disposal dwarfed those of Tynemouth priory. Moreover, in 1314 Edward II granted the bishop the right to load and unload merchandise wherever he wished on the Tyne and, in direct contravention of their rights, forbade the burgesses to coerce ships into using Newcastle. The matter was not allowed to rest there, of course, but after a series of further tussles, Richard II in 1383 granted the bishopric a charter permitting it to ship coal and other merchandise from the south bank, 'without impediment from the men of Newcastle and others'. An exasperated petition from the burgesses followed hard upon the heels of this grant, claiming that they had for time out of mind, as well as by charters of former kings, possessed the right to control the whole of the River Tyne, and they reciprocated by withholding the payment of their annual borough farm.[6] It was to no avail, and Newcastle's claims against the bishop were finally rejected in 1391. Moreover, in the course of the fifteenth century the city's rights were further eroded, especially in favour of Tynemouth priory which won an important Star Chamber case in 1512.[7]

---

[5] Fraser 1962, 210; Blake 1967, 24–5; Howell (ed.), *Monopoly*, 5.

[6] Brand 1789, ii. 12–13, 258–60; *CChR 1341-1417*, 290–1; *CCR 1381-5*, 573.

[7] A useful account of relations between Newcastle and Tynemouth priory is contained in I. S. Leadam (ed.), *Select Cases before the King's Council in Star Chamber, ii. A.D. 1509-1544*, Selden Society, xxv (1910), pp. xciii–xcvi, 68–74.

Significantly, in none of these disputes do we find Newcastle burgesses attempting to monopolize the sale of coal from the Tyne, rather they were seeking to route the trade through their city in order to benefit 'by impositions and heavy charges upon every chaldron of coals put on board'.[8] After a century and more of deterioration, however, their fortunes began to wax along with those of the coal trade. The first reference to the existence of the Hostmen's Company occurs in 1517, and in 1529 an act of Parliament was passed which repelled the encroachments 'of late divers great personages as well spiritual as temporal having lands adjoining', which had been likely to bring the city 'to utter decay and ruin', and restored to Newcastle all former rights over the trade of the Tyne, excepting only the trade in salt and fish granted to Tynemouth priory by Edward IV, and the victualling of passing ships.[9] Nor was this all, the burgesses had begun to lay claim to the coal trade, as a letter written by the chancellor of the bishopric to Wolsey during his tenure of the see, 1523-9, makes plain. It is pointed out therein that the Whickham coal-pits were potentially worth 500 marks a year (£333. 6s. 8d.) to the see, and that the liberties and privileges possessed by the bishop allowed him to ship coals from the Durham side of the river. The letter went on:

the merchants of Newcastle will be loathe to apply themselves thereunto, howbeit your privileges and grants be clear enough, and it is no reason that they should enforce your Grace to sell your coals only unto them at their own prices, and they utter the same at their own liberty both to Englishmen and strangers at prices unreasonable, as they have done heretofore.[10]

The position of the city was soon to be strengthened further by the dissolution of Tynemouth priory, its inveterate enemy, while its other adversary the bishopric of Durham was rendered largely impotent by the prolonged weakness of the bishops under Elizabeth I.

Incorporation and ascendancy

It is uncertain whether the Hostmen's Company was specializing in the coal trade when it is first mentioned in 1517,[11] but there can be no doubt that its involvement with coal grew step by step with the increase in the trade. Certainly the charter of 1600 which incorporated the Company

---

[8] CChR 1341-1417, 290.
[9] Statutes of the Realm, 2 Henry 8, c.18; Leadam, Select Cases, pp. xcv–xcvi.
[10] Galloway 1898, i. 84.
[11] Dendy (ed.), Merchant Adventurers, pp. xxi, 159, 160, 164.

stressed that it was confirming and extending the 'liberties, privileges, immunities, jurisdictions, uses and customs' already enjoyed rather than conferring new ones.[12] And the 'gild or fraternity commonly called Hostmen, for the loading and better disposing of sea coals and pit coals, and stones called grind-stones, rub-stones and whet-stones, in, upon and within our river or port of Tyne', is said in the charter to have existed in Newcastle 'from the time whereof the memory of man is not to the contrary', although it had never been formally established by charters or letters patent. The charter is frustratingly imprecise on exactly what 'liberties etc.' had hitherto been enjoyed by the Hostmen, and contains no explicit reference to a monopoly of coal sales on the Tyne, but there can be no doubt that the Hostmen had already arrogated those powers. This much is made explicit by both sides in the late sixteenth-century disputes concerning the Grand Lease and the price of coal. For example, in answer to a suit made to Elizabeth I in 1586 by a Mr Poynes, who had sought a monopoly of the export of coal from the realm, the mayor and burgesses openly stated that the town from 'time out of mind hath used to sell, ship and deliver coals by certain principal persons of that town, called *Oastmen*, to whom it only appertained to sell and convey coals from that port into any other port or place, within or without the realm'. Of even greater moment was the Privy Council pronouncement made in the same year as the charter of incorporation, which acceded to the Hostmen's claim, that 'the buying, selling and lading of coal' was theirs 'both by custom and prescription time out of mind'.[13]

The closing decades of the sixteenth century and the opening years of the seventeenth were a watershed in the development of both the Tyneside coal industry and the authority of the city of Newcastle. Against a backdrop of soaring demand and output, not only did the Hostmen come to enjoy a monopoly of the sale of coal, they increasingly dominated its production. But success was not easily won, and every step in their ascent was fiercely contested. Instrumental in securing the ascendancy of the Hostmen over the Tyneside industry was the passing of the collieries of Whickham and Gateshead, potentially the most productive and lucrative in Britain, from the diffident bishopric of Durham into the hands of an enterprising cabal of Newcastle merchants. In this way a giant share of the soaring coal trade was proffered into the hands of a 'few rich men of Newcastle'.[14] For a time the bishop's

[12] The charters granted to the Hostmen and the city are printed in full in Brand 1789, ii. 605–27, 659–62.   [13] Dendy (ed.), *Hostmen*, 9; APC 1586, 427–8.

[14] The phrase comes from BL Lansdowne, 62(23).

borough of Gateshead was annexed by Newcastle, and in order to restore its independence the bishop was obliged to grant a 450-year lease of the borough tolls and salt meadows to its mighty neighbour. Other gains followed. In 1606 the Newcastle corporation finally assumed full admiralty jurisdiction over the Tyne, and eight years later the conservancy of the river was also placed securely in its hands.[15]

The tale of the Grand Lease of Whickham and Gateshead collieries has been told many times, but it bears retelling here from our own perspective, so pivotal an event was it in the evolution of the 'lords of coal'.[16] English bishops suffered grievously after the Reformation from the plundering of monarchs and courtiers, and the death of Bishop Pilkington in January 1576 provided an opportunity for yet further despoliation of Durham, one of the richest sees. In February 1577 Elizabeth extracted a 79–year lease of the manors of Whickham and Gateshead from the new bishop, Richard Barnes, and this was converted five years later into a new 99–year lease. It appears that the queen secured the lease for Robert Dudley, earl of Leicester, and that it was he who passed it on to his servant Thomas Sutton. The rent of £110 payable to the bishop was well below market value when the lease was granted, and in enterprising hands in a time of soaring demand for coal it was soon rendered derisory. Sutton appears to have operated the mines himself for six years, and profited greatly. But he was unable to gain admission as a freeman and Hostman of Newcastle, and in 1583 he assigned the remaining ninety-eight years of the lease to Henry Anderson and William Selby, leading members of the Newcastle burgess aristocracy, probably for £5,500 but possibly for as much as £12,000. What happened thereafter is hard to divine among the plethora of charges and protestations concerning rightful ownership, but it is likely that the intention had been that Anderson and Selby should take the lease on behalf of the mayor and corporation of Newcastle, and that at least part of the money which purchased it came from the town treasury. It is also probable that such a route would have been followed because a direct transfer to the town would have aroused intense opposition in Parliament, the City of London, and the bishopric. But, instead of making the lease over to the corporation, Anderson and Selby merely took on a few major co-partners drawn from the upper reaches

[15] Welford 1884–7, ii. 292–9, 305–10; Nef 1932, ii. 127.

[16] See e.g. Galloway 1898, i. 93–9; Nef 1932, i. 151–6; Moller thesis 1933, 445–58. The account written by Ralph Gardiner in 1655 is valuable though not always reliable (*England's Grievance*, 13–14). A colourful account is contained in Trevor-Roper 1945–6.

of the merchant oligarchy of Newcastle, including William Jennison, Henry Chapman, William Riddell, Henry Mitford, Roger Nicholson, and George Farnaby, leaving the bulk of the burgesses with tiny shares or none at all.[17]

The chief protagonist for the interests of those who had been excluded from wealth and power was Henry Sanderson, a free burgess and royal customs officer. But in 1598 the Privy Council, having nominated a committee of inquiry into the whole affair, declared that the magistrates of Newcastle were 'unjustly charged' and that there was 'no just cause for complaint proved'. A desperate appeal by the tenants and inhabitants of the bishopric for the revocation of the Grand Lease fared no better, and the bishop found himself powerless even to enforce payment of the agreed rent of £110.[18]

Disputes between burgesses over the ownership of the lease and the right to share in the riches it bestowed were to persist for many years, while simultaneous complaints about the rising price and falling quality of the coal sent from Tyneside embroiled Newcastle in a heated dispute with London.[19] According to the City the source of their injuries lay in an oligarchy of a 'few persons, being men of great wealth', numbering eighteen or twenty, who held not only the collieries of Whickham and Gateshead but all the other collieries around the city of Newcastle, in order to be able to 'sell their seacoal at their own prices for their best advantage and the public detriment [and] by evil practice seek to increase their gain to the hurt of others, especially the poorer sort'.[20] The queen and Parliament were apt to be mindful of the needs of the capital, and the alleged increase in the price of a London chaldron from 4s. in 1577 to 9s. in 1595 was probably not much of an exaggeration. But after a prompt hearing before the Privy Council the City's case made painfully slow progress. The soaring revenues which the Crown derived from the collection of 12d. on every chaldron shipped from the Tyne effectively guaranteed its continuing support for the Hostmen and Newcastle, and it could have come as no surprise when the queen declared that the inflation of prices was due 'to the engrossing of the said coals by a few

[17] The Grand Lessees, responding to an accusation by the City of London that the lease was held by 3 or 4 coal-owners, replied in 1595 that there were 'above thirty that are interested and parties to this lease . . . and . . . some be widows and orphans, and of those some not having more than 144th part' (Dendy (ed.), *Hostmen*, 6).

[18] Nef 1932, ii. 124–5, 154; BL Lansdowne 66(86).

[19] BL Lansdowne 65(11); Harleian 6850(39); Dendy (ed.), *Hostmen*, 2–9; Moller thesis 1933, 452–8.

[20] BL Lansdowne 65(11).

persons in London and places near adjoining', rather than by the rigging of supplies on Tyneside.[21]

The incorporation of the Hostmen's Company and the conferring of the Grand Charter upon Newcastle in 1600 inflamed passions on Tyneside still further. For the bulk of Newcastle burgesses now found themselves excluded from membership of the all-powerful Hostmen's Company and the government of Newcastle, as well as from any share in the riches bestowed by the Grand Lease. The correlation between the Grand Lessees, the rulers of the Hostmen, and the rulers of Newcastle was very close indeed, and at times almost perfect. Between 1581 and 1591, for example, all the major Grand Lessees served as mayor. Moreover, the city charter of 1600 prescribed an archetypal form of oligarchic government, which enabled the Hostmen's dominance to grow yet stronger. The first ten members of the Company, as listed in their charter, were the ten aldermen of the city, and nine of the ten were also major partners in the Grand Lease; William Jennison was the first mayor under the new constitution and the first governor of the Hostmen; William Jackson was the new town clerk and the first clerk to the Hostmen. When James Clavering became the first sheriff in 1604, he was immediately admitted into the Company.[22]

Within the space of a couple of decades, or even less, the Hostmen's Company had assumed control of the city of Newcastle and of the output and sale of one of the nation's most vital commodities and fastest growing trades. From each test the Hostmen and their leadership had emerged triumphant and even stronger. The new century dawned with the 'lords of coal' in an apparently impregnable position.[23] Flushed with the new-found legitimacy bestowed by their royal charter, the Hostmen proceeded to embark upon a wide-ranging programme of internal legislation to extend and enhance control over its membership, and between 8 July 1600 and 23 July 1601 the Company's court passed twenty-six acts.[24] External threats to their newly won legal powers, in the form of bills in opposition to the charter of incorporation, were introduced in the Commons in 1604 and the Lords in 1606, but they soon perished.[25]

The strength of the monopoly which the Hostmen possessed was bolstered by a restrictive policy on admissions. It was laid down in the Great Charter of 1600 that the Company had 'the full authority and power from time to time at their pleasure, to choose, name, and ordain

[21] *APC 1601–4*, 67.   [22] Nef 1932, ii. 126; Welford 1884–7, iii. 420.
[23] The title is coined in BL Lansdowne 66(86).   [24] Dendy (ed.), *Hostmen*, 29–42.
[25] Welford 1884–7, iii. 163, 176; Nef 1932, ii. 128–9.

others, being inhabitants of the said town, and burgesses of the town of Newcastle upon Tyne, to be brethren of the aforesaid fraternity', and in accordance with customary practice in other guilds and companies only the sons and apprentices of members were to be admitted as of right, others were to be admitted 'as a matter of grace and favour'. The result was that only a small proportion of the burgesses of Newcastle were allowed to share in the benefits of membership, and this was greatly resented. Within months of incorporation a flurry of complaints followed the path blazed by Henry Sanderson, this time instigated by that rare beast, a mayor who was not a Hostman. The very first clause of the petition of complaint of the mayor and burgesses to the Council of the North encapsulated their major grievance: 'that their [i.e. the Company of Hostmen's] incorporation was granted for the benefit of the town, and procured at the costs of their common treasure, whereof the burgesses are more than five hundred, and the hostmen that reap the benefit thereof fewer than forty'. Restrictions upon admission were likewise prominent when the mayor and burgesses petitioned James I in 1603 that every free burgess should be able to become a Hostman upon request, as they had before incorporation. In their meticulous reply the Hostmen denied that entry had ever been so free, and asserted instead that it had normally been open only to those whose masters or parents had been Hostmen, or to 'such as had coalmines, or had coals of their own, and upon such fine as was reasonably agreed upon'. To their surprise the Hostmen were rebuffed, first by a decree of the Council of the North and then by a charter from the king. A series of constitutional reforms for the city and the Company was prescribed, including the requirement that every free burgess, who had attained that status by apprenticeship or patrimony, desirous of becoming a Hostman should be admitted upon payment of a maximum fine of 53s. 4d..[26]

Yet the Hostmen's Company had grown too powerful to be so easily thwarted, and although at first sight these prescriptions posed a severe threat, in practice they were able to be accommodated without too much discomfort. Whereas in the three years after incorporation only seven new members had been admitted to the Company, on 17 January 1604 fifteen new members were admitted, doubtless in speedy response to the decree of the Council of the North. But admissions thereafter soon returned to a trickle, as the Hostmen began interpreting the decree and charter as narrowly as possible.[27] Only those burgesses who

[26] Dendy (ed.), *Hostmen*, 19–27.
[27] Ibid. 265–74 lists the admissions of members from 1600 onwards.

had become free by service or patrimony were considered eligible, and then only if they were members of one of the twelve principal mysteries of the town. Moreover, outsiders were at best only granted life-membership, which debarred their widows, sons, and apprentices from membership.[28] That the decree of 1603 and the charter of 1604 had little or no lasting impact is evident from the failure of the membership of the Company to increase much if at all in size. If we may judge from the testimony of the Lord Mayor of London, there were about sixty 'free-hosts' in 1595, which accords well with the fifty-six names entered in the charter of incorporation of 1600. In 1629 it was reported that the whole fellowship consisted of at least sixty persons, but a year later the Hostmen themselves gave their membership as 'about fifty'.[29]

Burgesses striving to become Hostmen wished to share in the wealth that flowed from the exercise of the monopoly over the sale of Tyneside coal rather than to overthrow it, and it was not until 1621 that a further serious assault on the existence of that monopoly was mounted, this time with the fervent support of a non-free coal-owner, Robert Brandling, MP for Morpeth, 'a man hated of the town and he likewise hates them'.[30] But these were halcyon days for the 'lords of coal', and when in 1623 an act of Parliament was passed against monopolies it contained a special provision exempting the Hostmen's Company entirely and stating that it did not extend to, nor was it prejudicial to, any right whatsoever which the Hostmen enjoyed in the coal trade.[31] The revenues derived from Richmond's shilling, around £7,500 a year at this time, were too indispensable to the solvency of impecunious monarchs to be tampered with in the interests of free trade, or even lower coal prices.

The possession of monopoly rights, even when derived from the Crown and enforced through civic government, did not ensure that they could be effectively exercised. The history of guilds is littered with the debris of orders and by-laws expressing pious hopes rather than tangible authority, and Tudor and Stuart monarchs established a multitude of private monopolies with insufficient means of enforcement, thus bringing ruin rather than riches to the monopolists. The Hostmen, however, belong to quite a different species. The almost perpetual clamour from those close to coal who wished to share in or overthrow their privileges signals as much. A good independent yardstick of the strength of the Hostmen is also supplied by the experience of the ninth

---

[28] Dendy (ed.), *Hostmen*, p. xli.
[30] DN Syon QII 126.
[29] Moller thesis 1933, 538; Dendy (ed.), *Hostmen*, 2.
[31] 25 James I, *c*.3 (Dendy (ed.), *Hostmen*, 28).

earl of Northumberland, who owned a number of rich Tyneside collieries but failed lamentably in his attempt to make money from producing coal. Even though the earl was imprisoned in the Tower between 1605 and 1622, suspected of complicity in the Gunpowder Plot, he remained a powerful force in the north, and was allowed to retain possession of his estates and revenues. Voluminous correspondence surrounded the earl's foray into direct management, and it is possible to observe the reasons for the failure of this enterprise from within. The earl, like all great landowners, was instinctively a rentier, but a prolonged and bitter dispute with James Cole, a leading Hostman, over the payment of rent encouraged him to take Newburn and Tynemouth collieries into his own hands. When his steward, Captain Whitehead, wrote in January 1616 in the early stages of the venture, his letter tingled with alarm and suspicion. The 'Newcastle men' were discomfited by the earl working his own pits, and Whitehead had been unable to obtain the services of a borer, despite offering double pay. A letter of the same date from Nicholas Hardwick brought further matters of concern to the earl's attention. The 'Grandlease men' had lowered the price of their coal since the earl had begun working, with the intention of forcing him out of production, and pressure from Newcastle was keeping the viewer, William Bunting, from overseeing the work more than once a fortnight. When Hardwick wrote again on 18 February, it was to report that although Whitehead had managed to persuade a leading salter to purchase 200 tens, this had provoked yet further discontent in Newcastle.[32]

The earl had lent his support to the Hostmen in 1604 and 1606 by opposing the bills put forward to curb their powers,[33] but now he was seen as their enemy. Attempts in March 1617 to dispose of his coal using a fitter called Carr, probably the Hostman Leonard Carr, were not very rewarding. Although the coal was 'good and popular', Carr demanded an extra 5 chaldrons to the score, and when he came to load it was alleged that he put 78 chaldrons on board a ship which should have taken no more than 62, a bonus of no less than 8 in the score. At these discounts all profit was being lost to the earl, but finding any alternative means of selling coal was proving impossible. On 16 November a letter from Whitehead bemoaned that he found all 'the Newcastle men very loathe that your Lordship should come in amongst them and therefore no trust [was] to be reposed in any of them'. A week later he reported that only one man had offered to buy, and he seemed not only to be very

[32] DN Syon QII, 111; QXI 51, 52.   [33] Nef 1932, ii. 128.

poor and therefore capable of taking only a small quantity, but quite likely to prove incapable of paying the £3. 5s. a ten he had offered. A month later Bunting the viewer was counselling the earl that because 'the Newcastle monopoly' was so strong there was no alternative to reaching an agreement with a Hostman. By January, however, White-head reported that even Carr was reluctant to fit Northumberland's coal. Conditions did not improve in the summer, which should have been the peak selling period, and Whitehead wrote frequently of the resistance of the Hostmen. A realistic appraisal of the prospects was given to the earl by the experienced and knowledgeable William Bunting. 'We have many coals wrought and can get no vent for them', he wrote, 'for the magistrates of Newcastle have made such strict orders to bar unfreemen from venting any coals' that it was impossible to sell at a profit. 'This action', Bunting continued, 'is done chiefly to cross your Lordship's officers in the sale of their coals. For certain merchants that be freemen within the town, which had undertaken sale of them, have now refused, and dare not perform for fear of offence.'[34]

Despite all the portents Whitehead remained stubbornly optimistic, and vowed to resist offering the exorbitant quantities of gift-coals that were demanded by Hostmen. He encouraged the earl by reporting that Newburn coal was well liked at Hull, Yarmouth, and Dover, and at the end of September he held out hope that a freeman would take 100 tens off the staithe, and that he himself would be able to dispose of the rest on a selling expedition along the east coast, talking directly to ship-masters at Scarborough, Hull, Boston, and King's Lynn. We do not know whether this sales trip materialized, but conditions had not improved by the following summer. No Hostman could be found who would take less than five chaldron extra to the score, which would have meant that the earl would have received only £3 a ten. At this price the colliery's operating costs would not be met, and in desperation White-head begged the earl to reply to his letters and give him instructions. Salvation appeared right at the close of the selling season, in the form of Robert Anderson and Nicholas Tempest, two founder-members of the Hostmen's Company, who made an offer to purchase all the accumu-lated stocks and up to 400 tens of new production at £3. 3s. 4d. per ten. Whitehead applauded it as an unbeatable offer, and it was snatched up by a grateful earl, but it is difficult not to see it as the final step in a conspiracy to bring Northumberland to his knees. The terms were ungenerous, and Tempest and Anderson proved very slow payers.

[34] DN Syon QVI 75; QII 104; QVI 85, 88, 91, 100, 101.

Resistance to the Hostmen had proved very costly, even for so rich a man. In the very next year the victory of the Hostmen was complete, for Newburn flooded and the earl gave up the unequal struggle and abandoned the production of coal once and for all.[35]

The aims of the 'Newcastle men', of course, were not simply to force non-free coal-owners to sell their coal to them alone, but to force them to desist working their collieries and instead lease them to Hostmen. They sought not just a monopoly of sale but a monopoly of production as well. Whickham colliery at its peak was probably producing up to a third of the output of the whole of Northumberland and Durham and, as the ship-money assessment of 1636 reveals, Hostmen were also in possession of most of the other leading collieries on Tyneside. None the less, Hostmen had no special entitlement to purchase or lease collieries, only an advantageous position from which to do so. The abundance of potential mining-sites ensured that there could be no perfect monopoly, and throughout the period outsiders continued to mine coal. In 1610, for example, it was reported that 'there are divers free burgesses of Newcastle, who are not and will not be free of the fellowship of Hostmen, who have both coals and shipping of their own'. Some independent operators were men of considerable perseverance as well as substance. Robert Brandling, who proffered assistance to the earl, continued to operate collieries in defiance of the Hostmen for many years, and was followed by his son John; and Anthony Errington, of gentry stock, throve by mining coal at Denton and Sugley Common, adjacent to Newburn, and in 1622 he built a mansion overlooking his mines.[36]

But such men were exceptions. The success with which the Hostmen were able to stop unfree producers selling direct to the shipmasters, and to restrict entry into their Company, militated against the profitability of independent enterprises. Unfree producers could sell their coal cheaply to the salt-pans, and serve inland markets with limited quantities but, as Northumberland found, when attempting to sell to shippers they faced the prospect of heavily discounted prices and the loss of their profit to Hostmen fitters. It was for these reasons that the Hostmen were able to offer more for leases and, in those rare cases when collieries were sold, higher purchase prices. For all of Hugh Bird's fair promises of being able to find outsiders who would pay far more for

[35] Ibid. 106, 114, 116; QII 135; QVI 121, 122; QII 144, 145, 148.
[36] BL Lansdowne 169(46); DN Syon QII 126; Welford 1884-7, iii. 317-18; Nef 1932, ii. 128-30; Watts 1975, 54.

Northumberland's leases than Hostmen would, when it came to firm offers and hard cash it was the 'Newcastle men' who took possession. As Richard Wallis, a non-Hostman, was told when he sought the lease of a mine near the Tyne in 1622, 'I understand the Town of Newcastle are suitors for it, who are both able to give more than any man else, and have always engrossed into their hands as much as they have been able to get'. A pleasing irony occurred when Sir William Selby, the head of one of the most powerful coal-owning Hostmen dynasties, was obliged in 1638 to sell some of his interests in collieries to meet debts exceeding £11,000 contracted by his spendthrift son. Selby bemoaned that he could not obtain a satisfactory price because 'no man can make any gain by them but . . . a free hostman of Newcastle-upon-Tyne'. With engaging effrontery he petitioned the king that whoever might buy his colliery or any part of it, should be admitted, and also their heirs, 'as to the sale and vending of coals only to trade as free hostmen'. If this concession were granted, Selby maintained, he would be certain to find buyers.[37]

Such dominance inevitably led on occasion to the formation of cartels. There were very few periods of normal trading in the sixteenth and seventeenth centuries when demand outstripped supply, and the prime intention of such combinations was to mitigate the effects of glut by restricting competition between coal-owners and enabling them to present a united front to the shipmasters. The early years of the seventeenth century were a period of consolidation of demand, with signs of weakening prices, and within little more than two years of incorporation the 'lords of coal' on 26 February 1603 agreed to 'an order and agreement of partnership for the vent of coals', under which prices would be maintained and the available market shared in agreed portions between coal-owners. This was the first of a long line of 'Limitations of Vend', formal combinations of producers, which were to continue intermittently for centuries. The 1603 agreement was reached between twenty-nine coal-owners, about half the total membership of the Company, and ratified and promulgated by the Court. The vend of the coming year was estimated at 9,080 tens, each of ten chaldrons, amounting to some 236,000 tons. Each partner's expected output was specified, and then the partners were grouped into four approximately equal quarters. The groups were to sell coals in equal amounts, and sales within each group were to be conducted according to the specified shares; if any member had a surplus of coal he was permitted to sell it

[37] Nef 1932, ii. 20; Sweezy 1938, 12–13.

only to another member of his group who had a shortfall. Partners were exhorted to sell coals of good quality only, not to cause a scarcity, and to abide by the 'reasonable' prices of 8s. or less for a chaldron of 'mean coals', 9s. for the 'second sort', and not above 10s. for the 'best sort'.[38]

The 1603 agreement was headed 'For reformation of many great abuses and disorders heretofore practised by the general Company of the Hostmen of Newcastle upon Tyne, their servants and workmen, and also for the better ordering, disposing, uttering and loading of seacoals', while that of 1605 stressed how it might lead to the more efficient collection of customs duties.[39] Those who consumed coal, however, were not convinced that these were the true motives. The combination of 1603 had provoked spirited but ineffective protests from London; that of 1605 met the resistance of the shipmasters, which was to prove far more effective. Much of the profit of a voyage derived from the ability to bargain over price and the quantity of gift-coal allowed at Newcastle, and at a stroke the united front presented by the major coal-owners threatened to fix both prices and allowances. The shipmasters were enraged and, according to the Hostmen, by a 'sinister construing' of the agreements and 'upon a malicious and perverse forwardness, and upon peevish counsel amongst themselves', they organized a boycott which lasted for two months in the spring of 1605. The boycott inevitably produced shortages and high prices in London, and once again the City moved against the Hostmen, although this time their case was strengthened by a drastic fall in royal customs revenues. A bill was duly presented in the Court of Star Chamber, and the Privy Council acted swiftly to dissolve the combination since it was 'injurious and prejudicial to the King's Majesty's subjects'.[40]

There are no traces of any further attempts to form combinations of coal-owners during the ensuing twelve years. Although it is possible that covert associations were formed, it is probable that the tightening of the market and the resumption of an upward drift in prices rendered combinations unnecessary. They were also dangerous. The Hostmen had been duly chastened by the reprimand received from the Privy Council. Moreover, rising prices predictably sparked another howl of protest from London alleging price-rigging, to which the Hostmen responded by giving the City authorities a lecture on the basic principles of economics, maintaining that the chief cause of rising prices was that 'the use of seacoals in London and the other coast towns through the

[38] Dendy (ed.), *Hostmen*, 43–8.   [39] Ibid. 51–5.
[40] Welford 1884–7, iii. 76; Dendy (ed.), *Hostmen*, 56.

kingdom, is so increased above the quantity that formerly it was'.[41] Yet oversupply was a recurrent problem, and the Hostmen found the temptation to form cartels irresistible in 1617, 1622, and 1627. However, the generous quotas which were set make it clear that the primary aim was not the restriction of production, which may in any case have been impossible to reach agreement upon, but the sharing of the available market and the elimination of competition among themselves in their dealings with the shipmasters.[42] When challenged in 1603 the Hostmen had professed that the major benefit of the partnership to themselves was 'that every Hostman might sell and vent his coals alike, and that one of them might not be overborne in his sales by the riches of any other of them, and that the said trade might be indifferent between them all',[43] and the 1622 agreement specified that all sales of coal were to be channelled through seven nominated Hostmen. But the shipmasters had discovered a powerful form of self-defence, and representations to the Privy Council again produced the desired response. In May 1623 the combination was ordered to be dissolved, 'being a near monopoly tending to the great damage of the public'.[44]

The concern displayed by the Privy Council and City authorities with securing ample supplies of good quality coal at reasonable prices is eloquent testimony to the importance that this fuel had attained by the early seventeenth century. Indeed, so bitter did the controversy over the mixing of bad coal with good become that a group of Hostmen were briefly imprisoned in the Fleet in 1618.[45] Yet in 1627, in a defiant act, the Hostmen again reacted to a slump in shipments with yet another formal combination. This slump was of exceptionally severe proportions, with coastal shipments from Newcastle plunging from 378,000 tons in 1623–4 to just 218,000 tons in 1624–5 and 295,000 tons in 1625–6. However, the 1627 agreement included some important changes in format: centralized sales were abandoned, and each member was free to sell his own quota, with fines of 6 d. per chaldron for any excess sales, and compensation of 16 d. per chaldron, later 24 d., for those who were unable to meet their quotas. The overall quota was fixed at an extremely optimistic 366,000 tons, and actual trading conditions continued to be poor. After a few months of operation a memorandum was circulated pointing to widespread breaches in observance, possibly because the benefits which the combination promised through the bolstering of prices were outweighed

[41] Dendy (ed.), Hostmen, 58–61.
[42] Ibid. 63–71, 72–4.
[43] Ibid. 23.
[44] Nef 1932, ii. 114–15.
[45] Brand 1789, ii. 278.

by the penalties which flowed from an inability to sell as much as each Hostman wished.[46] Perhaps also, because owners were able to sell their own coal directly to the shippers, many did not abide by its terms. The combination in the event does not seem to have been effective enough to have provoked a response from either shippers or consumers. It was to be the last in the period covered by this volume, though the coal glut at the turn of the seventeenth century brought about the revival of combinations in the first decade of the eighteenth century.

The years prior to the Civil War were a time of upheaval and uncertainty in the coal trade, occasioned by a series of speculative ventures and new monopolies designed to enhance the revenues of an impecunious Crown. Charles I found the temptation to meddle with the coal trade irresistible, despite the fact that, unmolested, it already constituted 'the bravest farm the king has'. Using the model of the tin farm, by which he drew revenues from the pre-emption of the output of the stannaries of Cornwall and Devon, Charles's advisers drew up plans whereby the king would purchase the produce of all Tyneside collieries at a fixed price. The schemes also involved a new corporation of Hostmen and a Society of Coal Merchants, but predictably they were brought to a premature end by a boycott of shippers before they died of natural causes.[47]

Civil War and metamorphosis

At the height of their powers in the first half of the seventeenth century, the Hostmen attained a remarkable degree of control over the production and sale of coal from the leading British coalfield, but there had always been tensions within their ranks. Apart from wide differences in wealth, the membership was split into those who ran collieries and those who made their living from selling the coal of others to the shipmasters. In the early combination agreements perhaps no more than half of the Company were named as producers, and the core of leading coal-owning families was smaller still. In 1603, for example, the twenty-nine coal-owners who are listed have only eighteen different surnames, and the range of quotas allowed them runs from over 23,000 tons to just 4,000 tons. While such policies as restrictions on entry into the Company and on the ability of non-freemen to sell their coal direct to shipmasters could be supported by all, many members were fitters who

---

[46] Dendy (ed.), *Hostmen*, 72–4; Sweezy 1938, 14.

[47] Welford 1884–7, iii. 354–8; Galloway 1898, i. 140–1; Nef 1932, ii. 279–82; *CSPD 1638–9*, 250, 327.

were increasingly content to gain a living from selling the coals of non-freemen on commission. Nor was it always possible to gain unanimity among coal-owners on the form which combination agreements should take, for those with low costs of production had less to gain from the restriction of competition. As has been noted, the agreement of 1627 was not universally obeyed, and in 1637 a number of mine-owners 'so many as will vent near 3,000 tens [*c*.80,000 tons] of the best sort' refused to submit to the Company's orders.[48]

Attempts to regulate prices through the amount of 'gift-coals' given as enticements to shipmasters frequently met similar fates. Bonuses varied with the state of the trade, and they are generally heard of in the Hostmen's courts in times of slack trading when they threatened to reach unacceptably generous proportions. On 26 May 1651, for example, it was reported that some members 'for base ends, give away four or five chalder of coals at every twenty chalder of coals that they sell', and it was decided that henceforth all extra chaldrons and cash inducements should be prohibited. Ominously, less than a month later the ordinance was amended to permit gift-coals of one chaldron per score, and it seems to have lapsed completely soon afterwards. In October 1690, in extremely slack trading when as many as six extra chaldrons per score were being given, an attempt was made to revive the prohibition, and the court ordered 'that all gift coals be wholly taken of and none allowed for the future upon any pretence whatsoever'. In order to secure the conformity of the fitters, it was agreed that they should be paid 'one shilling per chaldron for all coals they shall so vend'. Significantly, Lionel Vane and four other freemen were deputed to consult on this matter with 'the unfreemen that vend coals in this affair'. The order was subsequently revoked in July 1692, only to be revived in February 1695. Inevitably, as we know from independent evidence, these orders were virtually impossible to enforce, as the Company finally admitted openly in November 1700. Regulating gift-coals was tantamount to regulating prices, and the Company was unable to stop individual members from gaining sales by breaking the rules.[49]

If ambitious attempts of questionable legality to control production and regulate sales by corporate action had eventually to be abandoned, the very essence of the Company's *raison d'être* also eventually came under threat from within. The sizeable number of fitters in the ranks of the Hostmen, whose livelihoods came from selling the coal of others

[48] Dendy (ed.), *Hostmen*, 74; Nef 1932, ii. 118.
[49] Dendy (ed.), *Hostmen*, 93–4, 146–50, 157.

rather than operating collieries, were greatly harmed by many of the rules which discriminated against non-free coal-owners. The rules of the Company regulating the sale of the coal of non-free coal-owners by Hostmen were clear, although they have sometimes been misunderstood by historians.[50] Non-freemen were allowed to sell their coal only to Hostmen, and Hostmen were perfectly at liberty to buy it. What Hostmen were not permitted to do was simply to 'colour' the coal of non-free producers; that is, to sell it on commission without first purchasing it. In the words of the Company by-law it was prohibited for any brother or sister to deal in the coals of a non-free person 'where the profit and loss of the coals and stones vended do not wholly and altogether accrue to the freeman in whose name the said coals and grindstones are cleared'.[51] Such an arrangement was, however, unlikely to suit either the non-free producer or the fitter. Coal-owners were resentful of the prospect of a substantial share of their profits going to middlemen who simply sold their coal in the Tyne, while for the majority of fitters the sums of money and the risks involved in purchasing large quantities of coal in a volatile market in order to sell it again were simply too great.

If the seeds of the decline of the authority of the Hostmen's Company were sown before the Civil War, this event and the political tenor of the Protectorate which followed provided an ideal environment for the process of germination. The occupation and reoccupation of Newcastle by the Scots, the manipulation of the coal trade first by the Crown and then by Parliament, the sequestration of the estates of royalists, and the physical damage sustained by collieries, all hastened change.[52] Perhaps most important of all were the overwhelming numbers of royalists among the coal-owning dynasties, men who stood to suffer greatly when Parliament assumed power. Included among these were such coal magnates as Sir Francis Anderson, Sir John Marley, Sir James Liddell, Sir Thomas Riddell, Sir Nicholas and Ralph Cole, Sir William Selby, Sir Francis Bowes, Sir Richard and William Tempest, and many lesser men and the heirs of the great. Indeed, Sir Lionel Maddison and John Blakiston appear to have been the only leading Hostmen who were deemed 'well-affected'. Yet the impact of the supremacy of the parliamentarian cause was cushioned by expediency. Driven by the desperate need for fuel in the south, as well as for the money which a

---

[50] e.g. Nef erroneously believed that Hostmen were forbidden to buy the coal of non-members (1932, ii. 21).

[51] Dendy (ed.), *Hostmen*, 91–2.

[52] An excellent account of Newcastle and the Civil War is contained in Howell 1967.

thriving trade would furnish, most of these 'notorious delinquents and malignants' not only survived but retained the ownership and management of the coal-mines upon which their families' fortunes depended. Few delinquents were expelled from the Hostmen's Company. Henry Marley, who had been a captain in the earl of Newcastle's army was deprived of his membership, but he was left in possession of his mines and was able to sell his coal through friendly members. Pragmatism was apt to triumph over principle when Londoners froze, the price of coal rocketed, and the revenues of the government from the shipment of coal assumed the proportions of a trickle rather than the desired flood. Those in power believed that there were simply too few expert 'well-affected' persons in mining to replace 'malignant' royalists, so skilful was the management of collieries and the coal trade considered.[53]

Yet, if the personnel running the Tyneside coal industry changed little, the context in which the Hostmen operated became far less sympathetic to them. Delinquents remained out of favour, and while a majority in Parliament was never obtained to support the abolition of the privileges of the Company, government assistance could no longer be relied upon to enforce them. Sir Lionel Maddison, a staunch Puritan and parliamentarian, took over as governor of the Company in 1645, and was followed in office by a succession of men who were either viewed as well affected or, at the least, free of the taint of delinquency. Although we can identify only two political appointees who were forced upon the Company, Edward Man and Robert Ellison, the increase in the numbers of admissions after the War is suggestive. Between 1617 and 1645 the Company had admitted an average of just over two new members annually, while from 1645 to 1660 the annual average was almost five.[54] The Hostmen's Company was admitting a greater number of Newcastle burgesses, gentlemen, and merchants, as well as those who had served their apprenticeships. In this way the processes of change within it were accelerated.

The stark divisions of wealth and function which had existed in the Company from the earliest days became ever more marked as the century progressed, and the fitters became numerically ever more dominant over the coal-owners. As they did so breaches of rules governing the sale of the coal of non-freemen became ever more frequent and ever more threatening to the viability of the Company.[55] There was a

[53] Dendy (ed.), *Hostmen*, 81–3. [54] Ibid. 266–74; Howell 1967, 276.
[55] See e.g. Dendy (ed.), *Hostmen*, 56–7, 79, 86, 91–2, 96, 97, 99, 100, 130, 142, 147–8, 153, 154, 157, 159, 160–3.

new air of defiance about many of the offenders appearing before the court, which was symptomatic of the broader challenges to authority which were being displayed in many other areas of the city's life.[56] Guild restrictions were under assault, and there were powerful pressures from below to sweep away ancient customs and to set trade free. Against the trend, the Company in 1654 decided to make a determined effort to stamp out the 'colouring' of coals, and it appointed a committee. Its report made alarming reading. Twelve non-free coal-owners were identified as selling their coal illicitly through the services of named members who acted as their fitters, and attention was also drawn to the existence 'of divers fitters who are unfree men yet buy coals for themselves and lade them in the names of freemen of this fraternity'. The unlawful dealings of Stephen Hutcheson, Hostman, on behalf of James Cole, unfree, were concealed, it was alleged, in an indenture dated 20 January 1652 which recorded the sale of 6,500 chaldrons (c.17,000 tons) by Cole to Hutcheson which was 'not real or *bona fide*'. Further, a shipmaster from Yarmouth declared that although he dealt through Henry Wall, who was a freemen, he subsequently bought the coal that was loaded on to his ship from Henry Marley, who was not, and paid all the purchase money to him.[57] Conflicts of interest within the fraternity between coal-owners and fitters meant that firm policies towards such offences could not be made effective. Expulsions were frequently threatened but rarely executed, even when dealing with the most flagrant breaches of the rules. Fines were levied, but not at a level sufficient to act as a deterrent. Hutcheson, for example, was fined £20, which was almost certainly far less than the commission he would have received for selling the 6,500 chaldrons in question.

Assaults upon the privileges of the Company and the city of Newcastle from without also assumed threatening proportions in the 1650s. The Civil War and the emergence of radical philosophies had helped to create a climate within which traditional structures and customary privileges could more readily be challenged. In such a climate the case of Thomas Cliffe, ably handled by Ralph Gardiner, an implacable enemy of the magistrates of Newcastle, mushroomed into a *cause célèbre*.[58] At the outset it was alleged that Cliffe's wife had been killed in a mêlée when a deputation from Newcastle forcibly stopped Cliffe and his workmen from repairing ships at Shields, but this proved to be merely the pretext for a wide-ranging attack on the monopoly

---

[56] Howell 1967, 278.   [57] Dendy (ed.), *Hostmen*, 99–101.
[58] The case is dealt with in detail in Howell (ed.), *Monopoly*.

rights of the city and the Hostmen over the Tyne and coal trade. Gardiner found willing allies among non-free coal-owners and disaffected shipmasters, and was able to address his case to parliaments which contained sympathetic and vocal minorities. Spurred on by the support he had obtained, Gardiner boldy proposed that the whole basis of Newcastle's prerogatives should be examined and revoked if found unacceptable. Barebone's parliament decided his appeal had merit, and an act supporting a free trade in coal and salt on the Tyne was proposed. Untimately, however, struggles between radical and conservative parliamentarians over a wide range of policies proved too destructive, and when Parliament's authority was surrendered back to Oliver Cromwell reform of the coal monopoly was shelved. But Gardiner's enthusiasm continued unabated, and he met with some further success in 1658, when a committee was established to investigate and reform abuses and monopolistic practices. In the following year the Hostmen were ordered to send representatives to London to answer Gardiner's complaints, and as a result the fraternity speedily set up its own committee 'to meet with the unfree coalowners of the counties of Northumberland and Durham, and to treat with them about an accommodation for the vending of their coals according to certain proposals made by the committee for the hearing of complaints against monopolies'.[59]

The Restoration in 1660 threw such liberalizing measures abruptly into reverse. Not only was hostile government action halted, the Company was encouraged swiftly to set about seeking to strengthen its constitutional position. A mere seven months after Charles II assumed the throne a committee was appointed to consider how the Company charter might be 'improved to their best advantage', and how the Sunderland coal trade might be brought into line with Newcastle's. The exemption enjoyed by Sunderland coal from the 1s. per chaldron duty exacted on shipments from Tyneside was a source of much grievance. Two months later counsel's favourable opinion on the right of the Company to levy heavy fines was received, and in May 1662 a commission was obtained from the mayor and burgesses authorizing the seizure of all coals that had been 'vended by unfreemen ... and laid aboard ships'. Having received legal confirmation of its powers, the Company's court embarked upon a fierce attack on the sales of coal by the non-free and the 'colouring' of coals by free fitters. But this was not all. So emboldened was the Company that it ventured to extend its control

[59] Dendy (ed.), *Hostmen*, 117.

into new areas: it forbade fitters to sell coal to shipmasters at Shields, it prohibited free fitters from any form of association with non-free fitters, and it sought to regulate the level of gift-coal conceded to shipmasters and to tighten the rules relating to apprenticeships.[60]

The governing faction of the fraternity clearly hoped for a return to the halcyon pre-Civil War days, but they hoped in vain. Time had moved on and a multitude of developments, both within the Company and without, rendered the past irrecoverable. It had become ever more common to load ships downstream as far as Shields, which was 'very prejudicial unto the brethren of this fraternity' because it was easy for illicit transactions to pass undetected,[61] while the progressive expansion of production in the Wear valley and on the North Sea coast rendered chimerical any lingering quest for comprehensive control of the output of coal by Hostmen. At the time of incorporation in 1600 the Tyne had accounted for perhaps 95 per cent of all shipments from the north-east; by mid-century the Tyne accounted for some 80 per cent, and by the last quarter for around 75 per cent. Perhaps of even greater moment, was the presence of non-free coal magnates of the substance of Charles Montagu and Lord Widdrington in the Tyne valley. As a consequence, the proportion of seasale coal which was produced by freemen may have fallen dangerously close to 60 per cent. Dominance of production had been lost, and dominance of trade was soon to be.

The correspondence conducted between Charles Montagu and various of his partners and agents reveals that in the later 1690s the outsider was enjoying far greater freedom and less discrimination and hostility than the earl of Northumberland had encountered some eighty years before. Montagu was using the services of free fitters to vend the output of Benwell and Gibside. He did so partly because he was unsure whether the Hostmen would seize his coal if he did not, and partly because trade was not buoyant and it was prudent to rely for the time being on experienced men with good contacts. One such 'cunning' fitter was Henry Milbourne, who according to Montagu was 'an errant noted K[nave], but is the oldest fitter and able to sell more coals than any man in Newcastle'. Even so Montagu's arrangements breached the rules of the Company, for there was no pretence that the fitters were purchasing the coal from him. They sold it for a straight commission of $8\frac{1}{2}$–$12d$ a chaldron.[62]

Montagu was, however, far from satisfied with the service he

[60] Ibid., pp. xxxiv–xxxv, 188ff.   [61] Ibid. 90, 123, 148.

[62] NeUL Montagu, Montagu to Baker 26/5/96, 30/12/97.

received, and began toying with the possibility of selling his coal directly to the shipmasters through his own employees. He also took steps to promote the good reputation of Benwell and Gibside coals in his native London. When he sought advice from coal-owning 'grandees' of the Hostmen's Company whether the Hostmen would seize his coals if they were 'led by an unfree man', one thought it a scandal and said that they might as well have a charter to seize country gentlemen's corn on the Tyne, and others said that a 10,000th share of a colliery held by a freeman made the whole colliery free. Most remarkable of all, Sir William Blackett, who had been governor of the Company in 1691 and 1692, is reported as saying to Montagu that all merchants had a right to be free of the Hostmen's Company and that he would bring in all the merchants and confound all the fitters by outnumbering them. Such assurances set Montagu thinking about schemes whereby he could make a freeman a partner in his collieries, 'with restrictive covenants', or use a merchant who could become free and thus 'qualify' his coals.[63]

By the late seventeenth century there was clearly little sense of corporate purpose within the fraternity. Even the fitters were not united, and it was a group of six fitters who were instrumental in commencing the process whereby the prerogatives of the Company to monopolize the sale of coal were ultimately overthrown. The case they fought is worth dwelling upon in some detail, for it gave formality and virtual finality to the withering of the Company's powers in these crucial areas. On 14 April 1703 the court heard a petition of complaint:

by divers of the company against Charles Atkinson, John Maddison, Jeremiah Hunter, Timothy Rawling, Thomas Forster and Francis Armorer, hostmen, for aiding and assisting gentlemen owners of coals not free of this Society who confederate with the lightermen and buyers of coals in the City of London to the ruin and prejudice of the hostmen and the coal trade in Newcastle.

On 5 May the six fitters were suspended from membership for six months, and a committee recommended that the dealings members had with London lightermen and coal buyers should be severely restricted, 'under the penalty of disfranchisement or fines of considerable amount'. Far from being settled, however, the dispute rapidly escalated, and on 20 May the governor reported that he had been served with six writs of mandamus from the Court of Queen's Bench at Westminster, ordering that the six suspended members should be restored to the full liberties and privileges of the Company. The fitters, who were clearly being

<hr />

[63] NeUL Montagu, Montagu to Baker 14/8/97.

sponsored by the non-free coal-owners for whom they worked, had obtained a devastating opinion from Mr Northey, the Attorney-General, on the powers which the Hostmen could derive from their charter. The Attorney-General had pronounced:

I am of the opinion that the members of the corporation by virtue of their charter are not nor can be entitled to the sole landing and disposing, carrying or shipping of coals on the River Tyne between the town of Newcastle and the place of Sparhawk, but the owners of coals may convey their coals on shipboard at Newcastle in such ways and with such assistance as they shall think fit.

Ominously, on the very same day as the writs of mandamus were being discussed, Thomas Grieve, another fitter, brought an action against various members who had seized coal for breaches of Company by-laws relating to dealings with non-free producers.[64]

The Company immediately secured a majority among the membership to fight on, and to join with the mayor and burgesses to preserve the custom of foreign bought and foreign sold. But it was mere bravado; the cause was lost. Nor was it lost simply because of a lack of a legal right to enforce claims. The long-standing and destructive split in interests between the coal-owners and the fitters who gained their living by selling the coal of others had become irreversible, and went to the very heart of the *raison d'être* of the Company. Moreover, although the coal magnates of the Tyne valley continued to be a small and select group up to the close of the century, and almost all were to be found among the ranks of the Hostmen, the dominance of the Tyne valley and the Hostmen was no longer absolute enough nor coherent enough for the policies of the past to be successfully pursued. The greatest coal-owner of all, Charles Montagu, whose collieries were producing well over 100,000 tons a year in the 1700s was an outsider. So too were Lord Widdrington and Mr Pitts, with perhaps 30,000 tons between them, to say nothing of the proprietors of the major seasale collieries of the Wear and the North Sea coast.

None the less, it is important to distinguish the declining fortunes of the Hostmen's Company from the still formidable powers of the leading coal-owners. The eighteenth century dawned with the revival of the long dormant 'Limitation of the Vend'. The policies adopted by the leading coal-owners in this time of slump were of venerable pedigree; what was new was that their combinations were no longer assembled solely from within the ranks of the Hostmen's Company.[65]

[64] Dendy (ed.), *Hostmen*, 160–4.   [65] See in particular Ellis 1981, 111–38.

ii. The London coal trade[66]

The price of coal sold wholesale in the Pool of London was, in normal years in the seventeenth century, some two and a half to three times higher than that which the colliery owners and fitters received from the shipmasters when they delivered it to their vessels on the Tyne and the Wear. In the last quarter of the century the ratio rose higher still with the imposition of substantial duties, first by the City and then by Parliament. In those years around the turn of the century when war was not disrupting trade, a Londoner could expect to pay well over 15s. a ton for coal which had cost the shipper at the very most 4s. on the Tyne or the Wear. It was disparities like this which had for centuries induced Londoners into believing that they paid far too much for their coal. In describing how coal reached the hearths of the capital's houses, Ralph Gardiner tells how 'the owners of collieries must first sell the coals to the magistrates of Newcastle, the magistrates to the masters of ships, the masters of ships to the woodmongers or wharfingers, and they to those that spend them'.[67] Gardiner unwittingly simplified the chain, omitting the dealings which often took place between the woodmongers and wharfingers and the lesser coal-merchants, notably the chandlers, who served the needs of the poor. He omitted also those employed at various stages to manhandle the coal from boat to ship, ship to boat, boat to wharf, wharf to cart and pack-horse, and finally from cart and pack-horse to cellar. He could also have mentioned the shares which some coal-owners and some London coal-dealers held in colliers.

Dependence upon coal, and the indispensability of fuel to everyday life, meant that any interruption to supplies was apt to induce panic and soaring prices. If suspicion was rife in normal years, in the seemingly interminable succession of disruptions which punctuated the trade in the seventeenth century complaints of profiteering repeatedly rose to a crescendo. 'I need not declare how the subjects are abused in the price of coals', wrote the anonymous author of the *Grand Concern of England* in 1673, nor 'how many poor have starved for want of fuel, by reason of the horrid prices put upon them, especially in time of war, either by the merchant [shipper], or the woodmonger, or between them both.'[68] It

[66] The London coal trade has received considerable attention from historians. In addition to lengthy discussions in Nef (1932, i. 405–10; ii. 78–89, 96–110) and Moller (thesis 1933, 577–97), modern accounts are given in Smith 1961 and Hausman 1981.

[67] *England's Grievance*, 205.

[68] *Grand Concern of England*, 59–60.

was not only the public who believed that they were the victims of conspiracy, this belief was shared by those in authority to whom they turned for help. Whether they were justified is hard to establish definitively, despite the mountains of 'evidence' produced by committees and commissions of inquiry. When complaints were investigated, contemporaries generally managed to find abuses somewhere along the supply chain, but their inquiries throw little light on the extent of abuses and even less on the impact which they had upon prices. The economics of transporting coal from Northumberland and Durham to the towns and cities of the east coast was little understood by consumers at large, and there was a persistent tendency to understate seriously the legitimate costs of the journey. By contrast, consumers were all too prone to overstate both the impact on prices and the strength and durability of the unlawful combinations and unrestrained greed which they saw lurking at every link in the chain. Historians, however, must have some sympathy for the confusion of contemporaries, for in a century which experienced so many years of war, the separation of the typical from the exceptional and the influences endogenous to the industry and trade from those which were exogenous, is a taxing task indeed.

The strength of the hold which the Hostman of Newcastle possessed over the production and sale of coal on Tyneside has been emphasized above, but it would be wrong to assume that it necessarily resulted in substantially higher coal prices. Indeed, despite soaring demand, coal was rarely in short supply in the north-east, and producer prices remained stable or fell over much of the seventeenth century. The disincentives which the Hostmen so successfully created for outsiders doubtless dissuaded some from entering into production, but the harm was limited in an environment where excess capacity was a recurring problem. Moreover, the very strength of the Hostmen had beneficial effects upon the performance of the industry, for they were adventurers *par excellence*, and whole dynasties of Newcastle families devoted themselves and the bulk of their fortunes to mining and selling coal.

It was in conditions of glut that the Hostmen occasionally sought to combine to regulate sales to the shipmasters. But such overt combinations occurred in only a handful of years, and even in these years the consensus among historians is that they had relatively little impact on retail prices.[69] The prime intention of the participants of cartels was

[69] Nef 1932, ii. 118; Moller thesis 1933, 529-30; Flinn 1984, 254-67, 300; Ashton and Sykes 1964, 211-25.

defensive rather than aggressive; to share out such trade as was available and to avoid an outbreak of cut-throat competition and a consequent collapse of prices. Limitations on production were attainable only in the most acute of crises, and then only briefly. The quotas that were placed upon sales were invariably generous, with permitted shipments as high or in excess of those of preceding years. Moreover, as the rapidity and strength of the responses of the shipmasters demonstrated, combinations and attempts to limit the quantities of gift-coals struck primarily at the shippers' profits rather than at the pockets of London and east coast consumers. The opportunities for higher profits which shipmasters perceived, or even the ability to adjust to changing trading conditions, were threatened by the defensive moves of the Hostmen, but when such moves seemed likely to prove successful the shipmasters themselves usually combined to thwart them.

In order to assess the efficiency with which the east coast coal trade was conducted, and whether it bestowed excess profits on shipmasters and London coal-merchants, it is essential to gain some understanding of the normal costs of transportation, including reasonable profits and the incidence of duties and tolls. Table 15.1 provides some guidance towards this end. It is based on Newcastle price data, information presented by knowledgeable contemporaries on the freight of coal under normal conditions, and the prices which were actually paid by Westminster College in London.

Differences in the manner in which contemporaries examined the coal trade, and in the perspective from which they viewed it, colour the figures they presented, and makes interpretation of them a matter of judgement. The prices paid by Westminster College varied during the course of the year, and those quoted in Table 15.1 are averages. Column 1 is based in part upon a reply made by the Lord Mayor to the Privy Council in 1601, in which he maintained that it cost 13s. to freight a chaldron of coal by Newcastle measure from the Tyne to the Thames; and we have assumed that this sum included all duties payable in Newcastle. The mayor also reported that coal could usually be purchased on Tyneside for 10s. a chaldron, although local evidence indicates that the price at this time could rise as high as 11–12s. Such figures would mean that the shipmasters would have to sell a London chaldron to the capital's coal-merchants at 12–13s. just to break even. Five years later, during which time Tyneside coal prices do not appear to have altered much if at all, the Attorney-General argued that it never cost the shipper more than 13s. 4d. to bring a London chaldron to the

Table 15.1 *The freight and prices of a London chaldron*

	1601	1606	1698–1700
Price on Tyneside	5s. 3d.–6s. 4d.	5s. 3d.–6s. 4d.	4s. 9d.–5s. 9d.
Freight and Newcastle duties	6s. 10d.	—	6s.
Break-even sale price for shippers in London	12s. 1d.–13s. 2d.	13s. 4d.	10s. 9d.–11s. 9d.
London duties	[nil]	[nil]	5s. 10d.
Lighterage, wharfage, and metage	1s.[a]	1s.[a]	4s.[b]
Minimum cost price to London merchants	13s. 1d.–14s. 2d.	14s. 4d.	21s. 7d.–22s. 7d.
Average price paid by Westminster College, including delivery	13s. 10d.	18s. 9d.	23s.–30s.
(Minimum delivery charge to Westminster College)	1s	1s.	2s. 6d.

Notes:

[a] Estimated cost: 4d. per chaldron was payable for metage.

[b] Ostensibly includes only the costs of ferrying the coal from the ships to the wharves in lighters, but probably also includes a measure of profit for the coal-dealer. At the beginning of the century ships were able to unload at the wharves, but later the coal had to be off-loaded on to lighters.

Sources: Nef 1932, ii. 89–92; Beveridge 1939, 193.

Thames. In addition to these costs, the dealer who purchased from the shipper had to pay 'metage' at 4*d.* per chaldron, and the charges of unloading and storing. Finally, the coal had to be transported to the premises of the consumer. The 13*s.* 10*d.* per chaldron delivered that Westminster College paid on average for the coal it burnt in 1601, and the 18*s.* 9*d.* it paid in 1606, after allowing for the 1*s.* per chaldron delivery charge, would appear to leave little scope for either the shipmasters or the London coal-merchants to have derived excessive profits.

In the closing years of the seventeenth century coal was being sold on Tyneside for around 9–10*s.* for a Newcastle chaldron, equivalent to 4*s.* 9*d.*–5*s.* 9*d.* for a London chaldron. According to evidence presented in a series of proposals made to encourage the Crown to take the coal trade into its own hands, freight to London, presumably including duties payable in Newcastle, was estimated at around 6*s.* for each London chaldron. Since under these proposals the shippers would not be investing or taking risks by buying and selling coal this must be seen as a payment purely for freight. When coal was unloaded at this time in London a further 1*s.* 6*d.* was payable on each chaldron for Church Duty, 4*d.* for Orphan's Duty, and 5*s.* for parliamentary taxation. In addition, the coal had to be measured, ferried to the shore, unloaded, and stored. These stages were called lighterage, wharfage, and metage, for which a further 4*s.* per London chaldron was usually allowed in contemporary estimates. It is likely that the 4*s.* also included an element of profit to the coal-merchant, although in 1696 the rate that the coalheavers were to be paid for handling each chaldron was increased from 9–10*d.* to 16*d.*[70] The prices paid by Westminster College for coal delivered between 1698 and 1700 would once again seem to leave little room in these normal years for the excessive profits so bitterly and persistently complained of.

Such findings are entirely consonant with the records of shipmasters and shipowners, which suggest that the returns on capital in the shipping trade were normally modest. Allowances, discounts, and overmeasures were rife, as those who engaged in the trade testified:

An inspection made by Edward Grey, during his time in the Coal Trade, about Gift Coal to the masters of ships, in the years following:

1682	This year was allowed and given away	1 cha. in every score
1683		2 cha.
1684		1 or 2 ch.

[70] Moller thesis 1933, 595–6.

1685	$1\frac{1}{2}$ or 2
1686	2 and sometimes 3
1687	3

1688 This year in the beginning was allowed 3 in the score and the rest of the year, no gift at all

1689	No gift coals
1690	4—some gave 5 & 6
1691	3 at the beginning, then none

1692 At beginning 2 & 3, all year after 4 & some 5 & 6[71]

Yet shipmasters receiving generous amounts of gift-coal when trade was poor could expect to meet depressed prices and demands for generous overmeasure in London. Even in buoyant years the dealers in the Thames expected to receive an 'ingrain' of at least one extra chaldron in every score. Moreover, despite contemporary claims to the contrary, it was difficult for the shippers to manipulate supplies on a continuous basis. London burnt around half a million tons of coal in the later seventeenth century, and it arrived in 2,000 or more separate shipments. Each shipment was individually priced on arrival, as a result of negotiation between the master of the vessel and a London coal-merchant. Although the shipmasters might seek to take advantage of poor weather and hostilities, and to force up prices by delaying their arrival in the capital, lengthy delays were also costly to them. What is more the bargaining position of shipmasters was weakened by the relatively small amounts of coal which they carried, the sheer numbers of ships engaging in the trade, and the competition which inevitably took place between them. An account of the trade of several colliers owned by a north country merchant in 1675–6 shows that profits could be as low as £1 per voyage, and the average revealed was only £3. Calculations from information supplied by participants in a controversy over the profitability of the trade in the first half of the eighteenth century suggest an annual return on capital of 8–9 per cent, when account has been taken of insurance risks. There is also much to indicate that by the close of our period there were too many ships participating in the trade, and that profits were being driven down. In July 1711 it was reported that few masters were clearing £10 profit on a voyage, the majority were making losses, and some were laying up their ships.[72]

Thus a trade which attracted hundreds of ships, part-time and occasional as well as specialist, was channelled through the narrow

[71] Ellis 1981, 100.
[72] Michell thesis 1978, 139; Hausman 1981, 234–46.

nexus of the Pool of London which, if we are to believe contemporaries, was dominated and manipulated by a few rich dealers. In 1558, when imports of less than 20,000 tons carried in 200 to 300 shipments arrived in the Thames from Tyneside, it was said that the wholesale coal business was largely in the hands of just fourteen citizens, 'who do much occupy and use the trade of buying and selling of seacoals'. They were drawn from a wide range of London guilds, including fishmongers, haberdashers, grocers, and leather-sellers, which suggests the unspecialized nature of the trade at this time.[73] Expansion encouraged more formal marketing and organization, and the woodmongers came to the fore as their original trade in firewood slumped. In 1605 James I granted the woodmongers a charter of incorporation, probably in return for a donation of £200 towards the Ulster Plantation fund. How real the strength of the Company of Woodmongers was at this time is difficult to assess, for although the charter included certain privileges in the vending of fuel, as well as in the provision of carts to carry it, a monopoly of the right to buy and sell coal in the capital was never given. Indeed, in 1607 when the Attorney-General brought charges against certain engrossers of coals, he named Thomas Bagshawe, fishmonger, Thomas Careless, wharfinger, Francis Clarke, ironmonger, and Thomas Morley as the greatest offenders. Of these only Morley was to become a prominent member of the Woodmongers' Company. Thereafter, however, woodmongers increasingly became the main focus of discontent, and it is possible to chart the tightening of their grip over the sale of coal in the capital by the vehemence and the diversity of the complaints levelled against them. In 1618, for example, woodmongers were singled out as a major cause of high prices, and it was said that they were buying coal from the shipmasters at 14s. a chaldron and reselling it at 22s.[74]

Times of crisis, when coal supplies were interrupted, may have been potentially profitable for those engaged in the coal trade, but they were also dangerous. So essential was coal for London's well-being that any major disruption was likely to provoke demands for legislation to control abuses in the trade, fix maximum prices, and even for the Crown to exercise a monopoly of the purchase, shipment, and sale of coal. The inquiries and interrogations which were conducted during such times provide informative memoranda on the structure of the London coal trade, the participants within it, and the many real and imagined abuses which lurked in every sector. Much can be learnt, for example, from

[73] Nef 1932, i. 405–6.   [74] Moller thesis 1933, 522.

those inquiries set in motion in the autumn of 1638, during the chaos caused by the threatened pre-emption of all north-eastern coal by Charles I, and the shipping boycott which followed. The Lords of the Council in the Star Chamber became concerned that the prescribed prices for coal, 17s. per chaldron in summer and 19s. in winter, were being exceeded, and they directed the justices of the peace to investigate all branches of the trade. The justices duly reported that there were some shipmasters or merchants who purportedly sold their loads at £19 the score, but in fact received an extra 40s. for every score of chaldrons for agreeing to sell at such a price, while others sold at whatever price they could obtain. Secondly, it was found that although the wharfingers and woodmongers pretended that their charges of 2s. the chaldron were for metage, lighterage, wharfage, and carriage, these charges were really met by an allowance of overmeasure from the shippers. Thirdly, although coal stocks were built up in the summer when prices were lowest, retailers always sold their coals at the latest and highest price. The justices also found that retailers sold coal by the peck and the half bushel to the poor at 8d. per bushel, 'which comes to 24s. a chaldron and is a great abuse'. Fourthly, the justices were convinced that the monopoly over the loading and carriage of coal within the City enjoyed by the Carmen was also conducive to an enhancement of prices.[75]

When prices soared in 1664 because of enemy ships in the North Sea, an act was passed through Parliament for regulating the price of sea coals through the medium of the justices of the peace. The City also began its own investigation 'concerning the enhancement of prices by retailers', which soon developed into a sustained assault on the Woodmongers' Company. What the investigators discovered to their own satisfaction was a thoroughgoing conspiracy to monopolize the trade and enhance profits. For example, they claimed that the Woodmongers had taken possession of many of the wharves suitable for coal, and persuaded the owners of those that they did not possess to refuse permission for their wharves to be used for the unloading and storage of coal. Other serious complaints found proved against the Woodmongers included the engrossing of all the coal coming on to the market, along with the carts to transport it with, and the use of fraudulent measures. In the highly charged atmosphere which surrounded the coal trade during the doleful succession of catastrophes between 1664 and 1667, the Woodmongers were deemed to have overreached themselves. The

[75] Dale 1923, 19–21.

Commons in 1667, after consideration of the report, revoked the Wood-mongers' charter and cancelled their jurisdiction over the Carmen.[76]

The revocation did not, of course, bring an end to price instability or to complaints of profiteering, nor did it bring about the immediate demise of the influence of the Woodmongers. Indeed, just three years later they were accused of going down the Thames to meet colliers, and there buying up great quantities of coal in order to resell it at excessive prices in the City.[77] But other elements were combining to accelerate the decline of the share of the wholesale market enjoyed by the Wood-mongers, most notably the lightermen. The ever greater numbers of colliers frequenting the Thames, and their rising bulk, meant that increasingly they had to be unloaded in the river rather than alongside wharves. This function was carried out by lightermen, who owned the boats which ferried the coal from ship to wharf, and often also supplied the labour to manhandle it. Within a few decades they had effectively supplanted the Woodmongers in dealing with shipmasters and, in the eyes of the public, they had also assumed the role of the chief instigators of exorbitant prices in London. The Queen's speech to Parliament in November 1703 mentioned the need for regulations for preventing excessive prices, and voiced suspicion that in the coal trade 'there may be a combination of some persons, to enrich themselves by a general oppression of others, and particularly the poor'. The committees which were set up by the House of Lords and the Court of Aldermen duly found that these suspicions were confirmed. Although part of the blame was found to lie in the lack of convoys to protect the colliers on their voyages from the Tyne and the Wear, and it was admitted that the threat of impressment was a discouragement to the seamen which manned them, the trade in London was found to be 'altered and restrained by a small number of lightermen'.[78] The alleged misdeeds had remained almost constant, but the perpetrators had changed.

Other significant developments were also taking place in the London coal-market in the later seventeenth century. A new class of middlemen called crimps or factors was emerging, who acted as agents interposing themselves between the shipmasters and the retailers, arranging sales and negotiating terms. As such they resembled the fitters of the north-east. Their precise origins are not clear, and the functions they performed were not standardized. Some were lightermen who also dealt in coal on their own behalf, while others ventured no money of their

---

[76] Dale 1923, 36–55; Smith 1961, 29–32.
[77] Smith 1961, 33.   [78] Ibid. 34–8.

own but gained a living by earning commission from their knowledge of market conditions, the handling of paperwork, and the settling of duties.

Direct contact was also being increasingly established between north-eastern coal-owners and the London market. The coal-owners were seeking to boost their sales by enlisting the assistance of the major London coal-dealers, sometimes entering into legal contracts with them and sometimes operating in partnership. It seems that the earliest initiatives were taken by men who were not members of the Hostmen's Company, and the Company itself attempted to restrict competition between members and forbade advertising. Charles Montagu, who resided in London, was very active in the promotion of coal from his Gibside and Benwell collieries, and in 1699 he can be found in partnership with Messrs Slyford, Tubner, and Oldner to market coal from two wharves.[79] More commonly contracts would be made whereby the coal-dealers would receive an agreed rate of commission for purchasing a particular coal-owner's coals from the shipmasters in the Thames. Richard Oldner was described in the Aldermen's report of 1703 as one of the leading lightermen or crimps, and, with his brother and son who were both named George, they were known by Henry Liddell as the 'fat Oldners'. The Oldners were particularly prominent in dealings with northern coal-owners. They made a seven-year contract in 1700 with Sir John Clavering, which required Clavering to pay them 4d. for every chaldron of Clavering Stella Main coal that they either bought in London or caused to be bought by shipmasters in the Tyne.[80]

iii. Conclusion

In the coal trade as elsewhere in the commerce of the sixteenth and seventeenth centuries there were serious market imperfections. Official and unofficial monopolies and restraints and restrictive practices operated on both a personal and a corporate level, but it would be unwise to join with contemporaries in finding in such imperfections the prime cause of high and unstable London prices. Indeed 'high' is a relative term, and Londoners seem often to have had unrealistic expectations. Even when sailings could proceed unmolested by hostilities or bad weather, the transporting of a ton of coal from the Tyne to the

[79] NeUL Montagu, Montagu to Baker 27/12/1698, 11/1/1699.
[80] HRO Cowper D/EPT 4854. For details of another contract see Willan 1938, 35.

Thames increased its basic cost by a factor of 3.5–4 in the late fourteenth century, and 2–2.5 in the seventeenth. When reasonable profits and customs dues were added, the price was in danger of appearing unreasonable to consumers. When shipping was disrupted prices in the eyes of Londoners rapidly became extortionate, and east coast shipping was chronically vulnerable to disruption. The very dependence of the capital on coal rendered the stopping of that trade a prime means of holding the country to ransom. Thus during the First Dutch War hostilities in the North Sea had forced up prices in London to double their normal level by November 1652, and to treble by the following April. The prolonged crisis which began in 1664 and persisted until 1667 involved a blockade of the coast by the Dutch, a massive epidemic of plague, the Fire of London, and a co-ordinated cessation of production by the major coal-owners. In 1663–4 over 525,000 tons had been shipped coastwise from Newcastle; in the following two years shipments plunged first to 329,000 tons and then to 223,000 tons. In 1666–7 they recovered partially to 282,000 tons, but it was only in the following year that they were restored to normal levels. Pepys, who felt the cold sorely and deeply resented having to pay for the means of banishing it, kept a mournful log of price movements in his diary: 44–49s. a chaldron in February 1664 and 70–100s. in the following month; 63s. a chaldron in December 1666 rising to 80s. in the following March, followed by a collapse to 23s. in April with the arrival of a large fleet of colliers. But by June, he recorded, prices had soared to 110–120s. a chaldron, only to plunge again by September to 28–29s.[81]

Distortions created by the manipulation of markets were, by comparison, of far less moment. Recurring instability doubtless dispensed occasional windfall profits to some fortunate shippers and merchants and opened up some opportunities for profiteering, but in general it was harmful. Disruption forced up the costs of shippers by raising the wages of seamen and imposing long periods of expensive inactivity. Moreover, when shipping ceased the Tyneside coal-owners were left with large stocks of unsold coal which deteriorated on the staithes or the banks of their collieries, and while the profit which London coal-dealers made on each chaldron of coal may have soared, there were far fewer chaldrons to buy and sell.

Overall the abundant capacity of the north-eastern coalfield undermined any sustained attempts at producers' cartels. Free entry and the

---

[81] Moller thesis 1933, 497.

participation of a multitude of ships on an occasional basis generally rendered the shipping of coal highly competitive, and in the later seventeenth century there are distinct signs here also of over-capacity and falling returns on capital. The wholesaling and retailing of coal within London, although subject to some abuse, was evidently sufficiently flexible and open to avoid any single group gaining effective control. There were no formal or legitimate monopolies of the sale of coal in London, and although cliques of rich and powerful merchants emerged from time to time which strove to dominate the wholesale trade, they always had to contend with numerous lesser rivals, as well as with a vocal and influential consumer lobby. Freedom to trade in coal meant that dealers continued to be drawn from a wide circle.

Finally, it would also be wrong to allow the clamour from consumers to colour our assessment of the efficiency of the east coast trade, for its achievements were commendable. While the amounts of coal that were shipped soared ever higher, the real costs of carrying it plummeted. Yet in the trade in coal, just as in its production, spectacular achievements can be shown to have rested upon simple yet strong foundations. Though gargantuan in aggregate, the trade was composed of thousands of voyages and multitudes of transactions, each one no more than modest in its scale. On average 700,000 tons of coal, which cost the shippers £125,000–130,000 to purchase, were shipped from the northeast annually in the last quarter of the seventeenth century. The costs the shippers incurred in transporting the coal to London and other east coast ports added at least as much again to their expenditure, probably bringing it to more than £250,000 each year. However, this vast quantity of coal, and the huge sums required to purchase and carry it, were divided into more than 5,000 parcels; for this is the number of sailings which took place each year. The cost of freighting even the largest of colliers was thus tiny by the standards of other branches of trade. Four hundred tons of coal could be loaded in Newcastle or Sunderland for the expenditure of no more than £75, voyages were short, and money could be turned over many times in a season.

In similar fashion, the ownership of each collier was split into many parts, enabling the investment required for the provision of shipping to be split into easily manageable parcels. The expansion of the collier fleet did not depend upon the grandees of London and Newcastle, who entered late into the business. As with the production of coal, the opportunity for profit brought forth ample supplies of money to be invested. The ownership of the ships which carried the coal was spread throughout the east coast ports from which they came, and lay in the hands of scores of provincial merchants and investors of relatively modest means.[82] Abundant coal and ample shipping helped to keep the coal trade, by the standards of the time, relatively free and competitive.

[82] Willan 1938, 38–40; Nef 1932, ii. 26–7. Metters thesis 1982 contains a thoughtful examination of evidence relating to the involvement of King's Lynn merchants in the coal trade.

CHAPTER 16

The Coal Industry and the Economy in Early Modern Britain

In the mid-seventeenth century a Tyneside poet proudly proclaimed that a new era had dawned, in which 'sterling' coal had supplanted gold as the most valuable commodity in the realm. So indispensable had coal become, and so fertile were the leading Tyneside collieries, that the wealth of the City of London was draining northwards. In the quest for its 'Soveraign' heat, the poet assures, the citizens would even be prepared to pawn their wives:

> Englands a perfect World! has Indies too!
> Correct your Maps: New-castle is Peru . . .
> For whatsoere that gawdy City boasts,
> Each Month derives to these attractive coasts,
> Wee shall exhaust their Chamber and devoure
> The Treasures of Guild-hall, the Mint, the Towre
> Our Staiths their morgag'd-streets will soon divide,
> Blathon owne Cornehill, Stella share Cheapside[1]

Nor were such panegyrics confined to the smug residents of thriving mining regions. In 1738 a French visitor to England who was captivated by the industry and prosperity that he encountered, reported to his native country that 'Coal is one of the greatest sources of English wealth and plenty [and] the soul of English manufactures'.[2]

It would not be taxing to fill a chapter with such encomiums, and the works of J. U. Nef provide a ready store of apposite quotations with which to embark on such a task. However, the very enthusiasm of such proponents, and the unbridled extravagance of many of their claims, have invoked a deep scepticism among recent generations of historians, and it has become customary to treat with great caution the words of those swayed by partisan interests or dazzled by novelty. But prudence should not lead to a failure to appreciate to the full the actual achievements of the coal industry. For anyone closely acquainted with the

---

[1] Thomas Winnard?, 'News from Newcastle' (1651).   [2] Quoted in Nef 1932, i. 222–3.

abundant sources, it would be hard to conceive of a seventeenth-century Britain without coal, so dependent had she become upon the heat which it produced. Every household had a natural desire to keep its members tolerably warm, to cook food, and to heat water for washing and laundering. For a very substantial proportion of those households, in town and country alike, coal provided the most economical source of heat. It was the pre-eminent fuel of town-dwellers, and almost without exception the greater towns were overwhelmingly dependent upon coal. In the model of urban supply enunciated by von Thünen, a nineteenth-century German disciple of Adam Smith whose hypotheses have recently become fashionable, after the first belt of land encircling a town had been devoted to market gardening and the production of perishables, high costs of transportation decreed that the next belt had to be devoted to woodland producing fuel and building materials for the inhabitants.[3] But while such a pattern of land use may well have obtained in classical wood-fuel regions, the availability of cheap coal in early modern Britain enabled agriculture to supplant arboriculture, thereby alleviating pressure on extremely scarce resources. In this way coal played an important enabling role in the progress of urbanization; not just in the constant growth of London during the sixteenth and seventeenth centuries, but also in the general expansion of cities and towns throughout the realm, which was a notable feature of the latter part of the period.

Cheap coal was similarly beneficial to Britain's industrial development, and well before the eighteenth century it had become the leading industrial fuel. With the notable exception of iron-making, coal was being burnt by all the major industries in which the provision of heat was a significant part of the production process, and it was virtually the sole fuel of the leading energy consumers. Moreover, coal was making a special contribution to the efficiency and competitiveness of an expanding list of industries, new and old, which were able to adopt new coal-burning technologies. The substantial benefits which accrued to the swelling ranks of manufacturers and processors who could abandon expensive wood or charcoal stimulated innovation and improved competitiveness, thereby encouraging the emergence of Britain as a 'mineral fuel economy' in advance of any other nation.[4]

Objectivity and balance are among the indispensable attributes of all historians, yet the devotion of many years of labour to the study of a

---

[3] J. R. von Thünen, *The Isolated State*, ed. P. Hall (Oxford, 1966).
[4] Harris 1974 and 1976; Wrigley 1988.

particular person, institution, trade, or industry heightens the difficulty of retaining a perfect sense of perspective. Human nature is likely to seek to reward effort with significance, and historians are often at their most vulnerable when assessing the value of the fruits of their own labours. At the same time, since energy is one of the prerequisites of economic activity, and heat is one of the basic requirements of human survival, it is difficult to avoid the conclusion that without an abundant flow from the coal-mines at prices often appreciably lower than those of other fuels, the development of Britain and the well-being of her population would have been severely impeded.

It is impossible to arrive at sound statistics for energy consumption in early modern Britain, and it is unlikely that we shall ever be able to proceed beyond educated guesswork. There are, however, a number of methods by which such educated guesses can be formulated. One such involves the comparison of the output of coal with that of other fuels. The best estimate of the extent of woodland, plantations, hedgerows, and non-woodland trees in late seventeenth-century England is appreciably less than three million acres.[5] Since it took the annual yield of more than one acre of well-managed coppiced woodland to produce on a sustainable basis the heat energy of a ton of coal, and most probably nearly two acres, we can conclude that even if the total annual growth of England's woodland and hedgerow trees had been exclusively devoted to the production of firewood it would scarcely have been able to match the calorific value of the 2–2.2 million tons of coal which English coal-mines were yielding at this time. But, of course, fire was only one of the manifold uses to which wood was put. Wood was an all-purpose raw material, essential to the building of houses, vehicles, and ships, and to the production of most furniture, tools, and machines. In Gregory King's opinion less than half, by value, of the wood that was cut was burnt.[6] This is not all; the actual yield of wood fell far short of the potential maximum. Poor management led to the productivity of a substantial part of woodland being very low, and remoteness ensured that a sizeable proportion of annual growth was never utilized. Thus, even if we make generous allowance for the contribution of peat and other combustible substances, and for the use of wood gathered from scattered local trees for firing, it is difficult to believe that coal was not supplying the major part of England's heat energy well before the start of the eighteenth century.

[5] I am extremely grateful to Dr Oliver Rackham for expert guidance on the extent and productivity of woodlands and trees.   [6] *Natural and Political Observations* (1804 edn.), 53.

If there had been no cheap coal the necessity to increase the supplies of firewood to meet the whole of Britain's fuel needs would have given a dramatic boost to the inflation of not only the price of wood but of the prices of all other products derived from the land, since vast acreages would have had to be converted from agriculture to arboriculture. Imports of firewood could have offered little salvation, for wood was already scarce and expensive overseas. Nor could supplies of turf, reeds, gorse, or other plant fuels have offered any but the most transitory assistance to the consumer. Moreover, despite the optimistic musings of Tim Nourse,[7] even if it had been possible to grow all the firewood that was needed to substitute for coal, it would not have been possible to fell, cut up, and transport it economically to the consumer. Unlike coal, where many hundreds of tons can be extracted from a single pit, the production of wood is a very extensive process. British woodland has always tended to be located away from the sea and rivers and, since wood was even more expensive to carry than coal, efficient transportation would have necessitated new plantations on land close to water communications. This in turn would have forced into reverse the economically rational trend of these centuries, which was to devote such conveniently located land to arable farming and market gardening.

These notions are purely speculative, of course, but for a concrete historical example of the power of the restraint which could be imposed upon industrial and commercial development by finite and ultimately scarce fuel supplies, there is the experience of The Netherlands. Here vast and conveniently located peat deposits provided very cheap fuel for the Dutch Republic throughout the seventeenth century, and helped to facilitate both urban and industrial expansion. Short canals were constructed to feed peat into the major towns, and fuel-intensive industries flourished as low-priced energy gave them a competitive advantage over the industries of neighbouring states. To this extent The Netherlands resembled Britain with its cheap coal. But it has been estimated very conservatively that 3–5 per cent of the entire workable peat reserves of the country were consumed on average in each decade of the seventeenth century and that, whereas in Britain seemingly limitless supplies of coal were able to be dug from the ground at modest marginal costs, The Netherlands in the eighteenth century faced the exhaustion of her peat supplies and an increasing dependence upon imported coal rendered expensive by high duties and transport costs. Rising fuel costs inevitably impacted adversely on the large industrial

[7] 'An Essay upon the Fuel of London', *Campania Foelix* (1700).

sector, as well as upon the disposable incomes of the Dutch people. One hesitates to go as far as a recent historian who has proclaimed a leading role for fuel supplies in both the promotion of the glorious efflorescence of the Dutch Republic in the seventeenth century, and the waning of its fortunes in the eighteenth, but it would be perverse to deny them significance.[8]

The multiplier effect on the economy at large of the growth of the British coal industry and trade has long been appreciated and, without any pretence to precision, further contributions can be made to the assessment of its scale. Calculations based upon the productivity data given in Chapter 10 indicate that output per man in the collieries may well have been in the region of 200 tons to 250 tons per annum. This in turn suggests that British coalmining would have given employment to the full-time equivalent of some 12,000 to 15,000 persons in the late seventeenth century, and it is likely that at least as much employment was generated in the transportation of coal and its distribution to the consumer. In the east coast trade, for example, those who produced the coal were greatly outnumbered by the carters, waggonmen, keelmen, seamen, lightermen, heavers, and coalmen who handled it on its way from pithead to hearth. On the basis of one seaman to every 25 tons of cargo, and an average of eight to ten voyages a year for a ship fully devoted to the coal trade, it would have taken just as many seamen to carry the coal down the coast from Tyneside and Wearside as it took colliers to dig it up. Appreciably looser approximations still can be postulated for the contribution of the coal industry to the national product. At an average pithead price of, say, 4s per ton, the annual production of some two and a half million tons attained by English and Welsh coalfields around 1700 would have had a value of £500,000, with retail prices averaging at least double and possibly nearly treble this figure.[9] If we accept the now conventional estimate of £50 million for the national product of England and Wales at this time, the share of the coal industry based on pithead prices would have worked out at some 1 per cent, and its share of the product of the commercial and industrial sectors at perhaps 3 per cent.[10] Significantly, the mining of

---

[8] J. W. de Zeeuw, 'Peat and the Dutch Golden Age: The Historical Meaning of Energy Attainability', *AAG Bijdragen*, 21 (1978). See also the criticisms made by R. W. Unger, 'Energy Sources for the Dutch Golden Age: Peat, Wind and Coal', *Research in Economic History*, 9 (1984).

[9] By way of comparison, total exports of woollen goods at this time were valued at around £3,000,000.

[10] R. Floud and D. N. McCloskey, *The Economic History of Britain since 1700* (2 vols., Cambridge, 1981), i. 64. A similar set of calculations a century later would produce a share for the

coal employed substantially less than 1 per cent of the total work-force.[11]

The example of sustained, spectacular expansion furnished by the coal industry in the later sixteenth and seventeenth centuries may have some broader relevance for understanding the nature of the British economy and the conditions under which growth and development could take place. It may also, in some small way, throw light on the nature of pre-industrialized economies in general. Detailed in the body of this work are many examples of how the stimulating conditions under which the coal industry operated created a forcing-house for profound advances in very many aspects of mining and trading, involving not just pure technology in the sense of 'gadgets' or scientific discoveries, but improvements in the organization of labour and business structure, in management, finance, and record-keeping, and in marketing, transportation, and the techniques of distribution. Yet, as has also been demonstrated, these advances were achieved largely through a multitude of strides rather than a few giant leaps. Indeed, perhaps most suggestive of all is the apparent smoothness, even ease, with which much of the massive growth of output was accomplished. Historians often display an unhealthy interest in the spectacular and the unique to the neglect of the Promethean forces which can be unleashed from the commonplace by successive generations of skilled practitioners responding on a daily basis to the demands of an eager market. Hence, when conducting perennial quests for the prerequisites and triggers of sustained economic development, too much time is often spent searching for awesome manifestations of such supply-side agents as the invention and dissemination of wholly new technologies, and the accumulation of large reservoirs of capital, and too little time observing the latent potential for advancement and growth existing in pre-industrialized economies.

The experience of the British coal industry during the sixteenth and seventeenth centuries had its unique features, but it also had much in common with the experience not just of the mining of other minerals but of leading manufacturing industries. Even the great collieries had some counterparts in other fields, while high rates of growth were

British coalmining industry of the national product of 2.2%, rising to slightly less than 3% by 1830 (Flinn 1984, 451). The 'value-added' of coal is very high since only insignificant amounts are spent on other commodities in the course of its production.

[11] Based upon data for population totals and age structure given in Wrigley and Schofield 1981, 528–9.

achieved in many branches of manufacturing by the simple proliferation of small units of production. Very substantial expansion of the output of cloth, for example, was able to be accommodated within the framework of the 'putting-out' or domestic system of production, which rested heavily upon the application of traditional procedures, albeit constantly improved and amended. Artisan workshops and putting-out arrangements, like the ubiquitous small-scale collieries producing a few thousand tons a year, were well suited to the conditions which generally prevailed in the economy. But occasionally the promise of exceptional returns elicited exceptional investments, which in turn resulted in extraordinary industrial structures. In the first half of the sixteenth century William Stumpe of Malmesbury and John Winchcombe of Newbury, who had made fortunes in the production of cloth using the domestic system, were seduced by trade booms and the promise of sustained high demand for their wares into setting up factories. Such short-lived and ill-starred ventures have rightly been termed 'boomtime freaks' but, on the positive side, they do show what was capable of being achieved when trading conditions permitted.[12] The special circumstance which lay behind the much more durable industrial enterprise which Ambrose Crowley established at Winlaton in the 1690s, incorporating factories, warehouses, forges, a slitting mill, and a steel furnace, was Crowley's ability to secure a virtual monopoly of Navy contracts. The government also lay behind some remarkably precocious industrial structures which emerged briefly in Devon at the turn of the thirteenth and fourteenth centuries and again in the later fifteenth century. Here the Crown and its lessees operated silver-lead mines which employed large diversified work-forces, sometimes running to many hundreds. Shafts were sunk through hard rock to depths many times greater than would have been justified by the extraction of lead alone, and systems of adits, soughs, and drainage pumps were created that would not have disgraced many a seventeenth-century colliery.[13]

In late Tudor and Stuart times capital and enterprise were frequently lavished on worthless projects, and they do not appear to have been lacking for ventures with a reasonable chance of success, as the ability of shipping capacity on the east coast to more than match the needs of the booming coal trade amply demonstrates. This is far from saying,

[12] Gough 1969, 36–44.

[13] Lewis 1965 edn., 192–7; L. F. Salzman, 'Mines and Stannaries', *The English Government at Work, 1327-1336*, iii. ed. J. F. Willard, W. A. Morris, and W. H. Dunham (Cambridge, Mass., 1950), 68–87.

however, that conditions were potentially ripe in seventeenth-century England for the 'take-off' of a whole series of major industries. There was simply neither the scale nor the constancy of demand to sustain widespread further industrialization. A thriving market for fuel existed because it was a basic subsistence commodity, and the consumption of coal soared because it was able to be supplied at competitive prices.

Nevertheless, even the market for coal was not infinitely extensible. The differing pace and patterns of growth in the various British coal-fields have been detailed above, and the tendency for supply to outstrip demand has been a recurring theme of this volume. Moreover, towards the close of the seventeenth century there are clear indications that in very many places there was a worsening glut of coal. From coalfield after coalfield comes abundant evidence that coal-owners were struggling under the existence or imminent threat of excess capacity. The pre-eminent challenge facing most British producers at this time was not the raising of coal but its sale, and when markets presented themselves output could often be boosted at breathtaking speed. Thus the building of a waggonway from Gibside colliery in 1699, which sharply reduced the costs of transport to the Tyne, enabled Charles Montagu to increase his vend in just three years from 27,000 tons to more than 105,000 tons. Similarly, the end of hostilities and the improvement of the seasale market to Ireland permitted the output of Sir John Lowther's Howgill colliery in Cumberland to rise from less than 16,000 tons to more than 32,000 tons in the three years from 1701 to 1703. But despite falling real producer prices, the market for the coal of Northumberland and Durham had peaked in the early 1680s, and the 75,000 or so extra tons which uttered forth from Gibside found a ready sale only at the expense of other Tyneside coal-owners, who found themselves unable to sell as much as previously. Likewise, the expansion of Howgill inflicted damage on coal-owners up and down the western seaboard.

Quite simply the potential capacity of the coal industry was progress-ing in leaps and bounds while, for a time at least, trends in the economy at large were combining to moderate the rate of growth in the demand for its product. By the close of the seventeenth century annual per capita consumption in Britain had risen to around half a ton, but in the absence of new uses for very substantial quantities of coal further rapid growth could only come from rising population. Instead the long upswing in numbers was halted and then reversed. The latest and most reliable estimate suggests that the population of England peaked around 1650 at five and a quarter millions, and fell modestly over the next half-century.

Moreover, the growth in the market for sea coal was further inhibited by wars which led to the frequent interruption of supply routes, and by increased customs duties which forced retail prices sharply upwards. There are also signs from the early 1650s, which proliferate after the Restoration, of an increasingly constructive concern with improving the supply of wood and timber, through the advocation of increased plantings and the devotion of more attention to preservation and the better management of woodlands.[14] As Evelyn exclaimed in his influential treatise, *Sylva*, published in 1664, 'Who would not preserve timber when within so few years the price is almost quadrupled'. The laws of economics, backed by intense government concern over the availability of shipbuilding timber, were eventually beginning to assert themselves.

The British coal industry at the turn of the seventeenth and eighteenth centuries was mature as well as large, and it was able to meet with comfort all the requirements which were then placed upon it. In the course of the first half of the eighteenth century annual output is thought to have been boosted by more than two million tons, which was disposed of at virtually constant real prices, and once again this achievement was not dependent upon revolutionary changes in structure or technology. The depth of shafts did not increase dramatically before the late eighteenth century, and the satisfactory ventilation of deep pits had to await the nineteenth century. The exception was the steam-engine, and by 1750 150 steam pumping-engines had been installed in British collieries. However, the steam-engine did not make a significant contribution to the winding of coal much before 1800, and although the output of the coalfields of Scotland, Cumberland, Lancashire, and Yorkshire is estimated to have grown by more than one million tons between 1700 and 1750, it did so with the assistance of only twenty-two steam pumping-engines.

The succeeding volume in this series demonstrates that the major turning-point for the British coal industry occurred in the second half of the eighteenth century. In the fifty years after 1750 population almost doubled, urbanization and industrialization proceeded apace, coal was universally adopted as the fuel for all stages of the production of iron, new uses were found for steam power, and the number of steam-engines built came to be counted in thousands rather than tens and hundreds. In such an environment the modern coal industry was born. In the twenty-five years after 1750 production rose by an amount which far exceeded

[14] *AHEW*, v, part ii. 309–10, 375–7; Sharp 1975.

the total output of 1700, and by the close of the eighteenth century over fifteen million tons of coal were being produced each year. Here was a watershed at least as decisive as that which had been experienced in the later sixteenth century. It is to be hoped that this volume has convincingly demonstrated that the superlative performance of the coal industry at the heart of the industrial revolution owed much to the firmness of the foundations which had been sunk in earlier times.

Appendix A
Weights and Measures

Coal is not a commodity [which] would pay its charge of a minute, nice admeasurement

Charles Montagu, 1699

The description and definition of the variety of weights and measures used in the medieval and early modern coal trade might at first sight appear to be a routine task requiring patience, perseverance, accuracy, and attention to detail in greater quantities than insight, powers of analysis, and imagination. Such a judgement would be quite erroneous. It would be tedious to attempt to convey a full appreciation of the labyrinthine complexities and the essential intangibility of this seemingly substantive topic, or of the succession of uncertainties, incongruities, and blatant contradictions that await any researcher who seeks to produce, from the measures used for coal, a set of consistent and logical relationships. Yet the portents are clearly in evidence for any aspiring historical metrologist to observe. Eloquent testimony to the difficulty of the task is furnished by the long succession of researchers, from Green in 1866 to Dendy (1902), Nef (1932), Mott (1962) and Dietz (1986), who have begun their expositions by pointing out the errors and misunderstandings of their predecessors. Moreover, immersion in the sources reveals that contemporary experts in the coal trade were at times scarcely less bewildered by the manifold measures in use, and the relationships which they bore to each other, than the historians who followed centuries after.

Many of the contributory agents of this doubt and confusion soon become apparent to the student. There is the baffling variety of measures in use, of which chaldrons, tens, keels, weys, tons, metts, vats, quarters, bushels, corves, scoops, rooks, dozens, works, fothers, and loads (cart-, wain-, waggon-, and, horse-) are but a small selection. Nor was a chaldron simply a chaldron. There were land chaldrons and sea chaldrons. Nor was a land chaldron simply a land chaldron, or a sea chaldron a sea chaldron. In the north-east each colliery using the chaldron as a measure of output, sale, or transport had its own standard of capacity. Newcastle sea chaldrons differed from London chaldrons, which in turn differed from those on the Forth, or in Lancashire or Hull. Nor were such measures necessarily constant over time. The Newcastle sea chaldron of the fourteenth and fifteenth centuries was very different from that of the seventeenth century, while the local land measures of individual collieries had a tendency to alter with the terms of leases, the capacities of the containers filled by the hewers, or the capacities of the vehicles by which the coal was conveyed from the pit. Colliery chaldrons carried in wains or waggons to the staithes were the basis upon which royalties were calculated for payment to the landlord, but they had to be converted into sea chaldrons when they were carried by keels to the shipmasters and when coal was assessed for the payment of customs duty. Such a conversion constituted 'making out', and according to Charles Montagu all the 'coal professors' believed that because 30 'led' chaldrons made 40 sea chaldrons a 'led' chaldron made out at 25 per cent, 'grounded on 10 being the fourth part of 40'. Whereas, he proclaimed gleefully, it was really one-third![1]

Coal was repeatedly transferred from container to container on its journey from colliery to consumer, and each of these had its own customary capacity. Yet, even when the precise dimensions of the container are known, there can be no certainty how much coal it carried. First because the coal in the containers was heaped, and second because coal is not homogeneous and does not have a uniform ratio of weight to volume. Even when in identical condition coal varies greatly in density, and of course it can exist in varying degrees of size and wetness, and varying states of purity. Therefore the amounts of coal contained in identical receptacles can differ widely in weight. But the practice of heaping is of no less significance, for the amount of coal in the cone, which formed the heap of measures of identical capacity when level, varied greatly according to the shape of the container and whether it was wide or narrow, deep or shallow.[2] Therefore, in order to calculate the amount of coal in a heaped measure, or to compare one heaped measure with another, it is essential to know not merely the capacity of the measures, usually defined by the number of gallons of water they held, but their precise shape and dimensions. A failure to comprehend these two fundamental truths has led many into making false comparisons and conversions.

Coal, in keeping with many other commodities, was almost invariably measured by volume rather than by weight, and its measures were defined, when they were defined at all, in bushels, quarters, gallons, pints, and suchlike. With the exception of Scottish coal, which was customed by the ton in London, it was not until the act of 1694 that coal was first required to be measured by weight rather than volume. Even then, however, measurement by weight was only for Northumberland and Durham coal destined for shipment, and when this coal reached its port of destination it was duly measured by volume. The reason for the universal dependence upon volume rather than weight was simply that for most commodities it was far easier and cheaper to

[1] NeUL Montagu, Montagu to Baker 17/8/97.
[2] A report into London measures in 1800 produced drawings of a coal bushel and a coal vat, with movable triangular bows or handles across the tops to determine the height and form of the heap. It was claimed that if the height of the heap were undefined it could allow with ease 10 bushels in the place of 9 (Smith 1961, 362-3).

administer. Weighing a low-value, high-bulk commodity like coal was, with the exception of utilizing the keel, impractical. Even measuring by volume was a time-consuming and relatively expensive process. Contemporaries therefore invariably dealt in volumes: the annual vend of Newcastle was reckoned in Newcastle chaldrons, the production of a midlands colliery in loads or rooks, the purchases of a London household in London chaldrons, quarters, bushels, or pecks. Yet, it is now customary to measure by weight, and in order to be intelligible medieval and early modern volumes need to be converted into tons.

Herein lies the rub. For, as the authorities increasingly came to appreciate, there was no single standard of conversion of weight to volume or vice versa. In the final analysis it is not possible to tell precisely what a particular chaldron of Newcastle coal weighed, even when it was in exact accordance with the act of 1678 and defined in terms of 'the bowl-tub of Newcastle containing two and twenty gallons and a pottle Winchester measure, and being seven and twenty inches diameter upon the top from outside to outside and no more, and allowing one and twenty bowls of coals to be measured by such bowl-tub by heap measure to each chalder and no more'. To discover its weight one would need to know the density of the coal, its moisture content, and the dimensions of each lump. No doubt this is why sixteen years later Parliament, having defined the Newcastle chaldron by volume, sought also to define it by weight. But inevitably, since there was no constant relationship between weight and volume, the statute of 1694 merely substituted one for the other.[3] These are basic facts of nature, but an appreciation of them can help to explain much of the confusion of contemporaries and historians alike on metrological matters.

The following commentaries are not intended to provide a comprehensive guide to the measures used in the coal industry and trade. When local and customary measures have been converted into tons in the tables and text of this book, the methods employed have been noted there. A lengthy discourse on the size of the load, chaldron, or corf in each of the collieries which used it as a measure would be inappropriate as well as inconclusive. Instead the intention has been to provide some general information on the most common measures. The exceptions are the Newcastle and the London chaldrons, which dominated the coal trade and which have warranted extended discussion.

i. The chaldron

The chaldron, also known as the chalder, was an ancient measure used for coal from at least the thirteenth century. It was, however, little more than a generic name given to a large quantity of coal; it was not standardized, and there were very many widely differing regional and local chaldron measures. Two were of prime importance: the Newcastle chaldron and the London chaldron. The Newcastle chaldron was the measure for all coal shipped from the ports of Northumberland and Durham coastwise and overseas; and the London

---

[3] *Statutes of the Realm*, 30 Charles II, c. 8; 6 and 7 William and Mary c. 10.

chaldron became the standardized wholesale measure for coal throughout virtually the whole of the east and south of England and, eventually, also on the western seaboard.

The quest to discover the weight of the Newcastle chaldron during the medieval and early modern centuries has proven to be a Herculean task for historians, for it is beset with obstacles, traps, and false clues. J. U. Nef assumed that, although the London chaldron remained stable in weight throughout the sixteenth and seventeenth centuries, the weight of the Newcastle chaldron was altered repeatedly. He maintained that it weighed 2,000 lb. in 1421, and that 'thereafter its weight was continually increased by the traders, in their efforts to reduce the burden of taxes on coal, until 1678, when the weight was fixed by statute at 52½ cwt., to be increased in 1694, by another statute, to 53 cwt.'. Nef established to his own satisfaction a series of dates when the weight of the chaldron was known, namely 18 cwt. in 1421, c.40 cwt. in 1616, c.52 cwt. in the period 1636–40, and 52.5–53 cwt. in the period 1678–94, and, 'for want of a better method' he postulated that the weight of the chaldron increased at a constant rate between these dates.[4] It was on the basis of these series of estimates that Nef converted the data that he was able to collect on the numbers of chaldrons shipped from Tyneside into tons, and arrived at his subsequently discredited conclusion that 'In less than a century and a quarter, shipments from Newcastle multiplied nearly nineteenfold, while imports at London multiplied more than thirtyfold'.[5] In the persistent and at times heated debate which has surrounded Nef's quantitative estimates of the growth of the east coast coal trade, the crucial issue of the changing rates at which he converted chaldrons into tons has scarcely been raised.

In 1962, however, R. A. Mott published two articles in which he attempted to correct Nef's estimates.[6] Mott argued that in 1368 the Newcastle and London chaldrons were identical at around 17 cwt., and that the statutory increase in the capacity of the bushel in 1497 pushed both chaldrons up to c.21 cwt. In 1530, he goes on, the Newcastle chaldron was doubled in size, and at about the same time the London chaldron was increased to 1.33 tons, at which weight it was to remain until it was abandoned as a measure in 1832. Mott put the date of the final change in the weight of the Newcastle chaldron at 1635, when it rose from 42 to 52.5 cwt. Thus although there is broad agreement between Nef and Mott that the Newcastle chaldron became c.52 cwt. in the 1630s, Nef would see this as a result of a gradual increase in size over many decades, while Mott would see it occurring at a stroke. The most recent examination of the capacity of the Newcastle chaldron was published in 1986 by B. Dietz.[7] Dietz concluded that the chaldron was constant before 1695, and he is therefore at considerable variance with both Nef and Mott. In a reworking of the data for both shipments from the north-east and the weight of the

[4] Nef 1932, ii. 368–70.	[5] Ibid., i. 20–1.
[6] Mott 1962a, 1962b.	[7] Dietz 1986.

London and Newcastle chaldrons, Dietz follows Nef and Mott in believing that the former remained fixed at 1.3 tons from an early date, but for the latter, before 1694, he adopts a compromise figure of 42 cwt.

The Newcastle chaldron

In most forms of historical research it is advisable to proceed from the known to the unknown, rather than vice versa, and in the pursuit of the chaldron it is essential. Accordingly we must begin with the statutes of 1678 and 1694, which were entitled 'An Act for the Admeasurement of Keels and Boats carrying Coals' and 'An Act for the better Admeasurement of Keels and Keel-Boats in the Port of Newcastle and the Members thereunto belonging' respectively. As their titles suggest both pieces of legislation were primarily concerned with regulating the size of the loads which keels carried to seagoing ships higher up the estuary. For the keel-load was used to determine the amount of customs and other duties which were payable and the amount of coal of which the ship-master was taking delivery. The quantity which the keel carried was indicated by nails, which were driven into the vessels at successive intervals at the water-mark as they lay in the water. The 1678 statute attempted to define the chaldron by volume, and required that nails be driven in at chaldron intervals after twenty-one bowls of coal of carefully specified dimensions had been thrown into the keel; while that of 1694 attempted to define the chaldron by weight and required that the nails be driven in at 53 cwt. intervals, according to 'a dead weight of lead or iron or otherwise'.

The first measuring and nailing of the keels was therefore a crucial exercise, for it determined the dimensions of all the subsequent cargoes which they carried. Although it had been the accepted method of gauging shipments since early times, it could never be more than rough and ready, as the repeated concern with the achievement of greater accuracy, expressed from the late fourteenth century onwards, amply demonstrates.[8] The procedure lent itself to manifold 'Frauds, deceits and abuses ... to the diminution of His Majesty's customs and the damage and prejudice of the sellers and buyers of coals', which could be practised both during measurement and in subsequent use, such as the heaping of coal in the middle of the keel so that more could be loaded before the water reached the nail, and the illicit removal and reposition-ing of nails. It was also an unavoidably inaccurate form of measurement in choppy water. But, perhaps most important of all, the capacity of all sub-sequent loads was dependent upon the nature and condition of the coal which had been used when the keel was first measured.

As has been noted, the statute of 1678 prescribed that the chaldron used for shipping coals from all north-eastern ports should consist of 21 heaped bowls, each bowl to be 27 in. in diameter and 22 gallons and a pottle Winchester

---

[8] *Statutes of the Realm*, 9 Henry V, 1 c. 10; *CPR 1381-5*, 499; *CPR 1389-92*, 30; *CPR 1416-22*, 394; *CPR 1452-61*, 608.

measure in capacity. It was further specified that each wain used to fill the keels should carry 7 heaped bowls and each cart 3 heaped bowls and 1 bushel, and that there were to be 3 wain-loads or 6 cart-loads to each chaldron, and no more. Care was also taken to specify that the coal used for measuring keels should be newly wrought and led to the staithe within three months of the 'Admeasurement', and that one-half used in the measuring should be wet and one-half dry. Just prior to the statute, in 1676, exact and even more detailed dimensions of the 'sealed bowl-tub' were sworn to in Newcastle by various collectors of customs, coal-meters, and the keeper of the bowl-tub, and their findings are contained in a document of hitherto unrecognized significance.[9] The bowl the officials found in use measured 26 in. from outside to outside across the top, and 24 in. on the inside; the diameter of the bowl across the inside at the bottom was 25 in., and the depth at the middle was $11\frac{1}{2}$ in. and at the side $11\frac{1}{4}$ in. It held 22 gallons and 1 pint by liquid measure, though it was previously thought to hold 22 gallons and a pottle. Fortunately, one of the inquisitors, Anthony Isaacson, then proceeded to calculate the weight of coal which it would hold when heaped. First he filled it with dry coals and having deducted the weight of the bowl found that it held 2 cwt. 13 lb.; he then repeated the process using wet coals and found that it weighed 3 cwt. 1 lb., a massive 42 per cent more. Taking half dry and half wet coals would produce a chaldron weighing 53 cwt. 91 lb. Isaacson concluded his calculations by remarking that in such matters there 'is no certain rule'.

It was right that he should be so circumspect. For a contemporaneous memorandum presented to Giles Dunstar, one of the General Surveyors of customs, claimed that although identical bowls were used in Sunderland and Newcastle, and 21 bowls went into each chaldron, half wet and half dry, 'exactly as is now practised', a chaldron at Sunderland was bigger than a chaldron at Newcastle. This the memorandum evidenced by stating that the same ship which could take in but 20 chaldrons at Sunderland, could take in 25, and sometimes 26 and 27, at Newcastle. Likewise the '20 chalder from Sunderland will make out at London 44 and 45, when 20 chalder from Newcastle will make but at London 31, 32, 33'. This 'knotty question', the memorandum goes on to relate, was due to a variety of factors, including the construction and working conditions of the keels of the two ports: which gave easier measure as time passed in Sunderland but worse measure in Newcastle; the differing state of the coal used in the measuring: which was newly dug, hard and round, and water resistant in Newcastle, and old, weathered coal which soaked up the water in Sunderland; and the contrasting qualities of the coal produced in the two regions: namely, hard and heavy, bad mixed with good, on Tyneside, and free and light on Wearside.[10]

    [9] NuRO Society of Antiquaries, ZAN M12/C23.6.
    [10] LCA NCB Swillington, memorandum to Giles Dunstar. See also PRO C.30/24/7/596; BoL Rawlinson A.241, fos. 79–82.

This memorandum thus stresses a crucial element often neglected by those who have studied the dimensions of the chaldron. Whereas keels were initially measured with chaldrons of carefully regulated volumes, thereafter they were loaded for shipping in accordance with the *weight* of the coal used for the first measuring. Which is to say, as much coal was thrown into the keel as was necessary to bring it up to the appropriate nails, rather than as much coal as was necessary to match the volume of the original coal. Thus, since coal of varying densities, size, and moisture content was shipped, so the volumes required to load the keel up to the conventional 8-chaldron marker inevitably differed, even though the statute might be rigorously adhered to. Moderately damp small coals from Tyneside have been found to be 10 per cent heavier than large dry lumps, and differences in the specific gravity of bituminous coals can affect the space–weight ratios by a similar margin.[11]

Not everything in this memorandum should be accepted at face value, however, for there was intense rivalry between the two northern coal ports, with Newcastle extremely resentful of the exemption of their neighbours from the 1s. per chaldron customs duty on coastwise shipments. But many of the issues it raises were real enough, and no doubt similar reasoning led to the adoption of weight rather than volume as the standard in 1694. The provisions of the 1694 statute were simple, the keel was to be marked according to 53 cwt. chaldrons rather than 21-bowl chaldrons, and those wains and carts which were used to load coal directly into keels were to be marked to contain $17\frac{1}{2}$ cwt. and $8\frac{3}{4}$ cwt. respectively.

In the light of Dr Dietz's conclusions our first task must be to consider whether the 1694 statute ordered an increase in the size of the Newcastle chaldron by around a quarter. The answer must be firmly negative. As Anthony Isaacson noted in 1676, when he conducted his experiments using the precise volumes specified in the 1674 statute, a chaldron of half dry and half wet coal weighed 53.8 cwt. Furthermore, neither the content of the statute of 1694, nor the proceedings in Parliament which preceded it, give any indication that the intention was to increase dramatically the size of the chaldron. On the contrary the stated intention was to maintain better its prescribed proportions. The 1694 statute draws attention to the new forms of frauds and deceits which were diminishing the king's customs revenues and, of course, these could only occur through the shipping of chaldrons of excessive size. Indeed the prosecutions which had been brought in the years preceding 1694 were against those who had moved the nails in keels so as to give excess measure as a bribe to shipmasters. These and other frauds and deceits the statute of 1694 hoped to stamp out, as the title states, by 'the better Admeasurement of keels and keel-boats'. Moreover, there is no indication whatsoever in the voluminous contemporary records of the north-eastern coal industry and trade of this time that the chaldron had been changed in size, and even a much smaller increase than 25

[11] Dietz 1986, 284–5.

per cent would have had repercussions which could be expected to have featured somewhere in the broad spectrum of contemporary records available to us. Nor is there any detectable sympathetic movement in either the price of a Newcastle chaldron, the number of chaldrons carried by vessels visiting the Tyne and the Wear, or the total numbers of chaldrons shipped, each of which one would have expected as an inevitable corollary of such an enlargement. It may therefore be safely concluded that the chaldron was not increased in size in 1694, and the same would appear to be true in 1678. Indeed both statutes are best explained in the context of the need to restrain the size of the chaldrons shipped from the north-east during gluts of coal and the proliferation of discounts and incentives to shipmasters.

The key to the size of the Newcastle chaldron lies in the bowl. That the statute of 1678 did not introduce the chaldron of 21 bowls is shown by a petition of 1663 from Newcastle coal-owners which speaks of '21 bowls to the chalder being the measure now established by law to ships'. Contemporaneous documents in the same collection also predicate a Newcastle chaldron one and three-quarters to twice as large as a London chaldron, which, since the latter can be shown to have remained fixed in size, strongly suggests that the former was of the order of 53 cwt.[12] Proceeding backwards in time, we find confirmation in the State Papers of 1638 of a 21-bowl chaldron then in use, and an Exchequer commission of inquiry into measures in the coal trade in 1616 found that the 'water-bowl' of Newcastle contained 22 gallons within the wood, and that 21 of these bowls 'being ringed and heaped' made a Newcastle water chaldron, 'by which all manners of coals that are sold and shipped to be transported out of the port of Newcastle or any of the members or creeks thereof into the ports beyond the seas or elsewhere'.[13] Thus the only change in the volume of a chaldron between 1616 and 1678 would appear to have been a contraction in the capacity of the bowl by a pint or a pottle (half-gallon), which constituted just 0.5–1.1 per cent, and was well within the margins of error of construction of the bowl or of changes occurring in its use. Moreover, experts in 1624 and 1618 worked on the premiss that the Newcastle chaldron was approximately double the size of the London chaldron.[14] Therefore, contrary to what has hitherto been claimed, there is no reason to believe that the volume of the standard Newcastle chaldron changed significantly during the course of the seventeenth century.

When we pass backwards beyond 1600 our task becomes more difficult and our conclusions must be more tentative. Yet the depositions of witnesses to the Exchequer commission of 1616 testified that the bowl was a customary measure that had been in use 'for sundry years', and among all the profusion of documentation on coal and the coal trade in the sixteenth century a single direct reference to a change in the size of the standard chaldron has yet to be

---

[12] PRO C.30/24/7/597.   [13] *CSPD 1637-8*, 347; PRO E. 178/4934.
[14] BoL Rawlinson, C. 784, fo. 1; Moller thesis 1933, 522 n.

discovered. What is more, in the second half of the century there were a series of well-recorded and tenacious inquiries into such closely related matters as the rising price of coal and the customs duties payable on shipments. Any change in the size of the measure used in the north-east would have been of direct relevance, but in none of the inquiries does any of the protagonists or witnesses raise the slightest suggestion that this had happened.[15]

None the less, although we can confirm the stability of volume of the standard Newcastle chaldron back to the 1570s, there is conclusive evidence from the fourteenth and fifteenth centuries that a substantially smaller sea chaldron was then in use. For example, the statute of 1421 sought to restrict the capacity of the measured keel to 20 chaldrons, whereas keels in the seventeenth century carried only 8–12 chaldrons.[16] References abound to the 20-chaldron keel in the later Middle Ages, but if each chaldron then was of the capacity of 53 cwt, they would have been carrying more than 50 tons. Such a proposition strains the bounds of credibility, for not only would keels of such burthen have been twice as large as later keels, they would have been as large, if not larger, than the sea-going craft of the time. The satisfyingly detailed account of the purchase of coal at Winlaton in 1366 for the king's building works in Windsor Castle throws considerable further light, for when delivered to London the 604 chaldrons purchased at Winlaton which had survived the voyage, the rest having been lost at sea, made just 561¼ chaldrons by London measure. That the Winlaton chaldrons were the same measure as those referred to in the 1421 statute and elsewhere is indicated by the fact that 20 of them were carried in each of the keels which ferried them from the colliery along the Tyne to the ships.[17]

Further specific information is available on chaldron sizes in the accounts of the bishop of Durham's mines at Whickham in the later fifteenth century.[18] We are told in the accounts of the 1450s and 1460s that the land chaldron, used to measure production, was 4 quarters, that the sea chaldron was 6 quarters and 4 bushels, and that each keel contained 18–20 chaldron or 30 fothers. At the Moyr pit at Whickham at the close of the century, 16 chaldrons 'by pit measure' equalled 12 chaldrons 'by water measure', 20 water chaldrons made a keel-load, and 1 water chaldron was equivalent to 1⅔ fothers. The coal was transported from the pits to the water in fother units, and, as later, we can be certain that a fother was a wain-load. The reported relationship between fothers and keels on the one hand and chaldrons on the other is thus again seriously at odds with that of the seventeenth century, when we know their

---

[15] See e.g. the long-running dispute between the City of London and Newcastle aldermen and coal-owners (BL Lansdowne 65(11); Harleian 6850(39); Dendy (ed.), *Hostmen*, 5–7), and the voluminous records generated by the succession of disputes following the granting of the Host-men's Charter and the imposition of the Queen's shilling (see above, Ch. 15(i)).

[16] See above, Ch. 13(iii).   [17] Taylor 1858, 208–9.

[18] DUDP Church Commission box 79.

dimensions. If the wain-load/fother was approximately the same as it was to be later, then the water chaldron would have been 26 to 29 cwt. In the seventeenth century a keel was capable of carrying around 27 to 32 tons; in the later fifteenth century, at 20 water chaldrons to a full load, keels would have carried 26 to 29 tons. Once again it is far more likely that chaldrons were around half the size of later chaldrons, than that wains and keels in the later Middle Ages were twice as large as they were to be in the seventeenth century.

Such reasoning is further substantiated by the numbers of chaldrons carried by ships engaging in the coastal and overseas coal trade. A series of Newcastle customs accounts from 1377 to 1391 reveals average shipments of between 43 and 46 chaldrons, with a few ships carrying in excess of 100 chaldrons. When in 1465–6 we next have data, the average shipment had risen to 50 chaldrons. Such average shipments, if chaldrons weighed over 50 cwt. each, would have been of the order of 115 to 130 tons, with the largest ships carrying 250 tons or more. Once again this is far too high to have been possible. It is generally thought that the vast majority of ships engaging in the east coast and North Sea trades in the later Middle Ages were of less than 50 tons burthen. At Yarmouth in 1513, for example, only 36 vessels out of the 157 registered were over 50 tons, and the average was a mere 39 tons.[19] Conclusively, in the opening decades of the sixteenth century, when a good spread of Newcastle Chamberlains' accounts and royal customs records are available, the average coal shipment was not 50 chaldrons but only 20.[20] Indeed, it was not until the seventeenth century that the average number of Newcastle chaldrons per ship began to exceed 20. If late medieval chaldrons weighed around 25 cwt., instead of over 50 cwt., however, the burthens of the ships which carried them would have been a more plausible 60 tons, which would also be compatible with the thesis that the size of ships engaged in the east coast trade declined in the late fifteenth and early sixteenth centuries.[21]

All this evidence, and much more besides, points indisputably towards a medieval sea chaldron of far smaller capacity than that in use from the sixteenth century. By the time of the earliest available Newcastle Chamberlains' account of 1505–6 and the first sixteenth-century royal customs accounts, a Newcastle chaldron of approximately double the size of that used for shipments in the Middle Ages was in use, and thereafter it appears to have remained approximately stable. There is no direct indication in the records of the early and mid-sixteenth century, any more than there is in those of the later sixteenth- or seventeenth-century, that the standard measurements were sub-

[19] Blake 1967, 17–20; Scammell 1961, 332–41; Burwash 1947, 145–90.
[20] TWRO 543/212; PRO E. 122/108/12, 109/1; Scammell 1961, 333.
[21] Scammell 1961 argues convincingly for a decrease in the average tonnage of east coast ships at the end of the Middle Ages, but his assumption that the size of the chaldron did not change between the mid-15th cent. and the later 16th cent. leads him to overstate the scale of the decrease.

sequently changed. Indeed the testimony of customs accounts, royal and local, with their details of cargo sizes and duty paid, and the pattern of wholesale and retail prices both in the north-east and at the points of consumption, all indicate stability in the units by which coal was transported and traded.

In conclusion, the amplitude of the variations between standard chaldrons and the actual chaldrons which were shipped must be stressed again. To those inconsistencies which inevitably flowed from the methods of measuring and the qualities of coal must be added the overmeasure which was illicitly given by sellers in order to connive in the evasion of customs duties and encourage shipmasters to buy when trade was slack. For these reasons the chaldrons shipped from the north-east could not have had a set volume or weight or a fixed conversion ratio into London chaldrons, even though the standard measurement was not altered. It is perhaps significant that the statutes of 1678 and 1694, which were seeking to limit the size of the chaldrons which were shipped, were introduced in a time of recurring glut, stagnant or falling prices, and massive allowances of gift-coals to shipmasters.[22] On the other hand, it is likely that the average size of chaldrons shipped from Tyneside in periods when demand threatened to outrun supply, as from time to time around the turn of the sixteenth and seventeenth centuries, conformed much more closely to the standard. Indeed it was claimed in 1600 that the wain which had for 'time out of mind' carried 8 bowls was now carrying scarcely 7.[23]

For these reasons previous assumptions of the changing size of the Newcastle chaldron cannot be sustained. A case cannot be upheld for either a progressive rise in the size of the Newcastle chaldron over the sixteenth and seventeenth centuries, or for a substantial increase in the seventeenth century following upon a long period of stability. While the size of chaldrons shipped from Tyneside and Wearside undoubtedly varied significantly in both weight and volume, these variations took the form of oscillations, fluctuations, and deviations rather than trends. As such it would be impractical to attempt to incorporate them formally into our statistical descriptions of the coal trade. Accordingly a weight of 25 cwt. has been adopted for the chaldron used for shipping coal from the north-east in the Middle Ages, and 53 cwt. for the Newcastle chaldron of the sixteenth and seventeenth centuries.

The London chaldron

Throughout the Middle Ages and the sixteenth and seventeenth centuries the London chaldron was a volumetric measure, with no fixed weight. The capacity of the chaldron was defined many times, and it can be shown to have remained fixed from at least as early as the mid-sixteenth century at 48 Winchester bushels. This capacity was arrived at by defining the chaldron as constituting 36 heaped coal bushels, with the heap constituting an additional third. According to the statute of 1664/5 'all sorts of coals commonly called

[22] See above Ch. 15(ii).   [23] Dendy (ed.), *Hostmen*, 38–9.

seacoals brought into the River of Thames and sold, shall be sold by the chaldron containing thirty six bushels heaped up, and according to the bushel sealed for that purpose at Guildhall in London'. More detail is forthcoming from the report of a committee appointed by Common Council in 1676 to consider the measures for sea coals, and in particular complaints by coal-merchants that the Guildhall bushel was not lawful and that it did not accord with the 'fatt' anciently used for measuring coal when it was offloaded from ships. The committee found all to be well, and concluded that 'in the said trial we found the said bushel to agree and answer the dimensions of the said *fatt*, the said *fatt* heaped with coals containing nine of the said bushels heaped with seacoals agreeing as near as art can make them'. The significance of the standard bushel residing at Guildhall rather than at the Exchequer was that it was a special coal bushel, and when measured by the committee it was found to contain 8 gallons and 1 quart of water, rather than the 8 gallons of the Winchester bushel.[24]

A number of references survive of the total volume of coal comprised by 4 heaped vats or 36 heaped bushels. In 1616 the Exchequer commission of inquiry found by experiment that a London chaldron contained 396 gallons of coal. William Gilpin, estates steward of Sir John Lowther, claimed in 1698 that the 'London chaldron exactly' was used to measure coal shipped from White-haven, that the bags or sacks used there contained 3 Winchesters (24 gallons), and that 16 such sacks produced a chaldron of the same size as 36 heaped coal bushels did in London. He also added that in London 'the heap reckoned one third of the strike'. The total volume of coal in the Cumberland chaldron was therefore 384 gallons, just 3 per cent less than the Exchequer commissioners had computed in London over eighty years before.[25]

A number of attempts were made at the turn of the seventeenth and eighteenth centuries, in a new spirit of enquiry, to weigh the coal which con-stituted such a volume. In 1698 William Gilpin weighed a sack of Whitehaven coal and 'found it very near 1 C. 3 quarters, that is 196 lb.', which would have resulted in a London chaldron of 28 cwt. This was exactly the weight found by a committee of the House of Lords, which conducted a series of experiments in 1703. When Sir Robert Southwell had conducted a similar experiment for the Royal Society in 1675, the coal he used weighed just under 29.5 cwt., and in 1697 Sir Charles Montagu, using Derwent coal, found that a London chaldron weighed 29 cwt. So novel did Montagu think his experiment, that he instructed his cousin to keep it 'from all flesh living'.[26] The close degree of agreement produced by these trials, a range of only 5 per cent, suggests that coals of very similar densities were used in them. A series of authoritative estimates made

[24] *Statutes of the Realm*, 16 and 17 Charles II, c. 2; Smith 1961, 361-2.

[25] PRO E. 178/4934; Hainsworth (ed.), *Sir John Lowther*, 578.

[26] Hainsworth (ed.), *Sir John Lowther*, 585; HMC *House of Lords*, v. 239-40; NeUL Montagu, Montagu to Baker 29/7/97; Birch 1756-7, iii. 207-10.

between 1793 and 1847 produced London chaldrons ranging in weight from 26.5 cwt. to 28.462 cwt.[27] Throughout this book London chaldrons have been taken to weigh 28 cwt.

ii. Notes on some common units of production and sale

The following notes are not definitive, nor are they intended as a comprehensive guide to the multitude of measures in use before the eighteenth century. Such a task would, in any event, be scarcely attainable, since although the names of measures were often widely disseminated, their capacities varied widely between collieries and localities. Many errors in the past have stemmed from the assumption that the precise information which had been obtained from one colliery on the size of the corf, chaldron, load, ten, etc., could be applied to the corves, chaldrons, loads, tens, etc. of other collieries. Discussions of the dimensions of particular measures are contained in the text and the footnotes, and may be consulted via the index. Lists and attempted definitions of the weights and measures used in the coal industry and trade are to be found in various works.[28]

Corves, bowls, and baskets

The containers used to convey coal from the face to the surface were naturally also often used to compute the output of collieries. They were also the units commonly adopted in the piece-rate agreements of hewers and putters. As might be expected the dimensions of the corf, bowl, or basket varied widely from colliery to colliery, and were dependent upon local working conditions and custom. Within each colliery, however, strict procedures were taken to keep them of uniform size.

Loads

Coal was very frequently sold in loads. The size of the load was variable and depended upon the capacity of the vehicles or horses used to carry the coal from the colliery. There was no standardization between collieries, although standard loads were often introduced in towns, as part of attempts by urban authorities to regulate the dimensions of the weights and measures of commodities sold within their jurisdictions. In the collieries the load was usually defined in terms of the number of corves or baskets of coal which it contained. Information concerning the precise size of the load in use in any particular colliery is only rarely available, but it is invariably obvious from the context whether reference is being made to a horse-load or a cart- or wain-load. A wain-load often approximated to a fother or a ton, and was rarely much larger. On Tyneside the wain-load for leading coal to the staithes was defined as 17.5

[27] Greenwell 1888, 17.
[28] Flinn 1984, 416–2; Nef 1932, ii. 367–78; Rees 1968, i. 129–32.

cwt. In Coventry the city corporation decreed that a 'wain load is to contain in measure being orderly and sufficiently stacked up to one full ell square in height, breadth and length, according to the usual manner heretofore used at other coalmines within the county of Warwick and the county of Coventry'.[29] At 45 in. to the ell such a quantity of coal might be expected to weigh just over one ton. Horses were generally capable of carrying 2–2.5 cwt., though the weight could vary according to the breeds of horses and the terrain they had to traverse.

Rooks

The rook was widely used as a measure of production and sales in the midlands' coalfields. It was based on the corf or basket in which coal was hauled to the surface, and therefore varied from colliery to colliery. We have two contemporaneous definitions: at Wollaton c.1610 a rook was defined as containing 18 'corve-fulls', and measuring '2 yards and a quarter high, and one yard square, close stacked', while at nearby Strelley in 1612 a rook was said to contain 13 'corve-fulls' and to be 'two yards high and a yard and a quarter square by measure'.[30] Such quantities of coal would be likely to have weighed between one and two tons. That the rook did contain more than a ton of coal, and more than most wains and carts could transport, is suggested by the sale of coal by collieries in 'three quarters' of a rook, also called a load, as well as in rooks.

Tens

The ten was a north-eastern measure. It has been the subject of much confusion, largely because of the failure to recognize that there were three distinct tens: the production of coal was often measured by 'getting tens'; coal carried from the colliery to the river was frequently measured in 'led tens', and the 'vending ten' was used for the sale and shipping of coal. That the 'vending ten' was quite simply ten Newcastle sea chaldrons can be demonstrated from innumerable sources, and poses few problems. The tens used to measure the quantities of coal that were dug or led to the Tyne were, however, highly variable and depended upon the receptacles in which the coal was raised and the vehicles in which it was carried. Thus on the earl of Northumberland's estates at Whitley colliery in the 1670s and 1680s, 16 scores of corves made a getting ten and 40 fothers (wain-loads) made a led ten, while at Whorlton Moor colliery in the same decades the getting ten consisted of 21 scores of corves and the led ten contained 60 fothers.[31] Led tens were generally appreciably larger than vending tens, often making 13–15 Newcastle chaldrons. The process of conversion was termed 'making out'.

[29] White thesis 1969, 196.
[30] HMC *Middleton*, 170, 175; HMC *Rutland*, iv. 484.
[31] DN Syon Cx 2*a* (1); 4*b* (1, 2).

Weys

The wey was in general use in South Wales, and occasionally also in other west coast ports. There are good reasons for believing that the seventeenth-century Glamorgan wey contained approximately 5 tons. There were 4 weys to a last.

Appendix B
Prices

they would desire but a reasonable Living-Price for Coals, and have all to
be Just to such an Established Current Price.

Compleat Collier (1708)

There can be no such thing as a national price series for coal during our period.
It would neither be feasible to attempt to construct one, nor meaningful if it
were able to be constructed. The factors which determined the prices at which
coal was sold from a landlocked colliery in, for example, the East Midlands or
Lancashire, often differed from those at work elsewhere on the same coalfields,
and had very little indeed in common with those prevailing in a city supplied
by sea from Tyneside. Moreover, since the dimensions of many weights and
measures are often known in only approximate terms, and transport costs
played such a leading role in the determination of consumer prices, any
attempt to conflate series drawn from a variety of locations would be doomed
to mislead. For these and other reasons the data are presented in this appendix
in as pure a form as possible, and they have been drawn only from those series
which inspire some confidence in their internal consistency.

i. Prices in the north-east

Knowledge of price movements on Tyneside is essential to an understanding
of the coal industry and trade, but, while there are many references to prices in
the north-east, there are no long-run series which derive from a single inter-
nally consistent source. The prices in Table B.1, as the references indicate, have
divers origins and, judged in the strictest terms, this series is one of the least
robust in this appendix. Yet the provenance of each of the prices which have
been included, with the exception of those for 1536–49, has been examined and
found worthy of inclusion. Moreover, the broad pattern of prices suggested by
this table is supported by an abundance of complementary material, including
that contained in Table B.2.

Table B.1 *Newcastle: prices paid by shipmasters per chaldron (53 cwt.), 1536-1703*

Period	Price	Context	Source
1536	2s. 6d.		
1548	2s. 6d.	Provenance unknown	Rogers 1866–1902, iv. 372
1549	2s. 10¾d.		
Before 1577	4s.	History of price movements before the making of the Grand Lease, during Sutton's tenure, and since	Dendy (ed.), *Hostmen*, 2
1577–83	6s.		
1595	9s.	assignment to the town of Newcastle. As asserted by the Lord Mayor of London, and not subsequently disputed by the Aldermen and coal-owners of Newcastle	
1603	8s. 'mean coals' 9s. 'second coals' 10s. 'best sort'	Maximum selling prices agreed among the Hostmen	Dendy (ed.), *Hostmen*, 47
1607	10s.	Current rate according to a leading London merchant	Nef 1932, ii. 396
1616	10s. 6d.–11s.	Current rate for best grade, reported in State Papers	Nef 1932, ii. 396
1618	10s.–11s.	Ruling prices for ship coal, reported in Star Chamber proceedings	BoL Rawlinson, C. 784
1624	10s. 6d.	Ruling prices for ship coal, reported in State Papers	Moller thesis 1933, 799
1632	10s. 6d.–11s.	Ruling prices recorded by Exchequer commission	Nef 1932, ii. 397
1637–8	10s.–11s.	Reported in State Papers and Star Chamber	Nef 1932, ii. 497; Moller thesis 1933, 799
1651	11s.	Minimum price set by Hostmen	Dendy (ed.), *Hostmen*, 194
1656	12s.	Raised from 10s. during past 2 years, as reported in State Papers	Nef 1932, ii. 397
1672	7s.	'The like never known before'	CSPD 1672, 230

Table B.1 (*cont.*)

Period	Price	Context	Source
1673	6s. 3d.	Prices reported in Hostmen's court	Dendy (ed.), *Hostmen*, 135
1696	9s.–10s.	Ruling rates according to a representative of the Customs Commissioners	Nef 1932, ii. 397
1701	10s.–10s. 6d.		Povey, *Unhappiness of England*, 8
1703	c. 10s.	Information received by the House of Lords	HMC *House of Lords*, v, 238–9

The price of small coal ('pancoal') sold to the salt-pans was normally approximately half that of 'ship-coal'.

Table B.2 *Tyneside: prices received by coal-owners, per chaldron (53 cwt.), 1674–1708*

Period	Price	Context	Source
1674–5	9s. 5d.	Average prices received by the Vanes for coal from their Stella colliery	NuRO Cookson, ZCO IV/47/1–33
1675–6	7s.		
1677–8	9s.		
1678–9	9s.		
1682–3	9s. 6d.		
1697	8s.–9s.	Prices which Montagu received, or realistically expected to receive, for his Gibside and Benwell coals	NeUL Montagu; NuRO Benwell, MBE/VI/1b
1698	8s.–8s. 6d.		
1699	8s. 6d.–9s.		
1700	8s.–8s. 6d.		
1701–2	8s.	Average prices received by the Claverings for coal from their Chopwell colliery	HRO Cowper D/EPT 4878, fos. 41–58
1702–3	8s. 1d.		
1703–4	8s. 3d.		
1708	8s.	'this Noble, this Main-Coal, was sold, as lately it was, or now is, for 8s. per chaldron'	J. C., *Compleat Collier*, 17

Table B.3 *Prices paid by Durham priory, 1300-1539*

Period	*d.* per chaldron		Period	*d.* per chaldron
1300–9	12		1420–9	24
1310–19	15		1430–9	21.25
1320–9	14		1440–9	20.5
1330–9	15.5		1450–9	20
1340–9	12		1460–9	20
1350–9	20		1470–9	20
1360–9	17.25		1480–9	20
1370–9	18		1490–9	17.5
1380–9	12.5		1500–9	17
1390–9	22		1510–19	—
1400–9	18		1520–9	16
1410–19	20		1530–9	16

Notes: Prices are inclusive of carriage to the priory. The chaldron consisted of 4 quarters. The Bursar's Accounts have been used to 1419, and the Almoner's Accounts subsequently. Coal prices were extracted from the Durham priory archives by the Beveridge price research team (LSE Beveridge, C1, C5) but the data they collected are unreliable because they often fail to deal appropriately with transport costs, make incorrect conversions from cart-loads and fothers to chaldrons, and assume incorrectly that the accountants used the long hundred. All the prices in this table are for purchases in chaldrons.

Sources: DUPK Bursar's Rolls and Almoner's Rolls.

ii. East coast prices

The bulk of coal prices at Hull listed in Table B.4 are derived from the account books of Hull Trinity House, which begin in 1461 and run into the eighteenth century. They were extracted and processed by D. M. Woodward. A new building was erected for Trinity House during the 1460s and 1470s to serve as both an administrative headquarters for the guild and an almshouse for thirteen old seamen or their widows, and in the seventeenth century the guild looked after a larger number of poor. Each year a quantity of coal and turf was bought to heat the premises. There is no doubt that the overwhelming bulk of the coal arriving in Hull came from the north-east. Only very occasional consignments came down river to Hull from the Yorkshire coalfield: in 1622–3 half a chaldron of coal 'from the West Country' was bought, and in 1652–3 the House bought two lots of 'Western Coals'. Similarly, a ton of Scottish coal was bought in the summer of 1624, and, at the height of the Civil War, in September 1643, the House purchased 14 tons of 'Scotch coals'. Coal was also purchased

Table B.4 *Coal prices at Hull, 1471-1700*

Period	Price per Hull chaldron (*c.*40 cwt.) in pence	Period	Price per Hull chaldron (*c.*40 cwt.) in pence	Period	Price per Hull chaldron (*c.*40 cwt.) in pence
1471–2	48	1550	96	1584	144
1473	43	1551	150	1585	144
1484	40	1552	100	1586	144
1485	40	1553	96	1587	160
1486	40	1554	88	1588	168
1487	40	1555	92	1589	—
1488	40	1556	93	1590	—
1488–9	46	1557	158	1591	150
1491–3	40	1558	135	1592	—
1493–5	40	1559	109	1593	188
1495–8	46	1560	120	1594	160
1499	42	1561	120	1595	189
1512–14	52	1562	110	1596	192
1521	52	1563	160	1597	177
1522	52	1564	114	1598	162
1523	60	1565	118	1599	162
1524	60	1566	119	1600	180
1525	60	1567	119	1601	184
1526	68	1568	—	1602	179
1527	64	1569	120	1603	164
1529	60	1570	151	1604	156
1530	56	1571	151	1605	186
1534	60	1572	144	1606	174
1535	60	1573	160	1607	185
1536	64	1574	180	1608	221
1539	60	1575	144	1609	197
1541	56	1576	160	1610	188
1542	59	1577	144	1611	189
1544	99	1578	156	1612	190
1545	82	1579	144	1613	198
1546	64	1580	160	1614	192
1547	67	1581	150	1615	193
1548	79	1582	156	1616	192
1549	112	1583	160	1617	186

Table B.4 (*cont.*)

Period	Price per Hull chaldron (*c.* 40 cwt.) in pence	Period	Price per Hull chaldron (*c.* 40 cwt.) in pence	Period	Price per Hull chaldron (*c.* 40 cwt.) in pence
1618	192	1646	260	1674	273
1619	180	1647	242	1675	256
1620	186	1648	216	1676	236
1621	180	1649	325	1677	219
1622	189	1650	258	1678	226
1623	192	1651	264	1679	212
1624	181	1652	240	1680	196
1625	186	1653	320	1681	202
1626	190	1654	275	1682	201
1627	186	1655	250	1683	201
1628	197	1656	308	1684	218
1629	214	1657	240	1685	210
1630	204	1658	270	1686	207
1631	176	1659	258	1687	204
1632	194	1660	246	1688	219
1633	189	1661	332	1689	229
1634	210	1662	216	1690	310
1635	210	1663	214	1691	281
1636	236	1664	219	1692	294
1637	231	1665	—	1693	—
1638	—	1666	—	1694	—
1639	217	1667	300	1695	312
1640	223	1668	245	1696	278
1641	—	1669	228	1697	—
1642	299	1670	204	1698	—
1643	384	1671	204	1699	274
1644	498	1672	310	1700	267
1645	400	1673	351		

Sources: HTH, Account Books, 1–4; HUA, Trinity House Vouchers, DTR/1/7; HCA, Accounts, BRF/3/20, 21; 6/87, 378, 497.

by the town council to heat the town hall and various *maisons dieu*, and the price of such coal has been added to the series.

The prices given in the table are those relating to coal on board ship at Hull. Customers also had to pay handling charges which stood at 4*d.* and 6*d.* a chaldron in the late fifteenth century, rose to between 14*d.* and 16*d.* in the 1590s and reached as high as 48*d.* during the Civil War, before stabilizing at around 45*d.* for the rest of the century. These charges included measuring the coal on board ship and paying a small civic due, shovelling the coal into a ketch, carrying it to the quayside, heaving it ashore, carting it to the Trinity House or Town Hall, and shovelling it into the coal-store.

Coal was frequently purchased on more than one occasion during the year, and often at different prices. The prices given in Table B.4 are the mean prices of all the coal which was purchased, and have been calculated by aggregating the cost of all the coal and dividing it by the total number of chaldrons purchased. The accounts cover a calendar year.

Whereas the London chaldron of *c.*28 cwt. was in general use on the east coast of England, a larger measure was used at Hull. This much is indicated by the level of prices paid for coal on board ship at the port which, having regard to differences in transport costs and duties, are significantly out of line with those ruling in King's Lynn, Cambridge, and London given in Table B.5. For confirmation we have the statement, in the Hull primages of 1671–2, that '22 London [chalder] is 15 chalder of coals [by Hull measure]', and a note in John Houghton's price report for 22 June 1693 which states that the chaldron at Hull was 63 bushels as against the 36 heaped or 48 stricken bushels of the London chaldron.

Table B.5 records coal prices operating in King's Lynn, Cambridge, and London from 1582 to 1702. The King's Lynn prices have been extracted from the Coal Stock Accounts and are for purchases made on board ship by the city corporation for resale to the poor. Those for King's and Trinity Colleges, Cambridge, are of purchases made on board barges at the quay adjacent to Magdalene College and Bridge. The additional costs of landing, measuring, and carting have not been included. In the early years officers of King's College sometimes made purchases in King's Lynn and arranged transport to Cambridge. In these instances the price quoted is the cost of purchase at King's Lynn plus the cost of transport to Magdalene Bridge. The series of prices extracted by Thorold Rogers from King's College muniments is unreliable because it does not always successfully distinguish between the costs of transport and of purchase. For Westminster College, London, prices are of purchases made for the college, supplemented in years when these are missing by purchases made for the brewery. Down to 1620 the prices of the two series are identical in all but two years and include delivery to the college. The prices for the Lord Steward's Department are for purchases made by the Messenger of the Great Wardrobe and delivered to the offices of that department in York

Table B.5 *Coal prices at King's Lynn, Cambridge, and London, 1582–1702*

Year	King's Lynn d.	Cambridge		London	
		King's d.	Trinity d.	Westminster d.	Lord Steward's Department d.
1582	—	160	—	—	
1583	—	160	—	—	
1584	106	165	—	—	
1585	—	160	—	—	
1586	—	151	—	189	
1587	—	167	—	188	
1588	—	162	—	186	
1589	—	166	—	233	
1590	—	186	—	213	
1591	—	152	—	177	
1592	—	152	—	157	
1593	—	180	—	153	
1594	—	154	—	183	
1595	130	162	182	163	
1596	—	179	—	203	
1597	138	160	160	191	
1598	129	160	—	171	
1599	—	162	—	168	
1600	122	150	—	—	

Year				
1601	166	160	170	131
1602	168	168	178	—
1603	166	—	183	—
1604	161	157	158	—
1605	150	—	159	—
1606	186	174	209	—
1607	206	—	180	152
1608	224	198	225	—
1609	224	178	183	134
1610	191	165	177	122
1611	190	—	171	129
1612	188	160	164	117
1613	194	—	165	—
1614	222	160	182	128
1615	222	169	171	135
1616	231	169	158	104
1617	229	—	162	—
1618	187	158	156	—
1619	186	—	156	130
1620	202	—	180	—
1621	197	163	170	134
1622	186	—	192	128
1623	186	—	173	132
1624	—	—	160	124
1625	—	—	163	
1626	218	—	209	
1627	238	—	186	

Table B.5 (cont.)

Year	King's Lynn d.	Cambridge		London	
		King's d.	Trinity d.	Westminster d.	Lord Steward's Department d.
1628	162	188	—	259	
1629	156	234	—	217	
1630	132	224	—	257	
1631	136	167	—	267	
1632	134	183	—	255	
1633	142	198	—	250	
1634	142	212	—	249	
1635	146	195	—	244	
1636	185	200	—	264	
1637	173	212	214	266	
1638	156	215	—	244	
1639	166	234	—	—	
1640	—	200	223	266	
1641	213	297	—	304	
1642	174	268	250	268	
1643	—	353	354	447	
1644	344	515	—	—	
1645	215	311	318	—	
1646	180	207	241	—	

Year					
1647	156	216	205	—	—
1648	176	202	239	—	—
1649	216	255	241	—	—
1650	—	210	234	—	—
1651	—	245	252	—	—
1652	—	260	230	—	—
1653	—	307	380	—	—
1654	—	252	290	—	—
1655	—	237	250	—	—
1656	—	267	267	—	—
1657	—	228	238	—	—
1658	—	240	244	—	—
1659	—	238	251	—	—
1660	—	218	221	—	—
1661	—	216	210	—	—
1662	—	216	—	—	—
1663	—	216	269	—	—
1664	—	216	—	—	—
1665	—	253	—	352	—
1666	—	228	305	392	—
1667	222	304	311	566	—
1668	—	260	234	390	292
1669	—	233	—	280	—
1670	—	216	226	—	323
1671	—	216	223	—	347
1672	—	258	288	—	344
1673	—	361	322	734	494

Table B.5 (cont.)

Year	King's Lynn d.	Cambridge		London	
		King's d.	Trinity d.	Westminster d.	Lord Steward's Department d.
1674	—	231	252	—	307
1675	—	357	249	330	325
1676	—	234	240	258	286
1677	—	234	250	312	285
1678	—	234	240	292	221
1679	—	228	234	317	—
1680	—	225	228	274	248
1681	—	225	240	—	259
1682	—	228	240	—	283
1683	—	222	228	252	298
1684	—	234	228	—	298
1685	—	228	240	252	—
1686	—	222	228	246	265
1687	—	216	228	—	252
1688	—	216	240	—	252
1689	—	240	240	300	361
1690	—	282	290	386	391
1691	—	284	285	372	368
1692	—	288	319	435	403

1693	—	308	327	386	403
1694	—	300	324	397	380
1695	—	310	332	343	410
1696	—	318	320	413	414
1697	—	312	270	328	414
1698	—	252	271	332	352
1699	—	252	268	264	328
1700	—	264	—	300	328
1701	—	295	—	292	358
1702	—	360	—	333	472

Note:

All prices are in pence per London chaldron (c.28 cwt.).

Sources: King's Lynn: Nor RO KL/C44 17–25; King's College: KC Mundum Books; Trinity College, LSE Beveridge, G2; Westminster College and the Lord Steward's Dept: Beveridge 1939, 173–7, 193–4, 399–404, 434–5. Beveridge adopted the unconventional method of dating his prices according to the opening Michaelmas of the accounts which he used. In this table the closing Michaelmas has been adopted in order to render the data comparable with the other series.

House and Great Queen Street. Purchases were usually made direct from the colliers in the Thames.

iii. Prices in the Thames valley

Table B.6 *Coal prices at Eton and Oxford, 1633-1702*

Period	Eton College d.	Oxford colleges d.
1633–42	—	588
1643–52	472	600
1653–62	290	455
1663–72	405	496
1673–82	335	417
1683–92	366	463
1693–1702	385	501

Note: All prices are in pence per London chaldron (*c.*28 cwt.)
Source: Rogers 1866–1902. v. 404–5.

iv. Pithead prices

The data in Table B.7 have been extracted from the accounts of a selection of landsale collieries, and are the prices at which coal was sold to customers who came to the pits with their own transport. Most collieries also raised small quantities of inferior coal called 'soft coal' or 'small coal', which was disposed of at appreciably lower prices. The sample of collieries included in the table has no claims whatsoever to typicality, and reflects instead the market conditions prevailing in the particular localities in which they operated. Comparisons between prices obtained at individual collieries are rendered especially difficult because of the likelihood of significant variations in the dimensions of the measures by which the coal was sold, even when they were given the same name.

Table B.7 *Pithead prices, 1520–1699*

Period	Wollaton (Notts.) d. per rook	Trowell (Notts.) d. per rook	Heanor (Derby.) d. per rook	Beaudesert (Staffs.) d. per dozen	Handsworth (Yorks.) d. per load	Sheffield Park (Yorks.) d. per load	Prescot (Lancs.) d. per cart-load	Whiston (Lancs.) d. per work
1520–9	18	—	—	—	—	—	—	—
1530–9	18	—	—	—	—	—	—	—
1540–9	18	—	—	—	—	—	—	—
1550–9	24	—	—	—	—	—	6	—
1560–9	32	—	—	—	—	—	—	—
1570–9	32	—	—	—	18	—	12	—
1580–9	40	—	—	—	—	24	14	—
1590–9	40	—	—	—	—	24	—	—
1600–9	—	—	—	—	—	—	—	—
1610–19	—	40–8	36	48	—	—	—	—
1620–9	54	40–56	—	60	—	—	—	—
1630–9	—	—	—	—	—	—	—	90
1640–9	—	72–89	52–64	60	—	—	—	90
1650–9	—	70–79	53–63	—	36	—	—	120
1660–9	—	69–81	—	—	36	—	—	120
1670–9	—	—	—	—	36	—	—	100
1680–9	—	—	—	—	36	—	—	—
1690–9	—	—	—	48	—	—	—	—

Note: Most collieries also produced small quantities of 'soft coal' or 'small coal', which was sold at appreciably lower prices.

Sources: NoUL Middleton Mi. Ac; NoRo Charlton of Chilwell; StRO Anglesey; SCL Wentworth-Woodhouse, Bright; BL Add. MS. 27352; SCL Arundel; LPL Shrewsbury. Dr John Langton kindly supplied prices for sales from Prescot and Whiston.

v. English prices, 1691–1702

The prices shown in Table B.8 are derived from those which were submitted to John Houghton by correspondents from around England, and published by him in his weekly paper. Houghton took care to ensure that the data sent to him were consistent, especially with respect to the chaldron measures in use. Although there can be no absolute certainty that the chaldrons in all places were of identical dimensions, the table does provide a useful guide to the range of prices to be found in England at the turn of the seventeenth and eighteenth centuries. The figures quoted are the means of the annual means of the prices which Houghton published. As might be expected relatively few correspondents managed to make complete returns for all four quarters of every year. A balance has been struck between the largest possible sample of towns and an adequate number of observations, by including in the table those towns for which Houghton received prices for four or more years between 1691 and 1703. It should be noted that 1s. 6d. per chaldron duty was payable in London up to 1694, 6s. 10d. in 1694–5, 1s. 10d. in 1696–8, and 6s. 10d. from 1698 onwards. A map based on these data is printed above, p. 52.

The figures in the third column of the table are the means of the indices of those annual prices which exist for each location as a percentage of London prices in those years. Price data exist for London for all relevant years.

Table B.8 *English prices, 1691-1702*

Town	Average price in shillings per London chaldron	Price as a % of London price
Bedford	22	74.4
Brecon	10	33.1
Brentford	33.7	121.6
Bury St Edmunds	22.6	66.3
Cambridge	27.8	90
Chichester	49.4	142.6
Colchester	26.1	79.0
Dartford	26.2	91.8
Devizes	29.2	95
Dunstable	42.4	125.5
Falmouth	27.8	87.0
Guildford	33.2	110.8
Kingston	22	74.4
Lewes	30.9	107.4
London	31.2	100
Monmouth	31.9	108.7
Newmarket	26.1	86.8
Northampton	39.4	114.4
Norwich	24.1	78.5
Nottingham	10	31.6
Oakham	20	67.1
Oxford	40.8	122
Pembroke	15.1	51.6
Plymouth	31.9	101.3
Reading	35.1	113
Rochester	35.4	108.7
Romford	32.7	104.2
St Albans	37.6	134
Sandwich	30.7	89.6
Southampton	34.8	111.7
Stamford	27.9	91.3

Bibliography

A. Manuscript sources

The manuscript collections used in this study are listed below under the archives in which they are housed.

Alnwick Castle, Northumberland
  Alnwick Castle MSS
  Syon MSS
Bangor University Library, Bangor
  Mostyn MSS
  Gwysaney MSS
Bodleian Library, Oxford
  Bankes MSS
  Rawlinson MSS
  Selden Supra MSS
Bolton Reference Library, Lancashire
  Bradford MSS
Bristol Reference Library
  Ellacombe MSS
British Library, London
  Additional MSS
  Egerton MSS
  Harleian MSS
  Lansdowne MSS
  Sloane MSS
  Stowe MSS
British Library of Political and Economic Science, London School of Economics
  Beveridge Price and Wage Collection
Brotherton Library, Leeds
  Arthington MSS
  Wolley Hall MSS
City of Coventry Record Office
  Hawkesbury MSS
Clwyd Record Office, Hawarden
  Glynde MSS
Corporation of London Records Office, Guildhall
  Alchin MSS
  Coal Meters' Accounts

Coal Duty Account Books
Orphans' Fund Coal Duties Account Books
Remembrancia MSS
Cumbria County Record Office, Carlisle
Lonsdale MSS
Derbyshire County Record Office, Matlock
Bowden MSS (Staveley colliery)
Durham Cathedral, Dean and Chapter Library, Durham
Sharp MSS
Durham County Record Office, Durham
Strathmore MSS
Whickham Deeds
Durham University, Department of Palaeography, Durham
Dean and Chapter Muniments
Durham University, Prior's Kitchen, Durham
Baker Baker Estate Papers
Bishopric Halmote Court Records
Church Commission Deposit
Gateshead Public Library, Gateshead
Cotesworth MSS
Ellison MSS
Glamorgan Record Office
Mackworth MSS
Gloucester County Record Office, Gloucester
Bledisloe MSS
Dyrham Park MSS
Lydney Park Estate MSS
Newton of Barrs Court MSS
Wills and Inventories
Gwent Record Office, Monmouthshire
Nantyglo and Blain MSS
Hatfield House, Hertfordshire
Salisbury MSS
Hertfordshire County Record Office, Hertford
Cowper (Penshanger) MSS
Hull City Archives
Accounts (BRF)
Hull Trinity House Archives
Account Books
Hull University Archives
Trinity House Vouchers (DTR)
Huntington Library, California
Hastings MSS

Kent Archives Office, Maidstone
  Cranfield MSS
King's College, Cambridge
  Mundum Books
Lambeth Palace Library, London
  Shrewsbury MSS
Lancashire County Record Office, Preston
  Bankes of Winstanley MSS
  Hesketh of Rufford MSS
  Kay-Shuttleworth Deposit
  Molyneux of Sefton MSS
  Trappes-Lomax MSS
  Wills and Inventories, WCW Infra and Supra
Leeds City Archives
  Gascoigne MSS
  Mexborough MSS
  NCB (Swillington Estate)
  Temple Newsom MSS
National Library of Scotland, Edinburgh
  Halkett of Pitfirrane Papers
  Wemyss of Bogie Papers
  MS 2263 Coal Customs
  Accession 5253
National Library of Wales, Aberystwyth
  Chirk Castle MSS
  Penrice and Margam MSS
Newcastle University Library
  Montagu Papers
Norfolk County Record Office, Norwich
  King's Lynn Coal Stock Accounts
North of England Institute of Mining and Mechanical Engineers, Newcastle upon Tyne
  Bell Collection
  Buddle Collection
Northumberland County Record Office, Newcastle upon Tyne
  Benwell Manor MSS
  Blackgate Deeds
  Cookson MSS
  Delaval (Hastings) MSS
  Ridley MSS
  Society of Antiquaries MSS
Nottinghamshire County Record Office, Nottingham
  Charlton of Chilwell MSS

Edge of Strelley MSS
Foljambe of Osberton MSS
Portland of Welbeck MSS
Savile of Rufford MSS
Nottingham University Library
Clifton of Clifton MSS
Galway of Serlby MSS
Middleton MSS
Newcastle of Clumber MSS
Public Record Office, London
Chancery.   C. 1–5 Chancery Proceedings
            C. 78
Exchequer. E. 101 Miscellaneous Accounts
            E. 122 Customs Accounts
            E. 134 Depositions
            E. 178 Commissions
            E. 190 Port Books
            E. 317 Papers of the Civil War and Interregnum
            E. 320 Augmentation Office
            E. 321 Court of Augmentation Proceedings
Court of Star Chamber: STAC 8, Proceedings James I
Special Collections: SC 6, Ministers' Accounts
                     SC 12 Rentals and Surveys
Palatinate of Durham: DURH
Forfeited Estates Commission: FEC 1
Shaftesbury Papers: C 30
State Papers: SP 15, 16
Sandbeck Park, Rotherham, Yorkshire
Lumley MSS
Scottish Record Office, Edinburgh
Airth MSS
Biel MSS
Buccleuch MSS
Cardross MSS
Clerk of Penicuik MSS
Dundas of Dundas MSS
Eglington MSS
Elphinstone MSS
Exchequer Rolls
Henderson of Fordell MSS
Kirkness MSS
Leven and Melville MSS
Mar and Kellie MSS

Musselburgh MSS
Pittenweem MSS
Register House Series
Whitehill MSS
Sheffield Central Library
Arundel MSS
Talbot MSS
Wentworth Woodhouse (Bright) MSS
Wharncliffe MSS
Shropshire County Record Office, Shrewsbury
Forester Papers
Willey Estate Papers
Somerset County Record Office, Taunton
Hylton of Ammersdown MSS
Phelips of Montacute MSS
Staffordshire County Record Office, Stafford
Anglesey MSS
Sutherland MSS
Tyne and Wear County Record Office, Newcastle upon Tyne
Hostmen's Company Records
Tyne Keelmen's Records
Jesmond Colliery Records
City Chamberlains' Accounts
University College of North Wales, Library, Bangor
Gwysaney MSS
Mostyn MSS
Warwickshire County Record Office, Warwick
Landor of Rugeley MSS
Newdigate MSS
Wigan Record Office
Haigh Colliery Orders
Bridgeman Ledger
William Salt Library, Stafford
Hand Morgan (Robins) MSS

B. Contemporary printed material

A comprehensive list of anonymous tracts, broadsides, etc., on matters concerned with coal was compiled by J. U. Nef (1932, ii. 338–40), and has not been included below. When these works have been referred to in the text full bibliographical details have been cited there.

Acts of the Parliaments of Scotland (1844 etc.).

AGRICOLA, GEORGIUS , *De Re Metallica,* 1556, ed. H. C. and L. H. Hoover (1912).

Anonymous, 'Copy of a Manuscript Account of Nottingham; Written by an Anonymous Author the year before the Civil War broke out', *Transactions of the Thoroton Society,* 2 (1898), supplement.

BATESON , M. (ed.), *Records of the Borough of Leicester,* i–iii. *1103–1603* (3 vols., Cambridge, 1899–1905).

BATHO , G. (ed.), *The Household Papers of Henry Percy, Ninth Earl of Northumberland (1564–1632),* Camden Society, 3rd ser., xciii (1962).

BOYLE, J. R., and DENDY, F. W. (eds.), *Extracts from the Records of the Merchant Adventurers of Newcastle-upon-Tyne,* i, Surtees Society, xciii (1895).

BRERETON , Sir WILLIAM , *Travels in Holland, the United Provinces, England, Scotland and Ireland, 1634–5,* Chetham Society Publications, i (Manchester, 1844).

BRINKWORTH, E. R. C., and GIBSON, J. S. W. , *Banbury Wills and Inventories, part two, 1621–50,* Banbury Historical Society, xiv (1976).

CAMDEN, WILLIAM , *Britannia: or, a Chorographical description of the Flourishing Kingdoms of England, Scotland and Ireland etc., 1586,* trans. and enlarged by Richard Gough, 1607 (3 vols., 1789 edn.).

DEFOE, DANIEL , *A Tour Thro' the Whole Island of Great Britain* (1726–6) (1968 edn.)

DENDY, F. W. (ed.), *Extracts from the Records of the Merchant Adventurers of Newcastle-upon-Tyne,* ii, Surtees Society, ci (1899).

—— *Extracts from the Records of the Company of Hostmen of Newcastle-upon-Tyne,* Surtees Society, cv (1901).

DICKINSON, H. T. (ed.), *The Correspondence of Sir James Clavering,* Surtees Society, clxxviii (1967).

DIGGES, THOMAS , *Pantometria* (1571).

DODDS, M. H. (ed.), *Extracts from the Newcastle-upon-Tyne Council Minute Books, 1639–56,* Newcastle upon Tyne Records Committee, i (1920).

DUDLEY, DUD , *Metallum Martis, or Iron Made with Pit-Coale, Sea-Coale etc.* (1665).

DUGDALE , Sir WILLIAM , *The Antiquities of Warwickshire* (1656).

EVELYN, JOHN, *Fumifugium: or the Inconvenience of the Aer and Smoak of London Dissipated* (1661) (Exeter, 1976 edn.).

—— *Sylva, or a Discourse of Forest-Trees and the Propagation of Timber* (1664).

FIENNES, CELIA , *The Journeys of Celia Fiennes, 1685–c.1712,* ed. C. Morris (1982 edn.).

FOWLER, F. J. (ed.), *Extracts from the Account Rolls of the Abbey of Durham,* 3 vols., Surtees Society, xcix, c, ciii (1898–1901).

FRASER, C. M. (ed.), *The Accounts of the Chamberlains of Newcastle upon Tyne, 1508–1511* (Newcastle upon Tyne, 1987).

FULLER, T., *The History of the Worthies of England* (1662), ed. J. Freeman (1952).

GARDINER, RALPH, *England's Grievance Discovered in relation to the Coal Trade* (1655) (Newcastle upon Tyne, 1796 edn.).

GERBIER, Sir BALTHAZAR, *Counsel and Advice to all Builders* (1663).

GRAY, WILLIAM, *Chorographia, or a Survey of Newcastle upon Tyne, 1649* (Hertford, 1970 edn.).

GREENWELL, W. (ed.), *Bishop Hatfield's Survey. A Record of the Possessions of Durham, made by order of Thomas de Hatfield, Bishop of Durham*, Surtees Society, xxxii (1857).

—— *Wills and Inventories from the Registry at Durham*, Surtees Society, xxxviii (1860).

HAINSWORTH, D. R. (ed.), *Commercial Papers of Sir Christopher Lowther, 1611–1644*, Surtees Society, clxxxix (1977).

—— *The Correspondence of Sir John Lowther of Whitehaven, 1693–98. A Political Community in Wartime* (Oxford, 1983).

HALL, H., and NICHOLAS, F. J. (eds.), *Select Tracts and Table Books of English Weights and Measures (1100–1742)*, Camden Society, 3rd ser., xli (1929).

HARRIS, Sir WALTER, *Remarks on the Affairs and Trade of England and Ireland* (1691).

HARRISON, WILLIAM, *The Description of England*, ed. G. Edelen (New York, 1968).

Historical Manuscripts Commission, *Reports and Calendars*, especially manuscripts of House of Lords, Lord Middleton, Marquis of Salisbury.

HODGSON, J. C. (ed.), *Wills and Inventories from the Registry at Durham, part iii*, Surtees Society, cxii (1906).

HOUGHTON, JOHN, *A Collection for the Improvement of Husbandry and Trade*. Weekly newsheet published by Houghton.

—— *A Collection for the Improvement of Husbandry and Trade*, ed. R. Bradley (4 vols., 1727–8).

HOUGHTON, THOMAS, *Rara Avis in Terris or the Compleat Miner* (1681).

HOWELL, R. J. (ed.), *Monopoly on the Tyne, 1650–58. Papers relating to Ralph Gardner*, Society of Antiquaries of Newcastle upon Tyne, record ser., ii (1978).

HUDLESTONE, C. R. (ed.), *Naworth Estate and Household Accounts, 1648–1660*, Surtees Society, clxviii (1958).

JAMES, M. E. (ed.), *Estate Accounts of the Earls of Northumberland, 1562–1637*, Surtees Society, clxiii (1955).

J.C., *The Compleat Collier: or, the Whole Art of Sinking, Getting, and Working Coal-Mines* (1708) (Newcastle upon Tyne, 1968 edn.).

Journals of the House of Commons (1742 etc.).

Journals of the House of Lords (1762 etc.).

KENNEDY, P. A. (ed.), *Nottinghamshire Household Inventories*, Thoroton Society, record ser. xxii (1963).

KING, GREGORY, *Natural and Political Observations upon the State and Condition of England* (1695) (1804 edn.).

KIRBY, D. A. (ed.), *Parliamentary Surveys of the Bishopric of Durham*, Surtees Society, 2 vols., clxxxiii, clxxxv (1971–2).

LELAND, JOHN, *The Itinerary of John Leland in or about the years 1535–1543*, ed. L. Toulmin-Smith (5 vols., 1907–10).

—— *The Itinerary in Wales of John Leland in or about the years 1536–1539*, ed. L. Toulmin-Smith (1906).

LLWYD, EDWARD, *Parochialia* (1697), ed. R. H. Morris, *Archaeologia Cambrensis*, supplements, 6th ser., ix, x (1909–10).

MACKWORTH, Sir HUMPHREY, *The Case of Sir Humphrey Mackworth, and of the Mine-Adventurers, with Respect to the Irregular Proceedings of several Justices of the Peace etc.* (1705).

MEIGE, GUY, *The New States of England under their Majesties King William and Queen Mary* (1691).

MOORE, J. S. (ed.), *The Goods and Chattels of Our Forefathers: Frampton Cotterell and district Probate Inventories* (1976).

NORTH, ROGER, *The Life of the Right Honourable Francis North, Baron of Guilford*, ed. M. North (1742).

NOURSE, TIM, *Campania Foelix . . . to which are added two essays (1) of a Country House (2) of the Fuel of London* (1700).

ORNSBY, G. (ed.), *Selections from the Household Books of Lord William Howard of Naworth Castle*, Surtees Society, lxviii (1878).

OWEN, D. M., *The Making of King's Lynn: A Documentary Survey* (1984).

OWEN, GEORGE, *The Description of Pembrokeshire* (1603), ed. H. Owen, Cymmrodorion Record Series, i (2 parts, 1892–7).

PEPYS, SAMUEL, *The Diary of Samuel Pepys*, ed. R. Latham and W. Matthews (11 vols., 1970–83).

PERCY, T. (ed.), *The Regulations and Establishment of the Household of Henry Algernon Percy, the Fifth Earl of Northumberland, A.D. 1512* (1770).

PHILLIPS, C. B. (ed.), *Lowther Family Estate Books, 1617–75*, Surtees Society, cxci (1979).

Philosophical Transactions of the Royal Society (1665 etc.).

PLATT, Sir HUGH, *A New and Cheape and Delicate Fire of Cole-Balles* (1603).

PLATTES, GABRIEL, *A Discovery of Subterraneall Treasure: viz. of All Manner of Mines and Minerals from the Gold to the Coale* (1639).

PLOT, ROBERT, *The Natural History of Staffordshire* (1686) (Manchester, 1973 edn.).

POVEY, CHARLES, *A Discovery of Indirect Practices in the Coal-Trade; or a Detection of the Pernicious Maxims* (1700).

—— *The Unhappiness of England as to its Trade by Sea and Land Truly Stated* (1701).

PRIMATT, STEPHEN, *The City and Countrey Purchaser and Builder* (2nd edn. 1680).

Public Record Office, *Acts of the Privy Council of England* (1890 etc.).

—— *Calendar of Charter Rolls* (1903 etc.).

—— *Calendar of Close Rolls* (1892 etc.).

—— *Calendar of Inquisitions Post Mortem* (1904 etc.).

—— *Calendar of Patent Rolls* (1891 etc.).

—— *Calendar of Proceedings of the Committee for Compounding, 1643–1660* (1888).

—— *Calendar of State Papers Domestic* (1856 etc.).

—— *Calendar of State Papers Venetian* (1864 etc.).

—— *Letters and Papers, Foreign and Domestic, Henry VIII* (1920 etc.).

RAINE, J. (ed.), *Wills and Inventories illustrative of the History, Manners, Language, Statistics etc. of the Northern Counties of England*, Surtees Society, ii (1835).

—— *The Priory of Finchale: The Charters of Endowments, Inventories and Account Rolls, of the Priory of Finchale in the County of Durham*, Surtees Society, vi (1837).

—— *The Durham Household Book: Or the Accounts of the Bursar of the Monastery of Durham from Pentecost 1530 to Pentecost 1534*, Surtees Society, xviii (1844).

—— *The Inventories and Account Rolls of the Benedictine Houses or Cells of Jarrow and Monk-Wearmouth, in the County of Durham*, Surtees Society, xxix (1854).

ROVENZON, JOHN, *A Treatise of Metallica* (1613).

Scottish Record Office, *Exchequer Rolls of Scotland* (1878 etc.).

—— *Register of the Privy Council of Scotland* (1877 etc.).

SINCLAIR, GEORGE, *The Hydrostaticks ... with a Short History of Coal* (Edinburgh, 1672).

STANNING, J. H., *The Royalist Composition Papers: Being the Proceedings of the Committee for Compounding, A.D., 1643–1660*, Lancashire and Cheshire Record Society, xxiv, xxix (1891–6).

Statutes of the Realm (9 vols., 1810–24).

STEER, F. W. (ed.), *Farm and Cottage Inventories of Mid-Essex, 1635 to 1749* (Chichester, 1969 edn.).

STEVENSON, W. H., and BAKER, W. T. (eds.), *Records of the Borough of Nottingham, 1155–1702* (5 vols., 1882–1900).

STOCKS, H. (ed.), *Records of the Borough of Leicester*, iv. *1603–88* (Cambridge, 1923).

STOW, JOHN, *The Annales or Generall Chronicle of England* (1615 edn.).

TAWNEY, R. H., and POWER, E. (eds.), *Tudor Economic Documents* (3 vols., 1924).

TRINDER, B., and COX, J. (eds.), *Yeomen and Colliers in Telford: Probate Inventories for Dawley, Lilleshall, Wellington and Wrockwardine, 1660–1750* (1980).

VAISEY, D. G. (ed.), *Probate Inventories of Lichfield and District, 1585–1680*, Collections of a History of Staffordshire, 4th ser., v (1969).

Valor Ecclesiasticus, temp. Henry VIII, auctoritate Regia Institutus, ed. J. Caley and
J. Hunter (6 vols., Record Commission, 1810–34).

WALLER, WILLIAM, *An Essay on the Value of the Mines late of Sir Carberry Price*
(1698).

WALTON, J. (ed.), *Calendar of the Greenwell Deeds in the Public Reference Library*
(Newcastle upon Tyne, 1927).

WELFORD, R. (ed.), *Records of the Committees for Compounding etc., with Delinquent Royalists in Durham and Northumberland during the Civil War, 1643–
1660*, Surtees Society, cxi (1905).

WILLAN, T. S. (ed.), *A Tudor Book of Rates* (Manchester, 1962).

YARRANTON, ANDREW, *England's Improvement by Sea and Land* (1677) (1698
edn.).

C. Theses

BLAKE, J. B., 'Some Aspects of the Trade of Newcastle-upon-Tyne in the Fourteenth Century' (Bristol University MA, 1962).

BULLEY, J. A., 'The Development of the Coal Industry in the Radstock Area of
Somerset from Earliest Times to 1830' (London University MA, 1952).

COX, R. M., 'The Development of the Coal Industry in South Yorkshire before
1830' (Sheffield University MA, 1960).

CROMAR, P., 'Economic Power and Organisation: The Development of the
Coal Industry of Tyneside, 1700–1828' (Cambridge University Ph.D., 1977).

EVANS, B. M., 'The Welsh Coal Trade during the Stuart Period, 1603–1709'
(University College of Wales, Aberystwyth, MA, 1928).

FROST, P. M., 'The Growth and Localisation of Rural Industry in South Staffordshire, 1560–1720' (Birmingham University Ph.D., 1973).

GOODMAN, K. W. G., 'Hammerman's Hill: The Land, People and Industry of
the Titterstone Clee Hill area of Shropshire from the 16th to the 18th Centuries' (Keele University Ph.D., 1979).

GRANT, E. G., 'The Spatial Development of the Warwickshire Coalfield'
(Birmingham University Ph.D., 1977).

GRIFFIN, C. P., 'The Economic and Social Development of the Leicestershire
and South Derbyshire Coalfield, 1550–1914' (Nottingham University Ph.D.,
1969).

GRUFFYDD, K. L., 'The Development of the Coal Industry in Flintshire to 1740'
(University College of North Wales, Bangor, MA, 1981).

GUY, I. 'The Scottish Export Trade, 1460–1599, from the Exchequer Rolls' (St
Andrews University M.Phil., 1982).

HALL, B., 'The Trade of Newcastle upon Tyne and the North-East Coast,
1600–1640' (London University Ph.D., 1933).

HARRISON, C. J., 'The Social and Economic History of Cannock and Rugeley,
1546–97' (Keele University Ph.D., 1974).

HOUSTON, R. A., 'Aspects of Society in Scotland and North East England, *c.* 1550–*c.* 1750: Social Structure, Literacy and Geographical Mobility' (Cambridge University Ph.D., 1981).

HUGHES, L. M., 'Politics, Society and Civil War in Warwickshire, 1620–50' (Liverpool University Ph.D., 1979).

LARMINIE, V. M., 'The Lifestyle and Attitudes of the Seventeenth-Century Gentleman, with special reference to the Newdigates of Arbury Hall, Warwickshire' (Birmingham University Ph.D., 1980).

LOMAS, R. A., 'Durham Cathedral Priory as a Landowner and a Landlord, 1290–1540' (Durham University Ph.D., 1973).

MAKEY, W. H., 'The Place of Whitehaven in the Irish Coal Trade, 1600–1750' (London University MA, 1952).

MARCOMBE, D., 'The Dean and Chapter of Durham, 1558–1603' (Durham University Ph.D., 1973).

METTERS, G. A., 'The Rulers and Merchants of King's Lynn in the Early Seventeenth Century' (University of East Anglia Ph.D., 1982).

MICHELL, A. R., 'The Port and Town of Great Yarmouth and its Social and Economic Relationships with its Neighbours on both sides of the Seas, 1550–1714: An Essay in the History of the North Sea Economy' (Cambridge University Ph.D., 1978).

MOLLER, A. W. R., 'The History of English Coalmining, 1500–1750' (Oxford University D.Phil., 1933).

ORMROD, D. J., 'Anglo-Dutch Commerce, 1700–1760' (Cambridge University Ph.D., 1973).

SMITH, R. S., 'The Willoughbys of Wollaton, 1500–1643: With Special Reference to Early Mining in Nottinghamshire' (Nottingham University Ph.D., 1964). Dr Smith kindly lent the author a copy of an expanded and revised version of his thesis, which is referred to in the footnotes as Smith MS.

WHITE, A. W. A., 'Sixty Years of Coalmining Enterprise on the North Warwickshire Estate of the Newdigates of Arbury, 1680–1740' (Birmingham University MA, 1969).

WILLIAMS, N. J. G., 'The Maritime Trade of the East Anglian Ports, 1550–1590' (Oxford University D.Phil., 1952).

D. Secondary printed works

This section includes all secondary works used in the preparation of this book and referred to only by author's name and date of publication in the notes. Works referred to only occasionally in the notes have their full citations given there. The place of publication is London unless otherwise stated. This does not aim to be a comprehensive bibliography of the history of coalmining before 1700; for that see Benson, Neville, and Thompson 1981. For the key to abbreviations of journal titles, see pp. xvi–xvii.

ANDERSON, D., *A Pictorial History of the British Coal Industry* (1982).

ARNOT, R. P., *A History of Scottish Miners from the Earliest Times* (1955).

ASHTON, T. S., and SYKES, J., *The Coal Industry of the Eighteenth Century* (Manchester, 1964 edn.).

ASHWORTH, W., *The History of the British Coal Industry*, v. *1946-1982: The Nationalized Industry* (Oxford, 1986).

ATKINSON, F., 'The Horse as a Source of Rotary Power', *Transactions of the Newcomen Society*, 33 (1960).

—— *The Great Northern Coalfield, 1700–1900* (Newcastle upon Tyne, 1977).

BAILEY, F. A., 'Early Coalmining in Prescot, Lancashire', *Transactions of the Historic Society of Lancashire and Cheshire*, 99 (1947).

BANKES, J. M., 'Records of Mining in Winstanley and Orrell, near Wigan', *Transactions of the Lancashire and Cheshire Antiquarian Society*, 34 (1939).

BARKER, T. C., 'Lancashire Coal, Cheshire Salt and the Rise of Liverpool', *Transactions of the Historic Society of Lancashire and Cheshire*, 103 (1951).

BARROWMAN, J., 'Slavery in the Coal-Mines of Scotland', *Transactions of the Federated Institute of Mining Engineers*, 14 (1897–8).

BEASTALL, T. W., *A North Country Estate: The Lumleys and the Saundersons as Landowners, 1600–1900* (Chichester, 1975).

BECKETT, J. V., *Coal and Tobacco: The Lowthers and the Economic Development of West Cumberland, 1660–1760* (Cambridge, 1981).

BENSON, J., and NEVILLE, R. G. (eds.), *Studies in the Yorkshire Coal Industry* (Manchester, 1976).

—— —— and THOMPSON, C. H., *Bibliography of the British Coal Industry* (Oxford, 1981).

BERNAN, W., *On the History and Art of Warming and Ventilating Rooms and Buildings* (2 vols., 1845).

BEVERIDGE, D., *Culross and Tulliallan or Perthshire on Forth: Its History and Antiquities with Elucidations of Scottish Life and Character from the Burgh and Kirk Sessions Records of that District* (2 vols., Edinburgh and London, 1885).

BEVERIDGE, W., *et al.*, *Prices and Wages in England from the Twelfth to the Nineteenth Century*, i. *Price Tables: Mercantile Era* (1939).

BIRCH, T., *A History of the Royal Society* (3 vols., 1756–7).

BIRRELL, J., 'Common Rights in the Medieval Forest', *P. & P.* 117 (1987).

BLACKWOOD, B. G., *The Lancashire Gentry and the Great Rebellion*, Chetham Society, 3rd ser., xxv (Manchester, 1978).

BLAKE, J. B., 'The Medieval Coal Trade of North-East England: Some Fourteenth-Century Evidence', *Northern History*, 2 (1967).

BLANCHARD, I. S. W., 'Commercial Crisis and Change: Trade and the Industrial Economy of the North-East, 1509–32', *Northern History*, 8 (1973).

BOWMAN, A. J., 'Culross Colliery: A Sixteenth-Century Mine', *Industrial Archaeology*, 7 (1970).

BRAND, J., *History of Newcastle* (2 vols., 1789).

BRIMBLECOMBE, P., *The Big Smoke: A History of Air Pollution in London since Medieval Times* (1987).

BROWN, E. H., PHELPS, and HOPKINS, S. V., *A Perspective of Wages and Prices* (1981).

BULMAN, H. F., and REDMAYNE, R., *Colliery Working and Management* (1912).

BULLEY, J. A., '"To Mendip for coal": A Study of the Somerset Coalfield before 1830', *Proceedings of the Somerset Archaeological and Natural History Society*, 97 (1952), 98 (1953).

BURWASH, D., *English Merchant Shipping, 1460–1540* (Toronto, 1947).

CHALKLIN, C. W., *Seventeenth Century Kent* (1965).

CHALONER, W. H., 'Salt in Cheshire, 1600–1870', *Transactions of the Lancashire and Cheshire Antiquarian Society*, 71 (1961).

CHURCH, R., *The History of the British Coal Industry*, iii. *1830–1913: Victorian Pre-Eminence* (Oxford, 1986).

CLARK, P. (ed.), *Country Towns in Pre-Industrial England* (Leicester, 1981).

—— *The English Alehouse: A Social History, 1200–1830* (1983).

CLAY, C. G. A., *Economic Expansion and Social Change: England 1500–1700* (2 vols., Cambridge, 1984).

CLAYTON, A. K., 'Coal Mining at Hoyland', *Transactions of Hunterian Archaeological Society*, 9 (1966).

CLIFFE, J. T., *The Yorkshire Gentry from the Reformation to the Civil War* (1969).

COLEMAN, D. C., *Industry in Tudor and Stuart England* (1975).

—— 'The Coal Industry: A Rejoinder', *EcHR* 2nd ser. 30 (1977).

CONNOR, A. D., *Weights and Measures of England* (1987).

CORFIELD, P. J., *The Impact of English Towns, 1700–1800* (Oxford, 1982).

COURT, W. H. B., *The Rise of the Midland Industries, 1600–1838* (1938).

CROFTON, H. T., 'Lancashire and Cheshire Coal Mining Records', *Transactions of the Lancashire and Cheshire Antiquarian Society*, 7 (1889).

CUNNINGTON, M. E., 'Mineral Coal in Roman Britain', *Antiquity*, 7 (1933).

DALE, H. B., *Coal and the London Coal Trade* (1912).

—— *The Fellowship of Woodmongers: Six Centuries of the London Coal Trade* (n.d. Reprinted from the *Coal Merchant and Shipper* (1923)).

DAVIS, R., *The Rise of the English Shipping Industry* (1962).

DIETZ, B., 'The North-East Coal Trade, 1550–1750: Measures, Markets and the Metropolis', *Northern History*, 22 (1986).

DONNACHIE, I., *A History of the Brewing Industry in Scotland* (Edinburgh, 1979).

DUCKHAM, B. F., 'Life and Labour in a Scottish Colliery, 1698–1755', *Scottish Historical Review*, 47 (1968).

—— 'Serfdom in Eighteenth-Century Scotland', *History*, 54 (1969).

—— *A History of the Scottish Coal Industry*, i. *1700–1813* (Newton Abbot, 1970).

DUNN, M., *An Historical, Geological and Descriptive View of the Coal Trade of the North of England* (Newcastle upon Tyne, 1844).

DYER, A. D., *The City of Worcester in the Sixteenth Century* (Leicester, 1973).

—— 'Wood and Coal: A Change of Fuel', *History Today*, 26 (1976).

DYER, C., 'The Consumer and the Market in the Later Middle Ages', *EcHR* 2nd ser. 42 (1989).

ELLIS, J. M., 'The Decline and Fall of the Tyneside Salt Industry, 1660–1790: A Re-examination', *EcHR* 2nd ser. 33 (1980).

—— *A Study of the Business Fortunes of William Cotesworth, c.1668–1726* (New York, 1981).

EVELEIGH, D. J., *Firegrates and Kitchen Ranges* (Aylesbury, 1983).

FLETCHER, I., 'The Archaeology of the West Cumberland Coal Trade', *Transactions of the Cumberland and Westmorland Antiquarian and Archaeological Society*, 3 (1878).

FLINN, M. W., 'The Growth of the English Iron Industry, 1660–1760', *EcHR* 2nd ser. 11 (1958).

—— *The History of the British Coal Industry*, ii. *1790–1830: The Industrial Revolution* (Oxford, 1984).

FRASER, C. M., 'The North-East Coal Trade until 1421', *Transactions of the Architectural and Archaeological Society of Durham and Northumberland*, 11 (1962).

GALLOWAY, R. L., *Annals of Coal Mining and the Coal Trade* (2 vols., 1898).

GODFREY, E. S., *The Development of English Glassmaking, 1560–1640* (Oxford, 1975).

GOUGH, J. W., *The Rise of the Entrepreneur* (1969).

GRANT, E. G., *A Warwickshire Colliery in the Seventeenth Century*, Dugdale Society Occasional Papers, 26 (1979).

GRANT, I. F., *The Social and Economic Development of Scotland before 1603* (Edinburgh and London, 1930).

GRASSBY, R., 'The Rate of Profit in Seventeenth-Century England', *EHR* 84 (1969).

GREEN, H., 'The Southern Portion of the Nottinghamshire and Derbyshire Coalfield and the Development of Transport before 1850', *Transactions of the Derbyshire Natural History and Archaeological Society*, NS 9 (1935).

GREEN, W., 'The Chronicles and Records of the Northern Coal Trade in the Counties of Durham and Northumberland', *Transactions of the North of England Institute of Mining Engineers Transactions*, 15 (1865–6).

GREENWELL, G. C., *A Glossary of Terms used in the Coal Trade of Northumberland and Durham* (1888).

GRIFFIN, A. R., 'Bell-Pits and Soughs: Some East Midlands Examples', *Industrial Archaeology*, 6 (1969).

—— *Coalmining* (1971a).

—— *Mining in the East Midlands, 1550–1947* (1971b).

GRIFFIN, C. P., 'Technological Change in the Leicestershire and South Derbyshire Coalfield before 1850', *Industrial Archaeology Review*, 3 (1978).

HALLAM, H. E. (ed.), *The Agrarian History of England and Wales*, ii. *1042–1350* (Cambridge, 1988).

HAMMERSLEY, G., 'Crown Woods and their Exploitation in the Sixteenth and Seventeenth Centuries', *Bulletin of the Institute of Historical Research*, 30 (1957).

—— 'The Charcoal Iron Industry and its Fuel, 1540–1750', *EcHR* 2nd ser. 26 (1973).

HARDY, S. M., 'The Development of Coal Mining in a North Derbyshire Village, 1635–1860', *University of Birmingham Historical Journal*, 5 (1955–6).

HARRIS, J. R., 'The Rise of Coal Technology', *Scientific American*, 231 (Aug. 1974).

—— 'Skills, Coal and British Industry in the Eighteenth Century', *History*, 61 (1976).

—— *The British Iron Industry, 1700–1850* (1988).

HART, C. E., *The Free Miners of the Royal Forest of Dean and the Hundred of St. Briavels* (Gloucester, 1953).

—— *The Industrial History of Dean* (Newton Abbot, 1971).

HATCHER, J., *English Tin Production and Trade before 1550* (Oxford, 1973).

HAUSMAN, W. J., *Public Policy and the Supply of Coal to London, 1700–1770* (New York, 1981).

—— 'The London Coal Trade, 1600–1911', in J. Chartres and S. Gyimesi (eds.), *The Structure of Internal Trade, 15th to 19th Century*, 9th Congress of the International Economic History Association (Berne, 1986).

HAVINDEN, M. A., 'Lime as a means of Agricultural Improvement: The Devon Example', in C. W. Chalklin and M. A. Havinden (eds.), *Rural Change and Economic Growth, 1500–1800* (1974).

HENSON, F. A., and SMITH, R. S., 'Detecting Early Coal Workings from the Air', *Colliery Engineering* (June 1955).

HEWITT, M. J., *Medieval Cheshire: An Economic and Social History of Cheshire in the Reigns of the Three Edwards* (Manchester, 1929).

HEY, D. G., *The Rural Metalworkers of the Sheffield Region* (Leicester, 1972).

—— *Yorkshire from A.D. 1000* (1986).

HINSLEY, F. B., 'The Development of Coal Mine Ventilation in Great Britain up to the End of the Nineteenth Century', *Transactions of the Newcomen Society*, 42 (1969–70).

HOPKINSON, G. G., 'The Development of the South Yorkshire and North Derbyshire Coalfield, 1500–1775', in J. Benson and R. G. Neville (eds.), *Studies in The Yorkshire Coal Industry* (Manchester, 1976).

HOSKINS, W. G., *Industry, Trade and People in Exeter, 1680–1800* (Manchester, 1935).

—— *The Midland Peasant* (1965 edn.).

HOUSTON, R., 'Coal, Class and Culture: Labour Relations in a Scottish Mining Community, 1650–1750', *Social History*, 8 (1983).

HOWELL, R., *Newcastle upon Tyne and the Puritan Revolution: A Study of the Civil War in North England* (Oxford, 1967).

HUGHES, E., *North Country Life in the Eighteenth Century*, i. *The North-East, 1700–50* (Oxford, 1952).

—— *North Country Life in the Eighteenth Century*, ii. *Cumberland and Westmorland, 1700–1830* (Oxford, 1965).

JACK, S. M., *Trade and Industry in Tudor and Stuart England* (1977).

JAMES, M., *Social Problems and Policy during the Puritan Revolution, 1640–1660* (1930).

JAMES, M. E., *Family, Lineage and Civil Society: A Study of Society, Politics and Mentality in the Durham Region, 1500–1640* (Oxford, 1974).

JENKINS, P., *The Making of a Ruling Class: The Glamorgan Gentry, 1640–1790* (Cambridge, 1983).

JENKINS, R., 'Coke: A Note on its Production and Use, 1587–1640', *Transactions of the Newcomen Society*, 12 (1931–2).

JENKINS, W. J., 'The Early History of Coal-Mining in the Black Country and especially around Dudley', *Transactions of the Newcomen Society*, 8 (1927–8).

KERRIDGE, E., 'The Coal Industry in Tudor and Stuart England: A Comment', *EcHR* 2nd ser. 30 (1977).

LANGTON, J., 'Coal Output in South-West Lancashire, 1590–1799', *EcHR* 2nd ser. 25 (1972).

—— *Geographical Change and Industrial Revolution: Coalmining in South West Lancashire, 1590–1799* (Cambridge, 1979*a*).

—— 'Landowners and the Development of Coal Mining in South-West Lancashire', in H. S. A. Fox and R., A. Butlin (eds.), *Change in the Countryside* (1979*b*),

LEE, C. E., 'The Waggonways of Tyneside', *Archaeologia Aeliana*, 24 (1951).

LEWIS, E. A., 'The Development of Industry and Commerce in Wales during the Middle Ages', *Transactions of the Royal Historical Society*, NS 17 (1903).

LEWIS, G. R., *The Stannaries: A Study of the Medieval Tin Miners of Cornwall and Devon* (Truro, 1965 edn.).

LEWIS, M. J. T., *Early Wooden Railways* (1970).

LIPSON, E., *The Economic History of England* (3 vols., 1956 edn.).

LYTHE, S. G. E., *The Economy of Scotland in its European Setting, 1550–1625* (Edinburgh and London, 1960).

—— 'The Economy of Scotland under James VI and I', in A. G. R. Smith (ed.), *The Reign of James I and VI* (1973).

—— and BUTT, J., *An Economic History of Scotland, 1100–1939* (Glasgow, 1975).

MALCOLMSON, R. W., '"A Set of Ungovernable People": The Ringswood Colliers in the Eighteenth Century', in J. Brewer and J. Styles (eds.), *An Ungovernable People: The English and their Law in the Seventeenth and Eighteenth Centuries* (1980).

MARSHALL, G. D., *Presbyteries and Profits: Calvinism and the Development and Capitalism in Scotland, 1560–1707* (Oxford, 1980).

MATHIAS, P., *The Brewing Industry in England, 1700–1830* (Cambridge, 1959).

—— *The Transformation of England: Essays in the Economic and Social History of England in the Eighteenth Century* (1979).

MILLER, E., and HATCHER, J., *Medieval England: Rural Society and Economic Change, 1086–1348* (1978).

Mining Association of Great Britain, *Historical Review of Coal Mines* (c. 1924).

MOLLER, A. W., 'Coal Mining in the Seventeenth Century', *Transactions of the Royal Historical Society*, 4th ser. 8 (1925).

MORIMOTO, N., 'The Coal-Mining of Durham Cathedral Priory from the Fourteenth Century to the Time of its Dissolution', *Keieishigaku*, 4 (1970).

MOTT, R. A., 'The Newcastle Coal Trade', *Colliery Guardian*, 204 (1962*a*).

—— 'The Newcastle and London Chaldrons for Measuring Coal', *Archaeologia Aeliana*, 4th ser. 40 (1962*b*).

—— and GREENFIELD, G. J. (eds.), *The History of Coke Making and of the Coke Oven Managers' Association* (Cambridge, 1936).

NEF, J. U., 'The Dominance of the Trader in the English Coal Industry', *JEBH* 1 (1929).

—— *The Rise of the British Coal Industry* (2 vols., 1932).

—— 'The Progress of Technology an the Growth of Large-Scale Industry in Great Britain, 1540–1640', *EcHR* 5 (1934).

—— 'Prices and Industrial Capitalism in France and England, 1540–1640', *EcHR* (1937).

—— *Industry and Government in France and England, 1540–1640* (Philadelphia, 1940).

Northumberland County History Committee (eds.), *A History of Nothumberland* (15 vols., Newcastle upon Tyne and London, 1905–40).

PALLISER, D. M., *Tudor York* (Oxford, 1979).

POLLARD, S., *The Genesis of Modern Management* (1965).

RACKHAM, O., *Ancient Woodland: Its History, Vegetation and Uses in England* (1980).

REES, W., 'Miscellanea', *South Wales and Monmouthshire Record Society*, 1 (1949).

—— *Industry before the Industrial Revolution, incorporating a study of the Chartered Companies of the Society of Mines Royal and of Mineral and Battery Works* (2 vols., Cardiff, 1968).

—— and WILLIAMS, G., *Glamorgan County History* (Cardiff, 1936–).

RILEY, H. T., *Memorials of London and London Life in the XIII, XIV and XV Centuries* (1868).

ROEBUCK, P., *Yorkshire Baronets, 1640–1760: Families, Estates and Fortunes* (Oxford, 1980).

ROGERS, J. E. T., *A History of Agriculture and Prices in England* (7 vols., Oxford, 1866–1902).

ROWLANDS, M. B., 'Industry and Social Change in Staffordshire, 1660–1760: A Study of Probate and Other Records of Tradesmen', *Lichfield and South Staffordshire Archaeological and Historical Society Transactions*, 9 (1967–8).

—— *Masters and Men in the Small Metalware Trades of the West Midlands* (Manchester, 1975).

—— 'Society and Industry in the West Midlands at the End of the Seventeenth Century', *Midland History*, 4 (1977).

—— *The West Midlands from A.D. 1000* (1987).

SALZMANN, L. F., *English Industries of the Middle Ages* (1913).

SCAMMELL, G. V., 'English Merchant Shipping at the End of the Middle Ages: Some East Coast Evidence', *EcHR* 2nd ser. 13 (1961).

SCHUBERT, H. E., *History of the British Iron and Steel Industry* (1957).

SHARP, B., *In Contempt of All Authority: Rural Artisans and Riot in the West of England, 1586–1660* (1980).

SHARP, L., 'Timber, Science, and Economic Reform in the Seventeenth Century', *Forestry*, 48 (1975).

SHUFFREY, L. A., *The English Fireplace and its Accessories* (1912).

SIMPSON, J. B., 'Coal Mining by the Monks', *Transactions of the North of England Institute of Mining Engineers*, 39 (1909–10).

SIMPSON, T. V., 'Old Mining Records and Plans', *Transactions of the North of England Institute of Mining Engineers*, 86 (1930–1).

SINGLETON, D., 'The Removal of Features of Early Coalmining from the Landscape', *East Midlands Geographer*, 31 (1969).

SMITH, R., *Sea Coal for London: History of the Coal Factors in the London Market* (1961).

SMITH, R. B., *Land and Politics in the England of Henry VIII* (Oxford, 1970).

SMITH, R. S., 'Huntingdon Beaumont: Adventurer in Coalmines', *Renaissance and Modern Studies*, 1 (1957).

—— 'England's First Rails: A Reconsideration', *Renaissance and Modern Studies*, 4 (1960).

—— *Early Mining around Nottingham, 1500–1650* (Nottingham, 1989).

SMOUT, C., *Scottish Trade on the Eve of the Union, 1660–1707* (Edinburgh, 1963).

STONE, L., 'An Elizabethan Coalmine', *EcHR* 2nd ser. 3 (1950–1).

—— *The Crisis of the Aristocracy, 1558–1641* (Oxford, 1965).

—— and FAWTIER STONE, J. C., *An Open Élite? England 1540–1880* (Oxford, 1984).

SUPPLE, B., *The History of the British Coal Industry*, iv. *1913–1946: The Political Economy of Decline* (Oxford, 1987).

SWAIN, J. T., *Industry before the Industrial Revolution: North-East Lancashire, c.1500–1640*, Cheetham Society, 3rd ser., xxxii (Manchester, 1986).

SWEEZY, P. M., *Monopoly and Competition in the English Coal Trade, 1550–1850* (Cambridge, Mass., 1938).

SYMONS, M. V., *Coal Mining in the Llanelli Area*, i. *16th Century to 1829* (Llanelli, 1979).

TAYLOR, T. J., 'The Archaeology of the Coal Trade', *Archaeological Institute of Great Britain and Ireland: Proceedings at Annual General Meeting held at Newcastle in 1852* (1858).

TELFORD, S. J., 'Early Industrial Development on the Northumberland Coast between Seaton Sluice and Cullercoats', *Industrial Archaeology*, 3 (1974).

TERRY, C. S., 'The Scottish Campaign in Northumberland and Durham between January and June, 1644', and 'The Siege of Newcastle by the Scots in 1644', *AA* 21 (1899).

THIRSK, J. (ed.), *The Agrarian History of England and Wales*, iv. *1500–1640* (Cambridge, 1967).

—— (ed.), *The Agrarian History of England and Wales*, v(i). *1640–1750: Regional Farming Systems* (Cambridge, 1984).

—— (ed.), *The Agrarian History of England and Wales*, v(ii). *1640–1750: Agrarian Change* (Cambridge, 1985).

THOMAS, B., 'Was There an Energy Crisis in Great Britain in the Seventeenth Century?', *Explorations in Entrepreneurial History*, 23 (1986).

TREVOR-ROPER, H. R., 'The Bishopric of Durham and The Capitalist Reformation', *Durham University Journal*, 38, NS 7 (1945–6).

TRIGG, W. B., 'The Halifax Coalfield', in 5 parts, *Transactions of the Halifax Antiquarian Society* (1930–2).

TRINDER, B., *The Industrial Revolution in Shropshire* (1973).

TROTT, C. D. J., 'Coal Mining in the Borough of Neath in the 17th and Early Eighteenth Centuries', *Morgannwyg*, 13 (1969).

TURNER, E. R., 'The Keelmen of Newcastle', *American Historical Review*, 21 (1915–16).

—— 'The English Coal Industry in the Seventeenth and Eighteenth Centuries', *American Historical Review*, 27 (1921).

Victoria History of the Counties of England, in progress (Oxford, 1900–   ).

WANKLYN, M. D. G., 'John Weld of Willey, 1585–1665: An Enterprising Landowner of the Early Seventeenth Century', *West Midlands Studies*, 3 (1969).

—— 'John Weld of Willey: Estate Management, 1631–1650', *West Midlands Studies*, 4 (1970–1).

—— 'Industrial Development in the Ironbridge Gorge before Abraham Darby', *West Midlands Studies*, 15 (1982).

WATTS, S. J., *From Border to Middle Shire: Northumberland, 1586–1625* (1975).

WEATHERILL, L., *The Pottery Trade and North Staffordshire, 1660–1760* (Manchester, 1971).

WEBSTER, G., 'A Note on the Use of Coal in Roman Britain', *Antiquaries Journal*, 35 (1955).

WELFORD, R., *A History of Newcastle and Gateshead* (3 vols., 1884–7).

—— *Men of Mark 'twixt Tyne and Tweed* (3 vols., 1895).

WHATLEY, C. A., *'That Important and Necessary Article': The Salt Industry and its Trade in Fife and Tayside c.1570–1850*, Abertay Historical Society (Dundee, 1984).

—— 'Salt, Coal and the Act of Union of 1707: A Revision Article', *Scottish Historical Review*, 46 (1987).

WHITE, A. W. A., *Men and Mining in Warwickshire*, Coventry and North Warwickshire History Pamphlets, 7 (1970).

WILCOCK, D., *The Durham Coalfield. Part I: the 'Sea-Cole' Age*, Durham County Library Local History Publications, xiv (1979).

WILLAN, T. S., *River Navigation in England, 1600–1760* (Oxford, 1936).

—— *The English Coasting Trade* (Manchester, 1938).

—— *The Inland Trade: Studies in English Internal Trade in the Sixteenth and Seventeenth Centuries* (Manchester, 1976).

WILSON, C., *England's Apprenticeship, 1603–1763* (1984 edn.).

WOOD, O., *West Cumberland Coal, 1600–1982/3*, Cumberland and Westmorland Antiquarian and Archaeological Society, extra ser., xxiv (1988).

WRIGHT, L., *Home Fires Burning: The History of Domestic Heating and Cooking* (1984).

WRIGHTSON, K., and LEVINE, D., 'Death in Whickham', in J. Walter and R. Schofield (eds.), *Famine, Disease, and the Social Order in Early Modern Society* (Cambridge, 1989).

WRIGLEY, E. A., 'A Simple Model of London's Importance in Changing English Society and Economy, 1650–1750', *P. & P.* 37 (1967).

—— *Continuity, Chance and Change: The Character of the Industrial Revolution* (Cambridge, 1988).

—— and SCHOFIELD, R. S., *The Population History of England, 1541-1871: A Reconstruction* (1981).

ZUPKO, R. E., 'The Weights and Measures of Scotland before the Union', *Scottish Historical Review*, 56 (1977).

—— *British Weights and Measures: A History from Antiquity to the Seventeenth Century* (Madison, Wisc., 1977).

Index

colliers:
characteristics of 307–8, 377–8; boys 385, 401–2; free miners of Dean 173–5; mobility of 152, 159, 176, 208, 308, 312–13, 381; serfdom in Scotland 310–16; women 308, 384–5

earnings and allowances, 319, 391–405; bonuses 313, 394–5; coal allowances 289, 309, 318, 395–6; drinking money 313, 395; free ale and tobacco 396; housing allowances 397; methods of remuneration 391–7; 'shoe silver' 313; sick pay and compensation 317, 319–21; 'strike-ale' 394

life-style of: absenteeism 309, 313, 314, 388–90, 403; consumption patterns 404–5; drinking habits 311, 313, 314; education and literacy 285, 314–15, 404–5; farming 402–4; health 233, 403–4

types of, see banksmen, firemen, haulers/ putters, hewers, sinkers/soughers, timbermen, winders/watermen

working conditions: accidents 232–3, 236–8, 318–19, 320–1, 401; bonds 309–10; continuity of employment 346–9, 387–90; hours of work 386–7; night-work 163, 288, 316–17, 387; productivity 344–6; punishment 308–9, 310, 311, 312, 316–17; rules governing 308–16; strikes and lock-outs 315, 317–18

colliers (ships) 114, 466
capacity of 114, 473–6, 566
manning levels, 479–80
ownership of, 545–6
see also shipping